Joaquin Miller, Henry T. Williams

The Pacific Tourist

Adams & Bishop's illustrated trans-continental guide of travel, from the Atlantic to

the Pacific Ocean - a complete traveler's guide of the Union and Central Pacific

railroads

Joaquin Miller, Henry T. Williams

The Pacific Tourist
Adams & Bishop's illustrated trans-continental guide of travel, from the Atlantic to the Pacific Ocean - a complete traveler's guide of the Union and Central Pacific railroads

ISBN/EAN: 9783337840068

Printed in Europe, USA, Canada, Australia, Japan

Cover: Foto ©Andreas Hilbeck / pixelio.de

More available books at **www.hansebooks.com**

Testimonials & Endorsements

OF

RAILROADS, THE PRESS, AND PUBLIC MEN.

• •

"UNION PACIFIC RAILROAD CO.,
OMAHA, NEB., May 30, 1876.}

Mr. Henry T Williams:

I consider THE PACIFIC TOURIST a very complete volume, indispensable to the overland passenger, and a book that every library should contain. The information it gives is correct and concisely stated, while the illustrations are very true and beautiful, forming a most attractive feature of the work. You should be liberally rewarded for the pains and expense you have been at in producing it.

J. J. DICKEY,
Superintendent Telegraph Department."

"OFFICE CHICAGO & NORTH-WESTERN RAILROAD, CO.,
CHICAGO, June 3, 1876. }

You have made a Guide that you should be proud of, and I trust that you will be amply repaid for your work. I sincerely hope for its success.

W. H. STENNETT,
General Passenger Agent."

" Office of U. S. Geological and Geographical Survey
of the Territories,
WASHINGTON, June 10, 1876. }

DEAR SIR:

Your Guide Book is splendid. Nothing like it ever got out on this Continent. It is a world of information in regard to the Far West. It will be useful, not only to the traveler, but to all others, as a condensed library of information about the West. Yours sincerely,

F. V. HAYDEN."

" MICHIGAN CENTRAL RAILROAD CO.,
CHICAGO, May 29, 1876. }

I thank you for an opportunity to see 'WILLIAMS' PACIFIC TOURISTS' GUIDE.' It makes a very creditable appearance, and will meet the wants of all who are searching for a correct guide to the many points of interest upon our GREAT TRANS-CONTINENTAL ROUTE. I wish you much success in the undertaking. Yours truly,

HENRY C. WENTWORTH,
General Passenger Agent."

' CHICAGO, BURLINGTON & QUINCY RAILROAD CO.,
BOSTON, June 1, 1876. }

Your Guide is very finely gotten up, and is ahead of anything of the kind I have yet seen.

E. P. RIPLEY,
General Eastern Agent."

" MICHIGAN CENTRAL RAILROAD.
BOSTON, June 6, 1876. }

I have examined your 'PACIFIC TOURIST,' and take pleasure in commending it to trans-continental travelers, not only as an accurate Guide Book, but as a work well calculated to while away hours which become too heavy for comfort. The work is well edited, and is worthy of a place, not only in the hands of the traveler, but on the shelves of the private library. I hope your labors will meet with satisfactory reward.

J. Q. A. BEAN,
General Eastern Agent."

" We are surprised at the amount of information it contains. The volume contains more matter than the combined issues of Nordhoff's California, Picturesque America, and Crofutt's book. Its illustrations of western scenery and travel, in numbers, beauty and accuracy, exceed those of any volume ever published. The railroad companies have unqualifiedly indorsed it as the most accurate and reliable guide ever seen."

AMERICAN BOOKSELLER, N. Y.

"The Pacific Tourist is singularly full and complete."

THE EVENING POST, N. Y.

"THE PACIFIC TOURIST is as its editor claims, the costliest and handsomest book of the sort yet issued. The descriptions are well written, and wood engravings after good artists are very handsome. Mr. Williams has done a great deal of traveling, spent a considerable amount of money in getting up the Guide, and has been very competently aided by tourists and journalists of experience."

SPRINGFIELD REPUBLICAN, (MASS.)

"It will not disappoint expectations in any respect, its only fault being that its contents are of so comprehensive a kind, that the intending tourist will, likely enough, suffer from an embarrassment of riches."

DAILY INQUIRER, PHILADELPHIA, PA.

" This Guide ranks among the very best efforts ever issued. Its richness and completeness in illustrations, information and descriptions, can only be realized by an examination of the work. The ground traveled over and described is immense. It is doubtful if any other work offers so much valuable and useful information to travelers in so succinct and attractive a form. We may say that it gives, indeed, too much for the money. The views are profuse and notably good. The amount of illustration in the book considering its cost, is absolutely marvelous, and the ability and energy Mr. Williams has shown in getting it up is something to be admired."

PUBLISHERS' WEEKLY, NEW YORK CITY.

" At last there is a Guide Book to the Pacific Coast, every way worthy of the wonderful scenery, and inexhaustible resources of the western part of the American Continent, and the sagacity, skill and money that have given us the Pacific Railroads.

THE PACIFIC TOURIST is edited by the one man in this country, who is competent to furnish such a Guide Book. Mr. Williams has, in personal travel and by various excursions, made himself personally familiar with the whole ground. The volume is filled with all possible information of value to those intending to travel to the Pacific, and is so interestingly written, and so lavishly and beautifully illustrated by the best artists, as to make it a volume worthy any library. Time and space utterly fail to describe details. The book only needs to be seen to be appreciated."

THE DAILY UNION, SPRINGFIELD, MASS.

" Indispensable to persons traveling in the West. It is brought out in excellent, even sumptuous style, and is very copiously illustrated with pictures of interesting places and characters.

Every sort of information useful and entertaining, is given in regard to the whole region of the Pacific Slope, thus making the book of the greatest value to tourists and business men."

THE DAILY GRAPHIC, N. Y.

THE PACIFIC TOURIST

An Illustrated Guide

TO

PACIFIC R.R. CALIFORNIA,

AND

Pleasure Resorts across the Continent

H. T. WILLIAMS, Editor.

ADAMS & BISHOP, PUBLISHERS,

New York.

HENRY W. TROY—DES. C. MEEDER & CHUBB—SC.

PALACE CAR LIFE ON THE PACIFIC RAILROAD.

The Pacific Tourist.

ADAMS & BISHOP'S
Illustrated Trans-Continental Guide

OF TRAVEL,

FROM

The Atlantic to the Pacific Ocean.

CONTAINING FULL DESCRIPTIONS OF

RAILROAD ROUTES ACROSS THE CONTINENT, ALL PLEASURE RESORTS AND PLACES OF MOST
NOTED SCENERY IN THE FAR WEST, ALSO OF ALL CITIES, TOWNS, VILLAGES,
U. S. FORTS, SPRINGS, LAKES, MOUNTAINS,

ROUTES OF SUMMER TRAVEL, BEST LOCALITIES FOR HUNTING, FISHING, SPORTING, AND ENJOY-
MENT, WITH ALL NEEDFUL INFORMATION FOR THE PLEASURE TRAVELER,
MINER, SETTLER, OR BUSINESS MAN.

A COMPLETE TRAVELER'S GUIDE

OF

The Union and Central Pacific Railroads,

AND ALL POINTS OF BUSINESS OR PLEASURE TRAVEL TO

CALIFORNIA, COLORADO, NEBRASKA, WYOMING, UTAH, NEVADA, MONTANA, THE MINES AND MINING
OF THE TERRITORIES, THE LANDS OF THE PACIFIC COAST, THE WONDERS OF THE
ROCKY MOUNTAINS, THE SCENERY OF THE SIERRA NEVADAS, THE COL-
ORADO MOUNTAINS, THE BIG TREES, THE GEYSERS, THE
YOSEMITE, AND THE YELLOWSTONE.

HENRY T. WILLIAMS, EDITOR.

WITH SPECIAL CONTRIBUTIONS BY

PROF. F. V. HAYDEN, CLARENCE KING, CAPT. DUTTON, A. C. PEALE, JOAQUIN
MILLER, J. B. DAVIS, F. E. SHEARER.

ILLUSTRATIONS BY

THOMAS MORAN, A. C. WARREN, W. SNYDER, F. SCHELL, H. W. TROY, A. WILL.
ENGRAVINGS BY MEEDER & CHUBB.

Price, $1.50 Railroad Edition, Flexible Covers, 332 pp.
" $2.00 Full Cloth, Stiff Covers, 364 pp.

NEW YORK:
ADAMS & BISHOP, PUBLISHERS.
1881.

Springfield Printing Company, Printers, Electrotypers and Binders, Springfield, Mass.

PREFACE.

NEW FIELDS OF TRAVEL.

Since the opening of the Pacific Railroad, there has been developed, not only an immense field of mining industry, but many new and remarkable Places of Wonderful Scenery and Pleasure Travel. The Attractions of the Rocky Mountains and Sierras have become world famous, and Regions unknown five or ten years ago, have been discovered which far transcend the liveliest imagination in their scenic beauty, and glorious enjoyment. Those who have ever crossed the Continent once in enjoyment of the Scenery of the Far West or in search of Health, can now return to the same line of travel, and spend their entire time in visiting Resorts, Mountains, Lakes, Springs, Canons, which were unknown before, but now are so easily accessible that an entire Summer can be spent in new and delightful fields of travel.

The Yellowstone,—with all its glories of Springs, Geysers, Jets, and the million of its fairy-like colors, and fountains is now open for Tourists, by a new Route, so easily accessible, that a journey is no more made with effort, but with ease. The recent extension of the Utah Northern Railroad from Ogden, Utah, to Montana, almost to the border of the Yellowstone Park, now opens this wonderful Park and its scenery to the world

The Colorado Mountains.—New Routes of Pleasure Travel in Colorado have also been opened, with still more wonderful scenery. *The Veta Pass,* the highest railroad point in America, with its views of the Spanish Peaks, has been brought to notice by the extension of the Denver and Rio Grande Railroad, also the Grandeur of the Mountains and Lakes of the *San Juan Mining Region.* The wonderful richness of the mines at *Leadville,* exceeding the riches of any hitherto known, are hardly greater than the beauties of the scenery, by which it is reached either from Canon City, or *Denver,* or Georgetown. By the opening of the Colorado Central Railroad, easy access is given to the wonders of *Clear Creek Canon,* the *Ascent of Grays Peak,* the *Middle Park,* the *Hot Sulphur Springs,* the *Beauties of Estes Park* and *Long's Peak,* all of which are of remarkable interest.

The New Big Trees.—By the opening of the new Stage Route via Madera, there is given a new Route to the Yosemite, including a visit to another group of Big Trees, of as great celebrity as any yet discovered.

Arizona.—By the extension of the Southern Pacific Railroad into Arizona, is opened a new world of mineral richness, and Silver Wealth.

Pleasure Resorts of Southern California. — The Health and Pleasure Resorts of Southern California, and the Sea Coast Sanitariums, are made more accessible than ever, by the completion of the Southern Pacific Railroad and its branches.

Santa Barbara, Los Angeles, Santa Monica, Santa Cruz, San Bernardino, all made more easy of access and doubly attractive as Health Resorts.

Mount Shasta.—The wonderful scenery around *Mount Shasta* and in Northern California, are now open for tourists, via the California and Oregon Railroad.—a new Region of unusual beauty.

Oregon.—The Attractions of Oregon, and Washington Territory, are now easily reached, and the "*New Empire of the North West*" invites a world of Tourists, and offers Homes for settlers.

The Springs of California, — are becoming widely known. Near *Clear Lake* are new regions of travel, and the invalid can rejoice in healing virtues and a new climate.

A full record of the wonders reached by the Pacific Railroads, it is difficult to condense into small compass. The 350 or 400 pages of this volume, have already required for the Editor and his Assistants, over ten years travel, and $20 000 in cost. This volume is before the Tourist as the result of this expenditure of time and money. To its pages special assistance has been given by the most eminent travelers and Governmental Explorers of the day.

Professor F. V. Hayden,—the celebrated leader of the United States Geological Exploring Expedition, has contributed special assistance in the work of making this Guide complete, and written an admirable account for Tourists of the Wonders of the *Yellowstone. Clarence King* has also given a description of the Shoshone Falls.

Thomas Moran, who more than any other artist has drawn sketches of the Wonders of the West, and Albert Bierstadt the most celebrated of painters of American Scenery, have each added to the Guide rich embellishments and illustrations.

Wishing every Traveler the utmost joy in his Tour, and a happy "voyage,"

We are sincerely,

ADAMS & BISHOP.

Pleasures of Overland Travel.

Wonders of Scenery of the Rocky Mountains,

PACIFIC COAST AND THE PACIFIC RAIL ROAD.

THE grandest of American scenery borders the magnificent route of the Pacific Railroads. Since their completion, the glorious views of mountain grandeur in *The Yosemite, The Yellowstone*, have become known. The sublimities of *Colorado*, the *Rocky Mountains*, canons of Utah, and the *Sierra Nevadas*, have become famous. The attractions of the Far West for mining, stock raising and agriculture have added millions of wealth and population.

The glorious mountain climate, famed for its invigorating effects have attracted tourists and health seekers from the whole world. The golden land of California, its seaside pleasure resorts, its fertile grain fields, fruit gardens and flowers, have given irresistible charms to visitors; until now, a tour across the Continent opens to the traveler a succession of scenes, worthy the efforts of a life time to behold.

Industries have arisen by the opening of this great trans-continental line which were never expected or dreamed of by the projectors; the richest of mineral discoveries and the most encouraging of agricultural settlements have alike resulted, where little was thought of, and strangest of all, the tide of travel from Europe to Asia, China, Japan and the distant isles of the Pacific Ocean, now crosses the American Continent, with far more speed and greater safety.

Palace Car Life on the Pacific Railroad.—In no part of the world is travel made so easy and comfortable as on the Pacific Railroad. To travelers from the East it is a constant delight, and to ladies and families it is accompanied with absolutely no fatigue or discomfort. One lives at home in the Palace Car with as much true enjoyment as in the home drawing-room, and with the constant change of scenes afforded from the car window, it is far more enjoyable than the saloon of a fashionable steamer. For an entire week or more, as the train leisurely crosses the Continent, the little section and berth allotted to you, so neat and clean, so nicely furnished and kept, becomes your home. Here you sit and read, play your games, indulge in social conversation and glee, and if fortunate enough to possess good company of friends to join you, the overland tour becomes an intense delight.

The sleeping-cars from New York to Chicago, proceeding at their rushing rate of forty or more miles per hour, give to travelers no idea of the true comfort of Pullman car life. Indeed the first thousand miles of the journey to Chicago or St. Louis has more tedium and wearisomeness, and dust and inconvenience than all the rest of the journey. Do not judge of the whole trip by these first days out. From Chicago westward to Omaha the cars are far finer, and traveling more luxurious, likewise the rate of speed is slower and the motion of the train easy than on roads farther east.

At Omaha, as you view the long Pacific train just ready to leave the depot for its overland trip, (often over 600 feet in length), giving an appearance of strength, massiveness and majestic power, you can but admit it is exceedingly beautiful and impressive; this feeling is still more intensified when a day or so later, alone out upon the upland plains, with no living object in sight, as you stand at a little distance and look down upon the long train, it seems the handsomest work of science ever made for the comfort of earth's people.

The slow rate of speed, which averages but sixteen to twenty miles per hour, day and night, produces a peculiarly smooth, gentle and easy motion, most soothing and agreeable. The straight track, which for hundreds of miles is without a curve, avoids all swinging motions of the cars; sidelong bumps are unknown. The cars are connected with the Miller buffer and platform, and make a solid train, without the discomforts of jerks and jolts. And the steady, easy jog of the train, as it leisurely moves westward, gives a feeling of genuine comfort, such as no one ever feels or enjoys in any other part of the world.

A Pullman Pacific car train in motion is a grand and beautiful sight too, from within as well as from without. On some lovely, balmy, summer day, when the fresh breezes across the prairies induce us to open our doors and windows, there may often be seen curious and pleasant sights. Standing at the rear of the train, and with all doors open, there is an unobstructed view along the aisles throughout the entire length. On either side of the train, are the prairies, where the eye sees but wildness, and even desolation, then looking back upon this long aisle or avenue, he sees civilization and comfort and luxury. How sharp the contrast. The first day's ride over the Pacific Railroad westward, is a short one to nightfall, but it carries one through the beautiful undulating prairies of eastern Nebraska, the best settled portions of the State, where are its finest homes and richest soil. Opening suddenly into the broad and ever grand Valley of the Platte, the rich luxuriant meadow-grass, in

the warmth of the afternoon sun, make even the most desponding or prosaī feel there is beauty in prairie life.

On the second day out, the traveler is fast ascending the high plains and summits of the Rocky Mountains. The little villages of prairie dogs interest and amuse every one. Then come in sight the distant summits of Long's Peak and the Colorado Mountains. Without scarcely asking the cause, the tourist is full of glow and enthusiasm. He is alive with enjoyment, and yet can scarcely tell why. The great plains themselves seem full of interest.

Ah! It is this keen, beautiful, refreshing, oxygenated, invigorating, toning, beautiful, enlivening mountain air which is giving him the glow of nature, and quickening him into greater appreciation of this grand impressive country. The plains themselves are a sight—most forcible; shall we call them *the bluntness of desolation?* No, for every inch of the little turf beneath your feet is rich; the soil contains the finest of food in the little tufts of buffalo grass, on which thousands and millions of sheep and cattle may feed the year through. But it is the vastness of wide-extending, uninhabited, lifeless, uplifted solitude. If ever one feels belittled, 'tis on the plains, when each individual seems but a little mite, amid this *majesty of loneliness.* But the traveler finds with the Pullman car life, amid his enjoyments of reading, playing, conversation, making agreeable acquaintances, and with constant glances from the car window, enough to give him full and happy use of his time.

Night time comes, and then as your little berths are made up, and you snugly cover yourself up, under *double blankets* (for the night air is always crisp and cold), perhaps you will often witness the sight of a prairie fire, or the vivid flashes of lightning; some of nature's greatest scenes, hardly less interesting than the plains, and far more fearful and awe-inspiring. Then turning to rest, you will sleep amid the easy roll of the car, as sweetly and refreshingly as ever upon the home-bed. How little has ever been written of "Night on the Pacific Railroad," the delightful, snug, rejuvenating *sleeps* on the Pacific Railroad.

The lulling, quiet life by day, and the sound, refreshing repose by night, are to the system the best of health restorers. Were there but one thing tourists might feel most gratitude for, on their overland trip, 'tis their enjoyment of the exhilarating mountain air by day, and the splendid rest by night. But as our train moves on, it introduces us to new scenes. You soon ascend the Rocky Mountains at Sherman, and view there the vast mountain range, the "Back Bone of the Continent," and again descend and thunder amid the cliffs of Echo and Weber Canons. You carry with you your Pullman house and all its comforts, and from your little window, as from your little boudoir at home, you will see the mighty wonders of the Far West.

It is impossible to tell of the pleasures and joys of the palace ride you will have—five days—it will make you so well accustomed to car life, you feel when you drop upon the wharf of San Francisco, that you had left genuine comfort behind, and even the hotel, with its cosy parlor and cheerful fire, has not its full recompense.

Palace car life has every day its fresh and novel sights. No railroad has greater variety and contrasts of scenery than the Pacific Railroad. The great plains of Nebraska and Wyoming are not less impressive than the great Humboldt Desert. The rock majesties of Echo and Weber are not more wonderful than the curiosities of Great Salt Lake and the City of Deseret. And where more grandly and beautifully could a tourist drop down and finish his tour, than from the grand, towering summits of the Sierras, and amid the golden grain fields of California, its gardens, groves, and cottage blossoms?

When the traveler returns home, nothing will impress him more strongly or beautifully than the loveliness of the Valley of the Platte. Coming eastward, first, he will leave behind the millions of acres of little short buffalo grass, so dry and yellow, and soon comes to a little green. How refreshing it is after days of dry, sere vegetation. Gradually there come other grasses, a little taller and more green; then nearer and nearer to the end of the journey, come the waving of the corn-fields, the vast meadows of tall green grass, and the happy little farms. So complete a transition from the solitude of the uplands to the lovely green verdure of the lowlands of the Platte, is an inexpressible charm to all. No traveler ever returns East but with the most kindly of memories of the grand, and yet simple beauty of the Platte Valley.

Think then, oh reader! of the joys that await thee from the window of thy palace car!

Practical Hints for Comforts by the Way.—To enjoy palace car life properly, one always needs a good companion. This obtained, take a section together, wherever the journey leads you. From Chicago to Omaha, the company in sleeping-cars is usually quiet and refined, but beyond Omaha, there is often an indescribable mixture of races in the same car, and if you are alone, often the chance is that your "*compagnon du voyage*" may not be agreeable. It is impossible to order a section for *one* person *alone*, and the dictum of sleeping-car arrangements at Omaha requires all who come to take what berths are *assigned*. But if you will wait over one day at Omaha, you can make a choice of the whole train, and secure the most desirable berths. When your section is once located, generally you will find the same section reserved for you at Ogden, where you change

cars to the Central Pacific Railroad; all through passengers having usually the preference of best berths, and about the same position as on the cars of the Union Pacific.

Fee your porter on the sleeping-car always— if he is attentive and obliging, give him a dollar. His attention to your comfort and care of your baggage and constant watch over the little articles and hand-satchel, against loafers on the train, is worth all you give him. Often larger fees are given. This is just as the traveler feels. The porters of both Pacific Railroads are esteemed specially excellent, obliging and careful.

Meals.—The trains of the Union Pacific Railroad are arranged so as to stop at excellent stations at convenient hours, for meals. In place of the usual dining station at Laramie, there is now a most comfortable and convenient eating station at Rock Creek, a little farther west. Its pleasant, cheerful room filled with plants, and the convenience of better hours for meals, add greatly to the pleasure of the overland trip. At Green River you will find the dining-room entrance fairly surrounded with curiosities, and the office filled with oddities very amusing. The meals here are excellent, considering all supplies are obtained at a great distance away.

Usually all the eating-houses on both the Pacific Railroads are very excellent indeed. The keepers have to maintain their culinary excellence under great disadvantages, especially west of Sidney, as all food but meats must be brought from a great distance.

Travelers need to make no preparations for eating on the cars, as meals at all dining-halls are excellent, and food of great variety is nicely served; buffalo meat, antelope steak, tongue of all kinds, and always the best of beefsteak. Laramie possesses the reputation of the best steak on the Pacific Railroad. Sidney makes a specialty, occasionally, of antelope steak. At Evanston you will see the lively antics of the Chinese waiters, probably your first sight of them. Also they usually have nice mountain fish. At Green River you will always get nice biscuit; at Grand Island they give all you can possibly eat; it has a good name for its bountiful supplies.

At Ogden you will be pleased with the neatness and cleanness of the tables and service. At Cheyenne the dinners are always excellent, and the dining-room is cheerful. To any who either have desire to economize, or inability to eat three railroad meals per day, we recommend to carry a little basket with Albert biscuit and a little cup. This can be easily filled at all stopping-places with hot tea or coffee, and a sociable and comfortable glass of tea indulged in inside the car. The porter will fit you up a nice little table in your section, and spread on a neat white table-cloth.

When the tourist reaches the Central Pacific Railroad he passes beyond the domain of the Pullman Car Company; nevertheless, the new coaches of the Central Pacific Railroad are just as elegant and convenient.

As the comforts of the new cars are far superior to the old ones, which still are used, it would be better to wait over at Ogden one day to make sure of them. The dining-stations of the Central Pacific Railroad are bountiful in their supplies; at all of them fish is given in summer-time with great freedom. Fish is almost always to be had; no game of value. The food, cooking and service by Chinese waiters is simply excellent. The writer has never eaten nicer meals than those served at Winnemucca, Elko, Battle Mountain and Colfax. The Humboldt Desert is far from being a desert to the traveling public, for its eating-stations always furnish a *dessert* of good things and creature comforts.

A little lunch-basket nicely stowed with sweet and substantial bits of food will often save you the pain of long rides before meals; when the empty stomach craves food and failing to receive it, lays you up with the most dismal of sick headaches; it also serves you splendidly whenever the train is delayed. To be well on the Pacific Railroad *eat at regular hours, and never miss a meal.* Most of the sickness which we have witnessed, has arisen from irregular eating, or injudicious attempts at economy by skipping a meal to save a dollar. We have noticed those who were regular in eating at every meal, passed the journey with greatest ease, most comfort and best health. Those who were irregular, skipping here and there a meal, always suffered inconvenience.

In packing your little lunch-basket, avoid *tongue, by all means,* for it will not keep over a day or two, and its fumes in a sleeping-car are anything but like those from "Araby the blest." Avoid all articles which have odor of any description.

Lunch counters are attached to all eating-stations, so that you may easily procure hot coffee, tea, biscuit, sandwiches and fruit if you do not wish a full meal.

The uniform price of meals at all stations overland, is $1.00 greenbacks. On the Central Pacific, at Colfax pay 75 cents in silver; at Lathrop pay 50 cents silver—the cheapest and best meal for the money, of your whole tour. For clothing on your overland trip, you will need at Omaha the first day, if it is summer, a light spring suit; the next day a winter suit at Sherman. Again, at Salt Lake City and the Humboldt Desert, the thinnest of summer suits, and at the summit of the Sierras, all your underclothing. We can only advise you as you have to pass through so many extremes of temperature, to always wear your underclothing, day and night, through the overland trip, and add an overcoat if the air grows chilly.

Beware of the quick transition from the hot ride over the San Joaquin Valley to the cold sea air on the ferry from Oakland to San Francisco. Invalids have been chilled through with this unexpected sea breeze, and even the most hardy do not love it. Keep warm and keep inside the boat. Thus, reader, we have helped you with kindly hints how to enjoy your trip. Now let us glance, as we go, at each scene of industry where our tour will take us.

HINTS.

1. *Baggage.*— All baggage of reasonable weight can be checked from any Eastern city direct to Omaha, but is there rechecked.

2. At Omaha all baggage is weighed, and on all excess of over 100 pounds, passengers will pay 15 cts. per pound. This is imperative.

3. *Railroad Tickets*—are easily procurable for the whole trip across to San Francisco. It is better to buy one through ticket than to buy separately. By returning a different route from Omaha, from the one you went, the tour will be much more interesting, and give you fresh scenery constantly.

4. Buy your tickets only at known railroad offices, and never of agencies. In the West, railroads have offices at the principal hotels. These are usually perfectly reliable.

5. *To Check Baggage*—be at every depot one-half hour or more before the departure of trains.

6. *Transfer Coaches.*— In all Western cities there is a line of transfer coaches, which, for the uniform price of fifty cents, will take you and your baggage direct to any hotel, or transfer you at once across the city to any depot. They are trustworthy, cheap, and convenient. The agent will always pass through the train before arrival, selling transfer tickets and checks to hotels.

7. At Salt Lake City, horse-cars run from the depot direct to the hotels; also there is an omnibus transfer. Price, fifty cents.

8. At San Francisco the Pacific Transfer and Baggage Company will take your baggage to any hotel or private residence for 50 cents. Their agent is on every train; you will save time by giving him your check. Hotel coaches charge $1.00. Horse-cars run from the wharf direct to all hotels.

9. Greenbacks are used for all railroad tickets and payment of sleeping-car berths for the entire distance to California; also for all hotels to and including Salt Lake City, greenbacks will be received same as silver or gold. Away from the Central Pacific Railroad, you will sometimes need gold for coin expenses. After reaching San Francisco, you can sell your greenbacks and buy coin as often as necessary. If much coin is needed, buy and use the gold notes which are current everywhere within 300 miles of the city; beyond that the coin only is used. Gold notes

can be bought at any Banking House in San Francisco.

10. The uniform prices of board in the West are $3.00 to $4.50 per day at Chicago, $3.00 to $4.00 per day at Omaha, Denver, and Salt Lake City. In San Francisco, $3.00 gold per day at all hotels. To secure good nice rooms in California, the tourist must submit to extra charges of $1.00 to $1.50 per day.

11. If traveling with ladies, it is good policy, when within 100 miles of each city, where you expect to stop, to telegraph to your hotel in advance, requesting nice rooms reserved, always mentioning that you have ladies.

12. Whenever disposed to take horses and carriage for a ride, look out with sharp eyes for the tricks of the trade; if no price or time is agreed upon, you will have to pay dearly, and the farther west you go, the hire of horse flesh grows dearer (though the value per animal rapidly grows less.) Engage your livery carefully at so much per hour, and then choose your time to suit your wishes. Ten dollar bills melt quicker in carriage rides than any other " vain show."

13. Without much exception, all railroad officers, railroad conductors, Pullman car conductors are gentlemen in manners, courteous and civil. No passenger ever gains a point by loud orders or strong and forcible demands. You are treated respectfully by all, and the same is expected in return. The days of boisterous times, rough railroad men, and bullies in the Far West are gone, and there is as much civility there, often more, than you will find near home.

14. Railroad tickets must always be shown when baggage is checked.

ROUTES.

Route No. 1 from New York.—Take the Pennsylvania Central Railroad which leaves foot of Desbrosses street, by ferry, to Jersey City. To engage a good berth in your sleeping-car, go to a proper railroad office, and secure your berth by telegraph. There are local telegraphs connecting with the principal Pullman office. Do this the previous night, or morning, as then the best berths can be secured. Pullman cars run on the Pennsylvania Railroad to Chicago and St. Louis, direct, without change. Three trains leave per day. To see the richest scenery, take the *morning* train and you will have a good view of nearly the entire State of Pennsylvania by daylight, the valley of the Susquehanna and Juniata, and the famous Horse-Shoe Bend by moonlight. The Pennsylvania Railroad is *"always on time,"* the most reliable in its connections.

Route No. 2 from New York.—Leave *via* the Erie Railroad from foot of Chambers or West 23d street. The advantages of this route are numerous. This is the famous Pullman line—which ran the first line of dining-cars—between New York and Chicago. The meals

are very fine and service excellent. The sleeping-cars on the Erie Railroad belong to the Pullman Company, and are the finest in the world, of extra width and extra comfort. The scenery along the Erie Railroad (by all means take the morning train) is specially fine, and at points is remarkably lovely. The sleeping and dining-cars accompany the train to Chicago. The route passes *via* Salamanca, Atlantic and Great Western and Chicago extension of Baltimore and Ohio Railroad, direct without change, to Chicago. Passengers also can take other sleeping-cars of the train, if they wish, which will convey them direct to Buffalo and Niagara Falls, where there is direct connection *via* the Lake Shore Railroad or Michigan Central to Chicago.

Route No. 3 From New York—is *via* the New York Central and Hudson River.

Route No. 4—is *via* the *Baltimore* and *Ohio* Railroad. Tourists by this route, to and from California, have many advantages. It is *the shortest* line from Chicago or Cincinnati to the National Capitol at Washington. Its scenery, on the mountain division, between Harper's Ferry and Parkersburg, is grand and full of historic interest. Its dining stations are exceedingly well kept, and the comforts of its parlor and sleeping-cars are equal to the very best. Pullman cars run through to and from St. Louis and Chicago.

California travelers choosing this route east, will include Washington, Baltimore, Philadelphia and New York on one ticket, with their numerous scenes and objects of interest.

From Philadelphia.—Tourists uniformly prefer the Pennsylvania Central, though many often wish to visit Baltimore and Washington, and thence see the scenery along the Baltimore and Ohio Railroad, and go westward *via* Cincinnati to St. Louis.

From Baltimore and Washington.— Tourists have choice of either the Northern Central with Pennsylvania Central connections, or the Baltimore and Ohio Railroad. Pullman cars run on either road.

From Boston.—Wagner sleeping-cars run direct over the Boston and Albany Railroad, to Rochester, N. Y., and usually through to Chicago. Though this is an exceedingly convenient route, yet it gives no scenery of consequence. Tourists who desire the best scenery will do well to come direct to New York, the ride by steamer being always pleasant; and from New York make their start, the pleasantest time for departure always being on the fast special express in the morning.

From Cincinnati,—tourists have choice of two routes; 1st, *via* Ohio and Mississippi Railroad, direct to St. Louis, passing over the famous St. Louis Bridge, with omnibus transfer to other railroads; or, 2d, *via* Indianapolis, Bloomington and Western Railroad, which run trains direct to Burlington, Ia., or to Chicago. Pullman sleeping-cars run on either route.

From Chicago,—three roads run across Iowa direct to Council Bluffs.

The Chicago, Rock Island and Pacific Railroad—crosses the Mississippi River at Davenport. The view from the Railroad bridge is very beautiful, and the scenery along the whole line, especially through Iowa, is very beautiful. It is the Central Line West from Chicago, and especially noted for excellent railroad management. The Palace sleeping Cars of this line are owned by the Company and unexcelled in comfort and beauty, while the charges between Chicago are less than routes of other Sleeping Cars. The Road Bed is extremely fine, being laid with Steel Rails.

An excellent feature consists in the Dining Cars, where meals are served of unexcelled merit and remarkable cheapness, price 75 cents, a great comfort and satisfaction to the traveler.

Through Sleeping Cars run from Chicago westward, morning and evening, to Council Bluffs, Leavenworth, Peoria, and connecting points with other Railroads.

The Chicago, Burlington and Quincy Railroad—crosses the Mississippi at Burlington, Ia., and passes through Southern Iowa. The Pullman Cars are very elegant, and the road popular.

The Chicago and North-western Railroad—crosses the Mississippi at Clinton, Ia. The eating stations on this route are all very fine. The Pullman cars are also very superior.

NOTE.—West of Chicago the Pacific Through Trains leave in the morning, with Sleeping Cars through to Council Bluffs without Change.

From St. Louis—two routes are open to the tourist. *The Missouri Pacific Railroad* runs up on the south side of the Missouri River, with Pullman cars, direct for Kansas City, and also The St. Louis, Kansas City and Northern, on the northern side of the river.

Both of these routes are in direct connection with the *Kansas City, St. Joseph and Council Bluffs Railroad*, run through sleeping-cars from St. Louis direct to Omaha. The sleeping-car between St. Louis and Omaha, runs direct from Omaha depot to Kansas city, and thence alternate nights over each Missouri railroad.

Council Bluffs, Iowa, Railroad Transfer Grounds.—This, as well as Omaha, is a transfer point for all passengers, and the starting point of all trains on the Union Pacific railroad. A recent decision of U. S. Supreme Court, fixes the terminus of the Pacific Railroad on the east side of the Missouri River. The company has complied with the decision, and the necessity for bridge transfer is now entirely removed. At Council Bluffs is also the western terminus of the Iowa Railroads. A Union Depot for all railroads has been erected and all passengers, baggage, mails, freight, etc., and trains for the West, start from this point, as well as Omaha. Passengers, however, usually prefer to go to Omaha for a visit. The city of Council Bluffs is located about three miles east from the Missouri river, and contains a population of 15,000. Its record dates from as early as 1804, when the celebrated explorers, Lewis and Clark, held a council with the Indians, which fact, together with the physical peculiarity of the high bluffs overlooking the town, has given it its name—Council Bluffs.

The city is one of great enterprise, with a large number of public buildings, stores, State institutions, and dwellings, and is the nucleus of a large trade from surrounding Iowa towns, and is supported by a rich agricultural community. It is intimately connected with Omaha—with frequent trains over the bridge, by a railroad ferry, attached to the dummy train, an invention of P. P. Shelby. It will doubtless come more largely hereafter into prominence as a railroad town, though the commercial importance of Omaha, and its trade with the far West, will doubtless be for a long time to come, far superior. The general offices of the Union Pacific Railroad Company will remain at Omaha.

At Council Bluffs the Union Pacific Railroad Company have reserved ample grounds, over 1,000 acres, to accommodate its own traffic and that of connecting railroads, and extensive preparations will be made to accommodate the vast traffic of freights, passengers, baggage and stock, which daily arrives and departs.

Here are also located the stock-grounds of the company, which in time will render the locality a large stock-market. The past year over 4,000 cars of stock were transferred over the bridge, and there is ample room for extension.

Sleeping-Car Expenses.—The tariff to travelers is as follows, with all companies, and all in greenbacks:

One berth, New York to Chicago, one and one-half days, by any route,	$5 00
One berth, New York to Cincinnati, one and one-half days, by Pennsylvania railroad,	4 00
One berth, New York to Cincinnati, one and one-half days, by other routes,	5 00
One berth, New York to St. Louis, two days, by any route,	6 00
One berth, Chicago or St. Louis, to Omaha, by any route,	3 00
One berth, Omaha to Ogden, by Pacific Railroad,	8 00
One berth, Ogden to San Francisco, by Central Pacific Railroad,	6 00

MEALS.

All meals at all railroad dining-stations east of Omaha,	$0 75
Except dinners on Erie and New York Central,	1 00
All meals on Union Pacific Railroad,	1 00
All meals on Central Pacific Railroad, first day, currency,	1 00
All meals on Central Pacific Railroad, at Colfax,	75
All meals on Central Pacific Railroad, Lathrop,	50

Curiosities of History.—To whom the honor belongs of first proposing the plan of a railroad to the Pacific. history can never fully determine. Whitney offered to build it for a grant of thirty miles in width along its track, and it was looked upon as the freaky fancy of a monomaniac. Benton, too, the famous statesman, was once aglow with enthusiasm over the subject, and began to agitate the project, but it was considered the harmless fancy of an old politician. And in 1856, when General Fremont was nominated, the Platform of the National Republican Party contained a clause in its favor—but it was regarded as a piece of cheap electioneering "buncombe," and decidedly absurd. Perhaps the earliest record of a devoted admirer of this project was that of John Plumbe, in 1836. He was a Welshman by birth, an American by education and feeling, a civil engineer by profession, and lived at Dubuque, Ia. He began to agitate the project of a railroad from the great lakes across the Continent to the Territory of Oregon. From that time to his death, in California, several years after the discovery of gold, he never failed to urge his project; earnestly and ardently laboring to bring it before Congress, and attempting to secure a beginning of the great work. To far-seeing statesmen, the idea naturally occurred that in course of time there would arise on the Pacific Coast another empire of trade and commerce and industry, either at San Francisco, or the Puget Sound, which would in time, become the rival of New York and the East, and at once the project was taken up and encouraged by Carver, Wilkes, Benton, Whitney, Burton and others; but all such ideas met with indifference and ridicule.

In 1844, when Fremont made his famous explorations across the plains, which has earned him 'so world-wide a reputation, so little was known of the geography of that country, that his reports were considered an immense acquisition to the collection of books of physical knowledge of our country. This section was fully 2,300 miles in distance, entirely vacant, no settlement, entirely occupied by roving bands of Indians, and the undisturbed home of the buffalo and antelope. In that year Chicago was but an obscure village, on a prairie without a single inhabitant. And not a single line of railroad was built from the Atlantic westward beyond the Alleghanies, and on the Pacific only one American flag covered a feeble colony. The discovery of gold in California had its effect in directing public attention to the unknown riches of its Western border; and at last Congress woke up to the need of thorough explorations and investigations. In March, 1853, Congress made its first appropriation to explore the Far West, and ascertain if there was really a practicable route to the Pacific. In 1854, Congress appropriated $190,000 additional; and, as a result,

nine surveying parties were organized and pursued their work. Ten routes were surveyed between the 32d and 49th parallel of latitude; the eastern ends ranging all the way from Fulton, Ark., to St. Paul, Minn.,—and the western terminal points from San Diego to Puget Sound. The lengths of these routes varied from 1,533 to 2,290 miles.

The continued gold discoveries brought an immense flow of population to the Pacific Coast, and California, more alive to the necessities of such roads than the East, after numerous agitations, at last really made the first initiatory experiment. Early in 1861 there was organized at Sacramento, Cal., the Central Pacific Railroad Company, who by the appointment of T. D. Judah, as chief engineer, began the first and most thorough railroad survey ever made on the Sierras.

Congress then woke up, and in July, 1862, the first national charter was granted. As a curious fact in the act—the utmost limit of time allowed for the completion of the road was fixed at July 1, 1876. In October, 1863, the preliminary organization of the company was completed. A capital of one hundred million dollars authorized, and the first contract for construction begun in 1864, but no practical progress was made till 1865, when on the 5th of November, the first ceremony of breaking ground, at Omaha, was celebrated. Then was begun the great work ; the rapid progress of which afterward was a world-wide sensation, astounding engineers, capitalists and even governments, with the almost reckless daring of construction.

Necessity and Benefits to the Government.

From 1850 to 1860, the population of the far Western States and Territories increased from a mere handful to the large number of 554,301 persons, and in the whole area of 2,000 miles there had been built only 232 miles of telegraph, and 32 miles of railway. The United States Government had established forts and trading stations, and the year 1870 saw the completion of the Pacific Railroad line, Congress and the whole country were astonished to see the rapid rate of development, and the enormous expense of government military service. In that year the population had increased to 1,011,971, there had been built over 13,000 miles of telegraph lines ; there were completed over 4,000 miles of railroad ; all representing the gigantic capital of $363,750,000. In the reports of distinguished statesmen to the United States Senate, occur these remarks which show the spirit of the times then Senator Stewart of California, says :

"The cost of the overland service for the whole period, from the acquisition of our Pacific Coast possessions down to the completion of the Pacific Railroad was $8,000,000 per annum, and constantly increasing."

As a curious fact of national economy, these figures will show the result of the Pacific Rail road in saving to the United States Government:

Since the building of the road, the cost of transportation to the government has been as follows:

Amount cash paid to railroad companies for one-half charge of transportation per year, about $1,200,000 per annum, say for 7 years—1869 to 1876,	$8,400,000
The cost to the government of military transportation in 1870, was $8,000,000 per annum, and increasing over $1,000,000 per year. In 1876, would have been over $11,000,000. Average for 7 years, at $10,000,000 per year,	$70,000,000
Total saving in 7 years to United States Government,	$62,600,000
The actual amount of interest during this time paid by the United States Treasury on bonds issued in behalf of the railroad, average interest, $3,897, 129 per year. Total for 7 years,	$27,279,906
Net profit over all expenses to United States,	$42,320,094

These figures do not include vast amounts of incidental items which would have been of incalculable trouble, or immense expense to the United States, such as the indemnities constantly being paid by the United States for destruction of life and private property by Indians; also depredations of Indians on property in government service, increased mail facilities and decreased mail expenses, prevention of Indian wars, the rapid sale of public lands, and the energetic development of the mining interests of all the Territories.

If these can all be correctly estimated, the net gain to the United States by the building of the Pacific Railroad, is over *fifty millions of dollars.*

Hon. Henry Wilson, in a speech before the Senate, Thirty-seventh Congress, boldly said: " I give no grudging vote in giving away either money or land. I would sink $100,000,000 to build the road, and do it most cheerfully, and think I had done a great thing for my country. What are $75,000,000 or $100,000,000 in opening a railroad across the central regions of this Continent, that shall connect the people of the Atlantic and Pacific, and bind us together? Nothing. As to the lands, I do not grudge them."

It is a significant fact, that while the heat and activity of Congressional discussion was most earnest in aid and encouragement of the project, the following sentiments were unanimously entertained by all the members of Congress:

1. That the road was a *necessity* to the government, and if not built by private capital, must be built in time with public funds alone.

2. To encourage the capitalists of the country to come forward and aid the project, the government were willing to give one-half the funds necessary as a loan, and were then merely doing the least part of the whole.

3. That no expectations were entertained that

the road would ever, from its own means, be able to refund the advance made by the United States, and no other thought was ever entertained, save of the benefits to accrue to the public from the opening of this grand highway of national interest. No expectations were formed of the ability of the company to pay or repay the interest on the loan, but one thought was considered, that the building of the road was ample compensation and service in its vast aid to industry, and its saving in transportation.

As editor of this Guide, knowing well the resources of the Far West, we positively assert that the government has already, in seven years, realized in both savings and sales, enough money to liquidate one-third the whole principal, and accrued interest of the government loan, and in less than twenty years from the opening of the road, the government gain will be greater than the whole of the financial aid it has ever given. The Pacific Railroad is the right-hand saving power of the United States.

Discouragements. — Notwithstanding all that the government had done to encourage it (by speeches), the work languished. Capitalists doubted it. The great war of the rebellion attracted the attention of every one, and the government, after its first impulses, grew indifferent. A few bold men determined to work incessantly for its completion. And one of the results of the great war was the conviction in the minds of every one — of a closer Union of the States. " *Who knows,*" said one, " *but California and the whole Pacific Coast may secede, and where are we then? We can do nothing to retain them. The Pacific railway must be built. It shall be built to keep our country together.*"

The chief engineer of the railroad, Gen. G. M. Dodge, in complimenting the directors on the day of the completion of the last mile of track, says:

" The country is evidently satisfied that you accomplished wonders, and have achieved a work which will be a monument to your energy, your ability, and to your devotion to the enterprise, through all its gloomy, as well as bright periods, for it is notorious that notwithstanding the aid of the government, there was so little faith in the enterprise, that its dark days—when your private fortunes, and your all was staked on the success of the project—far exceeded those of sunshine, faith and confidence."

The lack of confidence in the project, even in the West, was so great that even in localities which were to be specially benefitted by its construction, the laborers even demanded their pay *before* they would perform their day's work, so little faith had they in the payment of their wages, or in the ability of the company to succeed in their efforts.

Probably no enterprise in the world has been so maligned, misrepresented and criticised as this, but now it is, by unbiased minds, pronounced, almost without exception, the best new road in the United States.

Rapid Progress.—Though chartered in 1862, yet the first grading was not done until 1864, and the first rail laid in July, 1865. At that time there was no railroad communication from the East; a gap of 140 miles existed between Omaha and Des Moines, and over this it was impossible to get supplies.

For 500 miles westward of the Missouri River, the country was completely destitute of timber, fuel, or any material with which to build or maintain a road, save the bare sand for the road-bed itself, everything had to be transported by teams or steamboats, hundreds and thousands of miles. Labor, and everything made by labor, was scarce and high.

Railroad ties were cut in Michigan and Pennsylvania, and shipped to Omaha at a cost, often, of $2.50 per tie. Even the splendid engine, of seventy horse-power, used at Omaha for the company's works, was transported in *wagons* across the prairies from Des Moines, the only way to get it. Shops had to be built, forges erected, and machinery put in place, and the supplies, even, for the subsistence of the laborers had to be brought by river from the East; yet it was all done.

As the Westerners concisely express it, "*The wind work had all been done, and grading now began.*"

In 1865, 40 miles of track were laid to Fremont. In 1866, 260 miles were laid. In 1867, 240 miles were laid, which included the ascent to Sherman. By January 1, 1868, there had been completed 540 miles. In 1868, to May 10, 1869, 555 miles more were laid, and the road finished—seven years in advance of the time set by Congress, and the time actually spent in construction was just *three years, six months, and ten days*.

To show the enormous amount of materials required in the Union Pacific Railroad alone, there were used in its construction 300,000 tons of iron rails, 1,700,000 fish-plates, 6,800,000 bolts, 6,126,375 cross-ties, 23,505,500 spikes.

Fast Building.—Day after day the average rate of building rose from one to two, three and five miles. Many will remember the daily thrill of excitement as the morning journals in the East made the announcements of so many more miles nearer the end, and as the number of completed miles, printed in the widely circulated advertisements of the company, reached 1000, the excitement became intense, as the rival roads now were fairly aglow with the heat of competition, and so near each other. In previous months there had existed a little engineering rivalry, good natured, but keen, as to the largest number of miles each could lay in one day. The Union Pacific men laid one day *six* miles; soon after the Central followed suit by laying *seven*,

The Union Pacific retaliated by laying seven and a half; to this the Central sent the announcement that they could lay ten miles in one day; to this Mr. Durant, the vice-president, sent back a wager of $10,000 that it could not be done. The pride and spirit of the Central Pacific had now been challenged, and they prepared for the enormous contest, one of extraordinary magnitude and rapidity. The 29th day of April, 1869, was selected for the decision of the contest, as there then remained but 14 miles of track to bring a meeting of the roads at Promontory Point.

Work began; the ground had already been graded and ties placed in position, and at the signal the cars loaded with rails moved forward. Four men, two on each side, seize with their nippers the ends of the rails, lift from the car and carry them to their place; the car moves steadily along over the rails as fast as they are laid. Immediately after follows a band of men who attach the plate and put the spikes in position; next a force of Chinamen who drive down the spikes solid to their homes, and last another gang of Chinamen with shovels, picks, etc., who ballast the track. The rapidity of all these motions, which required the most active of exercise and alert movements, was at the rate of 144 feet of track to every minute. By 1.30 P. M., the layers had placed *eight miles of track in just six hours.* Resuming work again, after the noon rest, the track-laying progressed, and at 7 P. M., exactly, the Central men finished their task of 10 miles, with 200 feet over. Mr. James Campbell, the superintendent of the division, then seizing a locomotive ran it over the ten miles of new track in forty minutes, and the Union men were satisfied. This was the greatest feat of railroad building ever known in the world, and when it is known how vast the materials required to supply this little stretch of ten miles, the reader is fairly astonished at the endurance of the laborers. To put this material in place over 4,000 men had been constantly employed. The laborers on that day handled 25,800 cross-ties, 3,520 iron rails, 55,000 spikes, 7,040 fish-plates, and 14,080 bolts, the weight of the whole being 4,362,000 pounds. Upon both roads, for a year previous, there had been remarkable activity.

A total force of 20,000 to 25,000 workmen all along the lines, and 5,000 to 6,000 teams had been engaged in grading and laying the track or getting out stone or timber. From 500 to 600 tons of materials were forwarded daily from either end of the lines.

The Sierra Nevadas suddenly became alive with wood-choppers, and at one place on the Truckee River twenty-five saw-mills went into operation in a single week. Upon one railroad 70 to 100 locomotives were in use at one time, constantly bringing materials and supplies. At one time there were 30 vessels *en route* from New York via Cape Horn, with iron, locomotives, rails and

SCENES IN OMAHA.

1. General View of Omaha and the Missouri Valley. 2.—Post-Office. 3.—High School Building.
4.—Grand Central Hotel. 5.—Missouri River Bridge.

rolling stock, destined for the Central Pacific Railroad; and it is a curious fact, that on several consecutive days, more miles of track were ironed by the railroad companies than it was possible for an ox-team to draw a load over. And when at last the great road was completed, the fact suddenly flashed upon the nation that a road once so distrusted, and considered too gigantic to be possible, was constructed an actual distance of 2,221 miles, in *less than five years*, of which all but 100 miles was done between January 1, 1866 and May 10, 1869—*three years, four months and ten days.*

OMAHA.

Railroads.—The first railroad that reached this city from the East was the Chicago and North-Western,—the first train over it arriving on Sunday, January 17, 1867. Then followed the Kansas City, Council Bluffs and St. Joseph, the Chicago, Rock Island and Pacific and the Burlington and Missouri River of Iowa (operated by the Chicago, Burlington and Quincy.) After these came the Sioux City and Pacific, the Omaha and North-Western and the Omaha and South-Western, and the Omaha and Republican Valley. The Omaha and South-Western is now operated by the Burlington and Missouri River Railroad in Nebraska. The latter extends to Lincoln the capital of the State; then westward uniting with the Union Pacific at Kearny Junction. It has a branch from its main lines from Crete to Beatrice, a thriving town near the southern boundary of the State. It also controls another line running from Brownville on the Missouri River, north to Nebraska City, thence west through Lincoln (where it connects with the main line) to York in the central part of the State. The Omaha and North-Western is completed about 40 miles, and follows the Missouri on the west side of that river, north from Omaha. It is being extended every year, and its claim that it will soon be one of the favorite routes to the Black Hills, as its tendency is towards the beautiful valley of the Elkhorn, one of the garden-spots of Nebraska. Other railroads are contemplated, among them the Nebraska Trunk Railroad down the west bank of the Missouri from Omaha to Atchison. When completed it will form close connection with the Missouri Pacific, giving a competing route to St. Louis and the seaboard. At Atchison it will connect with the Atchison, Topeka and Santa Fe, forming an almost direct route through Kansas to the mines of Southern Colorado, New Mexico and Arizona. As the Atchison road is being extended to meet the Southern Pacific, Omaha will have another outlet to the Pacific Coast. Another line is the St. Louis, Chillicothe and Omaha, commonly called "the Chillicothe route." The indications are that it will be fin-

ished soon, which will shorten up the distance to St Louis about 65 miles. The Omaha and Republican Valley operated by the Union Pacific Company, runs from Omaha to David City about 100 miles west, and it is already doing a large and increasing business. It will be extended westward as the country develops, and population increases. A branch of this line is contemplated from Valparaiso to Lincoln.

Besides these railroads, Omaha has the Missouri River on her front, giving the city cheap steam communication from the center of Montana to the Gulf of Mexico, and with the whole Mississippi valley and its tributaries as far East as Pennsylvania. The city has become the most important railroad center west of Chicago and St. Louis, and as the greatest popular "travel center" on the Missouri river, stands unrivaled. As a matter of interest we mention the fact that in 1875 there were 55,000 local arrivals and departures. In 1876 there were 70,000, and in 1878, 73,330. The city is the Eastern gateway of the mineral bearing regions of the West, and the products of British Columbia, the Pacific Coast, the Sandwich Islands and Asia find their way through her limits to the eastern markets. Within a circle having a radius of five hundred miles of which Omaha is the center, there are upwards of 12,000,000 people and 26,000 miles of railroads radiating in every direction. Within this circle is the Black Hills region, whose rapid development is already attracting attention. Beyond this limit on the west, are Western Colorado, the greater part of Wyoming, Utah, Idaho, Montana, Nevada and California. Omaha already has a controlling influence over the greater part of the mineral trade of these States and Territories, of which we shall speak hereafter.

The general offices of the Union Pacific are located here. They are in an elegant building which catches the eye of the traveler as one of the notable objects as he approaches the city. It was completed in 1878, at a cost of $858,453.74, and the citizens are very proud of this fine structure. The general offices of the Burlington and Missouri River in Nebraska, the Omaha and North-Western, the Omaha and South-Western and the Omaha and Republican Valley Railroads are also located here. In addition to these the general agencies of the Chicago, Sioux City, St. Louis and Eastern lines, have handsome offices, which are located in the Grand Central Hotel building. The Blue, Red, Empire and other fast freight lines are represented in the city, and it is probable that the Baltimore and Ohio, Wabash and other competing lines will push their fast freight lines to a connection with the Union Pacific and secure a proportion of the immense trans-continental traffic.

The Omaha and Republican Valley Railroad have taken steps looking to the early completion of a series of railroad lines that will "gridiron" the State. One line will run to Atchison, Kansas. Another to Lincoln, another into the Republican Valley, another to Grand Island and up the Loup Fork, and another to the Nebraska River in the north.

Manufactures.—In manufactures Omaha is now the most extensive manufacturing point on the Missouri river, the amount for 1878 being in the neighborhood of $9,000,00). She has an oil mill which supplies the extensive demand for linseed oil and oil cake, and promotes the growth of flax in Nebraska, necessitating at an early day the erection of flax mills in the city for the manufacture of that article; extensive white lead works, completed in the spring of 1878, a safe factory, several breweries, two distilleries, foundries and machine shops, carriage and wagon shops; three packing houses, flour mills and other manufactories in active operation or contemplated. Among the latter, are a nail mill, starch factory, etc., etc. Among the principal establishments in operation are the machine shops, car works and foundry of the Union Pacific Railroad, and the Omaha smelting works. The shops of the railroad occupy, with the roundhouse, about thirty acres of land on the bottom adjoining the table land on which most of the city proper is built. Their disbursements amount to $2,60),000 per annum for labor and material, while for office and manual labor alone the Union Pacific pays out annually in Omaha over one million dollars. The value of this business and the location of these shops to the city can therefore readily be seen, and are no small factors in Omaha's prosperity.

Business of Omaha — Facts Interesting and Curious.—When Omaha was first entitled to the honor of a post-office, the story is told that the first postmaster (still living in the city) used his hat for a post-office which he naturally carried with him wherever he went delivering the mail to anxious individuals who were waiting eagerly for him, or chased and overtook him. Twenty years after, Omaha possesses a handsome stone post-office and custom house worth $350,000, (in which there is a bonded warehouse,) and the finest building west of the Mississippi river. The post office has frequently handled twenty tons of overland and local mail matter per day. The total receipts at this post-office for 1878 were about $1,500,000 and the total number of letters, newspapers, and postal cards collected and delivered was 1,695,668. In 1861, the first telegraph reached Omaha, and its only office was, for several years, the terminus of the Pacific Telegraph. Now there are thirty telegraph wires radiating in all directions; fifteen offices, employing forty operators. The number of messages per day averages 4,600, of which one third relates to Pacific Railroad business, and including press dispatches, local and

Pacific coast, 17,800,000 words were repeated. The total value of school property in Omaha is $430,975, and the city is growing so rapidly that several more buildings are needed.

Omaha is the headquarters of the army of the Platte, and disburses about $1,000,000, besides an annual transportation account with the Union Pacific Railroad of $650,0,0. The office of Internal Revenue Collector for Nebraska is also located here. In 1865, Omaha did not have a single manufacturing establishment. In 1877, her manufactures amounted to about $9,000,000, the annual increase being from twenty to twenty-five per cent. Here are located the largest smelting and refining works on the North American Continent; the Omaha smelting works, who employ 150 men and do an annual business of $5,500,000. Seven breweries turn out 20.000 barrels of beer. One distillery pays the government $532,000 per year, and there are upward of fifty smaller enterprises, among which is a notable industry, the manufacture of brick: over 500,000,000 brick being turned out of four brick yards. The bank capital and surplus exceed $820,000. In overland times before the building of the Pacific Railroad, or just at its commencement, the wholesale trade of Omaha was wonderful. Single houses handling as much as $3,000,000. Since that time the courses of trade have been so divided, that the largest sales now of any wholesale establishment do not exceed $1.500,000.

Perhaps the best index of the enormous trade Omaha is gaining is in the increase of the shipments and receipts of live stock, grain, currency, precious metals, etc., etc.

The receipts of cattle at Omaha were as follows:

	NO.	INCREASE.
During 1876,	60,300	
" 1877,	95,590	35,200

The estimates place the receipts at 150.000 for 1879, and large stock yards will be built the present year. In 1874. the grain business amounted to about 300,000 bushels per annum. In six months ending March, the receipts amounted to 2,250,000 bushels and the corn crop of the last year had not then begun to move. Omaha has two grain elevators, but the greatest need of the trade is an elevator with a storage capacity of 1,000,000 bushels.

As to the movements of the precious metals into and through Omaha, we find that the Black Hills ores are appearing freely in the city, and since the opening of the Colorado Central Railroad from Cheyenne to Denver, the Union Pacific is getting its share of the ore and base bullion of that state. It is a noticeable fact that all of the shipments of fine gold and silver from New Mexico now find their way to the eastern cities through Omaha. The gold and silver product of the country west of Omaha is steadily increasing as will be seen by reference to these statistics :

GOLD AND SILVER PRODUCT OF THE WEST.

1869,	$61,500,000	1874,	$72,428,206
1870,	66,000,000	1875,	75,789,057
1871,	66,663,000	1876,	85,835,173
1872,	63,943,877	1877,	93,336,504
1873,	71,642,523		

Showing an increase in the gold and silver production in 1877 over 1869 of $31,836,504. In 1877, the estimated lead yield was $5,085,250, of which the Omaha smelting works manufactured $1,500,000 into lead bars for shipment east. This amount being equal to the lead yield of Illinois and Missouri combined.

In tracing the routes over which the precious metals of Colorado, New Mexico, Utah, Nevada and the West come, they must not be considered *possible and temporary*, but as the actual and permanent routes over which these metals have been passing into and through Omaha, viz. :

MOVEMENT OF BULLION AND ORES.

During	1873,	$21,500,000
"	1874,	41,907,090
"	1875,	49,848,542
"	1876,	56,733,100
"	1877,	50,060,368

Showing an increase in 1877 over 1873 of $28,560,368.

The increase in the eastward flow of gold in 1877 over 1876 was $5,227,102. The decrease in silver for the same time owing to the Asiatic demand and the coinage of trade dollars at San Francisco, was $11,890,834. Had not these influences been at work, it is safe to assume that the passage of gold and silver into and through Omaha for 1877 would have amounted to $64,000,000 or two-thirds of the entire product of the country. This does not include the amount contained in the ore, base bullion and lead passing over the Union Pacific roads :

During	1875,	64,429,400 pounds.
"	1876,	71,758,352 "
"	1877,	111,006,050 "

Showing an increase in 1877 over 1875 of 46,576,650 pounds. Of the amount in 1875, the Omaha smelting works received 29,638,826 pounds. The gain being proportionate for the two succeeding years. In 1875, not a car load of ore or bullion was handled at Kansas City from the Kansas Pacific Railroad. In 1877 the receipts of ore in that city were 23,964,250 pounds, mostly for shipment east.

The Omaha smelting works are the largest on the Continent, as previously stated. They are being constantly enlarged to meet the increasing demands of business. In 1875 the works in Colorado reduced $1,650,000 of ore and bullion. In 1874, the Omaha works reduced $$2,135,000. In 1875, $4,028,314. In 1876, $4,832,000. In 1877, $5,500,000. For 1875-76-77 their lead manufacture amounted to 35,262 tons or 70,524,000

pounds, so that Omaha now produces about one sixth of all the lead used in the United States. Heretofore this lead has been shipped east, but the new white lead works will use a large portion of it and in the near future there is no reason why Omaha may not be one of the principal lead manufacturing markets in the country. The statement of currency received at and shipped from Omaha is as follows, viz. :

In	1873,	$21,944,807.20
"	1874,	27,431,000.00
"	1875,	34,466,700.20
"	1876,	33,655,215.00
"	1877,	39,993,260.00

Showing an increase in 1877 over 1873 of $18,048,452.80

There was deposited in the Omaha banks, viz. :

During	1874,	$55,308,960.48
"	1875,	63,333,492.06
"	1876,	72,808,500.00
"	1877,	80,548,485.50

Showing an increase in 1877 over 1874 of $25,239,524.52.

Exchange sold by the same :

During	1874,	$25,768,426.92
"	1877,	38,181,671.38

Showing an increase in 1877 over 1874 of $12,413,244.46.

The public improvements show this record :

During	1875,	$360,000
"	1876,	238,000
"	1877,	785,000

An increase in 1877 over 1875 of $425,000; over 1876, $547,000. Careful estimates place the improvement record of this year at no less than $1,000,000. Judging by the tide of immigration now rushing into Nebraska through the efforts of eastern colonization societies and others, the realization will go beyond that figure, as the trade of the city is rapidly extending in every direction and the indications are that the present will be the most prosperous year in the history of the West.

In 1860, the transportation trade of Omaha amounted to 732,000 pounds. In 1877, the receipts and shipments from and to the West passing into and through Omaha were 2,172,720,000 pounds. In 1875, the Omaha merchants imported 17,450 carloads of merchandise.

The mercantile and manufacturing trade of the city in round numbers is as follows :

In	1875,	$17,000,000
"	1876,	25,000,000
"	1877,	30,000,000

This increase of $13,000,000 in two years was during a period of universal depression. But notwithstanding the hard times, Omaha has become the chief commercial city of the Missouri valley.

The "Omaha Union Stock Yards" were incorporated May 4, 1878, and began at once the erection of large and well arranged yards, on their grounds located on the Union Pacific track near the city limits. A dummy car line extending from the Union depot to Hanscom Park, connects the yards with the hotels and banks of the city. The packing, slaughtering and canning of beef is destined to grow into immense proportions at this point, as also undoubtedly will tanning and glue manufacture. The officers of the Union Stock Yards are Wm. A. Paxton, President ; Herman Kountze, Vice-President ; Jas. L. Lovett. General Manager : W. J. Broatch, Treasurer, and W. C. B. Allen, Secretary.

The U. P. R. R. Bridge Across the Missouri River.—The huge bridge, which spans the Missouri, is a fitting entrance to the wonders beyond—a mechanical wonder of itself, it fills every traveler with a sense of awe and majesty, as the first great scene of the overland journey.

The last piece of iron of the last span which completed the bridge was fastened in its place on the 20th of February, 1872. Previous to that time, all passengers and traffic were transferred across the treacherous and shifting shores of the Missouri River in steam-boats with flat keel, and with the ever-shifting currents and sand-bars, safe landings were always uncertain. The bridge comprises 11 spans, each span 250 feet in length, and elevated 50 feet above high water-mark. These spans are supported by one stone masonry abutment, and 11 piers with 22 cast-iron columns; each pier is 8 1-2 feet in diameter, and made of cast-iron in tubes one and three-fourths inches in thickness, 10 feet in length, with a weight of eight tons. As fast as the tubes of the columns are sunk, they are fitted together, seams made air-tight, and process continued till the complete depth and height is attained. During the building of the bridge from February, 1869, when work first commenced, until completion in 1872 (excepting a period of eight months suspension), about 500 men were constantly employed. Ten steam-engines were in use for the purpose of operating the pneumatic works to hoist the cylinders, help put the superstructure into position, to drive piles for temporary platforms and bridges, and to excavate sand within the columns. The columns were sunk into the bed of the river after being placed in correct position by the following method : The top of the column being made perfectly air-tight, all water beneath is forced out by pneumatic pressure. Then descending into the interior, a force of workmen excavate the sand and earth, filling buckets which are quickly hoisted upwards by the engines. When the excavation has reached one or more feet, the column sinks gradually inch by inch, more or less rapidly, until a solid bottom is reached.

The least time in which any column was sunk to bed rock from the commencement of the pneumatic process was seven days, and the greatest single depth of sinking at one time was 17 feet.

The greatest depth below low water which was reached by any column, at bed rock, was 82 feet. The greatest pressure to which the men working in the columns were subjected, was 54 pounds per square inch in excess of the atmosphere. When solid foundation is once obtained, the interior of the columns are filled with solid stone concrete for about 25 feet, and thence upward with cement masonry, till the bridge is reached.

The total length of the iron structure of the bridge is 2,750 feet. The eastern approach is by an embankment of gradual ascent one and a half miles in length, commencing east of the Transfer grounds, and almost at Council Bluffs, and thence ascending at the rate of 35 feet to the mile to the bridge.

Metumwa.—The old depot grounds of the Union Pacific Railroad were on the bank of the river immediately beneath the bridge. When this was constructed, in order to connect the bridge and main line of the railroad, it was necessary to construct, directly through the city, a branch line of road 7,000 feet in length, and construct a new depot on higher ground, of which as a result, witness the handsome, new structure, and spacious roof, and convenient waiting-rooms. From the first abutment to the bank, a trestle-work of 700 feet more, 60 feet in height was constructed; thus the entire length of the bridge, with necessary approaches, is 9,950 feet. Total cost is supposed to be about $2,650,000, and the annual revenue about $400,000. The bridge has figured notably in the discussions of Congress, whether or not it should be considered a part of the Union Pacific Railroad. The recent decision of the United States Supreme Court has at last declared it so to be, and with this is done away entirely the "Omaha Bridge Transfer" of the past.

Preparing for the Westward Trip.—Having rested and visited the principal points of interest in Omaha, you will be ready to take a fresh start. Repairing to the new depot, finished, at the crossing of Ninth street, you will find one of the most magnificent trains of cars made up by any railroad in the United States. Everything connected with them is first-class. Pullman sleeping-coaches are attached to all express trains, and all travelers know how finely they are furnished, and how they tend to relieve the wearisome monotony of tedious days in the journey from ocean to ocean. At this depot you will find the waiting-rooms, ticket-offices, baggage-rooms, lunch-stands, news and bookstand, together with one of the best kept eating-houses in the country. You will find gentlemanly attendants at all these places, ready to give you any information, and cheerfully answer your questions. If you have a little time, step into the Union Pacific Land office adjoining the depot, on the east, and see some of the productions of this prolific western soil. If you have come from the far East. it has been a slightly uphill journey all the way, and you are now at an elevation of 966 feet above the sea. If the weather is pleasant, you may already begin to feel the exhilarating effect of western breezes, and comparatively dry atmosphere. With books and papers to while away your leisure hours, you are finally ready for the start. The bell rings, the whistle shrieks, and off you go. The road first winds up a little valley, passing the Bridge Junction 1.5 (one and five-tenths) miles to

Summit Siding,— 3.2 miles from Omaha; elevation 1,142 feet. This place, you will observe by these figures, is reached by a heavy up grade. You are 176 feet higher than when you first started, and but little over three miles away. Here is a deep cut through the hill, and beyond it you strike Mud Creek Valley with a down grade for a few miles. This creek and the road run south on a line nearly parallel with, and about two and a half miles from, the Missouri River until the next station is reached.

Gilmore.—It is 9.5 miles from Omaha, with only 10 feet difference in *elevation*—976 feet. The valley is quite thickly settled, and as you look out on the left

" GOOD-BYE."

side of the cars, about four miles from Omaha, you will see a saloon called Half-Way House. At about this point you leave Douglas County and enter Sarpy County. Gilmore was named after an old resident of that locality, now dead. Here you are some nine miles south of Omaha, but only about three west of the Missouri River. Here you will first see what are called the bottom lands of Nebraska. They are as rich as any lands on this Continent. as the remarkable crops raised thereon fully attest. From this station you turn nearly due west, and

pass over the lower circle of what is called the ox-bow.

Papillion,— 14.5 miles from Omaha ; *elevation 972 feet*, is the next station, and is a thriving little town (pronounced Pa-pil-yo). It derives its name from the creek on whose banks it is situated. This creek was named by Lewis and Clark in their expedition to Oregon, in 1804, and is derived from a Latin word which means butterfly. The main branch was crossed a little west of Gilmore. It empties into the Missouri River about one mile north of the Platte River. It is reported that the early explorers named, saw an immense number of butterflies in the muddy and wet places near its mouth, and hence the name. These gentlemen explored this stream to its source, near the Elkhorn River. The town was laid out in the fall of 1869 by Dr. Beadle, and is the permanent county-seat of Sarpy County. It has a fine brick court-house, and a brick school-house, hotels, flouring mills and a grain ware-house; is located as are all the towns on the first two hundred miles of this road, in the midst of a rich agricultural country. Sarpy County has two newspapers — one the *Papillion Times*, published weekly at this place, and the other. the *Sarpy County Sentinel*, published at Sarpy Center, some five miles in the country from this station. Sarpy is one of the best settled counties in Nebraska, and has a property valuation of over $3,000,000.

Millard—is named for Hon. Ezra Millard, president of the Omaha National Bank, who has considerable landed property here. The station-house is comparatively new, and there are a few other buildings recently erected. It is pleasantly located, and, like all western towns, has plenty of room to grow. It is 20.9 miles from

Omaha ; elevation, 1,047 feet. Evidences of thrift are everywhere visible as you cast your eyes over the rolling prairies, and yet there is ample room for all who desire to locate in this vicinity. You have again crossed the boundary line of Sarpy County, which is a mile or two south-east of Millard, and are again in the County of Douglas.

Elkhorn.—28.9 miles from Omaha, elevation 1,150 feet. This is a growing town, and does a large business in grain ; it has an elevator, grain warehouses, two stores, a Catholic church, good school-house, and a hotel. You are now near the famous Elkhorn Valley and River. By a deep cut, the railroad makes its way through the bluff or hill on the east side of this stream, about a mile from the station,

The elevation of Waterloo is laid down at 1,140 feet. The town has a fine water-power which has been improved by the erection of a large flouring-mill. It also has two steam flouring-mills, and a new depot. At this point you enter the Platte Valley, of which so much has been written and which occupies such a prominent place in the history of the country. The Elkhorn and Platte Rivers form a junction a few miles south of this point, and the banks of these streams are more or less studded with timber, mostly cottonwood. In fact, the Elkhorn has considerable timber along its banks.

Valley—is 35 2 miles from Omaha, and is 1,120 feet above the sea. It has a store and hotel, and is the center of a rich farming dis-

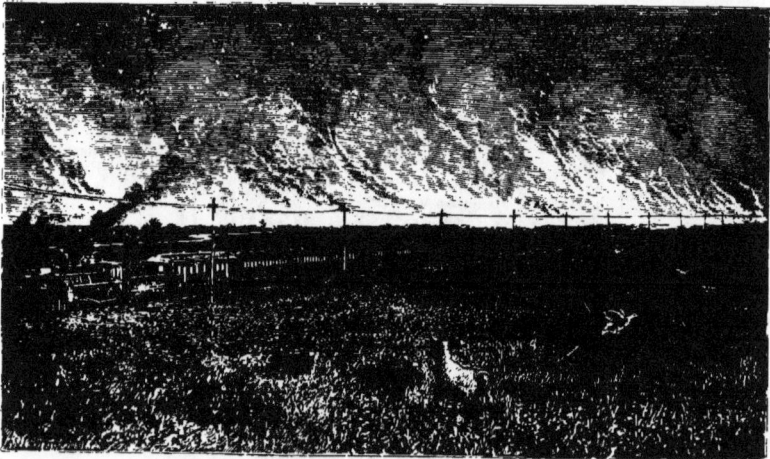

NIGHT SCENE. PRAIRIE ON FIRE.

and then on a down grade you glide into the valley. The rolling prairies are now behind you and south, beyond the Platte River, which for the first time comes into view. Crossing the Elkhorn River you arrive at

Waterloo,—30.9 miles from Omaha, and only two miles from the last station. A few years since, a train was thrown from the bridge spoken of, by reason of the high water of a freshet. This train had one car of either young fish or fish-eggs in transit ; the contents of this car were of course lost in the river, and since that time the Elkhorn abounds in pike, pickerel, bass, sunfish and perch. What the California streams lost by this disaster the Elkhorn gained, as these fish have increased rapidly in this stream, where they were previously unknown.

trict. The land seems low, and one would easily gain the impression that the soil here was very wet, but after digging through the black surface soil two or three feet you come to just such sand as is found in the channel of the Platte. In fact, the whole Platte Valley is underdrained by this river, and this is one reason why surface water from hard and extensive rains so quickly disappear, and why the land is able to produce such good crops in a dry season. Water is obtained anywhere in this valley by sinking what are called drive-wells, from six to twenty feet. Wind-mills are also extensively used by large farmers, who have stock which they confine upon their premises, and which otherwise they would have to drive some distance for water. The Omaha and Republican Valley Railroad runs to Wahoo and David City, soon to be extended to Lincoln.

Riverside,—which is 4i.4 miles from Omaha, with an elevation of about 1,140 feet. It will eventually become a station, as many trains already meet and pass here.

Prairie Fires.—During the first night's ride westward from Omaha, the traveler, as he gazes out of his car window (which he can easily do while reclining in his berth) will often find his curious attention rewarded by a sight of one of the most awful, yet grandest scenes of prairie life. The prairies, which in the day-time to some, seemed dry, dull, uninteresting, occasionally give place at night, to the lurid play of the fire-fiend, and the heavens and horizon seem like a furnace. A prairie on fire is a fearfully exciting and fear-stirring sight. Cheeks blanch as the wind sweeps its volume toward the observer, or across his track. Full in the distance is seen the long line of bright flame stretching for miles, with its broad band of dark smoke-clouds above. As the train comes near, the flames leap higher, and the smoke ascends higher, and on their dark bosom is reflected the fires' brilliantly-tinged light. Sweeping away for miles towards the bluffs, the fire jumps with the wind, and the flames leap 20 to 30, or more feet into the air, and for miles brighten the prairies with tne awful sight. We have never seen anything of prairie life or scenery possessing such majestic brilliance as the night glows, and rapid advances of a prairie fire. Far out on the prairies, beyond the settlements, the prairie fires, (usually set on fire by the sparks from the locomotives) rage unchecked for miles and miles, but nearer to the little settlements, where the cabins have just been set up, the fire is their deadliest and most dreaded enemy. No words can describe, no pencil paint the look of terror when the settler beholds advancing toward him the fire-fiend, for which .he is unprepared and unprotected. When the first sign of the advancing fire is given, all hands turn out; either a counter fire is started, which, eating from the settler's ranch, in the face of the wind, toward the grander coming volume, takes away its force, and leaves it nothing to feed upon, or furrows are broken with the plow around the settler's home. The cool earth thrown up, and all the grass beyond this is fired, while the little home enclosed within, is safe. A curious feature of prairie fires is, that the buffalo grass, the next season, is darker and richer than ever before; and lower down, in sections where the prairie fires are carefully kept off, trees, shrubs, bushes, etc., of many varieties, grow up spontaneously,

which never were seen before. So long as prairie fires rage, nothing will grow but the little tufts of prairie grass. Wherever the prairie fire ceases or is kept restrained, vegetation of all description as far west as the Platte, is completely changed. In the fall of the year these fires are most frequent; and creating a strong current or breeze by their own heat, they advance with the rapidity often of a locomotive, 20 or more miles an hour, and their terrible lurid light by night, and blackened path left behind, as seen next day by the traveler, are sights never to be forgotten.

In the lower river counties a prairie fire often originates from the careless dropping of a match, or the ashes shaken from a pipe. The little spark touches the dry grass like tinder—the constant breeze fans the little flame, and five minutes after it has covered yards. The loss to tillers of the soil is often appalling. One of General Sherman's veterans, in describing a prairie fire to a visitor, raising himself to his full six feet height, and with eye flashing as in battle excitement, said : " Mr. C., if I should catch a man firing the prairie at this time, as God helps me, I would shoot him down in his deed." A traveler riding on the prairie said, " only a few miles from me an emigrant, traveling in his close-covered wagon "*with the wind,*" was overtaken by the flames coming down on him unseen. Horses, family, wagon, were all destroyed in a moment, and himself barely lived long enough to tell the tale. Nearly every night in autumn the prairies of the boundless West, show either the near or distant glow of a fire, which in extent has the appearance of another burning Chicago.

" BUSTED."

Pike's Peak or Bust.—This expression has become widely known, and received its origin as

REPRESENTATIVE MEN OF THE UNION PACIFIC RAILROAD.

follows:—At the time of the opening of the Pike's Peak excitement in gold diggings, two pioneers made themselves conspicuous by painting in large letters on the side of their wagon cover:—"*Pike's Peak or Bust.*" In their haste to reach this, the newly discovered Eldorado, they scorned all safety and protection offered by the " train " and traveled alone, and on their "own hook."

For days and weeks they escaped the dangers attending their folly, and passed unharmed until they reached the roving ground of the bloody Sioux. Here they were surrounded and cruelly and wantonly murdered; their bodies were driven through with arrows, and pinned to the earth, and left to the sunshine and storms of the skies.

Fremont—is 46.5 miles from Omaha, and has an elevation of 1,176 feet. It is the county-seat of Dodge County, and has a population of full 3,000. In the year 1875, over $100,000 were expended in buildings in this growing young city. It has never, so far as population is concerned, experienced what may be called a great rush—its growth having been slow and steady. It is located near the south-east corner of the county. Originally the town comprised a whole section of land, but was afterwards reduced to about half a section. The town company was organized on the 26th day of August, 1856, and in that and the following year, thirteen log houses were built. John C. Hormel built the first frame house in 1857. The Union Pacific reached the town on the 24th day of January, 1866, nearly ten years after it was first laid out, and trains ran to it regularly, though the track was laid some 11 miles beyond, when work ceased for that winter. The Sioux City and Pacific road was completed to Fremont late in the fall of 1868. In the expectations of the residents, it was then to become a railroad center, and lots were sold at large prices. This last-named road runs from Blair on the Missouri River, where it crosses said stream and forms a junction with the Chicago and North-western. It then runs north on the east side of said river, to Sioux City. The Elkhorn Valley Railroad completed the first ten miles of its track in 1869, and the balance, some 50 miles, was finished to Wisner in the following year. This road is one of the natural routes to the Black Hills, and it is now stated that it will soon be extended in that direction. It will continue up the Elkhorn Valley to near its source, and then crossing the divide, will strike into the Niobrara Valley, thence westward until the Black Hills are reached. This road is a feeder to Fremont, and very valuable to its trade. The Atchison and Nebraska Railroad, is to be extended from Lincoln to this place, during the present year (1876). The city will then have a direct line to St. Louis and the South, with two direct lines to Chicago and the East. Other railroad

projects are contemplated, which will make this place in reality a railroad center.

Fremont has a large, new hotel, the Occidental, and several smaller ones ; has the finest opera house in the West, and the largest and finest dry-goods house in the State. It has five or six church edifices, and an elegant public school building, two banks, three or four elevators, a steam flouring mill, extensive broom factories, and two or three manufacturing establishments where headers are made. It also has a foundry and machine-shop. It is now a regular eating station on the railroad, all passenger trains east or west stopping here for dinner, which is really most abundant and excellent.

Fremont is virtually located at the junction of the Elkhorn and Platte Valleys, and from its position naturally controls a large scope of country. Its people are industrious, wide-awake and energetic. It is in the midst of a thickly-settled region, and its future prospects are very flattering.

Fremont has two newspapers — the *Fremont Herald* (daily and weekly), and the *Fremont Tribune* (weekly). The latter was first established, and probably has the largest circulation. The enterprise of newspapers in these western towns, contribute very largely to their growth and prosperity. The town is the fourth in size and population in the State.

The Elkhorn Valley is between two and three hundred miles in length, is well timbered and remarkably fertile, and the railroad which is to do the carrying business of this valley, has its terminus at Fremont.

The Great Platte Valley.—You have now passed over a few miles of the great Platte Valley. At Fremont it spreads out wonderfully, and for the first two hundred miles varies in width from five to fifteen miles. Through nearly all its eastern course, this river hugs the bluffs on its southern side. These bluffs as well as those more distant on the northern side of the valley, are plainly visible from the cars. Before the road was built, this valley was the great highway of overland travel to Colorado, Utah, California, and Oregon. Immense trains of wagons, heavily freighted, have passed over it, in their slow and tedious journeyings towards the setting sun. Leaving the Missouri at different points, the routes nearly all converged in the Platte Valley, and thence westward to their destination. The luxuriant grasses, and the proximity to water, made this the favorite route. It has also been the scene of deadly conflicts with the savages, and the bones of many a wanderer lie bleaching in the air, or are buried beneath some rough and hastily-made mound near the beaten road. But a wonderful change took place with the advent of the road. The " bull-whacker," with his white-covered wagon and raw-boned oxen—his slang phrases, and profane expressions, his rough life, and in many instances violent death—the crack of his long lash that would ring out in the clear morning air like that of a rifle, and his wicked goad or prod—an instrument of torture to his beasts—with all that these things imply, have nearly passed away. Their glory has departed, and in their place is the snorting engine and the thundering train.

The remarkable agricultural advantages of this valley are everywhere visible, and it is rapidly filling up with an industrious and thrifty class of farmers. The land grant of the Union Pacific Company extends for twenty miles on either side of the road, and includes every alternate section of land that was not taken at the time it was withdrawn from the market, for the benefit of the company. If you pass a long distance in the first two hundred miles of this valley without observing many improvements, it is pretty good evidence that the land is held by non-resident speculators, and this fact has a great influence in retarding the growth of the country. Around many of the residences are large groves of cotton-wood trees that have been planted by industrious hands and which give evidence of unusual thrift. In fact, the cotton-wood in most every part of this region is indigenous to the soil, and will thriftily grow where other kinds of timber fail. Trees sixty feet high and from eight to ten inches in diameter, are no uncommon result of six to eight years' growth. The banks of the Platte and the many islands in its channel, were formerly very heavily timbered with cotton-wood, but that on its banks has almost entirely disappeared, together with much that was upon the islands. The favorable State and national legislation in regard to tree planting will cause an increase in the timber land of Nebraska in a very short time, and must of necessity, have an influence upon its climate. Many scientists who are familiar with the circumstances attending the rapid development of the trans-Missouri plains and the elevated plateau joining the base of the Rocky Mountains, assert that this vast region of country is gradually undergoing important climatic changes—and that one of the results of these changes is the annually increasing rainfall. The rolling lands adjoining this valley are all very fertile, and with proper tillage produce large crops of small grain. The bottom lands are better adapted for corn, because it matures later in the season, and these bottom lands are better able to stand drouth than the uplands. The roots of the corn penetrate to a great depth, till they reach the moisture from the under-drainage. One of the finest sights that meets the eye of the traveler, is the Platte Valley in the spring or early summer; to our eastern farmer, it is fairly captivating, and all who are familiar with farms and farming in the

Eastern States, will be surprised; no stumps or stones or other obstacles appear to interfere with the progress of the plow, and the black surface-soil is, without doubt, the accumulation of vegetable matter for ages. The Platte Valley must be seen to be appreciated. Only a few years ago it was scarcely tenanted by man, and while the development has been marked, it will not compare with that which is sure to take place in the near future. There is ample room for the millions yet to come, and the lands of the Union Pacific Company are exceedingly cheap, varying in price from $3 to $10 per acre. The alternate sections of government land for the first two hundred miles of this valley are nearly all taken by homesteaders, or under the preemption laws of congress. Much of it, however, can be purchased at a low price from the occupants, who, as a general thing, desire to sell out and go West still. They belong to the uneasy, restless class of frontiers-men, who have decided objections to neighbors and settlements, and who want plenty of room, with no one to molest, in order to grow up with the country. A sod house near a living spring of water is to them a small paradise. They might possibly suffer from thirst, if they had to dig for water, and the labor required to build even a sod house, is obnoxious. But this will not hold good of all of them. There are many occupants of these sod houses in the State of Nebraska, and other parts of the West, who, with scanty means are striving for a home for their wives and children, and they cling to the soil upon which they have obtained a claim with great tenacity, and with sure prospects of success. They are worthy of all praise in their self-sacrificing efforts. A few years only will pass by before they will be surrounded with all the comforts and many of the luxuries of life. These are the experiences of many who "bless their stars" to-day that they have sod houses—homes—in and adjoining the great Platte Valley.

Shooting Prairie Hens.—This is a favorite scene, often witnessed September mornings in the far West. The prairie is covered with its grass, and wild flowers, which last all the season through. Here and there is a stubble field of oats, wheat, or acres on acres of the golden corn, swaying gracefully in the breeze, and perhaps there is a little music from the meadow larks or bird songsters of the fields. The dogs with keenest of scent, hunt out and stir up the game, and as they rise on wing, the ready gun with its aim, and deadly shot, brings them back lifeless. This is probably the most attractive way to look at a prairie hen, for we must confess that after a slice or two of the meat, as usually served at the eating stations of the railroads, from which we escape with danger to our front teeth, and unsatisfied stomachs, we can only exclaim "distance lends enchantment." However tough the meat, if served on the table when first killed, yet if kept till it grows gradually more tender, there is a wild, spicy flavor, which make them very agreeable eating. Buffalo meat and prairie hens are not altogether reliable as viands of the railroad dining stations, still every one must try for himself, with here and there a chance of finding sweet and tender morsels.

good an illustration as any, of the rapid growth of some of the western towns and counties. The county was organized in the spring of 1869, two years after the railroad had passed through it,—with Schuyler as the county-seat. In the spring of the present year, 1879, it has an assessed valuation of nearly $1,000,000, and a population of

HUNTING PRAIRIE HENS.

Ames—At present simply a side track, 53.5 miles from Omaha, and 1,270 feet above the sea. This was formerly called Ketchum; but bears its present name from Oliver Ames, Esq., one of the builders of this railroad. Observe the size of the trees in the cotton-wood groves and hedges near this place—all planted within the memory of the oldest inhabitant.

North Bend—61.5 miles from the eastern terminus of the road, and 1,250 feet in elevation, a little less than the preceding station. This is a thriving little town, with several stores, hotel, lumber-yard, grain elevator, etc. It has a pontoon bridge across the Platte River, which will materially increase its trade with Saunders County on the south. The opening of many farms in its vicinity have made it quite a grain market. The town is so named from a northward bend in the river, and it is the northernmost point on the Union Pacific in the State of Nebraska. The population is about 300.

Rogers—is a side-track, will eventually become a station; is in the midst of a rich farming country; is 68.5 miles from Omaha, and has an elevation of 1,359 feet.

Schuyler.—The county-seat of Colfax County. It is 75.9 miles from Omaha, with an elevation of 1,335 feet. This town and county, perhaps, is as

1,000 or more. Evidences of substantial growth are everywhere visible. The town has about twenty stores, of all kinds, two hotels, a substantial brick court-house, five churches, a beautiful school-house, grain elevators, etc. New buildings to accommodate its increasing trade, or its new residents, are constantly going up. There are three flouring-mills in the county, on Shell Creek, a beautiful stream fed by living springs, which runs nearly through the county from west to east, and from one to five miles north of the railroad track. The land in this county is most excellent, especially the rolling up-land north of Shell Creek. Some of the finest crops of spring wheat raised in the West are grown in this vicinity. The people are turning their attention to stock-raising more than formerly, and several flocks of sheep and herds of cattle are now kept in the county, by some of its enterprising stock-men. All of this accomplished in about six years. Schuyler is the third town west of Omaha that has a bridge across the Platte, Fremont being the first. These bridges are very advantageous to the trade of the towns in this valley.

Richland.—A small station 83.7 miles from Omaha, with an elevation of 1,440 feet. Up to a late period the land surrounding this station has been mostly held by speculators, but a change

26   THE PACIFIC TOURIST.

having been effected, the town has brighter prospects. Lots are freely given away to parties who will build on them. The location is a very fine one for a town, and it is surrounded by an excellent country. It is the last town west in Colfax County.

Columbus—is 91.7 miles from Omaha. It is 1,432 feet above the sea. A beautiful growing town, with a rich agricultural country to back it. It has seven churches, school buildings, brick court-house, grain elevator doing a large business. Good hotels and other building enterprises contemplated. It is located at the junction of the Loup Fork, with the Platte Rivers, and near where the old overland emigrant road crossed the first-named stream. It now has a population of about 2,000 people, and supports two newspapers which have large patronage and circulation; the *Journal*, which was first established, and the *Era*. Columbus has had two lives thus far. The first town-site was jumped by a party of Germans from Columbus, O., from which it takes its name. Afterwards the two interests were consolidated. It was the principal town west of Omaha until the railroad came. The old town, near the ferry crossing, was then moved to its present site near the station. The old town had two or three small stores, a blacksmith's shop, and saloons *ad libitum*. It was mostly kept alive by the westward emigration. At that time the Platte Valley was well supplied with ranches and ranchmen, only other names for whisky-shops and bar-tenders. During the week those concerns would pick up what they could from wagon trains, and Sundays the ranchmen would crowd into Columbus to spend it—the sharpers improving the opportunity to fleece the victims of their seductive wiles. At this time no attention whatever was paid to agricultural pursuits. On the advent of the railroad in 1866, the wood-choppers, the freighters, the ranchmen and others, lured by the charms of a frontier life, jumped the town and country. They could not endure the proximity to, and restraints of civilization. Then the second or new life of the town began. Farmers began to come in, and it was found by actual experiment that the soil was immensely prolific; that it had only to be tickled with the plow in order to laugh with the golden harvests. In the lapse of the few brief years of its second or permanent growth, it has become a great grain market and probably ships more car-loads each year (1,785 car-loads last year) than any other town on the line of the road. Men draw grain from seventy to eighty miles to this place for a market. It has access to the country south of the Loup and Platte Rivers, by means of good, substantial bridges; while the country north of it is as fine rolling prairie as can be found in any part of the West—well watered and adapted to either grazing or the

growing of crops. The men who first came to Columbus were nearly all poor, and it has been built up and improved by the capital they have acquired through their own industrious toil. The town has a good bank, without a dollar of foreign capital. It will soon have other railroads; one from Sioux City, and another to Crete and St. Joe, is projected; while in its immediate vicinity are large quantities of good lands which are held at low prices. These are only a few of the many advantages which Columbus offers to those in search of future homes.

How Buffalo Robes are Made.—George Clother is one of the proprietors of the Clother House at Columbus, Neb. It is one of the best home-like hostelries in the West. Mr. Clother is an old resident, having been in Columbus sixteen years. When he first came, the country was more or less overrun with wandering tribes of Indians, among whom were the Pawnees, the Omahas, the Sioux, and occasionally a stray band from some other tribe. In those days he was accustomed to traffic in furs and robes, and the business has grown with his increasing acquaintance, until it is now both large and profitable, though with the disappearance of both Indians and buffaloes, it is liable to decrease in the future. General Sheridan, we think it was, said that the vexed Indian question would be settled with the fate of the buffaloes—that both would disappear together. During the past few years, the slaughter of these proud monarchs of the plains, has been immense, and will continue, unless Congress interposes a friendly and saving hand. It is safe to say, that millions of them have been killed for their hides alone, or "just for fun," which in this case amounts to the same thing, as their hides have been repeatedly sold for less than a dollar, and regularly not more than $1.50. This slaughtering has taken place principally in the Platte, Republican, Solomon, and Arkansas Valleys, and where a few years since, travelers could see countless thousands of them from the car windows and platforms, on either the Union Pacific, Kansas Pacific or Atchison, Topeka & Santa Fe Railroads, they now, probably will see but few, if any. Their hides have been shipped East, where they make a poor quality of leather. Those only which are taken late in the fall and during the winter months of January and February, are fit for robes. The hair at this season of the year, is thick and firmly set.

About the time this killing process began in 1870, Mr. Clother entered upon the work of tanning robes, employing for this purpose the squaws of the Pawnee and Omaha tribes. The Pawnee reservation was only a short distance from Columbus, and the "Bucks" were glad of the opportunity of employment for their squaws. Labor is beneath their dignity, and they despise it. Besides this, tanning robes is hard and slow work, and in their opinion, just fit for squaws. For a

INDIAN TENT SCENE.

few years the squaws of both of the tribes named, have been engaged by Mr. Clother, but the departure of the Pawnees to their reservation in the Indian Territory, precluded the possibility of their employment, and hence in the winter of 1876, the Omahas seem to have a monopoly of the work, though there is not as much to do as formerly. We visited their camp to inspect the process of making robes. It was located in a body of heavy timber, with a thick growth of underbrush, on the narrow point of land where the Loup Fork and Platte Rivers form their junction. The low bushes made a perfect wind-break, and in the midst of the tall trees their Sibley tents were pitched. The barking of numerous dogs greeted our approach, and after making a few inquiries of one or two who could talk broken English, we crawled into the tent occupied by the "Bucks," whom we found intensely interested in gambling—playing a game with cards called "21." In this tent were nine "Bucks" and one squaw; three sat stolidly by—disinterested witnesses of the game; the squaw was engaged at some very plain needle-work, and occasionally poked the partly burned brands into the fire, which was in the center of the tent, and over which hung a kettle of boiling meat; the remaining six, sitting upon a blanket à la Turk, were shuffling and dealing the cards. Of course they play for money, and before them were several quarters in currency, and several silver quarters as money, and which enabled them to keep an account with each other, of the gains and losses. During this game they passed around, several times, a hollow-handled tomahawk, which was used as a pipe. One would take three or four whiffs, then pass it to the next, and so on, until it had been passed around several times. One of these "Bucks" was called "Spafford." He could talk English quite well. After a while we asked "Spafford" to show us some robes, but he pointed in the direction of his tent, and indicated where they could be found. He said he could not leave the game just then. We went to his tent where we found his mother, who showed us two robes, one of which was hers—a smaller one which she held at six dollars. Spafford had previously told us that $12.00 was the price of his robe. We then began to look for other robes, and saw them in various stages of completion. The process of tanning is simple, and yet, Indian tanned robes far excel those tanned by white men, in finish and value. When the hides are first taken from the animals, they must be stretched and dried, flesh side up; if they are not in this condition when the squaws receive them, they must do it. After they are thoroughly dried, the squaws then take all the flesh off, and reduce them to an even thickness, with an instrument, which, for want of a better name, may be termed an adze; it is a little thin piece of iron, about two inches long on the edge, and two and a half inches deep. This is firmly tied to a piece of the thigh bone of an elk, and is used the same as a small garden hoe, by eastern farmers in cutting up weeds. When the requisite thickness is obtained, the flesh side is covered with a preparation of lard, soap and salt, and the robe is then rolled up and laid by for two or three days. It is then unrolled and again stretched on a frame, like a quilt, with flesh side to the sun; in this shape it is scraped with a thin, oval-shaped piece of iron or steel, resembling a kitchen chopping-knife without the handle; this process usually lasts about two days. The robe is then taken from the frame, and drawn across a rope stretched between two trees, with the flesh side to the rope, until it becomes thoroughly dry and soft. This last process makes it very pliable, requires a good deal of time and strength, and renders the robe ready for market. Before the Indians came in contact with civilization, they used sharpened pieces of bone, instead of the pieces of iron we have named, and in place of the preparation of lard, soap and salt, they used buffalo brains, which are considered altogether preferable to this mixture; the brains of cattle are also used when they can be obtained; but the robes are taken out on the plains, or in the Platte and Republican Valleys, and brought here by wagon or rail, and of course the brains cannot very well be brought with them. The squaws laughed when we pulled out our note-book and began to write, being evidently as much astonished and interested as we; they looked with wonder at the book, pencil, and the words we wrote. While the lazy "Bucks," sit in their tents and gamble, the squaws are laboring hard to secure means for their support. An Indian is constitutionally opposed to labor. He is evidently tired all the time.

Jackson—So called from a former road-master of the Union Pacific—is 99.3 miles from

Omaha, with an elevation of 1,470 feet. The Loup Valley is just over the hills to your right, and the magnificent Platte bottom lands are still stretching out before you. It has one or two stores and bears a thrifty appearance; at one time it was supposed that this place or Columbus would be made the end of a division, but nothing has been developed on this subject within the past few years.

Silver Creek—109.4 miles from Omaha, and 1,534 feet above the sea. It is the first station in Merrick County, as Jackson was the last in Platte County. North of this station is the Pawnee reservation, one of the finest bodies of land yet unoccupied in the State. This once powerful tribe, between whom and the Sioux a deadly hostility exists, has dwindled down to small numbers, and during 1875, they abandoned their reservation entirely and went to the Indian Territory. An attempt was made a short time since to sell a part of this reservation at an appraised valuation, but it was not successful, and efforts are now being made to bring it into market under the preemption laws of the government at a fixed price, ($2.50 per acre) the proceeds of which are to go to the tribe on their new reservation. When this takes place Silver Creek will have a great impetus to its growth and trade, as it is the nearest railroad station to this reservation.

Clark.—Named after S. H. H. Clark, general superintendent of the Union Pacific; it is sometimes called Clark's, Clarksville and Clark's Station. It is 120.7 miles from the eastern terminus of the road, with an elevation of 1,610 feet. It has three stores, school-house, church, shops and dwellings, and is doing a fine trade; with a rich country around it, and the Pawnee reservation soon to be opened on the north, it is destined to become a thrifty town.

Central City.—The county-seat of Merrick County; has two or three churches, several stores, a brick court-house, school-house, hotels and numerous other buildings. Here is a bridge across the Platte. Population 600. The Nebraska Central Railroad is expected to form a junction with the Union Pacific, here. Local dissensions have injured the town in the past, and must operate to retard its growth in the future. About three miles west of this place a new side track has been put in. It is yet unnamed, though it will probably be called Lone Tree, and it is expected that a post-office with the same name will be established Merrick County has two flouring-mills, both of which are run by water, taken from the Platte River. The identical "lone tree," from which the place was named, has long since disappeared, but numerous groves of cotton-wood are everywhere visible. For 40 miles here the railroad track is perfectly straight.

Chapman.—112.3 miles from Omaha, and 1,760 feet above the sea. It is named after a former road-master of the Union Pacific. The town has two stores, school-house, and other buildings, and is in the midst of a fine, thickly settled country.

Lockwood—is 147.8 miles from Omaha, with an elevation of 1,800 feet. It is a side track where trains meet and pass. A store has recently been opened where a lively trade is done.

Grand Island.—The end of the first division of the Union Pacific Railroad, 153.8 miles from Omaha. and 1,850 feet above the sea. The town is named after an island in the Platte River, which is some forty miles long, and from one to three miles in width. It was first settled by a colony of Germans from Davenport, Ia., in 1857. The island is thickly settled, nearly every quarter section being occupied by a thrifty farmer. The soil is wonderfully prolific, being composed of a black vegetable mold, and is especially adapted to corn raising. The old town site of Grand Island was south of the present site, on the old emigrant road. The first three years of this town were very severe on the settlers. They had to haul all their supplies from Omaha, and part of this time they were obliged to live on short rations. They immediately began the cultivation of the soil, but at first had no market for their crops. This was soon remedied, however, by the opening of a market at Fort Kearny, some forty miles west, where they obtained good prices for everything they could raise. In a short time, the rush to Pike's Peak began, and as this was the last place on the route where emigrants could obtain grain and other supplies, the town grew, and many who are now in good circumstances, then laid the foundations of their prosperity. In this vicinity stray buffaloes first appeared to the early settlers of the valley. They never came in large herds, but when hunted by the Indians further west and south in the Republican Valley they would be seen wandering near this place. While the war was in progress, the settlers frequently saw war parties of the Sioux pass to and from the Pawnee camp on the high bluffs south of the Platte River, and opposite Fremont. When they returned from their attacks, they would exhibit the scalps they had taken, and manifest great glee as they swung them through the air, dangling from their spears. In the early spring of 1859, the stages from Omaha began to run. At first they came once a week, then twice, and later. daily. Then the telegraph line was put up. Meanwhile the trans-continental railroad was agitated. and as it became more and more talked about, the settlers here fondly hoped that they were on the exact spot where the three converging lines, as first proposed, would meet. But they were doomed to disappointment. The Union Pacific, Eastern Division. now the Kansas Pacific, grew into an independent line, while the Sioux City & Pacific had its course changed, finally uniting with the

Union Pacific at Fremont. But the railroad came at last in 1866. The heavy bodies of timber on the islands in the river and between the Platte and Wood Rivers were nearly all taken for cross-ties. It was only cotton-wood, but it would hold the spikes and rails for a few years until others could be obtained. Then the buildings on the old town site were moved up to the railroad and the town began to grow. The round-house for the steam-horses was built, and the town was made the end of a division of the road. An eating-house was erected, and stores, shops, and dwellings followed in quick succession. It is the county-seat of Hall County, and the first station in the county from the east. It has a fine large brick court-house, three church edifices, school-house, hotels, bank, and one of the largest steam flouring-mills in the State. This is one of the regular dining-stations on the road. Last year, 1875, the company put up an elegant hotel for the accommodation of the traveling public, at which all passenger trains stop for meals. It is exceedingly well kept, and under its present management will command the patronage of the public. Like all other towns of any importance in this valley, Grand Island hopes and expects more railroads. A road to connect with the St. Joe & Denver, and the Burlington & Missouri at Hastings, twenty-four miles south, is nearly all graded, and will probably soon be finished. A line is also projected to the north-west, and one to the north-east to reach Sioux City. Its present population is about 1,200, and its prospects for the future are flattering.

The country in this immediate vicinity is well settled by a thrifty class of German farmers, who have dug wealth from the soil, and when rations were scarce and border scares frequent, still hung on to their claims. The road came in 1866, and gave them communication with the outer world. The location of the roundhouse and necessary repair shops, for the division, is a great help to the town, as they give employment to quite a number of skilled mechanics. It is also the location of the government land office for the Grand Island land district. It has two weekly newspapers, the *Times* and *Independent,* both of which are well conducted. The new eating-house, elsewhere spoken of. is the finest on the road, though less expensive than many. It cost about $15,000. This is a breakfast and supper station, and the company has furnished ample accommodations for the patrons of this house.

After leaving Grand Island, a magnificent stretch of prairie country opens to view. The same may be said of the entire valley, but the view in other places is more limited by bluffs and hills than here. After passing Silver Creek, there is a section of the road, more than forty miles, in a straight line, but the extent of prairie brought into vision there is not as large as here. Up to this point, you have doubtless witnessed

EMINENT AMERICAN EXPLORERS AND ARTISTS.

1.—Gen. Custer. 2.—Gen. Fremont. 3.—Lieut. Wheeler. 4.—Prof. F. V. Hayden. 5.—Albert Bierstadt.
6.—Maj. J. W. Powell. 7.—Thomas Moran.

many groves of cotton-wood around the numerous dwellings you have passed, but they begin to diminish now—nearly the last of them being seen at

Alda,—the next station, some eight miles west of Grand Island, 161.5 miles from Omaha, at an elevation of 1,907 feet. There are one or two stores, a school-house, and several dwellings. It is two miles east of Wood River, which is spanned by the first iron bridge on the line. All regular passenger trains stop at this station and receive and deliver mails. In other parts of the country, Wood River would be called a rivulet or small brook, but such streams are frequently dignified with the name of rivers in the West. It forms a junction with the North Channel of the Platte River, just south of Grand Island. Its rise is in the bluffs across the divide, north of Plum Creek, and its general course is due east. The road runs along its southern bank for several miles, and in several places it is fringed with timber. When the road was first built through here, it was well timbered, but it was nearly all taken for construction purposes and fuel. In early days, say in 1859–60, this valley was the frontier settlement of the West, and a few of the old pioneer log houses are still standing, though very much dilapidated. The settlers had a few "Indian scares," and lost some stock, but beyond this, no great depredation was done. Fort Kearny was their first market-place to which they hauled their surplus grain and provisions. Though Wood River is so small, it nevertheless supplies three fleuring-mills with power for grinding, and there are several mill sites unoccupied. The first mill is near the iron bridge already spoken of, and the others will be noticed further on.

Wood River—is the name of the next station. It has two or three stores, several dwellings, and a new depot building. It is 169.6 miles from Omaha, and 1,974 feet above the sea. The old station was two miles further west, and the Catholic church still remains to mark the place where it stood. The country around here was first settled by some Irish families; they are industrious and worthy citizens, and have developed some fine farms. Prairie, or blue joint-grass has been principally seen thus far, but now you will observe patches of buffalo grass which increase as you go west, and of which we shall speak hereafter. This is the last station in Hall County.

Shelton—comes next—a side track, depot, a few dwellings, and another of those flouring-mills spoken of. In January, 1876, the water in Wood River was sufficient to keep three run of burrs going in this mill for about twenty out of every twenty-four hours. The flour made at nearly all the mills on the Union Pacific finds a ready market in the mountain towns west, to which it is usually shipped. Shelton was named

after the present cashier of the Union Pacific road at Omaha. It has an elevation of 2,010 feet, and is 177.4 miles from the eastern terminus of the road.

Successful Farming.—The little farms which now fill up the Platte Valley as far as North Platte are occupied by people who came from the older States, with very little cash capital, and by homesteading or warrant or purchase from the railroad on time, they have made many a snug home. To show what has been done by real industry, we quote from actual records the figures of the success of a farmer in Platte County. Beginning with the year 1867, and up to the year 1874, seven years, he cultivated in wheat and corn, an average of sixty to eighty acres wheat, and fifty acres corn; total 130 acres. His receipts from these two crops only, in seven years, was $13,314.05; expenses, $4,959.92; profits, $8,354.13. besides increase of value of land, which is fully $2,000 more. This is what was done with a capital of less than $2,000.

Tree Planting in Nebraska.—The Nebraskans celebrate a special day in the spring months as a holiday, in which the entire population join hands in a hearty exercise at tree planting; this is called *Arbor Day.* Travelers will notice from the car windows on their first day's ride westward from Omaha, quite a number of pretty groves of trees, planted both as windbreaks for their farms, and also for timber plantations. The tree most popular is the cottonwood, which grows very easily, sure to start, and is quite luxuriant in foliage; however it is valuable for shelter and stove-wood only, not for manufactures. As an instance of rapidity of growth, there are trees in the Platte Valley, which planted as cuttings, have in thirteen years measured 22 inches in diameter. Little boys are tempted by large premiums from their parents to test their capacity at tree planting on Arbor Day, and astonishing rapidity has occasionally been known, one farmer in one day having planted from sunrise to sundown, 14,000 trees, and in the course of one spring season, over 200,000. Settlers, as fast as they arrive, aim to accomplish two things. First, to break the sod for a corn field; next, to plant timber shelter. The winds which blow from the west are very constant, often fierce, and a shelter is of immense value to stock and fruit trees. Hedges of white willow, several miles in length, have been laid, which at five years from cuttings, have made a perfect fence 15 feet high; one farm alone has four miles of such continuous fence, which at four years of age was a complete protection. The rapidity of growth in the rich alluvial soil of the Platte Valley reminds one of tropical luxuriance. A grove of white ash, in twelve years, has grown to an average of 26 inches in circumference, and 30 feet high. Walnut trees, in eight years, have measured 22 inches in circumference, and 25 feet high. Maple trees, of twelve years, measure 43 inches around four feet from the ground. Elms of fourteen years, show 36 inches in girt, and a foot in diameter. Honey Locusts, eleven years of age, are 30 feet high, and 30 inches around. Cotton-wood trees, of thirteen years, have reached 66 inches in circumference, and 22 inches in diameter. White willow, same age, 45 inches in circumference. Nebraska planted 10,000,000 trees in 1878.

Gibbon,—the last station on Wood River, is 182.9 miles from the Missouri by rail, and has an elevation of 2,016 feet. It was formerly the county-seat of Buffalo County, and had a fine brick court-house erected. But the county-seat was voted to Kearny Junction in 1874, and the building is now used for school purposes. It has a hotel, several stores, and another of those flouring-mills, in plain sight from the track. The Platte River is some three miles distant, to the south, and glistens in the sunlight like a streak of silver; the level prairie between is studded with farm-houses, and in the late summer or early autumn numerous stacks of grain and hay are everywhere visible around the farmers' homes. The bluffs, south of the Platte, rear their low heads in the distance, and your vision is lost on prairie, prairie, prairie, as you look to the north. Beautiful as these prairies are in the spring and early summer, their blackened surface in the fall, if burned, or their dull drab color, if unburned, is monotonous and wearying.

Shelby—has an elevation of 2,106 feet, is 191.3 miles from Omaha. The town is named Kearny, and takes its name from General Kearny, who was an officer in the regular army during the Mexican war. Old Fort Kearny was located near this station, south of the Platte River, and the military reservation of government land still remains, though it will probably soon be brought into market. The rights, if they have any, of "squatter sovereigns" will here be tested, as nearly every quarter section in the whole reserve is occupied by them, some of whom have made valuable improvements in the shape of buildings, etc. It was formerly a great shipping point for cattle, but the advancing tide of settlements has driven stock-men, like the Indians, still further west. Occasionally, however, Texas herds are grazed near here, and the herders sometimes visit Kearny Junction, a few miles west, and attempt to run the town; they murdered a man there in 1875, in cold blood—shot him dead on the threshold of his own door—and this so incensed the inhabitants in the vicinity that they will not, probably, allow them to visit the town in future. The murderer was arrested, has been convicted, and time will tell whether he will be hung or not. Texas herders, as a class, are rough fellows, with long hair and beard, wide-rimmed hats, best fitting boots they can get, large spurs jingling at their heels, a small arsenal, in the shape of

Colt's revolvers, strapped to their waists with a careless *negligee* appearance. Their chief pleasure is in a row; their chief drink is "whisky straight," and they usually seem to feel better when they have killed somebody. Houses of prostitution and tippling saloons follow close in their wake. They are generous to their friends, dividing even the last dollar with a comrade who is "broke;" cowardly, treacherous and revengeful to their enemies. Human life is of but little account with them. Their life is one of constant exposure, and very laborious. They are perfect horsemen—usually in the saddle sixteen out of every twenty-four hours—and their great ambition seems to be to become "a devil of a fellow." generally. Nor does it require much care or effort on their part, to fill the bill. Thousands of them on the plains in their native State, in Kansas, Colorado, Wyoming, and Nebraska "have died with their boots on," and we suppose thousands more will perish the same way. Living violent lives, of course they meet with violent deaths. They are a peculiar race, answering, perhaps, a peculiar purpose. The community in which they live, and the country generally, will be better off when they have passed away, for almost ninety-nine out of every hundred goes

> " Down to the vile dust from whence he sprung,
> Unwept, unhonored and unsung."

Kearny has now nothing but a side track, depot and water-tank, with a section-house and the remains of an old corral from which cattle used to be shipped. The reservation included not only land on both sides of the river, but a large island which extends east and west quite a number of miles. The fort was south of the river, and scarcely a vestige now remains to mark the spot where the buildings formerly stood. This fort was built in 1858, by Colonel Charles May, of Mexican war fame. Three miles west of the old fort was Kearny City, which was a considerable town in the old overland times, but it disappeared with the advent of the railroad. The southern part of the reservation is covered with sand-hills, and useless, except for grazing. Notice how the buffalo grass appears and how its extent is increased as you go further west. The new houses around the station, especially those of the squatters on the reservation, are increasing, which indicates that the country is fast settling up.

Kearny Junction.—A lively, enterprising town, 195.3 miles from Omaha, with an elevation of 2,150 feet. It is the junction of the Burlington and Missouri Railroad only, and owes its rapid development to this fact more than to anything else. Formerly the St. Joe and Denver Railroad ran trains to this place, using the track of the Burlington and Missouri from Hastings, a smart little town twenty-four miles south of Grand Island. But this has been abandoned and it is supposed the road will build an independent line to some point on the Union Pacific. Grand Island and Kearny Junction both hope to get it. Kearny Junction was laid out by the town company in September, 1872, about the same time the Burlington and Missouri Railroad arrived; the first house was built in August, 1872, and the town has grown very rapidly ever since; it now has a population of 1,000 souls, six church edifices, one daily newspaper, the *Press*, one weekly, *The Times*, two brick bank buildings and other brick blocks, with hotels, numerous stores, school-house, court-house, etc. It has a daily stage line to Bloomington, a thriving town some sixty miles south in the Republican Valley, and quite an extensive trade from it and the South Loup Valley on the north; some of the stores here do quite a wholesale trade. The town is finely located on a gradual slope, and from the hills or bluffs on its north side the land in seven counties can be distinctly seen; it has the vim and energy which usually characterizes Western towns; it is an aspirant for the capital if it is ever moved from Lincoln, and has ground on the hill reserved for the location of the State buildings; it also expects a railroad from Sioux City, and one from the Republican Valley; altogether its future prospects are bright. Splendid crops of wheat, corn, oats, barley, broom-corn, potatoes, cabbages, and onions are raised in this vicinity during favorable seasons, but we regard the stock business as the best paying and surest investment for settlers; the buffalo grass, to our mind, is a sure indication of it. Kearny Junction is very healthy, and invalids would here find an agreeable resting-place.

Stevenson—has an elevation of 2,170 feet, and is 201.2 miles from the Missouri River. It is simply a side track with a section-house near by. The way settlers have pushed up this valley during the last five years, is marvelous.

Elm Creek—is 211.5 miles from Omaha, with an elevation of 2,241 feet. In the first 200 miles of your journey, you have attained an altitude more than a thousand feet above Omaha, where you started, and yet the ascent has been so gradual that you have scarcely noticed it. Elm Creek was so named after the creek which you cross just after leaving the station going west. It was formerly heavily timbered with elm, ash, hackberry and a few walnuts and cotton-woods; but the necessities of the road when it was built required it all and more too. The town has one or two saloons, stores, school-house and a few dwellings. The creek rises in the bluffs north-west, and sluggishly worries through them and the sand, till it is finally swallowed up by the Platte. But little timber remains in this vicinity. The next station, some nine miles west of Elm Creek, called

Overton—has the usual side track, school-house, a store and some few dwellings. This

valley, to this point and beyond, would have been thickly settled long before this but for climatic reasons which we need not name. The Platte Valley extends on either side here nearly as far as the eye can reach. The town is 220.5 miles from Omaha, at an elevation of 2,305 feet.

Josselyn,—A side track; will eventually become a station; named after the pay-master of the Union Pacific Road. It is 225.1 miles from Omaha, with an elevation of about 2,330 feet above the sea.

Plum Creek.—So named from a creek on the south side of the river, which flows into the Platte nearly opposite the town. The stage-station, on the old overland road was located on this creek and in those days it was considered quite an important point It was the scene of a number of conflicts with the savages—in fact one of their favorite points of attack; eleven white persons were killed and several wounded during one of these attacks. Four miles west of the present town-site they captured and burned a train of cars in 1867; one of the train men was scalped and recently was still living in or near Omaha; one was killed, and the others, we believe, made their escape. The nature of the bluffs here is such that they had a good opportunity to attack and escape before the settlers and emigrants could rally and give them battle. The creek rises in a very bluffy region, and runs north-east into the Platte. Plum Creek is the county-seat of Dawson County; has about 500 inhabitants; a fine brick court-house with jail underneath, one church edifice, school-house, two or three hotels, stores, warehouses, etc. It is a point where considerable broom-corn is purchased and shipped; has a semi-weekly stage line across the Republican Valley to Norton, in the State of Kansas, and a weekly newspaper. There is a substantial wagon bridge across the Platte River, nearly three-quarters of a mile in length. It is located in the midst of a very fine grazing country, though in favorable seasons crops have done well. With irrigation, perhaps they might be made a certainty. This town also enjoys quite a trade with the upper Republican Valley. It was formerly a favorite range for buffaloes, and large quantities of their bleaching bones have been gathered and shipped by rail to St. Louis and places east. It is 231.4 miles from Omaha, with an elevation of 2,370 feet.

Battle with the Indians at Plum Creek.—While the railroad was being built, the engineers, graders and track-layers were frequently driven from their work by the Indians. Not only then, but after the track was laid and trains running, it was some times torn up and trains ditched, causing loss of lives and destruction of property. One of these attacks took place near Plum Creek, as we will now relate. In July, 1867, a train was ditched about four miles west of the above-named station. It was by a band of southern Cheyennes, under a chief called Turkey Leg, who now draws his rations regularly from Uncle Sam, at the Red Cloud agency. He is a vicious looking fellow, his appearance naturally suggesting him as a fit subject for a hanging bee. At a small bridge, or culvert, over a dry ravine, they had lifted the iron rails from their chairs on the ties—raising only one end of each rail—about three feet, piling up ties under them for support, and firmly lashing the rails and ties together by wire cut from the adjoining telegraph line. They were pretty cunning in this arrangement of the rails, and evidently placed them where they thought they would penetrate the cylinder on each side of the engine. But not having a mechanical turn of mind exactly, and disregarding the slight curve in the road at this point, they missed their calculations, as the sequel shows, as one of the rails did no execution whatever, and the other went straight into and through the boiler. After they had fixed the rails in the manner described, they retired to where the bench or second bottom slopes down to the first, and there concealed themselves in the tall grass, waiting for the train. Before it left Plum Creek, a hand-car with three section men was sent ahead as a pilot. This car encountered the obstacle, and ran into the ravine, bruising and stunning the men and frightening them so that they were unable to signal to the approaching train. As soon as the car landed at the bottom of the ravine, the Indians rushed up, when two of the men, least hurt, ran away in the darkness of the night—it was little past midnight—and hid in the tall grass near by. The other, more stunned by the fall of the car, was scalped by the savages, and as the knife of the savage passed under his scalp, he seemed to realize his condition partly, and in his delirium wildly threw his arms out and snatched the scalp from the Indian, who had just lifted it from his skull. With this he, too, got away in the darkness, and is now an employe of the company at Omaha.

But the fated train came on without any knowledge of what had transpired in front. As the engine approached the ravine, the head-light gleaming out in the darkness in the dim distance, fast growing less and less, the engineer, Brooks Bowers by name, but familiarly called "Bully Brooks" by the railroad men, saw that the rails were displaced, whistled "down brakes," and reversed his engine, but all too late to stop the train. The door of the fire-box was open, and the fireman was in the act of adding fuel to the flames within, when the crash came. That fireman was named Hendershot, and the boys used to speak of him as "the drummer boy of the Rappahannock," as he bore the same name, and might have been the same person whose heroic deeds, in connection with Burnside's attack on Fredericksburg, are now matters

of history. He was thrown against the fire-box when the ravine was reached, and literally roasted alive, nothing but a few of his bones being afterwards found. The engineer was thrown over the lever he was holding in his hands, through the window of his cab, some twenty feet or more. In his flight the lever caught and ripped open his abdomen, and when found he was sitting on the ground holding his protruding bowels in his hands. Next to the engine were two flat cars loaded with brick. These were landed, brick and all, some thirty or forty feet in front of the engine, while the box cars, loaded with freight, were thrown upon the engine and around the wreck in great disorder After a time these took fire, and added horror to the scene. The savages now swarmed around the train and whooped and yelled in great glee. When the shock first came, however, the conductor ran ahead on the north side of the track to the engine, and there saw Bowers and Hendershot in the position we have described them. He told them he must leave them and flag the second section of the train following after, or it, too, would be wrecked. He then ran back, signaled this train, and with it returned to Plum Creek. Arriving there in the middle of the night, in vain did he try to get a force of men to proceed at once to the scene of the disaster. No one would go. In the morning, however, they rallied, armed themselves and went out to the wreck. By this time it was near ten o'clock. The burning box cars had fallen around the brave engineer, and while the fiery brands had undoubtedly added to his agony, they had also ended his earthly existence. His blackened and charred remains only told of his suffering. The rescuing party found the train still burning—the Indians had obtained all the plunder they could carry, and left in the early morning. In the first gray dawn of the morning they manifested their delight over the burning train in every possible way, and their savage glee knew no bounds. From the cars not then burned they rolled out boxes and bales of merchandise, from which they took bright-colored flannels, calicos, and other fancy goods. Bolts of these goods they would loosen, and with one end tied to their ponies' tails or the horn of their saddles, they would mount and start at full gallop up and down the prairie just to see the bright colors streaming in the wind behind them. But the end of this affair was not yet. The avenging hand of justice was on the track of these blood-thirsty villains, who, for some inscrutable reason, are permitted to wear the human form. In the spring of that year, by order of General Augur, then in command of the military department of the Platte, Major Frank North, of Columbus, Neb., who had had no little experience in the business, was authorized to raise a battalion of two hundred Pawnee Indians, who were peaceable and friendly

THE PACIFIC TOURIST.

towards the whites, and whose reservation is near Columbus, for scouting duty. It was the old experiment of fighting the devil with fire to be tried over again. These scouts were to fight the various hostile bands of the Sioux, Arrapahoes, and Cheyennes, and assist in guarding the railroad, and the railroad builders. At the time this train was attacked, these scouts were scattered in small detachments along the line of the road between Sidney and the Laramie Plains. General Augur was immediately notified of it, and he telegraphed Major North to take the nearest company of his scouts and repair as soon as possible to the scene of the disaster. At that time, Major North was about fourteen miles west of Sidney, at the end of the track, and his nearest company was some twelve miles further on. Mounting his horse, he rode to their camp in about fifty minutes, got his men together, and leaving orders for the wagons to follow, returned, arriving at the end of the track at about four o'clock in the afternoon. By the time these men and horses were loaded on the cars, the wagons had arrived, and by five o'clock the train pulled out. Arriving at Julesburg, they were attached to a passenger train, and by midnight, or within twenty-four hours after the disaster took place, he arrived at the scene. Meanwhile other white troops, stationed near by, had arrived. In the morning he was ordered by General Augur to follow the trail and ascertain whether the attack had been made by northern or southern Indians. With ten men he started on the scout. The sharp-sighted Pawnees soon struck the trail. They found where the hostile band had crossed the river, and where they had abandoned some of their plunder. They followed the trail all that day, and found that it bore south to the Republican Valley. From this fact, and other indications that only Indians would notice, he ascertained that the attacking band were southern Cheyennes. Returning from this scout, after about thirty-five miles' travel, he reported to the commanding officer at Omaha, and received orders to remain in the vicinity, and thoroughly scout the country, the belief being generally entertained among the officers that, if not followed, the Indians would soon return on another raid. Subsequent events proved this belief to be true, and they had not long to wait. In about ten days, their camp being at Plum Creek, one of the scouts came running into camp from the bluffs south of Plum Creek, and reported that the Indians were coming. He had discovered them in the distance, making their way in the direction of the old overland stage station, which they soon after reached. Arriving here, they unsaddled their horses and turned them loose in an old sod corral to feed and rest. They then began preparations to remain all night. The scouts, however, proposed to find out who and what they were before the evening approached.

Major North first determined to go with the company himself, but at the urgent solicitation of Capt. James Murie, finally gave him charge of the expedition. There were in the command, two white commissioned officers—Lieut. Isaac Davis, besides the Captain—two white sergeants, and forty-eight Pawnees. The company marched from their camp straight south to the Platte River, which they crossed; then turning to the left followed down its bank under the bushes to within about a mile and a half of the creek. Here they were discovered by the Cheyennes. Then there was mounting in hot haste—the Cheyennes at once preparing for the fray. There were one hundred and fifty warriors to be pitted against this small band of fifty-two, all told. But the Cheyennes, up to this time, supposed they were to fight white soldiers, and were very confident of victory. Forming in regular line, on they rushed to the conflict. Captain Murie's command, as soon as they found they were discovered, left the bushes on the river bank and went up into the road, where they formed in line of battle and were ordered to charge. As the order was given, the Pawnees set up their war-whoop, slapped their breasts with their hands and shouted " Pawnees." The opposing lines met on the banks of the creek, through which the scouts charged with all their speed. The Cheyennes immediately broke and fled in great confusion, every man for himself. Then followed the chase, the killing and the scalping. The Indians took their old trail for the Republican Valley, and put their horses to their utmost speed to escape the deadly fire of the Pawnees. Night finally ended the chase, and when the spoils were gathered, it was found that fifteen Cheyenne warriors had been made to bite the dust, and their scalps had been taken as trophies of victory. Two prisoners were also taken, one a boy of about sixteen years and the other a squaw. The boy was a nephew of Turkey Leg, the chief. Thirty-five horses and mules were also taken, while not a man of the scouts was hurt. After the chase had ceased, a rain-storm set in, and tired with their day's work, the trophies of their victory, they returned to camp. It was about midnight when they arrived. Major North and a company of infantry, under command of Capt. John A. Miller, had remained in camp guarding government and company property, and knowing that a battle had been fought, were intensely anxious to learn the result. When the Pawnees came near, it was with shouts and whoops and songs of victory. They exhibited their scalps and paraded their prisoners with great joy, and spent the whole night in scalp-dances and wild revelry. This victory put an end to attacks on railroad trains by the Cheyennes. The boy and squaw were kept in the camp of the Pawnees until late in the season, when a big council was held with the

Brule Sioux. Spotted Tail's band, at North Platte, to make a new treaty. Hearing of this council, Turkey Leg, chief of the Cheyennes, sent in a runner and offered to deliver up six white captives held in his band for the return of the boy and the squaw. After the necessary preliminaries had been effected, the runner was told to bring the white captives, that the exchange might be made. The boy held by the scouts was understood to be of royal lineage, and was expected to succeed Turkey Leg in the chieftaincy of the tribe. After the exchange had taken place, the old chief would scarcely allow the boy to leave his sight—such was his attachment to him, and manifested his delight in every possible way over his recovery. The white captives were two sisters by the name of Thompson, who lived south of the Platte River, nearly opposite Grand Island, and their twin brothers; a Norwegian girl taken on the Little Blue River, and a white child born to one of these women while in captivity. They were restored to their friends as soon as possible.

The Next Attack.—The Indians were not willing to have the iron rails that should bind the shores of the continent together laid in peace, and made strenuous and persistent efforts to prevent it. On the 16th of April, 1868, a "cut off" band of Sioux, under a scalawag chief, named Two Strikes, attacked and killed five section-men near Elm Creek Station, taking their scalps, and ran off a few head of stock. They were never pursued. On the same day, and evidently according to a pre-arranged plan, a part of the same band attacked the post at Sidney. They came up on the bluffs north of the town and fired into it. But no one was injured from their shooting at that time. Two conductors, however, named Tom Cahoon and William Edmunson, had gone down the Lodge Pole Creek, a little way to fish. They were unobserved by the Indians when the firing took place. Hearing the reports they climbed up the bank to see what was going on, and being seen by the Indians, they at once made an effort to cut them off, though they were only a mile or so from the post. The savages charged down upon them, and shot Cahoon, who fell forward on the ground. The Indians immediately scalped him and left him for dead. Mr. Edmunson ran towards the post as fast as he could, and drawing a small Derringer pistol, fired at his pursuers. Thinking he had a revolver and would be likely to shoot again if they came too close, they did not venture up as they had done, but allowed him to escape. He got away with some eight or nine arrow and bullet wounds, together and carrying four arrows sticking in his body. He was taken to the hospital, and rapidly recovered from his wounds. After the Indians had gone, the citizens went after the body of Mr. Cahoon, whom they supposed dead, but to their

surprise he was still alive. They brought him into the post, where he recovered, and is now running on the road.

Attack at Ogalalla.—In September of the same year, the same band of Sioux attempted to destroy a train between Alkali and Ogalalla. They fixed the rails the same as at Plum Creek. As the train came up the rails penetrated the cylinders on each side of the engine, as it was a straight track there; the engine going over into the ditch, with the cars piling up on top of it. The engineer and one of the brakemen who was on the engine at the time, were thrown through the window of the cab, and were but little hurt. The fireman was fastened by the tender against the end of the boiler, and after the train had stopped, there being no draft, the flames of the fire came out of the door to the fire-box upon him, and the poor fellow was literally roasted alive. He was released after six hours in this terrible position, during which he begged the attendants to kill him, but lived only a few moments after his release. All the trains at this time carried arms, and the conductor, with two or three passengers, among whom was Father Ryan, a Catholic priest of Columbus, Nebraska, seized the arms and defended the train—the Indians meanwhile skulking among the bluffs near the track, and occasionally firing a shot. Word was sent to North Platte, and an engine and men came up, who cleared the wreck. Meanwhile word was sent to Major North, then at Willow Island, to take one company of his scouts and follow the Indians. He came to Alkali and reported to Colonel Mizner, who was marching from North Platte with two companies of cavalry, all of whom started in pursuit. They went over to the North Platte River, crossed that stream and entered the sand-hills, where the scouts overtook and killed two of the Indians; the whole party going about thirty-five miles to a little lake, where the main body of Indians had just left and camped, finding the smouldering embers of the Indian fires still alive. That night some of the white soldiers let their camp fires get away into the prairie, and an immense prairie fire was the result. This, of course, alarmed the Indians, and further pursuit was abandoned, much to the disgust of the scouts. Colonel Mizner also claimed that his rations were running short, but from all the facts we can learn, he lacked the disposition to pursue and capture those Indians. At least, this is a charitable construction to put upon his acts.

In October of the same year (1868), the same band of Indians attacked the section-men near Potter Station, drove them in and ran off about twenty head of horses and mules. Major North and his scouts were immediately sent in pursuit. Leaving camp at Willow Island, the command was soon on the ground. It was evidently a small raiding party, and Major North sent a

Lieutenant and fifteen of his men after them. They struck their trail, followed them to the North Platte River, which they crossed, followed and overhauled them in the sand-hills, killing two, recapturing a part of the stolen horses, and returned without loss. The Indians have made some efforts to ditch a few trains since that year, but have effected no serious damage. Their efforts of late have mostly been confined to stock stealing, and they never seem so happy as when they have succeeded in running off a large number of horses and mules. When the road was first built it was their habit to cross it, going south and north, several times in each year. They roamed with the buffaloes over the plains of Nebraska, Colorado, Wyoming and Kansas. The effort of the government of late has been to confine them on their reservations, and the rapid disappearance of the buffaloes from the regions named have given them no excuse for hunting in the country now crossed by railroads and filling up with settlers.

Coyote—is the next station, simply a side track with a section-house near by. But little timber is visible at this place, though the bottom lands begin to widen, giving an extended view. This is not a timber country, and wherever it is found, the traveler will please bear in mind that it is the exception and not the rule. The islands in the river doubtless have some timber, but the most of it has long since disappeared. Occasionally you may see a few scattering trees which have been left by the prairie fires, and which stand in inaccessible places. This side track is 230.1 miles from Omaha, and 2,440 feet above the sea. The next station is

Cozad—so named after a gentleman from Cincinnati, Ohio, who purchased about 40,000 acres of land here from the railroad company; laid out the town; built quite a number of houses; induced people to settle here; has resold a good deal of his land, but still has about 20,000 acres in the immediate vicinity. Along the railroad track, west of Plum Creek, the traveler will notice that the buffalo grass has been rooted out by what is called prairie or blue-joint grass. This last is an annual grass and is killed by frost, after which it resembles dark colored brick—a reddish brown appearance. It has but little nutriment after the frost comes, but if cut and cured in July or August, makes an excellent quality of hay. The buffalo grass is just over the divide a little way, but is giving way to that just named. Some men of capital near Cozad, are interesting themselves in sheep raising, and frequently from this place west you will see large herds of cattle. Cozad is 245.1 miles from Omaha, with an elevation of 2,480 feet. It has two or three stores, school-house, hotel, several large dwellings, and with favorable seasons for growing crops in the future, will become quite a town. The Platte Valley at this point is about twenty miles wide.

Willow Island—is the next station; so named from the large number of willow bushes on the island in the river near by. It is 250.1 miles from the Missouri, and has an elevation of 2,511 feet. The prairie or blue-joint grass still continues along the side of the track, and the bluffs on the south side of the river seem more abrupt. They are full of ravines or "draws," and these sometimes have timber in them. At this station a large quantity of cedar piles and telegraph poles are delivered. They are hauled some forty miles from the cañons in the South Loup Valley. There is a store at this station and a corral near by where stock is kept; with a few old log and mud buildings, rapidly going to decay in the vicinity. The glory of this place, if it ever had any, has long since departed, but it may, nevertheless, yet become the pride of stock-men, who shall count their lowing herds by the thousand.

Grand Duke Alexis' First Buffalo Hunt.

During the visit of the Grand Duke Alexis of Russia, to the United States, the imperial party were escorted to the plains, and enjoyed the excitement of a buffalo hunt, over the western prairies. Connected with the chase were some incidents of rare curiosity and pleasure. As the only representative of the great Russian nation, he has seen the novelty of military life on the frontier; shaken hands with partially tamed Indian warriors, and smoked the pipe of peace in ancient style. Among the company were Buffalo Bill, a noble son of the wild West, and Generals Sheridan and Custer. The red men appeared in a grand pow-wow and war-dance, and indulged in arrow practice for his particular benefit.

The party started from camp Alexis, Willow Creek, Nebraska, in January, 1872. For the hunt the Duke's dress consisted of jacket and trowsers of heavy gray cloth, trimmed with green, the buttons bearing the Imperial Russian coat-of-arms; he wore his boots outside his trowsers, his cap was an Australian turban, with cloth top; he carried a Russian hunting knife, and an American revolver recently presented to him, and bearing the coat-of-arms of the United States and of Russia on the handle.

General Custer appeared in his well-known frontier buckskin hunting costume, and if, instead of the conical sealskin cap he wore, he had only had feathers fastened in his flowing hair, he would have passed at a distance for a great Indian chief.

Buffalo Bill, the famous scout, was dressed in a buckskin suit trimmed with fur, and wore a black slouch hat, his long hair hanging in ringlets down his shoulders.

Game was sighted in a long cañon with broken sides and high hills on either side, forming a magnificent arena.

The Grand Duke and Custer started off, and as they went Custer pulled out his revolver, and said, " Are you ready, Duke ? " Alexis drew off his glove, grasped his pistol, and with a wave of his hand replied, " All ready now, General." Buffalo Bill had been selected to show the Grand Duke how the buffaloes would stand at bay when suddenly attacked. A cow was singled out to show him how fleet of foot the females are, and the speed and skill essential to overtake and kill them. As soon as she espied them she started off at full speed, the Duke and Custer after her. Finding herself hard pressed, she ran up a steep declivity on the right side of the canon, and gaining a footing on the slope, kept along the narrow ledge, while the Duke and Custer followed in a line along the bottom of the canon. The chase was most exciting, and the Grand Duke, exhibiting an enthusiasm and daring which the most

elevation of 2,637 feet, and 268.4 miles from the eastern terminus of the road. The island in the river, from which the station is named, is quite large, and formerly had considerable timber for this country. An occasional tree may yet be seen.

McPherson—is 277.5 miles from Omaha, and 2,695 feet above the sea. It is the station named after the fort which is located south of the Platte River, on a military reservation, and nearly opposite the station. There is a wagon bridge across the river connecting the two places. The fort is about seven miles from the station, and is located near some springs formerly called "Cotton-wood Springs." It bears the name of the gallant general who fell before Atlanta, in 1864, in the war for the preservation of the Union. But few soldiers are now kept at this

GRAND DUKE ALEXIS KILLING HIS FIRST BUFFALO.

experienced western hunter could not have surpassed, pressed his game until she turned upon him. Describing a semi-circle with his horse, he dashed to the other side of her, and taking deliberate aim, discharged the contents of his revolver into her fore shoulder, as quick as a flash of lightning. The buffalo fell dead upon the instant. Thus, as he telegraphed to his father, the Czar of Russia, he killed the first wild horned monster that had met his eye in America. The sport continued for two days, and ended with a series of Indian festivities.

Warren—is a side track 260.4 miles from Omaha, and 2,570 feet above the sea. A section-house stands near by. The valley here narrows, and the bluffs on both sides come near the river.

Brady Island—is the next station, with an

fort, though at the time the war was in progress, and afterwards during the building of the road, and in the years of Indian conflict that raged on the frontier, it was a post of considerable importance. Immense quantities of hay are annually cut near this place, with which government and private contracts are filled. A part of the Seventh Iowa Cavalry, under Major O'Brien, camped on the site of the fort in 1866, and afterwards troops from the regular army were stationed here.

Gannett—named after J. W. Gannett, Esq., of Boston, and present auditor of the Union Pacific Railroad—is a side track with adjacent section-house; is 285.2 miles from Omaha, and 2,752 feet above the sea. All the stations for from fifty to a hundred miles east of this, are located in an excellent grazing country, and cattle and sheep are coming in to occupy it.

Five miles from Gannett, the railroad crosses the North Platte River on a pile bridge. There is a side track and two section-houses just east of the river, the side track for hay cars, and one of the section-houses near the bridge for the watchman, who walks its entire length after the passage of every train. The bridge is planked by the railroad company, and rented by Lincoln County, so that wagons, teams and stock have free passage. After leaving Cozad, the number of settlers' cabins and houses diminishes till you come to the North Platte Valley. South of the river between Fort McPherson and North Platte, there are quite a number of homesteaders, who have farmed it for a few years, with indifferent success, having to contend with drought and grasshoppers. The soil has been proven to be prolific, but some plan of irrigation will have to be adopted, before agriculture can be made a paying investment. In choice locations, however, such as pieces of low bottom land near the river, crops of potatoes and "garden truck" have been successfully raised for several years.

We have now entered upon the great stock-growing region of the continent, where cattle and horses can be grown and kept the year round without hay, and where the buffalo grass, excepting along the streams, affords the rich nutriment that produces fat, and renders cattle ready for market without grain.

The North Platte River will be crossed again at Fort Steele. It has its source in northern Colorado, west of the Medicine Bow Mountains. The Laramie River, which you cross just beyond Laramie City, and the Sweetwater, which rises in the Wind River Mountains north of Point of Rocks, and runs through the great South Pass, are two of its principal tributaries. It drains an immense region of country, and is fed by innumerable streams and springs from the Black Hills of Wyoming, the Wind River Mountains, the Medicine Bow Mountains, the Sweetwater Mountains, the Big Horn Mountains, Rattlesnake Hills and other elevations. The traveler must not be confused by the term "Black Hills." The Black Hills of Wyoming are those which you cross between Cheyenne and Laramie City, the summit of which you reach at Sherman. These are not the Black Hills of which so much has been said of late, in connection with the discovery of gold and the Sioux Indians. They are called the Black Hills of Dakota, and the nearest point to them on the railroad is Sidney. From the immense amount of water which runs into the North Platte River, it is a mystery what becomes of it all, as the river is shallow and sluggish where it is crossed near its mouth. Its treacherous bottom of ever varying and shifting quicksands, like that of the South Platte, does not make it a good fording stream for wagons,

though the water, except in certain seasons of the year, is the smallest obstacle. Up to the spring of 1875, this river was the southern boundary of what the Sioux Indians claimed as their reservation, and it was only by the payment of a special appropriation of $25,000, that they relinquished the right to hunt as far south as this river. The principal military posts on the stream, are Forts Fetterman, usually occupied by but few troops, and Laramie. The latter is at present the principal military depot for both troops and supplies off the line of the railroad, in this part of the West. It is 90 miles from Cheyenne, its nearest railroad station, and the point from whence nearly all the frontier expeditions into northern Wyoming, western Dakota, and the Big Horn and Powder River countries, start. The Laramie River and the North Platte form a junction near the fort.

The South Platte, which the railroad still follows for about eighty-five miles, is similar to the North Platte, so far as external observations go. It rises in the mountains south and west of Denver, receives a large number of tributaries; the chief of which is the Cache La Poudre, which forms a junction with it at Greeley, and then pursues a due east course to the Missouri River. The junction with the North Platte is formed a few miles below the bridge just spoken of. On neither of these streams, nor on any of their tributaries can agricultural pursuits be carried on without irrigation, and not always with success with irrigation. The hand of the Almighty has placed its ineffaceable mark upon all this vast region of country—that it is His pasture ground and adapted, so far as is known, to no other purpose. Millions of buffaloes have ranged over these bleak and desolate-looking plains for ages past, and from the short grass which grows in abundance thereon, have derived a rich sustenance. They have gone or are fast going, and the necessities of the civilization which follows, calls for beef and mutton. These plains must become the great beef-producing region of the continent. They are the Almighty's pasture grounds, and if there are not a thousand cattle upon a hill, there will surely be "cattle upon a thousand hills." The numerous tributaries to these two rivers are from ten to fifteen miles apart, with high rolling prairies between—affording abundance of water with adjacent pasture, and this pasture is the home of the richest natural grasses.

Before you reach the North Platte River, you will see conclusive evidence of the adaptability of these plains to stock-raising, and from this time on to where the river is again crossed, you will see numerous herds of cattle and flocks of sheep. The snows of winter in these elevated regions are dry, and not frequent. Driven by fierce winds, they will fill the hollows and small ravines, while the hills are always left bare, so that cattle and sheep can always obtain access to

CROSSING THE PLATTE, BY EMIGRANT TRAIN, IN OLD OVERLAND DAYS.

the ground, and the buffalo and bunch grasses with which it is covered. While hay must be cut for the sustenance of sheep during the few days storms may last, and for the horses and cattle that may be kept up; the vast herds, whether of cattle or horses, will go through the most severe winter that has ever been known in this region without hay or shelter, except that afforded by the ravines. The experiment has been repeatedly tried, and the vast herds that are now kept in this region, attest the success of that experiment. In Lincoln County, of which the town of North Platte is the county-seat, there are probably 60,000 head of cattle alone. Eastern farmers and stock-raisers will see that the attempt to provide hay for this vast number would be useless, and if required would render the keeping of so many in a single county unprofitable. The expense of providing hay would in the first place be great, and the expense of confining the cattle and feeding it out would be still greater. And if the buffaloes have lived in this country year after year, during the flight of the centuries without hay, why may not cattle and horses do likewise? The stock-grazing region to which allusion is here made, comprises in fact all the country west of the 100th meridian of longitude, to the base of the Rocky Mountains, and the elevated plateaus or great parks lying between the eastern and western ranges of the same mountains; while the extent north and south reaches from the Gulf of Mexico to the northern boundary line of the United States. Three great railroad lines already penetrate this vast stock range, and a decade will hardly pass away before other lines will follow. A ready outlet to the best stock markets in the country is therefore always accessible and always open.

But with all the natural advantages of this region, not every one who may be captivated with the idea of a stock ranche and lowing herds, can make it a success. The business requires capital and care—just the same attention that is given to any other successful business. Nor can it be safely entered upon under the impression that a fortune can be made in a day or in a year. It is a business liable to losses, to severe winters, unfavorable seasons and a glutted market. It does not run itself. By reason of a single hard winter, one man in the stock business has been known to lose a hundred thousand dollars, and the losses that same winter were proportionally severe upon those who were not as able to suffer them. It is a business which, if closely attended to, promises large returns upon the capital invested, and which, at the same time, is liable to heavy losses. It is more sure than mining and more profitable than agricultural or dairy-farming. But we shall have more to say of this hereafter, with specific illustrations as to what can be done in both sheep husbandry and cattle raising. Returning to the two rivers, one of

which we crossed near their junction—the vast area of bottom lands continue to widen, and for a long distance each has its broad valley. Leaving the North Platte here we shall ascend the South Platte to Julesburg. About one mile west of the bridge, we arrive at

North Platte—the end of another division of the Union Pacific Railroad. It is 291 miles from Omaha, and 2,789 feet above the sea. It is a thriving city, and outside of Omaha has the most extensive machine and repair shops on the line of the road. The roundhouse has twenty stalls, and it, together with the machine and repair shops, are substantially built of brick. In these shops engines and cars are either repaired or entirely built over,—a process which cannot hardly be called repairing, but which nevertheless renders them as good as new. The engine-room for the machine-shops, is a model of neatness; everything in and around it being kept in perfect order.

The town has about 2,000 inhabitants, two wide-awake newspapers; the *Republican* being a weekly, and the *Western Nebraskian* being a semi-weekly, together with several wholesale and retail stores and shops of various kinds. The Railroad House is the largest and leading hotel. About 150 men are given constant employment in the shops. There are also one or two companies of troops stationed here, not to protect the railroad from the savages, for that necessity has passed, but for economy in keeping and convenience for frontier duty. The town also has two or three church edifices, a brick court-house and brick school-house, both new, and both presenting a fine appearance. There are also several elegant private residences. It is beautifully located, and has excellent drainage. The bluffs or hills are in near view, both north and south, and give quite a picturesque appearance to the country in the immediate vicinity. The Black Hills excitement, in regard to the discovery of gold, has had some effect upon the town, and a railroad off to the north-west is talked. It is the home of some of the leading stock-men of this section of country. Near this city, in 1875, Col. E. D. Webster and Mrs. A. W. Randall, wife of the late ex-postmaster-general Randall, formed a copartnership to engage in the dairying business, and erected a cheese factory. During the year they manufactured about 30 tons of cheese, which brought them a fair return. Colonel Webster claims that the experiment has demonstrated that the business can be carried on with profit, and he believes it will eventually become the leading feature of this part of the country. He further says that the only drawback at present is the scarcity and unreliability of help, it being difficult to obtain a sufficient number of "milkers" at a reasonable price to milk a large number of cows. In 1876 the firm proposes to make cheese from the milk of from one to two hundred cows, and the balance of their herd—some five hundred—will be devoted to stock-raising. This dairy establishment is one of the new enterprises of North Platte, and, if successful in the future, will make it the prominent cheese-market of the West.

The town has abundant attractions for invalids needing rest—there being antelope and deer in the hills, fish in the streams, and an abundance of pure air to invigorate the body. It has a bright future and is destined to become one of the leading towns on the line of the railroad. Formerly it was an eating-station, but as now run, trains pass it in the night. The road was finished to this town in the fall of 1866, from which time until the following June it was the point where all overland freight was shipped. It was a rough town then, but this state of affairs did not last long, and the character of the place rapidly improved with the arrival of permanent settlers. There were a few Indian scares, but no serious attack was made by the savages upon the town. Two or three trains were ditched and wrecked, both east and west, but this was the extent of the damage done by them. Of this, however, we shall have more to say in another place.

Chimney Rock.—Near North Platte is the far-famed Chimney Rock, two and a half miles from the south bank of the Platte River. It is composed of a friable yellowish marl, which can be cut readily with the knife. It rises in the form of a thin, perpendicular shaft above a conical mound, whose base slopes gradually out toward the plains. It appears to be the renewal of the old chain of hills and rocks which bounded the valley, but which, from their softness of material, have been disintegrated by wind and weather. This possessing harder material has withstood these effects, although it is steadily yielding. In the days of Fremont's expedition, it was estimated that it was over 200 feet in height, but other travelers and explorers who had seen it years before, stated that its height had been as great as 500 feet. In those days it was a landmark visible for forty or fifty miles; now it is hardly 35 feet in height. Around the waist of the base runs a white band

CHIMNEY ROCK, NEAR NORTH PLATTE.

which sets off its height, and relieves the uniform yellow tint. It has often been struck by lightning.

The Overland Pony Express.

The Pony Express (of which few now remember those days of excitement and interest) was started in 1860, and the 3d of April, that year, is the memorable date of the starting of that first trip. In those days, the achievements of the Pony Express were attended with an eager excitement hardly less interesting than the building of the Pacific Railroad itself. "*Overland to California in thirteen days,*" was repeated everywhere as a remarkable achievement. The first company organized was formed in California in 1858 or 1859, under the name of the Central Overland California and Pike's Peak Express. At that time, with no telegraph or even stage line across the continent, this attempt was considered extraordinarily audacious. The services planned and executed by the company were a pony express, with stations sixty miles apart, the entire distance from St. Joseph, Mo., to Sacramento. The time occupied between ocean and ocean was fourteen days, and from St. Joseph to San Francisco, ten days. And the schedule of the company required the pony express to make trips in the following time:

From St. Joseph to Marysville,	12 hours.
From St. Joseph to Fort Kearny,	34 hours.
From St. Joseph to Laramie,	80 hours.
From St. Joseph to Fort Bridger,	108 hours.
From St. Joseph to Salt Lake,	124 hours.
From St. Joseph to Camp Floyd,	128 hours.
From St. Joseph to Carson City,	119 hours.
From St. Joseph to Placerville,	226 hours.
From St. Joseph to Sacramento,	232 hours.
From St. Joseph to San Francisco,	240 hours.

An express messenger left once a week from each side with not more than ten pounds of matter. The best of riders were chosen from among trappers, scouts and plains men, familiar with all the life of the route, fearless, and capable of great physical power, endurance and bravery. The ponies were very swift and strong, a cross between the American horse and Indian pony, and after each run of sixty miles, waited till the arrival of the messenger from the opposite direc-

OVERLAND PONY EXPRESS PURSUED BY HIGHWAYMEN.

tion, when each returned. The riders were constantly exposed to dangers from Indian attacks and pursued by highwaymen; and to compensate them for this risk they received the large salary of $1,200 a month each; and the modest price charged for the conveyance of business letters was $5.00, gold, per quarter ounce. At the time of the departure of the first messenger from St. Joseph, a special train was run over the Hannibal and St Joseph Railroad to bring the through messenger from New York, and a " *Pony Express Extra* " was issued of two pages, by the St. Joseph *Daily Gazette*, containing telegraphic news from all parts of the world, with a heavily leaded account of the new enterprise, and sending greetings to the press of California.

The route from St Joseph, after reaching the Platte Valley, followed just north of the present track of the Pacific Railroad to Laramie, then up the Sweet Water to Salt Lake, and down the Humboldt to Sacramento. Night and day the messengers spurred their ponies with the greatest speed each could endure. Often on arriving at an express station the messenger, without waiting to dismount, tossed his bag to another already waiting, and each were off at once, back again, and thus for eight days the little express bag traveled, arriving at the rail terminus, rarely a minute behind the prescribed time, a total distance of 2,000 miles.

For two years this system was kept up, until the telegraph line was finished in 1862, when the company dissolved with a loss of $200,000. As an instance of rapid speed, once, very important dispatches—election news—were carried from St. Joseph, Mo., to Denver City, Col., 625 miles, in sixty-nine hours, the last ten miles being made in thirty-one minutes. On this and next page, we give two illustrations characteristic of these times. One engraving is taken from a painting of G.

OLD PONY EXPRESS STATION AT CHEESE CREEK, NEBRASKA.

G. M. Ottinger, of Salt Lake City, which represents the express rider dashing along and cheering the telegraph men who were erecting the poles. This is an actual scene, as, in the summer of 1862, while the telegraph was under construction, the flitting by of the Pony Express was an almost daily occurrence. An illustration is also given of one of these express stations at Cheese Creek, Neb., which was soon afterwards abandoned as a thing of the past. The government mails were carried by special contract of the Overland Mail Company with the United States government, which was started in 1858, who cont'acted with them to run a monthly mail from San Francisco to the Missouri River for a consideration of $650,000 annual compensation. Of this company, John Butterfield who drove the first coach, was president. The route chosen was the Ox Bow, via. Santa Fe, but in 1860 the Indians became so

the driver may be heard shouting loudly, or with terrific whoop—a mile or so before his station is reached the keepers have heard it—and as his stage rattles up, the new relay of horses is ready, and in two or three minutes the stage is on its way again. After a few days' journey, the travelers become used to the swinging motion of the stage, and sleep as naturally as if made for such a life.

A Word with Invalids.

Thousands of invalids, especially consumptives, visit the mountains and California coast, every year, in search of health, and to try the effect of a change of climate in restoring them to activity and vigor. There can be no question but that many have been benefited by the change, and it is a fact equally patent that many have left good homes,

PONY EXPRESS SALUTING THE TELEGRAPH.

troublesome that the route was changed to that of the Pony Express, and soon afterwards a daily mail was established at an expense of $1,000,000 annually. The incidents of overland stage life have been repeated over and over again in books of Western adventure. Here and there were lonely post-offices away out on the distant prairies or plains. No passengers to set down or take up, the driver throws out his mail-bag, catches the one thrown to him, and whirls on without stopping, or scarcely checking the speed of his team. Morning, noon or night comes the inevitable "refreshment station," such as it is, where the weary passengers, well shaken up, were glad to regale themselves on pork and beans, corn bread, and "slumgullion"—the Far Western name for tea. Toward the middle of the night, perhaps,

kind friends, and plenty of care—to die alone and among strangers. With this last class the main trouble is, they wait too long in the East before starting. The disease, more or less rapid in its strides, gets too firm a hold upon the system—becomes too deeply rooted to be easily thrown off; then they start for health and rest that cannot be found, and most always go too far in search of it. There are a few words of advice to these people, which are the result of years of observation and experience on the plains and among the mountains.

First, the discovery of a tendency to lung and throat diseases should be a sufficient incentive to prompt one to an immediate change of climate. Do not wait until a change becomes hopeless because of the advanced stages of the disease.

Second, *do not at first go too far.* This is another mistake frequently committed by those who finally get started.

Third, *do not go too fast.* Remember the railroad from Omaha, in less than two days, will take you to an altitude of more than 8,000 feet, and this is a severe test on a pair of healthy lungs, to say nothing of its effect upon weak ones. First go as far as Grand Island, and stop. This place is 1,850 feet above the sea, and you are in the midst of a fine prairie country, with a generally clear atmosphere and balmy breezes. Here are good hotel accommodations, in a thickly settled region, where you can obtain plenty of fresh milk, cream and eggs, and such

either along the stream or on the adjoining highlands, still camping out, until you reach North Platte. Then take another rest, look around the country, mount your horse and ride out to the cattle ranches and live with the herders for a time. Do not be in a hurry to get away, and after you have been here a month or six weeks, if you still improve, or even hold your own with the character of the life herein prescribed, it will be safe for you to go still farther, and in the same manner. But if you are not benefited by the trip thus far, it will be better for you to return to your homes and friends, where loving hands can smooth your pillow and administer comfort during your declining days.

BUFFALO HUNTING.

other articles of diet as are necessary and conducive to your welfare. Ride or walk out from town; go around among the farmers, and if, after a month or so, you improve and wish to go farther, buy a team and wagon, and from this place go along leisurely overland, camping out if the weather is favorable. There are opportunities for hunting and fishing, along the road, which will afford amusement and recreation. When you get to Kearny Junction, stop a few weeks. Notice the effect of your new mode of life and the climate upon your health, and if you simply hold your own, it is safe for you to take another step up the Platte Valley in your westward journey. Leisurely pursue your way,

If the journey has benefited you, pursue it overland and camping out, to Sidney or Cheyenne, up the Lodge Pole Valley and along side of the railroad, or at Julesburg go up the South Platte Valley to Greeley. You are now, if at Cheyenne, over 6,000 feet above the sea, and between 5,000 and 6,000 feet at either Greeley or Denver, in the midst of a rarified and dry atmosphere. If your health is regained, do not think of returning, for this is almost sure to bring on a relapse, which is usually sudden, and from which there is no escape; your safety depends upon your remaining in these high altitudes, and on the high and dry plains of the West. A trip down in New Mexico, and across the plains to

Arizona, will also prove beneficial. In the old overland times, thousands of consumptives regained their health in driving teams, and by slowly crossing the plains, who would have died if the same journey had been taken on the cars. By the latter mode, the change from a damp and heavy atmosphere in the East, to the rarified and dry air of the plains and mountains, is too sudden; and after all, if the disease has become thoroughly seated, it is doubtful if any change will be effectual. It is an experiment which should only be tried with all possible safeguards thrown around it.

Buffalo Grass.—After you have passed the stations of North Platte and Sidney, you will observe the entire country carpeted with a short, dried up grass growing in little bunches. This is the famous buffalo grass which covers thousands of miles of the plains northward and southward and westward. Though it gives to the country a dried look, as if the very appearance of desolation and sterility, yet it is the richest grass ever known in the world. The entire State of Nebraska is famous for its remarkable variety of grasses. The Platte Valley is the home of no less than 149 varieties, all native to the soil, and were it not for the extraordinary beauty and luxuriance of the green carpet the grasses make, the Valley of the Platte would be almost wholly devoid of interest. The buffalo grass is rarely over two to three inches in height, and its seed is produced on flowers almost covered by leaves close to the ground. It grows in little tufts, broad and dense, and is exceedingly rich and sweet, having no less than 3 6-10 per cent. of saccharine matter. When making its first growth in the spring, it is green, then dries on its stem and remains the rest of the year like cured hay on the open ground, retaining all its sweetness. Without a single exception, horses, mules and stock of all descriptions, will forsake all other kinds of grass until all the buffalo grass within reach has been consumed. While the buffaloes roamed over this country it was their natural food, but with their disappearance and the coming of the white man, it is disappearing to give place to others. Leaving North Platte, the next station is

Nichols.—299.4 miles from Omaha, and 2,882 feet above the sea. It is simply a side track with section-house near, in the midst of the level bottom lands between the two rivers, both of which are in sight. Before reaching North Platte it will be observed that the bottom narrows, and that the bluffs or sand-hills in some instances approach the river's bank. But after leaving the town, for nearly twenty miles west, the level prairie between the rivers spreads out in view, with bluffs on either side beyond. Between North Platte and this station there are a few settlers, but the territory is mostly occupied as the winter range of Keith & Barton's herd of cattle,

as they are easily confined between the rivers with little help.

O'Fallon's—is the next station. It is 307.9 miles from Omaha, with an elevation of 2,976 feet. It is a telegraph station. O'Fallon's Bluffs are plainly visible south of the South Platte River, which they closely approach; at this point we lose sight of the Valley of the North Platte—a ridge of low hills jutting down from the west, while the railroad follows the south river. The railroad reached this place late in the fall of 1866, but North Platte was the terminal station until Julesburg was reached in 1867. If there was any timber on the streams in this vicinity, it has long since disappeared. On an island in the South Platte the Indians used to camp, and from their hiding places in the sand-hills and bluffs, frequently attacked emigrants and trains, but as before remarked, with the buffaloes, the Indians disappear.

Dexter—is simply a side track where trains occasionally meet and pass. It is 315.2 miles from Omaha, and has an elevation of 3,000 feet. The bluffs here come very near the river, and they are utilized in the building of a corral—the rocky ledge answering all the purposes of a fence. The monotony of the scenery up to this point now passes away, and the traveler will always find something in the ever-varying views of rocks, bluffs, streams and plains that will interest him in the journey.

Alkali.—A telegraph station, 322.4 miles from the Missouri River, and 3,038 feet above the sea. The alkali spots which have been witnessed in the soil since we left Omaha, are now more frequent, and the station naturally takes its name from these characteristics. This station has a small depot, side track and section-house; is in the midst of a fine grazing country, and opposite an old stage station south of the river.

Roscoe.—Simply a side track, 332.0 miles from Omaha, with an elevation of 3,105 feet. Just before reaching this place, and in this vicinity, the railroad passes through more sandy bluffs that approach the river.

Ogalalla—is the next station, 341.6 miles from Omaha. Elevation 3,190 feet. It is the county-seat of Keith County, Nebraska, and is destined to be the Texas town on the line of the Union Pacific. The regular trail for driving cattle from Texas may be said to terminate here. It has a depot, water tank, side tracks, cattle chutes, store, one or two boarding-houses, saloon, etc. It is the head-quarters and outfitting place of a large number of ranchmen, who have herds of cattle in this vicinity. It is some twelve miles from the North Platte River, where a number of herds find ample range. In 1875, it is claimed that nearly 60,000 head of Texas cattle were driven to this point, and afterwards distributed to various parties to whom they were sold. A large number of them were taken to the

Indian agencies at Red Cloud and Spotted Tail. There will be numerous buildings erected soon to accommodate the growing necessities of the town. Leaving Ogalalla we next come to

Brule,—so called from the Brule Sioux, a band of which Spotted Tail is the chief. Red Cloud is chief of the Ogalalla Sioux. This is probably the most powerful tribe of Indians now existing in the country, and when all united they are said to be able to raise at least 10,000 warriors. Those of them who have been taken east to Washington and other eastern cities, seem to have lost their belligerent feelings toward the whites, and will not probably go to war with them unless misled by tricksters or influenced by some other powerful motive. The young "bucks" who have remained on their reservations, however, think they can whip the whole country in a very short time if they should once get at it. This station was a favorite crossing place with this band of Sioux during the years when they used to hunt on the rivers south, or go on their scalping and horse-stealing expeditions. Brule is 351.2 miles from Omaha, and has an elevation of 3,260 feet. North of this place, on the North Platte, is Ash Hollow, a celebrated camping ground for Indians and the scene of a great victory over them by General Harney, in 1859. The whole tribe of Sioux probably have a greater admiration for General Harney, to-day, than for any other living American. Physical force is the only power which they can be made to respect and fear. Next comes

Big Spring,—which is 360.9 miles from the eastern end of the road, with an elevation of 3,325 feet. It is so named from large springs which break to the surface of the ground at the foot of the bluffs, on the right-hand side of the road going west, and in plain sight of the cars. The water tank, at this station, is supplied from these springs. The water is excellent, and the station is quite a camping place for those who continue to journey overland. This is a telegraph station.

Barton,—called after Hon. Guy C. Barton of North Platte. It is 368.7 miles from Omaha, and 3,421 feet above the sea—simply a side track where trains meet and pass. Beyond this station, a short distance, the old town of Julesburg can be seen across the river. Late in 1875, a stray herd of about six hundred buffaloes quietly passed over the old town site to and from the river, where they went for water. It will probably be their last visitation to this part of the country.

Julesburg,—377.4 miles from Omaha, and 3,500 feet above the sea. It was named after Jules Burg—a frontier character who was killed by one Jack Slade, another rough, in the old overland stage times. The old town was across the river, some four miles below the present station, and was a pretty rough place. The station

is opposite old Fort Sedgwick, now abandoned, and was the proposed junction of a branch railroad up the South Platte River by way of Greeley to Longmont, from which a railroad is completed to Denver. This branch is graded nearly the entire distance, and bridged part of the way. By an agreement made in 1875, the Union Pacific, or men in the company, relinquished the proposed and completed roads in Colorado to the Kansas Pacific, and the latter road relinquished its through business to the Pacific coast, and its efforts to compel the Union Pacific to pro rate with it from Cheyenne west. This arrangement effected the entire suspension of all efforts to complete this branch, and Julesburg is now, as formerly, a way-station on the Union Pacific. It is, however, quite a place for shipping stock, has one or two stores, some adobe houses and stables, with cattle-yards and chutes. The completion of this branch road would have been of great benefit to the Union Pacific, and to the entire State of Nebraska, by reason of the coal which is found in large quantities near Boulder, and which, if obtained there, would save some three or four hundred miles in hauling over very heavy grades, as is now done. It is doubtful if it is ever completed. At this point the Union Pacific passes through the north-eastern corner of Colorado, and here it leaves the South Platte River and ascends Lodge Pole Creek to within a few miles of Cheyenne.

The early pioneers who went to Utah, California and Oregon overland, usually crossed the South Platte River at this place, and followed up the Lodge Pole to Cheyenne Pass. In fact, there were many routes. One up the North Platte, one up the South Platte, one up the Lodge Pole, and others. The northern route passed through what is known as the Great South Pass, about 65 miles north of the Point of Rocks. The Lodge Pole route crossed the Black Hills at Cheyenne Pass, and the South Platte route followed up the Cache La Poudre and Dale Creek, until it struck the great Laramie Plains south-west of Sherman.

Fort Sedgwick, of which we have spoken, was established in May, 1864, and was named after the gallant commander of the Sixth Corps, army of the Potomac, who was killed at the battle of Spottsylvania Court-House while sighting a gun, and whose loss was greatly lamented by the entire army, and especially the corps he commanded. Among "the boys" he was familiarly spoken of as "Farmer John."

Incidents in the History of Julesburg.

The overland stage company had quite an important station at Julesburg, south side of the river, and about a mile east of the location of Fort Sedgwick. It was in 1865, before any rails had been laid on the Union Pacific. The stage company had accumulated a large quantity of supplies at this station, and the Indians knowing this, and ever hostile to the travel of the whites through this region, had their cupidity aroused. Troops were scattered all along the route, and frequently had to escort the stages from one station to another. At Julesburg, the road crossed the South Platte, followed the Lodge Pole up to Sidney, and then crossed over to the North Platte, which it ascended to Fort Laramie and beyond. Capt. N. J. O'Brien was in command at the fort, with one company of the Seventh Iowa Cavalry, and two pieces of artillery. On the 7th of January, 1875, the Sioux and Cheyennes, one thousand strong, discovering the small force to defend it, attacked the fort with great bravery. They had previously run the stage into the station, killing one man and one horse. When their presence was discovered,

but leaving their dead comrades to fall into the hands of the blood-thirsty foe. The Indians perceiving their disposition to fail back, redoubled their efforts, and endeavored to cut them off from the fort. They attacked with greater fury and boldness than ever, and came very near effecting their purpose. The men, however, fell back in good order, and were successful in gaining the fort. The Indians now surrounded this, but the artillery was brought out and served with good effect, so that they were kept at bay, and eventually night put an end to the conflict. In the night the Indians withdrew, and when the morning broke, not one was in sight. But now comes the most horrible part of this incident. The men went out to find, if possible, the bodies of their dead comrades. They found them, but

INDIAN ATTACK ON AN OVERLAND STAGE.

Captain O'Brien made the best disposition possible with his small force. He left a sergeant with some twelve men in the fort, to handle the artillery, and mounting the rest, thirty-seven men and one officer, besides himself, went out to meet the savages. The charge was sounded, and in they went. About a mile from the fort there is a projecting hill in the bluffs, back of and around which the main body of the Indians were concealed. As the men neared the top of this hill, they saw the large force opposed to them, but never flinched. The Indians charged upon them with great fury, and for quite a time the unequal contest was continued. But his ranks having become depleted by the loss of fourteen of the thirty-seven enlisted men, the captain ordered them to fall back, which they did in good order,

nearly all were beyond recognition: stripped of every vestige of clothing, mutilated beyond account, cold and stark they lay, in the places they had fallen; their fingers, toes and ears cut off, their mouths filled with powder and ignited, and every conceivable indignity committed upon their persons. Sorrowfully they gathered up these remains, and conveyed them to the fort, where they were decently buried; but the recollections of that awful night, did not fade from the memories of the survivors of that company. In subsequent battles with the savages, their courage was quickened and their arms nerved to deeds of daring, which cost many a warrior his life, and gave him a sudden exit to his happy hunting grounds. The loss of the savages in this battle, could not, at the time, be accurately ascertained, but from the best information since obtained, admitted by the Indians themselves, they had sixty-three warriors killed in this engagement. None were found on the field, as they always carry their dead away with them.

On the second day of February, less than a month from the above attack, they appeared in the vicinity of the fort again, and attacked and burned the station house of the stage company, other out-buildings and stores, and one or two houses adjoining. Five miles below the station was a ravine called the Devil's Dive, through which the stages passed. Captain O'Brien and four or five men were escorting the coach with three or four passengers, one of whom was a lady. As he ascended the bank of the ravine going toward the fort, he saw a smoke, and riding up to the top of a hill, he saw Indians. Returning to the coach, he had every man, passengers and all, carefully examine his arms, and caused the coach to proceed slowly along. Soon the road neared the bank of the river, and here he met some teamsters with wagons, who, beyond a pistol or two, were unarmed, and who had left the station for some object, less than a half hour before. They now became aware of the situation, and were greatly alarmed. These men the captain ordered to return and keep near the stage, which they did, all moving slowly toward the station and fort. Meanwhile the heads of Indians were popping up quite frequently, over the bluffs in the distance. Arriving near one of these, the captain boldly rode to the top, and taking his blanket swung it three times over his head. The Indians saw this, and supposed he had a large force in the rear, which he was signaling to come up, and they began to fly. The river was frozen, and sand had been scattered over two roadways on the ice. They took everything they could from the burning station and houses, and beat a retreat across the river. At the first sign of their leaving, the stage-driver and teamsters put their animals to their utmost speed, and ran into the fort, the captain arriving there in time to give the Indians a few parting shots from his artillery as the last of them ran across the river. The shots ricocheted along the ice, and caused the Indians to drop some of their plunder, though doing no further damage, as we could learn.

These are only two of the many incidents in our frontier history, that will soon be beyond the reach and knowledge of either the present or future generations.

The Great Indian Battle at Summit Springs.

On the divide south of the South Platte River, and about midway between old Fort Morgan and old Fort Sedgwick, opposite to which Julesburg now stands, there are some fine springs—the only good water in quite a region of territory. They are now called Summit Springs; and are

near the summit of a divide from which the water, when there is any, runs north and south.

In the winter of 1869, Major Frank North, before alluded to, received orders to recruit his scouts for the summer campaign. He organized one company in February, and two the following April, the total number in the three companies being one hundred and fifty men, exclusive of their white officers. In April of that year, General Carr, taking two of these companies and eight of the Fifth Cavalry, then stationed at Fort McPherson, was ordered to scout the country in the Republican, Solomon and Saline Valleys and their tributaries, and strike any marauding bands of Indians he might find. At that time, the Indians were raiding the advanced settlements in the lower Republican and Solomon Valleys, burning houses, killing and scalping men, women and children, and stealing all the horses they could find. The third company of the scouts had not then been organized. As soon as this was done, Major North was ordered to take them across the country from Fort Kearny, and join General Carr's command, at the mouth of Prairie Dog Creek, in the Republican Valley. This he did, effecting a junction about the 5th of May. After scouting the country between the Republican and Solomon for about a month, the command returned to the Republican, where it met a supply train, which had been sent out from Fort McPherson, and then proceeded up the valley. On arriving at the mouth of Medicine Creek, they struck the trail of a large village. This was on the first day of July, and they continued to follow it up the river for about one hundred and twenty-five miles. The trail then left the valley, and bore off to the North, until it struck Frenchman Creek, then up that creek to its source, and then over a divide to Summit Springs, about thirty-five miles from the headwaters of the Frenchman. The Indians of this village kept pickets out as a sort of a rear-guard, but did not think of an attack from another quarter. The Pawnee scouts were constantly in the advance, and kept the command well informed of the condition and disposition of the Indians. They had discovered the rear-guard of the Indians, without being themselves seen, reporting their situation, and telling just how the attack should be conducted, in order to be successful. A wide detour would have to be made, and the Indian village, encamped in a ravine near the springs, would have to be approached and attacked from the west. Every precaution was taken to conceal the movements of the troops. The attack was made on the 11th day of July. The heavy wagon train was left in the rear, and the best horses with their riders, were selected for the march, which was supposed to be, with the detour mentioned, at least fifty miles. The command arrived within about a mile and a half of the Indians undiscovered, at

4

about three o'clock, P. M., but before the disposi-
tions and arrangements for making the final
charge had been fully completed, one company of
cavalry unnecessarily exposed itself, and this precipitated the attack. The Indians were Sioux,
forty lodges, Cheyennes, forty-five lodges—eighty-
five in all. They had been in the raids together,
and were to separate the next day. They had
evidently concluded to take one day at these
splendid Springs, for the enjoyment of their fare-
well pow-wow, but it proved to be a "bad medicine day" for them. When they saw the company of cavalry that had unfortunately been
exposed to their view, they ran out to gather in
their horses, which were quietly feeding in the

the chief. He was seen, as the troops approached,
mounted upon his horse, with his wife and child
behind him, trying to escape, but when he found
his retreat cut off, he ran into a "pocket" or
"draw," in the side of a ravine, with almost perpendicular sides, where some fifteen other warriors had taken refuge. He had a very fine horse,
which he led to the mouth of this "pocket" and
shot dead. He then took his wife and child and
pushed them up on the bank of the "pocket,"
telling her, as he did this, to go and give themselves up, perhaps their lives would be spared.
The squaw and her child, a beautiful girl, went
straight to Major North, and raising her hands
in token of submission, drew them gently over

INDIAN COSTUMES.

vicinity of their camp, a mile or more away.
There was no time for delay. The troops and
scouts charged down upon them with all their
speed. The scouts, as usual, set up their infernal
war-whoop, and went in with a rush. The Indians were wholly unprepared for the attack, and
some of them were quietly lounging in their
tents. In fact it was nearly a complete surprise.
They were all under the lead of Tall Bull, a noted
Cheyenne chief and warrior, and numbered about
five hundred men, women and children—nearly
or quite two hundred being warriors. Seventeen
squaws and children were taken prisoners, and
as near as could be estimated, one hundred and
sixty warriors were slain, among them Tall Bull,

his face and down his form to the ground, where
she sank upon her knees, her child standing beside her. While Major North can talk Pawnee
like a native, he could not understand what she
said, but as all Indians use sign language to a
great extent, he readily interpreted her motions
to mean that she surrendered, and wanted him to
spare their lives. He motioned her to rise, which
she did, and told her by signs to go a little way,
sit down and stay there, and she would not be
harmed. She then, by signs, indicated that
there were seven living braves still in the
"pocket," and asked him to go in after them,
doubtless thinking that her husband might be
saved with herself. He declined this request,

especially as the Indians were shooting every one they could see from their concealed position, it being simply a question of life for life, and further told her that the braves in the ravine would all be killed. The troops and scouts staid around this "pocket," until satisfied that there were no living Indians there, and, on entering, found sixteen dead warriors and one dead squaw, lying close together, among whom was Tall Bull. In their raids in the Solomon Valley, they had captured two white women, whose lives they had spared for purposes worse than death, and at the time this attack was made, they were still alive. One of them had been taken by the principal Sioux chief, and the other was appropriated by Tall Bull, whose wife, doubtless from motives of ignorant jealousy, was accustomed to give her severe whippings, at least six days out of every seven, and her body showed the marks where she had been repeatedly bruised and lacerated by Tall Bull's squaw. The white woman who was appropriated by the Sioux chief, when he found she was likely to be rescued, was shot dead by him, and only gasped for breath a few times after being found by some of the officers, unable to

PAWNEE CHIEF IN FULL DRESS.

utter a word. As near as could be learned, her name was Susanna. It was afterwards ascertained that she was a Norwegian woman, and General Carr, in his report of the battle, calls the Springs, Susanna Springs, after this woman, and near which she was decently buried, and which name they ought to bear now.

When the charge was first begun, Captain Cushing of the scouts, passing by the lodge of Tall Bull, entered it. The chief, as before stated, had fled with his wife and child at the first approach of danger, but in his lodge there remained the other captive woman, whom he had shot and evidently left for dead. She was a German woman, unable to speak English, and up to this time, had supposed, from the presence of the scouts, that the fight was between Indians, and that whatever the result, there would be no change for the better so far as she was concerned. As the captain entered the lodge, he saw this woman in a sitting posture, nearly denuded, with the blood running down her waist. When the chief left the tent, he had shot her in the side, aiming at her heart, but the bullet struck a rib, glanced, passed part way around her body, and came out near the spine. As the fight had just commenced, Captain Cushing told her by motions and as best he could, to stay there and she would be taken care of, but not comprehending his meaning, and now, for the first time, realizing that white men were engaged in the battle, she thought, as he started to go, that she was to be left, and with the most pitiful moan ever uttered by human lips, she lifted her arms, clasped him around his limbs, and in every possible way, begged him not to leave her with the savages. Others passing by, he called them in, and the woman was partially made to understand that she would be cared for. He disengaged himself from her embrace, and after the fight had ended, returned and took her to the surgeon, who saw that her wounds were not fatal, that they were properly dressed, and provided for her as best he could on the return march to Fort Sedgwick, opposite where Julesburg now stands, where she was placed in the hospital and soon recovered. A few months later, having no home or friends where she was taken captive, she was married to a soldier, who was discharged by reason of expiration of service. The troops and scouts captured in this fight, nearly six hundred head of horses and mules, all the tents of the two tribes, an immense quantity of buffalo meat and robes, fifty guns of various kinds, with pistols, fancy Indian head-dresses, trinkets, etc., and $1,900 in twenty-dollar gold pieces, which the Indians had taken from this German woman's father at the time she was captured. About $900 of this gold was restored to the woman, and if the white soldiers had been as honest and generous as the brave Pawnee scouts, when the appeal for its restoration was made, every lost dollar would have been returned. Of the 8000, the scouts gave up over 860). The seventeen prisoners taken, included Tall Bull's wife and child. They were first carried to Fort Sedgwick, then sent to Omaha, where they were kept under guard for about six weeks, and then sent to the Whetstone Agency, on the Missouri River above Yankton. The widowed squaw married a Sioux Indian at the Red Cloud Agency, where she is now living.

Prairie Dogs.—The little villages of prairie dogs which are seen frequently by passengers from the car windows, soon after leaving Sidney, and line the track for many miles, are full of curious features of animal life. Ladies clap their hands, and children shout with glee at sight of these cunning little creatures. It is a pretty little animal, curious in shape, always fat, grayish red color, about sixteen inches in length, and always lives with a multitude of its companions in villages. It has a short, yelping sound, which it is very fond of uttering, and has some resemblance to the bark of a young puppy. The curious mounds or burrows are of considerable dimensions, dug in a sloping direction at an angle of forty-five degrees with the surface of the ground. After descending two or three yards they make a sudden turn upward, and terminate in a spacious chamber.

In the same hole with the prairie dog is found frequently the *burrowing owl*, and often upon the summits of their little burrows may be seen the solemn owl on one side of the hole in stately silence; while on the other side is the lively little prairie dog, squatted on the fattest part with head bobbed up, and fore paws hanging down, ready at the slightest noise to dart headfirst into his hole. In some of these holes rattlesnakes have been found. What harmony or congruity there can be in the lives of these three diverse species of creatures to help form a happy family, no one can give the reason, but all accounts seem to agree that the stately owl and the treacherous snake make their home with the little dogs, to abuse the hospitality of their four-footed friends by devouring their young.

The scene presented by one of these dog villages is very curious. The prairie dog is no less inquisitive than timid. On the approach of an intruder, the little creature gives a sharp yelp of alarm, and dives into its burrow, its example being at once followed by all its neighbors. For an instant the village appears to be deserted; but soon their curiosity gets the better of their prudence, and their inquisitive little noses are seen protruding from their burrows, to ascertain the cause of the alarm, a curiosity which often costs them dear. The prairie dog is remarkably tenacious of life, and unless shot in the head is sure to escape into its hole. The writer has often seen attempts to shoot them from the train as it passes. Away scampers the little dog,

stomach so full that it touches the ground, while little feet pulled for dear life for its own hole, and by its side or under it traveled the livelier bullet, each tearing up a stream of dust quicker than the eye can follow. Attempts have been made to tame them as pets, but they rarely ever live long, and have too apt a way of biting off fingers. They live only on the roots of grasses, not being flesh eaters.

Burton, an early traveler across the continent in 1861, was immensely interested in his examination of a prairie dog village. The Indians call them "*Wish-ton-wish*," from some slight resemblance to this cry.

"Wish-ton-wish" was at home, sitting posted like a sentinel upon the roof, and sunning himself in the mid-day glow. It is not easy to shoot him; he is out of doors all day, but timid and alert; at the least suspicion of danger he plunges with a jerking of the tail, and a somersault quicker than a shy young rabbit, into the nearest hole. peeping from the ground, and keeping up a feeble little cry, (wish-ton-wish!) more like the notes of a bird than a bark. If not killed outright, he will manage to wiggle into his home. The villages are generally on the brow of a hill, near a creek or pond, thus securing water without danger of drowning. The holes, which descend in a spiral form, must be deep, and are connected by long galleries, with sharp angles, ascents and descents, to puzzle the pursuer. Lieutenant Pike had 140 kettles of water poured into one without dislodging the occupant. The precincts of each village are always cleared of grass, upon which the animals live, as they rarely venture half a mile from home. In the winter time they stop the mouth of their burrows, and construct a deeper cell, where they live till spring appears.

The Indians and trappers eat the flesh, declaring it to be fatter and better than that of the squirrel. If the meat is exposed for a night or two to the frost, all rankness will be corrected. In the same hole are found rattlesnakes, the white burrowing owl, tortoises and horned frogs, the owl often gratifying his appetite by breaking open the skull of a young dog, with a smart stroke of his beak."

Iliff, the Late Cattle King of the Plains,

Had a range 150 miles long, a herd of 26,000 head, and was called the Great Cattle King of the plains, and had the "boss ranche" of this western country. This ranche is in northern Colorado. It begins at Julesburg, on the Union Pacific Railroad, and extends to Greeley, 156 miles west. Its southern boundary is the South Platte River; its northern, the divide, rocky and bluffy, just south of the Lodge Pole Creek. It has nearly the shape of a right-angled triangle, the right angle being at Greeley, the base line being the South Platte River. The streams flowing through it are, first,

PRAIRIE DOG CITY.

the river just named, Crow Creek, and other small creeks and streams which take their rise in living springs, in and near the bluffs of the divide mentioned, and flow in a southerly direction into the South Platte River. It includes bottom and upland ranges, and has several camps or ranches. The chief ranche is nearly south of Sidney, and about forty miles from Julesburg. At this ranche there are houses, sheds, stables, and corrals, and more than two sections of land fenced in. All the cattle bought by the late Mr. Iliff were rebranded and turned over to him at this place. Here are the private stock yards, with corrals, chutes, pens and all necessary conveniences for handling cattle. It is near the river, and of course has fine watering facilities, while from the adjoining bottom lands plenty of hay may be cut for the use of the horses employed in herding. He cut no hay for his cattle; they live the entire year on the rich native grasses on the range, and with the exception of a severe winter, now and then, the percentage of loss is not very great.

Mr. Iliff was a thorough cattle man, and from his long experience had a perfect knowledge of the business. He began in 1860, and during the war had government contracts to fill, in New Mexico and other frontier territories. He supplied most of the beef to the contractors who built the Union Pacific Railroad, and brought immense herds of cattle from Texas and the Indian Territory which were driven along the line of the road to supply the army of laborers with beef. He had been engaged in the stock business in Kansas, New Mexico, and in Colorado, and thought that this location was admirably adapted to it, if the sheep men would only keep out. Cattle and sheep will not do well on the same range together. Success in either requires separation. Mr. Iliff purchased and owned more than twenty thousand acres of the range occupied which, of course, included the choice springs and watering places within its limits.

He had more than 40,000 head of cattle, of all ages, sizes and conditions. The number of calves branded on his ranche one year, reached nearly 5,000 head, and his sales of three and four-year-old steers and fat cows, reached nearly the same number. He realized about $32 per head, net, on these sales. At this rate, 4,000 head would bring the snug little sum of $128,000. To take care of this immense herd, he employed from twelve to thirty-five men — very few, usually in the winter months, and the largest number during the "round ups" in the spring. During the shipping season of 1875, he had twenty-four men who were employed in cutting out of his herd the four-year-old steers that were ready for market, some fat three-year-olds, and such fat

cows as were no longer fit for breeding purposes. While engaged in this work, the same men gather the cows with unbranded calves, which they put into the corrals near by, and after the calves are branded they are turned loose with the herd again. By the introduction of thorough-bred Durham bulls, his herd was rapidly graded up. In addition to the cattle raised on his ranche, he dealt largely in Texas and Indian cattle, and advertised for 20,000 head of Texas cattle to be delivered on his ranche during the driving months of 1876. These cattle must be yearlings, two and three-year-old steers, and for them he had to pay $7, $11 and $15 per head, respectively. This is, at least, 10 per cent. advance on the prices paid for the same kind of cattle in 1875, and indicates their growing scarcity in Texas. Oregon and Montana cattle, are now beginning to come East, and 50,000 head were driven down for the season of 1878 to various points.

Mr. Iliff estimated the increase of cattle from his home herd—outside of purchases and sales—to be about 70 per cent. per year, and about equally divided as to gender. He did not separate his bulls from the herd, but allowed them to remain with it the entire year. In this part of his management, we believe he made a mistake, as the percentage of increase would be much larger if no calves were born during the severe winter and spring months of each year. The loss in calves at these times must be very great. The shipping points for his ranche were at Pine Bluffs and Julesburg, on the Union Pacific, and at Deers' Trail on the Kansas Pacific. The most of his cattle, however, were shipped over the first-mentioned road.

Lest any one should come to the conclusion that this business is all profit, and that the expenses and losses do not amount to much, let us further state that Mr. Iliff's policy was to keep his expenses as low as possible, having the keeping and safety of his cattle constantly in view. In 1875, the expenses of herding, cutting hay for horses, etc., amounted to less than $15,000. But the loss 's from thefts and death, some years, are frightful. The winter of 1871-2 was very severe. There were deep snows over his range that remained on the ground a long time, and the storms were incessant. In the midst of these storms, Mr. Iliff visited the ranche, and found his cattle literally dying by thousands. On the islands in South Platte River, he found and drove off into the sand-hills and bluffs on the south side, after great exertion, some 2,700 head, and of this number less than half were recovered. Their bleaching bones now whiten the plains in the vicinity where they were frozen and starved to death, and those finally recovered were found in two different States and four different Territories in the Union. More than $20,000 were expended in efforts to find them; nor was this all. It was impossible to tell, for a number of years, how great the loss had been. His books showed more than 5,000 head unaccounted for. No trace of them, beyond skeletons, could be found. At last, in the spring of 1874, this number was charged to profit and loss account, and the books balanced for a new start. Could they have been sold the fall previous, they would have averaged at least $18 per head, and at this rate would have amounted to $90,000.

It will thus be seen that the cattle business is not all profit; that it is liable to losses the same as any other business. Taking the years togeth-
er, with ordinary care and judgment, the busi-
ness will pay large profits and prove a desirable investment. We would not, how-
ever, advise every man to undertake it. It is a business that must be learned, and to succeed in it men must have experience, capital, and a good range. Mr. Iliff had all of these, and hence met with correspond-
ing success. The 26,000 head he had, he thought on an aver-
age, were worth $18 per head. This rate would place the capital he has invested in cattle at the sum of $468,000. In addition to this he has 160 head of horses and mules, worth at least $10,000, which are used, principally, in herding, together with wagons, horses, fences, corrals, sheds, stables, mowing-machines, tools and implements, and the large track of land before mentioned. Half a million dollars is a low estimate to name as the sum he had invested in this business, and yet from its very nature he was liable to lose half of it in the next year. Like other business ventures, if a man goes into it, of course he takes the chances,

but with care and good management we see no reason why he should not, in nine cases out of ten, win every time. Let the facts speak for themselves. Ordinary men can't raise a half million dollars, every day, for such an invest-ment, and if they could command that amount, very few would desire a stock ranche and the cattle business.

Bullwhackers.—A curious character of over-land life, when the plains were covered with teams, and long trains of freight-wagons, was the bullwhacker. He is in size and shape usually of very large proportions; very strong, long, un-
kempt hair, and face covered with the stiffest of beards. Eight or ten yoke of oxen were usually attached to each wagon, and often two wag-
ons were doubled up; i. e., the tongue of the second wagon passed under the body of the wag-
on just before it, and then secure-
ly fastened. By the side of his wagon hung his trusty axe and ready rifle, and on the tops of the wagons were spread the red blankets used for their cover at night. Of the bullwhacker, it is said that his *oath* and his *whip* are both the longest ever known. The handle of the ordinary whip is not more than

THE BULLWHACKER OF THE PLAINS.

three feet in length, but the lash, which is of braided rawhide, is seldom less than twenty feet long. From the wooden handle, the lash swells gradually out for about six feet, where it is nearly ten inches in circumference (the point called the "belly"); from here it tapers to within a foot of the end, which terminates in the form of a rib-bon-shaped thong. This is called by some face-tiously a "persuader," and under its influence it will make the ox-team progress at the magic rate of twenty miles per day. The effect on a refractory ox is quite forcible. The lazy ox occasionally receives a reminder in the shape of a whack in the flank, that causes him to double up as if seared with a red-hot iron.

The bullwhacker is universally regarded as the champion swearer of America. He is more profane than the mate of a Mississippi River packet, and his own word is good to the effect that he "*kin drink more whisky.*" The writer who heard this, says that "accompanying this statement were *some of the most astounding oaths that ever fell on the ear.*"

General Sherman humorously tells a story in defence of the extremely profane mule-driver who kept his trains so well closed up during the long marches of the army under his command. It is to this effect: "One of the members of a freighting firm in St. Louis desired to discourage the continual blasphemy of the bullwhackers in their employ. Orders were accordingly issued to their train-masters to discharge any man that should curse the cattle. The wagon-masters were selected more for their piety than for any extensive knowledge of their duties in the handling of trains. The outfit had not proceeded more than a hundred and fifty miles, before it was stuck fast. A messenger was dispatched to the firm with the information that the cattle would not pull a pound unless they were *cursed as usual.* Permission to do this was requested and granted, after which the train proceeded to Salt Lake, to which place good time was made."

The bullwhacker is astonishingly accurate with his lash. One of his favorite pastimes is to cut a coin from the top of a stick stuck loosely into the earth. If the coin is knocked off without disturbing the stake, it is his; if the stake is disturbed, the thrower loses the value of the coin. A curious incident is told of a bullwhacker, noted for the accuracy with which he throws his lash. He bet a comrade a pint of whisky that he could cut the cloth on the back of his pantaloons without touching the skin beneath. The bet was accepted. The individual put himself in position, stooping over to give fair chance. The blow was delivered carefully but in earnest, and thereon ensued the tallest jump ever put on record. The owner being minus a portion of his skin, as well as a large fragment of his breeches, and the bullwhacker's sorrowful cry, " *Thunder, I've lost the whisky.*"

Chappell,—387.4 miles from Omaha. Elevation 3.702 feet. It is a side track with section-houses near by. Trains meet and pass here, but passenger trains do not stop unless signaled.

Lodge Pole—has an elevation of 3,800 feet, and is 396.5 miles west of Omaha. The creek from which this station is named, rises in the Black Hills of Wyoming, west of Cheyenne, and is fed by springs and numerous small streams near its source. It generally has water in its

channel the entire year. In occasional places it sinks into the sand, runs a distance under-ground, and then reappears on the surface again. The valley of the Lodge Pole is quite narrow—the bluffs on either side at times approaching near the track. The whole region of country upon which we have now entered, is covered with buffalo grass, and affords both winter and summer grazing for immense herds of cattle and flocks of sheep. Stockmen claim that both cattle and sheep will do better in this region than farther east, for the reason that the native grasses are more nutritious, and that there is less snow in the winter.

Colton,—406.5 miles from Omaha, and 4,022 feet above the sea. It is simply a side track, named in honor of Francis Colton of Galesburg, Ill., and formerly general ticket agent of the road.

Sidney—is 414.2 miles from the Missouri River, and 4,073 feet above the sea. It is the end of a sub-division of the road, and has a roundhouse and machinery adequate for making minor repairs. The railroad reached and passed here in August 1867. The rocky bluffs which jut up close to the town, were quarried by the railroad men, and stone obtained for various construction purposes. It is now a regular eating-station, where all passenger trains stop for breakfast and supper. The railroad hotel is kept by J. B. Rumsey, and passengers may be assured of good meals, with plenty of time to eat, as the train stops thirty minutes. Sidney is the county-seat of Cheyenne County, Neb. The military post here known as Sidney Barracks, was laid out in 1867, and built in January, 1868, by Colonel Porter. The town has several stores, hotels, saloons and general outfitting establishments. It is the nearest railroad point to the Black Hills, it being only 185 miles by actual measurement to Harney's Peak, and the adjacent gold fields, over an excellent wagon road, with wood and water convenient of access. It has become a great outfitting depot for the Black Hills. A daily stage line and freight train now run regularly, reaching Custer City in thirty hours, and Deadwood in forty-eight hours. It is the point where large quantities of military and Indian supplies are shipped to the agencies and military posts adjoining. It also has a weekly newspaper, *The Sidney Telegraph,* which is quite an enterprising sheet. The town still has the characteristics of a frontier place, and not a small number of roughs have died here "with their boots on." In December, 1875, a man was found hanging to a telegraph pole one morning, who had shot another in cold blood, and without provocation. He was taken from the jail and jailer by masked men and　　ung up as aforesaid. The town was begun　　　 the time the railroad passed through. D.　　gan, now probate judge of the county, and J.　es and

Charles Moore being the first settlers. James Moore was the post trader here for a long time. He is now dead. In the time of the Pony Express he made the remarkable trip of 280 miles in fourteen hours and three-quarters. The town has had trouble with Indians, and was once attacked by them, as related in another place. Even after the trains were running regularly, the Indians would seek for revenge in ditching them and in killing all the employes they could. Section-men always went armed, ready to defend themselves in case of attack. In April of 1869, the Indians attacked two section-men who had gone to the creek for water, and one of them, Daniel Davidson, was killed—his body being literally filled with arrows. Right north of the town, where the traveler can see a small column of stones, was an old fort or breastwork, the remains of which are still visible, which was used as a place of defense in case of Indian raids. A bridge across the North Platte River, on the road to Spotted Tail's Agency, would largely increase the trade and importance of the town. In 1875, the assessed valuation of Cheyenne County was about $1,250,000. There are a large number of stockmen in the county.

Beautiful Cloud Effects.—Artists and all travelers, as they get nearer and nearer to the summit of the Rocky Mountains, will often have fine opportunities to see some magnificent cloud effects. The most glorious sunset ever witnessed by the writer, was one beautiful evening in passing down the line of the Denver Pacific Railroad from Cheyenne. Long's Peak, grand in its sublimity of snow, was surrounded with a collection of clouds, so poised that the rays of the setting sun showed us each side of them. On the hither side the fleecy clouds were lighted up with the grandest of crimson and golden colors; in their midst opened little circular or oval windows, which, letting light upon their upper portions, seemed to be of molten silver; while in their depth of deep azure blue—more beautiful than we can describe—there seemed to glow the intense colors and reflections from the bosom of a mountain lake. Every few minutes the clouds, at our distance from them, changed their position, and new colors, forms, and rays came and went, and when at last the sun itself dropped slowly behind the very point of the peak, and it shone out in startling clearness with the grand display of rainbow-colored clouds above; the sight seemed like a heavenly vision. The editors of the New York and Eastern Editorial Excursion Party of 1875, who witnessed the scene, expressed but one sentiment of admiration, that it was far the most superb cloud and sunset scene ever witnessed. Such scenes are very frequent, and exceedingly captivating to those who have a true artist's eye and appreciation of colors and effects.

An English traveler (to whom beautiful sunsets are unknown) when once traveling from Ogalalla toward Laramie, over the plains, says, "As we journeyed, the sun approached the horizon, and the sky and numerous clouds assumed columns of strange and wonderful beauty. The 'azure vault' itself was of all possible shades of light green, and also of clear light blue; some of the clouds were of solid masses of the deepest indigo, while a few were black, some were purple, and others faintly tinged with crimson and gold. Two days before, I had witnessed cloud effects almost equally fine. There is no monotony in the glorious dawns or beautiful sunsets, which are the rule on these elevated plains, and which go far to relieve the tameness of the landscape.

"As evening approached, on my journey to Laramie, and I neared my destination on the great mountain plains, I saw hovering over one of the snow-capped peaks, a richly colored cloud, so curious in form, and withal so perfect that it might well have been considered a miraculous omen, in the superstitious days of old. It was a most accurate representation of a long waving ostrich plume, in varying tints of crimson and purple and gold; I gazed on it with pleasure and wonder till it faded away."

Sunset in a Storm.—The Earl of Dunraven, in an account of his travels, mentions with wonder these extraordinary sunset scenes : "Just before sundown, the gorgeous flaunting streamers of bright yellow and red that were suddenly shot out across a lurid sky were most wonderful to behold. If the vivid colors were transferred to canvas with a quarter of their real brilliancy, the eye would be distressed by the representation, and the artist accused of gross exaggeration and of straining after outrageous effects.

"These stormy American sunsets are startling, barbaric, even savage in their brilliancy of tone, in their profusion of color, in their great streaks of red and broad flashes of yellow fire; startling, but never repulsive to the senses, or painful to the eye. For a time the light shone most brilliantly all over the western hemisphere, breaking through a confused mass of dazzling purple-edged clouds, massed against a glowing, burnished copper sky, darting out bright arrows through the rifts and rents, and striking full upon the mountain top.

"But not long did this glorious effulgence last. The soul of the evening soon passed away ; as the sun sank, the colors fled. The mountains became of a ghastly, livid greenish color, and as the faint rose light paled, faded slowly upward and vanished, it really looked as though the life were ebbing away, and the dull gray death-hue spreading over the face of a dying man."

Sunset Scene on Mount Washburne.—The Earl of Dunraven ascending, in the summer of 1874, the summit of Mt. Washburne was rewarded at sunset with a scene of extraordinary magnificence, which he relates as follows : " The sun was getting very low, and the valleys were already steeped in shade. To the east all was dark, but in the western heavens long flaming streaks of yellow were flashing across a lowering sky. The masses of black clouds were glowing red with an angry flush. The clear white light of a watery sun had changed into broad streaks of flaunting saffron. Across all the hemisphere, opposed to it, the setting orb was shaking out the red and yellow folds of its banners, challenging the forces of the storm, which was marshaling on the horizon its cloud warriors resplendent in burnished gold.

"The sun sank behind a cloud, and I turned away to descend; but as we went, the sun, though invisible to us, broke through some hidden rift in the clouds, and shone out bright and strong, splashing its horizontal rays full against the opposite slope, and deluging the lower portions of the valley with a flood of intense cherry-colored lurid light. The hills reddened as if beat upon by the full glare of a great furnace. It was a sight most glorious to see. The beauty of it held us and forced us to stop. The glow did not gradually ripen into fullness, but suddenly, and in all its intensity, struck upon a prominent ridge, lighting up the crags and cliffs, and even the rocks and stones, in all their details, and then by degrees it extended and spread on either side over the foot-hills, bringing out the projecting slopes and shoulders from deep gloom into clear light, and throwing back the valley into blackest shade. Every rock and precipice seemed close at hand, and shone and glowed with such radiance that you could trace the very rents and crevices in the cliff faces, and mark the pine trees clinging to the sides, while in comparison the deep recesses of the chasms and cañons seemed to extend for miles back into dark shadow. As the sun sank, so rose the light, rushing upward, surging over the hills in a wave of crimson mist, really beautiful to behold, and illuminating the great bulk of the range, while the peaks were still darkly rearing their sullen heads above the tide, and the valleys were all filled with gray vapors. At last the glare caught the mist, and in an instant transformed it from gray cloud into a gauzy, half-transparent veil light, airy, delicate exceed ingly, in color like the inner petals of the rose. Then, as the sun dropped suddenly, the light flashed upon the summit, the peaks leaped into startling life, and the darkness fell."

Brownson.—Simply a side track. Elevation 4,200 feet above the sea. Distance from Omaha, 424.2 miles. The station was named after a former general freight agent of the Union Pacific. From Sidney, and in this vicinity, the bluffs are rugged, and look like fortifications or the old castles that we read about. They are simply indications of the grand scenery which is to follow.

Potter.—433.1 miles from Omaha. Elevation 4,370 feet. It is a telegraph station. West of Potter you cross the bed of a dry creek, which leads into the Lodge Pole.

Bennett.—Another side track, at which passenger trains do not stop. There is a fine stock ranche near by, and the grazing in this vicinity is excellent. The station is named after Colonel Bennett, the efficient superintendent of the Pullman Palace Car Company at Omaha. It is 442.3 miles from the eastern terminus of the road, with an elevation of 4,580 feet.

Antelope.—451.3 miles from Omaha. Elevation, 4,712 feet. A telegraph and coal station, with side tracks and section-house. In November, 1875, the Indians, who have a liking for good and fast horses, equal to that of Bonner, the *New York Ledger* man, went to the ranche of Mr. Jones, a Kentuckian, about twenty miles south of this station, and stole some forty head of blooded horses and mares which he had there for breeding purposes. They are supposed —believed—to have gone north, and if Uncle Sam's Indian agents would withhold rations from the tribe until they were brought back, or make a thorough search for them, they could undoubtedly be found. Many of the animals were thoroughbreds, and very valuable. Here is another violation of the Sioux treaty. Mr. Jones will have to pocket his loss, while Uncle Sam will, of course, pocket the insult. Antelope is the home of some old hunters, and if the traveler desires to hear their experiences, let him stop a day and interview Jack Evans, who has a ranche here, and Mr. Goff, who has been engaged in the business some fourteen years.

Landscape of the Colorado Plains.—There is a charm in life on the great plains. To one who visits it for the first time, it seems lonely indeed, and yet it is never wearisome.

Now come great rolling uplands of enormous sweep, then boundless grassy plains, and all the grandeur of vast monotony and desolation. Sometimes the grand distances are broken by rugged buttes and bluffs. As they rise in sight, the traveler is as eager in his curiosity as the sea voyager just catching his first view of the distant shore. Over all these plains there is a sparkling, enthusiasm giving atmosphere, crisp, strong, magnetic, and a never-failing breeze; even in the hottest days, or portions of the day, the air is bracing, and rarely ever is the sky long cloudless.

That vastness of solitude, boundless plains, and boundless sky, that stretch of blue, that waste of brown, never a tree, river, bird, or animal, home or life of any nature, who can describe the sensations, which are so overpowering.

As you approach the mountains, the Colorado plains assume more verdure, as they are better watered by the little streams from the foot-hills, or bedewed by the mountain showers. In summer time the landscape is green, and the plains covered with flowers, while in autumn, with the yellow of the prairie grass, the flowers ever stay, new ones coming as old ones disappear. The sunflower is the most profuse of all the species of vegetation that spring up wherever the soil is opened. For thousands of miles, wherever the railroad or a wagon route has made its way across the country, there spring up parallel rows of the ever-living sunflower. In the eastern portions of the plains of Nebraska and Kansas, near the Missouri River, may be seen square miles of sunflowers, 7 to 9 feet high; as we travel farther west, they gradually dwindle until they are, in Colorado, only 3 to 9 *inches* in height, the oddest little plant in nature, yet perfect in shape and growth.

years yet to come, to be only the grazing-field of thousands of buffalo or herds of cattle. Water is scarce, irrigation is impossible, rains uncertain, and in many parts the soil is full of soda and alkali. The western march of settlement practically ends at the one hundredth meridian of longitude—North Platte.

Coyotes. — Pioneers, Indians and drivers, unite in the most thrilling exclamations of their detestations of this, the meanest of the animal tribe that infest the plains. Just after twilight, if you happen to be encamped on the plains, you will hear not far off the quick bark of a single coyote. This is the first call, the bugle cry. Then come answers, and the pack of wolves assemble rapidly; and just as darkness closes down, you have but one enjoyment left, to listen to the most

COYOTES.

Into this vast area of plains, which reaches from east to west 500 miles, and north to south 1,000 miles, there can be poured nearly all the population of Europe and Asia. Swallowing up by the thousands, the plains, with open mouth, wait with insatiate appetite for more. Into this area can be put the whole of India. It is twice as large as Hindostan, and as large as the whole of the United States east of Chicago.

Agriculture is certain as far west as the three hundredth mile from the Missouri River; from thence westward, to the immediate vicinity of the mountains, no crops can at present be raised. This reach of 200 miles or more is, for many

dismal of howling matches. As each new comer arrives he is welcomed with a howl. Each howl is short, and by the band there seems to be a chosen few who execute them in proper manner, with all the variations. After these few have performed some of their most "striking airs," a silence of a few moments' duration follows, and then the whole band breaks out with the most unearthly noises, which are second to no other noises of plains and mountains. Kit Carson once said of these howls, "that it was only a little dispute as to which coyote had, as the winner of the match, the right to take the stakes (steaks)." A traveler says of them: "It is quite impossible to do full justice to this wolf music. There is no racket known to the inhabitants of the more civilized sections of our country which will compare with it. All the felines in the neighborhood would not make a noise which would begin to equal wolf music." Strange as it may seem, the rough pioneer esteems this music his sweetest lullaby, for as one of the old " rough and readies" says: " If any redskin should take it under his scalp to look about camp, every cuss of them coyotes would shut up his trap and wake the fellows up with the *quiet.*" So long as the coyote cries there is no danger from Indians—the moment he ceases, danger is near—so the pioneer esteems their music his best lullaby, and their bark his safety. Occasionally the pack, toward early morning, will make a raid into the traveler's camp, and grab any edibles or pieces left within reach; even sometimes seizing the very haversack upon which the sleeper's head is pillowed, but seldom ever touching the persons of the campers. As morning approaches, they retire to a safe distance from camp, and squatted on their haunches like dogs, wait till the party leaves.

The *plains men* have an old saying, " That the coyotes can smell a *States feller*, and then you will not see a coyote anywhere within sight of camp." The explanation for which is supposed to be as follows, given also by the old plains men : " States fellers shoots at any live thing as jumps in their sight, whether it is any 'count to them or no."

Adams. — A side track 457.3 miles from Omaha; elevation 4,781 feet. The country here is considerably broken, and between the bluffs on either side huge boulders crop out.

Bushnell, — 463.2 miles from Omaha, and 4,860 feet above the sea. It is simply a side track with water tank. In coming up this valley the railroad crosses the Lodge Pole Creek, or its little branches, several times. Near Bushnell is a trestle bridge across the creek.

Hailstorms.—This region of country is frequently, in summer, visited with hailstorms and cloud-bursts. In the summer of 1875, a train was overtaken by one of these hailstorms, and not a whole pane of glass was left in the side of the cars toward the storm. The glass in skylights on the top of the cars was broken, and many of the hailstones, as large as a man's fist, bounded through the cars on the opposite side. The wooden sides of the cars were dented, and the sheet-iron casing of the engine-boiler looked as though it had passed through a violent case of the small-pox. When these cloud-bursts occur, the drops of rain seem as large as walnuts, and come so fast that the entire surface of the ground is covered—the surplus water not having time to run off. In such storms the road is liable to washouts, and great care is necessary in the running of trains to avoid accidents.

Bushnell is the last station in Nebraska. Just across the line, between it and Wyoming, comes *Pine Bluffs,*—473.2 miles from Omaha; elevation 5,026 feet. The little station takes its name from the stunted pines along the bluffs. Pine timber once was plenty here, but it disappeared when the road was built. It is the great trail and crossing point for Indians passing from the buffalo grounds on the Republican to Horse Creek and North Platte River. Was several times attacked by Indians during construction of road, several were killed and large amounts of stock stolen. It is now the head-quarters of Judge Tracy's cattle ranche, and several carloads of cattle are shipped each year. Muddy Creek is just west of station, has water most of the time, yet Lodge Pole Creek, beyond Egbert, sinks in the sand. Water can be found in the bed of the stream by digging 3 to 9 feet. This is a telegraph station, with side track, cattle-yards and chutes.

Tracy,—478.8 miles from Omaha; elevation 5,140 feet. It is a side track named in honor of Judge Tracy of Cheyenne.

Egbert,—484.4 miles from Omaha; elevation 5,272 feet. It is a side track with water tank. Three miles south of this side track runs the Muddy, which has quite a settlement of ranchemen. The Lodge Pole at this point is still dry, and the company dug thirty-two feet for the water which supplies their tank. The road here leaves the main valley of the Lodge Pole, to the right, and runs up a branch, in which the bed of a creek is visible, but which never has water in it except after the cloud-bursts spoken of.

Burns,—490.7 miles from the Missouri River, with an elevation of 5,428 feet. The grade is now quite heavy as we are going up on to the divide between the Lodge Pole and Crow Creek. Burns is simply a side track where trains occasionally meet and pass.

Hillsdale,—a telegraph station with side track and section-house. The place takes its name from a Mr. Hill, who was killed here by the Indians at the time the road was located. He belonged to the engineer corps of the road. The company's well here, which supplies the water tank, is 72 feet deep. North and south of this station numerous sheep ranches have been opened. By looking straight west, up the track, you can here obtain the first glimpse of the Black Hills of Wyoming—and they will come into plain view as you ascend the heavy grade toward the divide. Hillsdale is 5,591 feet above the sea, and 496.4 miles from Omaha. Notice the grade indicated by the elevations as you pass these stations.

Atkins,—502.6 miles from Omaha, and 5,800 feet above the sea. It is a side track, simply, with water tank and section-house near by. The well which supplies this station with water is over 200 feet deep. Here the traveler obtains a good view of the Black Hills stretching off to the right. Still up the grade you go, reaching the summit of the divide in the first snow shed on the line of the road just beyond

Archer,—which is 508 miles from the starting place, with an elevation of 6,000 feet above tide-water. This station is a side track with section-house near by. A short distance farther, you

makes its way through the bluffs off to the left. Soon we come to a deep cut through the spur of a bluff, passing which, we cross a bridge over a dry ravine, and then continue up the hill to the "Magic City" of the plains, called Cheyenne.

Long's Peak.—Travelers will notice, a few

LONG'S PEAK FROM ESTES PARK.

enter the shed; it seems like passing through a tunnel. In the distance there are mountains "to the right of you," and mountains "to the left of you," but we shall see more of them here-after. Leaving the snow shed we are now on a down grade into Crow Creek Valley, which

hours before reaching Cheyenne, the snow-clad summit of this bold peak, rising above the dis-tant horizon. It is about sixty miles south-west of the Union Pacific Railroad, and the highest mountain in northern Colorado. The view we here give is taken from Estes Park; a beautiful little park on its north-western slope, and about twelve miles distant from the summit. This park is about four miles wide, and six miles long, is well sheltered, easy of access, and beautifully covered with pine and spruce trees, scattered easily about over the grassy surface, which gives to it a true park-like loveliness. It is partially occupied by a few families who have taken up permanent homesteads, and has been for a long time an excellent pasture for large herds of cattle which live here the entire year. It is also becoming quite a pleasure resort, and has many attractive features to interest the health seeker and tourist. Excellent fishing, in lovely little trout streams, can be found all over the vicinity. From this valley is the only practicable route for ascending the peak. Long's Peak is 14,271 feet in elevation, and about 6,300 feet above the park. Its construction is of the boldest and most decided character, with great walls, deep canons; and on its sides there are gorges and caverns among the grandest on the continent. Its summit is divided into two sharp crests, the western one being the highest and most difficult of ascent. It is a famous landmark for a stretch of country of more than a hundred miles from north to south.

Buffaloes.—Buffalo hunting is a pastime tourists can now have little hope to indulge in. Few or no buffaloes ever appear within sight of the car windows of the overland trains, and the vast herds which once roamed for thousands of miles and continually up and down the great plain, are passing away, or disappearing from their old haunts to find some nook or corner more quiet and secure. Thousands of them have been killed during the past two or three winters for commercial purposes. The hides are stripped off and sold for as low prices as $1.50, while the bones are gathered in heaps near the railroad station and freighted eastward to be used for commercial fertilizers. In one winter it is estimated that on the lines of the Union and Kansas Pacific Railroad there were killed over 100,000 head.

A Smart Indian Trade. — The Indians which in olden times used to visit the military posts, were noticeable for their great anxieties to trade, and for their great shrewdness, which had often the spice of humor.

At one of the posts a Kiowa chief endeavored to consummate a bargain for an officer's wife, by offering as an equivalent a large number of *fat dogs;* the number was so large that the Indians present thinking it was impossible for the officer to withstand so tempting an offer, made haste to express their willingness to *help eat the dogs,* if there were more than the white man could manage for himself.

But it is among the Indians themselves that the sharpest species of trading is seen. In the great passion of the Indian for "fire-water"—

whisky—there comes out, in their trade for it, all the possible shrewdness and cunning of the races.

At one time, as a military officer relates the story, there was a Kiowa village, beautifully located for the winter near a grove of old cottonwood trees. The fact that the village was rich in buffalo robes and other skins became known to a band of the Cheyenne tribe. Stealing would not answer, as there were too many Kiowas and too few Cheyennes. But the shrewdness of the Cheyennes appeared soon in the shape of a bottle of whisky; how they obtained it was a mystery not explained.

With their whisky, the Cheyennes proceeded to the Kiowa village, exhibited their bottles, and distributed around a few judicious smells of the refreshing corn juice; every now and then giving the bottle a shake, so that the aroma should be thoroughly appreciated by *their friends the Kiowas.*

The smells were freely accepted, and there was an uncommon desire manifested to know more (i. e., get better acquainted) of the Cheyennes. Pipes were produced and duly smoked; after which the visitors announced their willingness to trade, as they said.

"They had not brought much whisky, as they did not know that their brothers, the Kiowas would like to see it. The little that they had with them was good and very strong," (with water) "when the Kiowas had tasted of it they would see." The Cheyenne was liberal, "he would give so much," (holding up the bottle and marking with the thumb something like half an inch of the whisky). "But seeing that the Kiowas were not in haste to trade, the Cheyennes would smoke with them." Meanwhile a kindly disposed bottle-holder was dispensing smells of the whisky to a few Kiowas, who were loud in their announcements of the number of fine robes which they possessed. This second smoke was quickly finished, and the Cheyenne again exhibited the *fire-water,* marking it as before by the location of the thumb on the bottle.

A general exclamation followed, for to the Kiowa's eye the position of the thumb on the bottle was so very much higher (i. e., so much less whisky than before). To this Cheyenne had no consideration; the trouble he said, was with the eyes of the Kiowas, which could not be expected to see big like those of a Cheyenne. Another smelling time ensued, which was followed by an instantaneous exhibition by the Kiowas of tin cups and robes, and the Cheyennes began to pour out the whisky.

While pouring out the promised grog, the position of the thumb on the bottle was regarded by each Kiowa with the most exact scrutiny, which effectually prevented all attempts to shove up the gauge. And it was noticeable by the care of the bottle-holders, that when the bottle was held up after each pass, no Indian could detect the

THE DOME OF THE CONTINENT, GRAY'S PEAK, COLORADO.

slightest variation between the whisky mark and the position of the finger on the bottle.

The Kiowas did not get drunk, and the Cheyennes left the village with all their ponies loaded with robes, having as they freely remarked, made a "*heap smart trade.*"

Astonishment of Indians at the Locomotive and Telegraphs.—When the first locomotive was seen passing over the plains, an Indian guide in the employ of the United States, exclaimed with inexpressible surprise, "Good Medicine *good medicine.* Look look," at the tu-te (toot). As he passed under the telegraph wires which then were stretching along the Platte, through which the wind as it swept, made the whirr and singing sound of a *prairie harp,* this guide heard the sound, and directly declared that they were talking "*medicines.*" This was supposed to be the creations of the *great spirit,* and everything of supernatural nature was "*medicine.*"

The Indians have rarely ever molested the telegraph wires which spanned the continent. Perhaps the following incident may have much to do with their respectful and distant attitude :— Shortly after the wires were erected, the attaches of the Telegraph Company invited a number of Indian chiefs to meet them at a given point, and from thence to travel, one party East and the other West.

When they had reached a distance of 100 miles apart, each party was invited to dictate a message to the other, which was sent over the wires. Then turning backward, they rode rapidly toward each other, and two days later met and compared notes. They were greatly astonished, and expressed themselves convinced that the "*Great Spirit*" had talked to them with the wires. They decided from that time it would be well to avoid meddling with the wires.

Soon after a little incident happened, which, in the minds of the Indians, seemed to settle forever the opinion that the telegraph belonged to the Great Spirit. A young Sioux Indian was determined to show that he had no faith in the Great Spirit's connection with the wires, so he set to work with his hatchet to cut down one of the telegraph poles. A severe thunder-storm was going on at a distance ; a charge of electricity being taken up by the wires, was passed to the pole which the Indian was cutting, and resulted in his instant death. After that the tribe never molested the telegraph again.

An Indian Prayer.—The following actual translation of an Indian prayer will give an idea of their feelings and longings, and the extent of their moral sentiments. It is a prayer to the Great Spirit by a Crow Indian :

"I am poor ; that is bad."

"Make me a Chief ; give me plenty of horses ; give me fine clothing. I ask for good spotted horses."

"Give me a large tent ; give me a great many horses ; let me steal fine horses ; grant it to me."

"Give me guns by cheating ; give me a beautiful woman ; bring the buffalo close by."

"No deep snow ; a little snow is good."

"Give me Black Feet to kill or to die ; close by, all together."

"Stop the people from dying, it is good."

"Give instruments for amusements, blankets too, and fine meats to eat."

"Give the people altogether plenty of fine buffalo, and plenty to eat."

CHEYENNE.

"*Magic City of the Plains,*"—516 miles from Omaha ; elevation, 6,041 feet. Thus truly is it named, for it is at present the most active and stirring city on the entire line. Travelers will here take a dinner in comfortable style at one of the best kept hotels between the two oceans. It is a good place to rest after a tiresome journey, and it will pay to stop a few days and enjoy the pure air and genial sun in this high altitude. The hotel is owned by the railroad company, and is 150 feet long by 36 wide, with a wing 25 feet square. It has an elegant dining-hall, around which hang the heads of antelope, deer, elk, mountain-sheep, black-tailed deer, buffalo, etc., all nicely preserved and looking very natural. It is two stories high, and the upper floor being well furnished with sleeping-rooms for guests. Cheyenne is the capital of Wyoming and the county-seat of Laramie County. Cheyenne has had its ups and downs. Once very lively when the road was building, then it fell dead and motionless. Now it has arisen again, and is the largest town on the railroad between Omaha and Salt Lake City, having a population of fully 4,000, and rapidly growing. There are two causes for this growth. First, the stock interests which center here, and second, the recent gold discoveries in the Black Hills. It is the terminus of the Denver Pacific Railroad, and of the Colorado Central completed, 1877, giving two routes to Colorado and New Mexico. During the last two years there has been a large increase in the permanent buildings of the city. In 1875, the Inter-Ocean hotel was completed — a fine brick structure three stories high, and other large and elegant brick blocks with iron and glass fronts. In proportion to its population, Cheyenne has more elegant and substantial business houses than most any other western city. Its inflation period has long since passed away, and its future growth, like its present, will be substantial and permanent. The town has a fine court-house and jail, which cost $40,000, a large public school building, a good city hall, and a brick opera-house. This is a wonderful change for a place known the world over by its fearful sobriquet of "Hell on Wheels." Churches have come where gamblers once reigned; and in five years as many edifices for religious purposes have been erected. The Episcopalians, Methodists, Presbyterians, Congregationalists and Catholics have all comfortable church buildings. The school accommodations, owing to the rapid growth of the city, will soon have to be enlarged. At first sight the traveler would naturally inquire, what there was to build and sustain a town here? The soil is not prolific, nor is the country around it. Crow Creek bottom is quite narrow, and in the most favorable seasons, by irrigation, "garden truck" may be raised, but beyond this everything looks barren and desolate. The soil has a reddish appearance, and appears to consist of decomposed granite underlaid in the valleys with sand and on the uplands with rock. In fact, a man who attempts to farm it for a living in this region of country is simply fooling away his time.

Stock Interests.—The rich nutritious grasses with which the great plains are covered are here found in all their excellence, and the large territory east at the base of the Black Hills, north as far as the North Platte River and south to the Gulf of Mexico, is now sustaining millions of sheep and cattle. Cheyenne is located in the midst of one of the best sections of this territory, and all around it are the ranches of stockmen—men engaged in growing cattle, sheep, horses and mules for market. With the exception of sheep, no hay is cut for these animals except for those kept up for use. Winter and summer they thrive and fatten upon nothing but the native grasses. Cheyenne is the central and natural trading-point for these ranchmen and stock growers. Another large and valuable element of its prosperity is the railroad trade—the company having here quite extensive machine and repair shops, with a commodious roundhouse. Hunting and exploring parties also supply themselves with outfits at this place, and immense quantities of military and Indian supplies also pass through here for the posts and Indian agencies north.

To give an idea of the stock business which centers here, and its rapid increase, let us state that 375 cars of cattle were shipped in 1874. which represent 7,500 head. In 1875, the shipments increased to 525 cars, or 10,500 head, with prospects for a large increase in 1876 and future years. It may be well to state here, the shipments from other points in this grazing belt of the country:

North Platte in 1875 shipped 96 cars, or 1,920 head.
Ogalalla, " " 207 " 4,140 "
Julesburg, " " 216 " 4,320 "
Sidney, " " 93 " 1,860 "
Pine Bluffs, " " 208 " 4,160 "

This statement does not include the cattle marketed at home or supplied to the Indian agencies in the north. Sixty thousand head of cattle, seventy thousand sheep and four thousand horses and mules are the estimated number owned and

held in Laramie County alone. The development of the cattle and stock interests of this vast upland region is something never thought of nor entered the heads of the projectors of the railroad. In 1867, when the railroad first arrived, there was not probably a hundred head of all kinds owned in the whole territory, outside of those belonging to contractors and stage lines. Now it is a leading interest, and represents millions of dollars. Like all other frontier towns, Cheyenne has a history, and it is similar to that of others. It was once a very fast town, and it is not very slow now. On the 1st day of July, 1867, it had one house built and owned by Judge J. R. Whitehead, on Eddy street, between Sixteenth and Seventeenth. That house stands to-day, and is known as the Whitehead block. It was built of logs and smoothly plastered, outside and in.

Rough Times.—When it was known that this was to be the winter terminus of the road, there was a grand hegira of roughs, gamblers and prostitutes from Julesburg and other places down the road to this point, and in the fall of that year and winter of '68, Cheyenne contained 6,000 inhabitants. Habitations sprang up like mushrooms. They were of every conceivable character, and some were simply holes in the ground, otherwise termed "dug-outs." Town-lots were sold at fabulous prices. Every nation on the globe, nearly, was represented here. The principal pastimes were gambling, drinking villainous rot-gut whisky, and shooting. Shooting scrapes were an every-day occurrence. Stealing anything from anybody was the natural habit of the thieving roughs. Knock downs and robberies were daily and nightly amusements. But these things had to come to an end, and their perpetrators, some of them, to a rope's end. The more respectable portion of the citizens became weary of the depredations on property and life. Vigilance committees were organized, and "Judge Lynch" held court, from which there were neither appeals nor stay of executions. Juries never disagreed, nor were there vexatious delays and motions for a new trial. Witnesses were unnecessary and demurrers of no account. Nor would "the insanity dodge" avail. The victims were known and "spotted" beforehand, the judgments of the courts were unerring and generally righteous. No gallows were erected, because telegraph poles and the railroad bridge across Crow Creek were convenient of access. When Cheyenne was only six months old, so frequent were the murders and robberies, and the city authorities so powerless, that a vigilance committee was organized. The first knowledge of its existence happened thus: Three men were arrested on the 10th day of January, 1868, charged with having stolen $900. They were put under bonds to appear before the court on the 14th of the same month. On the morning of the day after they were arrested, they were found on Eddy street, tied together,

5

walking abreast with a large piece of canvas attached to them, on which the following words were conspicuous: "$900 *stole*; $500 *returned*; *thieves—F. St. Clair, W. Grier, E. D. Brownville. City authorities please not interfere until 10 o'clock a. m. Next case goes up a tree. Beware of Vigilance Committee.*" Within one year after its organization, the "vigilantes" had hung and shot twelve desperadoes and sent five to the penitentiary. Since that time Cheyenne has been ruled by the law-and-order party, though even these may seem rather lax to eastern people not accustomed to the manners and customs of the frontier. Yet the people enjoy "peace."

On the 13th day of November, 1867, the track layers reached the city limits, and on the 14th the first passenger train arrived. The arrival of the track layers was greeted with music, a display of bunting, while the inhabitants turned out *en masse* to meet them. On the 14th an enthusiastic meeting of citizens was held to extend a public greeting to the railroad officials who had arrived on the first train, among whom were Sidney Dillon, Esq., now president of the company, and General Casement of Ohio, the champion track layer of the continent.

The first city government was organized, by the election of officers, on the 10th of August, 1867. The first newspaper was issued on the 19th of September, called the *Cheyenne Leader*, and has maintained its existence ever since—publishing daily and weekly editions. Other papers have since been started, but they were short-lived, until the publication of the *Cheyenne Daily News*, which is a spicy little daily. As the town is now able to support two papers, the *News* (just merged into the *Daily Sun*,) will continue to flourish.

Cheyenne is well laid out, with broad streets at right angles to the railroad, and has an abundant supply of pure water. Irrigating ditches run through the streets. A ditch was dug from Crow Creek to some natural "hollows" or reservoirs north of the town, which form beautiful little lakes. From these the water for the streets is taken by ditches. As a result, trees and shrubbery will soon ornament the streets and yards of the city, which will greatly add to its attractiveness and beauty. There are a few local manufactories already in existence and more will follow, and on a larger scale. With the wool which is soon to be annually shipped from this place, we should think a woolen factory would be a great desideratum.

Precious Stones.—In the adjacent mountains, on the hills and bluffs near by, and in the valleys of the streams in this vicinity, a large number of curious and precious stones, gems rich and rare, have been found. They are very plenty in their natural state, their chief value being in the cost of cutting by a lapidary and mounting by a jeweler. In the immediate neighborhood of Cheyenne the following are found: Moss-agates, in

great profusion; topaz, in colors; garnet or mountain ruby; they are usually found in the little heaps of sand thrown up by ants; opals variegated, rare as yet, and valuable; petrifactions of wood and shells, which when cut, polished and mounted, are splendid; amethysts, onyx, black and white, for cameos and jasper. All of these have been found in this vicinity, though some are rare. The most beautiful moss-agates are found about halfway to Fort Laramie, on Chugwater Creek. Messrs. Joslyn & Park, an old and reliable firm of manufacturing jewelers, in both Cheyenne and Salt Lake City, have made this business a specialty, and possess the largest and finest collection of stones in the country. Some of them are exceedingly beautiful. Fine specimens of petrified palm-wood may be seen at their store. They are both beautiful and rare. The fact that petrified palm-wood and petrified bones of the rhinoceros have been found in this territory, shows that some six million years ago—comparatively recent—there was a tropical climate in this region of country, when the palm flourished in luxuriance, and the rhinoceros sported in the warm streams or cavorted around on their sunny banks. Travelers who are willing to omit their dinner can improve the half hour allowed by the railroad, by a hurried run over to this store, which is but a block away.

Prospects.—At present, the greatest cause of the growth and prosperity of Cheyenne is the discovery of gold in the Black Hills of Dakota. This cause will last until, if that country will warrant it, a railroad is built there. The discoveries of gold seem to be extensive and inexhaustive, and the building of a railroad from some point here or on the Union Pacific or Missouri River, will rapidly follow. The Colorado Central Railroad newly opened gives to Cheyenne very flattering prospects, and its business men are reaping a rich harvest from their investments. The opening of northern Wyoming to settlement, the development of the vast mineral resources of the territory, and the continued prosperity of her stock interests, will give to the "Magic City of the Plains" the trade, growth and influence which her location demands.

Health.—As a resort for health-seekers, Cheyenne has superior advantages. It is about a thousand feet higher than Denver, with an atmosphere not only rarefied but dry. It has good hotels and livery accommodations. Ponies are cheap, and invalids can purchase them and ride over the hills and dales at pleasure. There is also an abundance of game in the vicinity—antelope, rabbits, deer, etc. A bear weighing over 1,500 pounds, was killed near here in 1875. It is the largest one we ever saw. Its skin has been preserved, and the bear has been mounted in good shape. Frequent excursions can also be taken in the warm summer weather to Fort Laramie, Cheyenne Pass, and other places which will expand the lungs

SCENES IN THE BLACK HILLS.

1.—Golden Park.   2.—Genevieve Park.   3.—Custer Park.   4.—Limestone Peak.   5.—Harney's Park.

and invigorate the body. The results of several years' observations at the United States Signal Station here, show that the temperature is more even, taking the years together, than in many places East or on the Pacific coast. The hottest days do not equal those which frequently occur in the East, and in the summer months the nights are deliciously cool, assuring the invalid good sleep under plenty of blankets. We predict a great rush of invalids and health-seekers to this place and vicinity, in the near future. Although Cheyenne is a good place to sleep, yet the people are wide-awake and "owly" nights.

Rapidity of Business at Cheyenne.— On the 22d of July, 1867, the first lots were offered for sale by the Union Pacific Railroad Company at Cheyenne—66 by 132 feet for $150. Thirty days after, these lots sold for $1,000 each, and in two to three months thereafter, the same lots were again resold at $2,000 to $2,500. On the 15th of July, 1867, there was but one house at Cheyenne. Six months thereafter, there were no less than *three thousand*. The government freight which was transported over the plains to Cheyenne, from November, 1867, to February, 1868, four months, amounted to 6,000 tons, and filled twelve large warehouses, and for a long time subsequently averaged 15,000,000 to 20,000,000 pounds annually.

During the fall and winter, there were three forwarding companies whose business in transporting goods, exclusive of government supplies, averaged 5,000,000 pounds per month. Stores were erected with marvelous rapidity. One firm constructed an entire store, 25 by 55 feet, quite substantial, in just forty-eight hours; three hundred firms were in operation that winter, doing mostly a wholesale business; of this number, over seventy made sales of over $10,000 per month each, and with some firms sales reached over $30,000 per month.

The first post-office was established October 30, 1867; salary $1.00 per month. In two months the United States mails had increased so enormously as to average 2,600 letters per day, and in two months more this was doubled, and salary increased to $2,000 per year. Though business declined as soon as the terminus of the road was moved, yet it now has a solid business. The population in 1879 is about 6,000, and there was invested in new buildings, in the single year of 1875, no less than $430,000.

The Black Hills Gold Discoveries.

For several years the impression has obtained that there was gold in the Black Hills of Dakota, and every exploration under the auspices of the government has tended to encourage and strengthen this impression. In 1860, Colonel Bullock, now a resident of Cheyenne, was an Indian agent and trader where Fort Laramie now stands. He saw a squaw in his store, one day,

with something in her mouth. He said, "Let me see that." She gave it to him, and it proved to be a nugget of gold, worth about three dollars. He said, "Give that to me." She told him she would, for some raisins and candy. These he gave her, and afterwards gave her coffee and sugar to its full value. He showed the gold to his interpreter, and requested him, if possible, to find out where it came from. The interpreter did his best, but the squaw would only say that it was picked up in the bed of a creek, and that the Indians would kill her if she told where it was. During his long experience as a trader with the Indians, Colonel Bullock frequently saw small nuggets of gold, but could never find out where the Indians obtained them, and the inferences he drew from all the information he could obtain were to the effect that the Bear Lodge country, nearly north of the Inyan Kara mountain, was the region where this gold came from. According to the most recent information on the subject, the eastern boundary line of Wyoming strikes the Black Hills nearly in the center,—that about one-half are in Dakota and the other half in Wyoming. Harney's Peak and Dodge's Peak are in the former, while the Inyan Kara and Bear Lodge Mountains are in the latter territory. The question of the existence of gold there and other precious metals, can no longer be doubted. The official report of Professor Jenny sufficiently establishes this fact. It also establishes the fact that in a small portion of the country which he examined, it is found in paying quantities. It remains, therefore, for the hardy miners and sturdy pioneers to demonstrate still further whether it is there in large quantities. Thus far every thing has been against them, and they even now are upon forbidden ground, liable at any moment to be driven out of the Hills by United States troops. But there is an implied understanding and belief now becoming quite prevalent that they will be allowed to remain,—that the government will not molest them again. If only this result can be obtained, it will be satisfactory to the miners. They do not fear the Indians; they only ask, if the government will not protect them, that it will not interfere with their mining operations nor destroy their property. Nor will they attack the Indians,—they are safe if they keep away and do not disturb them. If, however, they are attacked, self-defence will require vigorous measures for protection. The law of the case, as we understand it, is simply this: that the reservations agreed upon by the treaty of 1868 are in Dakota territory; that a part of the Black Hills only are in that territory, nor is there any evidence or indications that they ever occupied this part beyond the cutting of a few lodge-poles. The facts are that the Indians are in Nebraska instead of Dakota, and that they are really afraid of the Black Hills because of the terrific storms that visit them, when, "from peak to peak, the rattling crags among, leaps the live thunder," and the pranks of livid lightning are fearful to behold. They have a superstitious reverence for these Hills, and believe them to be the home of the Great Spirit. The treaty only gives them the right to hunt in Wyoming, as far west as the crests of the Big Horn Mountains, whenever there is sufficient game to warrant the chase. With the exception of this proviso, therefore, the whole territory of Wyoming is open to exploration, settlement and development. The next question is,—Will the government protect the pioneers in their explorations? or must they protect themselves in going where they have an undoubted right to go?

The Black Hills are mainly confined to a region of territory lying between the forks of the Cheyenne river. In addition to the gulch and placer diggings, already discovered, there have been a few discoveries of what appears to be rich quartz lodes of gold and veins of silver. This region is about one hundred miles long and eighty miles wide. French Creek, Spring Creek, Rapid Creek, Box-elder Creek, Elk Creek and others head in these Hills, and flow mainly in an eastern direction, emptying into the south fork of the Cheyenne. The north fork seems to hug the hills pretty closely with small creeks and streams, yet unexplored, heading in the mountains and flowing into it. The north fork heads in Pumpkin Butte, a mountain a little north-west of Fort Fetterman, on the North Platte river. West of the northern portion of the Black Hills, there are several ranges of mountains and several streams which flow north into the Yellowstone River. All accounts of this region of country, as far west as the Big Horn Mountains, unite in the report of its rich min-

AGNES PARK.—BLACK HILLS.

eral character, and we believe the richest mineral discoveries ever known on this continent will be made here in the next few years.

How to get to the Black Hills.—Within the past years of 1876 to 1879, there have been opened three distinct routes to the Black Hills, and it is now easy of access. The principal routes are via the Union Pacific Railroad, and stage line from either Sidney or Cheyenne. A longer route is occasionally used by steamers up the Missouri River to Sioux City, Yankton and Port Pierre, and thence by wagon across the plains and "bad lands" of Dakota. This route is long and circuitous, with not as good wood, water or grazing, as the Southern route. From Cheyenne there is a good natural road, which runs to Fort Laramie, a distance of 90 miles, over which the U. S. mails have been carried for many years. It passes through a country with good ranches, at convenient distances apart. From Fort Laramie to Custer and Deadwood City, there is a good wagon road, which has recently been shortened 60 miles, so that the entire distances are as follows:

Cheyenne to Fort Laramie 93 miles; to Custer City, 260 miles; Hill City, 275 miles; Golden City, 295 miles; Rapid City, 315 miles; Elizabeth City, 347 miles; Deadwood, 318 miles; Crook City, 360 miles.

The Cheyenne and Black Hills Stage line now runs regularly, daily trips over the road with a superior outfit for transportation of all classes of passengers. Hitherto the Cheyenne route has been the principal one since it has been the depot of supplies. It is the only route used by the Government Supply trains, is in the proximity of four government military forts and stations, and along the entire route there is an ample supply of wood, water and grain. It is also the line of the telegraph to the Black Hills, which connects Deadwood and Cheyenne. The time occupied in stage travel to the principal places of the Black Hills is from 48 to 60 hours.

Sidney has also become a large outfitting point, and there is now invested nearly $100,000 capital in transportation, equipments for passengers and freight to the Black Hills mines.

Stages leave Sidney every morning at 8 o'clock, and make the distance in following time:

Red Cloud Agency in 20 hours; Buffalo Gap (the point of intersection with stage for Custer, 30 miles West) in 30 hours, and reaches the entire distance to Deadwood in 48 to 60 hours.

By the Sidney route distances are as follows: To Red Cloud Agency, 109 miles; Buffalo Gap, 171 miles; French Creek, 184 miles; Battle Creek, 196 miles; Rapid River, 214 miles; Spring Valley, 228 miles; Crook City, 246 miles; Deadwood, 285 miles. The advantage of distance in favor of the Sidney route is nearly one-fourth less than by any other route.

Result of the Opening of the Black Hills.—During the past season of 1878, the yield of the gold mines was over $3,000,000. Cheyenne bankers are said to have bought above $900,000 worth of gold dust, and various amounts have been forwarded in other ways, besides what has been kept in the Hills. This result has been entirely from *placer mining.* One mining party known as the Wheeler party, has realized nearly $500,000 in one season. Extraordinary success attended their work; $2,600 were cleared in only 42 hours' work, and in general, on Deadwood Creek, the average to the miners on each claim was $300 to $700 per day. Nearly all the yield of the Black Hills in 1876 was gleaned in the vicinity of Deadwood and Whitewood gulches.

Quartz mining has been attempted. First assays were but $38 per ton, and the average of the ores thus far experimented upon, vary from $30 to $50 per ton. During the past year 1,000 stamping mills have been erected.

Miners with mortar and pestle have taken ore from some of these quartz lodes, and realized as high as $15 per day. Since the settlement of Deadwood, prices of living have gradually declined, until good day board now averages only from $7 to $10. Freight from Cheyenne and Sidney now costs but $3 to $4 per 100 lbs. The width of the mineral belt is now definitely ascertained to be but 10 to 15 miles, but it stretches 100 miles long. The agricultural value of the Hills is beyond all words of expression. The valleys have been found to be surpassingly fertile, the rain-fall regular and constant, and were any one dissatisfied with mining, still there is room for thousands of farms and peaceful homes.

A statement is made, apparently of unquestioned accuracy, of an explorer on Spring Creek, who, with three others, and one day's sluicing, took out $38 coarse gold, the pieces varying from

three cents to three dollars in value. One man prospecting on Iron Creek, sixty miles farther off, took out $23.67 from one pan of dirt. Mr. Allen, the recorder of mining claims, took from his claim four pounds of coarse gold in one month, and all reports agree in an average of seven to twenty-five cents per pan, which will turn out per day $7 to $50 to each man.

As a proof of the existence of gold, it is but necessary to quote from the authority of Professor Jenny's report of a visit in July, 1875, whereof writing to the Department of the Interior at Washington, he announces the discovery of gold in paying quantities near Harney's Peak; deposits very rich, with plenty of water in the streams: "The gold is found in quartz ledges of enormous dimensions. Whether the mines be valuable or not, there is a vastness of future wealth in the grass lands, farms and timber. The soil is deep and fertile; the rain-fall more abundant than any other point west of the Alleghanies." In the summer of 1875, an expedition headed by General Custer visited this region, wherein he describes finding an abundance of wild fruits, strawberries, raspberries, gooseberries in wonderful profusion; and frequently the wild berry was larger and more delicious flavor than the domestic species in the Eastern states.

A miner writing from personal view thus speaks of the richness of the section thus far discovered: "I found several miners working their claims, as yet in a crude and primitive manner. Some of them working with a Chinese rocker cleaned up from five to seven pennyweights of gold, the result of but three hours' work. Twenty-five miles north-west of Spring Creek, I found the largest vein of gold quartz I have ever seen, being from 300 to 600 feet in width, and traceable for over 40 miles in length. I also found a vein of white crystallized quartz about four feet in width, in which gold was plainly visible. I obtained some specimens, fabulously rich; one piece was sent to the Omaha smelting works which averaged $42,000 to the ton. At Rapid Creek the prospects are still better than in Spring Gulch. Castle Creek is the richest found in the Black Hills. One claim has been worked to the bed-rock, in the channel, which paid $6.00 of gold to one cubic foot of gravel."

The best mines have proved by the latest discoveries to be on the west side of the Hills, and aside from the value of the precious metal, the superb salubrity of the climate, and the natural richness of the soil, make it extraordinarily attractive. An explorer describes the country as "the richest ever seen or heard of between the Missouri River and Central Oregon. Excellent timber in the greatest abundance; as fine pasturage as I ever saw; rich black loam soil; splendid water; showers every few days; no disagreeable winds; a delicious, bracing atmosphere to either work or rest in; a splendid diversity of hill and valley; prairie and timber forest; a landscape of which the eye never tires."

During one week, 800 miners passed through Hill City, *en route* for the mines of Whitewood and Deadwood. In most of the creeks the bedrock lies 15 to 20 and 40 feet below the surface. On the 1st of March, last year, there were estimated to be over 20,000 people in the Black Hills, and rapidly accumulating at the rate of 1,000 per week, but since the rich Colorado discoveries at Leadville, the excitement has decreased.

A Terrible Thunder-Storm.—The Black Hills of Dakota are the fear of Indians, because of the frequent thunder-storms. Col. R. I. Dodge, United States Commander of Black Hills Expedition, 1874, states that in this region "thunder-storms are quite frequent, terrific in force and power, and fearful in the vividness, the nearness of the lightning. Scarcely a day in summer that there is not a thunder-storm in some part of the hills.

"One afternoon, from the top of one of the high mountains, near Harney's Peak, I saw five separate and distinct storms, occurring at the same instant in different parts of the hills. One of these struck our party with fatal results.

"A heavy rain-storm coming on, two soldiers and the boy took refuge under a tall pine. All three were seated on a rock about six feet from the trunk of the tree, and each held in his hand the reins of his horse's bridle. At the flash, the three persons and horses were thrown to the ground, one of the soldiers being pitched quite a distance, alighting on his head. The surgeon was promptly on hand. Each person had been struck on the check bone, just under the eye. The fluid passed down the person of each, going out at the ball of the foot, boring a hole in the shoe sole as clean and round as if made by a bullet, and raising a large blood blister on the bottom of the foot. Neither had any other mark whatever. Skipping from the men to the horses, the flash prostrated all, striking each just over the eye. Two soon recovered their feet, and the third was killed.

"During this storm, which lasted scarce half an hour, more than twenty trees were struck by lightning within a radius of a few hundred yards.

"At another time, I witnessed another curious and unaccountable phenomenon. I was on a high mountain of the Harney Group. Within four miles of me, in different directions, were three thunder-storms, their clouds being probably 500 or 1,000 feet below me. Though I could see the vivid and incessant flashes of lightning, *not a sound of the thunder could be heard.* Throughout the Hills the number of the trees which bear the mark of the thunder-bolt is very remarkable, and the strongest proof of the violence and frequent recurrence of these storms. The electric current acts in the most eccentric way. In some cases it will have struck the very top of a

LIGHTNING SCENE ON THE PRAIRIES.

lofty pine, and passed down, cutting a straight
and narrow groove in the bark, without any apparent ill effect on the tree, which remains green
and flourishing; at other times the tree will be
riven into a thousand pieces, as if with the blows
of a giant axe, and the fragments scattered a
hundred feet around."

Rainbows.—" The rainbow of the Black
Hills is a marvel of perfection and beauty. Two
or three times wider than the rainbow of the
States, it forms a complete and perfect arch, both
ends being, sometimes, visible to the beholder,
and one so near and distinct that there would be
little difficulty in locating the traditional 'pot of
gold.' Very frequently the rainbow is doubled,
and several times I saw three distinct arches, the
third and higher being, however, a comparatively
faint reflex of the brilliant colors of the lower."

867 feet at base, 297 feet at top. It rises 1,127
feet above its base, and 5,100 feet above tide-
water. Its summit is inaccessible to anything
without wings. The sides are fluted and scored
by the action of the elements, and immense
blocks of granite, split off from the column by
frost, are piled in huge, irregular mounds about
its base. The Indians call this shaft " *The Bad
God's Tower.*"

Game.—The Hills are full of deer, elk, bears,
wolves, cougars, grouse, and ducks. The streams
have an abundance of fish, although of but few
sorts.

After careful investigation General Dodge
closes with this expression of careful judgment:

Opinion of General Dodge.—" I but express my fair and candid opinion when I pronounce the Black Hills, in many respects, the

DEVIL'S TOWER—BLACK HILLS.

Mountains. — Harney's Peak is 7,440 feet
above tide-water, the other peaks are

Crook's Monument,	7,690 feet elevation.
Dodge's Peak,	7,300 feet elevation.
Terry's Peak,	7,200 feet elevation.
Warren's Peak,	6,900 feet elevation.
Custer's Peak,	6,750 feet elevation.
Crow Peak,	6,200 feet elevation.
Bare Peak,	5,200 feet elevation.
Devil's Tower,	5,100 feet elevation.

The *Devil's Tower* is one of the most remarkable peaks of the world. General Dodge describes it thus: " An immense obelisk of granite,

finest country I have ever seen. The beauty and
variety of the scenery, the excellence of the soil,
the magnificence of the climate, the abundance
of timber and building stone make it a most desirable residence for men who want good homes.

" As a grazing country it can not be surpassed,
and small stock farms of fine cattle and sheep
can not fail of success.

" Gold there is every-where in the granite—gold
enough to make many fortunes, and tempt to
the loss of many more.

"Here is a country destined, in a few years, to be an important and wealthy portion of the great American Republic."

There is little doubt that in a few years this section, from the Black Hills of Dakota to and across the Big Horn region, and all northern Wyoming, will be a rich field of industry, as have been Colorado and Utah. The illustrations we give are from photographs taken by General Custer in his famous Black Hills Exploring Expedition of 1875, and represent this country to be of great scenic beauty.

COLORADO.

Pleasure Resorts.—Colorado is an empire of itself in enterprise, scenic beauty and abundance of pleasure resorts. In 1870, few or none of these were known, and towns were small in number and population. Since that time, it has become a center of great railroad activity, has grown in wonderful favor as an attractive region for summer travel; and as a country for health-giving and life-giving strength, it has drawn thither thousands who have made it their permanent home.

THE COLORADO CENTRAL RAILROAD.

Tourists to Colorado will find a journey over this new Railroad Line just opened, of special interest and attractiveness. Through Sleeping Cars from Omaha run direct over this line to Denver, simply changing trains at Cheyenne, and all trains make connections from Denver for Union Pacific Trains East. The route for the first 50 or more miles South passes at the base of the Rocky Mountains, in grand view of their sublime snow-capped summits. The equal of this ride is not found in any Railroad in the Far West. At Fort Collins the railroad crosses the famous *Cache la Poudre Valley*, one of the finest and most lovely regions of agricultural wealth in the State. Wheat and all kinds of grain are here cultivated in large farms, and yield luxuriant crops.

Estes Park is a place of superb scenic attraction, which will afford a most pleasurable resort for the overland Tourist to visit. It is reached by stage from Longmont, distance 36 miles, contains a very superior mountain hotel, and a wide expanse of park scenery, with magnificent views of Long's Peak, and the snowy caps of the neighboring peaks; also there is abundance of trout fishing. For a health resort to any one seeking rest and recuperation, a sojourn here will be found particularly enjoyable.

Longmont is in the midst of a thriving agricultural country, with large and rich farms—the country is nearly level—yet the supply of water is abundant for irrigating purposes, and the farming advantages of the country are good.

Some of the little farms are gems in their neatness. The railroad here is at its greatest distance from the range; hence they seem smaller, and lower in elevation, with less snow, though here and there is an opening in the range which reveals the glorious form of some tall snow covered Monarch.

The population is about 400.

Boulder is most prettily located at the entrance to the famous Boulder Canon, and immediately in a little cove at the base of the mountains. The valley is the most fertile in the State, the water supply is unsurpassed, the climate is the warmest of any country, and the crops are much earlier than any place for 100 miles from Denver. Tourists will find numerous mines near here worth visiting, also most interesting rides up Boulder Canon, Bear Creek Canon, and a trip to Caribon Silver mines. The railroad, as it passes Southward and rises out of the valley to the upland, reveals, as you cast a glance back, a wondrously beautiful view of landscape charms. The mountain view is sublime; the near peaks being dark, while the distant ones, well covered with snow, afford startling contrast and are beautiful in the extreme.

From Boulder to Golden Junction, and thence to Denver, the railroad crosses alternately high upland, then descends into and crosses the valley of many streams flowing from the mountain, which irrigate a region of wonderful agricultural fertility. Upon these uplands, there is a magnificent and exhilarating breeze, constantly blowing from the mountains. Dark Canons appear and disappear as the Tourist travels on. The afternoon sun often reveals glorious displays of sunset colors on the clouds, thunder storms with lightning often give wild and thrilling effects. And at each descent from the upland into each little valley, the view is one of beauty and pleasure.

The railroad as it turns East from Colorado Junction, reveals at the right, the busy town of Golden, a mile distant, over it, towers a peak of 1,000 feet high and down the little valley of Clear Creek, the route passes till your terminus at Denver.

This route of reaching Denver from the East must be specially advantageous to Tourists.

The *Denver Pacific Railroad* also runs direct from Cheyenne, southward, to Denver, and trains connect with the mid-day trains of the Union Pacific Railroad. The distance, 106 miles, is mainly over a vast level plain, covered only with the short gray buffalo grass, but parallel with the main range of the Rocky Mountains, and 20 to 30 miles from their eastern base.

Greeley.—Named in honor of Horace Greeley, and settled in May, 1870. The colony passess about 100,000 acres of fine alluvial soil in the Valley of the *Cache La Poudre* River. Irrigat-

WILLIAMS' CANON, COLORADO SPRINGS.

BY THOMAS MORAN.

ing ditches have been constructed, and there is an abundance of water for all agricultural purposes. The town for several years has increased with steady rapidity, and the population is slightly over 2,000. At this place are located some of the finest grist-mills of the entire West. The place has achieved considerable reputation as a temperance town.

Denver—is the capital of the State. This has become a large railroad point. From it diverge the Kansas Pacific, 636 miles eastward to Kansas City, the Denver and Rio Grande Railroad, Narrow Gauge, southward, to Canon City, Pueblo and Trinidad, and Port Garland; also the various branches of the Colorado Central to Georgetown, Idaho Springs, Central City, and the mines of the mountains.

Its population exceeds 20,000, and its location is most advantageous for easy trade and communication with all the principal points of the Territory. Located on an open plain, about thirteen miles from the Rocky Mountains; here is a grand view of the entire range from Long's Peak on the north to Pike's Peak on the south. While eastward, northward and southward stretches the vast upland plains which is so impressive with its boundless extent. The city is full of thrift, of life; and trade is always splendid. The buildings which grace the principal streets are made principally of brick, and in general appearance, are superior to those of any city west of the Missouri River. Daily, weekly and monthly newspapers thrive. Here is a branch of the United States Mint, gas-works, water-works, horse-railroads, and a multitude of hotels. The best of which are the Grand Central, Inter-Ocean, American, Sargent, Broadwell and Villa Park. From this point the traveler can radiate in all directions in search of pleasure resorts.

Notes to Tourists.—The uniform railroad fare in the Territory averages ten cents per mile. Stage routes run all through the mountains, fare from ten to twenty cents per mile. The uniform rate of board is four dollars per day, and almost every-where can be found excellent living; the nicest of beef steak, bread and biscuit. In many of the mountain resorts plenty of good fishing can be found, and delicate trout are common viands of the hotel tables. The best season of the year for a visit to Colorado is in July and August. As then the snow has nearly disappeared from the mountains, and all the beautiful parks and valleys are easily approachable. Those who wish to include both Colorado and California in a pleasure trip will do well to visit California first, during April May and June, and then on return spend July and August leisurely in the cozy little home resorts of Colorado. Although it must be confessed that the scenery of the Colorado mountains is far the most impressive and most beautiful when *first seen*, before reaching the greater magnificence of the Yosemite and Sierras.

Living in Colorado is more nearly like New England customs than in California, and to those who seek Western travel, for health, the climate of Colorado is much more favorable than that of California.

The Denver and Rio Grande Railroad—will carry the traveler southward from Denver, along the base of the Rocky Mountains, to some of the most noted pleasure resorts of the territory. This little narrow gauge is a wonder of itself, representing nearly $1,000,000 of capital, and operating over 200 miles of road, it has developed a traffic exceeding $500,000 per year, where six years ago the stage route did not realize $1,000 per month, and the prospects for the future for its trade with the miners of the San Juan Country, Trinidad, Sante Fe, are most encouraging, as the new gold discoveries become better developed. Seventy-six miles south of Denver, on this line, are clustered three little places of resort, practically one in interest, Colorado Springs, Colorado City, and

Manitou Springs.—The former is the railroad station, a lively town, which in five years has risen from the prairie to a population of 3,000. Six miles distant from the Springs at Manitou, are collected several elegant hotels, and in the vicinity are numerous soda springs—iron springs and medicinal baths—of great virtue. The location of this resort, with its wonderful collection of objects of natural interest and scenery, have earned for it the title of "Saratoga of the Far West." Travelers find here beautiful scenery in the Ute Pass—Garden of the Gods—Glen Eyrie, numerous beautiful canons, Queen Canon —Cheyenne Canon, grand and impressive, and towering over all is the lofty summit of Pike's Peak, 14,300 feet high, up which ascends a trail to the government signal station, the highest in the United States. Travelers, who frequently ascend this peak are rewarded, when on a clear day, with a glimpse of grand and glorious views of the peaks and mountains, southward and westward.

In this vicinity is located a pretty little canon about 15 miles in length, with walls of rock rising to uniform height of 600 and 800 feet above a very narrow foot pass below. This canon was discovered and named, in 1870, by a party of editors, *Williams' Canon*, in honor of H. T. Williams, their commander. This was the first visit of an Eastern party, of any notoriety, at the Springs. No railroad was then built, and not a house was to be seen, nor even a rancheman's cabin. The scenery of this canon, (*see illustration*), is at various points wild in the extreme, and the colossal walls of rocks are of such shape and formation that they give to the observer an excellent general idea of the characteristic canon scenery of the mountains. The canon has never been fully explored, and at present is the scene of fifty or more claims of gold discoveries.

GATE-WAY TO THE GARDEN OF THE GODS.

Pleasure travelers are uniformly glad that they have made a visit to these points, as they excel in interest any other points in the Western trip. Southward from Colorado Springs, the next most noted resort is Canon City and the *Grand Canon of the Arkansas.*—This is a scene of remarkable beauty and magnificence; at one point can be seen the river winding its way for ten miles, at the base of huge perpendicular rocks which rise fully 1000 and 2000 feet above the current. This is the grandest canon view in Colorado. Westward from Colorado Springs is the South Park, a noted route for travelers who enjoy camping out, and a fine drive through the mountains.

Garden of the Gods. — The Beautiful Gate.—This is also a famous pleasure resort at Manitou, near Colorado Springs. Midway between the Station and Springs is located one of the most beautiful and curious little parks, and upheaval of rocks that Western scenery can display. Descending from parallel ridges into a little park, the traveler sees in front of him a beautiful gate of two enormous rocks, rising in massive proportion to the height of 350 feet, with a natural gateway between of 200 feet in width, with a small rock in the center. Standing a little eastward, the observer gets the view illustrated in our engraving. At the right is another parallel ridge of rocks, pure white, which contrasts finely with the dark red of the rocks of the gate. Through the gate, in the long distance is seen the summit of Pike's Peak, eighteen miles away. Around these rocks is a little grassy park of fifty or more acres, in which according to the mythological stories of the people, the "gods" found such lovely times in play that they christened it a garden. These two parallel ridges of white and red rocks extend for many miles at the foot of the mountains, and form other curious formations at Glen Eyrie, Monument Park and Pleasant Park, although much less in size and impressiveness. The locality is the most famous in all Transcontinental travel.

The Dome of the Continent—Gray's Peak.—Westward from Denver, 65 miles, and 14 from Georgetown, Colorado, rises the grandest and most beautiful of the mountains of Colorado. The way thither is one of easy approach, through valley and mountain roads of gradual ascent, past Idaho Springs, one of the most charming of summer resorts, and past all the mines of Golden, Empire, Georgetown, and the silver mines of the Palisades. Near to the summit are two very successful mines, Baker and Stevens, which are dug out of the perpendicular face of a rock fully 200 feet in height. Rising above all the ranges of the Colorado Mountains of north Colorado, Gray's Peaks are the grand Lookout Points, from which to view to advantage all the vast mountain range. In a clear day the observer can embrace in his range of vision a distance of 100 miles, in each

direction, northward, southward and westward, and even eastward to over the plains east of Denver. From this point are plainly discernible Pike's Peak, 80 miles away, Mount Lincoln, 50 miles; Mount of the Holy Cross, 60 miles; Long's Peak, 50 miles; the City of Denver, 65 miles, and even the summit of the Spanish Peaks, 150 miles southward, and the higher ranges of the Uintah Mountains, 150 miles westward. The total range of the vision being not less than 200 to 250 miles. Beneath them at the foot, lie the beautiful rivers and lakes of Middle Park; southward the vast extended plains of South Park, and everywhere near at hand multitudes of little grassy parks, like valleys dotted with the groves of spruce and pine, as if planted for a grand pleasure ground. The height of the Peak is 14,351 feet, and is the easiest of access of all the mountains of Colorado. Travelers and pleasure tourists who desire one grand sight, never to be regretted, must not fail to include this in their Western visit for the sublimity and grand exaltation as from so lofty a height one views a sea of huge mountains, is a thing always to live in one's memory. There is a fine road to within three miles of the summit, through charming verdure-clad canons and valleys and the rest of the way can be made over a fine trail by horseback, even to the summit.

Westward from Denver are Idaho Springs, Georgetown, Gray's Peak, Middle Park, Clear Creek, and Boulder Canons, with the mining attractions of Central City, Georgetown, Empire, Caribou, and Black Hawk, where the observer can witness sights of extraordinary beauty. We can not possibly describe the attractions of these resorts. They are at once terrible, overpowering, lonely, and full of indescribable majesty. Amid them all the tourist travels daily, imbibing the life-giving, beautiful, fresh air full of its oxygen to quicken and stimulate the system; the eye drinks in the wealth of scenery, and loves to note the beauties of the wonderful glowing sunlight, and the occasional cloud-storms, and wild display of power and glory.

We know of no country better worth the title of the "*Switzerland of America*" than Colorado, with its beautiful mountain parks, valleys, and springs. Go and see them all. The tour will be worthy of remembrance for a life-time.

The editor of this Guide expects soon to issue *The Colorado Tourist,* devoted more especially to the attractions of Colorado, as the limits of this Guide can not begin to possibly describe a hundredth part of the objects of interest within that little region—a *world of pleasure travel by itself.*

Of Life in Colorado,—a prominent writer has said: "At Denver I found, as I thought, the grade of civilization actually higher than in most Western cities. In elegance of building, in finish, in furniture, in dress and equipages, that city is not behind any this side of the Atlantic border. The total absence of squalidity and vis-

MOUNTAIN OF THE HOLY CROSS, COLORADO.

ible poverty, and I may also say of coarseness and rowdyism, impressed me on my visit very strongly, as did the earnestness, activity and intensity of life which is everywhere so apparent." P. T. Barnum once said of Colorado, in a lecture: "Why, Coloradoans are the most disappointed people I ever saw. Two-thirds of them came here to die, and they can't do it. This wonderful air brings them back from the verge of the tomb, and they are naturally exceedingly disappointed."

The average temperature is about 60° the year round—the air is bracing, winter mild, and days almost always full of clear skies and bright warm sunshine. The purity and dryness of the atmosphere are proverbial.

Mountain of the Holy Cross.—The name of this remarkable mountain is renowned to the ends of the earth, and is the only one with this name in the world. It is the principal mountain of the Sawatch Range, just west of the Middle Park of Colorado, and exceedingly difficult of access. The Hayden party were several days in merely finding an accessible way of travel to reach its base. The characteristic features which give it its name is the vertical face, nearly 3,000 feet in depth, with a cross at the upper portion, the entire fissures being filled with snow. The cross is of such remarkable size and distinct contrast with the dark granite rock, that it can be seen nearly eighty miles away, and easily distinguished from all other mountain peaks. The snow seems to have been caught in the fissure, which is formed of a succession of steps, and here, becoming well lodged, it remains all the year. Late in the summer the cross is very much diminished in size by the melting of the snow. A beautiful green lake lies at the base of the peak, almost up to the timber line, which forms a reservoir for the waters from the melting snows of the high peaks. From this flows a stream with many charming cascades. The height of the mountain is 14,176 feet above tide-water. The perpendicular arm of the cross is 1,500 feet in length, and fully 50 feet in breadth, the snow lying in the crevice from 50 to 100 feet in depth. The horizontal arm varies in length with the seasons, but averages 700 feet. The mountain was ascended by the Hayden party only with the greatest difficulty, after 5,000 feet of climbing—fifty pounds of instruments on each back, and obliged to pass thirty hours on the summit, with no shelter, protection, fuel or provisions, except one pocket lunch.

New Pleasure Resorts in Colorado.

Overland tourists, desiring to behold the grandest scenery in America should stop at Cheyenne, and visit some of the following newly opened resorts. In every respect the title of THE

AMERICAN SWITZERLAND is well deserved, for the wild, weird, majestic and colossal, are so mingled with scenes of valley loveliness or Alpine sublimity, as to be beyond description. You should not fail to visit

Estes Park,—a little gem of parks, the prettiest in Colorado,—easily reached by stage on every side. The view as you reach the rim of the park, and look down is *glorious in the extreme.* We have seen none of Bierstadt's paintings to equal it. A cozy hotel is found in the park, nice living, cheap prices, saddle horses and abundance of trout fishing. A few days can be spent in the midst of most enchanting park and mountain scenery. A rim of snow-capped mountains surrounds the valley, which in appearance very much resembles an English park.

Clear Creek Canon.—Do not fail to visit this, one of the *wonders of Colorado.* A little narrow gauge railroad from Denver to Golden, thence pushes its way right up the course of the canon, where it makes its way between the torrent of the rapid creek, and the walls of stupendous rocks. These rocks rise 1,000 to 2,000 feet in elevation of almost perpendicular direction, and succeed one another in the most inconceivable wildness, tortuosity and extreme sublimity, alternating with extreme wildness,—a scene of splendor and wonder. The grade of the railroad averages over 100 feet to the mile. Upon this road are three places worth special visits, *Central City* where are rich gold mines, and where horses can be obtained for the ascent of James Peak,—or Boulder Pass one of the most magnificent views in all the West, — *Idaho Springs* is celebrated for its *Soda* and *Sulphur Springs* which are great help to invalids.

Georgetown,—is the scene of rich mines, and from this place are many routes to famous points of scenery. Here horses can be engaged for the ascent of *Grays Peak,* a tour of a lifetime, the grandest of all mountains in Colorado. Its ascent is very easy, and costs but trifling. No tourist should omit it, as you can behold in a clear day a sea of mountains, and a vision of 500 miles before your astonished gaze.

The Middle Park. — From Georgetown also is a splendid wagon road to the *Hot Sulphur Springs, Middle Park.* These are excellent for all who feel the need of health,—a grand place for camping parties. West of here is rich fishing and hunting, and the *scenery* of the *Canon of the Grand,* on the west, or Grand Lake on the east, is very attractive. From this place one can travel on horseback the entire distance across the mountains to Utah, with little inconvenience, trails already existing in the valleys of rivers.

Scenery of Southern Colorado,—requires more staging, but is still more grand than that of Northern Colorado. Here are the richest mines recently discovered, which produce *half a million dollars per week.* This sec-

THE UINTAH MOUNTAINS.—SCENE NEAR GILBERT'S PEAK.

tion of country is divided into two parts. The first being via the *Denver, South Park, and Pacific Railroad* which is the principal route to *Leadville* the new mining Eldorado. The scenery near here is most inspiring. The canons traversed by the R. W. are full of rugged beauty, while ascending the *Platte Canon*, the grade is often 140 feet to the mile, and the gorges between the mountains are often 2,000 feet high. The stage ride to Leadville is very easy, across the South Park, in view of the glorious mountains. At Fairplay you can take horses for an ascent up *Mount Lincoln*, 14,299 feet high. The view here is finer than from Pike's Peak. Around is seen a sea of snow capped peaks and at its base a little gem of a lake.

The second route to the scenery of Southern Colorado is via the *Denver and Rio Grande Railway*. From Canon City, no finer ride is possible than an excursion to *Rosita*, and return, thence a trip to the Grand Canon of the Arkansas, and a stage ride up the Arkansas valley to Twin Lakes would be most glorious. A person visiting Leadville may enter this route and return by the other and *vice versa*.

Another tour over this railroad is via Pueblo to *Trinidad and Garland*.

Scenery of Veta Pass.—This is the highest railway point in *America*, 9,339 feet elevation. The scenery is extremely peculiar. The little railroad ascending a pretty canon, beautifully timbered, for several miles, suddenly turns, crosses, and returns on the opposite side ascending in a steep grade of 211 feet average to the mile, until as it reaches the extreme crest of the summit of the Dump Mountain, there bursts before the astonished visitor a glorious vision. To the south the Spanish Peaks, to the north, Veta Mountain, and to the north-west, the immense form of *Mount Blanca*, the highest of the range. The railroad from this crest immediately turns and follows back on the ridge only a few feet from its track on the other side, and then ascending, amid timber passes over the summit of the divide into the San Luis Park, whence it terminates at Almosa on the Rio Grande River. Stages here leave for the *San Juan Mountain Country*, about 100 miles distant, where is not only the grandest of mountain scenery, but also infinite riches of mineral wealth.

Powder River Country.— The Powder River, so named from the dark powder-colored sand in its bed, rises in the Big Horn Mountains, north and north-west of Old Fort Casper, and runs in a general north-easterly direction till it empties into the Yellowstone River. It drains an immense area of country, flows through a large region of fine grazing lands, and has in the mountains and hills on either side, untold treasures of rich metals and precious gems. It has hitherto been forbidden ground to white men, but those who have passed through it give glowing descrip-

tions of its luxuriant fertility, its grand scenery and its mineral wealth. It will be one of the finest grazing-regions in the country, producing vast herds of cattle, sheep and horses. There are also heavy bodies of timber on the hills and mountains which border this river. Its wonders are just beginning to be told.

The Tongue River Country.—This is similar to that borderin the Powder River, but the soil is more fertile and better adapted to agricultural pursuits. The Tongue River rises in the Big Horn Mountains, in the central portion of northern Wyoming, and runs north into the Yellowstone River. It abounds in the usual varieties of fish, and game is abundant along its banks. It is a very crooked stream.

Hazard—is 522.4 miles from Omaha, with an elevation of 6.325 feet. It is the junction with the Colorado Central Railroad. As you leave Cheyenne, looking off to the right, you will see the Black Hills of Wyoming stretching to the north, and you will wonder how you are to get by them. To the left Long's Peak rears its snow-capped summit high into the air. It is one of the famous mountains of Colorado, and you have a better view of it on the Colorado Central than from the Union Pacific. It is always crowned with snow and frequently obscured by clouds. How grand it looks, and how huge it appears in the distance.

Otto,—530.6 miles from Omaha, and 6,724 feet above the sea. Every opportunity for obtaining the mountain views, both to the right and left, should be observed and taken advantage of. This is the usual passing place where the express trains meet from East and West.

Granite Canon—is the next station, 535.6 miles from Omaha, and 7,298 feet in altitude. You approach this station high upon the side of a ravine, and through deep cuts in granite spurs. Stunted pines, like lone sentinels, are seen on the bleak hills. Here are large quarries of stone from which the railroad company's buildings at Cheyenne were constructed. The cuts, through a reddish granite, are short but very heavy. Snow sheds are now quite frequent.

Buford,—542.5 miles from Omaha; elevation, 7,780 feet. It is a telegraph station. As you leave it on your left, the "Twin Mountains," two peaks in the Black Hills, lift their rocky heads above the barren waste around them. Near these mountains the noted desperado, Jack Slade, once had his retreat The country here is covered with short buffalo grass, cut with ravines and draws, abounding in fine springs, and in places, covered with pine trees. The dark hues of the pine give the hills their name, "black," and in places the timber is quite heavy. A short distance to your right, Crow Creek rises and winds its way among the hills to the plains below. Four and a half miles north from Buford, near the valley of Crow Creek, mines of copper

6

and silver have been discovered. The ore assays over $50 per ton, but is very refractory. Notice on north side of road the signboard, "Summit of the Mountains."

Sherman—is 549.2 miles from Omaha, at an elevation of 8,242 feet. At the time the road was completed here, it was the highest railroad point in the world, but there are higher places now reached by rail in South America. It has been reached by an ascent so gradual that you have hardly noticed it. In the past few years there have been many changes in grade of the Union Pacific, and wherever possible, the track has been raised above the cuts, so the snow, unless in immense quantities, now causes but little impediment to travel. At Sherman, the snow never falls very deep, but there is a con-

mile, and the maximum grade of any one mile is 90 feet. From Sherman to Laramie, the distance is 23.4 miles; the average grade is 50 feet to the mile, while the maximum grade of any one mile is the same as on the eastern slope—90 feet to the mile. These grades indicate why this route across the Black Hills was selected in preference to others where the altitude was not as great—the approach on either side being more gradual, though the elevation is greater. Nearly all trains between Cheyenne and Laramie have two engines attached so that they may be easily controlled. It is a steady pull to the summit, from each side, and the heavy down grades from it require a great deal of power to properly control trains. About ¼ mile west of Sherman on the left side of the road, is "Reed's Rock," so

SKULL ROCKS, NEAR SHERMAN.

stant breeze, that most Eastern people would pronounce a gale, and the snow is constantly drifting and packs so hard wherever it finds lodgment, that it is exceedingly difficult to displace, requiring an immense power of snowplows, engines and shovelers. As you approach Sherman, you will see the balanced rocks, and to the right of the station, about one-quarter of a mile, is a rugged peak, near which are graves of some who are quietly sleeping so near heaven, and a solitary pine tree, like a sentinel keeping guard over them. Sherman is a telegraph station, has a hotel, one or two saloons, several houses, and a roundhouse where an engine is kept for use in cases of emergency. The difference in elevation between this place and Cheyenne is 2,201 feet, and distance nearly 33 miles. The average grade from Cheyenne is 67 feet per

called from one of the civil engineers who laid out the road. Something like two hundred feet to the eastward of the station, and on the north side of the track, there may be seen a post, bearing the important announcement that this is the *"Summit of the Rocky Mountains."* Station is named after General Sherman.

Dale Creek Bridge—is about two miles west of Sherman. This bridge is built of iron, and seems to be a light airy structure, but is really very substantial. The creek, like a thread of silver, winds its devious way in the depths below, and is soon lost to sight as you pass rapidly down the grade and through the granite cuts and snow sheds beyond. This bridge is 650 feet long, and nearly 130 feet high, and is one of the wonders on the great trans-continental route. A water tank, just beyond it, is supplied with water

DALE CREEK BRIDGE.

from the creek by means of a steam pump. The buildings in the valley below seem small in the distance, though they are not a great way off. The old wagon road crossed the creek down a ravine, on the right side of the track, and the remains of the bridge may still be seen. This stream rises about six miles north of the bridge, and is fed by numerous springs and tributaries, running in a general southerly direction, until it empties into the Cache La Poudre River. The old overland road from Denver to California ascended this river and creek until it struck the head-waters of the Laramie. Leaving Dale Creek bridge, the road soon turns to the right, and before you, on the left, is spread out, like a magnificent panorama,

The Great Laramie Plains.—These plains have an average width of 40 miles, and are 100 miles in length. They begin at the western base of the Black Hills and extend to the slope of the Medicine Bow Mountains, and north beyond where the Laramie River cuts its way through these hills to join its waters with the North Platte. They comprise an area of over two and a half millions of acres, and are regarded as one of the richest grazing portions of country. Across these plains, and a little to the left, as you begin to glide over them, rises in full view the Diamond Peaks of the Medicine Bow Range. They are trim and clear-cut cones, with sharp pointed summits—a fact which has given them their name, while their sides, and the rugged hills around them, are covered with timber. Still farther in the shadowy distance, in a south-westerly direction, if the atmosphere is clear, you will see the white summits of the Snowy Range—white with their robes of perpetual snow. Even in the hottest weather experienced on these plains, it makes

one feel chilly to look at them they are so cold, cheerless and forbidding.

In the hills we have just passed, there is an abundance of game, such as mountain sheep, bear, antelope, and an occasional mountain lion, while Dale Creek and all the little brooks which flow into the South Platte River are filled with trout. The speckled beauties are not found however, in the streams which flow into the North.Platte. This is a well-established fact, and we have yet failed to discover any satisfactory reason for it, though some of these brooks, flowing in opposite directions, head not more than fifty yards apart.

Skull Rocks.—These rocks, found near Dale Creek, are excellent samples of the granite rocks which are so abundant in this section, and show how they bear the effects of the severe weather. All the massive rocks, which, like the ruins of old castles, are scattered all over the Black Hills, were once angular in form, and square masses, which in time have been worn to their present forms by the disintegrating effects of the atmosphere.

Tie-Siding.—555.2 miles from Omaha; elevation, 7,985 feet. This is a telegraph station, A well-worn and much traveled road leads hence across the prairies southward to the mountains of Diamond Peaks, in the neighborhood of which are obtained ties, fence-poles and wood. There are a few houses, and the inevitable saloon—houses occupied mostly by woodchoppers and teamsters—while the saloons generally take the most of their money. A short distance from this station two soldiers of an Iowa cavalry regiment were killed by Indians at the overland stage station, in 1865. The pine board and mound which marks their resting-place will soon disappear, and there will be nothing left to mark the spot where they fell. Near Tie-Siding are extensive ranches occupied by sheep during the summer. The general direction of the traveler is now north. In fact, after leaving Dale Creek bridge, you turn towards the north, and continue in that direction, sometimes even making a little east, until you pass Rock Creek Station, a distance of about seventy miles by rail. We have now fairly entered upon the great Laramie Plains. The next station is

Harney,—simply a side track, 559.3 miles from the eastern terminus, with an elevation of 7,857 feet. We are going down grade now pretty fast. The old stage road can be seen to the left, and the higher mountains of the Medicine Bow Range shut in the western view.

Red Buttes,—near the base of the western slope of the Black Hills—is 563.8 miles from Omaha; elevation, 7,336 feet. So-called from the reddish color of the Buttes between Harney and this place, on the right side of the track. This red appearance of the soil on both hill and plain, indicates the presence of iron. It would seem that at some remote period the whole valley was on a level with the top of these Buttes, and they, composed of harder and more cohesive substance than the soil around, have withstood the drain and wash of ages, while it has settled away. They are of all sorts of shapes. The nearest about half a mile from the track, and excite no little interest from their peculiar forms, in the mind of the traveler who is at all curious on such subjects; some of them are isolated, and then again you will see them in groups. There are quite a number in sight from the car windows, and their close inspection would warrant the tourist in stopping at Laramie and making them and other objects in the vicinity a visit. Red Buttes is a telegraph station, with a few settlers in the neighborhood. These plains have been called the paradise for sheep; but of this subject we will speak in another place.

Fort Sanders,—570.3 miles from Omaha; elevation 7,163 feet. This is a station for the military post which was established here in June, 1866, by Col. H. M. Mizner of the 18th United States Infantry. Its buildings for both officers and men are mainly of logs, and many of them are both substantial and comfortable. The post can be seen from a long distance in every direction; is close to the track and on the old military road leading across the Black Hills by way of Cheyenne Pass to Fort Walbach at the eastern base of the hills, now abandoned, and to the military posts near Cheyenne. It will probably be abandoned in a short time.

Laramie—is 572.8 miles from Omaha, and 7,123 feet above the sea. It is the end of a division of the Union Pacific Railroad, one of the largest towns on the road, has large machine and repair shops, and is destined to become from its mining and manufacturing capacities yet unde-

veloped, the largest city on the road in Wyoming. It is located on the Laramie River, in the midst of the Laramie Plains, has fully 4,000 people, is the county-seat of Albany County, has numerous churches and schools, several public buildings, brick and stone blocks, with streets regularly laid out at right angles to the railroad; is well watered from one of the mountain streams in the vicinity, and altogether is one of the most promising towns on the line of the road. It is called the "Gem city of the Mountains," and its altitude and close proximity to the hills behind it give it a fair show for the name. The rolling mills of the company, giving employment to from 150 to 300 men, are located and in operation here, in the northern limits of the city. It is expected and understood that a foundry and smelting works for reducing iron ore will soon be established in connection with the rolling mills. At present these mills have all they can do in re-rolling the worn out rails of the track, which are brought here for that purpose. The water-power in the Laramie River will also soon be utilized in the erection of woolen mills and factories for refining soda and other minerals with which this country abounds. The mineral resources of Wyoming have not been developed. The slight explorations which have thus far been made only demonstrate the fact of their existence in untold quantities. Laramie, for instance, has within a radius of thirty miles the following named minerals : Antimony, cinnabar, gold, silver, copper, lead, plumbago, iron, red hematite iron, brown hematite, specular iron, sulphate of soda, gypsum, kaolin or porcelain clay, fire clay, brick clay, coal, sand, limestone, fine quality, sandstone for building purposes within two miles of the city, and good wagon roads to all the places where these materials are found. Laramie, from its location and surroundings, must become a manufacturing city, and upon this fact we base the prophecy of its future greatness and prosperity. There are lakes of soda within the distance named that must soon be utilized. A simple chemical process only is required to render this article into the soda of commerce—immense quantities of which are used in this country annually, and most of it comes from foreign countries. It is expected that a soda factory will be started at Laramie within the next year.

Sheep-Raising.—We have before remarked that the Laramie Plains were a paradise for sheep. The success which has attended sheep husbandry on these plains sufficiently attests this fact. It is true, first efforts were not as successful as they should have been, but this is reasonably accounted for in the lack of experience of those who engaged in it, and a want of knowledge of the peculiarities of the climate. It has generally been claimed that sheep will live and do well where antelope thrive. While this theory holds good in the main, it has nevertheless been ascertained that sheep on these plains require hay and shelter in order to be successfully carried through the storms of winter. It is also true that this hay may not be needed, or but a little of it used, but every preparation for safety requires that it should be on hand to be used if necessary. The winter is rare indeed, in this locality, that makes twenty successive days' feeding a necessity. Usually the storms last two or three days, perhaps not as long, when hay and shelter are required. Another fact about this business is that the climate is healthy, and seems especially adapted to sheep. If brought here in a sound and healthy condition, they will remain so with ordinary care, and the climate alone has been effectual in curing some of the diseases to which they are subject. Within the last few years a great number of men have invested capital in sheep husbandry in the vicinity of Laramie, and without an exception they have done well where their flocks have received the requisite attention and care. Among the shepherd kings of the plains may be mentioned the firms of Willard & Kennedy, King & Lane, Rumsey & Co., T. J. Fisher & Co., and others. The firm first named have about 6,000 in their flock, and have accommodations at their different ranches for 10,000 sheep. They place this number as the limit of their flock. Their home ranch is on the Laramie River, about twenty miles due west from the city, and is worthy of a visit from any traveler who desires information on the subject. They are Boston men, and are meeting with success because they give their personal care and attention to the business. Their sheep are divided into flocks of about 2,500 each; this number is all that can be well cared for in a flock. One man, a pony and one or two good shepherd dogs are all that are necessary to care for a flock, though some flocks are cared for without the pony or dogs. Mexican herders or shepherds are considered the best, and usually cost about $25 per month and board. They have long been accustomed to the business in New Mexico, and the most of them don't know enough to do anything else. The wool of graded sheep will usually more than pay all the expenses of the flock, leaving the increase as clear profit, and the increase depends to a large extent on how well the flock is managed; it is ordinarily 80 per cent. Some have had an increase of their flocks as large as 90 per cent, others as low as 60 per cent. Some of the successful sheep men have begun their flocks with Spanish Merinos, others with French Merinos, others with Cotswolds, others still with Mexican sheep. These last are very hardy; have small bodies and coarse wool. The ewes are usually good mothers, and all of them will hunt and dig through the snow for grass, while other breeds would not. Mexican sheep will live and thrive where tenderly raised eastern sheep will die. They are cheap and easily graded up.

On the other hand, when once acclimated, graded sheep cost no more care than others, and their wool will bring double the price in the market. Each class of sheep has its advocates on these plains, and each class has been successful. As an illustration of what care and attention will do in the sheep business, we call attention to the facts and figures in the case of T. J. Fisher & Co., quoting from memory. In August, 1873, Mr. Fisher bought some 600 ewes. At the end of the first year he had a few over 1,300 sheep and lambs, together with the wool clip from the original number purchased, in the spring of 1874. At the end of the second year, in August, 1875, he had over 1,900 sheep and lambs, together with the wool clip in the spring of that year. His sheep being graded, the wool more than paid all expenses of herding, cutting hay, corrals, etc. His ranche is on the Little Laramie River, some fourteen miles from the city. While nearly all who have entered upon this business have been remarkably successful, so far as we are able to learn, Mr. Fisher has been the most successful, in proportion to the capital invested. Tourists desiring further information on this subject will do well to visit his ranche and inspect his method of conducting the business. Messrs. King & Lane, and Rumsey & Co., have some very fine Cotswold and Merino sheep, and a visit to their flocks will abundantly reward any one who desires further information on the subject.

Stock Statistics. — The total number of stock grazing on the plains of Laramie County, at last estimate, was as follows :

Sheep,	78,322 head, worth $3,	value,	$234,966
Horned cattle,	87,000 "	" 20,	" 1,740,000
Horses and mules, 2,600	"	" 50,	" 130,000
Total,			$2,104,966

The average weight of fleece of sheep sheared last spring, was 9 lbs. per sheep. The average increase in flocks is 60 to 90 per cent. per annum, and the average increase of capital, is 50 to 60 per cent. per year.

Sheep husbandry is destined to become the feature of the Laramie Plains, and the wool which will soon be raised in this vicinity will keep thousands of spindles in motion near the very place where it is produced, thus saving to both producer and consumer vast sums which are now lost in transportation.

Early Times. — In April, 1868, the first town lots in Laramie were sold by the railroad company. There was a great rush for town lots— excitement ran very high, and the history of Cheyenne in this respect, where men made fortunes in a day, was repeated here. In fact, a month or two prior to the beginning of the sale, the town site was covered with tents, wagons, dugouts, etc., of parties waiting for the day of sale. With that sale, the settlement of the town began. The first week, over 400 lots sold and building began rapidly. In less than two weeks something over 500 buildings and structures of some kind had been erected. This was an example of western growth that would astonish the slow-going denizens of the Atlantic States. It is true these structures were of a peculiar character, and such as were usually found in the towns for the time being made the business terminus of the road. Some were of logs, some of cross-ties, others were simply four posts set in the ground with canvas sides and roofs. Others still were made of boards, in sections, and easy to be moved when the next terminus should be made known.

The iron rails that were soon to bear the iron horse were laid past the town on the 9th day of May, 1868, and on the day following, the first train arrived and discharged its freight. Laramie maintained the character of all these western towns in the early days of their settlement. The same class of human beings that had populated and depopulated North Platte, Julesburg, Cheyenne, and other places, lived and flourished here until the next move was made. They were gamblers, thieves, prostitutes, murderers—bad men and women of every calling and description under the heavens, and from almost every nationality on the globe—and when they could prey upon no one else, would, as a matter of course, prey upon each other. The worst that has ever been written of these characters does not depict the whole truth; they were, in many cases, outlaws from the East—fled to escape the consequences of crimes committed there, and each man was a law unto himself. Armed to the very teeth, it was simply a word and a shot, and many times the shot came first. Of course those who were respectable, and who desired to do a legitimate business could not endure for a long time, the presence and rascalities of these border characters. There being no law in force, the next best thing was a resort to "lynch law." This was the experience of Laramie.

Laramie is now an orderly, well-governed city, where the rights of person and property are respected, and forcibly reminds one of the quiet towns in the East. All saloons and other places of like character, are closed on the Sabbath, the churches are well attended, and the schools are liberally patronized. It is one of the most attractive towns on the line of the Union Pacific road, and offers many advantages to those who desire, for any reason, a change of location.

In addition to other public institutions else-

EARLY MORNING SCENE ON THE LARAMIE PLAINS.

where mentioned, Laramie has the location of the territorial penitentiary, a small wing of which is already constructed, and which is plainly visible only a short distance west of the railroad track. A good hotel is kept at the old depot. For years it was a regular dining station, and is still one of the most important and interesting places on the Omaha route, but the dining station has recently been transferred to Rock Creek, fifty-two miles farther west, the better to accommodate the hour of dining to the wants of travelers. A manufactory for soda is talked of, and if the mines of this article are properly developed, Laramie will soon supply the world with soda enough to raise, not only biscuits and bread, but no small sum of money as a return for the investment. The rolling mills and machine and repair shops of the company are sources of perpetual trade and income. and must of necessity increase with the annually increasing business of the company. A visit to the soda lakes, gold mines, Iron Mountain, Red Buttes and other places of interest in the vicinity, together with good hotel accommodations, will surely lure the traveler to spend a few days in this "Gem city of the Mountains."

Laramie Peak.—This is the highest peak of the Black Hills Range in Wyoming and Colorado, north of Long's Peak, and is about 10,000 feet high. The Hayden exploring party, who were encamped at its base, describe witnessing a sunset scene of rare beauty. The sun passed down directly behind the summit of Laramie Peak. The whole range of mountains was gilded with a golden light. and the haziness of the atmosphere gave to the whole scene a deeper beauty. The valleys at the base of the Cottonwood and Laramie Rivers are full of pleasant little streams and grassy plains. Sometimes these valleys expand out into beautiful oval park-like areas, which are favorite resorts of wild game, and

HUNTING IN THE ROCKY MOUNTAINS.

would be exceedingly desirable for settlements. Emigrants would find here beautiful scenery, pure air and water, and a mild and extremely healthy climate. Cereals and roots could be easily raised, and stock-raising could be made a source of wealth to them and the whole community.

The Windmills of the Union Pacific Railroad.—The traveler notices with interest the ever frequent windmills which appear at every station, and are such prominent objects over the broad prairies. They are used for supplying the locomotives and station houses with water. Probably no finer specimens exist in the United States than are found on the lines of this road.

In these tanks is a large hollow globe floating in the water. These globes are so connected with levers that when the water has reached a certain height, the slats or fans are thrown in line with the wind, and the machine stops. As the water is drawn off for supplying the locomotives, the ball falls, and the machine is again put in motion. They are thus self-regulating and self-acting. The water is thrown up by a forcing pump. A curious fact may be here mentioned. These tanks, when closely covered. have thus far proved that there is enough caloric in the water to prevent it from freezing.

Wind River Mountains.—These mountains, seen on the map and just north of the railroad, are destined soon to celebrity, for their mining value, although as yet but partially explored. Two well-known peaks rise among them, Fremont's Peak and Snow's Peak, the latter being the highest; its elevation is given by Fremont as 13,570 feet. The mountains are filled with a dense growth of a species of the nut pine, which furnishes food for innumerable birds and squirrels, and supplies the Indians with their favorite food.

Indian Burial Tree.—Among the Indian tribes there are quite a number whose custom is to honor their dead with burial places in the tops of favored trees. The Comanches, Apaches, Cheyennes, Arrapahoes and Kiowas all do this. After an Indian is dead, his corpse is securely wrapped like a mummy; with it are put food, arms, tobacco, etc.,—which its spirit is supposed to want in his trip to the happy hunting ground,—and the whole covered with an outer covering made of willows. All the Indians of the tribe celebrate mourning both before and after this is done; then the body is placed upon a platform, constructed in some old tree, usually a large cotton-wood. The feet of the departed Indian are turned with care to the southward, for thither resides the Great Spirit,—so the Indians say—and thither he is going. In some of their favor-

Wyoming. They are really the first range of the Rockies. They begin at the valley of the North Platte River, directly south of Fort Fetterman, and unite with the Medicine Bow Range in northern Colorado, south-west from Sherman. Laramie Peak and Reed's Peak, north of the Laramie Canon, are the highest peaks in this range. The waters which flow from them east of the Black Hills, and those which flow west from the Medicine Bow Range, all unite in the North Platte River, which describes a half circle around their northern extremity, and then flows eastward to the Missouri River. This range of mountains, as before stated, is crossed at Sherman. They have not been prospected to any great extent for the precious metals, but gold, silver, copper, iron and other minerals are known to exist. Iron is found in large quantities.

INDIAN BURIAL TREE, NEAR FORT LARAMIE.

ite groves, as many as eight or ten bodies have been found in a single tree. Another mode of burial is to erect a scaffold on some prominent knoll or bluff. These customs are prevalent among those Indian tribes which are most roving, and live in the saddle. "Foot Indians," those which inhabit the plains, and are peaceable, most invariably bury their dead in the ground—always, however, accompanied with such good things as he will need in his trips thereafter in the new hunting-grounds.

The Black Hills of Wyoming, and the Medicine Bow Range.—In going west, the first range of real mountains the traveler meets with are what are called the Black Hills of

About 18 miles north-east from Laramie is Iron Mountain, on the head of Chugwater Creek. It is said to be nearly pure, and will some day be developed. There has been talk of a railroad from Cheyenne with a branch to this mountain, but nothing has been done yet. In searching for a route for the Union Pacific Railroad, a survey of the Laramie Canon was made, but it was found to be impracticable for a railroad. It, however, has grand scenery, and will become a place of resort, by tourists, as soon as the Indian question is settled. The Black Hills virtually connect with the Medicine Bow Range at both extremities, bearing to the left around the circle of the North Platte, and to the right south

MEDICINE BOW MOUNTAINS, FROM MEDICINE BOW RIVER.

of Sherman. The canons of both the Laramie and Platte Rivers are rugged and grand. Laramie Peak has an elevation of 10,000 feet, and lies in plain view off to the right from Lookout to Medicine Bow Stations.

Crossing the Black Hills, the road strikes the Laramie Plains, and then the Medicine Bow Range rises grandly before you. At Laramie City—the road running north—you look west and behold Sheep Mountain in front, whose summit is 10,000 feet above the sea; to the left of this is Mt. Agassiz, so named in honor of the distinguished scientist who gave his life to the cause he loved so well. To the right of Sheep Mountain, which is in the Medicine Bow Range, you discover what seems to be a large depression in the mountains. This is where the Little Laramie River heads, and across it, to the right, still other peaks of this range lift their snowy heads. The range is now on your left until you pass around its northern bend and into the North Platte Valley again at Fort Steele. On the northern extremity, Elk Mountain looms up, the best view of which can be obtained as you pass from Medicine Bow Station to Fort Steele, provided, of course, you look when the foot hills do not obscure your vision. The Medicine Bow Range is also full of the precious metals, mostly gold, but has not been developed. The Centennial Mine, located by a party of gentlemen from Laramie, on the first day of January, 1875, is on the mountain just north of one of the branches of the Little Laramie River, and in a clear day, with a good glass, can plainly be seen from Laramie City. Nearly all the streams which head in the Medicine Bow Mountains will show "color" to the prospector, but the lodes are mostly "blind," and can only be found by persistent search. This range is also heavily timbered, and abounds in game, and except the highest peaks, is free from snow in the summer. The timber is mostly pine, and immense quantities are annually cut for railroad ties, telegraph and fence poles and wood. Nearly every ranche on the Laramie Plains is supplied with poles for corrals, sheds and fences from the Black Hills or Medicine Bow Range. The Laramie Plains is the great basin between these two ranges, and the road has to pass northward a long distance in order to find its way out. Leaving the grand views of these mountains, the traveler enters upon a vast, dreary and unproductive waste—fitly called a desert. Still its rough and broken appearance with rocks, hills, and mountains on either side afford a strange and pleasant relief from the dull monotony of the eastern plains.

Leaving Laramie City, the track passes close to the company's rolling mills, from the tall chimneys of which there are huge volumes of black smoke and occasional flames, constantly belching forth. We soon cross the Laramie River on a wooden truss bridge, and run along near its banks to

Howell,—which is a side track, eight miles from Laramie, and 580.8 miles from Omaha; elevation, 7,000 feet. Passing over the plains, walled in by mountains on either side, we reach the next station,

Wyoming,—over fifteen miles from Laramie, and 588.4 miles from Omaha; elevation, 7,068 feet. Having reached the highest altitude on the line of the road between the two oceans, at Sherman, you see we are now going down hill a little, and from this time until we cross the Sierras, there will be a constant succession of "ups and downs" in our journey. Wyoming is on the Little Laramie River, which empties into the Laramie River near the station. It is a telegraph station with a few houses in the vicinity —in the midst of a fine grazing country, with sheep and cattle ranches in sight. Leaving Wyoming, the aspect of the country soon changes. A bluff on the right lies near the track, the country becomes more undulating as we pass on, and the grass seems to grow thinner except on the bottom near the stream. Sage brush and greasewood, well known to all frontier men, begin to appear. We have seen a little of sage brush before in the vicinity of Julesburg, and Sidney, and now strike it again.

Cooper's Lake,—598.9 miles from Omaha, with an elevation of 7,044 feet It is a telegraph station with the usual side track and section-houses. The station is named from the little lake near by, which can best be seen from the cars at the water tank, beyond the station. It isn't much of a lake, nor can much of it be seen from the car windows. The water is said to look very green in the summer, and to differ but little in appearance from the green grass which surrounds it. The lake itself is about half a mile wide, and a mile and a half long, and about two miles from the track, though it does not seem half that distance. It is fed by Cooper and Dutton Creeks, but has no visible outlet.

Lookout,—607.6 miles from Omaha, and about thirty-five miles from Laramie; elevation, 7,169 feet. The road left what may be called the Laramie bottom at the last station, and now winds through a rolling country, which soon becomes rough and broken, with the sage brush constantly increasing. Notice the changes in the elevation as you pass along.

Miser,—615.9 miles from Omaha; elevation, 6.810 feet. Near here coal has been found. It is in the vicinity of Rock Creek, which is said to be the eastern rim of the coal fields discovered on this elevated plateau, in the middle of the Continent. From the last station to this, and beyond, you have fine and constantly changing views from the moving train, of Laramie Peak, away off to the right, and of Elk Mountain to the left. Sage brush is the only natural production of the soil in this region, and is said to be eaten by antelope and elk in the absence of grass or anything better. It is also said that sheep will feed upon it, and that wherever antelope live and flourish, sheep will do likewise.

Rock Creek,—so called from a creek of the same name, which the road here crosses; 624.6 miles from Omaha; elevation, 6.690 feet. This is a regular eating station, instead of Laramie. The dining-room is beautifully decorated with flowers, vines and horns of game, a pretty Bay window with blooming flowers and walls covered with vines, and the display of hanging baskets, making the meal one of the most agreeable on the road. Hotel is kept by Thayer and Hughes.

The government is surveying a new road to Fort Fetterman, to start from Rock Creek, instead of Medicine Bow.

Rock Creek rises in the north-eastern peaks of the Medicine Bow Range, and runs in that direction to this station, near which it turns toward the west and unites with Medicine Bow River, near Medicine Bow Station.

Wilcox.—A side track for the passing of trains, 632.3 miles from Omaha, and 7,033 feet above the sea. The next station is

Como,—named after Lake Como, which the

road here passes. One peculiarity of this lake is that it is near Rock Creek—separated from it by a ridge of hills estimated at 200 feet high,—with no visible outlet. The station is 640.2 miles from Omaha, and 6,680 feet above the sea. The lake has been estimated to be 200 feet above the surface of Rock Creek, from which it is separated as above stated. It is fed by warm springs, which also supply the water tank of the company at the station. In a cold day the steam from these springs can be seen at some distance. It is also a great resort for ducks, and sportsmen can obtain fine shooting here in the proper season. If lizards are fish with legs, then we have fish with legs abounding in this lake and vicinity. These animals are from 6 to 18 inches in length, with a head a good deal like that of a frog, and tufts or tassels where the gills would be on a fish. They have four legs and crawl around to a certain extent on the land. There are two kinds of these lizards, one differing from the other in size and color more than in shape, and either kind are devoured by the ducks when they can be caught. The lake is about one mile wide in the widest place, and two and a half miles long.

Valley of the Chugwater.— The Chugwater Valley is about 100 miles long. It has been for many years a favorite locality for wintering stock, not only on account of the excellence of the grass and water, but also from the fact that the climate is mild throughout the winter. Cattle and horses thrive well all winter without hay or shelter. The broad valley is protected from strong cold winds by high walls or bluffs. The soil everywhere is fertile, and wherever the surface can be irrigated, good crops of all kinds of cereals and hardy vegetables can be raised without difficulty.

In this valley and near the source of the Chugwater, are thousands of tons of iron ore, indicating deposits of vast extent and richness, which can be made easily accessible whenever desirable to construct a railroad to Montana.

Medicine Bow—is 647.3 miles from Omaha; elevation, 6,550 feet. The river, from which the station is named, was crossed a short distance before we reached the station. It rises directly south, in the Medicine Bow Mountains, and runs nearly north to the place where it is crossed by the railroad, after which it turns toward the west and unites with the North Platte, below Fort Steele.

There is a roundhouse of five stalls, in which one or more engines are kept, to assist trains up and down the steep grades between here and Carbon. It is also a point from which a large quantity of military supplies for Fort Fetterman and other posts are distributed. The government has a freight depot here. There are one or two stores, with the inevitable saloon and several dwellings, in the vicinity. There is a good wagon road from this place to Fort Fetterman, distance ninety miles, and it is by far the nearest route to the gold fields in the Black Hills of Dakota, for passengers and miners from the West. The Indians were disinclined to leave this region and even now hardly know how to give it up. In the summer of 1875, they came here and stole a herd of between three and four hundred horses that were grazing on Rock Creek. Some of these horses have been seen and recognized at the agencies of Red Cloud and Spotted Tail; and when demand was made for them, the owners were quietly told by the Indian agents to make out their claims and present them to the proper authorities to be paid. But the cases of their payment are like angels' visits, few and far between. Some of the horses stolen belonged to Judge Kelly, member of Congress, from Pennsylvania. Medicine Bow is in the midst of a rough, broken country, over which millions of antelope and jack rabbits roam at pleasure. When the road was built here immense quantities of ties and wood were cut in the mountains south, and delivered at this place.

Curiosities of Indian Life and Character.—The entire country, from North Platte over as far as the western border of Laramie Plains, has been for years the roving ground of the Indians, of whom we could tell many interesting facts respecting their life and the curious interviews the overland scouts, trappers, etc., have had with them. To a man, every scout will unite in denunciation of their treachery. Jim Baker,—an old Rocky Mountain trapper,—once told, in his characteristic manner the following, to General Marcy:

"They are the most onsartainest varmints in all creation, and I reckon thar not mor'n half human; for you never seed a human, arter you'd fed and treated him to the best fixins in your lodge, just turn round and steal all your horses, or anything he could lay his hand on.

"No, not adzackly! he would feel kinder grateful, and ask you to spread a blanket in his lodge if ever you passed that way. But the Indian, he don't care shucks for you, and is ready to do you a heap of mischief as soon as he quits your feed. No, Cap'," he continued, "it's not the right way to give 'um presents to buy peace; but ef I was governor of these yeer United States, I'll tell you what I'd do. I'd invite 'um all to a big feast, and make believe I wanted to have a big talk, and as soon as I got 'um all together, I'd pitch in and scalp half of 'um, and then t'other half would be mighty glad to make a peace that would stick. That's the way I'd make a treaty with the dog-ond, red-bellied varmints; and, as sure as you're born, Cap, that's the only way.

"It ain' no use to talk about honor with them, Cap.; they hain't got no such thing in 'um; and they won't show fair fight, any way you can fix it. Don't they kill and scalp a white man, when'ar they get the better on him? The mean varmints, they'll never behave themselves until you give 'um a clean out and out licking. They can't onderstand white folks' ways, and they won't learn 'um. and ef you treat 'um decently, they think you're afeard. You may depend on't, Cap., the only way to treat Indians, is to thrash them well at first, then the balance will sorter take to you and behave themselves."

Indian observations on the character of the American and English people, are often pretty good. An Indian once describing to an English-man the characteristics of the different people he knew, said as follows, most naively:

"King George man, (English) very good; Boston man, (American) good; John Chinaman, not good; but the black man, *he no better than a dog.*"

They are particularly curious about negroes, as they do not feel certain whether the black goes all through. Some years ago, a party of negroes escaping from Texas, were captured by some of the Comanches, who *scraped their skin to settle this question.*

At the time of the presidency of Lincoln, an Indian, while conversing with an English mis-sionary, asked him who was the chief of the English. He was told. "Ah! Queen Victoly," for they can't pronounce it. "Is she a woman?" "Yes." "Who is the chief of the Boston men, (American)?" "Mr. Lincoln." "Ah! I thought so; but another Indian once told me that it was Mr. Washington. Are Mr. Lincoln and the English woman-chief good friends?" "Yes, excellent friends." He thought for a moment, and, finally, said eagerly: "Then if they are so good friends, *why does not Mr. Lincoln take Queen Victoly for his squaw?*"

The Indians are very fond of card-playing, and, perhaps in no other way can their natural treachery be so well illustrated, and desire to take advantage of others by cheating.

An Indian once, while at a wayside village, near the mines, and with a natural born swin-dler, explained to his white hearers how he could manage to cheat while dealing the cards.

While playing in the open air, in some valley, near some rocks, with a young Indian, while dealing the cards, he would shout out as if he saw some lovely forest maid passing near or ascending the rock or sides of the hill: "Aah, nanich skok tenans klatchmann (Hallo! look at that young woman!)" While the Indian looked around, "old Buffalo" immediately took the opportunity of dealing double to himself, or of selecting an ace or two before his opponent turned around.

A semi-civilized Indian, named Black Beaver, once visited General Marcy at St. Louis, and on his return back to his native camp, he prided himself not a little on his knowledge of cities and

men, white and civilized. Camping one night with a Comanche guide, the General overheard the two in an apparently earnest and amicable talk. The General inquired of him afterward what he had been saying.

"I've been telling the Comanche what I've seen among the white folks. I tell him 'bout the steamboats, and the railroads, and the heep o' houses I see in St. Louis, but he say lz—— fool. I tell him the world is round, but he keep all o' time say, 'Hush, you fool, do you spose I'ze child? Haven't I got eyes? Can't I see the prairie? You call him round? Maybe so; I tell you something you not know before. One time my grandfather he made long journey that way (West), when he got on big mountain, he see heep water on t'other side, just so flat as he can be, and he see the sun go straight down on t'other side. S'pose the world flat he stand still?'"

General Marcy attempted to explain to him the telegraph, but there he was nonplussed. "What you call the magnetic telegraph?" He was told, "You have heard of New York and New Orleans?" "Oh, yes." "Very well; we have a wire connecting these two cities, which are 1,000 miles apart, and it would take a man thirty days, on a good horse, to ride it. Now, a man stands at one end of this wire in New York, and by touching it a few times, he inquires of his friend in New Orleans, what he had for breakfast. His friend in New Orleans touches the other end of the wire, and in ten minutes the answer comes back, *ham and eggs.*"

Beaver was requested to tell this to the Co-manche, but he remained silent, his countenance all the time covered with a most comical, puz-zled expression. Again he was asked to tell him, when he declared, "No, Captain, I not tell him that, for I don't b'lieve that myself."

He was assured that it was a fact, but no amount of assurances could induce him to pin his faith on such a seemingly incredible state-ment. All he would reply was simply, "Injun not very smart; sometimes he's big fool, but he holler pretty loud; you hear him, maybe, half a mile; you say 'Merican man he talk thousand miles;' I 'spect you try to fool me now, Cap'n. *May be you lie.*"

Polygamy is quite frequent among many of the Indians of the plains, and some amusing stories are told of the way they get their wives. One such is told of an Indian boy of only eight-een, whose father, considering that he had ar-rived at the years of discretion, presented him with a lodge, several horses, and goods enough to establish him in life. The first thing the pre-cocious youth did was to go and secretly bargain with a chief for his daughter, enjoining secrecy, and then to a second, third and fourth, the re-sult of which was, that on a fixed day, he claimed all four ladies, to the astonishment of the tribe

THE PACIFIC TOURIST. 93

and the indignation of the fathers. But he obtained his wives and marched them off to his wigwam. Not only this, but the chiefs determined that a youth who could do so bold an act, must be a person of discretion, and deserved and gave him a seat in the council among the warriors and the medicine men.

Of the want of books and writing among the Indians, they give the following explanations: "It is impossible. The Great Spirit at first made a red and a white boy; to the red boy he gave a book, and to the white boy a bow and arrow, but the white boy came round the red boy, stole his book, and went off, leaving him the bow and arrow, and, therefore, an Indian could not make a book."

Carbon,—656.5 miles from Omaha, with an elevation of 6,750 feet. A station of great prominence for coal mining. Population 700. This is the first station on the line of the road, where the company obtains a supply of coal. A shaft about 120 feet deep has been sunk, and veins of coal opened about six feet thick. The coal is hoisted to the surface by means of a stationary engine, and dumped into cars by means of chutes, or into large bins from which it is taken to supply passing engines. From 50 to 150 men are employed in these mines, and a good many of them live in board shanties, adobe houses, and dug-outs along the side of the track. The coal is mostly used by the company—but little being sold as it is not as good for domestic purposes as the coal found at Rock Springs. Leaving Carbon we pass through a rugged country, with scenery sufficiently attractive to keep the traveler on the constant lookout, to

Simpson,—a side track, with section-house, 663.5 miles from Omaha, and an elevation of 6,898 feet. Passenger trains do not stop and on we go to

Percy,—668.1 miles from Omaha, and 6,950 feet above the sea. From Simpson to this station, you can obtain the finest view of Elk Mountain on the left. We have not been able to ascertain its elevation, but its comparative short distance from the road causes it to look high and grand. It can be seen from a long distance, either east or west, and is the noted peak of the Medicine Bow Range. It seems to jut out from the main ridge, and looking from the west, stands in bold relief against the sky. The station is named in honor of Colonel Percy, who was killed here by the Sioux Indians, when the road was being surveyed. At this station passengers who desire to visit Elk Mountain, and the region in its immediate vicinity will leave the cars. During the construction of the road large quantities of wood and ties with timber for bridges, were cut in the mountains and foot hills, and hauled to this station. At the foot of Elk Mountain stood

Fort Halleck now abandoned, and a station of the Overland Stage Company. There were many skirmishes with the Indians in this vicinity in those days, and now and then you will be able to find an old settler who will entertain you for hours, in the recital of wild adventures and hairbreadth escapes. A visit to the site of the old fort and the region of country around, together with a close view of the grand scenery of the mountains, will amply repay the traveler for his time and money. About four miles south of Percy, fine veins of coal were discovered in 1875, but they have not been opened or tested. One is nine and the other over twenty feet in thickness. Notice a suggestive sign as you pass the station. It is "Bowles's Hotel," and of course, indicates that everything is perfectly "straight" within.

South of this station there is some very fine grazing land, mostly in the valleys of the little streams that head in the Medicine Bow Range, and flow westward into the North Platte River, and a considerable quantity of hay is cut during favorable seasons.

A Curious and Exciting Race.—Engineers have told of a curious scene on the Pacific Railroad not far from the Laramie Plains, of a race between the locomotive and a herd of deer. At daybreak, the locomotive, with its long train of carriages and freight cars, entered a narrow valley or gorge, where runs quite a rivulet of clear and cold mountain water. On the banks of this stream a large herd of red deer were standing, occasionally lapping the refreshing element. The timid creatures, startled by the presence in their midst of the "iron horse," knew not what course to pursue in order to get away from it. The engineer, to add to their evident perplexity, caused the whistle to send forth its loudest and most discordant shriek. This was enough for the deer. To get beyond reach of this new enemy, they started up the road, taking the course the locomotive was pursuing. The race became exciting. It was a superb trial of steam and iron against muscle and lung. The engineer "put on steam," and sent his locomotive with its burdensome train, whirling along the track; but for many miles—six or seven it was estimated—the frightened animals kept ahead, fairly beating their antagonist. At last the pursued and pursuer got into a more open country. This the deer perceiving, they sprang on one side, and, with unabated speed, ran to a safe distance, where beyond reach of locomotive or rifle, they stood and gazed with dilated eyes—their limbs trembling from unusual exertion, and gasping for breath—at their fast receding enemy.

Dana—is the next station—simply a side track. It is 674.2 miles from Omaha; elevation, 6,875 feet. The rugged, broken character of the country with cuts for the track, and fills in the

DEER RACE WITH TRAIN ON THE U. P. R. R.

valleys, will interest the observing tourist if he passes by in daylight.

St. Marys,—681.7 miles from Omaha, with an elevation of 6,751 feet. It is a telegraph station with accompanying side tack, section-house, etc. From this station to the next, the bluffs are rugged and wild, the road passing through a short tunnel and several deep cuts. There is nothing but the changing scenery as you move along with the train, to relieve this country from its desolate appearance. Sage brush and greasewood continue to be the only products of the soil.

Walcott,—a side track 689.5 miles from the Missouri River, and 6,800 feet above the sea. After leaving this station, the road winds around the bluffs, passing through some very deep cuts, near one of which there is a stone quarry from which stone is taken by the company for road purposes at Green River. A side track to the quarry has been laid and stone easily loaded on the flat cars used for their transportation. Suddenly bursting through one of these cuts we enter the valley of the Platte, through what is called Rattle Snake Pass, by the railroad men, and arrive at

Fort Steele,—which is 695.3 miles from Omaha, 122.5 miles from Laramie, and has an elevation of 6,840 feet. It is a telegraph station, and the site of the government post of the same name. We cross North Platte River just before arriving at the station, and are 4,051 feet higher than when we crossed the same stream at North Platte City, near the junction of the two Plattes in the State of Nebraska. Fort Steele was established on the last day of June, 1868, by

Col. R. I. Dodge, then of the Thirtieth United States Infantry. It is considered a good strategic point, as well as a convenient base of supplies, in case of a campaign against the Indians. The buildings are mostly of logs, and none of them very comfortable. In 1875, the government finished a fine stone hospital building here. The station also does considerable government business, and there is a government depot for receiving and storing supplies near the track. The valley of the North Platte at this upper crossing is quite narrow, without the broad and fertile bottom-lands we were accustomed to see below as we whirled along its banks. From the head of this river in the North Park of Colorado, to a point as far down as Fort Laramie, its route describes the form of a horseshoe. Its tributaries from the east mostly rise in the Medicine Bow Range, and flow westward. They are principally Douglas Creek, Fresh Creek, Brush Creek, Cedar Creek, Spring Creek, and Pass Creek. They are beautiful streams with fine grass valleys and partially wooded banks. Its tributaries from the west are Beaver Creek, Grand Encampment Creek, Cow Creek, Hot Spring Creek, Jack Creek, and Sage Creek. Hot Spring Creek is so named from the hot sulphur springs which are found near its mouth. All the streams which rise in the Medicine Bow Range, and flow into the North Platte, show the "color" of gold where they have been prospected, and some rich diggings are said to have been discovered at the head of Douglas Creek. We believe it will not be long before the Medicine Bow Mountains will develop into a rich mining country. The waters of the Hot Springs referred to are claimed to possess remarkable medicinal virtues, and are from 40 to 45 miles from Fort Steele, up the right bank of the river. The wonders of even these desolate plains do not begin to be known, and when they are fully realized, the world will be astonished at the results. About three miles west of Fort Steele is the site of Benton—the town that was—now wholly abandoned. For a short time it was the business terminus of the road, while its construction was going on, and possessed all the characteristics of the railroad towns in those days. At one time it had a population estimated as high as five thousand souls. Old iron barrel hoops, rusty tin cans, a few holes in the ground, a few posts and stumps, and nearly or quite a hundred nameless graves in close proximity, are all that

perior satisfaction it would give. The railroad reached and passed Benton in July, 1868. The valley of the N. Platte River begins to be occupied by cattle men, as stock can be carried through the severest winters, thus far experienced, without hay. It has superior advantages, not only for grazing, but its numerous "draws" or ravines afford friendly shelter in case of storms.

View on the North Platte, near Fort Fred Steele.—The Platte River here is over 700 miles from its mouth near Omaha, and has an elevation of 6,845 feet. Upon the plains it was a wide, shallow stream, with sand-bars and shifting currents. Here it is a deep, clear, cold stream, and but little distant from its source among the perpetual snow banks of the Rocky Mountains.

Grenville—is the next station, 703.7 miles from Omaha with an elevation of 6,500 feet

VIEW ON THE PLATTE, NEAR FORT FRED STEELE.

now remain to mark the place where Benton was. It grew in a day, and faded out of sight as quickly. But it was a red-hot town while it lasted. A death, sometimes two or three of them, with corresponding burials, was the morning custom. Whisky was preferred to water because it was much easier to obtain, and unrestrained by civilized society or wholesome laws, the devil in men and women had full sway, and made free exhibitions of his nature. The town was three miles from the North Platte River, where all the water was obtained and hauled in, price ten cents per bucket, or one dollar per barrel. In that town, a drink of regular old "tangle-foot" whisky, at "two bits" (twenty-five cents) would last a good deal longer than a bucket of water, to say nothing of the su-

above the sea. It is simply a side track for the meeting and passing of trains. Passenger trains seldom stop. The next station and the end of a subdivision of the road is

Rawlins,—named in honor of Gen. John A. Rawlins, General Grant's chief of staff and his first secretary of war. The springs near here bear the same name, but it has been incorrectly spelled. heretofore. This station is 137.9 miles from Laramie, and 710.7 miles from Omaha. It has an elevation of 6,732 feet. We are going up hill again. The town has a population of over 700 souls, a large majority of whom are railroad employes. The company has erected a hotel for the use of its employes and the traveling public, and has a roundhouse and machine-shops which are kept pretty busy in the repair of engines.

The water used by engines on this division is
strongly impregnated with alkali and other substances, which form scales on the inside of the
boiler and adhere to the flues. The engines are,
therefore, carefully watched and every precaution
taken to guard against accidents. North of the
town, is what might be called in some countries,
a mountain. Near the east end of this mountain valuable beds of red hematite—iron ore—
have been found. This ore is very pure, and,
when ground, makes a very hard and durable
paint. It is said to be water and fire-proof when
used in sufficient quantities. The dark red
freight and flat cars which you see on the line of
the road belonging to the company, have been
painted with this material, and it is rapidly
growing into public favor as its merits become
known. There are two mills here for the manufacture of this paint, and a large quantity is
always on hand. Forty miles due north from
Rawlins are the Ferris and Seminole mining districts. These mines were visited, in 1875, by
Professor Hayden and Professor Thompson.
The lodes operated by the Vulcan Mining Company, indicated gold, silver and copper, mixed
with iron. This company is composed mostly of
mechanics and employes of the Union Pacific.
They first sunk a shaft on the vein and
obtained ore at about 60 feet from the surface
that assayed well and gave indications of a rich
mine. They then commenced a tunnel, and from
their monthly wages, during nearly two years or
more, contributed and expended about $24,000.
At a distance of about 365 feet, they struck the
vein, and have a large body of rich ore in sight
and on the dump. A mill will soon be put in,
when the company will begin to realize something for their outlay. The Elgin Mining Company have also put in a tunnel, and are reported
to have struck a rich vein. The developments,
thus far made, indicate that the copper and silver
will soon run out, and that the mines will be
essentially gold-bearing. South of Rawlins about
60 miles, on the Snake River Region, are fine
grazing fields, already occupied, to a certain extent, by cattle men, and mining country yet
undeveloped. Placer diggings have been found
and worked to some extent, and indications of
rich quartz lodes are prevalent, some having
already been discovered. A colony of farmers
and miners from the vicinity of Denver, Col.,
have settled in that region, and more are constantly going in. About a mile and a half from
Rawlins, east, is a large sulphur spring. It is
untaken, as yet. We could not ascertain
whether the waters had been analyzed or not,
though they are claimed to possess the usual
medicinal qualities of water from similar springs.
The springs frequently alluded to as Rawlins
Springs, are on the left of the track, and a little
west of the town. The small creek which passes
through the place, is known as Separation Creek,

and empties into the North Platte River north
of Fort Steele. There are, also, immense beds
or lakes of soda, tributary to this station, some
of which is nearly pure. When they are utilized,
as they doubtless soon will be, and the industry
is developed, employment will be given to many
laborers now idle, together with fortunes to those
who have the nerve and capacity to successfully
carry it on. We are informed that from twelve
to fourteen millions of dollars are annually paid
in customs duties on the article of imported soda,
alone. Rawlins is in the midst of a broken, desolate country, and depends upon railroad impor-
tations for nearly everything upon which its
people live, though there is a fine country reported both north and south. In addition to the
other buildings named, it has the usual quantity
of saloons, together with several stores, at which
a thriving trade is done. The future of the
town will depend largely upon the developments
in the mining districts spoken of.

Summit.—A side track, nearly seven miles
from Rawlins, and 717.4 miles from Omaha;
elevation, 6,821 feet. Heavy grades now for
quite a distance.

Separation.—One would naturally suppose
from the name, that the waters flowing east and
west, divided or separated here, but such is not
the fact. It is reported that a party of engineers
who were surveying and locating the road,
separated here to run different lines—hence the
name. It is a telegraph station, 724.1 miles from
Omaha, and 6,900 feet above the level of the
sea. The artesian well at this station, which
supplies the water tank is 860 feet deep. The
water from these wells is not always pure—frequently having a brackish or alkali taste.

Fillmore,—named in honor of a former division superintendent of the road, now in the
stock business, with ranche at Wyoming. It is
731.6 miles from Omaha; elevation, 6,885 feet.
Simply a side track in the midst of a barren,
broken country.

Creston.—738.6 miles from the eastern terminus of the road, and 7,030 feet above the sea.
It is a telegraph station, with the usual side
tracks and section-house. Three miles farther
west, and we reach the summit of the divide
which separates the waters of the two oceans
This is the crowning ridge in the backbone of the
Continent, and a desolate place it is. It is the
summit of the Rocky Mountains. "What was
this country made for?"—We asked a fellow-
traveler. "To hold the rest of it together"—
was the ready reply. That is good; the best
reason for its existence we've had. It is of some
use after all. Allowing 60 feet grade for the
three miles west of Creston, to the actual summit
of the divide, and we are then 1,122 feet lower
than at Sherman. It is true there are no lofty
peaks here, with snowy crests the year round,
but an immense roll, over which we glide and

never think that we are crossing the summit of the rock-ribbed Rockies. At this divide a short distance north of the track, a pole was once erected with a flag to mark the spot, but it has fallen before the fierce gales which sweep over this elevated ridge, and which seem to have withered everything they touched. Standing on the rear platform of the train, looking east you notice the undulations of the road as it passes beneath you; Elk Mountain of the Medicine Bow Range, and the far distant Black Hills rise grandly in view as you approach the crest, but suddenly you have passed to the other side, and a stretch of country two hundred miles long drops from your view in an instant. On this part of the road the most difficulty with snow is usually experienced in the winter. There is a constant breeze here, and frequent storms, though a few miles farther it may be clear and pleasant. In the great snow blockade of the winter of 1871-2, the telegraph poles were frequently buried in the drifts. The Western Union Company had their wires elevated on poles planted in the snow in several places, to keep them above the drifts. In that blockade, the worst ever known since the road was built, there were seventeen days without trains. Since then the track has been raised, snow fences planted, sheds erected and every possible appliance used to insure the safe and speedy passage of trains. Looking again to the north you can see the snowy heads of the Wind River Mountains, with the peak named after Fremont, the gallant Path-finder of the West, towering against the sky. Notice the dark shades of the timber lines as they press against the eternal snows with which they are covered. Looking forward to the west, if you have a chance, Pilot Butte, north of Rock Springs, one of the great landmarks of the plains, is clearly visible. To the south you behold the mountains where the tributaries of the Snake River rise, and whence they flow into the Pacific Ocean. *Notice on north sign-board*, "CONTINENTAL DIVIDE."

Latham, — 746.1 miles from Omaha, and 6,900 feet above the sea. Passenger trains do not stop as it is only a side track. On we go to

Washakie, — so called after a Shoshone chief, reputed to be friendly to the whites, whose tribe fights the Sioux when there is opportunity. Here is an artesian well, 638 feet deep, flowing 800 gallons per hour.

Red Desert. — The country near is reddish in appearance, but the place is named after the *Red Desert*, near which is an immense basin of its own, similar to the Salt Lake basin. It lies 500 feet below the level of the country, has no outlet, and extends from the South Pass on the north, to Bridger's Pass on the south, and east from summit of the divide to Tipton on the west, a very singular depression right on the divide of the Continent. The little stream just seen before reaching this place, flows south and is lost in this

basin. The country near is alkali, and subject to high water and heavy rains, giving great difficulty to preserve the security of road-bed and track. Station is 763 miles from Omaha; elevation 6,710 feet.

Tipton, — a side track for meeting and passing trains. It is 769.6 miles from the "Big Muddy," with an elevation of 6,800 feet. We have been going up hill again — leaving the valley of the Snake River. The snows of winter leave heavy drifts along here, but the railroad men have learned by experience how to manage them quite successfully. When the drifts have reached the top of the fences in height, they go along and raise the fences to the top of the drifts, fastening them as best they can in the snow. This they repeat as often as necessary, and thus, the snow, in many instances, is kept away from the track, but the drifts become pretty high.

Table Rock, — named from a rock resembling a table south of, and about six miles from the station. It is 776.3 miles from Omaha, and 6.890 feet above the sea — is a telegraph station. There is a long, evenly cut bluff south of the track, estimated to be 600 feet in height. On what appears to be the north-west corner of this bluff a square, table-like, projection rises — the table — and presents a very odd appearance. It can be seen for quite a distance, as you look to the left from the cars. The table projects about 60 feet above the bluffs adjoining, though it does not seem half that distance. Next we come to

Agate, — 781.3 miles from Omaha, and 6,785 feet above the sea. South of this station and to a certain extent, in its immediate vicinity, moss agates are found. The stones, however, are not clear and well-defined. They are smoky and dark, rendering them nearly valueless. Agate is only a side track where trains seldom stop. Down the grade we pass to

Bitter Creek, — a telegraph station, 786.3 miles from Omaha, with an elevation of 6,685 feet. At this station, we first strike the well-known Bitter Creek Valley, through which we shall pass to Green River. About four miles below this station, on the south side of the track, the old overland stage and emigrant road struck the valley, as it came in from Bridger's Pass, and across the Snake River Valley. The railroad reaches Bitter Creek through a "draw" or dry ravine which unites with the valley proper, at the station. The old stage-road struck the creek farther south, and before it reaches the railroad. This was formerly quite a station, and the end of a passenger division. It has a small roundhouse, with ten stalls and turn-table, upon which the engines and snow-plows are turned. Between this station and Rawlins, as has been observed, are very heavy grades, requiring two engines to pull a train. These extra engines come with trains as far as this station, and then assist eastward bound trains back again. A large quan-

SCENES ON GREEN RIVER.
1.—Flaming Gorge.   2.—Brown's Hole.   3.—Looking up the Valley of Green River.

tity of bridge timber is also kept here, ready for any emergency. In the great washout at the foot of this valley, in the spring of 1875, large quantities were used. Bitter Creek is rightly named. Its waters are so strongly impregnated with alkali that they are almost useless. Nevertheless, at the head of this creek, where it is fed by cold, clear springs, for more than ten miles from the station, trout have been caught, though they are small. The rugged scenery along this valley will interest the traveler, as the views are constantly changing. There are no machine-shops for repairs here, only the five-stall roundhouse. The creek has been dammed for the purpose of supplying the water tank, though the water is not the best for boilers. The whole region of country, from a point east, as far as Rock Creek to Green River, is underlaid with coal. It frequently crops out in this valley. The coal is lignite and will not "coke" like the bituminous coal. There are also indications of iron and other minerals, in the immediate vicinity of the valley. Occasionally, you will see little shrub pines on the bluffs—but no timber. These pines have tried to grow, but the sterility of the soil is against them. They find it almost impossible to "take root." Sometimes it seems, as you pass down the valley and look ahead, as though the train was going square against the rocks, and would be dashed in pieces; but a sudden curve, and you have rounded the projecting bluffs, and are safely pursuing your journey. Again, it seems as though the bluffs were trying to shake hands across the chasm, or making an effort to become dovetailed together. They assume all sorts of shapes, washed out in places by the storms of ages—smoothly carved as if by the hand of the sculptor—and again, ragged and grotesque. The geology of the Bitter Creek and Green River Valleys, will afford a chapter of curious interest, and will amply reward him who searches thoroughly after the knowledge. Professor Hayden and Major Powell have the best reports on the formation and geology of this region.

Black Buttes—is the next station, 795.4 miles from Omaha, and 6,600 feet above the sea. It is a telegraph station with accompanying side tracks. Formerly there was a coal mine worked here, said to belong to Jack Morrow, now of Omaha, and quite a noted frontier character in his day. It furnishes excellent coal, easily accessible, the vein being from six to eight feet thick. As you approach the station, notice the balanced rock north of the road and within 50 feet of the side track. The buttes from which the station

is named are south of the creek, and plainly visible.

Hallville,—named after a noted contractor who graded the road through this part of the valley. A few posts and adobe walls are all that remain of the camp. It is simply a side track, 800.9 miles from Omaha, with an elevation of 6,590 feet.

Point of Rocks—is a station with a history. It was formerly quite a town, but its glory has departed with the causes which brought it into existence. It was formerly the point of departure and the outfitting place for the Sweetwater Gold District, South Pass City, Atlantic City, Camp Stambaugh, and other places in the region of the Great South Pass at the foot of Wind River Mountains, and is the nearest railroad point to those places. to-day, with a good wagon road not much traveled. Distance to South Pass City, 65 miles. The rocks from which this place is named are on a high point south of the track, and a little east of the station. They seem in the distance like faint outlines of huge perpendicular columns, not very high, but really 365 feet perpendicular above their base surroundings. Their summit is about 1,100 feet above the track. At the base of the rocks proper, and about 735 feet above the track, seven sulphur springs break out, three of which are large ones, the balance being small.

North of the track, and three-fourths of a mile west of the station, is an iron spring, reputed to possess remarkable medicinal qualities, several invalids, especially females, having been highly benefited by drinking and bathing in its waters. Four miles north of the station is a huge sulphur spring, with water pouring forth from the ground. The artesian well, which supplies the water tank here, is 700 feet deep. Water is pumped out by steam power. Wells & Fargo's Overland Express Company had a station here, and their old adobe buildings, rapidly going into decay, may still be seen across the creek, at the base of the bluffs. In the "piping" times of the town several buildings were commenced, but the collapse was so sudden that they were never completed. This station is 806.7 miles from Omaha, and 6,490 feet above the sea. It is now a place of large coal interests, over one hundred car loads per day being shipped. There is also an artesian well one thousand and fifteen feet deep.

Thayer,—simply a side track, 812 miles from Omaha, with an elevation of 6,425 feet. The moving trains will give the tourist an ever-varying view of the grand and beautiful scenery of this valley.

Salt Wells,—818.2 miles from the eastern

terminus of the road, and 6,360 feet above the sea. It is a telegraph station, and in the construction period of the road, was a place where considerable timber, wood, etc., was delivered. The water from the well here has a saltish, alkaline taste, hence the name. Three and one-half miles north, there is a salt or alkali basin, which has no visible outlet in which the brackish waters stand the most of the year.

Baxter,—826.2 miles from Omaha; eleva-

its entire line. Rock Springs coal for domestic purposes is only surpassed by anthracite. It has but little of the sulphurous smell of other soft coal, burns into ashes without clinkers, and without the black soot which characterizes other coal. These mines, with others, were formerly operated by the Wyoming Coal Company. Their product is annually increasing; wherever the superior merits of the coal have become known it speedily supplants other kinds in use. In 1875 the company mined 104,427 tons, or

CASTLE ROCK.

tion, 6,300 feet—A side track where passenger trains do not stop. The valley narrows in this vicinity, and the rugged rocks with their ragged edges, if possible become more interesting to the observer.

Rock Springs,—831.6 miles from Omaha, and 6,280 feet above the sea. This is the great coal station on the line of the Union Pacific Road. The company not only furnishes the finest lignite coal to be found, for its own use, but supplies the market at every point along

10,442 cars allowing the usual ten tons per car. They did not, however, ship this number of cars as considerable coal is furnished to all the engines that pass, and consumed by the people living in the town. They are now working two veins, one six and the other about nine feet in thickness. The Artesian well here is 1,145 feet deep.

Lawrence,—840.6 miles from Omaha, with an elevation of 6,200 feet. A side track for passing trains between Rock Springs and *Green River,*—which is the end of the Laramie division of the road, 273.8 miles from that place, and 846.6 miles from Omaha, with an elevation of 6,140 feet. This is a regular eating-station, breakfast and supper, and *is now* one of the best kept hostelries on the road. This place will eventually be a popular resort for those who are seeking for fossiliferous remains, and those who delight in fishing. Here is the outfitting point for hunting and fishing parties who desire to go either north or south, and here is the head center for Rocky Mountain specimens, fossils, petrifactions, etc., and travelers would like to know beforehand just what accommodations they can obtain. Mr. Kitchen is able to provide for all, in elegant style, at reasonable prices. Here, also, he has on exhibition and for sale the specimens alluded to—such as beautiful moss agates, fossil fish, petrified shells and wood, with others which we are not able to name. Par-

others to reclaim the soil, but thus far with indifferent success, though Mr. Fields was quite successful, in 1875, with a crop of potatoes, cabbages, turnips, radishes, and other "garden truck."

Stages leave here for the Big Horn Waters and other towns tri-weekly. The old mud huts are beginning to find occupants again. The Desert House is the only hotel, a pleasant place with its flowers, ferns, and pictures.

The high projecting tower north of the track, crowning a bluff, is 625 feet higher than the river level below, and about 615 feet higher than the track. Other rocks, as "The Sisters" and "The Twin Sisters" will be readily recognized by the passing traveler.

"Wake up, wake up," said an old lady to her husband, as the train approached the station one

THE TWIN SISTERS, GREEN RIVER.

ties of men are employed to search the hills, mountains and valleys in this vicinity, for these specimens, and when found, to bring them in. The stock is, therefore, continually replenished with rich and rare gems and fossils, and they may here be obtained at any time.

Being the end of a division, Green River has a large roundhouse with fifteen stalls, and the usual machine and repair shops. The railroad bursts into the valley through a narrow gorge between two hills, then turns to the right and enters the town, crossing the river beyond on a wooden truss bridge. The old adobe town, remains of which are still visible, was on the bottom-land directly in front of the gorge.

Green River is now the county-seat of Sweetwater County, Wyoming, and has a population of nearly 1,000 persons. Efforts have been made by Mr. Fields and a few

morning last year; "here is Solomon's temple petrified," said she, as she gave him another shake. The old gentleman rubbed his eyes, gave another yawn, and finally looked out, to see what excites the curiosity of every traveler, as he arrives at this place. Sure enough: it seems as though some great temple once stood here, or several of them, and in the wrecks of time, left their gigantic pillars standing, as a reminder of their former greatness.

The Green River.—The peculiar color of this river is not owing to the fact of any discoloration of the water; that, when the banks of the stream are not filled by freshets of itself or some of its tributaries, is very pure and sweet, and of the usual color of clear water, but is owing to the green shale through which it runs, and which can readily be seen in the bluffs in the vicinity and for quite a distance up Black's Fork, and

PETRIFIED FISH CUT, GREEN RIVER.

WEST BANK GREEN RIVER, LOOKING EASTWARD.

which is supposed to contain arsenic or chloride of copper, which becomes detached by drainage and fastens itself to the pebble stones and bottom of the stream, causing the water, as you look into it, to bear the same color. This river rises in the Wyoming and Wind River Mountains, is fed by numerous tributaries, and flows in a general southerly direction, until it unites with the Colorado River. The scenery along its banks, most always rugged, in some places is sublime. Where it is crossed by the railroad, its valley is narrow, enclosed on either side by high bluffs, which have been washed into numerous fanciful shapes by the storms of time, and which are crowned, in many instances, by columns, or towers, forcibly reminding one of the towers, battlements and castles, spoken of in the old feudal times. Its tributaries, nearly all have narrow fertile valleys, which are being occupied by stockmen, and which afford both hay and shelter for stock. South of the railroad, it winds through the famous Colorado Cañon, so well and grandly described by Major Powell, the explorer. The river and its surroundings must from their very nature, always be a source of interest to the scientist, and will soon become a popular resort for fossil hunters, gem searchers and sportsmen.

Brown's Hole.—This is a beautiful scene just below Red Cañon, the water is calm, quiet, and peaceful, like a mirror, with wonderfully distinct reflections. Here is the last quiet stretch of the river ere it enters into the turbulent passage of the deeper, gloomier, and larger cañon

below The sandy beach, at the left, shows the foot-prints of numerous deer, bears, and elk that frequent the bank.

Brown's Hole is an expansion of the valley of Green River, and is about five miles wide and thirty miles long. This is a name given by the old trappers,—40 years ago, or more—and has been a favorite wintering place for stock. Little or no snow falls in the valleys, and they are so well surrounded by high mountains, that the bleak winds of winter cannot reach them. The valley is covered with wild sage and bunch grass—and at the time of the visit of the Hayden Exploring Party, there were 2,200 head of Texas cattle, just driven in, to fatten for the California market. In the north sides of the valley, the beds of rock have, by the action of the weather, become shaped into innumerably beautiful, architectural forms, like the ruins of pyramids.

Giant's Club.—This is fairly a giant in dimensions,— as its proportions are really colossal. It rises with almost perpendicular sides, and is impossible to scale by ascent. The rock is valuable for its curious composition, as it bears evidences of having once existed at the bottom of a lake. The rock lies in regular strata, all horizontal, and most of these contain fossils of plants and fishes. The plants are all extinct species, and closely allied to our fruit and forest trees ; among them, however, are some palms, which indicated this to be, in original times, when the deposit was formed, a very warm climate. Professor Hayden, in examining this rock, and others near, found the plants in the upper part of the rock, and about a hundred feet lower down, discovered the remains of fishes, all of them belonging to fresh water, and all extinct species. They were imbedded in oily shales, and insects were found with them, in a remarkable state of preservation. With the fishes were also found feathers of birds, and a few reeds.

Peculiarities of the Green River Rocks. —To the curious formation of rocks which give all this region its characteristic features, is given the name of the Green River Shales; the sediments are arranged in regular layers, mostly quite thin, but varying from the thickness of a knife-blade to several feet. These peculiar layers, or bands, are quite varied in shades of color. In some of the thin slabs of shale, are thousands of beautiful impressions of fish, sometimes a dozen or so within the compass of a square foot. Impressions of insects and water plants are also sometimes found. At Burning Rock Cut, the road is cut through thin layers of a sort of cream-colored, chalky limestone, interspersed with strata of a dark brown color, saturated with petroleum as to burn freely. The Cut derives its name Burning Rocks, from the fact that during the building of the road the rocks became ignited and burned for some days, illuminating the labor of the workmen by night—and filling the valley with dense clouds of smoke by day.

Curious Scenes along the Green River. —At the mouth of Henry's Fork there is a view on Green River of great beauty, which derives its principal charm from its vivid colors. The wa-

ters of the river are of the purest emerald, with banks and sand-bars of glistening white. The perpendicular bluff to the left is nearly 1,500 feet above the level of the river, and of a bright red and yellow. When illuminated by full sunlight, it is grand, and deserves its full title "The Flaming Gorge." It is the entrance to a gateway to the still greater wonders and grandeurs of the famous Red Canon that cuts its way to a depth of 3,000 feet, between this point and its entrance into Brown's Hole.

Leaving Green River the railroad crosses the bridge, turns to the right, and runs along under the bluffs—the highest being about 350 feet high, and almost over the river in one place—for about three miles, when it again turns to the left, passing the divide where there is an un-

GIANT'S CLUB, GREEN RIVER.

GIANT'S TEA-POT, GREEN RIVER.

named side track, and along a hilly, broken country.

The Sweetwater.—This stream rises in the Wind River Mountains, directly north of Point of Rocks and Salt Wells, in the great South Pass, discovered by General Fremont, and runs in a general easterly direction uniting with the North Platte River about 80 miles north of Fort Steele. South of it is the Sweetwater Mountain Range. North of it lay the Rattlesnake Hills, which are said to be one continuous chain of broken ragged rocks heaped upon each other in confused masses. They are utterly barren and desolate, and beyond the snakes which give them their name, are avoided by almost every living thing. Near the mouth of this river, Independence

Rock, a noted landmark of the plains, rises. It is on the line of the Indian trail, to the upper North Platte Region, and near it has been found immense deposits of soda in lakes which are said to be nearly pure, and which are soon to be worked. The valley of this stream is rarely covered with snow in winter, and affords excellent grazing for stock the entire year. Were it not so exposed to Indian raids in summer, it would soon be occupied. The care of stock requires horses and beyond the killing of a few head for beef occasionally, the Indians do not trouble it; the horses are what they want, and what they come after and scalps will be taken, if necessary to obtain them. Placer, gulch and quartz gold has been discovered in the Wind River Mountains, near the Great South Pass, and fortunes have been made and lost in that mining district in a very short time. They have been made by the mining sharks, who sold their mines to the inexperienced and uninitiated from the East, and lost by the parties who were "taken in." There are however valuable mines in this vicinity (nearly all gold), which will some day be developed. To the east of the Wind River Mountains is the Shoshone or Snake River Indian reservation has been laid off. The principal towns are Atlantic City, South Pass City and Miner's Delight, a mining town. Near Atlantic City is Camp Stambough and still farther north on the east side of the same mountain, is Camp Brown, the latter being near the boundary line of the Indian reservation referred to. Very fine hot mineral springs have been found on or near this reservation, which will eventually be extensively patronized. The main road by which these places are reached, leads out from Bryan and Green River. From the latter place four-horse coaches are run tri-weekly, while from the former a great quantity of government freight is annually shipped. The road crosses the river near the mouth of Big Sandy Creek, and follows up this stream, and its south branch to Pacific Spring, after which it crosses a low divide to a tributary of the Sweetwater. While the road from Point of Rocks is much shorter yet this route is said to be the best as it follows the valley of a stream all the way, and avoids sand-hills which are very trying to stock. From Green River the road at present traveled, passes up the valley until it strikes the Big Sandy, where it intersects the road from Bryan. The nearest peaks seen on the north side of the track, as you pass the divide just west of Creston, are those of the real Rocky Mountain Range, and extend in a north-westerly direction to the head of the Wind River Mountains, from which they are only divided by the Sweetwater Valley. Before the Lodge Pole Valley Route was discovered via the Cheyenne Pass, the North Platte and Sweetwater Route via the South Pass and Big Sandy was the main, in fact the great overland

route, traveled by the Mormons and California emigrants. At the time the railroad was built, however, the Lodge Pole Route was the one mainly traveled. The vast region north of the railroad between the Black Hills and Green River Valley, contains within itself the germs of a mighty empire, only waiting for the united efforts of capital and labor for development.

Bryan,—over 13 miles from Green River, and 860 miles from Omaha, with an elevation of 6,340 feet or just 200 feet higher than at Green River. This station was formerly a division terminus at which time it was a place of considerable importance. The government has a depot here, where its freight for Camp Stambaugh, Camp Brown and other places is received. The majority of the freight for the Sweetwater Mining District and the settlements at the base of the Wind River Mountains, South Pass City, Atlantic City, etc., is also shipped from this place, the distance to the latter city being 90 miles. Bryan is the first station where the railroad strikes Black's Fork of the Green River. This fork rises in the Uintah Mountains, directly south of Piedmont, and runs in a north-easterly direction till it reaches Bryan, then turns toward the south-west and unites with Green River some twenty miles below the town of Green River. The valley at Bryan is quite broad in places, and thickly covered with sage brush and greasewood. The soil is said to be fertile and capable of producing large crops with irrigation.

Fort Bridger, eleven miles south of Carter Station, is on this stream, and at that place over 300 bushels of potatoes have been raised from a single half acre of ground. This shows what this virgin soil can do if irrigated. The table-land on the elevated benches that the traveler will observe on either side of the road, is said to be equally rich, and would be equally as prolific if it could be irrigated. As you approach Bryan, look away to the south and south-east, and you will behold the towering peaks of the Uintah Mountains, 70 or 80 miles off. They do not look so distant, but then distance is very deceptive in this country. Bryan is a telegraph station with a store, saloon, and a few houses—all that's left to tell the story of its better and departed days. Its early history is the same as all the railroad towns we have mentioned, with roughs, cut-throats, gamblers, villains, etc., and their cleaning out by vigilance committees, under law administered by "Judge Lynch."

We now pursue our way up the valley of Black's Fork. Four miles west of Bryan, the road first crosses this stream which it follows to Church Buttes.

Marston—is the next station—a side track 21 miles from Green River, and 867.6 miles from Omaha; elevation, 6,215 feet. From the apparently level plains which the road crosses, abrupt buttes or bluffs rise as if built by human hands as mounds to conceal some treasure, or to perpetuate some remarkable incident in history. They form a curious study, and awaken no little interest in the mind of an observing traveler. To the left of the track there are a number of low buttes as you approach

Granger,—the next station, 877.2 miles from Omaha, and 6,270 feet above the sea. It is a telegraph station, named in honor of an old settler here, and is the principal shipping point on the line of the Union Pacific, for Montana and Idaho cattle. These cattle are driven to this point from the territories named, and the shipments are increasing every year. Yards and chutes have been erected for their accommodation and use. Near the station are one or two stone houses. The road here crosses Ham's Fork, a tributary of Black's Fork, which rises some 70

to Evanston, in great profusion. The most of them, however, are valueless, but occasionally specimens of rare beauty are picked up. On what are called "the bad lands," about 7 miles south of the road, however, the finest agates, with other beautiful gems, are obtained with little difficulty. In Ham's Fork water agates, creamy white, and amber colored, may be occasionally picked up. They are quite rare, and when cut by the lapidary, are held to be of considerable value.

View of Uintah Mountains.—The view we give an illustration of, on page 80, is one of the finest in the Far West. The scene is taken from Photograph Ridge, at an elevation of 10,829 feet. In the foreground is a picturesque group of the mountain pines. In the middle distance flows Black's Fork. The peaks or cones

CHURCH BUTTES ON BLACK'S FORK.

miles north-west, and which, the old settlers say, is really the main stream of the two. The banks of this stream, as far as you can see, are lined with bushes, and farther up, its valley produces luxuriant grass, from which hay is cut, and upon which numerous herds of cattle feed. An oval peak rises on the north side of the track, beyond which, in the distance, may be seen a range of bluffs, or mountains, which rise up between Ham's Fork and Green River. From Granger to the next station, are buttes on both sides of the track, while, to the left, the high peaks of the Uintah Range tower up in the distance, affording one of the grandest views on the line of the road. This is the region of moss agates, gems of various kinds, and precious stones. Agates are found all along the line of the road from Green River

in the distance have their summits far above the limits of perpetual snow, and from 1,500 to 2,000 feet above the springs that are the sources of the streams below. These cones are distinctly stratified, mostly horizontal, and there are frequently vast piles of purplish, compact quartzite, which resemble Egyptian pyramids on a gigantic scale, without a trace of grit, vegetation, or water. One of these remarkable structures stands out isolated from the rest, in the middle of the Valley of Smith's Fork, and is so much like a Gothic church, that the United States Surveying Party gave it the name of Hayden's Cathedral, after the leader of the exploration.

Church Buttes,—887.7 miles from Omaha; elevation, 6,317 feet. The particular buttes, from which the station derives its name, are about 10 miles south of the station, on the old overland stage road, but buttes rise up from the level plains in this vicinity in every direction. They are, however, fast washing away. The annual increase in rain-fall on this desert, since the completion of the railroad and the stretching of five telegraph wires, is remarkable, and is especially noticed by the old settlers. These rains, with the frosts of winter, are having a noticeable effect on the buttes. Isolated peaks have disappeared entirely—and prominent projections have been materially lessened. There are still a large number, however, chiseled by the action of frosts and rains into fantastic shapes which will excite the attention and rivet the gaze of the traveler, as he passes by; but, if their annual diminution continues, in less than half a century, they will have lost their interest. Near this station is the last crossing of Black's Fork, which now bears away to the left, while the road ascends another of its branches, called the Big Muddy. What has been said in reference to agates, etc., of the other stations, will apply to Church Buttes with equal force.

Curious Scientific Explorations. — Church Buttes is a curious formation, located on the line of the old overland stage route, about one hundred and fifty miles east from Salt Lake, and at this point having an elevation of 6,731 feet. The formation is part of the *Mauvaises Terres*, or Bad Lands, and consists of a vast deposit of sedimentary sandstones, and marly clay, in perfectly horizontal strata, and contain within their beds, some very remarkable paleontological remains. The peculiar effects of stormy weather and flood, in the past, has carved the bluff-lines into the most curious and fantastic forms—lofty domes and pinnacles, and fluted columns, these rocks resembling some cathedral of the olden time, standing in the midst of desolation.

Professor Hayden, in speaking of them says, "Distance lends a most delicious enchantment to the scene, and the imagination can build many castles from out of this mass of most singular formation. A nearer approach dispels some of the illusions, but the mind is no less impressed with the infinite variety of detail and the scattered remains of the extinct life of some far distant age."

In this section are found "moss agates," in the greatest abundance, being scattered all over the surface of the country. Standing upon one of the summits of the highest point of the " Bad Lands," Hayden says, "as far as the eye can reach, upon every side, is a vast extent of most infinite detail. It looks like some ruined city of the gods, blasted, bare, desolate, but grave, beyond a mortal's telling." In 1870, a geological expedition, headed by Prof. O. C. Marsh, of Yale College, and known as the " Yale College Expedition of 1870 " — visited the " Bad Lands " and made a geological examination. They were accompanied

by Buffalo Bill, a military troupe, and ten Pawnee Indians, as guides. On the way, Professor Marsh endeavored to explain the mighty changes of geology and the grand discoveries they would make—and as Buffalo Bill intimated, some of them were "*pretty tough yarns.*" The desolation of the country can only be imagined, not described—hour after hour the party marched over burning sand-hills, without rocks or trees, or signs of water, while the thermometer stood at 110° in the shade of the wagons. After fourteen hours in the saddle, one of the soldiers, exhausted with heat and thirst, finally exclaimed : "*What did God Almighty make such as this for ?*" "*Why,*" replied another more devout trooper, "*God Almighty made the country good enough, but it's this deuced geology the professor talks about, that spoiled it all.*"

For fresh water the party had to thank the favor of a thunder-shower, during which they drank from the rims of each other's hats. Their researches resulted in the discovery of the remains of various species of the camel, horse, mammals, and others new to science. A branch of this expedition exploring the canons and plains of Northern Colorado, discovered a large deposit which contained great quantities of fossil turtles, and rhinoceros, birds, and the remains of the *areodon,*—a remarkable animal combining the characteristics of the modern sheep, pig and deer. The remains of another monster, the *Titanotherium,* were found of such vast proportions, that a lower jaw measured over *four feet* in length. At Antelope Station, in one of these areodon beds, remains were found of several species of horse :—one a three-toed animal, and another which, although full grown, had attained the height of but two feet. In an exploration near Green River—the expedition found petrified fishes in abundance, and a small bed, containing fossil insects, *a rare discovery.* Here were beetles and dragons, flies and grasshoppers; a gigantic fossil mosquito, and an extinct flea of great dimensions were also discovered. At Fort Wallace, Ks., the party found a trophy in the form of a skeleton of a sea serpent nearly complete, which alone required four days to dig out and bring to the camp. This monster when alive could not have been less than 60 feet. It had a slender eel-like body and tail, with mouth like a boa-constrictor.

Among the curious incidents which happened, was the discovery of a genuine Sioux Indian burial ground. The dead were reposing on platforms of boughs elevated above the ground, and supported at the four corners by poles about eight feet in height. On one of these tombs lay two bodies,—a woman, decked in beads and bracelets, and a scalpless brave, with war paint still on the cheeks, and holding in his crumbling hand, a rusty shot-gun, and a pack of cards. Several incidents occurred from the abundance of rattle-snakes. Several animals were bitten by them, and the country at some places fairly swarmed with them. Numbers were killed every day by the horses' feet, and while members of the party would occasionally bathe in the river, these reptiles would bask upon the bank of the stream near their clothes, as one of them says, "Their humming soon became an old tune, and the charm of shooting the wretches wore away for all but one, who was collecting their rattles as a necklace for his lady love."

Hampton,—a little over 50 miles from Green River, 897.1 miles from Omaha, and 6,500 feet above the sea. It is simply a side track where, occasionally, trains meet and pass. Approaching this station, two large buttes lift themselves above their fellows on the left side of the track, while beyond, a low, dark ridge may be seen covered with cedars. In this ridge is an abundance of game and good hunting at almost any season of the year. The game consists of elk, coyotes, wolves, deer, bears, etc. About three miles before you reach the next station, you will notice off to the right of the track, a long, low, dark ridge. It is also covered with cedars, and it strikes the road near Bridger Station. There are also plenty of cedars in the bluffs to the left before you reach

Carter,—the next station, which is 904.6 miles from Omaha, and 6,550 feet above the sea. The station is named in honor of Col. Dick Carter, whose home is here, and who has lived here since the completion of the railroad. It is the nearest railroad station to Fort Bridger, which is located on Black's Fork, 11 miles due south, and reached by daily stages from this point. Colonel Carter is about to try the experiment of raising crops at this station. He has built a dam across the creek and dug a ditch nearly 2,000 feet long, which will irrigate the ground he proposes to till. Near Carter, also, one can hardly go amiss of moss agates and other curious specimens. About 20 miles a little north-west of this station, is a mountain of coal on a tributary of Little Muddy. In this mountain are found three splendid veins of coal, of total thickness of 87 feet, which can be traced over ten miles, also layers of slate 25 to 30 feet in depth. The coal resembles cannel coal, and makes excellent coke for smelting purposes. Seven miles north of Carter, a white sulphur spring was discovered in the summer of 1875, whose waters will equal, if not surpass those of the celebrated springs of Virginia. Within about a hundred yards of these sulphur springs, and at the same time, a chalybeate spring was also discovered, but its waters have not yet been analyzed, though their medicinal qualities are said to be excellent. There is also, a fine fresh water spring near by. A branch railroad from Carter would pass these

springs, and reach the mountain of coal in a distance of 24 miles.

Smith's Fork, a branch of Black's, is about five miles south of Fort Bridger, and Henry's Fork, of Green River, is some 25 miles still farther south, and is noted for its rich grazing. It is mostly occupied by stockmen as a winter range, and large numbers of cattle are annually wintered without hay in its valley. Smith's and Henry's Forks are filled with trout, and afford fine fishing, while there is an abundance of game, such as elk, deer, antelope and bear to attract the hunter and sportsman. A plenty of sage hens give fine shooting in the summer months. Carter is a telegraph station, and has a store from which ranchemen, hunters, and others obtain supplies. It was formerly an eating-station on the road and was renowned for the splendid trout which were served up by Colonel Carter, who was its proprietor. A government road to Fort Ellis, Montana, and the Yellowstone Park, has been surveyed from this station by way of Bear River Valley and the Soda Springs in Idaho. It is some 80 miles nearer than by Ogden or Corinne, over a fine route, and will probably be opened in a year or two.

Bridger,—914.1 miles from Omaha, with an elevation of 6,780 feet. It is a telegraph station named in honor of Jim Bridger, who was a noted hunter and guide, for government and other expeditions. Since leaving Bryan, we have been going up hill all the time, and our ascent will now be rapid until we pass the divide between Piedmont and Aspen. Near here is a cliff five hundred feet high, called "*Pluto's Outlook.*" Can be seen on left of track three miles west.

Leroy,—is the next station. It is 919.1 miles from Omaha, and 7,123 feet above the level of the sea. In passing over only five miles of road, we have ascended nearly 350 feet. Leaving this place, you will observe old telegraph poles still standing on the left of the track. They mark the line of the old overland road. About two miles west of Leroy, at the base of a hill or bluff, south of the track, are some excellent Soda Springs. They are near the road, and trains sometimes stop to enable passengers to drink the water. In 1875, an emigrant train stopped at these springs a few minutes, when one of the passengers, on the way to the springs, picked up a most beautiful moss agate, in which there were six clearly defined, conical shaped trees, each one perfect in shape and form. The hills and valleys in this vicinity continue to abound in agates and other curious specimens, while soda, iron and fresh water springs, are numerous, sometimes in close proximity to each other.

Piedmont.—Here the road, after crossing it, leaves the Muddy, which comes in from the south. This station is ten miles from Leroy, 929.1 miles from Omaha, and has an elevation of

7,540 feet. In summer, the scenery along this part of the road is delightful, while in winter the storms are severe, the wind blowing almost a constant gale, while the snow drifts mountains high. There are several snow sheds along this part of the road, the longest being on the summit, 2,700 feet in length. The road having to wind around the spurs and into the depressions of the hills, is very crooked, in one place doubling back on itself. We are now crossing a high ridge in the Uintah Mountains, and the second highest elevation on the Union Pacific. Off to the left these mountains in higher, grander forms, lift their summits toward the clouds, and are most always covered with snow, while their sides are lined with dark green—the color of the pine forests, which partially envelop them. While the road was being built, large quantities of ties, telegraph poles and bridge timber, were cut on the Foot Hills, near these mountains, and delivered to the company. About two miles northwest of Piedmont, is a wonderful Soda Spring. The sediment or deposits of this spring have built up a conical-shaped body with a basin on the top. In this basin the water appears, to a small extent, and has evidently sometime had a greater flow than at present; but, as similar springs have broken out around the base of this cone, the pressure on the main spring has, doubtless, been relieved, and its flow, consequently, lessened. The cone is about 15 feet high and is well worthy of a visit from the tourist. At Piedmont, the traveler will first observe the permanent coal pits, built of stone and brick, which

INTERIOR OF SNOW SHEDS, U. P. R. R.

are used in this country for the manufacture of charcoal for the smelting works of Utah. There are more of them at Hilliard and Evanston, and they will be more fully described then.

Leaving Piedmont, the road makes a long curve, like a horse-shoe doubling on itself, and, finally, reaches the summit of the divide in a long snow shed, one of the longest on the road. Aspen,—the next station. It is 938.5 miles from Omaha, and has a reported elevation of 7,835 feet. It is not a great distance—only about two miles —from the summit. Evidences of change in the formation of the country are everywhere visible, and the change affords a marked relief to the weary monotony of the desolate plains over which we have passed. Down the grade we now pass rapidly, with high hills on either side of the track—through a lovely valley, with an occasional fill, and through a deep cut, to the next station.

Hilliard,—a new station, opened for business in 1873, is 943.5 miles from Omaha, with an elevation of 7,310 feet. The town owes its importance to the Hilliard Flume & Lumber Company, which has extensive property interests here, and in the vicinity. In approaching the town from Aspen, the road passes down a "draw" or ravine, through a cut on a curve, and near this place enters the Bear River Valley, one of the most beautiful, and so far as has been demonstrated, fertile valleys of the Rocky Mountains. Two things excite the curiosity of the traveler if he has never seen them before; one is the coal pits, and the other is the elevated flume under which trains of cars pass. This flume, built of timber and boards, is 24 miles long, and is 2,000 feet higher where it first takes the water from Bear River, than where it empties the same at Hilliard. The greatest fall in any one mile is 320 feet. The timber which is brought to the station by this flume, is obtained in large amounts in the foot hills of the Uintah Mountains, or on the mountains themselves and is mostly pine. The saw-mill of the company, erected at the head of this flume, has a capacity of 40,000 feet in 24 hours, with an engine of 40 horse-power. Over 2,000,000 feet of lumber were consumed in the construction of this flume, and its branches in the mountains. Through it cord-wood, lumber, ties and saw-logs are floated down to the railroad. The cord-wood is used for charcoal. You will observe the conical shaped pits in which it is made, near the railway track, on the right, as you pass westward. There are 29 pits or kilns at Hilliard, nineteen small ones, and ten large ones. The small kilns require twenty-six cords of wood at a filling, and the

ROCK CUT, NEAR ASPEN.

large ones forty cords. The small ones cost about $750, each; the large ones $900. These kilns consume 2,000 cords of wood per month, and produce 100,000 bushels of charcoal as a result, in the same time. There are other kilns about nine miles south of the town, in active operation. There are fine iron and sulphur springs within three-fourths of a mile of the station. The reddish appearance of the mountain we have just passed indicates the presence of iron in this vicinity in large quantities, and also begins to crop out in different places as we go down the valley. Bear River is renowned for its trout. They are caught south of the road in the mountain tributaries, and north of Evanston, in Bear River Lake. Though the country has somewhat changed in appearance, and a different formation has been entered upon, we have not passed the region of agates and gems, precious and otherwise. They are found in the vicinity of Hilliard, in large quantities, together with numerous petrifactions of bones, etc., with fossilized fish, shells, ferns and other materials.

Twenty-five miles a little south-west of Hilliard are found two sulphur mountains. The sulphur is nearly 90 per cent. pure, in inexhaustible quantities.

The scenery of the Upper Bear River is rugged and grand. About 20 miles south of Hilliard is a natural fort which was taken possession of by a gang of horse thieves and cutthroats, under the lead of one Jack Watkins, a genuine frontier ruffian, who, with his companions, for a long time resisted all attempts at capture.

The hills and mountains in this vicinity abound in game, and offer rare inducements to sportsmen. The country around both Hilliard and Evanston is the natural home for bears, elk, deer, catamounts, lynx, wolves, coyotes, wolverines, beaver, mink, foxes, badgers, mountain lions, wild cats, jack rabbits, etc., grouse sage hens, quails and ducks in the spring and fall. Not far north of Evanston, on Bear River, is *Bear Lake*, ten miles in length, and from five to eight in breadth. The boundary line between Idaho and Utah passes directly across the lake from east to west.

Soda Springs.—Farther north, at the Big Bend of Bear River, the most interesting group of soda springs known on the Continent, occupy some six square miles. To those graced with steam vents, Fremont gave the name of Steamboat

Springs, from the noise they make like a low-pressure engine. Near by is a spring with an orifice brightly stained with a brilliant yellow coating of oxide of iron, from which the water is thrown up two feet.

Independence Rock.—This has long been a noted landmark, for travelers on the old overland wagon route. Its base is literally covered with names and dates, some of them even before Fremont's expedition crossed the Continent—many more well known. The Sweetwater River flows immediately along the southern end of it, and on the opposite side of the stream is another ridge similar to it, continuing from the south-west, which was once connected with it. It is a huge example of disintegration; its rounded form resembles an oblong hay-stack, with layers of rocks lapping over the top and sides of the mass. Thin layers

INDEPENDENCE ROCK.

have been broken off in part, and huge masses are scattered all around it. On some portions of the sides they lap down to the ground, with so gentle a descent that one can walk up to the top without difficulty. The rock has a circumference of 1,550 yards. The north end is 193 feet in height, and the opposite end, 167 feet, with a depression in the center of 75 feet.

Devil's Gate on the Sweetwater.—Following up the valley from Independence Rock, and five miles north, is another celebrated natural curiosity. The Devil's Gate, a canon which the Sweetwater River has worn through the Granite Ridge cutting it at right-angles. The walls are vertical, being about 350 feet high, and the distance through is about 300 yards. The current of the stream through the gate is slow, finding its way among the fallen masses of rock, with gentle, easy motion, and pleasant murmur.

Fifteen miles farther above the Devil's Gate, is

another conspicuous landmark,—the *Twin Peaks,* which really are but one high peak in the ridge, cleft down the centre, dividing it in two, nearly to the base.

View in the Uintah Mountains.—The view we give on page 80, is taken from Photograph Ridge, elevation, 10,829 feet, — by the Hayden Exploring Expedition, and is one of the grandest and most perfect mountain views in the West. The traveler, as he passes rapidly through Echo and Weber Canons, and casually notices the chain of mountains at the south, can form no idea of their beauty and grandeur. Professor Hayden says of this view "In the foreground of our view is a picturesque group of the mountain pines. In the middle distance, glimmering in the sunlight like a silver thread, is Black's Fork, meandering through grassy, lawn-like parks, the eye following it up to its sources, among the everlasting snows of the summit ridge. The peaks or cones in the distance, are most distinctly stratified and apparently horizontal or nearly so, with their summits far above the limits of perpetual snow, and from 1,500 to 2,000 feet above the springs that rise from the streams below."

Gilbert's Peak.—is one of the highest peaks of the Uintah Mountain Range, named after General Gilbert of the U. S. A. It has near its summit a beautiful lake of 11,000 feet, and above this rises the peak abruptly 2,250 more. Total, 13,250 feet.

Throughout these mountains are very many lakes,—which gather among the rocks bordered with dense growth of spruce trees, and form a characteristic feature of the scenery.

Bear River City.—After leaving Hilliard, the road, as it continues down the valley of Sulphur Creek, passes the site of Bear River City, a once famous town, but which now has not a single building to mark where it once stood; a mile and a half west of Hilliard will be seen the headboards of the graves of early-day rioters. The city was laid out in 1868, and for a time there was high speculation in lots, and once the population reached as high as 2,000 persons. Frequent garrotings, deaths and robberies, led to the organization of a vigilance committee, who hung three of the desperadoes. An active fight afterwards ensued between the citizens and the mob, who had organized to revenge the death of one of their number. The citizens were well protected by the wall of a store, and by active firing killed 16 of the rioters, with other losses, never known. From that day the place was dropped by the railroad, and it faded entirely away.

Millis — is the next station, 947.5 miles from Omaha, with an elevation of 6,790 feet. It is an unimportant side track, where trains occasionally pass. Its location is about a mile and a half below or west of the site of Bear River City. Leaving Millis the road soon crosses Bear River over a low trestle-work—an opening being left in the embankment for the passage of surplus water in time of freshets. The entire valley here has been known to be covered with water in the spring.

Evanston.—957 miles from Omaha; elevation, 6.770 feet. It is the county-seat of Uintah County, Wyoming Territory, and the last town going west, in Wyoming. It contains about 1,500 people, and is a thriving business place, owing to proximity of the coal mines, its lumber interests and the location of the division roundhouse of twenty stalls, with car and machine-shops—giving constant employment to a large number of men. The town is located on the western bank of Bear River, and has abundant water power that might be utilized in various manufactories. A large saw-mill, run by a lumber company, gets its logs from the mountains toward the head of the stream. They are rolled into the river, and floated down to the mill. This place, also, has a few charcoal kilns—lumber, coal and charcoal, being the principal products of the town. Evanston is a regular dinner station—trains from the east and west stopping thirty minutes for dinner. You will dine at the "Mountain Trout Hotel," a well-kept house, where everything is scrupulously neat—the food being plainly, but well cocked. At this house, the traveler will find regular Chinese waiters, dressed in Chinese costume, quick, polite and attentive, and you can here gratify your curiosity by seeing and talking with them. Game and trout will usually be found on the tables, in their season. The proximity of this eating-station, and the one kept at Green River, to the great trout-fishing regions of the Rocky Mountains, creates an expectation, on the part of the traveler, that he will usually find the speckled beauties served up at these stations, nor is he often disappointed, in the proper season of the year.

THE DEVIL'S GATE ON THE SWEETWATER.

The town has good schools, three or four churches and an excellent court-house. A daily and weekly newspaper—"*The Evanston Age*," is published here. Bear River, which runs through this place, rises in the Uintah Mountains, on the south, and runs in a general northerly direction to the great soda springs in Idaho, about 120 miles directly north of Echo City. It then turns to the south-west and empties into Great Salt Lake, near Corinne. Its valley is pretty well settled by Mormons, and others, all the way round its great bend. Near the location of these soda springs, and at the northern extremity of Bear River Mountains, evidences of volcanic action are everywhere visible, and extinct craters are no u n c o m m o n thing.

Evanston is built mostly on the left side of the track, as you enter the town, the valley rising into the hill behind it. This hill, were it not for the hard winds and deep snows of winter, would afford some very fine building spots, and for summer residences must be delightful. In winter, however, some of the little houses that skirt the hill on the western borders of the place, are literally covered with snow which drifts over the hills from the south. The agricultural prospects of the valley, lower down, are said to be flattering —the Mormon farmers producing fine crops. Near Evanston there are a number of cattle ranches where hay is cut, and cattle have to be fed and sheltered during the winter. There have also been some successful experiments in raising potatoes, cabbages, turnips, parsnips, radishes, lettuce, onions and other "garden truck," while oats, barley and wheat can undoubtedly be raised in favorable seasons. Notice the altitude of this place, and then the traveler can form the best opinion as to whether agriculture, as a steady busi-

ness, can be made successful. Candor compels us further to say that frosts may happen during every one of the summer months.

Sporting.—Evanston, however, possesses all the attractions which delight the sportsman. The mountains to the north and south, and the high hills in the immediate vicinity, are full of game, while Bear River is renowned for its trout. The streams flowing into Bear River, on either side, both north and south of the town, are full of trout, and afford excellent sport in those seasons of the year when their catching is not prohibited by law, while Bear Lake, some sixty miles north, from all that we could learn about it, is the chosen home of trout and the very paradise of fishermen. Sporting parties can obtain guides, outfits, and accommodations at Evanston, from which place they can hunt, fish, visit the Sulphur Mountains, and search for fossils, etc., to their heart's content. It is one of the most favorable points on the line of the road for recreation and amusement, and will, eventually, become a noted resort for tourists.

Chinamen begin to thicken as you proceed west. At Evanston they have quite a settlement, the shanties and buildings on the right of the track and opposite the depot being "China Town." Here they have their "Joss" house, saloons and residences. *Ah Say*, their head man, speaks very good English, has his Chinese wife with him, and with the exception of the inevitable "cue," dresses and appears like the Americans, with whom he has now lived for about fifteen years.

About three miles from Evanston, on the east side of Bear River, is Alma, the coal miners' town. Here coal mines belonging to the Central Pacific, the Union Pacific, and to S. H.

LAKE LAL, OR MOORE'S LAKE, HEAD OF BEAR RIVER.

Winsor are worked. Mr. Winsor is just opening his mine—which is nearest to Evanston—while the other mines have been worked for some time. "The Rocky Mountain Coal Company." is the name of the corporation which supplies the Central Pacific with coal. In 1875, this company mined 98,897 tons, or 9,890 cars of coal. They have three mines open. In one year, not long since, they mined about 150,000 tons, or 15,000 cars. The Union Pacific having other mines along their road do not, of course, mine as much here as does the Rocky Mountain Company.

A Mountain on fire.

Do not be startled at this announcement, yet this is a genuine fact; the companies operating these mines, have been put to immense labor and expense to keep under control an immense fire in their coal veins. These mines took fire from spontaneous combustion in this way. They perhaps took out too much coal in the first place, that is, did not leave pillars enough to support the overhanging walls; what is called "slack"—coal that has crumbled by action of air—was also allowed to accumulate in the mine. The vein of fire clay next above the vein of coal fell down on this slack, and caused spontaneous combustion of the coal underneath it. A fire with a perpetual supply of fuel is rather a hard thing to master, and in a coal mine generally awakens no small amount of anxiety. In fact, it is very dangerous. As soon as it was discovered, and its location fixed, the company immediately began to wall around it; they ceased all operations in its immediate vicinity, and with rock, lime and sand, made their air-tight walls along "the slopes," between "the rooms" and across "the air passages," until the outside air was completely shut out, and the fire entirely shut in, and awaited further developments. Occasionally it breaks out over a piece of this wall, and then they begin farther back and wall again. But the fire is not extinguished and probably never will be. Water will not quench it, its action on the fire clay only increases the difficulty. Inside of these fire walls, pillar after pillar of the coal left standing to support the roof has been consumed, and the earth and rocks above have fallen into the cavity, leaving great craters on the side of the mountain, and the rock-ribbed pile itself has seamed and cracked open in places above the burning fires. Air has thus got in and the rains and melting snows of spring run into these fissures and craters, dissolving the fire clay, and thus add to the extent of the burning mass. But everything goes on around the mine without excitement, and as though nothing had happened. Watchmen are kept on duty all the time, and the first appearance of the fire near the walls is detected and a new wall built. And

thus while the smouldering fires are burning up the coal in one part of the mine, men are taking it out unconcernedly in another part, to supply the locomotives with the power to generate steam.

How long the fire will burn no one can tell. It will only stop when the fuel upon which it feeds is exhausted, and this can only be cut off by mining all around it, taking out the full thickness of the vein—26 feet—and thus exhausting the supply. It will then cave in and the rest of the mine can be saved. Coal mining has its dangers, not the least of which are "slack and waste" which result in fires. In Mine No. 1, of the Rocky Mountain Coal Company, the fire is confined in a space 250 by 600 feet. In Mine No. 2, owned by same company, it is confined by a space 175 by 1,100 feet.

A Valuable Coal Mine.

—Leaving Evanston, in about two miles the branch to Alma turns off to the right, and the town with hoisting works of the coal companies can be plainly seen, together with a beautiful view down the Bear River Valley. On what is called Twin Creek, down this valley, the Wyoming Coal & Coke Company, have discovered and located a coal mine 41 miles due north from Evanston. The mine is on the east side of Bear River. This company has what it claims to be a mountain of coal. The veins on the ground level are four and one-half feet thick, above it there are about six feet of slate; then a ten foot vein of coal; then sandstone about five feet thick—what miners call "Winn rock;" then three feet of fire clay; then two feet of coal; then alternate layers of fire clay and coal 26 feet; then 125 feet of solid fire clay; then sandstone, limestone, etc., to the summit, it being about 400 feet above the level surface around it. A shaft has been sunk from the ground level, and another vein of coal struck ten feet below the surface. We are minute in giving this description of this coal mine, because it is claimed that the coal it furnishes will coke, that it will give 50 per cent. coke, and coke is the great demand of the smelting furnaces in the mining regions of this part of the Continent. It is claimed that the tests which have been applied to this coal, establish conclusively its coking qualities and ovens for coking purposes have been put in. The work of the present year will, satisfactorily determine the question whether coking coal can be found in the Rocky Mountains. The history of rich mineral-producing regions is that the metals are usually (because cheaper) brought to the fuel instead of carrying the fuel to the metal. Hence if these coal mines are proved to produce good coke, a town of smelters must spring up near by.

Wahsatch,—a telegraph station, on the divide between Bear River Valley and Echo Canon. It

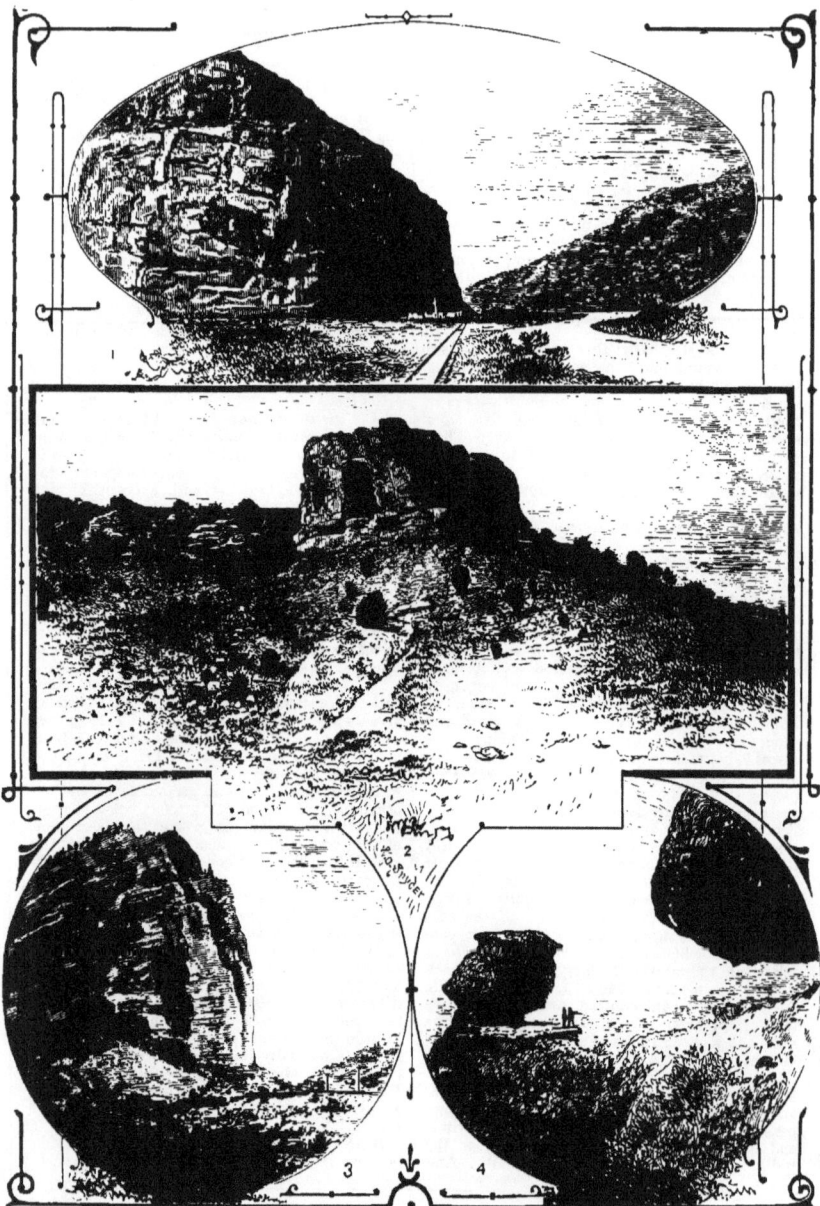

ROCKS NEAR ECHO CITY.

1.—Bromley's Cathedral. 2.—Castle Rock. 3.—The Great Eastern. 4.—Hanging Rock.

is 968 miles from Omaha, and reported to be 6,879 feet above the level of the sea. The road here crosses a low pass in the Wahsatch Range of Mountains. As you ascend the beautiful valley leading to this station, the grim peaks of the Uintahs tower up in the distance on your left, while the adjoining hills shut out the higher elevations of the Wahsatch Range, on the north. Leaving Evanston, the road turns abruptly to the left, and the town and valley are soon lost to sight. Four miles out, on the left side of the track, the traveler will notice a sign put up on a post—the east side of which reads, "Wyoming," the west side, "Utah." Wahsatch was formerly a terminus of a sub-division of the road, and contained the regular dining-hall of the company, with roundhouse, machine and repair shops, etc. The water in the tank is supplied from a mountain spring near by, and a "Y" for turning engines, and a small house to shelter one, is about all that is left of a once famous town.

Artesian Wells.—It has been our candid opinion that the great plains, basins and alkali deserts which lie between the Rocky Mountains and Sierras can all be reclaimed and soil made fertile by the sinking of artesian wells. The entire Humboldt Valley can be made productive by this means alone. As a proof of the success of sinking artesian wells, we can mention several along the Union Pacific Railroad. Commencing at Separation and terminating at Rock Springs, a distance of 108 miles, the Union Pacific Railroad has sunk successfully six artesian wells:

One at Separation, 6,900 feet above sea level, is 1,180 feet deep, the water rising to within 10 feet of the surface.

At Creston, 7,030 feet elevation, the well is only 300 feet deep, furnishing abundant supply of water at that point.

At Washakie, 6,697 feet elevation, the well is 638 feet deep. The water rises 15 feet above the surface, and flows at the rate of 800 gallons per hour.

At Bitter Creek, 6,685 feet elevation, the well is 696 feet deep, discharging at the surface 1,000 gallons per hour, and with pumping, yields 2,160 gallons per hour.

At Point of Rocks, elevation 6,490 feet, the well is 1,000 feet deep, and the supply of water abundant, although it does not rise to the surface nearer than 17 feet.

At Rock Springs, at an elevation of 6,280 feet, the well is 1,150 feet deep, and discharges at the surface 960 gallons per hour, or at 26 feet above the surface, 571 gallons per hour.

As the elevation of all these places is 2,000 feet or more above the Salt Lake Valley, and also the Humboldt Valley, there is every probability that the sinking of artesian wells in these valleys would result in an immense flow of water.

Chinese Workmen.—The Chinese are emphatically a peculiar people, renowned for their industry and economy. They will live comfortably on what the same number of Americans would throw away. Their peculiarities have been so often described that a repetition of them to any great extent is not needed here. Nevertheless a sight of them always awakens a curiosity to know all there is to be known concerning their customs, habits, social and moral relations, etc. A great deal that they do is mysterious to us, but perfectly plain and simple to them. In their habits of eating, for instance, why do they use "chopsticks" instead of forks? "Same as 'Melican man's fork" said one as we watched its dextrous use. Their principal articles of diet seem to be rice and pork. They reject the great American fashion of frying nearly everything they cook, and substitute boiling instead. In the center of a table, or on a bench near by, they place a pan filled with boiled rice. To this each one of the "mess" will go and fill his bowl with a spoon or ladle, return to the table and take his "chopsticks"—two slender sticks, about the length of an ordinary table knife, and operate them with his fingers as if they were fastened together with a pivot, like shears, lifting the bowl to his mouth every time he takes up the food with the "chopsticks." The pork for a "mess" will be cut into small pieces and placed in one dish on the table from which each one helps himself with these "chopsticks." In other words "they all dive into one dish" for their pork. They are called "almond-eyed celestials"—but did you ever notice how much their eyes resemble those of swine?

The first gang of Chinamen you meet with on the road are employed near Table Rock; formerly they extended to Rawlins, but they are inefficient laborers, although industrious, especially in the winter. We shall see more of them by the time we reach the Pacific Coast. Rock Springs as a town is mostly composed of dugouts, shanties, holes in the ground, etc., occupied by miners, including Chinamen, together with a few substantial buildings, such as the company's store, a good school-house, two or three ordinary hotels and the customary saloons. The importance of the town is wholly due to the coal trade, otherwise it would be nothing.

ECHO AND WEBER CAÑONS.

And now, with full breath and anxious heart, repressed excitement and keen zest,—we anxiously scan the scenes from car windows or platforms, and prepare for one grand, rushing descent into the glories of Echo Cañon. The writer will never forget the feelings of overwhelming wonder and awe, as with the seal of admiration in both eye and lips, the ride through this famous cañon was enjoyed. Rocks beside which all eastern scenes were pigmies, rose up in astounding abruptness and massiveness—colossal old Titans of majestic dimensions, and sublimely soaring summits, and perpendicular sides,—succeeded each other for miles, and the little company of spectators, seemed but an insignificant portion of the handiwork of the Almighty. The train of cars, which, on the plain, seemed so full of life, and grand in power, here was dwarfed into baby carriages; and the shriek of the whistle, as it echoed and resounded along the cliffs and from rock to rock, or was hemmed in by the confines of the *amphitheatre*, appeared like entering the portals to the palace of some *Terrible Being*. Into the short distance of sixty miles is crowded a constant succession of those scenes and objects of natural curiosity, which form the most interesting part of the road, and have made it world-wide in fame. It seems hard, after nearly a week of expectation and keen anxiety for a glimpse of such scenes of grandeur, and after more than two days of steady riding over the smooth surface of the rolling upland plain, to find all the most magnificent objects of interest crowded into so short a space, and passed in less than three hours.

Travelers must remember, however, that the scenes witnessed from the railroad are but a very little portion of the whole. To gather true refreshing glimpses of western scenery, the tourist must get away from the railroad, into the little valleys, ascend the bluffs and mountains, and views yet more glorious will greet the eye. Echo Canon is the most impressive scene that is beheld for over 1,500 miles, on the overland railroad. The constant succession of rocks—each growing more and more huge, and more and more perpendicular and colossal in form—make the attractions of the valley *grow upon the eye* instead of decrease.

The observer enters the canon about on a level with the top of the rocks, and even can overlook them, then gradually descends until at the very bottom of the valley the track is so close to the foot of the rocks, the observer has to elevate his head with an upward look of nearly 90°, to scale their summits. Let us now prepare to descend, and brace ourselves eagerly for the exhilaration of the ride, the scenery of which will live with you in memory for years.

Entering Echo Canon. — Leaving Wahsatch we pass rapidly down grade, into the canon, and we will point out, in detail, all objects of interest as they are passed, so that travelers may recognize them. From Wahsatch, especially, you want to look with all the eyes you have, and look quick, too, as one object passes quickly out of sight and another comes into view. About a mile from Wahsatch, you will notice what is called the "Z" canon where the road formerly zigzagged down a small canon, on the left, and passed through the valley of the creek to near Castle Rock Station, where it united with the present line. Two miles farther on,

over heavy grades and short curves, you enter tunnel No. 2, which is 1,100 feet long. Passing through the tunnel, the high reddish rocks, moulded into every conceivable shape, and frequent side canons cut through the walls on either side of the road. You reach at last *Castle Rock Station,*—about eight and one-half miles from Wahsatch, 976.4 miles from Omaha with an elevation of 6,290 feet. It is so called from the rock a little east of the station which bears the same name. Notice the arched doorway on one corner of the old castle just after it is passed, with red colored side pieces, and capped with gray. In close proximity are some needle rocks—sharp-pointed—one small one especially prominent. Still nearer the station is a shelving rock on a projecting peak. Opposite the water tank are rocks worn in curious shape. Further on, about half a mile, is a cave with rocks and scattering cedars above it. Next comes what is termed "Swallows' Nest," because of the numerous holes near the top, chiseled out by the action of both water and wind, and in summer sheltering a large number of swallows. Toward it in summer months,

"The Swallows Homeward fly."

Then comes a honey-combed peak with a shelving gray rock under it, after which we pass through, what the railroad boys call "gravel" or "wet cut"—the sides being gravel, and springs breaking out in the bottom by the track. Then Phillip's Canon juts in from the right with yards for cattle at its mouth. See the curious formations along the side of this canon as you pass it. About four miles from the last station, are other castle rocks similar in appearance to those already passed, and rocks with caps and slender little spires like needles. Then comes a singular perpendicular column jutting out in front of the ledge, with outstretched wings as if it would lift itself up and fly, but for its weight. This is called the "Winged Rock." If there was a projection in front to resemble a neck and head, the rock would appear very much like an eagle or some other large bird, with pinions extended just ready to fly. A little below this, are the "Kettle Rocks" huge gray-looking boulders, nearly to the top of the ledge, looking like immense caldron kettles. Behind them are some sharp-pointed projections like spires. These rocks are capped with red, but gray underneath. Then comes "Hood Rock" a single angular rock about half way to the top of the ledge, worn out in the center, and resembling the three-cornered hoods on modern ulster overcoats. About a mile before reaching the next station, the rocks are yellow in appearance and rounding a point you will notice sandstone layers with a dip of more than 45 degrees, showing a mighty upheaval at some period in the remote past.

Hanging Rock,—a little over seven miles from Castle Rock, and 983.7 miles from Omaha; elevation, 5,974 feet. The descent has been very rapid since we struck this canon. This station is wrongly named. All books and guides which represent the rocks of Echo Canon overhanging the railroad, are erroneous. Nothing in the shape of a hanging rock can be seen, but as you pass the station, you will notice how the elements have worn out a hollow or cavity in one place, which is bridged by a slim gray rock, nearly horizontal in position, forming a natural or hanging bridge across the cavity, about 50 feet in depth. It can be seen as you pass around a curve just after leaving the station. Going a little farther, you notice what is called "Jack-in-the-Pulpit-Rock," at the corner of a projecting ledge, and near the top thereof. A round gray column, flat on the surface, stands in front; this is the pulpit, while in close proximity rises the veritable "Jack" himself, as if expounding the law and gospel to his scattering auditors. Then comes the

North Fork of Echo Canon,—down which more water annually flows, than in the main canon. Now bending around a curve, if you look forward, it seems as though the train was about to throw us directly against a high precipice in front, and that there was no way of escape; but we keep onward and finally pass safely on another side. We now approach what are called "the narrows." The rocky sides of the canon seem to draw together. Notice the frame of an old rickety saw-mill on the left, and a short distance below, still on the left, see a huge, conical-shaped rock rising close to the track. We are particular in mentioning these, because they are landmarks, and will enable the traveler to know when he is near the ledge on the right of the track, upon which the Mormons piled up stones to roll down on Gen. Albert Sidney Johnson's army, when it should pass here, in 1857. The canon virtually becomes a gorge here, and the wagon road runs close to the base of the high bluffs, (it could not be made in any other place) —which the Mormons fortified after a fashion. Now you pass these forts; high up on the top, on the outer edge or rim you will still see small piles of stones which were gathered there for offensive operations, when the trains and soldiers of the army went by. They look small—they are so far off, and you pass them so quickly—not larger than your fist—but nevertheless they are there. They are best seen as they recede from view.

At the time we speak of, (1857) there was trouble between the Mormons and the United States authorities, which led to the sending of an army to Salt Lake City. It approached as far as Fort Bridger, where — the season being late—it went into winter quarters. it was ex-

pected to pass through this canon, however, that same fall, and hence the preparations which the Mormons made to receive it. Their army—the Nauvoo Legion, *redivivus*, under the command of Gen. Daniel H. Wells, had its camp near these rocks, in a little widening of the valley below, just beyond where you pass a "pocket" of boulders, or detached parts of the ledges above, which have sometime, in the dim past, rolled into the valley. The rocky fort being passed, with the pocket of boulders and the site of the old camp, the traveler next approaches "Steamboat Rock," a huge red projection like the prow of a big propeller. A little cedar, like a flag of perpetual green, shows its head on the bow, while farther back, the beginning of the hurricane deck is visible. It slopes off to the rear, and becomes enveloped in the rocky mass around it. By some, this is called "The Great Eastern," and the one just below it, if anything, a more perfect representation of a steamer, is

SENTINEL ROCK, ECHO CANON.

called "The Great Republic." They are really curious formations, and wonderful to those who look upon them for the first time. "Monument Rock" comes next. It is within a cove and seems withdrawn from the front, as though shunning the gaze of the passing world, yet in a position to observe every thing that goes by. If the train would only stop and give you more time— but this cannot be done, and your only recourse

ROCK SCENES NEAR ECHO CITY.

1.—Witches Rocks. 2.—Battlement Rocks. 3.—Egyptian Tombs. 4.—Witches Bottles. 5.—Needle Rocks, near Wahsatch.

is to pause at Echo and let it pass, while you wait for the one following. This will give you ample opportunity to see the natural wonders congregated in this vicinity. We have almost reached the mouth of Echo Creek, and the Weber River comes in from the left, opposite "Bromley's Cathedral," in front of which stands "Pulpit Rock," on the most extended point as you turn the elbow in the road. This "Cathedral" is named in honor of J. E. Bromley, Esq., who has lived at Echo since 1858, and who came here as a division superintendent of Ben Holladay's Overland Stage and Express Line. It extends some distance —a mile or more —around the bend in the mountain, and has numerous towers and spires, turrets and domes, on either side. "Pulpit Rock" is so called from its resemblance to an old-fashioned pulpit, and rises in plain view as you go round the curve into Weber Valley. It is a tradition among a good many people, that the "Prophet of the Lord," who now presides over the church of "The Latter Day Saints," in Salt Lake City, once preached to the assembled multitude from this exalted eminence; but, while we dislike to spoil a story that lends such a charm to the place, and clothes it with historic interest, nevertheless, such is not the fact. The oldest and most faithful Mormons we could find in Echo, know nothing of any such transaction. Our cut is a faithful representation of this remarkable rock. It is estimated to be about sixty feet high—above the track. You will desire to know how high the ledges are, which have been so rapidly passed. We are informed that Mr. S. B. Reed, one of the civil engineers who constructed this part of the railroad, stated that the average height of all the rocks of Echo canon, is from 600 to 800 feet above the railroad.

As you approach the elbow referred to, there is an opening through the mountains on the left, and in close proximity to "Pulpit Rock," the waters of Echo Creek unite with those of Weber River, which here come in through this opening. If not the southernmost point on the line of the road, it is next to it. You have been traveling in a south-westerly direction since leaving Evanston; you now round the elbow, turn toward the north-west, and arrive at *Echo,*—a beautiful spot—a valley nestled between the hills, with evidences of thrift on every hand. This station is nearly nine and a half miles from Hanging Rock, 993 miles from Omaha, and 5,315 feet above the level of the sea. The town and the canon are rightly named, for the report of a gun or pistol discharged in this canon will bound from side to side, in continuous echoes, until it finally dies away. "Bromley's Cathedral" rears its red-stained columns in rear of and overshadowing the town, while opposite is a lofty peak of the Wahsatch Range. To the right the valley opens out for a short distance like an amphitheatre, near the lower extremity of which, "The Witches," a group of rocks, lift their weird and grotesque forms. They are about half way to the summit of the

PULPIT ROCK, ECHO CANON—LOOKING WESTWARD.

ledge behind them. Weber Valley, from its source to the Great Salt Lake, is pretty thickly settled with Mormons, though quite a number of Gentiles have obtained a foothold in the mines and along the line of the railroad.

Upper Weber Valley.—From this station there is a narrow gauge railroad up the Weber Valley to Coalville, seven miles in length. The town has two or three stores, hotels, saloons, etc., and a school-house is to be built this year. Accommodations for fishing parties, with guides, can here be obtained. The Echo and Weber Rivers, with their tributaries, abound in trout, while there is plenty of game, elk, deer, bear, etc., in the mountains. Richard F. Burton, the African explorer, visited this canon and Salt Lake City in 1860, and wrote a book called "City of the Saints," which was published by the Harpers, in 1862. He speaks of the wonders of this valley as follows: "Echo Kanyon has but one fault; its sublimity will make all similar features look tame."

Weber River rises in the Wahsatch Mountains, about 50 miles in

PULPIT ROCK AND VALLEY.—LOOKING SOUTHWARD.

a south-eastern direction from Echo, flows nearly due west to Kammas City, when it turns to the north-west and passes in that general direction into the Great Salt Lake, not far from Ogden. Going up this river from Echo, Grass Creek flows in about two and a half miles from the starting point. This creek and canon runs very nearly parallel to Echo Creek. Very important and extensive coal mines have been discovered from two to four miles up this canon. It is not as wild or rugged in its formation as Echo Canon. The mines are soon to be developed. Two and a half miles above the mouth of Grass Creek is

Coalville,—a town of about 600 people, with a few elegant buildings, among which are the Mormon bishop's residence and a fine two-story brick court-house, which stands on an elevation near the town, and can be seen for a long distance. The town is situated on the south side of Chalk Creek where it empties into Weber River. This creek also runs nearly parallel with Echo Canon, and rises in the mountains near the head of the Hilliard Lumber Company's flume. It is called Chalk Creek from the white chalky appearance of the bluffs along its banks. Coalville is a Mormon village, and its inhabitants are nearly all employed in mining coal from two to three miles above the town where the railroad ends. This road is called the Summit County Railroad, and is owned by some of the wealthy Mormons in Salt Lake City. Four miles farther up the Weber, and you come to Hoytsville, another Mormon village. It is a farming settlement. The town has a grist-mill. Four miles still farther is located the town of Wanship, named after an old Ute chief. It has about 400 inhabitants, with a hotel. It is located at the junction of Silver Creek with the Weber. Still going up the Weber, in about three miles there is another Mormon settlement called Three Mile. It has a "co-op" store, bishop's residence, and a tithing office.

Peoa.—Leaving Three Mile, and pursuing the course still up one of the most beautiful valleys in the country, the tourist will reach Peoa, a nice little farming town, in five miles travel. Evidences of thrift and of the successful cultivation of the soil, are visible all along the valley, but it is a wonderful matter to eastern

SCENE AT MOUTH OF ECHO CANON.

men who know nothing of the characteristics of the soil, and see nothing but sage brush and greasewood growing thereon, how crops can be raised amidst such sterility. Irrigation has done it all. The labor to accomplish it has been immense, but thirty-five to forty bushels of spring wheat to the acre attest the result. The soil has been proved to be very prolific.

Kammas City.—Next on this mountain journey comes Kammas City, eight miles beyond Peoa, on Kammas Prairie. This is an elevated plateau about four miles by ten, and affords some very fine grazing lands and meadows. It is nearly all occupied by stockmen. Here the Weber makes a grand detour; coming from the mountains in the east, it here turns almost a square corner toward the

north, and then pursues its way through valleys
and gorges, through hills and mountains to a
quiet rest in the waters of the Great Salt Lake.
Above this prairie the river cuts its way through
a wild rocky canon, lashing its sides with foam
as though angry at its confinement, out into the
prairie where it seems to gather strength for its
next fearful plunge in the rocky gorges below.
In the lofty peaks of the mountains, east of
Kamas Prairie, in the frigid realms of perpetual snow, the traveler will find the head of Weber
River, and the route to it will give him some of
the grandest views to be found on the American
Continent.

Parley's Park.—The old stage road to
the "City of the Saints," after leaving Echo
passed up the Weber to Wanship, at the
mouth of Silver Creek; thence nine miles
to Parley's Park, a lovely place in summer,
where a week or two could be whiled away
in the beauty of the valley and amidst the
grandeur of the mountains. There are three
things in nature which make a man feel small—
as though he stood in the presence of Divinity.
These are the ocean, with its ceaseless roar; the
mighty plains in their solitude, and with their
sense of loneliness; and the mountains in their
towering greatness, with heads almost beyond
the ken of mortal vision, and crowned with
eternal snows. Parley's Park is nearly round in
shape, about four miles in diameter, and almost
surrounded by the rocky domes of the Wahsatch
Range. The old stage road leaves Park City to
the left, and reaches the summit on the west side
of the divide; thence, it follows down Parley's
Canon to Salt Lake City, forty-eight miles, by
this route, from Echo. The mountain streams
along this road abound in trout, while elk, deer
and bear, will reward the hunter's toil. There
are ranches and 1 small farms by the way, which
will afford abundant stopping places for rest and
food; there are mines of marvelous richness, to
reward one's curiosity, if nothing else will do it;
and, in fact, there is probably nothing which can
be gained along the line of the Union Pacific,
which will afford so much gratification, at so little expense, of either money or time, as a leisurely jaunt of a week or two up the river and
its tributaries from Echo.

*Characteristics of Echo and Weber
Canons.*—The massive rocks which form Echo
Canon, are of red sandstone, which by the steady
process of *original erosion* and subsequent weather,
have worn into their present shape. Their
shapes are exceedingly curious, and their average height, 500 to 800 feet. At the amphitheatre, and the Steamboat Rock, the height is
fully 800 feet to the summit. There is a bold
projection in the wall of rock near the Pulpit,
called Hanging Rock; but it is composed of a
mass of coarse conglomerate, which is easily
washed away, and is not very easily noticed.

Pulpit Rock overlooks Echo City and the valley of the Weber, through which flows a pure
beautiful mountain stream. In one of our
illustrations is shown a railroad train passing
through this valley and descending to the entrance of Weber Canon just below. This is the
sketch of the special excursion train of the New
York and Eastern Editorial Excursion Party
of 1875, who, at this part, the center of the valley, midway between the two canons, were profuse in their exclamations of delight at the
scene of beauty.

A curious feature of Echo Canon is that its
scenery is entirely on the right or north side,
and that the Weber Canon has, also, upon the

MONUMENT ROCK.—ECHO CANON.

same side, its wildest and most characteristic
scenery. The entrance and departure from
each canon is distinguished with great abruptness and distinctness. Travelers who can enjoy
the fortunate position of the lowest step on the
platform of each car, can witness all the scenes
of Echo and Weber Canons, to the best advantage. The view is particularly fine,—as when
the train describes the sharp turn, under and
around Pulpit Rock, the view from the last platform includes the whole length of the train on
the curve,—and overhead the jutting point of
the rock, and, farther above, the massive Rock
Mountain, the overlook to the entire valley. Just
as the train rounds at Pulpit Rock, passengers

THE CLIFFS OF ECHO CANON, UTAH.

BY THOMAS MORAN.

on the south side of the train, will have a pretty little glimpse of the upper portion of Weber River, with its green banks and tree verdure—a charming relief to the bare, dry plains, so constant and even tiresome. A curious feature of this little Weber Valley, are the *terraces.* Near Echo City is a low, narrow bottom, near the river; then an abrupt ascent of 30 feet; then a level plain or bottom of 200 to 400 yards; then a gentle ascent to the rock bluffs.

The Weber River is exceedingly crooked in its course,—originally occupying the entire width of the little space in the canon—and in constructing the railroad at various points, the road-bed here has been built directly into the river, to make room for the track. The average angle of elevation of the heights of Weber Canon is 70 to 80 degrees,—and the height of the summits above the river is 1,500 to 2,000 feet. In this canon is found a thick bed of hard, red sandstone, of great value for building stone,—which can be wrought into fine forms for culverts, fronts of buildings, caps, sills, etc. Emerging from the mouth of Weber Canon—and turning to the right, every vestige of rugged canon scenery vanishes, and the scene is changed into one of peace and quietness of valley life. Here the Weber River has a strong, powerful current—with heavy and constant fall over beds of water-worn stones, and fallen rocks of immense size. In the spring and summer months, it is swollen by the melting of snow from the mountains, and is of great depth,—though usually it averages but four to six feet in depth and its width, at the mouth of the canon, is usually 120 feet.

The remainder of its course to the Great Salt Lake, is through a large open bottom of increasing breadth, along which gather little villages, grain fields, meadows, brilliant with flowers of which the Indian Pink, with its deep scarlet clusters, is most luxuriant. The hills are smooth in outline, and as we approach Ogden, the grand summit of the Wahsatch Mountains, with snowy peaks, arise behind, in front, and northward, around us bold and impressive. This is the range of mountains which border the east side of the Salt Lake Valley, and will accompany us, as we go southward to Salt Lake City.

Rocks of Weber Canon.—Returning to the road; after leaving Echo you will soon notice, on the north side of the track, two curious formations. The first is a group of reddish-colored cones of different sizes and varying some, in shape, but on the whole remarkably uniform in their appearance. These are known as Battlement Rocks. They are about one mile, perhaps not that, below Echo. Next come the wierd forms of " The Witches "—looking as though they were talking with each other. These are gray, and about this place it seems that the formation changes—

the red-colored rocks disappearing—dark gray taking their place. How these columns were formed will ever be a question of interest to those who are permitted to see them. One of the Witches especially looks as though she was afflicted with the "Grecian bend" of modern fashion, a fact which does not at all comport with the dignity or character of a witch. Worn in fantastic shapes by the storms of ages, and capped with gray, they stand as if "mocking the changes and the chance of time." Four miles below Echo, we round a rocky point, nearly opposite to which lies the little Mormon Village of Henniferville, on the left side of Weber River, with its bishop's palace—the largest brick building in sight—and school-house, also of brick, nestled under the mountains which lift up rugged peaks in the background. The valley now narrows to a gorge, and we approach Weber Canon proper. It has high bluffs on the left, with a rocky castle towering up on the right. If Echo Canon was a wonderful place in the mind of the traveler, wonders, if possible more rugged and grand, will be revealed to his gaze here. High up on the face of a bluff to the left, as you pass through the gorge, see the little holes or caves worn by the winds, in which the eagles build their nests. This bluff is called "*Eagle nest Rock.*" Every year the proud monarch of the air finds here a safe habitation in which to raise his young. It is beyond the reach of men, and accessible only to the birds which fly in the air. Passing this home of " Freedom's Bird," before we have time to read these lines hardly, we are at the

Thousand Mile Tree, Devil's Slide, &c., —on the left side of the track. There it stands, spreading its arms of green, from one of which hangs the sign which marks the distance traveled since leaving Omaha. It is passed in a moment, and other objects of interest claim your attention. High upon rocks to the right, as you peer ahead, see how the winds have made holes in projecting points through which the light and sky beyond can be observed; now looking back see another similar formation on the opposite side— one to be seen looking ahead, the other looking back. Now we come to Slate Cut—where photograph rocks without number are found. The rocks are so called from the pictures of ferns, branches of trees, shrubs, etc., which are seen traced in them. They remind one of moss-agates, only they are a great deal larger—magnified a thousand times, and are not in clear groundwork like the agates. *Lost Creek Canon* now puts in from the right, and around the curve you can see the houses of the little Mormon Town, Croyden. It is only seven miles from Echo. This canon runs parallel with Echo Canon for quite a distance, and is said to be rich in the scenery characteristic of this region, with a narrow valley of great fertility when cultivated. But right here on the left side of the road, pushing out from the side of the mountain, is the "*Devil's Slide*"—one of the most singular formations to be seen on the entire route from ocean to ocean. It is composed of two parallel ledges of granite, turned upon their edges, serrated and jutting out in places fifty feet from the mountain side, and about 14 feet apart. It is a rough place for any one; height about 800 feet.

Weber Quarry,—1,001.5 miles from Omaha, and 5,250 feet above the sea. It is a side track where fine reddish sandstone is obtained for building purposes, and for the use of the road. The sandstone is variegated, and is both beautiful and durable when cut, or polished. The gorge still continues, and devils' slides on a smaller scale than the one noticed, are visible on both sides of the road. A little below this station, *Dry Creek Canon* comes in on the right. The road now passes round short curves amidst the wildest scenery, when it is suddenly blocked to all human appearance; yet tunnel No. 3 gives us liberty. Crossing a bridge observe the terraced mountain on the right, and by the time it is well in view, we enter and pass through tunnel No. 4, after which comes *Round Valley,* where a huge basin in the mountains is formed, and where man again obtains a foothold. On the right of the mountain, as you enter this valley, there is a group of balanced rocks, that seem ready to topple over into the valley below. Still rounding another point farther down, and we arrive at

Weber,—1,008.5 miles from Omaha, an elevation of 5,130 feet. It is a telegraph station in a thrifty looking Mormon village. The valley here widens out—the narrows are passed—and scenes of surpassing beauty, especially in the summer, enchant the eye. To the left the mountains gradually recede, and *East Canon Creek,* which takes its rise in Parley's Park, be-

fore mentioned, cutting its way through the rocky hills, comes into the valley of the Weber. This station is the nearest point on the Union Pacific Road to Salt Lake City. The town and cultivated farms in the valley seem like an oasis in the midst of a desert. Here, for the first time on the road, the traveler will see the magic sign, "Z. C. M. I.," which, literally translated, means "Zion's Co-operative Mercantile Institution," their dry goods, groceries, notions, etc. The Mormon name for this station is Morgan City. As you leave this station, the same query broached before, rises in the mind of the traveler—how are we to get out? We seem entirely surrounded by hills and mountains, and, while there is a depression visible off to the right, it does not seem low enough for a railroad to pass over. But we follow the river down, and notice the result. Bending first to the right, then to the left, and again to the right round a curve like an elbow, and nearly as short, we reach

Peterson, —1,016.4 miles from Omaha; elevation, 4,963 feet—another telegraph station, near which

THOUSAND MILE TREE.—WEBER CANON.

a wagon bridge crosses the river on the left. It is convenient to a Mormon village called Enterprise, near by, and within a few miles of another, called Mountain Green. Just below Peterson, *Cottonwood Creek* puts in from the right, while immediately in front, Devil's Gate Mountain rears its snowy crest. You now begin to see where we are to get out of the basin. A huge gap in the mountains opens before you. It is the *Devil's Gap* with the *Devil's Gate* and several other odd characteristics about it. It is one of the most remarkable places on the line of the road. The waters of Weber River, as if enraged at their attempted restraint, rush wildly along. now on one side of the road, and now on the other, and now headed off completely by a projecting ledge before them, turn madly to the right, determined with irresistible strength to force their way through the mountain; foiled in this, they turn abruptly to the left, still rushing madly on, and at last find their way out to the plain beyond. If Echo was grand, and the narrows grander—this Devil's Gate pass is surely grandest of all. Just before you enter the deep cut, you will notice the old wagon road winding along the bed of the stream, cut out of the mountain's side in some places, and, in others, walled up from the river. In the midst of all this majestic grandeur, the train passes, but seldom stops at a station appropriately named

Devil's Gate. —1,020.4 miles from Omaha, and 4,870 feet above the sea, —and so we pass rapidly on. The gap begins to open in the west, and we soon emerge from one of the grandest scenes in nature, into the lovely valley below, reclaimed by the hands of men from the barren waste of a desert, and made to bud and blossom as the rose. We have now passed the Wahsatch Range of mountains, though their towering peaks are on the right, and recede from view on the left, as we leave their base and get

DEVIL'S SLIDE.—WEBER CAÑON.

out into the plain. We are now in the Great Salt Lake Basin, or Valley; and, though the lake itself is not in sight, the mountains on its islands are. These mountains, back of Ogden, are almost always crowned with snow, and frequently have their summits enveloped in clouds. They are storm-breeders—every one, and the old Storm King sometimes holds high carnival among them, when

> "From peak to peak, the rattling crags among,
> Leaps the live thunder."

The winds and storms of winter occasionally fill the craggy gap through which we have passed with snow, to such an extent that it slides like an avalanche down over the track, and in the river below, where the rushing waters give it a cordial greeting, and where it soon melts in their embrace.

Uintah.—1,025.3 miles from Omaha; elevation, 4,560 feet. This was formerly the stage station for Salt Lake City, but the completion of the Utah Central Railroad from Ogden, took away its glory. While it was the stage terminus it was a lively place, though it never possessed indications of being a town of any great size. Approaching the town, the valley opens out like a panorama, and neat little houses with farms and gardens attached, greet the eyes of the traveler in a wonderful change from the scenes through which he has just passed. Looking off to the left you will notice the first bench of land across the river, with a higher bench or terrace in the rear. Upon this first bench, the Morrisite massacre took place in 1862, an account of which we shall give in another place. Leaving Uintah, the road pursues its way in a general northerly direction along the base of the mountains, till it arrives at

Ogden,—the western terminus of the Union Pacific Railroad, 1,033.8 miles from Omaha, and 4,340 feet above the level of the sea. By agreement between the two roads, it is also the eastern terminus of the Central Pacific Railroad. The place is one of considerable importance, being the second city in size and population in the Territory of Utah. It is regularly laid out, is the county-seat of Weber County, has a court-house of brick, which, with grounds, cost about $20,000, two or three churches and a Mormon tabernacle. The town may properly be divided into two parts — upper and lower Ogden. The upper part is pleasantly situated on an elevated

SCENES IN WEBER CANON.

1.—Ogden, Utah. Wahsatch Mountains in the distance. 2.—Devil's Gate and High Peaks of Wahsatch Mountains.
3.—Heights of Weber Canon. 4.—Tunnel No. 3, Weber Canon.

bench adjoining the mountains. This bench breaks rather abruptly, and almost forms a bluff, and then begins lower Ogden. The upper part is mostly occupied for residences, and has some beautiful yards with trees now well grown. The lower portion—that which is principally seen from the railroad, is mostly occupied by business houses. One peculiarity of the towns in these western or central Territories, is the running streams of water on each side of nearly every street, which are fed by some mountain stream, and from which water is taken to irrigate the yards, gardens and orchards adjoining the dwellings. Ogden now has fully 6,000 people, and has a bright future before it. It is not only the terminus of the two great trans-continental lines before mentioned, but is also the starting-point of the Utah Central and Utah Northern Railroads. These four companies have united in the purchase of grounds, on which a large Union depot will soon be built, nearly east of the present building, and nearer the business portion of the city. It is the regular supper and breakfast station of the Union Pacific and Central Pacific Railroads—passengers having one hour in which to take their meals and transfer their baggage. The Central Pacific Road has numerous machine and repair shops here which are wooden buildings of a temporary character, and which will soon be replaced by more permanent structures. In addition to their freight depots the Union Pacific has only a roundhouse for the shelter of engines—their buildings for the sub-division of the road being located at Evanston.

Ogden is the last town on the Weber River before it empties into the Great Salt Lake. This river takes its name from an old mountaineer and trapper, who was well known in these parts during the early days of the Mormon settlement. The town is named for Mr. Ogden, another old mountaineer who lived and died near or in the city. Ogden is destined to become a manufacturing town of no small importance. Vast quantities of iron ore can be obtained within five miles of the city, and iron works on a large scale have been commenced, but owing to want of proper foresight, the company ran short of means before their works were completed. An effort is now being made to resuscitate them, and with additional capital carry them on to completion. The freight on all iron brought into the Territory is so large in amount, that an iron manufactory here, with coal and iron ore bearing 60 per cent. of pure iron of an excellent quality, near by, will prove a paying investment and materially facilitate the development of the Territory. Discoveries of silver have also been made on the mountains back of the city, but the mines have not, as yet, been developed. These discoveries have been made up in Ogden Canon, about five miles from the city.

On the mountain directly east of the town, ex-cellent slate quarries have been discovered and worked to some extent. It is said to be equal to the best found in the Eastern States.

Ogden River rises in the Wahsatch Range of Mountains, some 40 miles east of the city. It has three forks—north, middle and south—all of which unite just above the canon and fairly cut their way through one of the wildest and most romantic gorges on the Continent.

Ogden Canon.—This lovely little canon contains views quite as pretty as either Weber or Echo Canons. Visitors should stay over at Ogden and spend a day in a drive hither.

A fine creek, about 30 feet wide, and three to five feet deep, has cut through the mountain and its ridges. As it comes out of the mountain on the west side, it opens into a broad, grassy valley, thickly settled with farmers, and joins the Weber River about five miles distant. The scenes, as the traveler passes through the narrows of the canon, are wild in the extreme. The rocks rise from 500 to 2,000 feet almost perpendicularly, and the width averages less than 100 feet for a long distance. In this canon, geologists have found evidence sufficiently satisfactory to indicate that the entire Salt Lake Valley was once a huge fresh water lake, whose surface rose high up on the sides of the mountains, even covering the highest terrace.

Five miles up the canon, which runs eastward, there is a beautiful little valley, with table-like terraces, 30 to 50 feet above the bed of the creek, wherein a little Mormon village is located. The situation is a lovely one—the sides of the hills which enclose the valley, are 800 to 1,000 feet high, smoothly rounded and sloping, covered with coarse bunch grass and small bushes.

In addition to the railroad hotel before spoken of—which, by the way, is a first-class house and popular with the traveling public—Ogden has several hotels, prominent among which are the Utah Hotel, an up-town establishment, convenient for commercial men, and the Beardsley House which caters for railroad travel. It is also supplied with two newspapers, the *Daily Junction*, a small seven by nine sheet—the organ of the church, and published by one of the bishops, a Mormon poet, etc. The other is a weekly, styled the *Ogden Freeman*, the organ of the opposition. The city water-works are supplied with water taken from Ogden River, at the mouth of Ogden Canon. The road through the canon is a dugway along the stream, and sometimes built up from it, while the wall rocks on either side tower up thousands of feet. The water in the river goes rushing madly on over huge rocks and boulders lying in the bed of the stream, as though it would push them out of the way. In some places the rocks almost hang over the road, and as you round some point they seem as though they would push you into the stream. In some places the formation and dip of the rocks is very peculiar. They seem to be set up on end, in thin layers, and with a slight dip, while the wash of ages has worn out a channel for the river. About two miles up the cañon, Warm Spring Cañon comes in on the right. It is not much of a cañon, but high up on the mountain side, near its source, are warm springs from which it takes its name. About half a mile farther are some hot sulphur springs, on the left side of the river, in the midst of a little grove of trees. This is a charming resort for the tourist, and he will never cense admiring the wild and rugged in nature, as exhibited in this canon. The canon is about six miles long, and the stream which runs through it is filled with "the speckled beauties" which are so tempting to the fisherman and so satisfactory to the epicure. As you look to the top of the mountain you will see pine trees that appear like little shrubs. These trees are from 50 to 80 feet in height, and are cut and brought down to the valleys for their timber. Accommodations for pleasure parties for visiting this wonderful canon, and for fishing and hunting, can be obtained in Ogden, and no excursion party from ocean to ocean should fail to visit it.

NARROWS OF OGDEN CANON.

Beyond the mountains, before the river gorges through, there is a fertile valley pretty well settled, and the road through the canon gives the people living there an outlet to the town. This road was built several years ago, and required a great deal of time and labor, and fitly illustrates the persevering industry of the Mormon people.

Fruit-growing is very common in the vicinity of Ogden, and a large quantity of the best varieties grown in the Territory are produced in this region of country. Utah apples, peaches and pears are finer in size, color and flavor than any grown in the Eastern or Middle States.

Hot Springs. — Northward from Ogden, about a day's ride, is a very interesting locality, known as the *Hot Springs.* Here is a group of warm springs, in the aggregate, a stream three feet wide, and six to twelve inches deep; the surface, for a space of 300 to 400 yards in extent, is covered with a deposit of oxide of iron, so that it resembles a tanyard in color. The temperature is 136°. They flow from beneath a mountain called Hot Spring Mountain, which is about five miles long and three wide. The elevation of the lake is 4,191 feet. The water of the spring is clear as crystal, containing great quantities of iron, and the supply is abundant. As there are plenty of cold springs in the vicinity, there is nothing to prevent this from being a noted place of resort for invalids. The medicinal qualities of this water are excellent for rheumatism, skin diseases, dyspepsia, and the climate is unsurpassed.

The Territory of Utah.

When the Mormons first located in Utah, in 1847, it was territory belonging to Mexico, but by the treaty of Guadaloupe Hidalgo, in March, 1848, it was passed over to the United States with New Mexico and the whole of upper California. The government of the United States was not very prompt in extending its jurisdiction over the newly-acquired Territory, and in

WILHELMINA PASS, WEBER CANON.

BY THOMAS MORAN.

the absence of any other government the Mormons set up one for themselves, which was called the State of Deseret. This was done in the spring of 1849. On the 9th of September, 1850, Congress passed a bill which ignored the State government of the Mormons, and organized the Territory of Utah, and on the 28th of that same month, Millard Fillmore, President, appointed Brigham Young,Governor of the Territory with a full complement of executive and judicial officers. Since that time the area of the Territory has been diminished, but it is still large enough for all practical purposes. It now extends from the 37th to the 42d parallels of north latitude, and from the 109th to the 114th degree of longitude, embracing over 84,000 square miles or over 54,000,000 of acres. The national census of 1870 showed a population of about 90,000, and a fair estimate would give the Territory about 125,000 people at the present time. The climate, as a general thing, is salubrious and healthy, and violent extremes of either heat or cold are seldom experienced. The area of land susceptible of cultivation is small as compared to that included in the whole Territory, and a large quantity of even desert land is now unproductive because of the presence of alkali and mineral substances. While all kinds of grain can be grown with more or less success—depending upon local causes—wheat is the great staple, and in favorable seasons and localities monstrous crops of the great cereal have been produced.

It may astonish eastern readers, but it is nevertheless a fact, that whole fields, producing from fifty to sixty bushels per acre of as fine wheat as was ever grown, are no uncommon thing in Utah. The land, of course, is irrigated, and there is no great danger of loss by rains during the harvest season. The average yield, it is true, is a great deal less than this, amounting to about twenty-five bushels per acre. On account of the high altitude and cool nights, corn will not do as well, though fair crops are raised. Vegetables of all kinds grow to an astonishing size, and are superior in quality. Corn will, as a general thing, do better in the valleys in the southern part of the Territory, where cotton is also grown to a limited extent, and some kinds of tropical fruits. The climate and soil are especially adapted to the production of apples, pears, peaches, plums, currants, strawberries, raspberries, blackberries, etc. It must constantly be borne in mind, that successful agricultural pursuits can only be carried on here with irrigation, and that, as a general thing, it costs no more to irrigate land here, nor as much, as it costs to drain and clear it in many of the Eastern States. The market for most of the products raised in this Territory, is at the mining camps and settlements, and in Nevada, Idaho and Montana. The explorations in the southern half of the Territory, have resulted in the discovery of

vast deposits of iron, coal, copper, silver, gold and lead. In the Strawberry Valley, coal veins over twenty feet thick, of excellent quality, have been discovered. In San Pete Valley, other magnificent coal deposits have been found, from which coke for smelting purposes has been made. East of the Wahsatch Range, in San Pete County, are the remains of the Moquis Village, of which much has been written. Iron County, still south, is so named from the vast deposits of this material found within its limits; and, in the spring of 1876, the most wonderful discoveries of silver were made near St. George, in what has been called the Bonanza District. There is horn silver around a piece of petrified wood in a sandstone formation. A part of this petrifaction was coal. The discovery of silver in such a formation, has upset many of the geological theories heretofore prevalent in the country. Ore from surface mines to the value of over fifty thousand dollars, has already been taken out. This discovery is one of the wonders of the country. A correspondent of the *Salt Lake Tribune,* recently spoke of these mines as follows: "The mines are in the rear of Bonanza City, and are certainly a new thing in the theory of geology and the mining world. Those in Silver Flat are found under and in sandstone, lying flat and about six to eight inches in width, showing rich chlorides, horn silver and sulphurets, carrying some mica. The manner of working the same has the appearance of quarrying rock." Judge Barbee, the discoverer of these mines, found several pieces of petrified wood ore, containing chlorides and horn silver. The specimen that we saw, said to have been brought from these mines, was carbonized to a certain extent—one side distinctly showing a thin vein of coal. There are two main ranges of mountains in Utah, running nearly parallel to each other. The easternmost range is the Wahsatch, and that farther west, the Oquirrh. Still farther to the west are broken ranges, parallel with those above named. Nearly all of these, so far as they have been prospected, are mineral bearing; and, in our judgment, the time is not far distant, when mines greater even than the Comstock, will be developed in Utah. They only await capital and the extension of railroads for their development. The Emma mine, which has filled the public prints, is thought to be one of the richest mines on the Continent, to-day, by the leading business men of Utah, who are familiar with the characteristics of the district in which it is located. In fact, Utah alone, has all the resources of an empire; and if it were only under a safe, stable and peaceful political local government, she would become the richest and brightest star in the coronet of the nation. It were well if certain pages in her eventful history could be forever obliterated.

Utah Central Railroad.—Ogden is the

northern terminus of this road. It is the pioneer line of Utah proper, though the Union Pacific and Central Pacific Roads were completed first through the magnificent generosity of the people of the United States. Early in May, 1869, the iron rails which bound the Continent together were joined near Promontory, some 50 miles west of Ogden. One week after this was done, work on the Utah Central began. The company was organized on the 8th of March previous, Brigham Young being president. A large quantity of material for building railroads was left on hand, when the Union Pacific was finished to Promontory, and this was purchased by the Utah Central Company. Brigham Young had entered into a contract for grading the former road, from the head of Echo Canon to Ogden, and successfully accomplished the work. If this had not been done, that road would have failed in its race across the Continent, and the Central Pacific would have built the greatest part of the trans-continental line. His contract was sublet to John Sharp and Joseph A. Young, the eldest son of the Mormon prophet. They crowded it with all possible speed, and obtained that experience in railroad building then, which has been of great advantage to the people of Utah since. In less than eight months from the time ground was broken for this new line of road, the last rail was laid, and on the 10th day of January, 1870, the first through train from Ogden, arrived in Salt Lake City. As elsewhere stated, this company is to unite with others in the erection of a Union depot at Ogden, work upon which will probably begin the present year. Their road now crosses the Central Pacific in Ogden, at nearly right angles, and their depot and freight houses are north of the Pacific Roads. Arriving at Ogden from the east, the traveler, looking ahead to the right, will see the engine and train of cars ready to take him to the City of the Saints. Entering elegantly furnished cars at about 6 o'clock P. M., and turning your back upon Ogden and the lofty mountain peaks behind it, you will soon be off. In less than a quarter of a mile, the road passes over the Weber River on a new and elegant iron bridge, just put up by the American Bridge Company of Chicago. It is a suspension bridge, 150 feet span, each end resting on a solid abutment of masonry. This bridge is so constructed that it will contract by cold or expand by heat as one body, one end being placed on rollers to allow self adjustment by the action of heat or cold. The bridge crossed, the road passes through a cut, and rises upon a bench or terrace of land from which, off to the right, the traveler obtains the first view of the Dead Sea of America—the Great Salt Lake. The general direction of the road is due south, and you pursue your way along the base of the foot hills and mountains, which form the first line looking

east, of the Wahsatch Range. As far as Kaysville, the road passes over a comparatively unsettled country, though in the dim distance on the right, the farming settlements of Hooper may be seen near the mouth of Weber River. We soon arrive at

Kaysville,—16 miles from Ogden. It is a telegraph station surrounded by a farming settlement, with its "co-op" store, blacksmith-shop and the usual buildings of a small country town. In entering and leaving, the road crosses several little creeks that flow down from the mountains, the waters of which are nearly all drank up by the dry earth in the processes of irrigation. Passing on, the traveler will notice a few houses and settlements, toward the lake and mountains, sometimes nearer the mountains; arriving at

Farmington,—the next station, 21 1-4 miles from Ogden. It is the county-seat of Davis County, and has, besides a court-house, the usual store and shops. This town is also located in the midst of a farming region, and nearly overshadowed by the mountains on the east. Davis County slopes to the west toward the lake, has a warm rich soil, and when irrigated, produces luxuriant crops of vegetables, melons, grain, etc., for the Salt Lake market. Leaving this station the road draws near to the side of this great inland sea, to

Centerville,—25 1-2 miles from Ogden,—a little farming town with its store, etc. Between the lake on one side and the mountains on the other, and the thrifty farms with orchards and gardens now on either side and all around him, the traveler will be kept pretty busy.

Wood's Cross—is the next station, 27 3-4 miles from Ogden. It is about midway between the mountains and the lake, and is located in what is called the best portion of Davis County. It is a telegraph station with usual side tracks, etc. The country gradually slopes into the lake toward the west with an occasional drift of sand near the shore, covered with the inevitable sage brush which we have had since leaving Laramie River. The cosy farm houses and the evidences of thrift everywhere visible, the growing crops and ripening fruits, if in the summer—all conspire to make a pleasant landscape, upon which the traveler can feast his greedy gaze, while the shadow of the mountains grows longer, and the twilight deepens into night as we arrive at

Salt Lake City,—the southern terminus of the road, 36 1-2 miles from Ogden. But of this city, more in another place.

The Utah Central has been a paying road from the start, and its business, as the years pass by, is destined to make it better still. We have not all the data at hand to show what it has done, but will give one or two illustrations. In 1873, its tonnage was as follows. Freights received, 233,533,450 lbs. Freights shipped, 55,387,754 lbs. In 1874, there was a slight falling off,

SALT LAKE CITY AND WAHSATCH MOUNTAINS

though it was not as large as expected from the business done in 1873, because of general depression of the mining interest of the Territory. In 1875, its business was as follows: Freights received, 184,158,526 lbs. Freights shipped 51,189,929 lbs. Its gross earnings for 1875 were $407,000. Its operating expenses were $162,000. This last sum does not of course include dividends on its stock of $1,500,000, nor the interest on its bonds amounting to $1,000,000. The passenger fare, first class, from Ogden to Salt Lake is $2. The controlling interest in this road is at present owned by stockholders in the Union Pacific, and it is one of the best paying roads in the country. The above figures prove it.

SALT LAKE CITY.

Its Discovery.—When Brigham Young, with his weary band of pioneers arrived here, in 1847, it was a dreary waste, nevertheless a beautiful site so far as location is concerned, for a city. It lies on a bench or gradual slope from the Wahsatch Mountains, which tower up behind it on the east, to the River Jordan, which bounds it on the west. It is recorded that when the pioneers came within a few days' march of the place, Orson Pratt and a few others went ahead of the party "to spy out the land" and select a place for camping, etc., convenient to wood and water. On the 22d day of July, 1847, he rode over this valley with his companions, and returning to the main body, reported the results of their observations. On the morning of July 24, 1847, this body arrived at the top of the hill, overlooking the site of the city, and the valley beyond, and were enchanted with the scene. They gave vent to their joy in exclamations of thanksgiving and praise to Almighty God, firmly believing they had found the land of promise, though it did not flow with "milk and honey," and the "Zion of the Mountains" predicted by ancient prophets. The Mormons are great on literal interpretation. Figurative language and expressions as viewed by them are realities. The Bible means exactly what it says with them. They had reasons, however, for being enchanted. From the canon through which they entered the valley, the view is simply magnificent. The Great Salt Lake glittered like a sheet of silver in the rays of the morning sun; the towering peaks of the mountain ranges, crowned with clouds and snow, lifted themselves high up toward the sky, and the valley, though a desert, was to them as lovely as a June rose. The party camped on a small stream south-west of the temple, and proceeded to consecrate the entire valley to the "Kingdom of God." On the 28th of the same month, the ground for the temple was selected—a tract of 40 acres, and a city two miles square was laid off. Streets eight rods wide were

staked out, and the blocks contained ten acres each. Orson Pratt took observations, and determined the latitude and longitude of the city. A large number of this pioneer party, after planting their crops returned for their families, and the last expedition for that year arrived on the last day of October, when they were received by those that remained with demonstrations of great joy. Brigham Young went back with the returning party, and did not find his way again to "Zion" until the next year. After the city had been founded, emigration from foreign countries, which had been suspended, was re-organized and came pouring into the Territory in masses. The city grew and the people spread out over the Territory, settling every available spot of land, thus contributing to its prosperity.

Beauty of Position.—The main portion of the city lies off to the left, as it is approached by the traveler, and presents a pleasing appearance. Its streets are wide, with streams of water coursing their way along the sides, while rows of beautiful shade trees line the walks; and gardens, and yards filled with fruit trees of various kinds, everywhere greet the eye. Visitors who are interested in beautiful gardens, will find the most interesting on Main Street, just west of the Walker House, at the residences of the Walker Brothers; also at Mr. Jennings, on Temple Street, near the depots. The city is now nearly thirty years old, and in that time the tourist can see for himself what wonderful changes have been made. The desert truly buds and blossoms as the rose. The city is admirably located for beauty, and at once charms its visitors. The tourist should engage a carriage and drive up and down the shaded streets, and see the wilderness of fruit groves and gardens. The first practical thing, however, with the traveler is to select his stopping place, during his visit. Of hotels there are two first-class houses that are popular resorts with the traveling public. The Walker House is a four story brick structure with 132 rooms. It is located on the west side of Main Street, has a frontage of 82 feet and a depth of 120 feet. It has lately been entirely renovated and handsomely furnished; also has had the addition of a passenger elevator. It is especially noted for its excellent table, which is abundant in game, fruits, fish, etc. The Townsend House is on the corner of West Temple and South Second streets, and has a fine shady piazza along the front. Both of these hotels face eastward, both are lighted with gas, and both are supplied with all modern conveniences and luxuries. There are, also, other good hotels in the city, which are considered second-class, and are largely patronized.

Sights for Tourists.—Having selected a stopping place, the next thing is a visit to the warm sulphur springs, for a bath. The street

OFFICES AND FAMILY RESIDENCE OF BRIGHAM YOUNG.

cars, running by nearly all the hotels, will take you there.

Warm Springs.—These are, to invalids, the most grateful and delightful places of resort in the city. Exceedingly valuable either for rheumatic or dyspeptic complaints, they are excellent in general invigorating properties, and specially efficacious in skin diseases. They are but about one mile from the hotel, reached either by horse-cars or carriage. Even a pleasant walk is preferable. Best times to enjoy them are early in the morning before breakfast, or immediately before dinner. Should never be taken within three hours after a meal. The springs issue from the limestone rock near the foot of the mountains, and the curious character of the rock is seen in the stones used for either fences or the foundation of the buildings. The following analysis has been made of the water by Dr. Charles S. Jackson of Boston, and is generally posted on the walls of the bathing-house.

"Three fluid ounces of the water, on evaporating to entire dryness in a platine capsule, gave 8.25 grains of solid dry saline matter.

Carbonate of lime and magnesia,	0.240	1.280
Peroxide of iron,	0.040	0.208
Lime,	0.545	2.907
Chlorine,	3.454	18.421
Soda,	2.877	15.344
Magnesia,	0.370	2.073
Sulphuric Acid,	0.703	3.748
	8.229	43.981

It is slightly charged with hydro-sulphuric acid gas, and with carbonic acid gas, and is a pleasant, saline mineral water, having the valuable properties belonging to a saline sulphur spring. The temperature is lukewarm, and, being of a sulphurous nature, the effects are very penetrating; at first the sensation is delicious, producing a delightful feeling of ease and re-

pose; but if the bather remains long, over fifteen minutes, there is danger of weakness and too great relaxation. These baths are now under control of an experienced gentleman, and fitted up with every modern convenience. Here are Turkish baths, Hot Air baths and Russian baths, in addition to the natural bath. The warm sulphur-water can be enjoyed in private

NEW MORMON TEMPLE.

rooms, or in the large plunge or swimming bath. Separate rooms for ladies and gentlemen, and a smaller building near by is fixed up for the boys, where they can frolic to their heart's content.

Hot Springs.—The tourist should take a

carriage, and, after visiting the Warm Springs and enjoying the bath, drive a mile farther north to where the mountain spur juts out to the very railroad—and, right at its base are situated the "*Hot Springs*," which are the greatest natural curiosity of the city. The water boils up, with great force, from a little alcove in the limestone rocks, just even with the surface of the ground. If you dare to thrust your hand in it, you will find it boiling hot, apparently with a temperature of over 200°. The finger can not be retained in the water for the best part of a minute ; yet the sensation, as it is withdrawn, is so soft and cooling, you will like to try it again and again—and, strange to say, rarely with any danger of scalding. If meat is dropped into this boiling water,

agriculture and vegetation for hundreds of yards within the vicinity. This lake is also supposed to be supplied, to some extent, by other hot springs beneath the surface. Strange as it may seem, the hot water does not prevent the existence of some kinds of excellent fish, among which have been seen some very fine large trout.

Analysis of Hot Sulphur Spring :

Chloride of Sodium,		0.8052
" " Magnesium,		0.0288
" " Calcium,		0.1096
Sulphate of Lime.		0.0806
Carbonate of Lime,		0.0180
Silica,		0.0180
		1.0602

Specific gravity, 1.1454.

The Museum—is located on the south side

INTERIOR OF OFFICE OF THE MORMAN PRESIDENT.

it is soon cooked. (though we cannot guarantee a pleasant taste) and eggs will be boiled, ready for the table, in three minutes Often a dense volume of steam rises from the spring. though not always. A very large volume of water issues forth from the little hole in the rock—scarcely larger than the top of a barrel—about four feet wide and six to twenty inches deep. Immediately near the rock is a little pool, in which the water, still hot, deposits a peculiar greenish color on the sides, and coats the long, wavy grass with its sulphurous sediment. Flowing beneath the railroad track and beyond in the meadows, it forms a beautiful little lake, called Hot Spring Lake, which, constantly filling up, is steadily increasing its area, and, practically, destroying all

of South Temple street, and directly opposite the Tabernacle Professor Barfoot is in charge, and he will show you specimen ores from the mines, precious stones from the desert, potteryware and other articles from the ruins of ancient Indian villages, the first boat ever launched on the Great Salt Lake by white men, home-made cloths and silks, the products of the industry of this people, specimen birds of Utah, a scalp from the head of a dead Indian, implements of Indian warfare and industry, such as blankets white people cannot make. shells from the ocean, and various articles from the Sandwich Islands, and other things too numerous to mention.

Formerly there were quite a number of living wild animals kept here, but some fiend poisoned

VIEW OF SALT LAKE CITY, LOOKING WESTWARD ACROSS THE JORDAN VALLEY.

the most of them. There are now living, however, a large horned owl, a prairie dog, and the owls that burrow with him, together with the rattlesnake; also other birds and reptiles which need not be named. This institution is the result of the individual enterprise of John W.

SIGN OF MORMON STORES.—SALT LAKE CITY.

Young, Esq., and for which he is entitled to great credit. A nominal sum, simply, is charged for admission, which goes for the support of Professor Barfoot, who has the care and direction of the Museum. Across the street, behind a high wall, is the Tabernacle, and near by it, on the east, enclosed within the same high wall, are the foundation walls of the new Temple. We shall not attempt a description of either, as a personal inspection will be far more satisfactory to the visitor. We advise every tourist to get to the top of the Tabernacle, if possible, and get a view of the city from the roof. Within the same walls may be found the Endowment house, of which so much has been written. In this building both monogamous and polygamous marriages take place, and the quasi-masonic rites of the church are performed. On South Temple street, east of Temple block, is the late residence of Brigham Young, also enclosed in a high wall which shuts out the rude gaze of passers-by, and gently reminds the outsider that he has no business to obtrude there. Nearly opposite to this residence is a large and beautiful house which is supposed to belong to the Prophet's favorite wife, Amelia — familiarly called *Amelia Palace*, probably the finest residence for 500 miles around. Returning to East Temple or Main street, we behold a large brick building with iron and glass front, three stories high, with a skylight its entire length. This is the new "co-op" store, 40 feet wide and 300 feet long, with all the modern improvements, steam elevator, etc. Nearly opposite this store is Savage's picture gallery, whose photographs of scenery and views along the road, are the finest of any ever issued in the Great West. Continuing on the same street south, and the elegant building of the Deseret National Bank greets our gaze, on the north-east corner of East Temple and First South streets. Diagonally across the street from this is the emporium of William Jennings, Esq. But it is needless to enumerate all the buildings in the city, be they public or p r i v a t e. We must not omit, however, the elegant private residence and beautiful grounds of Mr. Jennings, on the corner east of the depot. They are worthy of a visit, and so, also, is the elegant private residence of Feramor Little, directly east of the Deseret National Bank. The theater is open occasionally in the evening, where may be seen many of the leading Mormons and their families. The city is supplied w i t h gas, water, and street railroads. T h e water is brought from City Creek Canon, through the principal streets, in iron pipes, though in some seasons the supply is rather short.

Scenery Near the City.—North of the city, Ensign Peak lifts its head, the Mountain of Prophecy, etc. Its crown is oval in shape, and the mountain, etc, is said to have been seen in a vision by some of the Mormon dignitaries long before it was beheld by the naked eyes of the present settlers. The sight from this peak, or others near at hand, is grand and impressive. Under your feet lies the City of the Saints, to

the west the Great Salt Lake, to the south the valley of the river Jordan, the settlements along the line of the railroad, and the mountains on either side. Though the way to the summit requires a little toil, and will expand one's lungs to the fullest extent, yet the reward, when once the summit is reached, will amply pay for all the toil it has cost.

In the summer months only, the Tabernacle is open, and the services of the Mormon church are then h e l d there nearly every Sabbath. Behind the rostrum or pulpit is the great organ, made in the city, and said to be the second in size on the Continent.

East of the city there seems to be a withdrawal of the mountains and a part of a circle, formed l i k e an amphitheatre. About two miles east is Camp Douglas, established by General Connor during the late war. It is beautifully located on an elevated bench commanding t h e city, and at the base of the mountains. New buildings have been erected, and it is now considered one of the finest and most convenient posts the government has. It is supplied with water from Red Butte Canon, and has a great many conveniences.

INTERIOR OF MORMON TABERNACLE.—THE GREAT ORGAN.

Below Camp Douglas, Emigration Canon next cuts the mountains in twain. It is the canon through which Orson Pratt and his companions came when they first discovered the valley, the lake, and the site for a city—through which Brigham Young and the pioneers came, and was the route by which nearly all the overland emigrants arrived, on coming from the East. Below this, as you look south, is Parley's Canon, through which a road leads to Parley's Park and the mining districts in that region. Then comes South Mill Creek with its canon, through the towering peaks, and then the Big Cottonwood Creek and Canon. Between it and Little Cottonwood Canon, next on the south, is the mountain of silver—or the hill upon which is located some of the richest paying mines in the Territory. Here is the Flagstaff, the North Star, the Emma, the Reed & Benson, and others worth their millions. The Emma mine has become notorious in the history of mines, but there is not a practical miner in Utah who doubts the existence of large bodies of rich ore there, and, if it had been practically worked, would, in the opinion of many, have equaled, if not exceeded, the celebrated Comstock lode before this.

No visitor to Salt Lake should leave the city without a trip to the lake and a ride on its placid bosom—a trip, also, to the southern terminus of the Utah Southern Railroad, the mountains and canons along its line, and to the mountains and mines of Stockton, Ophir, Bingham, and above all, the Cottonwood districts. If you are further inclined to improve the opportunity, ride up to Parley's Park, go to Provo and spend a week, or a month even, in visiting the wonderful canons near there, and in hunting and fishing in the mountain streams and in Lake Utah. A trip to the summit of old Mount Nebo would afford you good exercise, and very fine views. With Salt Lake for headquarters, all these places can be taken in, and your only regret will be that you did not stay longer, travel farther, and see more of this wonderful land.

Gardening, Irrigation.—The city was originally laid out in large ten acre blocks, which were, in time, subdivided into house lots, most of which, having been liberally planted with

NEW RESIDENCE OF BRIGHAM YOUNG.—AMELIA PALACE.

fruit trees, have since grown with great luxuriance, and the city seems a vast fruit orchard and garden. Through all the streets run the little irrigating streams, and every part of the city has its chance, once or twice a week, to get a supply of pure water to wet the soil and freshen the vegetation.

The city is divided into wards. Every ward has its master, and he compels all the inhabitants to turn out and work on public improvements. There is no shirking. Every one has a responsibility to guard and watch his own property, take care of his own irrigating ditches, and keep his ward in perfect order. The city is one of perfect order and quietness.

Through all the streets of the city there is a universal and luxuriant growth of shade trees. These have been planted profusely, and grow with amazing rapidity. The locust, maple and box-elder, are the greatest favorites, the former, however, being most planted. In many cases the roots have struck the alkali soils, which contain an excess of soda and potash, and their leaves have turned from a bright or dark green to a sickly yellow—and often trees may be noticed, half green and half yellow.

This alkali has to be washed out of the soil by irrigation, and gradually grows less positive year by year. In nearly all the gardens are splendid apples, pears, plums and apricots, growing with exceeding thrift, and covered with the most beautiful blushing colors. Apricots which in the East are almost unknown, here have been so abundant as often to sell as low as $1.00 per bushel, and we have seen them as large as eastern peaches, from four to six and eight inches round.

Flowers are very abundant, and vegetables are wonderfully prolific. In the gardens of William Jennings, may be seen growing out doors on trellises, grapes, the Black Hamburgh, Golden Chasselas and Mission grape, varieties which are only grown in a hot-house in the East. Through all the gardens can be seen an abundance of raspberries, gooseberries and currants. In Mr. Jennings's garden, in summer, may be seen a pretty flower garden, 150 feet in diameter,—within the center of which is a piece of velvety lawn—the finest and most perfect ever seen—while from it, southward, can be caught a specially glorious view of the Twin Peaks of the Wahsatch Mountains, capped with unvarying snow.

Future of Salt Lake City.—The future of Salt Lake depends upon two things—the mines and the railroads. If the mines are developed and capital is thus increased, it will have a tendency to cause an immense amount of building in the city, and a corresponding advance in real estate. It is claimed that the city now has a population of 30,000 souls, but we think 22,000 a closer estimate. Many parties owning and operating mines make the city their place of residence, and some have already invested in real estate there. We heard the opinion of a wealthy capitalist—a gentleman operating in mines—to the effect that in ten years Salt Lake would number 250,000 people, but he was a little enthusiastic. If the Utah Southern is extended to the Pacific Coast, it will add largely to the wealth, population and influence of the "City of the Saints." The silent influence of the Gentiles and the moral power of the Nation has already had an effect upon the Mormons of the city, which will soon be felt throughout the Territory. The discovery and development of the mines will largely increase the Gentile population throughout the Territory, and their influence will then be each year more powerfully felt, and we question if Mormonism will be strong enough to withstand them.

Newspapers.—The press of Salt Lake is exceedingly peculiar. The *Daily News* is the recognized church organ; the *Daily Herald* is more lively. It is the organ of the so-called progressive Mormons. The *Daily Tribune* is a stinging, lively journal—the leading organ of the opposition to the priesthood and the theocracy. The *Mail* is an evening paper under Gentile influences, but not as bold or belligerent as the *Tribune*. The *Utah Weekly Miner* is a paper devoted to the development of the mineral resources of the Territory. There is another little evening paper called the *Times*, under church influences. Fortunes have been expended upon newspaper enterprises in Salt Lake, but with the exception of the three papers first mentioned, none have succeeded. The ground is now, however, fully occupied, and further efforts should

be directed toward improving those already established, rather than in new and costly experiments.

The Utah Southern Railroad.—This road is really a continuation of the Utah Central. It was begun on the 1st day of May, 1871, and completed to Sandy that same year. In 1872 it was extended to Lehi, about thirty miles from Salt Lake City. In 1873 it was extended to Provo, and its present terminus is at York, a little place just across the divide between Lake Utah and Juab Valley. It will probably be extended from a hundred to a hundred and fifty miles the present year. York is 75 miles from Salt Lake City, and 16 miles from Nephi, the next town on its proposed line of any importance. The stockholders of the Union Pacific Road, own a controlling interest in this, as also in the Utah Central. It will probably be extended to the Pacific Coast sometime. The following is the record of freight received and forwarded at the Salt Lake City Station for the year 1875. Freight received, 70,916,527 lbs. Freight forwarded, 71,969,954 lbs. Its gross earnings for same period, were $188,987.00,—and its operating expenses, were $120,650.87. The great bulk of its business is between Salt Lake City and Sandy, though travel and traffic are gradually increasing on the balance of its line, and will rapidly double up as soon as the road shall have reached the rich mining districts in the southern portions of Utah, which are at present comparatively undeveloped. Its general direction is southward from Salt Lake City, up the Jordan Valley to the Valley of Lake Utah, and thence across the divide as before mentioned. Travelers visiting this Territory should not fail to visit the towns, valleys and mountains on this line of road. The Valley of Lake Utah especially, entirely surrounded by mountains lofty and rugged, will compare favorably, so far as magnificent scenery is concerned, with anything of a similar character to be found either in Europe or America. Leaving Salt Lake City, we slowly pass through the limits of the corporation where cultivated fields and gardens, with farm houses and fine orchards of all kinds of fruit trees, giving evidences of thrift on every side, greet our gaze. Streams of water are constantly running through the irrigating ditches, and the contrast between the cultivated lands and the sage brush deserts, sometimes side by side, is wonderful. On our left, the everlasting mountains, with their crowns of snow almost always visible, stand like an impenetrable barrier to approaches from the east, or like eternal finger-boards, and say as plainly as words can indicate —"go south or north; you cannot pass us." On the right, the river Jordan winds its way to the waters of the great inland sea, while beyond, towering into the sky, are the peaks of the Oquirrh Range. You will need to keep your eyes wide open, and gaze quickly upon the rapidly changing scenes as they come into view, or swiftly recede from your vision; for, between the scenes of nature and the works of man in reclaiming this desert, you will hardly know which to admire the most, or which is the most worthy of your attention. Passing on, we arrive at the first station—

Little Cottonwood,—7 miles from the city. It is a way station at which trains do not stop unless flagged, or the signal is given from on board the train. All the canons and ravines in the mountains supply more or less water, which is gathered into canals and distributed through ditches as required for the fields, meadows and orchards. The well cultivated fields continue until we arrive at

Junction,— 12 miles from Salt Lake City, where the Bingham Canon & Camp Floyd Railroad intersects the Utah Southern. Passengers here change cars for Bingham Canon and the mining districts in that vicinity. This road is about twenty-two miles long and is extensively used in transporting ore, bullion, coke, coal and charcoal to and from the mines and smelting works and railroad. It is a narrow gauge (three feet) road and is now doing a fine business.

Sandy,—13 miles from the city and the point of intersection of the Wahsatch & Jordan Valley Railroad,—narrow gauge (three feet). This road turns off to the left and goes up Little Cottonwood Canon, which can now plainly be seen from the cars. The Big Cottonwood Canon is also in sight. There they are, with the mountain of silver between them. There is silver enough in that mountain to pay the national debt of the United States, with enough left to pay for a huge fourth of July celebration. This road has some very heavy grades, and, on the

SNOW SLIDE MOUNTAIN.—LITTLE COTTONWOOD CANON.

upper end of it, horses, instead of engines, are employed to haul the empty cars. These two narrow gauge roads are now under one management. The Little Cottonwood Road is about eighteen miles in length. Sandy is a flourishing little town. It has several smelters, or reduction works, where crude ore is converted into bullion. The celebrated Flagstaff mine has its smelting works here; its ore is brought down from the mine on the Wahsatch & Jordan Valley Railroad. Every visitor to Utah, who is at all interested in mines, or metallurgy, will obtain a great deal of information, and be amply repaid for the time and expense of a visit to its more celebrated mining districts. A visit to the Bingham and Little Cottonwood Districts, certainly should not be neglected. Leaving Sandy, we enter into a desert country again; the farmhouses are scattering, though the land on the right, toward the immediate vicinity of the Jordan, is still pretty well settled. The next station is

Draperville, —17 miles from Salt Lake City. It is an unimportant station, convenient to a little Mormon settlement. Leaving this station we soon cross South Willow Creek, and then follow the outer rim of the hills around the valley toward the right, like a huge amphitheatre. We have been going up hill, and, as we turn to the right, to get through a pass or gorge in the mountains, the valley below us with Sandy, Salt Lake City, Salt Lake itself, its islands, the mountains beyond and a vast scope of country is suddenly unrolled, like a beautiful panorama, to our view — a magnificent spectacle which never fails to excite and satisfy the beholder. Turning to the left again, we near the narrows, and, looking to the right, the river Jordan winds along beneath us; then, passing through

a deep cut, we suddenly emerge into the valley of Lake Utah, and at once become enchanted with the lovely view now spread out before us. The valley, cities and towns we have just left, are entirely shut out from our vision, and, in their stead, new wonders invite our attention. There is Lake Utah, with little villages and settlements between its shores and the base of the mountains, and those mountains thousands of feet in height, piercing the very clouds, around it. With an elevation about 500 feet higher than that of the Great Salt Lake, it lies nestled down among the lofty peaks, as though it would hide its beauty and shun the gaze of the outside world. But iron arms have forced their way through the rugged defiles, and now hold it in long and lasting embrace. Henceforth it will receive the homage of thousands, and become a place of worship to the multitudes who shall see in it and its surroundings, the Mecca of their pilgrimages—the gratification of their desires and the satisfaction of every hope. This is strong language, and the tourist himself shall be the judge of its truthfulness. This lake is virtually the head of the river Jordan. It winds its way, like a ribbon of silver, through the valley, passes through the gorge we have entered and becomes lost to view. Down into the valley of the lake we go and arrive at

Lehi,—the next station, 31 miles from the City of the Saints. It is located on Dry Canon Creek, though the creek furnishes water sufficient to irrigate the thrifty farms bordering the little village. A large portion of the bottom-lands around the lake are cultivated and irrigated with the water that flows down the mountain streams.

American Fork,—34 miles from Salt Lake City, is now reached. It is named from the creek and canon back of the town, which has cleft the mountains in twain, and left on their ragged edges the marks of the heroic and victorious struggle. From this town another narrow gauge railroad has been built up the canon to Deer Creek, some twelve miles, to accommodate the necessities of the mines which have been opened there. It will be extended whenever the increased productions of these mines shall demand it. Of the grand scenery of this noted canon we shall speak in another place. The town is about six miles from the mouth of the canon, and has every appearance of the industry which usually characterizes Mormon towns.

Pleasant Grove,—37 miles from the city, is the next station. It is a thriving farming settlement, and similar to all the little villages in the Territory. It was formerly called Battle Creek because of a fight which early settlers had with the Ute Indians. Leaving Pleasant Grove we soon arrive at

Provo,—48 miles from Salt Lake City, and the third town in size in Utah Territory, having a population of about 5,000 souls. After leaving the last station, off to the left, Provo Canon is visible, with Provo or Timpanogos River flowing through it. This river rises in the western spur of the Uintah Mountains, flows along the southern part of Kammas Prairie and then turns to the south-west, entering what is called Provo Valley, which lies east of the range of mountains on our left, and finally cutting through this range into the valley of Lake Utah. Observe, as you approach the town, how the strata of rocks in the mountains on each side of the canon dip toward each other. An immense body of water flows down this river, annually—more than passes through the river Jordan, the surplus being taken up by evaporation or drank by the thirsty soil. We cross the river as we approach the town, and for the first time since leaving Salt Lake, see small bodies of timber, mostly cottonwood, and a thick undergrowth of brush, etc.

Sporting.—Between the town and lake are low marshes and meadows which render this place a paradise for ducks, which fact the sportsman will do well to note. The streams which flow into the lake abound in fish, and the lake itself is full of trout, chub, suckers, etc. It is no unfrequent matter to catch trout here weighing from seven to ten pounds, though from two to five pounds is their usual weight. The trout ascend the streams in the proper season to deposit their spawn; the suckers follow to devour it, and sometimes they almost choke the river, so vast are they in numbers, and are caught in large quantities. The streams sometimes fall so rapidly that they are left in shallow places and die there as the water recedes. Measures should be taken to prevent this wholesale raid on the spawn of the trout, or it will soon be destroyed—at least materially lessened. If the suckers are masters of the situation, so far as the spawn is concerned. the reverse holds true with the trout in the lake, for there they attack the suckers without mercy, and the old adage that "the big fish eat the little ones," proves literally true. It is evident that the young suckers are relished by the larger trout in this lake.

The town of Provo is regularly laid out, has numerous school-houses, stores, grist-mill, tanneries, woolen factory, etc. Brigham Young has a private residence here, which he frequently visits, and which is occupied by one of his so-called wives. It has finely cultivated gardens, yards, orchards and small farms adjacent.

Springville,—53 miles from Salt Lake City. The little town lies back under the mountains, and will probably be the initial point of a narrow gauge railroad to the extensive coal fields in Strawberry Valley, some 60 miles east. This coal possesses coking qualities, and as a large amount of coke is now imported from Pittsburg, Pa., for the use of the numerous smelting works in the Territory, it at once becomes an object to manufacture it nearer home. Coke made from coal found in the San Pete Valley is already shipped from this point. Still rounding the eastern rim of the valley, we soon arrive at the next station, which is

Spanish Fork,—58 miles from Salt Lake City. To the left, the traveler will observe the canons and gorges which have cut their way through the mountains, and the lofty peaks of Mount Nebo, now nearly in front. Hobble Creek courses a canon through the range back of Springville, and now Spanish Fork does likewise. There is more of a depression in the mountain, however, where this river canons through. It has two main branches on the other side of the range—upon the northern, the proposed Denver Railroad comes in, while the southern branch heads in the divide that crosses San Pete Valley, east of Mount Nebo. Near Wales, in this valley, coking coal has been discovered, ovens erected, and the manufactured article is now delivered at Springville, being hauled nearly 60 miles by wagons. The projected railroad from Springville, will pass up the valley of the Spanish Fork River. The town is located on this river, a little distance from the road. We cross the river soon after leaving the station. A little village called Pontoun, is seen on the left at the base of Mount Nebo.

Payson,—66 miles from the City of the Saints. Iron ore is shipped from here to the smelters, where it is used for fluxing purposes in the reduction of ore. It is hauled some 14 miles by wagons. It is said to bear 60 or 65 per cent. of iron, and is known as brown hematite. At this station and the next, ore and bullion are hauled from the East Tintic Mining District, which is about 22 miles away. To our right, a mountain rises from the level plain around it, while the lake puts out an arm, as if to clasp it in fond embrace. Between this mountain and Mount Nebo, the road finds its way, and a little farther on, this arm of the lake can be seen west of the mountain.

Santaquin—is the next station, 71 miles from Salt Lake City. Stage lines leave here for the Tintic Mining District on the west. In one year this station received one million tons of ore. The road now passes through a low depression or valley, which divides the Wahsatch and Oquirrh Ranges, and across the divide between Lake Utah and Juab Valley, by easy grades, and we soon arrive at

York,—75 miles from the northern terminus, and the present southern terminus of the Utah Southern Railroad. The town is of no particular importance, and will lose its present significance as soon as the road is extended. In fact it is no place for a town, and there is no country around it to support one. Farther down the valley, streams from the mountains come in, water for irrigation can be obtained, and the desert, under the manipulations of labor, is made to bud and blossom as the rose. When the road is extended to Nephi, 16 miles, the traveler can pass into a beautiful and highly cultivated valley, and behold the towering form and giant outlines of Mount Nebo, from the south. It is one of the highest peaks in the Wahsatch Range of the Rocky Mountains, and its lofty head whitened by eternal snows, is frequently obscured by clouds. The elevation of the summit of this mountain, is given by the Engineer Department of the United States Army, at 11,922 feet.

Frisco Mines.— The railroad is to be extended this year 150 miles south to these mines, and thence in time to Arizona and California through new belts of mineral richness. Stages leave here daily for Pioche and St. George.

AMERICAN FORK CANON.

Of this canon, no less a writer than the late Charles Kingsley, Canon of the English Church in London, England, has given the most enthusiastic expression, and declares it " *The rival of the Yosemite.*"

It is by far the most wonderful of all the canons which are within convenient access to the Pacific Railroad, and tourists who value sights of grandeur and sublime rock scenery, must not omit it in their overland tour. In interest, beauty, and as a delightful pleasure trip, it will surpass either Echo, Weber, or Humboldt Canons, and not a little of the joy is attributable to the novel mode of ascent and descent.

Taking the cars of the Utah Southern Railroad at Salt Lake City, proceed southward to American Fork Station; there a little train is in waiting with narrow gauge cars and locomotive. If the party is large enough for a picnic, so much the better, as often flat cars are added, neatly trimmed with evergreen boughs. The railroad, after leaving the station turns directly toward the mountain range, and gradually ascends for the first six miles, a steady grade of 200 feet to the mile, until just before the mouth of the canon it reaches 296 feet. Nothing can describe the apparent desolation of sage brush and dry sterile appearance of the soil, but here and there wherever the little mountain brook can be diverted from its course, and its water used to irrigate the land, the richest of fruit trees, grass and grain spring up and give abundant crops. The little stream, with its rapid fall, follows us up the entire length of the canon. The upward ascent of the grade seems hardly noticeable, of so uniform a slope is the surface of the country, and it is not till the base of the mountains is reached, and the tourist looks back, he realizes his height,

AMERICAN FORK CANON.

BY THOMAS MORAN.

and sees in the distance the clear surface of Utah Lake considerably below him. Gathering now on the flat cars—where the scenery can be best observed—the little train slowly enters the canon. Scarcely 500 feet are passed over before there bursts upon the eye views of rock scenes of the most rugged character. The little valley is scarcely 100 feet broad, and in its widest part not over 200 feet, but from the very track and little stream, the rocks loom up into heights of startling distinctness and almost perpendicular elevation.

The color of the rocks is uniformly of very dark red and brown granite, apparently having once been heated in a terrible furnace, and then in melting had arranged themselves into rugged and fantastic shape more than mortal could conceive.

At the beginning of the canon, the rocks average about 800 feet in height, then, as the route ascends, the sides become more and more bold and erect,—the height greater, and the summits sticking up in jagged points seem like heaven-reaching spires,—often 1,500, 2,000, and 2,500 feet above the observer.

No pen can picture the sensations of the observer, as he passes slowly through these scenes—which are constantly shifting. Each turn in the road brings forward some new view, more entrancing than the last,—and on either side, front and rear, the vision is superb in the highest degree. We could not term these scenes better than to call them "*Rock Kaleidoscopes.*" For in this short distance of 12 miles, there is a constant succession of castellated heights, titanic monsters, spires, rock mountains of increasing height, sublime form and piercing altitudes, meeting us, crossing our path, and shooting up above and around us the entire distance,—it seems like a succession of nature's castles, far more rugged and picturesque than the castle covered rocks of the Rhine. Rocks of endless form and beauty, vistas of rocks, sky towering summits, bold crags, and flinty points jutting out from the mountain sides in most profuse, rugged, yet charming positions and combinations, that those eyes which once had no admiration for rocks—here confess with extreme enthusiasm, that there is beauty beyond the wildest imaginations.

While passing upward, the train is very slow, scarcely passing more than four or six miles per hour,—the traveler will see some rocks of curious formations at the left hand, about one-third of the way up; on the summit of one of the highest crags, will be seen a sharp-pointed rock, and in it a large distinct hole, through which can be seen the sky beyond. The contrast of the dark brown rock, and the clear blue of the sky is intense. This is familiarly called the *Devil's Eye.*

Farther up, the track passes under the jutting

edge of a rock mountain with a sharply cut alcove in its base. This is *Hanging Rock*—the roof of the rock which projects over the railroad, being about 20 feet outward.

Near the upper part of the canon, just before reaching the junction of two little valleys, the track reaches a huge rock mountain overlooking a little wilderness of trees and vegetation, in the center of which is located the *Old Mill.* It is now entirely useless, once used for sawing timber and ties for the railroad, but though it has left its field of usefulness behind,—it has remained to add a far more important help to art. The scene as viewed in our illustration, is one considered the most lovely and picturesque, not only of the entire canon, but also of all the Territory. In all that grand reach of country, of 2,000 miles from Omaha to the Sierras, not a single view is the equal of this delightful scene of the Old Mill. The dense growth of trees, the rippling water, the bold rock at the side, the soft shades of light in the distance, the luxuriant bushes along the stream, and the little silent deserted mill, situated exactly in the most beautiful site, make up a view which artists of keenest taste admit with rapture is unparalleled in beauty.

Beyond this, as the track ascends the canon, it is bordered with more shrubbery and trees,—and the rock views partially ceasing—the tourist will find his best vision looking backward, with a good view of the tallest mountain of the canon, *Lone Mountain,* or *Mount Aspinwall.*

At last the end of the track is reached at *Deer Creek,* though the canon continues six miles or more to the *Silver Lake Mine.* At Deer Creek, there is a little village with a comfortable inn and store, and a large collection of charcoal kilns. This business is quite large, there being ten pits of brick, which reduce each about 1,100 bushels of charcoal, for which the proprietor gets 25 cents per bushel,—a business of about $50,000 per year is done.

The Miller Mine has been estimated exceedingly rich, and is owned largely by New York capitalists, who work it steadily. It is said to yield, with lead, over fifty ounces of silver per ton. The American Fork Railroad was built originally to facilitate the carrying of ores, as well as the charcoal, but the grandeur of the scenery has given it a celebrity among tourists, far beyond that of any railroad in Utah.

At Deer Creek is a good hotel, The Mountain Glen House, and a lovely picnic grove, pure spring water, and for those of good wind and lovers of adventure,—an opportunity for mountain climbing.

The total length of the canon to this point, is 12 miles, and the total length of the railroad, is 16 miles,—cost about $400,000, and the most solidly built narrow gauge railroad in the United States. The total ascent in elevation for the whole railroad, is nearly 5,000 feet, and

10

SCENES IN AMERICAN FORK CANON.

1.—Mt. Aspinwall, or Lone Mountain. 2.—Rock Summits. 3.—Picnic Grove, Deer Creek.
4.—A quiet Glen. 5.—Hanging Rock. 6.—Rock Narrows.

the average grade of the railroad is 200 feet. The maximum grade is 296 feet. This is the steepest railroad grade in the United States, and the only grade over 200 feet ascended by a locomotive.

Tourists who have enjoyed so fine and glorious a ride up the canon hither, will perhaps expect that the return will be tame. They will be most pleasantly surprised and disappointed, for it is *the grandest of all railroad scenes they will ever witness*.

Detaching the locomotive from the train, the conductor stands at the little brake, and without a signal or help, the little cars of the train quietly start on their downward journey, alone. Gliding down with increasing speed, rounding the curves with grand and swinging motion, the breeze fanning your face, and the beautiful, pure mountain air stimulating your spirits to the highest limits of exhilaration, your feelings and body are in an intense glow of delight, as the rock scenes, crags and mountain heights come back again in all their sublimity, and your little car, securely held, glides swiftly down the beautiful valley. In no part of the country is there a scene to be compared with this. The entire being is fascinated, and when, at last, the little car turns swiftly into the broad plain, the tourist feels he has left behind him a land of delight. The little cars occupy but one hour in making the descent, and the writer has made the trip in forty minutes. This canon was first brought to the notice of the traveling public and pleasure travelers of the East, by the editor of "THE PACIFIC TOURIST," who conducted over it, in 1873, the first body of editors which had ever visited the locality. Since that time, its value as a road for mining purposes has become less valuable, yet the canon has become noted as a resort of grand and remarkable scenery.

NOTE.—Since the foregoing description was written, the railroad has been discontinued, but the tourist can visit it by horse from American Fork or Alta.

Lake Utah.—This beautiful sheet of water lies between the Oquirrh and Wahsatch Ranges of Mountains. These ranges and their foot hills come closely together between Drapersville and Lehi, and the River Jordan cuts through them there in a narrow gorge or canon. The lake and valley then suddenly burst upon the view of the traveler, and admiration grows into enthusiasm as he contemplates the lovely picture before him. The lake is about thirty miles long and six miles wide, is triangular in shape and composed of fresh water. Its elevation is about 4,482 feet, or nearly 300 feet greater than that of the Great Salt Lake. The railroad goes around the eastern side of the lake, turning an obtuse angle at or near Provo. The lake is fed by Provo River, American Fork, Hobble, Spanish Fork,

Peteetneet, Salt and a few other small creeks. Its outlet is the River Jordan which empties into Great Salt Lake, and supplies water for irrigating the numerous farms in its valley. As before stated the lake abounds in fish, and on its eastern and northern sides, has a large quantity of arable land. Its western shore is not very well watered, only one or two little creeks putting down into it from the Oquirrh Range of Mountains. It is well worthy of a visit from the tourist, or sportsman.

The Utah Western Railroad. — This road was first chartered on the 15th of June, 1874, with a capital stock of $800,000. The company is mostly composed of Utah men having their residence in Salt Lake City; John W. Young, a son of Brigham Young, being President, while Heber P. Kimball is Superintendent. The same year it was chartered, twelve miles were completed and opened for business on the 12th day of December, and, on the 1st of April, 1875, it was completed to Half-Way House, thirteen miles farther. An extension of fourteen miles is now under contract, which will doubtless be completed the present year. This last extension will take the road to within one and a half miles of Stockton, a prosperous mining town on the western slope of the Oquirrh Range of Mountains. Its business on twenty-five miles of completed road, for the year beginning February 10, 1875, and ending February 9, 1876, both days inclusive, was as follows: Freights received, 15,284,636 lbs.; freights forwarded, 5,276,619 lbs., one of the smelting works near Stockton, alone forwarding over 7,000,000 lbs. of bullion, ore, etc. The cash receipts for the same time were as follows: $49,186, and the operating expenses of the road, also, for the same period, were nearly $16,000. It is a narrow gauge road, (three feet) and has prospects for an extensive business in the future. Its general route is westward until it passes the southernmost point of the Great Salt Lake, and then southward, along the western base of the Oquirrh Range, and into the rich mining districts which have been developed on the western slope of those mountains. Leaving Salt Lake City, on a heavy downward grade of ninety-five feet to the mile, but which is short, the road crosses the River Jordan on a common pile bridge, and then over a barren sage brush country, until it reaches

Millstone Point.—near the base of the mountains, and 11 1-2 miles from Salt Lake City. This place is named from the fact that the first millstones used in grinding grain in Utah, were quarried from the mountains near this point. The old overland stage road from Salt Lake City to California passes along the line of the road, as does one line of the Western Union Telegraph Company, to the present terminus of the road. The station is of no partic-

THE OLD MILL, AMERICAN FORK CANON.

ular importance, and beyond the incident mentioned, is without a history. We are now at the base of the Oquirrh Range, and the first station of the Old Stage Company where they changed horses is pointed out to the traveler on the south side of the road. Beyond Millstone Point, about two miles on the south side of the track, is a large spring, which furnishes a good supply of water, and which has been utilized by a dairyman. A little beyond this spring on the same side of the track, there is, in the first point of rocks, quite an extensive cave which a shepherd uses as a shelter for his sheep, during the inclement season of the year. A rail fence with gate surrounds t h e entrance to the cave, and it is said to be large enough to turn a four horse team and wagon without difficulty. The extent of the outer part of the cave is about 40 feet, where a huge fallen rock precludes further access without inconvenience. The lake and its mountain islands, and the ranges beyond, now come grandly into view on the north side of the track. The next station is *Black Rock,* —17 1-2 miles from Salt Lake City,—a station named from a rock, dark enough to be called black, rising in the lake about 100 yards from the shore. It is nearly flat on the top, and with a little effort can be easily ascended. Jutting out from the shore, and a short distance from the station, is "Lion's Head" Rock. Beyond this is "Observation Point," from which the Goose Creek Mountains, 145 miles north, can be seen in a clear day, with their white peaks glistening in the sunlight. The northern point of the Oquirrh Range here comes close to the lake, and what seems to be a few scattering trees, or groves of trees, high up on the mountain, contain millions of feet of pine

LIONS HEAD ROCK.—GREAT SALT LAKE.

lumber, if it could only be made available. Right under "Observation Point," on the very edge of the lake shore stands a stone house, formerly kept as a hotel for pleasure seekers, but now the private property of John W. Young, Esq. Whoever occupies it hereafter, can very nearly be "rocked in the cradle of the deep," or, at least, be lulled to sleep by the murmur of the restless waves. Standing upon "Observation Point," before you, a little to the left, rises the rock from which the station is named; beyond and to the left still, Kimball's Island rises out of the sea twenty-two miles away; while off to the right is Church Island, 14 miles away: they do not look half the distance, but the rarified atmosphere of these elevated portions of the Continent is very deceptive as regards vision and distance. Promontory Point on the north shore of the lake is also visible at a distance of about eighty miles.

Lake Point, —20 miles from the city is the next station and the great resort for excursion parties and tourists in the summer. Near this station is "Giant's Cave" from which stalactites may be obtained, and other relics, said to be remains of Indians who were conquered and penned in until they died. A personal examination will satisfy the tourist as to the probable truth of this tradition. The company has a large hotel at Lake Point containing 35 rooms for guests, besides other necessary appurtenances to a good hotel. A wharf has been built into the lake, beside which, when not employed, the stern wheel steamer, "General Garfield," is moored. This steamer is employed for excursion parties and for transporting ore from the islands, and the west side of the lake, to the railroad. A bathing-house has been erected on the wharf, where conveniences for a salt water bath are kept. The waters of the lake are very dense, and it is almost impossible for bathers to sink. In former times three barrels of water would make by evaporation, one barrel of salt; now four barrels of water are required to effect the same result. A company has been organized in Salt Lake City, to manufacture salt from the waters of this lake near Millstone Point, and vats are to be erected the present year. An excellent quality can be made and sacked—ready for market for $1.50 per ton.

Half-Way House,—25 miles from Salt Lake City, and Tooele Station 37 miles are the next stations an l termini of the road. Grantville is one of the richest agricultural towns of Utah. Stages leave here for the mining camps on the western slope of the mountains, and a large amount of freighting is done with teams to and from the mines. The station will lose its importance as soon as the road passes beyond it. There are large springs of fresh water near the station, which supply a flouring mill and woolen factory with power. On the left side of the track, before you reach the station, is " E. T. City"—the initials being those of E. T. Benson, who was interested in the town. It is simply a settlement of Mormon farmers, nestled under the mountains. The woolen factory alluded to is a long, low stone structure, with approved modern machinery, about one and three-fourths miles from the station, north of the track. This route must prove very attractive to travelers, and one which will amply reward them in the pleasures it will afford. The rich mining districts of Rush Valley, Ophir and others, are reached by this line of road. The Hidden Treasure and other mines in these districts have already acquired a reputation and standing among the first mines in the country.

Social Life Among the Mormons.—Beyond the limits of Salt Lake City the uniform character of Mormon families is of exceeding plain ways of living, almost all being of very modest means, and even poor. What the better families have gained has been by the hardest and most persistent labor. It is said that when the city was first settled, there was not found over $1,000 in cash for the whole community, and for a long series of years thereafter money was little used, and the people lived and paid for their wants by barter, and a writer facetiously says : " A farmer wishes to purchase a pair of shoes for his wife. He consults the shoemaker, who avers his willingness to furnish the same for one load of wood. He has no wood, but sells a calf for a quantity of adobes, the adobes for an order on the merchant, payable in goods, and the goods and the order for a load of wood, and straightway the matron is shod.

" Seven water-melons purchased the price of a

ticket of admission to the theater. He paid for the tuition of his children, seventy-five cabbages per quarter. The dressmaker received for her services, four squashes per day. He settled his church dues in sorghum molasses. Two loads of pumpkins paid his annual subscription to the newspaper. He bought a ' *Treatise on Celestial Marriage*' for a load of gravel, and a bottle of soothing syrup for the baby, with a bushel of string beans."

In this way, before the advent of the railroad, fully nine-tenths of the business of the Mormon people was conducted. Now barter has given place to actual circulation of money.

While there is not what may be called distress or abject poverty in any part of the Mormon settlements, yet with many, especially the new emigrants, their means are so limited, and the labor so hard, it would be exceedingly discouraging to exist, but for the *grand confidence* all have in the joys to come promised by their religion and their leader.

Except in the cities there is little or no form of amusement, and the Sabbath is mainly the great day of reunion, when the population turn out *en masse* to the Tabernacle or other places of worship.

In the church services no one knows, until the speaker arises, who is to preach from the pulpit, or what may be the subject.

The subjects of sermons, addresses and exhortations are as wide as there are books. A writer has laughingly said : " In the Great Tabernacle, one will hear sermons, or advice on the culture of sorghum, upon infant baptism, upon the best manure for cabbages, upon the perseverance of the Saints, upon the wickedness of skimming milk before its sale, upon the best method of cleaning water ditches, upon bed-bug poison, upon the price of real estate, upon teething in children, upon the martyrs and persecutions of the Church, terrible denunciations of Gentiles and the enemies of the Mormons, upon olive oil as a cure for measles, upon the ordination of the priesthood, upon the character of Melchisedec, upon worms in dried peaches, upon abstinence from plug tobacco, upon the crime of fœticide, upon chignons, twenty-five-yard dresses, upon plural marriage, etc."

Portions of this are doubtless the extravagance of humor, yet it is true every possible thing, secular or spiritual, is discussed from the pulpit which the president thinks necessary for the instruction of the flock. We attended personally one Sunday a Sunday-school celebration in the Tabernacle, where the exercises were enlivened with a spirited delivery of " *Marco Bozarris.*" " *Gay You g Lochinvar,*" the singing of " Home, Sweet Home," and the gallery fronts were decorated with gay mottoes, of which there shone in great prominence, " *Utah's best crop, chil Iren.*"

REPRESENTATIVE MORMONS.

1.—W. Woodruff. 2.—John Taylor. 3.—Mayor Daniel H. Wells. 4.—W. H. Hooper. 5.—President Brigham Young.
6.—Orson Pratt. 7.—John Sharp. 8.—George Q. Cannon 9.—Orson Hyde.

The city Mormons are fond of the theater and dancing, and as their president is both the owner of the theater and its largest patron, the Saints consider his example highly judicious and exemplary, so the theater is crowded on all occasions. We were present, on one occasion, in 1869, when we witnessed over thirty of the children of one of the Mormons sitting in a row in the dress circle, and the private boxes filled with his wives. The most striking event of the evening was when one of the theatrical performers sung this ditty:

"If Jim Fisk's rat-and-tan, should have a bull-dog pup,
Do you think Louis Napoleon would try to bring him up?"

This elicited tremendous applause, and the performers, much to their own laughter and astonishment, had to repeat it.

A few years afterward, in witnessing a large body of Mormon children singing their school songs—we noticed the end of one of their little verses:

"Oh, how happy I ought to be,
For, daddy, I'm a Mormon."

As justifying their amusements, the Saints thus say, through one of their authorities:

" Dancing is a diversion for which all men and women have a natural fondness."

Dancing parties in the city are, therefore, quite frequent, and the most religious man is best entitled to the biggest amount of fun. Hence their religion should never be dull.

"As all people have a fondness for dramatic representations, it is well to so regulate and govern such exhibitions, that they may be instructive and purifying in their tendencies. If the best people absent themselves, the worst will dictate the character of the exercises."

Therefore every good Mormon, who can get a little money, indulges in the theater.

The Religion of the Mormons.—It is not the purpose of this *Guide* to express opinions of the religious aspect of Mormonism; but, as all visitors who come from the East, seeking either from curiosity to gain reliable information, or, having prejudices, expect to gratify them with outbursts of indignation, we can only stand aloof, and explain, calmly and candidly, a few facts as we have found them by actual contact and experience with both Mormons and Gentiles, and leave each reader to judge for himself the merits of this vexed question.

So thoroughly and implicitly have the masses of the Mormon people been led by their leader, that no one must be surprised to find that they are firm believers and obedient servants to all the doctrines and orders of the Church. *They believe just as they are told.*

Whatever, therefore, there is in their life, character and business, industry and enterprise, that is good and praiseworthy, to Brigham Young, their leader, belongs the credit. But for whatever there is wicked in their religion, life, faith,

deeds and church work—and for whatever is lacking in good, to the same powerful mind and willful hand, belongs the fearful responsibility.

Whether Mormonism be a religion or not—yet candor must confess, that if it fails to give and preserve peace, contentment, purity; if it makes its followers ignorant, brutal, superstitious, jealous, abusive, defiant; if it lack gentleness, meekness, kindness, courtesy; if it brings to its homes, sadness and discontent, it cannot be that *true religion*, which exists alone by sincere *trust in Christ* and *love for heaven.* If in all its doctrines, services, sermons, prayers, praise and church work, it fails to give the soul that seeks after rest, the refreshing, comforting peace it needs, it cannot be everlasting.

Mormonism has accomplished much in industry, and perseverance, in reclaiming Utah's waste lands and barren plains. It has opened a country, which now is teeming with riches inexhaustible and untold wealth is coming to a scene, once the very type of desolation. We give to the Mormons every worthy praise for their frugality, temperance and hard labor. No other class of people would have settled here. By patience they have reclaimed a desert,—peopled a waste, developed hidden treasures, have grown in thrift, and their lives bear witness to their forbearance, and complete trust and faith.

How The Mormon Church Influences Visitors.—The system of polygamy is not the only great question which affects the future of Utah. The more than all things else, it is the *Power of the Rulers of the Mormon Church.* It is natural that they should make efforts to maintain it by every use of power; gentleness if that will do the work, *coercion* if not.

It is unfortunate that in the spiritual services of the Church, they fail to impress visitors with proper respect. Their sermons, all eastern travelers have uniformly admitted, were remarkable in the absence of spiritual power. The simple truths of the Gospel rarely ever are discussed, the life of Christ, the Gospel of the New Testament, the "Sermon on the Mount"—the Cross are all ignored,—the Psalms of David, the life of Daniel, Solomon, and the work of the twelve Apostles are rarely referred to; instead, visitors are compelled to listen to long arguments justifying Mormonism and plural marriage, and expressions of detestation for their enemies.

We heard three of the elders talk at one of their Sabbath meetings, during which the name of Jesus Christ as the Saviour of the world, was scarcely mentioned. One talked of the wonderful conversion as he claimed, and baptism of some Lamanites (Indians), not one of whom today, can give a single intelligent reason for the course he has adopted. Another told of the time he was a local preacher in the East, of the Methodist Church, and of the trials and persecution they had endured there. The third was quite belligerent in tone, and gave utterance to what might possibly be interpreted as treasonable sentiments against the government of the United States. In the meantime the audience accepted all that was said with apparent relish. We thought of the saying of one of the popular humorists of the day, to the effect that " *if that kind of preaching suits that kind of people, it is just the kind of preaching that kind of people likes.*" Their preachers will often take a text from the sayings of the prophets, and give it a literal interpretation that would grate harshly upon orthodox ears, while the listener would be amused at the ingenuity displayed in twisting the word of God—making it mean anything desired.

It is exceedingly unfortunate for the cause of the Mormons, that such exhibitions of nature are made, the only result of which is to increase the prejudice of all visitors, and tend to gradually change the minds of those who would gladly be cordial, but feel they can not. We speak in candor; the efficacy of a religion is judged by its purity of life and speech. A true religion wins admiration from even its enemies. But Mormonism seems never to have made a friend of an enemy, and only returns even deeper resentment.

A religion which does not do as Christ commanded, " *Pray for them which persecute you, bless and curse not,*"—but treasures its resentments and fulminates its curses continually—can it be any religion at all ?

Inconsistencies. — Another circumstance, one very unfortunate for the Mormons, and always noticed by strangers, is the inconsistency of their history.

In the original revelation to Joseph Smith, there was not only no mention of polygamy, but in the Book of Mormon, such a practice was fiercely denounced. In the second chapter of the Book of Mormon, there originally appeared this warning to the Nephites:

" *Wherefore, hearken unto the word of the Lord, for there shall not any man among you have save it be one wife; and concubines he shall have none; for I the Lord God, delighteth in the chastity of woman.*"

The following comments and arguments based on the above, seem absolutely necessary, and impossible for any one to controvert:

1. *If Joseph Smith wrote this under the inspiration of the Holy Spirit, then present Mormon practices and doctrines, being wholly different, are not true nor worthy of confidence.*

2. *If Joseph Smith did not write this under the inspiration of the Almighty, then Joseph Smith did not receive a true revelation, was not a true Prophet, and what he has written has been entirely unworthy the confidence of his people.*

3. *If Mormonism since then has found a new*

revelation *totally opposed to the first, then the first must have been false.*

4. *If the first revelation was false, then the Book of Mormon is wholly false and unreliable, and Joseph Smith was an impostor.*

5. *If the first revelation was true, then (as the decrees of the Almighty once given, never change), the second revelation is not true, nor ever was inspired by God.*

6. *As History proves that Joseph Smith received and promulgated both the first and second revelations—as one of these must be false—as no Prophet could ever be falsely led, if instructed by the Almighty—it follows that Joseph Smith never received a true inspiration, was not a true Prophet—that Mormonism is not a revealed religion.*

Another inconsistency, fatal to the claims of the Mormon religion, is the curious act of Joseph Smith at Nauvoo. On the 12th of July, 1843, Smith received the new revelation. When it was first mentioned, it caused great commotion, and many rebelled against it. A few elders attempted to promulgate it, but so fierce was the opposition that at last, for peace, Smith officially made public proclamation *against it* in the Church paper as follows:

NOTICE.—As we have lately been credibly informed that an elder of the Church of Jesus Christ of Latter Day Saints, by the name of Hiram Brown, has been preaching polygamy and other false and corrupt doctrines in the County of Lapeer and State of Michigan,

This is to notify him, and the Church in general, that he has been cut off from the Church for his iniquity, and he is further notified to appear at the special conference on the 6th of April next, to make answer to these charges.

JOSEPH SMITH, } *Presidents of the Church.*
HYRUM SMITH, }

QUERY.—*What is the world to think of a religion, or a people, when their Prophet falsifies his own record, and denies his own revelation?*

Subsequent history shows that in less than three years from the publication of the above notice, the Mormon leaders were living in open and undisguised polygamy.

Would a Prophet who ever received a true revelation deny it, punish his followers for observing it, and then practice it for himself?

How appropriately the answer is given to this question when one takes up the Mormon Hymn Book, and finds among its verses, used in their church services, the following leading lines:

1. " The God that others worship is not the God for me."
2. " A church without a Prophet is not the church for me."
3. " A church without Apostles is not the church for me."
4. " The hope that Gentiles cherish is not the hope for me."
" It has no faith nor knowledge; far from it I would be."
5. " The heaven of sectarians is not the heaven for me."

The New Route to Montana and the Yellowstone, The Utah Northern R. R.

This new railroad has been lately pushed rapidly northward toward Montana. Upwards of 300 miles are expected to be finished this year.

VIEW OF GREAT SALT LAKE, FROM THE WAHSATCH MOUNTAINS.

BY THOMAS MORAN.

THE PACIFIC TOURIST.

155

Up-n this road are several points of very great interest, worth the special visit of tourists for one or two days. The road after leaving Ogden runs for a number of miles close to the foot of the Wahsatch Mountains. On its way it passes a Sulphur Spring where arises a dense cloud of vapor. The road gradually rises above the valley upward to the mountain range, giving grand views of the Great Salt Lake, and its islands, with the orchards and grain fields below. A backward look reveals the glories of the mountains. Reaching the *Summit*, there is a glorious view of an interior valley of the Bear River, with its villages and distant views of canons and peaks. The road then descends rapidly into the Cache Valley. The land is remarkably rich and well irrigated. Near Logan is a high plateau 300 feet above the town whence a fine view of the valley is obtained, and over fourteen villages seen, surrounded with a series of mountains capped with snow. The scene is most picturesque. Near Oneida and 30 miles distant are the famous *Soda Springs of Idaho*, which can now be reached by stage. A place where most remarkable cures have been effected. For tourists to the *Yellowstone*, this is now the *only available route*, saving over 300 miles horseback riding from any other point.

The Great Salt Lake.

In many respects this is the most wonderful body of water on the American Continent. It is the chief object of interest in the physical geography of the great basin in which it is located. Its waters are saline and brackish, unfit for use, and uninhabited by representatives of the finny tribes.

Its Discovery.—In his report on this lake, Captain Stansbury speaks of a French explorer, with an unpronounceable name, who left the western shores of the great lakes sometime in the seventeenth century, and proceeded westward for an undefined period, and made extensive discoveries on the Mississippi, Missouri, and other western rivers, and either saw, or heard from the Indians, of the Great Salt Lake. All accounts, however, are somewhat mixed, and not at all satisfactory. It is reported that John Jacob Astor fitted out an expedition, in 1820, to cross the Continent, meet a vessel he had sent round Cape Horn, and at some point on the Pacific Coast, form a town which should be to it what New York was to the Atlantic Coast, the greatest commercial emporium of that part of the country. This expedition, it is said, crossed the Rocky Mountains, near Fremont's Peak in the Wind River Range, and after reaching the Tetons separated into small parties, each one exploring on its own account. One of these, consisting of four men and commanded by a Mr. Miller, hunted around the vicinity of Snake River and

the Soda Springs, finally crossing into Cache Valley, a little north-west of Corinne. It is further reported that Miller, in one of his rambles, ascended the mountains south of this valley, and here, for the first time, beheld the waters of the great inland sea spread out before him. He returned to his party, and with them proceeded to the lake, and on further inspection concluded it was an arm of the ocean. This was its first discovery by white men. The next recorded visitation is that of John Bedyer, in 1825, and the next was by Captain Bonneville, in 1831, who saw it from the Red Buttes in the Wahsatch Range, and whose account was written up by Washington Irving. In 1832, Captain Walker first attempted to explore it with a party of forty men. He traveled around the northern and western boundaries, but was compelled to abandon the undertaking for want of water for his animals and men. Captain Stansbury afterwards explored it, and his report contains the only reliable information concerning this remarkable lake that has been published from official sources, though subsequent observation has revealed many facts and phenomenon concerning it which would be highly interesting if they could be collected and given to the world in tangible form. General Fremont also visited this lake, and has given some information about it.

Analysis.—The only analysis of its waters that we have been able to obtain is that given by Dr. Gale and recorded in Captain Stansbury's report. We quote: " It gives the specific gravity, 1.170; solid contents, 22.422 out of 100 parts. The solid contents when analyzed gave the following components:

Chloride of sodium,	20.196
Sulphate of soda,	1.834
Chloride of magnesium,	0.252
Chloride of Calcium, a trace.	
	22.282
Loss,	0.140
	22.422

A remarkable thing about this analysis is that the specific gravity, as here given, corresponds exactly with the mean of eight different analyses of the waters of the Dead Sea of Palestine, which is largely above that of the water of the ocean. This analysis reveals what is now generally known, that here is a source from which salt enough can be obtained to supply the Continent. When it is considered, however, that all the streams flowing into this lake are fresh water, draining the water-shed of a large area of country, and discharging from the springs, melting snows and rains of the great basin, an immense volume of water, the puzzling question very naturally arises as to the source of this abundant supply of saline matter. The various saline incrustations, however, at various points on the surrounding shores, indicate clearly that some portion of the earth is saturated with this ingredient. Still this lake is without any visible outlet, and with all the great influx of fresh water, annually, why does it remain so salty? The inference naturally follows that it washes some vast bed of rock salt or saline deposit in the bottom of the lake, hitherto undiscovered. Without facts, given at 4,851 this is a supposition which may or may not be true. The shores of this lake, especially toward the city bearing the same name, have now been settled nearly thirty years, and it would be strange indeed if the changes which have been gradually going on in this lake should not have been noticed. The elevation of the lake is given at 4,200 feet above the level of the sea. The elevation of Salt Lake City is given at 4,351 feet above the sea—difference of 151 feet. The figures here given as the elevation of the lake, we think, are based upon observations and calculations made several years ago, perhaps by Captain Stansbury. The observation of the old settlers is, that it is not correct—that the lake is from ten to fifteen feet higher now than it was in 1850, and that in proportion as the water rises it becomes less salty. Reliable citizens have informed us that in 1850, three barrels of water evaporated would make one of salt; now, four barrels of water are required for the same result. This fact leads to the opinion that the humidity of the atmosphere in this region of the Continent is increasing—in consequence of which there is less evaporation—evaporation being greater and more rapid in a dry than in a moist atmosphere—and the failure of evaporation to take up the surplus waters discharged into this lake has not only increased its volume and extent, but lessened its saline character. Since the settlement of this Territory, there has been a great increase of rain-fall, so much so that it is noticed and remarked upon by very many of the inhabitants, and the belief is very generally entertained that the Territory is gradually undergoing a great climatic change.

Speculations as to the Result.—The evaporation of the water in the lake growing gradually less, it will, of course, continue to rise and overflow its banks in the lowest places, but no fears need be entertained for the safety of any considerable portion of the country, or the inhabitants thereof. Notice the elevation of Salt Lake City, as herein given, being about 151 feet greater than the lake itself. If the rise continues it will be slower as the covered surface of the adjoining land becomes greater, on the principle that the larger end of a vessel fills more slowly with the same stream, than the smaller end. If it reaches a height of 15 or 20 feet above its present surface, it will first overflow a low, sandy and alkali desert on its western shore, nearly as large as the lake itself. In this case, its evaporating capacity will be nearly doubled in extent—a fact which will operate to retard

its rise. But if it continues to rise in th' years to come until it must have an outlet to the ocean, that outlet will be the Humboldt River, and a cut of 100 feet or less in the low hills of the divide, will give it. When, however, this event transpires, it will be—unless some convulsion of nature intervenes to hasten it—after the last reader of this book shall have finished his earthly labors and been quietly laid away to rest.

Boundaries and Extent.—Looking from Observation Point at the south end of the lake, to the north, it seems to be pretty well divided. Promontory Mountains on Antelope Island, those on Stansbury Island and Oquirrh Mountains are evidently parts of the same range—running from north to south, parallel with the Wahsatch Range. Their continuity is only broken by the waters in the lake or sink of the great basin. Promontory Mountains divide the northern end of the lake into two parts, or arms, the eastern being called Bear River Bay, and the western, Spring Bay—the latter being considerably the largest. The lake has numerous islands, both large and small. Fremont Island lies due west of the mouth of Weber River, and is plainly visible from the cars of the Utah Central Railroad. South of it and nearest to Salt Lake City, is Antelope Island. West of Antelope, and north-west from Lake Point, is Stansbury Island. A little north-west of this, is Carrington Island. North of these still, and in the western part of the lake are Hat, Gunnison and Dolphin Islands. Nearly south of Gunnison Island is a high promontory jutting out into the lake called Strong's Knob ; it is a prominent landmark on the western shore of the lake. Travelers on the Central Pacific Road can obtain a fine view of this great inland sea, near Monument Station. The extreme length of the lake is about 80 miles, and its extreme width, a little south of the 41st parallel of latitude, is about 50 miles. Promontory Mountains project into the lake from the north about 30 miles. Nearly all the islands we have named are rich in minerals, such as copper, silver, gold and iron. Excellent quarries of slate have also been opened, but neither it nor the mines have been developed to any great extent, because of the want of capital.

Incidents and Curiosities.—When Colonel Fremont first explored the lake in 1843, it is related by Jessie, his wife, that when his boat first touched the shore of Fremont Island, an oarsman in the bow of the boat was about to jump ashore, when Kit Carson, the guide, insisted that Colonel Fremont should first land and name the island,—"Fremont Island."

Tonic Properties.—A bath in the water of the Great Salt Lake, is one of the greatest delights a tourist can seek. We have personally indulged in its pleasure, and it is beyond question a splendid recreation. Upon the wharf near Lake Point, is a cozy bathing-house, wherein are bathing-suits, and large tubs filled with fresh water; donning the suits, you descend the steps and jump into the water. You are surprised at the buoyancy of it. The most vigorous effort and plunge will not keep your body under the surface. Clasping your hands and feet in the water, you can sit on its bosom with head and shoulders projecting above the surface,—and even then for but a short period, as the buoyancy of the water soon has a tendency to tip you over on your side. It is impossible to stand erect in the water, no matter how straight or rigid you place your limbs,—in a moment over goes your head, and up come your feet. Lying on your back, or side, or face, in any position—still you will always keep at the surface. But beyond this curious feature of impossibility of sinking, there is the better quality of the *toning and invigorating properties of the bath.* These are beyond all question, the finest of any spring along the Overland Route. In some warm summer day, take your bath in the lake,—spend, say half an hour in its water, and then returning to your bath-house, cleanse your skin from all saline material, which may adhere, by plentiful ablutions of pure water from the tubs, wash the hair and face thoroughly, then dress and walk up and down the wharf, or the cool piazza of the hotel,—and you are astonished at the wonderful amount of strength and invigoration given to your system, and with greater elasticity than ever you have possessed before, it seems like the commencement of a new life. Invalids should never fail to visit this lake, and enjoy its bath. Tourists who omit it,—will leave behind them the greatest curiosity of the Overland Tour, and it is no great effort of the imagination to conceive this fully the rival of the great ocean in all that can contribute to the attractions of sea-shore life. The cool breeze and delicious bath are all here.

In the summer time the excursion rates from Salt Lake City, are $1.50 per ticket, which includes passage both ways over the Utah Western Railroad, a ride on the steamer on the lake, and the privilege of a bath,—the cheapest and most useful enjoyment in the entire Territory.

The only life in or near the lake, is seen in the summer time by immense masses of little insects (*astemia fertiliso*,) which live on the surface of the lake, and thrive on its brine. These masses stretch out in curious forms over the surface. Sometimes, when small, they appear like a serpent, at other times like rings, globes, and other irregular figures. A gentle breeze will never disturb them, for their presence keeps the water a dead calm as if oil had been poured upon it. If disturbed by a boat passing through the mass, millions of little gnats or flies arise and swarm all over the vessel—anything but agreeable. Professor Spencer M. Baird, of the

Smithsonian Institute, Washington, believes the lake may yet sustain fish and other animal life. There seems to be plenty of insect food always on the surface,—occasionally with high winds, the surface of the lake is driven into waves, which dashing against the shore, shower the sage brushes near with salty incrustations, which, when dried in the sunlight, give a bright, glittering and pearly appearance, often furnishing splendid specimens for mineral cabinets.

Atmosphere.—The atmosphere which surrounds the lake, is a curiosity, always bluish and hazy—from the effects of the active evaporation, —in decided contrast to the purity and transparency of the air elsewhere. Surveyors say that it is difficult to use telescopes, and astronomical observations are imperfect.

The solid ingredients of the water have six and one-half times the density of those of the ocean, and wherever washed upon the shore, the salt dried, after evaporation, can be easily shoveled up into buckets and bags.

Burton describes a beautiful sunset scene upon the lake. "We turned our faces eastward as the sun was declining. The view had memorable beauties. From the blue and purple clouds, gorgeously edged with celestial fire, shot up a fan of penciled and colored light, extending halfway to the zenith, while in the south and southeast lightnings played among the darker mist masses, which backed the golden and emerald bench-lands of the farther valley. The splendid sunset cast a reflex of its loveliness upon the alkaline barrens around us. Opposite rose the Wahsatch Mountains, vast and voluminous, in stern and gloomy grandeur, northward the thin white vapors rising from the hot springs, and the dark swells of the lake."

The Great Desert West of Salt Lake City.—The overland stage, which traversed westward, followed a route immediately south of Salt Lake, and passed for several hundred miles through a desert, beside which the Humboldt Valley had no comparison in tediousness and discomfort. Captain Stansbury, an early explorer, in describing this section, describes large tracts of land covered with an incrustation of salt:

"The first part of the plains consisted simply of dried mud, with small crystals of salt scattered thickly over the surface; crossing this, we came upon another portion of it, three miles in width, where the ground was entirely covered with a thin layer of salt in a state of deliquescence, and of so soft consistence, that the feet of our mules sank at every step into the mud beneath. But we soon came upon a portion of the plains where the salt lay in a solid state, in one unbroken sheet, extending apparently to its western border. So firm and strong was this unique and snowy floor, that it sustained the weight of our entire train without in the least giving way, or cracking beneath the pressure.

Our mules walked upon it as upon a sheet of solid ice. The whole field was crossed by a network of little ridges, projecting about half an inch, as if the salt had expanded in the process of crystallization. I estimated this field to be, at least, seven miles wide and ten miles in length. The salt which was very pure and white, averaged from one-half to three-quarters of an inch in thickness, and was equal in all respects to our finest specimen for table use. Assuming these data, the quantity that here lay upon the ground in one body, exclusive of that already dissolved,—amounted to over 4,500,000 cubic yards, or about 100,000,000 bushels," And even this small area, is but a very little portion of the whole region, farther northward and westward.

The Wonders of Montana.

This new territory possesses very many remarkable features of wonderful scenery, agricultural wealth and mineral richness. In a few years it will be as famous and popular as Colorado.

Its Indian name is *Tay-a-he-shock-up,* or " *Country of the Mountains.*" To a larger extent than any Western Territory it is traversed by great rivers. The Missouri and Columbia with all their tributaries each possess nearly 2,000 miles of water, largely navigable within its borders.—and with the Yellowstone, any of them are larger than the Ohio River at Pittsburgh. Probably no state in America is as finely watered. The valleys of these rivers are wonderfully beautiful, usually a dozen miles in width or more, and all arable land. Were the fertile land of Montana placed by itself, it would form a country four miles wide and 4,000 long.

In addition to these valley lands, the sloping sides of the mountains are the natural home for grazing immense herds of cattle. The grass land and pastures of the Territory, being more famous in richness than any Territory of the Union.

The climate is very mild, although never as warm as in territories farther south, yet far more even and equable. In winter constant sunshine. The snow-fall is not as large as Michigan or Minnesota, and by actual test, the number of fine days in one year was 291,—or 100 more than the average of Chicago or Philadelphia. The average winter temperature is from 25° to 44°, which being in a dry climate is equal to that of 35° to 55° in an Eastern State. The average temperature for a year is 48°. The highest extreme of heat for six years was 94°—and lowest 19°—which is less than any Eastern State,—while the spring season opens a month earlier than at Omaha

These peculiarities of climate are due to the influence of the mildness of the winds of the Pacific Ocean, which blow across Oregon, and

up the valley of the Columbia, and so moderate the climate of this region that, while most northern in location, yet it is equal in mildness to one nearly 1,000 miles south. There are 16,000,000 acres of land suited for culture and less than 500,000 occupied, the last crops bringing about $3,000,000 in value.

The Territory is 550 miles long, east and west, and 300 miles wide from north to south. It is three times the size of New York, twice the size of the whole of New England, and will more than take Ohio and Indiana together within its borders.

Stock raising in Montana is attended with the greatest ease. A $30 Montana steer, costs but $3 to raise,—and while the mines continue to increase in productiveness, the demand for all farm and dairy products will be very great.

Montana is filled full with riches of gold, silver, iron, lead, copper, etc. Coal is extremely abundant. The entire mineral yield of the Territory to the present time is $145,000,000.

The financial condition is extremely lucrative. The average wealth of the people is $450, for every man, woman and child—the highest of any Western Territory. Its entire productions last year were $16,000,000. The freight, etc., paid for merchandise passing to and from its principal cities exceeded $10,000,000. The transportation business is immense, giving employment to over 2,500 wagons, 8,500 animals, 1,400 men, and an invested capital of $1,500,000, and the imports and exports exceed yearly 800,000,000 pounds or 40,000 tons. Employment is abundant, living cheap, no one is poor—for a *Poor Man's Paradise,* there is no home like one in Montana.

The average elevation of the Territory is 4,000 feet above the sea,—half that of Colorado. It is unlike Utah or Nevada, in that the country is *always green,* while the others are dry most of the year.

Helena City,—is about 500 miles north from Ogden, and has a population of 5,000. Its taxable wealth is $2,000,000—a beautiful city. Its business is very large. The three banks often exceed transactions of $300,000 per day. Several grocery firms each do business of over one million dollars per annum, and *half a million dollars* are paid for freight coming here.

Virginia City,—has about 1,000 inhabitants—elevation, 5,713 feet—very enterprising. A beautiful spring upon the mountain side flows through pipes into the place, which is there supplied at no cost to the people, who improve its use for pretty flower gardens and fruit farms. It is the principal outfitting place for the Yellowstone Park, distant 100 miles. A fine wagon road extends the entire distance.

Bozeman—is beautifully located, surrounded by mountains abruptly rising above the valley. Population 900, has many elegant residences.

THE PACIFIC TOURIST. 159

From here is an excellent route to the Yellowstone Park, about 75 miles away. Near Bozeman also are other places of attraction to tourists: *Mystic Lake*, distance 14 miles ; *Lund's Hot Springs*, eight miles ; *Rock Canyon*, five miles ; Bridger Canyon, three miles; Bear Canyon and Lakes, six miles ; Hunter's Hot Springs on the Yellowstone, 47 miles ; Middle Creek Falls and Canyon, 15 miles ; Mount Blackmore, 30 miles.

The mountains around are *The Sportsman's Home*, full of large game, and streams are crowded with trout.

The Deer Lodge Springs—are the principal Health Resort. Here are 40 springs, iron, soda, iodine, grouped together, with temperature of 115° to 150°.

The Central Pacific Railroad.

The record of the building of the Central Pacific Railroad is a description of one of the greatest trials of courage and faith the world has ever seen, and the actual results are, beyond doubt, the greatest marvel in engineering science, ever known in the United States. The heroic strength of character, the magnificent power and endurance, the financial intrepidity and the bold daring which defied all obstacles, overcame all difficulties, and literally shoved the mountains aside to make room for their pathway, are not equaled by any other achievement of the century. If ever an American can feel and express just admiration, it is to those *Samsons of the Pacific Coast*, who have hewn their way with the ponderous strength of their arms, and with invincible fortitude opened to the world the treasures of industry in the mountains and valleys of the Far West and the Pacific Coast. To one man, more than all others, is due the credit for the conception, survey and actual beginning of the great Trans-Continental Line. Theodore D. Judah—yet he did not live to see the completion of the railroad up the Sierras—and his successor Mr. S. S. Montague carried it through with great energy and success, and to them the nation and all California owe a debt of gratitude.

For years this brave and accomplished engineer had the subject of the road in his mind. It occupied his thoughts by day and was the subject of his dreams by night. The idea took a firm hold upon him, and he became completely absorbed in it. It energized his whole being and he was persistent and hopeful to the end. Sacramento, then a much smaller place than now, was the home of C. P. Huntington and Mark Hopkins, the former now Vice-President and the latter now Treasurer of the company, then hardware merchants under the firm name of Huntington & Hopkins. Their store became the headquarters of the little company that used to meet Judah there and talk over the enterprise. Judah's ideas were clear, his plans seemed practicable and his enthusiasm was contagious. The men who associated with him were led to make contributions for the purpose of partial payment toward a preliminary survey, and, in 1860, Judah and his assistants wandered over the gorges and canons of the Sierra Nevadas in search of a line for a railroad. The results of his summer's work were in every way encouraging—so much so that other contributions and subscriptions were obtained for work the following year. The summer of 1861 again found Judah and his party in the mountains. The work of the previous year was extended and further examination renewed the hope of the engineer and quickened the zeal of his followers. Success was certain if they could only enlist capital in the enterprise.

But right here was the difficulty. While the great majority of the people of California believed that the road would be built some day—it would not be done in their time. Some generation in the future might accomplish it, but it would be after they were all dead. The subject was broached in Congress, and finally, in 1862, the bill was passed. Huntington and Judah went to Washington with maps and charts, and rendered invaluable assistance to the friends of the measure in both houses of Congress, and the day of its passage was the day of their triumph. The news was sent to California with lightning speed, and caused great rejoicing among the people. The beginning of the end could now distinctly be seen. Though great difficulties had been surmounted, a comparatively greater one lay in the way. Capital which is proverbially timid, must now be enlisted in the enterprise. Forty miles of road must be built and accepted by the government, before the aid could be secured. Finally, with what local help they could get, and the assistance of New York capitalists and bankers, the work was begun at Sacramento, and the first section carried the line high up toward the summit of the Sierras. Their financial agents in New York, put their bonds on the market, and the funds for the further extension of the road were rapidly forthcoming. Leland Stanford, then as now President of the company, inaugurated the work at Sacramento, and also drove the silver spike, which completed the union of the two roads at Promontory on the 10th day of May, 1869. The progress of the road during each year, from the time of its commencement until its completion, is given as follows : In the years 1863-4-5, the company completed 20 miles each year. This might be called preliminary work. They were learning how, and their severest difficulties were to be overcome. In 1866 they built 30 miles, and the next year 46 miles. Now the rivalry between the two great corporations may be said to have commenced in earnest. In 1868, they built 364, and in 1869, up to May 10th, they closed the gap with 191 miles.

*Difficulties, Discouragements and La-
bor.*—Few travelers realize, as they pass so
easily and pleasantly over this railroad,—what is
represented by these long, smoothly-laid rails,
nor do they know of the early days of labor, and
intense energy.

Everything of every description of supplies had
to be shipped by water from New York, *via* Cape
Horn—to San Francisco, and then inland to
Sacramento. Thus months of delay occurred in
obtaining all needful material.

Even when the project was under full discussion at the little office in Sacramento, where gathered the six great brains which controlled the
destiny of the enterprise, (these were Governor
Leland Stanford, C. P. Huntington, Mark Hopkins, Charles Crocker, E. B. Crocker, and T.
D. Judah), everybody predicted its failure, and
few or none looked for its success. Very little
was known of the country it was to traverse,—and
that not satisfactory, and one prophesied that
this, the western end of the Great Trans-Continental Railroad, would be run up into the
clouds, and left in eternal snows.

Scores of friends approached Huntington in
those days and said, *" Huntington, don't go into
it; you will bury your whole fortune in the Sierra
Nevadas."*

Outsiders called it, after the first 40 miles were
built, *" The Dutch Flat Swindle; "* and the project was caricatured, abused by the newspapers,
derided by politicians, discountenanced by capitalists, and the credit of every one was impaired
who was connected with it.

Thus nobly did the Californians help this the
greatest enterprise of the State, and how much
more noble have they since been !

In a speech before the Senate Committee of
Congress by C. P. Huntington, he says:

" I suppose that it is a fact, the mercantile
credit of my partners in business and myself, was
positively injured by our connection with this
enterprise.

"The difficulties which confronted us then, are
now nearly forgotten, but they were intensely
vivid and real then. There were difficulties from
end to end; difficulties from high and steep
mountains; from snows; from deserts where
there was scarcity of water, and from gorges and
flats where there was an excess ; difficulties from
cold and from heat, from a scarcity of timber
and from obstructions of rock ; difficulties in
supplying a large force on a long line ; from Indians and want of laborers."

Of the princely subsidies voted by the United
States in its government bonds to aid the road—
what was the real case? From the individual
and private means of the five capitalists, they
were compelled to support a force of 800 men
one year—at their own risks—build 40 miles
before they were entitled to the government
bonds, and then were eleven months delayed in

receiving what was their due. To build the first
section of the road to the mountains, they were
obliged to call in private means, which out on
loan was yielding them two per cent. interest in
gold, per month—invest in the road and wait
for reimbursement. When the government
bonds were at last received, they vested into
gold at the high rate of premium then prevailing, (often taking $2 in bonds to buy $1.00 in
gold) to pay for labor and expense of construction, which, too, were excessively high for gold
prices.

The personal dangers of the builders were
great. The very surveyors ran the risk of being
killed by Indians, and some of them were; the
grading parties, at times, could only work under
military guard ; at all times all the track-layers
and the train hands had to be armed, and even
after construction the trains were often attacked.

The first 100 miles was up a total ascent of
7,000 feet, requiring the most skillful engineering and expenditures of vast sums of money in
excavation. At the height of 5,000 feet, the snow
line was reached, and 40 miles of snow galleries
had to be erected, at an additional expense of
$20,000 to $30,000 per mile, and for a mile or
more, in many places, these must be made so
strong that avalanches might pass over them and
yet preserve the safety of the track. Even after
passing the Sierras, the railroad descended into
a vast plain, dry, sere and deserted, where there
was not a sign of civilized life, nor any fuel.
For over 000 miles of the route, there was not a
single white inhabitant. For over 100 miles at a
stretch, no water could be found for either man
or machinery; and, even at the present day, in
many places the railroad company is obliged to
bring its water in artificial pipes for distances of
one to fifteen miles for the use of the engines.

Labor was almost impossible to get, and when
attained was almost impossible to control, until
the Chinese arrived, and to them is due the real
credit of the greatest help the road possessed.
Powder was one of the heaviest items of expense, which before the rise in prices of the war,
could have been had for $2.25 per keg—but then
was obtained with difficulty at $5.00. Locomo-
tives, cars, tools, all were bought at double prices.
Rails, now worth but $10.00 to $50.00 per ton,
then cost $80.00 to $150.00.

Every bar of iron and every tool had first to
be bought and started on a sea voyage round
Cape Horn, some four or six months before it
was needed.

Insurance on the sea voyages rose from 2 1-2
to 10 per cent.—freights increased from $18.00 to
$45.00 per ton.

Of the engineering difficulties of the construction on the Sierras, none can form a possible idea. A culvert would be built, the beginning of which was on the grade, while the other
end would be 50 feet or more below. At another

place is a bank 80 to 100 feet in height, covering a culvert 250 feet in length, then comes a bridge leaping a chasm of 150 feet in depth.

Next a cut of hardest granite, where, in the short space of 250 feet, would be working 30 carts and 250 workmen, thick as bees—while a little beyond is an embankment built up 80 feet, from whose top you can look down 1,000 feet.

The famous Summit Tunnel is 1,659 feet in length, cut through solid granite, and for a mile on either side there are rock cuttings of the most stupendous character, and the railroad is cut directly in the face of a precipice. The powder bill alone for one month was $54,000. Blasting was done three times per day, and sometimes of extraordinary execution. A hole of eight feet was once drilled and fired, and 1,440 yards of granite were thrown clear from the road-bed. Several more holes of same depth were drilled into a seam in the rock, which were lightly loaded and exploded until a large fissure was opened, when an immense charge was put in, set off, and 3,000 tons of granite went whirling down the mountain, tearing up trees, rocks, etc., with fearful havoc. One rock, weighing 70 pounds, was blown one-third of a mile away from its bed, while another of 240 pounds was blown entirely across Donner Lake, a distance of two-thirds of a mile. At one place, near Donner's Backbone, the railroad track is so constructed that it describes a curve of 180°, and runs back on the opposite side of the ridge only a few feet parallel to the course it has followed to the point, all at a grade of 90 feet to the mile.

But it is impossible to tell all the wonders of engineering, or the feats of skill; let active eyes watch the scene as the traveler passes over the railroad, and then give due credit and admiration to the pluck, skill, persistence and faith which has accomplished so much, and been productive of so much good.

The little beginning, in 1860, has now given place to the most astonishing enterprise of modern times. The pay-roll of the Central Pacific Railroad Company now exceeds 7,000 names of employes. The Southern Pacific Railroad, another grand enterprise, controlled in part by some of the same company, is building its road rapidly, with a force of 5,000 men, toward the fields of Arizona and New Mexico. All the important railroads and steamboats of California are now controlled by these gigantic corporations, and from the latest reports we quote figures of this financial capital of the greatest corporations in the United States:

CENTRAL PACIFIC RAILROAD COMPANY.

Capital stock actually paid in,	$54,275,500
Funded debt,	53,069,095
United States subsidy bonds,	27,855,680
Land grants of 11,722,400 acres at $2.50,	29,306,000
Value of lands in San Francisco, Oakland, and Sacramento,	7,750,000
Total value,	$172,256,275

SOUTHERN PACIFIC RAILROAD COMPANY.

Authorized capital stock.	$90,000,000
First mortgage bonds, authorized,	46,000,000
12,000,000 acres land grants, at $2 50,	30,000,000
Total value Southern Pacific Railroad Company,	$166,000,000
Total capital of Central Pacific and Southern Pacific Railroads,	$338,256,275
Number miles constructed and in operation by Central Pacific Railroad,	1,213
Number miles built and being built by Southern Pacific Railroad,	1,160

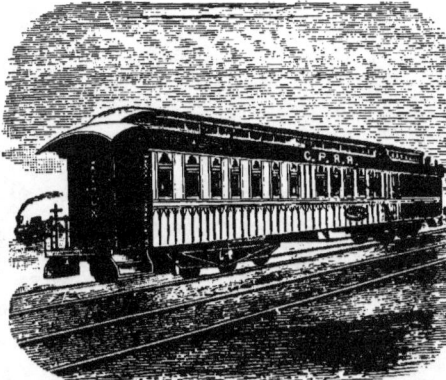

SILVER PALACE CAR, C. P. R. R.

Westward to San Francisco.

Travelers from the East, after dining at Ogden and having an hour in which to re-check their baggage, will board a train of silver palace cars belonging to the Central Pacific, in the evening, as the trains now run, and will soon be whirling away across the Great American Desert. As we pass out of the suburbs of Ogden, we cross Ogden River on a pile bridge, and leave it to pursue its turbulent way to the lake. We soon arrive at the point of junction before alluded to, but find no magnificent hotel, or other buildings, or any evidence of any. "Union Junction" is therefore a myth, and exists only in the fertile imagination. The land, such as it is, however, is there, and we soon pass the steaming Hot Springs on the right of the road and close to the track. These springs are said to be both iron

11

and sulphur, and from the red sediment which has been deposited over quite an area of surface near by, we judge that the iron springs predominate. Since leaving Weber Canon we have come nearly north and will continue in that direction until we approach Corinne. On our right are the towering peaks of the Wahsatch in close proximity. On our left are the irrigating ditches that supply the farms with water, an increasing growth of underbrush off toward the lake, and Fremont's Island in the distance with a towering rock, looking like a huge castle, upon one extremity of it. We soon pass a little town called North Ogden, at a canon through the mountains, which is sometimes called Ogden Hole, or North Ogden Canon. Before the road was built through Ogden Canon proper, this was the nearest source of communication with the valley the other side of the mountains. There are about nine miles of straight track here and we soon arrive at *Bonneville* —871 miles from San Francisco, with an elevation of 4,310 feet. It is merely a side track. The Mormons have some fine farms in this vicinity, and between the railroad and base of the mountains there are many cultivated fields and fine orchards of apple and peach trees. There are frequent canons through the range, at the mouth of which are little settlements or villages; the creeks from the canons supplying the water which irrigates their fields, gardens and orchards. The largest of these settlements or villages are called Willard City and Brigham City, and their business is now done almost exclusively with the Utah North-

ern Railroad, which runs parallel with the Central Pacific between Ogden and Corinne and nearer the base of the mountains. The next station is *Brigham,*—862 miles from San Francisco; elevation, 4,220 feet. A side track for the passing of trains. It is the station for Brigham City, which is some three miles away, though it does not look half that distance. Leaving this station we cross some alkali marshes near, and cross an arm of the lake or small bay, with the eastern part of the Great Salt Sea in full view, with Promontory Mountains beyond. Approaching Corinne we enter the celebrated Bear River Valley, crossing the river on a pile bridge and reach *Corinne,* —857 miles from San Francisco, with an elevation of 4,294 feet. It is the largest Gentile town in the Territory, and if not hated is cordially and effectually let alone by most of the Mormons in the surrounding settlements. The natural location is excellent, and when the thousands of acres of fertile lands in the Bear River Valley are settled, as they surely will be in time, Corinne will be the center of trade and influence to which her location entitles her. On the completion of the railroad through here—before it came, even—the Gentiles had taken possession of the town and determined to maintain an ascendency. From that time it has been an object of defamation by the Saints; and the lands in the broad valley which surround it, as rich as any in the Territory, are left with scarcely a settler. To-day these lands are open and in the market, and if enterprising farmers in the East desire farms in a healthful climate, near a

SHOSHONE INDIAN VILLAGE.

good market, with short winters and those seldom excessively cold, with the salt water breezes fresh from the lake, and in a country where the finest kind of fruit can be grown, we advise them to stop here, inform themselves as best they can, look the ground over thoroughly and decide for themselves, the question of choosing this place for a new home. This is one side of the picture. The other is want of water. All crops in this valley are raised by irrigation. A ditch has already been dug from Malad River, which supplies some farms on its line, and the town with water. A large flouring-mill is also supplied with water from this ditch.

Some of the finest wheat we ever saw was raised near Corinne, on irrigated land. It was

UTE SQUAW AND PAPPOOSE.

spring wheat and produced at the rate of nearly 50 bushels to the acre. The spring wheat of Utah far excels in quality, the best winter wheat produced in Eastern States. It has a large, plump, hard, white berry, and will rank as A No. 1 in any wheat market in the country.

Corinne in its early history, was "a rough town;" but the roughs have passed on, or sleep in unknown graves. The town now has three churches, a good school, a large flouring-mill, several commission and forwarding houses, stores of various kinds, etc. It was the old freighting point to eastern Idaho and Montana, before the Utah Northern Railroad was removed to Ogden. Corinne is about seven miles from Great Salt Lake.

The leading hotel is the "Central." Bear River abounds in fish, and in the proper season the sloughs and marshes bordering the river near the lake, are almost covered with ducks and wild geese, thus offering fine sport for the hunter and fisherman. The water-lines of the lake become, as we pass westward toward the mountains of the Promontory Range, visible high up on the side of the mountains. There are three distinct water-lines to be seen in some places near Ogden, and each one has left a bench or terrace of land or rock by which it may be traced.

The Indian as a Beggar.—As a beggar an Indian excels the laziest tramp. They have a free-masonry among themselves. Give an Indian anything and next day two Indians will call on you. The third day there will be three, the original beggar as one, and so on *ad infinitum.* A well known gentleman connected with the Union Pacific Railroad, seeing this propensity in the character of the Indian resolved to gratify it for his own amusement. Giving way to his charitable impulses he bestowed a nickel upon one of "Cooper's lords of the forest." Next day he was waited on by a committee of two. On the third day the first Indian made up the three. After the fourth day the thing became monotonous, and to get rid of his "friends" he locked his office door. No less than six Indians came down on him at once and looked in the windows. The gentleman concluded his finances were unequal to the strain, and that the attempt to support the whole tribe of that persuasion of Indians was useless.

Quarry,—a side track, with a huge, rocky, black castle on the right and back of it. The mountain on our right is called Little Mountain. As we pass beyond and look back, an oval-shaped dome rises from its northern end as the turret of a castle. Salt Creek rises in the valley above, and sinks into the sand on its way to the lake.

Blue Creek,—838 miles from San Francisco with an elevation of 4,379 feet. It is a telegraph station with a side track and turn-table. If we have a heavy train a helper engine is here awaiting our arrival, and will assist in pulling us up the hill to Promontory. Between this and the next station, are some very heavy grades, short curves and deep rocky cuts, with fills across ravines. Blue Creek comes rushing down from the mountains, and furnishes water for several stations along the road. Leaving this station we begin to climb around a curve and up the side of the Promontory Range, the road almost doubling back on itself. The old grade of the Union Pacific is crossed and recrossed in several places, and is only a short distance away.

As we wind into the depressions and round the points, gradually ascending to the summit of the divide, the view of the lake, Corinne, Ogden and the Wahsatch Mountains, is grand. The grade for a short distance, is said to be 110 feet to the mile. We pass the rock cuts where each road expend-d thousands of dollars, and where Bishop John Sharp, now President of the Utah Central, exploded a mine which lifted the rock from the grade completely out, and gave a clear track after the rubbish was cleared away.

Promontory,—804 miles from San Francisco; elevation, 4,905 feet. It is about 9 miles from Blue Creek, and in the first seven miles we ascend over 500 feet. While the road was under construction, this little place was quite lively, but its glory has departed, and its importance at this time, is chiefly historic. It has a very well-kept eating-house for railroad and train men, and large coal-sheds with a three-stall round-house and other buildings for the convenience of employes. The water used here is brought from Blue Creek. It is located between two peaks or ridges of the Promontory Range, one of which on the left, is covered with cedars, and a portion of the year crowned with snow.

This place is well known as the meeting of the two railroads.

The highest point on the left, is called "Peak" on Froiseth's Map of Utah, and from its summit a magnificent view of the lake and surrounding country can be obtained.

The Great Railroad Wedding—Driving the Last Spike.

American history, in its triumphs of skill, labor and genius, knows no event of greater, thrilling interest, than the scene which attended the driving of the last spike, which united the East and West with the bands of iron. The completion of a project so grand in conception, so successful in execution, and likely to prove so fruitful and rich in promise, was worthy of world-wide celebrity.

Upon the 10th of May, 1869, the rival roads approached each other, and two lengths of rails were left for the day's work. At 8 A. M., spectators began to arrive; at quarter to 9 A. M., the whistle of the Central Pacific Railroad is heard, and the first train arrives, bringing a large number of passengers. Then two additional trains arrive on the Union Pacific Railroad, from the East. At a quarter of 11 A. M., the Chinese workmen commenced leveling the bed of the road, with picks and shovels, preparatory to placing the ties. At a quarter past eleven the Governor's train (Governor Stanford) arrived. The engine was gaily decorated with little flags and ribbons—the red white and blue. The last tie is put in place—eight feet long, eight inches wide, and six inches thick. It was made of California laurel, finely polished, and ornamented with a silver escutcheon, bearing the following inscription :

" *The last tie laid on the Pacific Railroad, May 10, 1869.*"

Then follow the names of the directors and

officers of the Central Pacific Company, and of the presenter of the tie.

The exact point of contact of the road was 1,085.8 miles west from Omaha, which allowed 690 miles to the Central Pacific Railroad, for Sacramento, for their portion of the work. The engine Jupiter, of the Central Pacific Railroad, and the engine 119 of the Union Pacific Railroad, moved up to within 30 feet of each other.

Just before noon the announcement was sent to Washington, that the driving of the *last spike* of the railroad which connected the Atlantic and Pacific, would be communicated to all the telegraph offices in the country the instant the work was done, and instantly a large crowd gathered around the offices of the Western Union Telegraph Company to receive the welcome news.

The manager of the company placed a magnetic ball in a conspicuous position, where all present could witness the performance, and connected the same with the main lines, notifying the various offices of the country that he was ready. New Orleans, New York and Boston instantly answered " Ready."

In San Francisco, the wires were connected with the fire-alarm in the tower, where the heavy ring of the bell might spread the news immediately over the city, as quick as the event was completed.

Waiting for some time in impatience, at last came this message from Promontory Point, at 2.27 P. M. :

" *Almost ready. Hats off, prayer is being offered.*"

A silence for the prayer ensued ; at 2.40 P. M., the bell tapped again, and the officer at Promontory said :

" *We have got done praying, the spike is about to be presented.*"

Chicago replied : " *We understand, all are ready in the East.*"

From Promontory Point. " *All ready now; the spike will soon be driven. The signal will be three dots for the commencement of the blows.*"

For a moment the instrument was silent, and then the hammer of the magnet tapped the bell, one, two, three, the signal. Another pause of a few seconds, and the lightning came flashing eastward, 2,400 miles to Washington; and the blows of the hammer on the spike were repeated instantly in telegraphic accents upon the bell of the Capitol. At 2.47 P. M., Promontory Point gave the signal, " Done ; " and the great American Continent was successfully spanned. Immediately thereafter, flashed over the line, the following official announcement to the Associated Press :

Promontory Summit, Utah, May 10.—THE LAST RAIL IS LAID! THE LAST SPIKE IS DRIVEN! THE PACIFIC RAILROAD IS COMPLETED! *The point of junction is 1,086 miles west*

THE GREAT RAILROAD WEDDING.
1.—Driving the last Spike.   2.—Union of the East and West.   3.—First Whistle of the Iron Horse.

of the Missouri River, and 690 miles east of Sacramento City.

LELAND STANFORD,
Central Pacific Railroad.

T. C. DURANT, }
SIDNEY DILLON, } Union Pacific Railroad.
JOHN DUFF, }

Such were the telegraphic incidents that attended the completion of the greatest work of the age,—but during these few expectant moments, the scene itself at Promontory Point, was very impressive.

After the rival engines had moved up toward each other, a call was made for the people to stand back, in order that all might have a chance to see. Prayer was offered by Rev. Dr. Todd of Massachusetts. Brief remarks were then made by General Dodge and Governor Stanford. Three cheers were given for the Government of the *United States*, for the Railroad, for the Presidents, for the Star Spangled Banner, for the Laborers, and for those respectively, who furnished the means. Four spikes were then furnished,—*two gold* and *two silver,*—by Montana, Idaho, California, and Nevada. They were each about seven inches long, and a little larger than the iron spike.

Dr. Harkness, of Sacramento, in presenting to Governor Stanford a spike of pure gold, delivered a short and appropriate speech.

The Hon. F. A. Tritle, of Nevada, presented Dr. Durant with a spike of silver, saying : " *To the iron of the East, and the gold of the West, Nevada adds her link of silver to span the Continent and weld the oceans.*"

Governor Safford, of Arizona, presenting another spike, said : " *Ribbed in iron, clad in silver, and crowned with gold, Arizona presents her offering to the enterprise that has banded the Continent and webbed the oceans.*"

Dr. Durant stood on the north side of the tie, and Governor Stanford on the south side. At a given signal, these gentlemen struck the spikes, and at the same instant the electric spark was sent through the wires, east and west. The two locomotives moved up until they touched each other, and a bottle of wine was poured, as a libation on the last rail.

A number of ladies graced the ceremonies with their presence, and at 1 P. M., under an almost cloudless sky, and in the presence of about *one thousand one hundred people*, the greatest railroad on earth was completed.

A sumptuous repast was given to all the guests and railroad officers, and toward evening the trains each moved away and darkness fell upon the scene of joy and triumph.

Immediately after the ceremonies, the laurel tie was removed for preservation, and in its place an ordinary one substituted. Scarcely had it been put in its place, before a grand advance

was made upon it by the curiosity seekers and relic hunters and divided into numberless mementoes, and as fast as each tie was demolished and a new one substituted, this, too, shared the same fate, and probably within the first six months, there were used as many new ties. It is said that even one of the rails did not escape the grand battery of knife and hack, and the first one had soon to be removed to give place to another.

A curious incident, connected with the laying of the last rails, has been little noticed hitherto. Two lengths of rails, 56 feet, had been omitted. The Union Pacific people brought up their pair of rails, and the work of placing them was done by Europeans. The Central Pacific people then laid their pair of rails, the labor being performed by Mongolians. The foremen, in both cases, were Americans. Here, near the center of the great American Continent, were representatives of Asia, Europe and America—America directing and controlling.

It is somewhat unfortunate that all the scenes which characterize this place of meeting are passed over by the railroad trains at night, and travelers can not catch even a glimpse.

Leaving Promontory, a sugar-loaf peak rises on our right, and. as we near it, the lake again comes into view, looking like a green meadow in the distance. About three miles west of the station, on the left side of the track, a sign-board has been erected, stating that 10 miles of track were here laid in one day. Ten miles farther west a similar sign-board appears. This track was laid on the 29th of April, 1869, and, so far as known, is the largest number of miles ever laid in one day. (For a full description, see page 8.)

Rozel,—an unimportant station, where trains meet and pass ; but passenger trains do not stop unless signaled. The lake can now be seen for a long distance, and in a clear day, with a good glass, the view is magnificent. Still crossing a sage brush plain, with occasional alkali patches, closing in upon the shore at times, we soon arrive at

Lake.—There is an open plain to the north of these two stations, and north of Rozel especially, are salt wells. Between these two stations the second sign-board close to the track, showing the western limit of the 10 miles of track laid in one day, is seen. North of Lake Station about three miles, are Cedar Springs, which was quite a place during the construction of the road, and a great deal of wood, etc., was obtained near them, for use of the road. Leaving this station we pass across flats and marshes, with the old Union Pacific grade still well preserved, on our left. In places, however, it is partially washed away by the waves of the lake. Next comes

Monument,—801 miles from San Francisco ;

SALT LAKE FROM MONUMENT POINT.

MONUMENT POINT FROM SALT LAKE.

elevation, 4,227 feet. An isolated rock rises, like a monument, in the lake on the left, while the hill on the right is crowned with turrets and projecting domes. You have here a grand view of the lake, its islands and shores, with promontories, etc., which is correctly represented by our artist. The station itself is a mere side track and "Y," for the convenience of the road. When the strong south wind blows, the waves, dashing against the rocks on the shore, and the rolling white caps in the distance, form a beautiful view which the tourist, after passing the dreary waste, will appreciate. The road now turns to the right, and the view of the lake is shut out by a low hill that intervenes. On the west side of this hill are the Locomotive Springs which puff out steam at times, and which give them their name. A Mormon brother has a ranche at the springs, and seems to enjoy life as best he can with three wives.

The Overflow of the Great Salt Lake—Another theory as to its outlet.—Parties who profess to be well posted as to the nature of the country surrounding this great body of salt water, do not agree with the views elsewhere expressed, that in case its rise continues, its waters will flow into the Humboldt River. They assert that north of Monument Rock is an extensive arm of the lake, now dry, and that the divide between the northern extremity of this arm and the Raft River, a tributary of Snake River, is not more than from 50 to 75 feet high; and that, if the lake rises, this divide will be washed out— or a channel may be cut through it into Raft

River, and the surplus waters of the lake thus drained into the Pacific Ocean, through the Snake and Columbia Rivers. Next we pass

Seco,—which is an unimportant station in the midst of sage plains, and soon arrive at

Kelton,—790 miles from San Francisco, with an elevation of 4,223 feet. There have been no very heavy grades between this and Promontory. The town is located at the north-west corner of Salt Lake, and about two miles from it, with low marshes and sloughs intervening. This is a stage station, and passengers for Boise City and other points in Idaho, and points in Oregon as far as Dalles, will here leave the train and secure seats in the coaches of the stage line. The shipping of freight for Idaho, and the fact that it is the terminus of the stage line, are the principal causes for the growth and business of this place. It has a fair hotel, several stores, the usual number of saloons, and corrals for stock used in freighting. In 1875, 6,000,000 pounds of freight were shipped from this place to Idaho, or about 3,000 tons. The freighting business has gradually increased from year to year, and will continue to do so as the mines of the Territory are developed, and until the Portland, Dalles and Salt Lake Railroad is pushed forward into the Territory. Seven miles north of the town, at the foot of the mountains, are springs of clear, fresh water, from which water is conveyed for the use of the railroad and inhabitants. There is a good deal of stock grazed in the vicinity of this station, which feed on sage brush in the winter and such grass as they get, but find

good grazing in the summer. The surplus cattle
are shipped to the markets on the Pacific Coast.
Tourists will also bear in mind, that this is
the station nearest to the great Shoshone Falls.
These falls are 110 miles from Kelton. Passengers from the east will arrive at about 10 o'clock
P. M., and stay all night. Passengers from the
west will arrive at about two o'clock A. M. The
next morning they will take the stage
run by the North-western Stage Company, 100
miles to Rock Creek Station, which are made
over good roads in twelve hours. Here you will
stay over night, and take a team the next morning for the falls; distance ten miles over a lava
plain, with stinted sage brush. No sign of the
great falls is seen, until you reach a point one mile
from them, when they suddenly burst upon the
eye with a grandeur and magnificence truly
bewildering.

Travelers to the main falls can reach them on
foot very easily from the upper ridge. It will
abundantly repay visitors to go to the edge of
the river, and contemplate their silent grandeur.
A pathway or trail leads from the point where
wagons stop, and the distance is about one mile.

The Great Shoshone Falls.

BY CLARENCE KING.

In October, 1868, with a small detachment of
a United States Geological Survey, the writer
crossed the Goose Creek Mountains, in northern
Utah, and descended by the old Fort Boise Road
to the level of the Snake Plain. After camp and
breakfast, at Rock Creek, mounting in the saddle we headed toward the *Canon of the Shoshone.*
The air was cold and clear. The remotest
mountain peaks upon the horizon could be distinctly seen, and the forlorn details of their
brown slopes stared at us as through a vacuum.
A few miles in front, the smooth surface of the
plain was broken by a ragged, zigzag line of
black, which marked the edge of the farther wall
of the Snake Canon. A dull, throbbing sound
greeted us. Its pulsations were deep and seemed
to proceed from the ground beneath our feet.

Leaving the cavalry to bring up the wagon, my
two friends and I galloped on, and were quickly
upon the edge of the canon wall. We looked
down into a broad, circular excavation, three-
quarters of a mile in diameter, and nearly seven
hundred feet deep. East and north, over the
edges of the canon, we looked across miles and
miles of the Snake Plain, far on to the blue
boundary mountains. The wall of the gorge
opposite us, like the cliff at our feet, sank in
perpendicular bluffs, nearly to the level of the
river. A horizon as level as the sea: a circling
wall, whose sharp edges were here and there battlemented in huge, fortress-like masses; a broad
river, smooth and unruffled, flowing quietly into
the middle of the scene, and then plunging into

a labyrinth of rocks, tumbling over a precipice
two hundred feet high, and flowing westward in
a still, deep current, disappear behind a black
promontory. Where the river flowed around
the western promontory, it was wholly in shadow,
and of a deep sea-green. A scanty growth of
coniferous trees fringed the brink of the lower
cliffs, overhanging the river. Dead barrenness
is the whole sentiment of the scene.

My tent was pitched upon the edge of a cliff,
directly overhanging the rapids. From my door
I looked over the edge of the falls, and, whenever the veil of mist was blown aside, I could see
for a mile down the river. At the very brink of
the fall a few twisted evergreens cling with their
roots to the rock, and lean over the abyss of foam
with something of that air of fatal fascination
which is apt to take possession of men.

In plan, the fall recurves up-stream in a deep
horseshoe, resembling the outline of Niagara.
The total breadth is about seven hundred feet,
and the greatest height of a single fall about one
hundred and ninety. Among the islands above
the brink are several beautiful cascades, where
portions of the river pour over in lace-like forms.
The whole mass of the fall is one ever-varying
sheet of spray. In the early spring, when swollen
by the rapidly melted snows, the river pours over
with something like the grand volume of Niagara, but at the time of my visit, it was wholly
white foam. The river below the falls is very
deep. The right bank sinks into the water in a
clear, sharp precipice, but on the left side a narrow, pebbly beach extends along the foot of the
cliff. From the top of the wall, at a point a
quarter of a mile below the falls, a stream has
gradually worn a little stairway down to the
river: thick growths of evergreens have huddled
together in this ravine. Under the influence of
the cool shadow of the cliffs and the pines, and
constant percolating of surface-waters, a rare fertility is developed in the ravines opening upon
the shore of the canon. A luxuriance of ferns
and mosses, an almost tropical wealth of green
leaves and velvety carpeting line the banks.
There are no rocks at the base of the fall. The
sheet of foam plunges almost vertically into a
dark, beryl-green, lake-like expanse of the river.
Immense volumes of foam roll up from the cata-
ract-base, and, whirling about in the eddying
winds, rise often a thousand feet into the air.
When the wind blows down the canon, a gray
mist obscures the river for half a mile; and
when, as is usually the case in the afternoon, the
breezes blow eastward, the foam-cloud curls over
the brink of the fall, and hangs like a veil over
the upper river. The incessant roar, reinforced
by a thousand echoes, fills the canon. From out
this monotone, from time to time, rise strange,
wild sounds, and now and then may be heard a
slow, measured beat, not unlike the recurring fall
of breakers. From the white front of the cata-

SHOSHONE FALLS.

ract the eye constantly wanders up to the black, frowning parapet of lava. The actual edge is usually formed of irregular blocks and prisms of lava, poised upon their ends in an unstable equilibrium, ready to be tumbled over at the first leverage of the frost. Hardly an hour passes without the sudden boom of one of those rockmasses falling upon the ragged *debris* piled below. After sleeping on the nightmareish brink of the falls, it was no small satisfaction to climb out of the Dantean gulf and find myself once more upon a pleasantly prosaic foreground of sage. Nothing more effectually banishes the melotragic state of the mind than the obtrusive ugliness and abominable smell of this plant. From my feet a hundred miles of it stretched eastward. A half-hour's walk took me out of sight of the canon, and as the wind blew westward, only occasional, indistinct pulsations of the fall could be heard.

I walked for an hour, following an old Indian trail which occasionally approached within seeing distance of the river, and then, apparently quite satisfied, diverged again into the desert. When about four miles from the Shoshone, it bent abruptly to the north, and led to the edge of the canon. Here again the narrow gorge widened into a broad theater, surrounded as before by black, vertical walls, and crowded over its whole surface by rude piles and ridges of volcanic rock. The river entered it from the east through a magnificent gateway of basalt, and, having reached the middle, flows on either side of a low, rocky island, and plunges in two falls into a deep, green basin. A very singular ridge of the basalt projects like an arm almost across the river, inclosing within its semi-circle a bowl three hundred feet in diameter and two hundred feet deep. Within this the water was of the same peculiar beryl-green, dappled here and there by masses of foam which swim around and around with a spiral tendency toward the center. To the left of the island half the river plunges off an overhanging lip, and falls about 150 feet, the whole volume reaching the surface of the basin many feet from the wall. The other half of the river has worn away the edge, and descends in a tumbling cascade at an angle of about forty-five degrees.

The cliffs around the upper cataract are inferior to those of the Shoshone. While the level of the upper plain remains nearly the same, the river constantly deepens the channel in its westward course.

By dint of hard climbing I reached the actual brink in a few places, and saw the canon successively widening and narrowing, its walls here and there approaching each other and standing like the pillars of a gateway; the river alternately flowing along smooth, placid reaches of level, and then rushing swiftly down rocky cascades. Here and there along the cliff are disclosed the mouths of black caverns, where the

lava seems to have been blown up in the form of a great blister, as if the original flow had poured over some pool of water, and the hot rock, converting it into steam, had been blown up bubble-like by its immense expansion. I continued my excursions along the canon to the west of the Shoshone. About a mile below the fall, a very fine promontory juts sharply out from the wall, and projects nearly to the middle of the canon. Climbing with difficulty along its toppling crest, I reached a point which I found composed of immense, angular fragments piled up in dangerous poise. Looking eastward, the battlemented rocks around the falls limited the view; but westward I could see down long reaches of river, where islands of trachyte rose above white cascades. A peculiar and fine effect is noticeable upon the river during all the midday. The shadow of the southern cliff is cast down here and there, completely darkening the river, but often defining itself upon the water. The contrast between the rich, gem-like green of the sunlit portions and the deep-violet shadow of the cliff is of extreme beauty. The Snake River, deriving its volume wholly from the melting of the mountain snows, is a direct gauge of the annual advance of the sun. In June and July it is a tremendous torrent, carrying a full half of the Columbia. From the middle of July it constantly shrinks, reaching its minimum in midwinter. At the lowest, it is a river equal to the Sacramento or Connecticut.

Near the "City of Rocks" Station, in the Goose Creek Mountains, are found the "Giant Rocks," and over the little rise is the place that gives the name to the station. Dotting the plains are thousands of singular rocks, on which the weary pilgrims of 1849, have written their names in cart-grease paint. The old California road is still seen, but now overgrown with rank weeds. The view as you descend from the summit is sublime. Far away in the distance loom up the Salmon River Mountains, distant 125 miles, and in the intervening space winds the valley of the Snake River.

Kelton has from 250 to 300 inhabitants, nearly all supported by the Idaho trade, though it will eventually have some mining trade, as the recent discovery of mines in the Black Pine District, 25 miles north, will have an influence in this direction. Kelton is the nearest railroad station to these mines, and parties desiring to visit them will leave the cars here.

Idaho Territory.—This is one of the smallest of the Territories, as now constituted, and claims a population of about 15,000 people. There are three public lines of conveyance which lead into the Territory, or rather two, as one of them passes entirely through it. The stage line from Kelton passes the City of Rocks, and within ten miles of the Great Shoshone Falls, to Dalles in Oregon, by way of Boise City, 250 miles out; thence to Baker City, Oregon, 400 miles; to Union, 435 miles; to La Grande, 450 miles; to Unatilla, 510 miles, and to Walla Walla, 530 miles. At Boise City the line connects with stages for Idaho City, Centerville, Placerville and Silver City. Boise City is the territorial capital, a city said to contain 3,500 people, and located on the Boise River. There is not much agricultural land in the Territory, but a few of the valleys are cultivated and produce excellent crops of wheat, barley and oats, with potatoes and all kinds of vegetables. Crops are raised by

are quite a large number of Chinese in the Territory, mostly engaged in placer and gulch mining. They are industrious and frugal and will frequently make money from claims that have been abandoned as worthless by white men. So far as developed, the Territory has some rich mines, and those in the Atlantic District are becoming somewhat noted. It is claimed that the richest known gold mine in the country at present, is in this district. In addition to the supplies, etc., shipped from Winnemucca, over 6,000,000 pounds of freight were shipped from Kelton Station to this Territory in 1875, and more than this amount will be shipped the pres-

VIEW LOOKING DOWN THE SHOSHONE FALLS.

irrigation. Boise Valley, the settled portion of it, is about 60 miles long and four miles wide, and is the most thickly settled of any of the valleys in the Territory. The nights are so cool and the altitude of the valleys is so great that experiments in corn raising have not, thus far, turned out very well. The second line of public conveyance spoken of, runs from Winnemucca to Silver City.

It is claimed that this town is equal in population to Boise City. It is sustained by the mines located near it. At Rattlesnake Station there is also a connecting stage line for Rocky Bar, a mining camp, near which placer and gulch diggings have been discovered. There

ent year. Much of it has been, and will be, mining machinery. A railroad through the Territory is much needed, will aid greatly in the development of its mines, and will be a paying investment from the start, or, at least, in a very short time after its completion. The Snake and Salmon Rivers are among its principal streams. The Snake River rises in the mountains of the Yellowstone Region, and flows entirely through the Territory from east to west, and forms one of the tributaries to the Columbia River of Oregon. The scenery along its valley is varied, but in some places is grand. Idaho also has immense ranges where a large number of cattle are grazed both winter and summer, without hay. The stock interest is rapidly becoming one of the principal features of the Territory. Its future prosperity, however, depends largely upon the development of its mining interests.

Leaving Kelton, the road soon turns to the left, and, rising a heavy grade, reaches the divide between the Great Salt Lake and the valley beyond. The mountains for a distance are on our right, while, from the left, a magnificent view of the western arm of the lake can be obtained. Between the road and the lake are extensive salt plains, which in the sun glisten like burnished silver, while beyond are the green waters of this inland sea. Going up this grade, you will notice a ledge of rocks on the left side of the track, the lower end of which has been tunneled by the wind, forming a natural aperture like an open arch. We soon turn to the right, leave the lake behind us and wind along the side of the mountain. A dreary salt marsh or alkali plain is now seen on the left, and the low, isolated hill on the shore, which for a time obscured our vision is passed, giving us another view of the lake in the distance, and the mountains of the Wahsatch and Oquirrh Ranges beyond, as far as the eye can reach. Passing through a rocky cut from a projecting spur of the range we are passing, and looking to the right, a beautiful conical dome rises up, as a grim sentinel to guard the way.

Ombey,—simply a side track in the midst of a heavy gravel cut, 778 miles from San Francisco, with an elevation of 4,721 feet. At Kelton we were but little above the elevation of Salt Lake, 4,223 feet, and we are 500 feet higher here than when we left that place, the distance between the two being about 11 miles. From the frequent views of the Great American Desert which the traveler can obtain while passing over this portion of the road, he can form some idea of its utter barrenness and desolation, and the great sufferings of those who have attempted to cross it without adequate preparation, and the consequent burning thirst they and their animals have endured.

Matlin,—only a side track, 768 miles from San Francisco; elevation, 4,597 feet.

Terrace,—a railroad town on the edge of the Great American Desert. It is 757 miles from San Francisco, with an elevation of 4,544 feet. Here is a ten-stall roundhouse, and the machine and repair shops of the Salt Lake Division of the Central Pacific Railroad. Mr. R. H. Pratt, with head quarters at Ogden, is Superintendent of this Division, which extends from that place to Toano in Nevada. The town has about 300 people, which includes not only the railroad men and their families, but those who are here for the purpose of trade and traffic with them. The water tank here, as at a good many stations on this road, is supplied with water brought through pipes from the springs in the mountains.

The town has two or three stores, saloons and

an eating-house, where railroad men and emigrants take their meals. It depends wholly on its local trade at present; but the discovering and opening of the Rosebud Mines, about 10 miles north, will tend to increase its business, if they are developed. Terrace is the railroad station for the mines in the Newfoundland District, some 18 miles south. Miners for either of the above named districts, will leave the cars at this station. There are no stage lines to them, as yet, but private conveyances can be readily obtained. The desert with its dreary loneliness— a barren waste—still continues.

Leaving Terrace we have over 20 miles of straight road over which we soon pass. A spur of the Goose Creek Range of Mountains puts down on our right, while Silver Islet Mountain rises out of the alkali plain on our left, and Pilot's Peak, one of the lofty mountains of Nevada, and a noted landmark for many a weary pilgrim across the desert, looms up in the southwest.

Bovine,—an unimportant station, with side track for the convenience of passing trains, 747 miles from San Francisco, with an elevation of 4,317 feet. On our right are broken mountains, while there is an isolated peak one side of which seems to have settled away from the other, leaving it very rough and ragged. Next we come to

Lucin,—731 miles from San Francisco, with an elevation of 4,486 feet above the sea. Beyond Lucin, a short distance, we strike Grouse Creek, which rises in the hills north. This creek usually sinks in the sandy desert, and no water in it crosses the railroad, except in the spring when the snows are melting. On the right, east of the hills, and north of Lucin about 4 1-2 miles, are the Owl Springs which have an abundance of water. As we enter the pass in this low range of hills, we lose sight of Silver Islet Mountains, and the range close to the track is called the Pilot Range, or by the miners, Buel Range, after Buel City. Leaving Grouse Creek on our right, the road leads to the left again, and we enter the Thousand Spring Valley It virtually unites with the Grouse Valley, though its waters usually sink in the sand before they reach those of the creek mentioned. As we near Tecoma, the traveler will notice a small granite monument on the left side of the track, near the summit of the grade, supported by a heap of stones. This monument marks the Nevada State line and passing it, we enter the land of the "big bonanzas."

Tecoma,—Nevada, 721 miles from San Francisco, with an elevation of 4,812 feet. This is the nearest railroad station to the celebrated Tecoma Mines, one owned by Howland & Aspinwall of New York, and the other owned by a London company,—both mines bearing the same name. Tecoma is the railroad station for Lucin Mining District, and stages leave here every morning for Buel City, the mining town of the district, six miles south, in the foot hills of the range. It is the nearest railroad station also, to the Deep Creek District, 90 miles due south. The Goose Creek and Delano Districts have recently been opened about 35 miles north of this place and are said to contain rich prospects. The formation, however, is very much broken, and affords strong evidences of a mighty upheaval sometime. Within a mile or two of the town, north, a good view of the Thousand Spring Valley is obtained with its pasturage and hay lands. Tecoma has two or three stores, saloon, dwellings, etc., and will soon have a smelting works. It has a population of from 50 to 100; and the most of its business is with the mines and cattle men. Stock-yards convenient for shipping cattle have been erected here. There is a fine grazing country off to the north, where large herds of cattle are kept, and this has come to be a prominent business of this part of the country. As we approach Tecoma, on our left a bluff peak with perpendicular walls closes the northern end of Pilot Range, while Pilot Peak towers up to the heavens at the southern extremity. It is 20 miles from Tecoma to the base of this peak, though it does not seem half that distance. Tecoma is also the railroad station for the Silver Islet Mining District, and if the mines in its immediate vicinity are developed, it will become a place of considerable importance. Leaving Tecoma the railroad continues over a sage brush and greasewood plain to the left of the valley, with a part of the old Union Pacific grade on the right, and as we approach the next range of hills or mountains, we have a fine broadside view of grand old Pilot Peak, and do not wonder at its prominence, or the great regard in which it was held by the emigrants across this dreary desert.

Montello,—715 miles from San Francisco, with an elevation of 5,010 feet. At this station is a large water-tank supplied with water from a spring in the mountains on the right, some ten miles away. The mountain ranges this side of Ogden run from north to south, parallel with each other, and the railroad crosses them over low divides or passes, while the plains of the desert lay between them. To our right a point of the Pequop Range approaches the track, and shuts out our view of the Old Pilot, as we pass up the grade, and into the narrow defile.

It is generally understood that the mines of the Pilot Range are quite extensive, and that the ore, though of rather low grade, is nevertheless to be found in large quantities and is quite accessible. Buel City has a smelter erected which has reduced considerable ore.

Loray,—nearly on the summit of the divide. It is 704 miles from San Francisco, with an elevation of about 5,960 feet. It is a station of no particular importance to travelers. Wood and

timber, cut in the mountains for the use of the road, is delivered here.

Toano,—698 miles from San Francisco, with an elevation of 5,973 feet—the western terminus of the Salt Lake Division of the Central Pacific, and nearly 183 miles from Ogden. Toano has a roundhouse with 14 stalls and an adjoining shed where two engines can be sheltered. It has the usual side tracks, coal-sheds and buildings for the transaction of the business of the company. The town has about 250 people.

The following mining districts are tributary to this place, and transact the most of their business here: Silver Zone, distant 20 miles, mines mostly milling ore; Dolly Varden, 55 miles; Cherry Creek, 100 miles; Egan Canon, 105 miles; Shellburn, 110 miles; Mineral City, 130 miles; Ward, 140 miles. They are all south of the railroad, and connected with Toano by a good wagon road. Stages run regularly to Cherry Creek. A great deal of freight is carried to the mines, and ore and bullion hauled back. The road is destitute of water for a considerable part of the way, and wells, at a great expense, have been dug in some places, from which water is sold to freighters. The ore from some of the mines in these districts is very rich. Twenty cars of ore from the Paymaster Mine in the Ward District were shipped from here in January, 1876, nineteen of which averaged about $800 per ton, and one car averaged a little over $1,000 per ton, net. Not only the Ward, but others in this region are regarded as prosperous mining camps. In 1875, from 800 to 1,000 tons of base bullion were shipped from this place, the product of these mines. The valleys south have good ranges for stock, and some of them, as the Steptoe Valley, produce excellent crops of small grain and vegetables. The Toano Range of Mountains runs from north to south, and heads near this place. On the road to Pioche, about 180 miles from Toano, and about half a mile from the road, is the Mammoth Cave of Nevada. It has been partially explored, but its extent is not known. Beautiful specimens of stalactites and crystals have been found here, and the tourist would be highly interested in a visit to this cave, which in a short time must become a place of public resort.

North of Toano, the Goose Creek Range of Mountains, which divides Goose Creek and Thousand Spring Valley, are plainly visible. The Salmon Falls copper mines, on Salmon Falls River, are about 60 miles north, and are known to be rich in copper.

About 20 miles south of the town, a road to the Deep Creek Mining District branches off from the Pioche road, and part of the business of that mining camp is done here. The country immediately around Toano is barren and desolate in appearance—not very inviting to the traveler or settler.

On leaving Toano we have an up grade to Moore's Station, about 30 miles. In the winter great difficulty is experienced with snow over this distance, and in the summer the route is extremely beautiful and picturesque. Just west of the town, on the right, the low hills are covered with a scattering growth of scrub pines and cedars. The Pequop Range juts up to the town on the south, while on the north may still be seen the mountains of the Goose Creek Range. The road between this point and Wells is undulating, and full of short curves and heavy grades. Six snow sheds are passed, in rapid succession. As we look off to the right, the hill seems to descend into a large valley, with a range of mountains beyond. It is a dry, sage brush valley and continues in sight until we pass Independence.

Pequop,—689 miles from San Francisco, with an elevation of 6,184 feet. It is simply a side track, at which passenger trains do not stop. Passing this, we next reach the Otego telegraph station, which is only used in winter, to give notice of snow-blocked trains, etc.

Dead Man's Spring.—About five miles from Pequop, in the low hills off to the right of the track, is a spring which bears the above suggestive title. In the spring of 1873, the body of a dead man was found near it, with a bullet hole through his skull. The decomposition of the body had advanced so far that it was past recognition, and the questions as to who he was, and how he came to be killed, were not likely to be solved. In short, the man and his tragic end were wrapped in great mystery. The old adage, however, that "murder will out," was again verified in this case. It seems that a large drove of cattle came into this region of country, in the fall of 1872, and that two of the herders employed—one a Mexican, and the other a white man, were paid off near Wells, and started back for Colorado, where they were first employed. They camped together one night at this spring, and the next morning one was left cold and stark upon the bosom of mother earth, while the other, the Mexican, went on and in due time arrived in Denver, Col. He had murdered his companion, robbed him of his money, his watch and his horse, and with his plunder, with no one to witness the deed, thought himself secure. But a brother of the murdered man lived in Denver, and hearing nothing from the absent one for a long time, became somewhat alarmed about him, and began to institute inquiries and to search for his companion. His efforts were soon rewarded, and in a short time he heard that the Mexican,—who was known to have accompanied his brother in driving the herd to Nevada,—had returned, and had been seen in Denver. Furthermore, it was supposed that he had not left that city, and could be found somewhere in its immediate vicinity. His trail was finally struck, and followed until he was found. His account of the missing man was so confused, and his different stories so conflicting and improbable, that he was arrested and searched. The search revealed the watch and other trinkets of the murdered man, which were at once recognized by his brother. His horse was also found. The Mexican, now thoroughly suspected, was closely questioned, and the evidence against him was so strong, that, while confined in jail, he confessed the crime. This so exasperated the friends of the murdered man that they determined upon vengeance, and immediately organized to secure the death of the culprit. The villain was taken from his cell in the jail one night, and found the next morning hanging to a telegraph pole. Thus was the spring named.

Otego,—station and side track, which is 688 miles from San Francisco, with an elevation of 6,154 feet. The tourist may enjoy a magnificent view of hills and mountains, valleys and dales, as we pass on over some of the reverse curves in the road. The old Union Pacific grade is still seen in patches, on our right. Pequop Range, with Independence Valley, now looms grandly into view on our left, as we arrive at

Independence,—676 miles from San Francisco, with an elevation of 6,007 feet. We are now crossing a low divide between the valley on our right, above spoken of, and Independence Valley on our left. This station is on a heavy down grade, and trains going west seldom stop. The water tank is supplied from springs in the low hills off to the right, and the side track is a little beyond it. We now pass to the right around an isolated mountain that seems to guard the entrance to Independence Valley,—and then to the left, and as we turn to enter the pass in the mountains a lovely view of this beautiful valley is again obtained stretching away as far as the eye can reach. It is a great stock range, and thousands of cattle annually feed upon its rich nutritious grasses. Turning again to the right we enter what is called Cedar Pass. Passing a section-house at which there is a winter telegraph station for use of snow-bound trains, we soon reach the summit of the divide between Independence Valley, and the valley of the Humboldt, at

Moore's,—669 miles from San Francisco, with an elevation of 6,166 feet. It was formerly quite a town for wood-choppers and frontier men, when the railroad was being built; but its glory has departed and the stakes and posts of a few houses are all that remain to mark the spot. Down the grade we go into the far-famed Humboldt Valley, passing Cedar, a side track, where a camp of wood-choppers in the mountains on our left, deliver their wood.

Wells,—661 miles from San Francisco, with an elevation of 5,629 feet. Just as we enter the town, we pass the mountain spur on our left, and Clover Valley bursts into view. Its name is significant as it abounds in the natural clover so well known in the Eastern States. The town has about 200 inhabitants, with roundhouse for three engines, a hotel, stores, saloon, etc. The railroad water tank formerly supplied with water pumped from the wells, a little west of the town, is now filled from a mountain spring four miles away.

Humboldt Wells as they are called, give celebrity to this place. They are really springs about thirty in number, situated mostly in a low basin half a mile west of the station. There are no evidences of volcanic action about them as we could perceive, nor does a crater in this low place seem at all probable. They are very probably natural springs and from the nature of the porous soil around them, they do not rise and flow away as similar springs do in a more compact soil. The water, by residents here, is not considered brackish at all, nor is it particularly warm, though the springs have never been known to freeze over. They are also called bottomless, but no accurate knowledge has yet been published in regard to their depth. They are simply deep springs, but the opinion is here entertained that a lead and line would soon touch bottom in them. It was the great watering place in times of the old emigrant travel, and at least three of these roads converged to this point and united here. These were the Grass Creek, the Thousand Spring Valley and the Cedar Pass Roads. Emigrants in those days always rejoiced when they had passed the perils of the Great American Desert, and arrived at these springs where there was plenty of water, pure and sweet and an abundance of grass for their weary and worn animals. Hence it was a favorite camping ground. Visitors approching these springs in the summer, and springing on the sod can fairly shake the adjoining springs, a fact that leads to the opinion entertained by some, that they are really openings of a lake, which has been gradually covered over by the accumulation of grass and grass roots and other luxuriant vegetation, which abounds along and around the basin. The fact that the ground around these springs is so elastic, and the known incidents in history, where luxuriant vegetation has frequently caused islands in rivers and lakes, confirms this opinion in our mind, and we believe a thorough investigation will establish this theory as correct. There is then in this basin simply a covered lake, and the springs are openings to it. The conformation of the land around the basin also tends to convince us of the truth of this theory. The basin is the receptacle of the drainage of a large water-shed, and there are high mountains nearly all around it. These springs abound in fish—the little minnows that are so common in the brooks and small streams in the Eastern States. Other kinds there may be, but these only have been caught. The

apertures differ in size, and the openings to some are much larger than the openings in others. If they were on a side-hill every body would call them springs, but inasmuch as they are in a low basin, they are called wells. Their depth and surroundings also convey this impression.

Mr. Hamill, a merchant of Wells, says that he took a piece of railroad iron and tied some lariat ropes to it (about 160 feet), and could find no bottom in the deepest springs which he sounded with that length of rope. He further says that a government exploring party, under command of Lieutenant Cuppinger, visited Wells in 1870 and took soundings of the springs to a depth of from 1,500 to 1,700 feet and found no bottom. These soundings were of the largest springs or wells, and while his statement may be true, even soundings to this depth does not render them bottomless.

How to see them and know where they are, is the next thing of consequence to the traveler. As you pass west of the station, notice the end of a piece of the old Union Pacific grade; next the graves surrounded by painted fences; then off to the right a heap of stones, where the engine-house was built—the engine being used to force water from the well, which is just beyond this heap of stones, to the tank along side of the track. The heavy growth of grass around the place will indicate where this well is in summer, and the accumulated deposits of this grass has raised a little rim around this particular well.—and the same is true of others in its immediate vicinity.

Travelers will take notice that a mail and express stage line leaves Wells tri-weekly—Mondays, Wednesdays and Fridays—in the morning, for Sprucemont, 40 miles, and Cherry Creek, 95 miles distant. At Cherry Creek this line connects with stages for Egan Canon, on the line of the old overland stage route, Mineral City (Robinson District) and Hamilton, the county-seat of White Pine County. At Mineral City, conveyances can be easily obtained for Ward's District, 20 miles distant. The Spruce Mountain Mining District is said to contain some very good mines, and a company has recently been organized in San Francisco, to continue the work of development. Sprucemont is the mining town of the district, and is beautifully located on an elevated bench in the midst of groves of pines and cedars. Stages also run 100 miles south to Shellburne, also to Bull Run.

There are estimated to be about 40 ranches in Clover Valley, and as many in Ruby Valley. These ranchemen are engaged in agriculture and stock growing. They raise wheat, barley, oats, and splendid vegetables. Wells has extensive stock-yards, to accommodate the large shipments of cattle, annually made from these ranches. The valley in this immediate vicinity is the scene of the annual "round-ups," every spring. Cedar Pass Range is the range on our left, as we come through by Moore's Station. West of this range and south of Wells, is Clover Valley. The tourist will see "Castle Peak" on the further side of this valley as the train pauses at the station, and this peak is on the northern end of Ruby Range, and it is always covered with snow. Ruby Valley is nearly due south of the "Castle" which you see in the mountain, and is divided from Clover Valley by a spur of this range, which turns into it like a hook. Ruby Range is about 150 miles long, and we only see its northern extremity at Wells.

North of Wells, across the first range, lies the Thousand Spring Valley—then across another low divide, you - will strike a valley whose waters flow north-west through the Columbia River, to the Pacific Ocean. Fishermen will bear in mind that salmon trout are caught in this valley in the spring of the year. The stream is a branch of the Salmon Falls River, which empties into Snake River, about 120 miles north of this station.

A proposed railroad has been talked of, to connect this point with Callville, on the Colorado River, and the route is said to be very feasible. Wells is also the connecting point for a direct "cut off" to Salt Lake City, should such a road be built.

It may be well to remark here, that the mountain ranges in Nevada, as in Utah, generally extend from north to south—and the only exception to this rule, is where there are broken or detached ranges, or isolated peaks. Leaving Wells, the foot hills on our left, in a short distance, obscure a view of the high peaks in the Ruby Range ; but they soon reappear as we pass down the valley, and are our constant companions, only a short distance away, until we leave Halleck. Between the Humboldt River and the base of these mountains, there is an elevated bench covered with the usual sage brush and greasewood, while in the valley and along the borders of the stream, grass land predominates. An extensive stock-dealer, when asked about the qualifications, etc., for growing cattle, said that "there was about one acre of grass to seventy-five acres of sage brush," and a limited observation of this part of the State, at least, proves that he was not far out of the way. As we descend the river, however, a gradual increase in grass lands will be observed, while in places, the greasewood which, so far as we know, is entirely useless, grows in astonishing luxuriance.

Tulasco,—654 miles from San Francisco, with an elevation of 5,482 feet. The valley seems to widen out as we descend it, and bushes grow in bunches along the banks of the stream as if the old earth, under the most favorable conditions, was trying to produce trees to beautify and adorn these barren plains. Soon Bishop's Valley can

be seen on our right. Looking to the left, we see the canon in the mountain side, down which rushes Trout Creek, when the snows are melting in the spring and early summer. This creek abounds in " speckled beauties," and unites with the Humboldt about a mile and a half below Bishop's Creek, which we soon cross, through a covered bridge.

Bishop's—is another side track station, but on we glide through the valley as it widens out into magnificent proportions. It is 649 miles from San Francisco, and has an elevation of 5,412 feet. Another little creek and valley now appear on our right, and we soon arrive at

Deeth,—642 miles from San Francisco ; elevation, 5,340 feet. It is a telegraph station, and has a few buildings around it. The valley seems very broad as we approach this station, and evidences of settlement and cultivation begin to appear. The bushes and willows along the banks of the stream increase, and it is a paradise for ducks and geese.

Halleck—is the next station, 630 miles from San Francisco, with an elevation of 5,230 feet. It is named from Camp Halleck, which is located at the base of mountains, 13 miles from the station, and across the river. A few troops are usually kept here—two or three companies,—and all the freighting and business of the post is done from this station. The town itself has a post-office, hotel, a small store and the usual saloons where "lingering death," or "blue ruin," the common terms for whisky, is doled out to soldiers, and others who patronize them. It is probable that good crops of wheat, barley and oats could be raised here by irrigating the land, but it is mostly occupied as stock ranges. Camp Halleck is not plainly seen from the railroad, though a few buildings a little removed from it, will point out its locality. A regular mail ambulance runs daily between it and the station. Leaving Halleck, Elko Mountain seems to rise on our right close to the track, but the road soon turns and we pass this landmark on our left. The Ruby Range which we have seen away to the left, from Wells to the last station, is now left in the rear as we turn westward again, and pass down one of the Humboldt Canons. The camp is delightfully located, well watered and is surrounded with thriving groves of cottonwood trees.

Peko—is the next station, merely a side track, and section-house at the head of the first canon on the river. It is 626 miles from San Francisco, with an elevation of 5,204 feet. We are now at the head of the Humboldt Canon, the first one through which the river passes. It is not wild and rugged but nevertheless sufficiently so to make it interesting. A short distance below Peko, the North Fork of Humboldt comes in. It is about as large as the main body and is a peculiar stream. It rises nearly north of Carlin, some distance west of this point, and runs to the north-east for a distance, then nearly east, and finally turns toward the south-west, and unites with the Humboldt at this point. The road through this canon is full of short curves, and winds like a serpent through the hills. Now it seems as though the train would be thrown into a heap at the base of the hill we are approaching, but a turn to the right or left saves us from such a calamity. Once or twice before we reach Osino, the valley opens out between the hills, and where the North Fork enters there is an abundance of grass which is monopolized by a rancheman. At the next station,

Osino,—614 miles from San Francisco, with an elevation of 5,132 feet,—a mere side track, we enter upon an open valley, and for about nine miles pass over a nearly straight track. The valley is all taken up by ranchemen and farmers, and good crops are raised by irrigation. The water is taken from the Humboldt above, brought down in a ditch, from which it is taken and distributed among the farms.

Elko,—606 miles from San Francisco, with an elevation of 5,063 feet. It is the regular breakfast and supper station of the road, and passengers get an excellent meal in a neat house, kept by Mr. Clark, the most genial and accommodating landlord on the road. The table is usually well supplied with fruits, fish and game.

Elko is the county-seat of Elko County—the north-eastern county of the State. It has a population of about 1,200, and is destined to become one of the important commercial and educational centers of the State. It has a large brick court-house and jail, one church, an excellent public school, and is the seat of the State University. This institution has 40 acres of ground on a bench of land overlooking the city, in plain sight of the cars on the right, just before reaching the town. Its buildings have thus far cost about $30,000, and it was first opened in 1875. The money paid for freights consigned to this place and the mining districts which are tributary to it, in 1875 amounted to nearly $400,000, and the first year the railroad was completed ran up to over $1,000,000. The town has numerous retail stores and two or three wholesale establishments, with a bank, a flouring mill, brewery, hotels, etc. Water taken from the Humboldt River some 17 miles distant, and brought here in pipes, supplies the city. It has three large freight depots, for the accommodation of its railroad business, and is the location of the United States Land office for the Elko Land District. The city is rapidly improving, brick and wooden structures taking the place of the canvas houses that were formerly prevalent. Altogether it has a bright and promising future. Indians, mostly the Sho-

shones, of all sizes and of both sexes, hover around the town and beg from the trains of cars. They still bedaub themselves with paint, and strut around with feathers in their hats in true Indian style.

Elko is destined to become famous as a watering place. About one and a half miles north of the river, and west of the town, are a group of mineral springs that are already attracting the attention of invalids. There are six springs in this group, three hot, and one of them, called the "Chicken Soup Spring," has water which, with a little salt and pepper for seasoning, tastes very much like chicken broth. We regret that no analysis of the waters of these springs has been made, which we could furnish to our readers. Tourists in search of wonderful curiosities will not fail to visit these springs and observe the craters of those which are now extinct. The sediment or incrustations formed by the water into some kind of porous rock, accumulated around the apertures until at length they were raised, in one instance, about three feet above the surface of the ground, with a hollow basin, at least one foot in diameter on the top. Other extinct springs are not as high as this one, but show the same formation and have the same peculiarities. Of the hot flowing springs—said to be white sulphur—two are quite large, and one of them is said to contain a large solution of iron. A bathing-house has been erected a short distance away, to which the water is conducted, and in which there are private bathing-rooms supplied with both hot and cold water from the springs. There is also a large swimming bath near by, with dressing-rooms adjoining. A large hotel is to be erected the present year for the accommodation of guests. There is a public conveyance running between the city and the springs for the accommodation of visitors. In the absence of an analysis of the waters we will simply state that they are claimed to be a certain cure for rheumatism and all diseases of the blood; to have a remarkable effect in paralytic cases; to have a good effect on consumptives, when the disease is not too far advanced; to cure fevers of all kinds, and the leaded cases of miners who become poisoned with the lead disease, by working among antimonial ores. The uniform temperature of the hot springs has been further utilized in hatching chickens, and the experiment, if carried to perfection, will beat all the setting hens in the country. Poultry breeders will make a note of this fact. A competent physician who is a good judge of temperaments and diseases should be located at the springs, and additional facilities for the accommodation of invalids will make it a place of great resort.

The following mining districts are tributary to Elko, and will in the future, far more than in the past, contribute to its growth and prosperity: Lone Mountain, 30 miles distant; Tuscarora, 50 miles; Grand Junction, 55 miles; Cornucopia, 70 miles; Aurora, 80 miles; Bull Run, lately changed to Centennial, 80 miles; Cope, 100 miles; Island Mountain placer diggings and quartz mines, 75 miles; Bruno, 80 miles; Hicks, 110 miles; Mardis, 100 miles. Nearly all the business done in these mining districts is transacted through Elko, and adds not a little to its bustling activity. These districts are north of the town, and located mostly in the ranges of mountains that border or lie between the forks of the Owyhee River, a stream that flows into the Snake River of Idaho. Lieutenant Wheeler, in his report of the United States Exploring Expedition, which made a partial survey of the lands and features of Nevada, describes this mineral belt as about 160 miles long, and as one of the richest in the country. It has been but partially prospected, however, and we believe the developments which are now in progress and which are hereafter to be made, will astonish the nation as to the unparalleled richness of the mines of Nevada. Up to the spring of 1876, greater developments had been made in the mines in Tuscarora and Cornucopia Districts than in most of the others. Tuscarora is the principal town in the mining district of the same name. It has about 500 inhabitants, and by September of the present year is anticipated to have 1,500. The principal mines of this district are Young America, Young America North, Young America South, Lida, De Frees, Star, Grand Deposit, Syracuse and others. The most work thus far done, is on the Young America, Young America South, and De Frees. On the first named of these three there is an inclined shaft of 190 feet, and carries free ore from surface to end of development. In sinking, levels have been run to full extent of the ground, 800 feet, and the ledge is from 20 inches to five feet wide.

It is easily worked, no explosions being required, and the ore is said to average from $80 to $100 per ton in gold and silver, without assorting. The development on the De Frees Mine is as follows: A tunnel has been run from side of hill and ledge struck, about 40 feet from the surface; an incline shaft has been sunk from level of this tunnel to a depth of 95 feet, showing fine ore all the distance, the extreme bottom showing the best ore. This ore has averaged from $90 to $150 per ton, in gold and silver. Steam hoisting works have been erected on the Young America, and a twenty-stamp mill will soon be finished, for the reduction of the ores from this mine. A twenty-stamp mill will soon be finished for the De Frees Mine, and it is expected that these mills will do some custom work for the mines being developed in the vicinity. Other mines in the district are said to be very prom-

ising. The mines in the Tuscarora and Cornucopia Districts are in a porphyry formation, with free milling ore; those in the Bull Run or Centennial District are in porphyry and lime, and the ores have to be roasted before they are milled.

Cornucopia District is about 25 miles north of Tuscarora District, and contains a population of 500. Its mines are upon the same range of mountains as the Tuscarora. The principal mines in this district are the Leopard; the Panther, the Tiger, the Hussey, and the Consolidated Cornucopia. Principal developments are on the Leopard and Hussey. The former has been largely opened, and has been running a twenty-stamp mill for the past year or more, producing about $1,000,000. The ore is said to average about $150 per ton, all silver.

The Centennial District has a population of about 200. Its principal mine is the Blue Jacket, which supplies a twenty-stamp mill with ore. A Buckner furnace for roasting is also used in connection with the mill. The ore is said to average $70 per ton, and the vein is very large, frequently 20 feet between the walls. Other districts are said to contain promising mines, but miners and those interested in mines, are always so full of hope—always expecting to strike something rich—and nearly always having a good thing in the "prospects" already found, that it is extremely difficult to determine, in a short investigation, which is the most promising district, or where are the best undeveloped mines. In a developed mine the daily product of bullion will show what it is worth.

Elko has a daily stage route north, which carries the mail and express and supplies the following places : Taylors, Tuscarora, Independence Valley, Grand Junction, Cornucopia, Bull Run and Cope. These places are generally north and north-west of Elko. At Cope, the route ends. There is a weekly mail, stage and express line to the Island Mountain District, 75 miles due north. This is a placer gold field, discovered in 1873, and it is estimated that $100,000 in gold-dust, were taken out in 1875. Three miles north of the Island Mountain District, is the Wyoming District, where valuable silver mines are said to have been discovered. The chief lode is known as the Mardis, which is owned by a Chicago company. A stamp mill is now being erected there. The mineral belt before alluded to, begins at the north end of the Goose Creek Range, and runs south-west about 160 miles. It is about 60 miles wide. Tuscarora is also somewhat noted as a placer field, while Aurora, a new district west of Cornucopia, is said to be very promising. It is 10 miles from the last named place to Aurora.

In the vicinity of the mining districts spoken of, there are rich agricultural valleys where all kinds of grain, but corn, are extensively raised,

MOUNTAIN SCENE IN THE RUBY RANGE.

and vegetables and melons grow to a great size and excellence. There are, also, vast stock ranges—all of which are tributary to Elko.

South from Elko there is a semi-weekly stage, mail and express route to Bullion City, the town of the Railroad Mining District. This town has about 150 people, and is distant 25 miles from Elko. The ores of this district are smelting ores, and the town has two large furnaces for the reduction of this ore. The principal mines are owned by the Empire Company of New York.

There is also a weekly stage line into the South Fork and Huntington Valleys—two rich agricultural valleys, which are thickly settled with farmers and stockmen. In addition to the two valleys last named, there are the Star, Pleasant and Mound Valleys, all rich agricultural districts, and all tributary to Elko. Elko has one daily and two weekly papers which are well supported. The *Post* is a weekly, Republican in politics, and the *Independent*, daily and weekly, is Democratic in politics—though party ties do not seem to be drawn very tightly, and men, regardless of their personal political affiliations, frequently receive the support of all parties.

We will now take leave of this city, and, refreshed with food and rest, renew our journey westward. The valley of the Humboldt continues to widen as we leave Elko for a few miles, and if it is winter or cool mornings of spring or autumn, we will see the steam rising in clouds from the Hot Springs across the river near the wagon bridge, on our left. The pasture and meadow lands, with occasional houses are soon passed, and we arrive at

Moleen,—501 miles from San Francisco, with an elevation of 4,982 feet. It is simply a side track station, with no settlements around it, and trains seldom stop. The same general appearance of the valley and low ranges on either side continue to this place. Occasionally as we have glanced to the left, the high peaks of the Ruby Range have lifted themselves into view, overtopping the nearer and lower range that borders the river on the south.

Passing Moleen, the valley begins to narrow, and the river gorges through the Five Mile Canon. Close to the bluffs we roll along and suddenly, almost over our heads, the beating storms of ages have washed out the softer and more porous parts of the ledges, leaving turrets and peaks, towers and domes standing along in irregular order. We could not learn that this peculiar formation had any local name; they are known in this vicinity as the "Moleen Rocks," and with this name we must be satisfied. The road curves to conform to the line of the earth now one way and now another. The scenery here is not grand and sublime, but just enough peculiar to be interesting. The towering ledges in this canon or, in the one below, are not a thousand or fifteen hundred feet high,—for accurate measurements have placed them at about 800 feet. This canon is soon passed and the valley opens out again. We soon cross Susan's Creek, and then Maggie's Creek, then Mary's Creek, and we are at

Carlin,—585 miles from San Francisco, at an elevation of 1,897 feet. It is a railroad town, the terminus of a freight division of the road and the location of the roundhouse, machine,

car and repair shops of the Humboldt Division of the Central Pacific Railroad. It is the headquarters of Mr. G. W. Coddington, the Division Superintendent. The division extends from Toano to Winnemucca, and this place is about half way between them. The town has no business outside of the railroad shops and employes, and numbers about 200 people. The roundhouse has 16 stalls for engines, and the repair shop, six pits. It is in Elko County. The old emigrant road divided just before reaching Carlin, one branch going south of the river, and the range of mountains bordering the same, and the other going north of the hills on the north side of the river. These two roads came together below, near Gravelly Ford. In the vicinity of Carlin the four little creeks come in from the north. In the order in which they are crossed, they are called Susie, Maggie, Mary and Amelia. Tradition says in regard to these names, that an emigrant was crossing the plains with his family at an early day, and that in this family were four daughters in the order given, and that as the party came to these streams, they gave the name of each one of the daughters to them—a very appropriate thing to do, and their names have been perpetuated in history. Just east of Moleen Station, the tourist looking off to the left, will notice the break or gorge through the low hills, on the south side of the river. Through this gorge the South Fork of the Humboldt comes in. This stream rises in the Ruby Range of Mountains and flows in a general westerly direction, uniting with the main river at this point. We will here state that nearly all the people in the vicinity, call the range of mountains last alluded to "Ruby," and we have followed the custom; but Lieutenant Wheeler's Map speaks of it as the Humboldt Range, and according to the custom of the people along this valley, nearly every range of mountains in sight, from one side of the State to the other, is called "Humboldt Range," or "Humboldt Mountains." As to the fertility of these and other valleys in this part of the State, it all depends upon irrigation. A sage brush plain indicates good soil, but water must be obtained to raise a crop. An effort has been made to make Carlin the shipping point to the mining districts on the north, but without much success thus far. The iron horses are changed here, and with a fresh steed we pass down the valley. It is quite wide here, but will soon narrow as we enter the Twelve Mile Canon. Like the former, the road winds around the base of the bluffs and almost under the bluffs, with the river sometimes almost under us. The peaks and ledges seem to have no local name, but some of them are very singular. In one place, soon after entering the canon, the ledges on the right side of the track seem to stand up on edge, and broken into very irregular, serrated lines,—the teeth of the ledge being uneven as to

SCENES IN THE HUMBOLDT DESERT.

1.—The Sink of the Humboldt. 2.—Mountain Scene near Death. 3.—Group of Piute Indians. 4.—Humboldt River.
5.—Great American Desert, East of Elko. 6.—Wadsworth.

length. The height of the bluffs and of the palisades below, is about the same as in the former canon—800 feet. In some places the palisades are hollowed out like caves or open arches, and the debris that has crumbled and fallen from their summits during the ages, obscures their full form and height from view.

Twelve Mile Canon, in the Palisades, was graded in six weeks by the Central Pacific Railroad Company, one cut herein containing 6,600 cubic yards. Five Mile Canon just eastward, was graded in three weeks, with a force of 5,000 to 6,000 men.

With the perpendicular walls rising on each side of us, we glide around the curves, and in the midst of these reddish lines of towering rocks, arrive at

Palisade,—576 miles from San Francisco, with an elevation of 4,841 feet. It is the initial point of the Eureka & Palisade Railroad, is a growing little place between the wall rocks of the river, and has a population of from 150 to 200 souls. It has one or two hotels or lodging-houses, stores, saloons, two large freight depots, and the machine and repair shops of the Eureka & Palisade Railroad. This road is a three feet gauge, and we shall speak of it more fully hereafter. A new station-house, ticket and telegraph office has been constructed here,—the finest on the road—to be occupied and used by both the Central Pacific and Eureka & Palisade Roads. The town is located about half the distance down the canon, and the rocky, perpendicular walls give it a picturesque appearance. The lower half of the canon is not as wild and rugged, however, as the upper half. All freight, which is mostly base bullion, that is shipped from Eureka and other points on this branch road, has to be transferred here, and the traveler may sometimes be surprised, in passing, at the immense piles of bullion which may here be seen on the platform of the railroad companies. On a hill to the right is a wooden reservoir supplied by springs, from which the water used in town is taken. The canon above was not used for the purposes of travel before the passage of the Central Pacific Road—not even a horseman venturing through it.

Shoshone Indian Village.—Just below the town is what Fenimore Cooper would doubtless call an Indian Village, but it requires a great stretch of the imagination on the part of the practical American, or live Yankee, now-a-days, to see it. A dozen or so tents, discolored with smoke and besmeared with dirt and grease, revealing from six to ten squalid beings covered with vermin, filth and rags, is not calculated to create a pleasing impression, or awaken imaginary flights to any great extent. Between Ogden and Battle Mountain, the Indians now seen on the line of the road are mostly Shoshones. Their reservation proper, for this part of the country, is at Carlin,

but very few of them are on it. For some reason, best known to themselves, they prefer to look out for themselves rather than receive the small annual amount appropriated by the government for their maintenance. They are all inveterate gamblers, and a group of squaws will sit on the ground for hours, around a blanket stretched out, and throw sticks. There are usually five of these flat sticks, from four to six inches in length, one side of which is colored slightly. Each one has a rock, a piece of coal, or some other hard substance by her side, and slightly inclined toward the blanket. She will then gather the sticks in her hand and throw them upon this rock so that they will bound on to the blanket, and the point of the game seems to be, which side of the sticks, the colored or plain, comes up in falling. It seems to be a perfect game of chance, and the one who throws so that the sticks all fall colored side up, seems to have some advantage in the game. There is said to be some improvement in their methods of living during the last fifteen years; some of them have been employed on ranches, and some of the squaws are employed in doing the plainest kinds of housework; the children and younger members of the tribe are most all becoming acquainted with the English language, and all, so far as they are able, are gradually adopting the civilized customs of dress, etc., though they invariably, thus far, paint their faces.

Leaving Palisade, the traveler will notice the railroad bridge, a short distance out, on which the narrow gauge crosses the river on its way south as it enters Pine Valley. We soon enter gorges in the canon, and on the left side of the river a high bluff rises. After passing this, and looking back about half way up the side, a column is seen jutting out in front of the bluff, and crowned with what appears like a finger. We have called it "Finger Rock." The channel of the river has been turned from its bed by a heavy embankment—a work rendered necessary to avoid a short curve, and on we go over a very crooked piece of road for nearly six miles, when we cross the river and the valley again opens. We have now passed through the Twelve Mile Canon, and soon arrive at

Cluro,—a way-station 565 miles from San Francisco, with an elevation of 4,785 feet. Trains do not stop unless signaled. The valley becomes wider, the hills more sloping and less high as they border the valley, but away to the left are the higher peaks of the Cortez Mountains. We now enter an open basin, and on the right we see the old emigrant road making up the hill from Gravelly Ford. One branch of this road, leading to the same ford, we also cross, but the old roadway, plainly visible from the cars, up the hill on the north side of the river, marks the locality of the ford itself. The river here spreads over a wide, gravelly bed, and is

THE PALISADES ON THE HUMBOLDT.

BY THOMAS MORAN.

always shallow so that it is easily crossed. The emigrants, in the days of ox and mule trains, took advantage of this crossing to send letters, either one way or the other, by outward bound or returning trains. They would split a willow sprout by the side of the road and put their letters in it, which would be taken out by some one in the first train and carried to the nearest post-office on the route.

In 1858, it is said, that an Indian massacre took place here, in which 18 emigrants were killed; and other skirmishes with the gentle red men, were frequently in order. The old emigrant road is fairly lined with the graves of emigrants, who perished on their way to the land of

finally come to believe it themselves; and this may account for the many wonderful stories that have been palmed off on some book-makers, and by them, in turn, hashed up for the traveling public. Travelers can always hear all they choose, but it is well to be a little cautious about believing all they hear.

The Maiden's Grave.—There is hardly an old resident on this coast, but who has some incident to relate in reference to Gravelly Ford. It was not only an excellent crossing place, but it was also a fine camping place, where both man and beast could recruit after the weary days on the dreary plains. There were wide bottomlands that offered excellent grazing for stock,

ENTERING HUMBOLDT CANON.

gold, or in returning from the same. There are, also, many of the Shoshones and Piutes now living, who have been made cripples in these battles and skirmishes with the emigrants. They will talk about them with their acquaintances, and say "heap of white men killed there," but can seldom be induced to say how many Indians were slain in the same conflict. Indeed, parties representing each side of the contending forces have become well acquainted, and now frequently meet each other on friendly terms. There is a disposition, also, among these old plainsmen "to spin yarns," equal to any old navigator that ever lived, and one has to be extremely cautious as to what he believes. These old story-tellers are like old Jim Bridger—they will tell a lie so often and so earnestly, that they

and the small brush along the banks of the stream gave excellent shade and firewood. On a low point of land that juts out toward the river on the south side of the track, and just below this ford, is the Maiden's Grave. Tradition has it that she was one of a party of emigrants from Missouri, and that, at this ford, while they were in camp, she sickened and died. Her loving friends laid her away to rest in a grave on this point of land, in plain sight of the ford and of the valley for miles in either direction. But while her remains were crumbling into dust, and she, too, was fading from the memory of all, perhaps, but her immediate relatives, the railroad builders came along, and found the low mound, and the decayed head-board which marked her resting-place. With that admiration of, and devotion to woman, which characterizes American citizens of even humble origin, they made a new grave and surrounded it with an enclosure—a picket fence, painted white—and by the side of it erected a cross, the emblem of the Christian's faith, which bears on one side, this legend—"The Maiden's Grave"—and on the other, her name, "Lucinda Duncan." All honor to the men whose respect for the true woman led them to the performance of this praiseworthy act—an act which would have been performed by no race under the heavens, but ours: and not by them, indeed, to the remains, under similar circumstances, of a representative of the sterner sex. The location of this grave is near Beowawe, and the point is now used as a burial ground by the people living in the vicinity. Passing the point where the grave is located, an extended valley comes in from the left, south of which extends the Cortez Range of Mountains. We now arrive at

Beowawe,—556 miles from San Francisco, with an elevation of 4,695 feet. It has a hotel, a few dwellings, and is the station where the business of the Cortez Mining District is transacted. There is no regular stage line to this district, but private conveyances may be obtained. The mines are reported looking well—are mostly individual property. They are 30 miles from the station and a tri-weekly mail is carried by some parties who are interested in the matter. A reduction mill has been erected there, which is producing bullion regularly. There is a beautiful signification attached to the name of this station, which will be more fully realized after the station is passed, than before. It means "gate," or "the gate," and as you look back from below, the conformation of the hills on either side of the valley is such, that the station seems to stand in an open gateway, up the Humboldt Valley to the canon beyond. The valley is occasionally dotted with farm-houses, or ranches, and besides stock raising, which is one of the principal features of this part of the country, there is considerable done in the way of agriculture, barley being the chief crop—yielding immensely when the land is properly irrigated and the crops taken care of. At Beowawe an immense stretch of valley land can be seen away to the right, with a range of mountains, which seems to be an extension of the Reese River Range, north of the Humboldt, west of it. As the river bends northward to meet these valleys, it receives the waters of Boulder and Rock Creeks, which come in from the north and northeast. These creeks open up a vast country, which is well occupied by ranches and stockmen. Leaving Beowawe, we cross a large valley and sage brush plain—the valley coming in from the south. A few miles out, we notice, if the weather is at all cool, steam rising from the side of the mountain, while colored streaks, caused by the sediment of the springs, can clearly be

seen from the passing train. This steam comes from the Hot Springs on the mountain side, and the sediment marks their locality. The water in some of these springs is boiling hot, and partakes strongly of sulphur. We could not learn that any analysis had been made, nor could any one inform us of the exact temperature. There is a vast field for geological exploration in this State, and the general government should enter upon the work at once. The springs also are impregnated with iron, but no one knows the quantity, nor just in what proportion these mineral waters are mixed. To the inhabitants in this immediate vicinity, of course, they have ceased to be a wonder; but to the majority of travelers, they will ever be clothed with interest. A creek of alkali water comes down from the springs and we cross it on the flat alluded to, and the wide valley off to the right is still better seen as we approach and pass

Shoshone,—516 miles from San Francisco; elevation, 4,636 feet. It is simply a side track station. Rock Creek, before spoken of, comes into the Humboldt nearly opposite this place, and the broad valley continues, on the right of the road. The station is called Shoshone Point by the people in the valley, because a mountain, or high ridge, pushes out into the valley, like a promontory. This is one of the landmarks on the dividing line between the Shoshone and Piute tribes of Indians; but the line we consider purely imaginary, from the fact that Indians, as a general thing, go where they please in this country, lines or no lines. The wide basin spoken of, continues below and off to the right of this station, and, as we pass on, a long line of board fence will be noticed stretching, from a point high up on the mountain, across the track and valley toward the Humboldt River, on the right. This is the eastern line of Dunphy & Hildreth's stock ranche. In seven miles we shall pass the western line, or fence. We have before spoken of Iliff, as the cattle king of the plains, and, while this is true east of the Black Hills of Wyoming, he will have to yield the crown to some of the cattle kings of the Pacific Coast. This firm has 20 miles of fencing in these two lines: They have over 20 thousand acres fenced in. Their fences, made of redwood posts and Oregon pine boards, cost them a little over $900 per mile. They have, altogether, about 40,000 head of cattle, mainly in two herds—one here and the other north, on the Snake River. They have purchased of the State, government and Central Pacific Railroad and now own about 30,000 acres of land. Most of their cattle are shipped to, and find a market in San Francisco.

The immense range fenced in at this point is occupied by a select herd of graded stock, and some of the best blooded animals in the country are annually purchased to improve the grades.

The system they have adopted for grading up their herds, is such that in a very few years they will have the largest herd of high graded stock in the country. They also cut large quantities of hay on the meadow lands near the banks of the Humboldt, which they feed to all their weak cattle, and to those which they intend for late winter, or early spring market. The Humboldt Valley and its tributaries constitute the best part of the State for stock ranges. The snow seldom falls very deep; does not stay long, and the grass makes its appearance early in the spring. The purchase of large tracts of land by these foresighted cattlemen, will give them a monopoly of the business in the future.

Argenta,—535 miles from San Francisco; elevation, 4,518 feet. It is simply a side track station, where considerable hay is shipped. This station is immediately surrounded by alkali flats, near the base of the Reese River Mountains. The road continues for a few miles along the base of these mountains, when, suddenly, a broad valley opens out, on the left. It is the valley of Reese River. We turn to the right, cross the valley and the river—all there is left of it—and arrive at

Battle Mountain,—524 miles from San Francisco, with an elevation of 4,511 feet. It is located at the junction of the Reese River and Humboldt Valleys. The mountain which gives it its name is about three miles south of the station, where there are magnificent springs from which water is conducted to the town, supplying the railroad and inhabitants with water. Battle Mountain is the regular dinner station on the line of the road, and the passenger will dine at a very cosy and attractive place. In the midst of a surrounding desert he will observe the flowing fountain and patches of green grass which rest here greet his eyes, together with the evident taste and care which is manifested about everything connected with the house. Travelers will occasionally have a great deal of fun in listening to the talk of the Chinese waiters.

The town is mostly on one street south of the railroad. It has several quite extensive stores, a public hall, an excellent school-house, two large freight depots, a first-class hotel. It has an extensive and rapidly increasing trade with the surrounding country, and newly developed mining districts in its neighborhood. It is the business center of a large number of stockmen, and the trading point for a large number of mining districts—districts considerably scattered over quite a large part of the State. The town is located in Lander County, but is not the county-seat. Austin, 90 miles away, claims that honor.

Daily stages, carrying the mail and express, leave here for Austin, Belmont and other places south, immediately on the arrival of the trains from the west. The distance to Austin, 90 miles, is made by about 6 o'clock on the morning of the

day after departure, and, of course, takes in an all night stage ride. Belmont, about 90 miles from Austin, is reached in the evening of the day after departure.

The following mining districts, south of the railroad, are reached by stages to Lewis and Tuscarora: commencing on the east side of the Reese River Range, first is the Lewis Mining District, 16 miles distant from Battle Mountain. It is located on the northern extremity of the range. At the southern extremity of this range is the Austin District. The mountain range between these two districts, is said to contain mines, but it has not been thoroughly prospected. Austin, the head-quarters of the Austin District, is a very nice town with a population of about 3,000 souls. It is said to possess a good deal of public spirit, and is active and enterprising. It has a fine court-house, three churches, a large brick public school building, some elegant residences, and other appearances of thrift. The Reese River Valley is about 160 miles long, traversed its entire length by the river of the same name, though it cannot be called much of a river where the railroad crosses it, near Battle Mountain. The upper portion of the valley, about 50 miles in length, is a very fine agricultural district, is quite well settled, and is tributary to Austin. The valley is also settled in places where mountain streams come into it, between Battle Mountain and Austin. The Manhattan Company, composed of New York capitalists, own and operate nearly all the mines in the Austin District. They are reported to possess some excellent mines with milling ore, some of which is high grade. There are other mining districts around Austin, and tributary to it—such as the Jefferson, Ione, Belmont, etc., which are favorably spoken of.

On the west side of the Reese River Valley, and immediately south of Battle Mountain, are the following districts: Battle Mountain District, 7 miles distant; Galena District, 16 miles; Copper Canon, 18 miles, and Jersey, 55 miles. The copper mines are owned by an English company—which is now putting in concentrating machinery—and are said to be rich. The Jersey District produces smelting ore, and has one or two furnaces already erected which are turning out bullion.

North of Battle Mountain are the Cornucopia and Tuscarora Districts which are said to do some business from this place, and are regarded as tributary to it. Several stations on the line of the road are competing for the trade of these mining districts, and all claim it, and also claim to be the nearest railroad point, with the best wagon roads, etc.

Battle Mountain—not north of the Humboldt River, but about three miles south of the station—is reported to have been the scene of a conflict between a party of emigrants camped near the springs heretofore spoken of, and a band of redskins who had an innate hankering after the stock of the said party of emigrants. The losses of this battle are said to have been quite severe on both sides, considering the numbers engaged. It is generally conceded, however, that the redskins got the worst of it, though they say "A heap white men killed there."

The opening, or valley directly opposite and north of Battle Mountain, is without water in its lower portion, and is a desert of sand and sage brush. The range of mountains at whose base the town is situated, and south of it, on the west side of Reese River Valley, is sometimes called the Battle Mountain Range, and sometimes the Fish Creek Range, from a creek that rises in it about 25 miles south of Battle Mountain, and runs into Reese River Valley.

About 25 miles south of Battle Mountain, are some very fine hot springs. There are nearly 60 of them, covering about half a section of land. The largest one is about 60 feet long by 30 feet wide, and at times rises and falls from three to five feet. These springs are on the stage road to Austin, and are something of a wonder to travelers in that direction.

How Ore is Reduced.—We visited the reduction works of the Lewis District, and to those who are not familiar with the way in which ores are handled, the following account may be of some interest. The ore from the mine in this district is neither free milling nor smelting ore. It has to be dried before it can be milled, and then roasted before it can be separated and amalgamated. The following is our account of the process in taking the silver from the ore: The ore, as it comes from the mine, is first run through a crusher—a machine which has two heavy pieces of iron coming together like the human jaws in chewing. It is then passed either onto drying pans, heated by a fire from some furnace, or into a revolving dryer where all the moisture is extracted. From this dryer it passes through a large iron tube or pipe into the milling hoppers below. These hoppers, holding the crushed and dried ore, are similar to those seen in old fashioned grist-mills, and from them the ore runs on to the stamp mill. The stamp mill is a series of upright iron shafts with a heavy iron or steel hammer on the lower end of each shaft. By machinery, these shafts are lifted up very rapidly and dropped—a process repeated by each one from sixty to ninety times per minute. As they fall, they stamp or crush the ore to powder. In fact it leaves this mill pulverized like dust, and is conveyed by a horizontal screw to an adjoining room, where it is taken by elevators, just like those used in flouring mills to a bin or tank above. In the room where this elevator and bin are, is the cylindrical roaster and furnace. From the tank the pulverized ore is taken as required, through an iron pipe into a large horizontal revolving roaster. About one and one-half tons of ore dust are required to charge the roaster, to which is added from eight to ten per cent. of salt. The heat and fire from the furnace pass through this roaster as it slowly turns around, the ore now mixed with salt, falling of course, from side to side at each revolution, across and through the flames. It is kept in this place about seven hours, or until it is supposed to be thoroughly chloridized. It is a sulphuret ore as it comes from the mine, but becomes a chloride ore by passing through this process. It comes out of the roaster at a white heat, is then wet down and cooled, and taken to an amalgamating pan which is agitated with a muller, which revolves in the pan from 60 to 70 times per minute—in other words, it is a stirring apparatus. One and a half tons of ore are put into these pans, to which is added about 350 lbs. of quicksilver. Water is then turned in and the mixture stirred a little, to the consistency of thick paste. Then hot steam is let in upon the mass, and while in process of agitation it is heated to a boiling heat. The pulp, as it is now called, is kept in this pan and constantly agitated or stirred for about seven hours. A plug is then drawn from the bottom of the tank or pan, and the pulp passes into "a settler" or "separator" where it is again agitated in water—the amalgam, meanwhile, settling to the bottom of the "settler," the quicksilver—with the silver—being drawn into a little receiver, from which it is dipped into sacks and strained. The quicksilver being thus nearly all taken out, the balance is called dry amalgam, and this is taken to an iron retort, cylindrical in shape, about five feet long and 12 inches in diameter. This cylinder is charged with about 900 lbs. of this dry amalgam, then thoroughly sealed, after which it is heated from a furnace underneath. The quicksilver remaining in the amalgam, volatilizes under the action of heat, and passes through an iron tube surrounded by cold water, where it is condensed and saved. The quicksilver being expelled by the action of the heat, leaves the crude bullion (silver in this case) in the cylinder. The dry amalgam remains in the retort some six or seven hours,—requiring two or three hours additional to cool. The base bullion is then taken out, cut into small pieces and placed in a black lead crucible, and melted over a charcoal fire. While in this crucible the dross of course rises to the surface of the molten metal and is skimmed off. In the crucible it is thoroughly stirred with a long iron spoon, and a sample poured into cold water for assaying purposes. This is done just before the hot metal is poured into the molds and becomes bars. The assay determines its fineness and value, which is stamped upon it, and it is then shipped and sold. It goes into the mill ore from the mine, and comes out silver in bars.

The Great Plains and Desert.

BY JOAQUIN MILLER.

Go ye and look upon that land,
That far, vast land that few behold,
And none beholding, understand ;
That old, old land, which men call new,
That land as old as time is old :

Go journey with the seasons through
Its wastes, and learn how limitless,
How shoreless lie the distances,
Before you come to question this,
Or dare to dream what grandeur is.

The solemn silence of that plain,
Where unmanned tempests ride and reign,
It awes and it possesses you,
'Tis, oh, so eloquent.

        The blue
And bended skies seem built for it,
With rounded roof all fashioned fit,
And frescoed clouds, quaint-wrought and true :
While all else seems so far, so vain,
An idle tale but illy told,
Before this land so lone and old.

Lo ! here you learn how more than fit,
And dignified is silence, when
You hear the petty jeers of men,
Who point, and show their pointless wit.
The vastness of that voiceless plain,
Its awful solitudes remain,
Thenceforth for aye a part of you,

And you are of the favored few,
For you have learned your littleness.

Some silent red men cross your track ;
Some sun-tann'd trappers come and go ;
Some rolling seas of buffalo
Break thunder-like and far away,
Against the foot hills, breaking back,
Like breakers of some troubled bay ;
But not a voice the long, lone day.

Some white tail'd antelope flow by,
So airy-like ; some foxes shy,
And shadow-like shoot to and fro,
Like weaver's shuttles as you pass—;
And now and then from out the grass,
You hear some lone bird chick, and call,
A sharp keen call for her lost brood. •
That only make the solitude,
That mantles like some sombre pall,
Seem deeper still, and that is all.

A wide domain of mysteries,
And signs that men misunderstand !
A land of space and dreams : a land
Of sea, salt lakes and dried up seas !
A land of caves and caravans,
And lonely wells and pools.
        A land
That hath its purposes and plans,
That seem so like dead Palestine,
Save that its wastes have no confine,
Till pushed against the levell'd skies.

How the Piutes Bury their Dead.—
There seems to be a very irregular custom in
practice among this tribe of Indians, in reference to the disposition they make of their dead.
When one of their number is sick, the services
of a Medicine Man, as he is called, are made
available, and all his arts and skill are exhausted
to effect a recovery if possible. The Medicine
Man comes, and goes through a system of con-
tortions, which would rack the frame of a white
person till it was unjointed, makes passes with
the hands over the body of the sick one, and
keeps up a continual howl that must grate very
harshly upon the nerves of a sensitive person.
Amidst these motions and groans and passes, the
victim to disease lingers, until death puts an
end to his sufferings. When the final dissolu-
tion has occurred, the body hardly has time to
become cold, before it is wrapped in a blanket,
or old cloths, and preparations are made for the
burial. This is done in secret, and, strange as
it may appear, though many have died since the
advent of the whites into this country, not a
single person, so far as we could learn, knows of
the burial place of a Piute Indian. The Indians
will scatter in small parties, some of whom, it is
supposed, will dig a grave, or perhaps several of
them ; and though their actions may be closely
watched, they somehow manage to spirit away
the body and conceal it in its final resting-place
so completely, that its location is unknown.
Whether the immediate relatives of the deceased
are made acquainted with the burial place, we
could not learn, but judge not, from the fact
that all traces of the grave are obliterated from
human view. This custom of concealing their
dead, so very strange to us, is said to be universal among this tribe. Another singular custom
among them, is to remove the tent, or wick-ee-up,
at once, as soon as the body is taken away.
They claim that an evil spirit has cursed the
spot, and that it would be dangerous for them to
remain in the "wick-ee" longer, or on the
ground where it stood. They hasten into this
work as if actuated by the greatest fear, and,
ever afterwards, seem to regard it with suspicious
awe.

How the Piutes Catch Fish.—Nearly
all the Indians seen on the line of the road between Battle Mountain and Reno, are Piutes.
They are great rabbit-hunters, and very successful in fishing. They make hooks from rabbit
bones and greasewood, which are certainly superior to the most improved article made by the
whites. This hook is in the shape of what
might be called the letter "V" condensed; that
is, the prongs do not spread very far. A line,
made of the sinews of animals, or the bark of a
species of wild hemp, is attached to this hook at
the angle, and baited with a snail or fresh water
bloodsucker. Several of these hooks are tied to
a heavier line, or a piece of light rope, one above

the other, so far that they will not become tangled or snarled. A stone is then tied to the end
of the heavy line, and it is cast into the stream.
The fish take the bait readily, but Mr. Indian
does not "pull up" when he feels one fish on the
line. He waits until the indications are that
several fish are there—one on each hook—and
then he pulls out the heavy line, with fish and all.
It seems that the hooks are so made that they
can be swallowed easily enough with the bait, but
as soon as the fish begins to struggle, the string
acts on both prongs of the hook, pulling it
straight, the ends of the letter "V" hook, of
course, piercing its throat. It can neither swallow it, nor cast it forth from its mouth. The
more it pulls and struggles, the more straight-
ened the hook becomes. Besides the superiority
of this hook, one fish being caught, others are
naturally drawn around it, and seize the tempting bait upon the fatal hook. In this way an Indian will catch a dozen or so fish, while a white
man, with his fancy rod and "flies" and
"spoons," and other inventions to lure the finny
tribes and tempt them to take a bait, will catch
not one.

Leaving Battle Mountain we have a straight
track for about 20 miles, across a sage brush
plain, the river and a narrow strip of bottom-
lands, on our right.

Piute,—519 miles from San Francisco, with
no elevation given, and

Coin,—511 miles from San Francisco, are
simply side track stations where trains meet and
pass, but of no importance to the traveler. There
was no Indian battle fought near Piute, nor does
the Reese River sink into the valley here. What
battle there was, was fought, as before stated,
about three miles south of Battle Mountain Station, and what the sands in the valley do not ab-
sorb of the waters of Reese River, may be seen—
a little alkali stream—flowing across the railroad
track, east of Battle Mountain, to effect a junction with the Humboldt River.

Stone House,—504 miles from San Francisco, with an elevation of 4,422 feet. This was
not an old trading post, but a station in former
times of the Overland Stage Company, and the
house, built of stone near some very fine springs,
was one of the eating-houses on their line, where
travelers could relish square meals of bacon and
coffee with safety. There is no particular ravine
near the old ruins which the traveler would
notice as an impregnable fortress. Quite a
number of skirmishes are reported to have taken
place near this station, however, and the graves
yet distinguished in its vicinity tell of the number who were killed near this place, or died here
on their journey to the golden shores of the
Pacific. Stone House Mountain, as it is now
called, rears its head just back of the crumbling
ruins, and from its summit a most extensive and
beautiful view of the neighboring valleys and

surrounding country can be obtained. On the western slope of this mountain, and about seven miles from the station, are some hot springs similar to others found in the Great Basin. But these springs are no more peculiar than those found at Golconda, a few miles below, nor different from those found near Beowawe, which have already been mentioned. A gentleman who camped four days near them, while in pursuit of a marauding party of Indians, informs us that there are four springs at the place alluded to, that they vary in temperature, and that only one is boiling hot, from which steam simply rises in the cool mornings of the season. The waters of this particular spring are very fine for drinking, when cooled. These springs are not in sight from the railroad, nor can the steam therefrom be seen. About the only way one can become scalded is to tumble into it. In such a case, something more than "simple cerate and the prayers of friends" will be required. During the passage of the Humboldt Valley we cross several dry valleys, between ranges of mountains, that seem to be cut in twain by the river. These valleys are mostly covered with sand and sage brush; occasionally have streams flowing down from the mountains which soon sink in the sands. There is a wide valley of this description north of the track as we approach

Iron Point,—191 miles from San Francisco; elevation, 4,375 feet. This station is near the point of a low ridge, with barren sides and rocky summit; the rocks a little reddish, indicating the proximity of iron. It is a shipping point for cattle, and has extensive stock-yards, though there are no other accommodations near by. This ridge was formerly considered the boundary line between the Shoshones and Piutes, and a trespass by either party has been the cause of many an Indian war. The wasting away of these tribes, however, renders the line simply imaginary, and the rights of either party to exclusive privileges on either side are no longer regarded. The valley now narrows, and we pass through a sort of a canon, with high bluffs on both sides of the road. We wind round numerous curves, and after the canon is passed, we shall see the remains of an old irrigating ditch that was started here by a French company to take water from the Humboldt and carry it down the valley quite a distance for irrigating and mill purposes. A great amount of labor and money was expended upon this enterprise, but it was finally abandoned. We believe a small outlay, comparatively, would now make it a success. The ditch began at an adobe house, just as we are through a short canon and as the valley again begins to widen. This pass was called 'Emigrant Canon' in the days of wagon travel.

Golconda,—478 miles from San Francisco, with an elevation of 4,385 feet. The little town here has one or two stores, a hotel, several adobe houses and the usual railroad conveniences. Golconda is favorably located, as regards two or three important mining districts, and will eventually do considerable business with them. It is also the location of some eight or ten hot mineral springs, which are passed on the right side of the track, just after leaving town. These springs vary in temperature from cool, or tepid water, to that which is boiling hot. The swimming bath —an excavation in the ground—is supplied with tepid water, and is said to be very exhilarating. The Boiling Spring—exact temperature and analysis unknown—is utilized by the farmers in the valley in scalding their swine. The water is said to be hot enough to boil an egg in one minute. Here clouds of steam can be seen when the weather is cold, rising from the hot water and warm soil surrounding.

One of the springs near this station is also a curiosity, and should be visited by tourists. It is conical in shape, like an inverted tea-cup, four or five feet high, with a basin about three feet in diameter on the top. Formerly, the water came in at the bottom of this basin and bubbled over the rim; but a few years since, it was tapped from below, and the water now flows out at the side, leaving the basin and cone as it was formed, by the sedimentary incrustations and deposit. The water flowing from the hot spring is used for irrigating purposes, and the owners of the spring have a monopoly of early vegetable "garden truck," raising early radishes, lettuce, onions, etc., before their season, by the warmth produced from the hot water. It is expected that the springs will be improved this year by the erection of a suitable bathing-house and hotel for the accommodation of guests.

Gold Run Mining District, south of Golconda, is tributary to the place. The mines are reported rich in large bodies of ore, but not of a very high grade. They are, however, easily accessible, and not more than 10 or 15 miles from the railroad, with good wagon roads the entire distance. The ore in this district is both smelting and milling—but requires roasting if it is to be milled. Three prospects are now being worked. About three miles from town is a small four-stamp mill, which is running on ore from this district.

Paradise District of gold and silver mines, is about 18 miles north of Golconda. The ore is said to be a rich milling variety, but the prospects are not yet sufficiently developed to determine the true value of the district.

Tule,—530 miles from San Francisco, with an elevation of 4,313 feet. It is simply a side track of no importance to travelers, and trains seldom stop. After leaving Golconda, we look toward the north and see the opening of Eden Valley. East of this valley, and to our right, is the Soldier's Spring Range, a broken range of mountains. Eden Valley extends north to the Little

Humboldt River. In fact, this river flows through the upper portion of the valley, and rises in the range just named, and flows in a south-westerly direction through Paradise Valley and unites with the Humboldt, nearly opposite, north of Tule. Paradise Valley is a fine agricultural basin, thickly settled, about 30 miles north. Paradise Valley is the name of the post-office—a semi-weekly line of mail stages connecting it with Winnemucca, the county-seat of Humboldt County. This valley is shaped like a horseshoe, and produces superior crops of barley, wheat, rye and all kinds of vegetables. It seems to have a depression in the center, and, while it is nearly all cultivated, the best crops are raised on the slopes toward the mountains. The soil is a black, gravelly loam, and sage brush grows on the slopes to enormous size. Experiments in fruit culture have been tried, but, thus far, with indifferent success. Paradise Valley has a flouring-mill, store and dwellings, and gives every indication of thrift. Its name indicates the high esteem in which it is held by the settlers. It is nearly surrounded by mountains, and the numerous streams flowing down from them, afford ample water for irrigation. Most of these streams sink in the ground before they reach the Little Humboldt. Five miles beyond Tule, we reach

Winnemucca,—463 miles from San Francisco ; elevation, 4,332 feet. It is named in honor of the chief of the Piute tribe of Indians. The name itself means " chief," and is given to any member of the tribe who holds that office. The Piutes are divided into several bands, each under a chief they call " Captau," thought here to be derived from the Spanish, and to mean the same as our English word, "captain." Winnemucca is now about 70 years old, and lives on the Malheur Reservation, in Oregon—a reservation occupied by the Piutes and Bannocks. He is very much respected — almost worshiped by his dusky followers.

The town is the county-seat of Humboldt County, and has a population of about 1,200 people, among whom are some Indians, and quite a number of Chinamen. It is the western terminus of the Humboldt Division of the Central Pacific, has a large roundhouse, two large freight depots and the usual offices, etc., for the accommodation of the railroad business. An elegant brick court-house has been erected, together with several stores, hotels, shops, a large flouring-mill, a foundry, a ten-stamp quartz mill, with a capacity for crushing ten tons of ore every 24 hours, and other public improvements completed, or in contemplation. The town is divided into two parts—upper and lower; the latter being built on the bottom land near the river, and the upper, on a huge sand-bank, adjoining the railroad. Most of the buildings are frame, though a few are built of brick, or adobe, which, in this western country, are called " dobe," for short.

There is a school-house with accommodations for about 150 pupils—two apartments, and no churches. It is also quite a shipping point for cattle and wool. About 9,000 head of cattle were shipped to the San Francisco market from this place, in the months of January and February of the present year. In the spring of 1875, over 500,000 lbs. of wool were shipped to New York and Boston markets. It is also the shipping point to Camp McDermott, near the northern line of the State; to Silver City and Boise City, Idaho ; and to Baker and Grant

WINNEMUCCA, THE NAPOLEON OF THE PIUTES.

Counties, in south-eastern Oregon. The stage lines are as follows : Daily stage and mail line to Silver City and Boise City, Idaho,—distance to Silver City, 210 miles, extension to Boise, 65 miles farther. The same line supplies Camp McDermott, 85 miles distant. Semi-weekly line, Mondays and Fridays, to Paradise Valley, 45 miles. Weekly line—soon to be made daily and to carry the mail to Jersey, 65 miles, (south) leaving at present every Wednesday. There is also an immense freighting business done with the mining districts in the vicinity, and with Idaho Territory. Regular freight lines are on the road between this place and Silver City. The following mining districts are tributary to Winnemucca and located in Humboldt County; beginning north of the railroad—there are placer mines west of Paradise Valley and settlement; at Willow Creek about 60 miles distant from Winnemucca. Bartlett Creek Mines, gold and silver, 100 miles distant. Varyville is the town of this camp. It has about a hundred inhabitants, and is north-west of this city. Two quartz mills are in operation there, controlled by a Chicago company. Pueblo District—copper mines, about 100 miles distant. Winnemucca District—silver, two miles west of town, mines owned and operated by the Humboldt Mining Company, which has a ten-stamp quartz mill in town, supplied in part with ore from their mine, and run on custom ore at times. The ores in this vicinity have to be roasted, and this mill has a drop furnace—the ore dropping through the flaming fire instead of being turned in a revolving heated cylinder.

Central District in Eugene Mountain, southwest of town, produces silver ore and has a quartz mill.

South of the railroad there is Jersey District and town, 65 miles distant. The business of this mining camp is divided between Battle Mountain and this place—both claiming it. The town has about 200 people. The ore is argentiferous galena, rather above the average grade, and is found in large quantities. A smelting furnace has been erected and a considerable amount of base bullion has been turned out. The smelter has a capacity of 25 tons per day. The shaft in the mine has been sunk to a depth of 130 feet, and levels run about 300 feet. It is claimed to be a very promising mining district.

Antimony District is 80 miles due south of Winnemucca. Slabs of that mineral, weighing three tons, and averaging 70 per cent. pure antimony, can be obtained in this district. Near it is the Humboldt Salt Marsh, where salt, 95 per cent. pure, can be shoveled up by the wagonload. This salt deposit is very extensive, and the supply seems to be exhaustless. Underneath the surface deposit, rock salt, or salt in large cakes or slabs, is taken out, in the driest part of the season, by the ton.

In the valley leading to the above-named district are some very fine hot springs, but they are so common here as to be no curiosity. Twelve miles out, in the same valley, is a rich agricultural district, thickly settled, where not only grain and vegetables have been successfully cultivated, but the experiments in fruit culture have also proved successful. At the county fair, held in this city during the fall of 1875, fine specimens of apples, peaches, pears and plums were exhibited which were raised in this valley.

Bolivia District, silver ore, 70 miles away. Ore from this district is shipped to various points; some to the mill here that is claimed to average $500 per ton. Comminsville Camp, in

Sierra District, produces gold and silver ore. A ten-stamp mill is erected there.

As the tourist walks the platform at this place, looking across the river to the right, he will see Winnemucca Mountain, but a short distance away, overlooking the town. To the left, he will observe the peaks of the Franklin or Sonoma Range. To the east, and somewhat distant, are the ragged summits of the Soldier's Spring Range, while a little to the south-west, but apparently in front, Eugene Mountain lifts itself up as a landmark to guide the traveler on his way. This mountain will be passed on our left as we continue the journey.

Winnemucca has two newspapers, *The Daily Humboldt Register* and the *Daily Silver State*. Both are energetic little sheets, and fitly illustrate the enterprise of these western towns. Across the river, over a wooden bridge, is located the cemetery, in which the remains of the dead are enclosed. It is on an elevated, sandy bench, the second terrace or step from the river level. By it winds the stage road to Idaho and the north. The Piutes have their tents scattered on all sides of the town, to which the euphonious name of "Wick-ee-ups" is given. They serve to remind one of the departing glory—if they ever had any—of the Indian race. In this tribe, to their honor be it said, licentiousness among their women is very rare, and virtue is held in high esteem. But very few half-breed Indians can be found, or are they known in the State. This tribe, with the Bannocks, were especially hostile to the whites in an early day, and fought for many years with desperation and cruelty to prevent the settlement and development of this country. Their courage and deadly enmity has been displayed on many a hard-fought field, and if there are families in the East, or on the Pacific Coast, who still mourn the loss of missing ones, who were last heard of as crossing the plains, some Indian warrior, yet living, might be able to explain the mystery which has enveloped their final doom. For a number of years, with ceaseless vigilance, they hung around the trains of emigrants, eager to dispatch a stray victim, or upon the borders of settlements, ready to strike down the hardy pioneer at the first favorable opportunity. At present, overpowered by numbers, they live upon the bounty of their former enemies, and are slowly, but surely learning, by example, the ways of civilization. As a class, however, they are still indolent, dirty and covered with vermin. But they begin to learn the worth of money, and know already that it has a purchasing power which will supply their scanty wardrobe, and satisfy their longing appetites.

The mines on the top of Winnemucca Mountain are plainly seen, and the road that leads to them, from the cars, and the tourist from this will be able to understand something of the difficulties attending the process of getting out ore.

As we pass westward, a grand view of a distant range is obtained between Winnemucca and Black Butte. The last named mountain is an isolated peak, and stands out like a sentinel on guard. As we approach the higher peaks of the East or Humboldt Range, we pass

Rose Creek,—453 miles from San Francisco, with an elevation of 4,322 feet. It is an unimportant station, with side track, etc. You will have to look sharp to see the creek, or the roses, and, by way of variety, you will discover plenty of sage brush. It is a staple article, in this country. The river still winds its way along our right, and there is an occasional ranche on the mountain slope, where the water from some spring, or little creek, can be obtained for irrigation.

Raspberry, —443 miles from San Francisco; elevation 4,327 feet. If roses were few and far between, at the last station, raspberries are less frequent here. But these names are tantalizing and suggestive in the places they are applied to. Having turned the point of East Range, we bear off to the left. Eugene Mountain is now on our right, across the Humboldt River.

Mill City,—435 miles from San Francisco, with an elevation of 4,225 feet. This was once a town with great prospects. It was to be the terminus of the irrigating ditch, which we have seen beyond Winnemucca and Golconda, and this ditch, by a small expenditure of money, could now be made available, as far as Winnemucca. The Humboldt Mining Company, owning the stamp mill at that place, already alluded to, also own this ditch. The French capitalists, who put their money into the enterprise, long since abandoned it. Mill City, in their imagination, was to be the seat of empire—a mighty city of the plains, of influence and power. The banks of the canal they partially dug, were to be

lined with factories and mills. The mineral bearing ore of the State was to be brought to these mills, for reduction. Their ideas were grand, and could have been made successful, under other circumstances; but they were in advance of the times—ahead of the age in which they lived. In the mutations of time, the town has become a great shipping-point for cattle—100 cars being shipped last year—a number which is greatly exceeded in some years. It has a steam foundry in operation,—mostly employed in the manufacture and repair of mining machinery,—and is the railroad point where the business of several mining districts is done. Ore from Dun Glen, Unionville and Star City, comes here for shipment, and, once per week, bullion comes over from Unionville. This last place was formerly more lively than at present. It is a town of about 300 people—has four quartz mills in operation, and is connected with Mill City by a daily stage line, which passes by Star City—distance to Unionville, 20 miles; to Star City, 10 miles; to Dun Glen, 8 miles. The general course of the railroad being east and west, these places are all south of it. The mining districts, including the towns named, which are tributary to this place, are Unionville, Star and Indian Districts—all tributary to Mill City. Mill City has a neat little hotel, a livery stable and several dwellings. It may possibly be the junction of a railroad to Oregon—surveys of which have been, and are now being made.

Leaving Mill City, we pass rapidly by an opening or gap in the mountains on our left, while a broad extent of valley opens out on our right, as Eugene Mountain sinks into the plain. The river recedes from our view, and winds along across an alkali flat some six or seven miles away. Through this opening on our right, the proposed branch railroad to Oregon will pass.—

R. R. STATION, HUMBOLDT, NEVADA.

13

Surveys have already been made, and it is supposed the men in the Central Pacific Company will build it, and the junction with this road will be either here or near here. Through this gap travelers in the old emigrant times, turned off to go by the Honey Lake Route to Northern California and Southern Oregon. A natural road with easy grades is claimed for this route. In coming down this valley from Mill City, we pass a high mountain on our left,—said to be the highest peak in Nevada—8,000 feet high. It is called Star peak. The elevation given is the common rumor in the vicinity. It is certainly a high mountain, and its lofty towers are nearly always covered with snow. Opposite this mountain is

Humboldt,—423 miles from San Francisco, with an elevation of 4,236 feet above the sea,—nearly the same as the Great Salt Lake. We have been coming down hill all the way from Wells, and yet we are no lower than when we left Ogden. We have now arrived at

An Oasis in the Desert.

The traveler from the East, will be especially delighted with this spot. It will remind him of things human, of living in a land of cultivation again. The first growing trees since leaving Ogden will be seen here, with green grass, shady bowers and flowing fountains. Humboldt House is a regular breakfast and supper station, at which all passenger trains stop for meals. The proprietors have been here quite a number of years, and seem to delight in making their house, and surroundings beautiful and attractive to the traveling public. A fountain surrounded with an iron fence, springs up in front of the house, while gold-fish swim around in the basin below. East of the house, trees, locusts and poplars are growing finely, while the ground is covered with a thick matting of blue-grass. At first this lot was sown to alfalfa, which grew very rank and strong. Blue-grass seed was afterwards sown, and now it has rooted everything else out and grows luxuriantly. A field south of the road toward the mountain, has produced 18 tons of alfalfa at one cutting, and has been cut from five to seven times a year. In the garden north of the house, toward the valley, all kinds of vegetables grow luxuriantly. The average yield of potatoes is 300 bushels to the acre, of the very best quality. We were, however, particularly interested in the experiments made in fruit growing. Here in the midst, almost, of the Great Nevada Desert, with barrenness and desolation spread out on every hand—with a high rocky mountain on one side, and a huge alkali flat on the other, nestled under the towering cliffs as though it would claim shelter and protection, is this Oasis in the desert,—this reminder of more genial climes and a more kindly soil—this relief from the wearisome,

dreary views, which have everywhere met our gaze, over the largest part of the journey. The experiments so successful here prove, beyond a doubt, that the desert can be reclaimed and "made to bud and blossom as the rose." Grit, labor and above all, water, will do it. Here is an orchard of apple trees five years old, bearing not only fruit as beautiful to the eye as that raised in California, but superior in flavor—in fact retaining the flavor of eastern apples. These apple trees of all varieties are prolific bearers, and the same is true of the peaches, pears, plums and cherries. In the orchard and opposite the water tank, is a fish-pond some 25 or 30 feet in diameter. In it are trout, great speckled fellows, very thick and very shy. Rocky coves have been built for them in the bottom and center of the basin, and here they hide—seeking shade from the rays of the hot summer's sun, and also from those of the silvery moon. The experiments first made with these fish were costly, but have at last proved successful. This place and its surroundings cause the traveler not only to rejoice over the scene which here greets his gaze, but serves to remind him of home—of "God's country" either in the far East or, at this point, in the nearer West. In the fish-pond mentioned, there are a couple of wild geese, and a Mandarin duck said to be from Japan. It is a beautiful little creature with tufts of feathers on each side of its head, and finely colored plumage. The proprietors of the Humboldt House, seem to strive to offer attractions to their guests in both their indoor accommodations, and outside arrangements.

The station has shipped a large number of cattle, and is the shipping point for the sulphur or brimstone, that is manufactured some thirty miles north-west of the place. The old emigrant road spoken of as leading to Northern California and Southern Oregon, winds around the base of Eugene Mountain and near a low butte, resembling a haystack, which can be seen in the distance across the alkali flats. This road was laid out by General F. W. Lander, who was killed in the war of 1861, and is said to be one of the best wagon routes to the regions named. The Humboldt House is the place of resort for tourists who desire to visit the sulphur mines, Star Peak, or the mining districts in the Humboldt Range, Eugene Mountain, and the Antelope Range. The latter is a low range on our right, beginning as we leave this station. In front and south-east of the Humboldt House, is the Humboldt District, four to six miles distant. Humboldt Canon opens in the mountain side, in which was formerly located Humboldt City. Mines were first discovered in the rocky gorges of this range in 1861, and there was a great rush here from all parts of the country. The "City" sprang up as if by magic, and at one time contained about 500 people. Several substantial buildings were erected, a few of which still remain. The mines were diligently prospected, but not rewarded with immediate success, the expenses of living and building being very great, together with the determined hostility of the Indians, the people left it as suddenly as they came. The district remained idle until 1874-5, when work was again begun by a few individuals, and the mines are now being re-opened with rich developments and every prospect of success. The ore is gold, silver and argentiferous galena.

Antelope District is 16 miles away, in a westerly direction; Geneva District is 21 miles distant, in a north-westerly direction; both of these are but little developed.

one and one-half miles distant from the McWorthy Mines. They were formerly known as the Wright and Egbert Mines. This company have a new patented process for refining the crude ore, which they claim has a capacity of ten tons per day, and producing an article which they further claim is superior to that manufactured by any other process yet known. The ore, as it comes from the mine, is a mixture of sulphur, clay, gypsum, water, etc., and the trouble has heretofore been to separate them perfectly and cheaply. This company fuses the crude or mixed ore by heat, and then separates them by a chemical process which is claimed to be very simple, producing the "brimstone" of commerce, nearly 100 per cent. fine. The deposits lie in the hills,

TWO BITS TO SEE THE PAPPOOSE.

The sulphur mines are 30 miles away, in a north-westerly direction. Very large deposits of native sulphur are found in these mines which will average nearly 75 per cent. pure. There are two mines opened. One called the McWorthy Mine, located and developed by Mr. McWorthy, is now operated by a San Francisco company. The product of this mine is refined by retorts, three in number, which are now in active operation, and which are capable of producing about three tons per day of twenty-four hours. The mines of the Pacific Sulphur Company are about

and are found from 20 to 100 feet thick. They are also found in some of the adjoining valleys, but are not as pure in the valleys as in the hills. They are covered with ashes and mixed with extraneous matter. In fact, wherever these deposits come to the surface, they are covered with ashes, nearly white in color, indicating that at some period, they were on fire, and that the fire was extinguished—smothered—by the accumulation of these ashes. When "the elements shall melt with fervent heat," the vast sulphur deposits of Nevada will add fuel to the flames and greatly accelerate the melting process. Humboldt is the business center of the mining districts named, and has bright prospects for the future.

The Oregon branch of the Central Pacific Railroad, which was surveyed in 1875, will leave the main line of the Central Pacific, between Mill City and Humboldt, cross the Rabbit Hole Mountains, Mud Lakes, thence northerly to Goose Lake, then on to Klamath Lake, and across the Cascade Mountains near Fort Klamath, to intersect the completed railroad in Oregon. This road is to be constructed by an Oregon company, is not a part of the Central Pacific Railroad, but will be a feeder to it, and it is understood that some of the principal owners of the Central Pacific Railroad are giving it some of their support. It is expected to be in progress next year, and completed between Humboldt and some point on the California and Oregon Railroad, near Eugene City, a distance of 450 miles, within five years.

Immediately to the north-west of these mines, and in close proximity around them, is a vast alkali desert covering a large area of ground. Of all the dreary wastes to be seen in this section of the country, this desert is one of the most forbidding and desolate.

About half a mile west of Humboldt, on our right, is a sulphur deposit. It seems to be near the remains of what was once, evidently, a sulphur spring, long since dried up. It is not worked for the reason of its impurities—a far better article of crude is being obtained elsewhere. The river, still on our right, seems to have cut a deeper channel in the valley, and is seldom seen from the cars. On our left are the towering peaks of the Humboldt Range. The valley itself becomes more undulating, but still retains its dull monotony.

A Vigilance Committee Incident.—The following incident which happened in one of the Nevada mining towns, is vouched for by Clarence King:

Early in the fifties, on a still, hot summer's afternoon, a certain man, in a camp of the northern mines, which shall be nameless, having tracked his two donkeys and one horse a half mile, and discovering that a man's track with spur marks followed them, came back to town and told "the boys," who loitered about a popular saloon, that in his opinion some Mexican had stolen the animals. Such news as this demanded, naturally, drinks all round.

" Do you know, gentlemen," said one who assumed leadership, " that just naturally to shoot these greasers aint the best way? Give 'em a fair jury trial, and rope 'em up with all the majesty of the law. That's the cure."

Such words of moderation were well received, and they drank again to " Here's hoping we ketch that greaser."

As they loafed back to the veranda, a Mexican walked over the hill brow, jingling his spurs pleasantly in accord with a whistled waltz. The advocate for the law said in an undertone, " That's the cuss."

A rush, a struggle, and the Mexican, bound hand and foot, lay on his back in the bar-room. The camp turned out to a man. Happily such cries as " *String him up !*" "*Burn the doggoned lubricator !*" and other equally pleasant phrases fell unheeded upon his Spanish ear. A jury was quickly gathered in the street, and despite refusals to serve, the crowd hurried them in behind the bar.

A brief statement of the case was made by the *ci-devant* advocate, and they showed the jury into a commodious poker-room where were seats grouped about neat green tables. The noise outside, in the bar-room, by and by died away into complete silence, but from afar down the canon came confused sounds as of disorderly cheering. They came nearer, and again the light-hearted noise of human laughter mingled with clinking glasses around the bar.

A low knock at the jury door, the lock burst in, and a dozen smiling fellows asked the verdict. A foreman promptly answered, " *Not guilty.*"

With volleyed oaths, and ominous laying of hands on pistol hilts, the boys slammed the door with " *You'll have to do better than that.*"

In half an hour the advocate gently opened the door again.

" Your *opinion*, gentlemen ? "

" Guilty."

" Correct, you can come out. We hung him an hour ago."

The jury took theirs next, and when, after a few minutes, the pleasant village returned to its former tranquility, it was " *allowed* " at more than one saloon, that " Mexicans'll know enough to let white men's stock alone after this." One and another exchanged the belief that this sort of thing was more sensible than " nipping 'em on sight."

When, before sunset, the bar-keeper concluded to sweep some dust out of his poker-room back-door, he felt a momentary surprise at finding the missing horse dozing under the shadow of an oak, and the two lost donkeys serenely masticating playing-cards, of which many bushels lay in a dirty pile. He was then reminded that the animals had been there all day.

Rye Patch.—411 miles from San Francisco, with an elevation of 4,257 feet. In early days, in the canons that put down from the mountains near here and along the banks of the little creeks flowing through them, there were large patches of wild rye, which the station took its name. The increase, however, in the herds of the stockmen has destroyed its native growth, and it is now seldom seen. It is a small station with a store and saloon, freight-house, side track, etc. It is the location of a ten-stamp mill owned by the Rye Patch Mill and Mining Company, and which is supplied by ore taken from the company's mine in the mountains on our left. This mine is about four miles distant from the station. The Rye Patch Mining District, and the Eldorado Mining District, six miles away, are tributary to this place. The train stops but a moment, and as you look to the mountains, on the left, two high peaks are seen—the left one being Stark Peak, and the right one Eldorado Mountain. This is the best view of these mountains that can be obtained. Leaving this station, the mountains of the Humboldt Range gradually dwindle into hills, and a conical or isolated little peak across the range is seen. It seems fully as prominent as a wart on a man's nose. It is called Black Knob—a very appropriate name—and near it is Relief Mine and mill. There is no stage to this mining district, and its principal business point is

Oreana,—400 miles from San Francisco, with an elevation of 4,181 feet. The descent from Humboldt has been quite rapid, and we will soon be at the lowest elevation in this great basin. The Antelope Range continues on the north-west, and the Humboldt Range on the left, though the peaks in these ranges grow smaller as we pass this place. Oreana is the railroad and business point for the following mining districts : in the Antelope Range is the Trinity District, seven miles away. ore principally milling. The Governor Booth Mine has the most development thus far, though other prospects are said to be looking well. Some of the ore found in this district is claimed to be very rich. Adjoining this is the Arabia District, five miles from the station; it has smelting ore. Three miles from the mine and two miles from the station, on the Humboldt River, which has been dammed at this point, are the smelting furnaces, where the ore is reduced to base bullion. There is also a small stamp mill at this point. The principal mines thus far developed in this district are the Vanderbilt, Montezuma and Hurricane, and the ore is said to average 33 per cent. metal,—lead, antimony and silver. South of the railroad first comes the Sacrament District, seven miles away. It has milling ore but the prospects are not yet developed. Spring Valley District is next, 12 miles distant. The ore is gold and silver, and the Eagle Mine has a fifteen-stamp mill in operation reducing the ore. Relief District follows, 16 miles from Oreana. It has milling ore and a five-stamp mill. At the south end of this district, is a very superior mine of antimony, the ores of which are brought to this station and shipped to San Francisco. Bolivia District is 40 miles away, and abounds in copper ore. Tidal Wave is the name of the principal mine; Kellogg's Mine is next in importance. Conveyances to these

mining districts can be obtained at Oreana. The region round about the station is occupied by stockmen, and large numbers of cattle and horses are grazing upon the extensive ranges in the vicinity. No traveler will be able to see what they live on, but stockmen claim that they relish the white sage which abounds here, and that they will grow fat upon it. The very air is heavily perfumed with sage.

Leaving Oreana, we pass round a curve where the Humboldt River bends in toward the hills on our left, and soon cross the river which makes its way into Humboldt Lake. After crossing the river, the large growth of sage brush and greasewood shows that the soil in this vicinity is very rich and that, properly cultivated and well supplied with water, it will produce immense crops.

Lovelock's,—389 miles from San Francisco, with an elevation of 3,977 feet. It is a side track station with a telegraph office, a store, post-office and a few adjoining buildings. The Humboldt River near here, spreads out over considerable territory—a fact which renders irrigation comparatively easy. It has also caused the formation of a large body of natural meadows, from which immense quantities of hay are cut and shipped to different points along the line of the road. It is also a fine grazing region and large herds of cattle are fattened here upon the rich native grasses and the white sage. There are three varieties of the sage brush to be found on the plains and on the deserts. The largest kind is used as fuel for the engines at several stamp mills; white sage is considerably smaller and affords grazing for both cattle and sheep; the clover sage, still smaller, is not as plentiful as the former kinds, but is highly relished by sheep. Thus we have at last found the uses to which this shrub is applied. Even greasewood, when it first starts up in the spring, and before it hardens, is a favorite food with sheep and swine.

There is quite a settlement of farmers near Lovelock's. The station itself is named after a gentleman who lives near it. and who is an old settler in this part of the country. Farms are being cleared of sage brush and greasewood, irrigating ditches are being dug, and the success which has hitherto attended the growing of barley and potatoes, induces quite a number to engage in the business, and a black, rich soil gives every promise of encouragement. Before the railroad came, the meadow or pasture lands here were renowned among the emigrants, parties of whom recruited their stock after the wearisome journey across the plains. Upon the Humboldt meadows are now grazing nearly 400,000 head of cattle. After leaving Rye Patch, the Humboldt Mountains on our left dwindle considerably, and are neither ragged nor formidable after reaching this place. The same is likewise true of the

Trinity Range on our right They are low, barren, tinged with reddish brown; the evidences of volcanic action become more apparent as we pass, and the broken lava of the desert, the cinders and *scoria*, visible in places, speak of the time when the mountain ranges near here, were seething volcanoes and vomited forth smoke, flames, fire and lava with great profusion. Passing Lovelock's we soon arrive at a point, where a glimpse can be obtained of the waters of Humboldt Lake, just under the mountain ridge on our left. We have also passed by the richer soil that surrounds the last station, and entered upon the barren desert again.

Granite Point,—380 miles from San Francisco, with an elevation of 3,918 feet. Approaching the sink in this great basin, it will be seen that our elevation is decreasing, but this will only last for a short distance, and then it will be up hill again. On the right of the station, which is merely a side track, there is a ragged, broken mountain, which undoubtedly gives the place its name. It is the only thing curious or interesting to be seen from the cars. As we leave this place the lake comes int) full view—a beautiful sheet of water with white, salty incrustations all around it, like a cloud fringed with a silver border. The waters on the shore nearest the road, are said to be far more brackish and saline in character than those on the farther side. The channel through the lake is on that side, and probably the cause of the difference. The lake abounds in fish but they are mostly in the fresh water channel, and at the proper season it is a great resort for pelicans, wild geese and ducks. We approach nearer the shore as we pass to

Brown's,—373 miles from San Francisco, with an elevation of 3,929 feet. It is a coaling station, and engines sometimes take water from the tank, pumped from the lake, though it is poor stuff to make steam with. Above the nearer range of mountains, just across the lake, can be seen the tops of a farther and higher range in the distance. This higher range runs south of the Humboldt and Carson Sink, and looms into view as the nearer range gives way. Humboldt Lake was not as large formerly as now,—in fact it was a simple widening of the river as it entered the gateway of the sink below. At the foot of the lake a ridge of land extends nearly across the valley, and there was something of a gorge through which the outlet passed. The opportunity to build a dam was thus improved, and what was formerly a little widening in the river, has now become a lake about 35 miles long and from 16 to 18 miles wide in the widest places. It is filled with islands caused by this rise, and the head or volume of water thus accumulated serves to run a stamp mill, located a few miles below the station and under a reddish bluff across the valley. Ore for

this mill has been found in the mountains near it, and some is brought from the range on the north. You will notice an island nearly opposite the station, and may be interested to know that it was part of the main land before the dam was built. The mountains on each side of the track, now become high hills though, occasionally, a ragged peak is seen, to relieve the monotony of the journey. We pass over the ridge of land before spoken of, and fairly enter upon what is the beginning of the Humboldt and Carson Sink. We pass down on the low alkali flats which are whitened with salt, and which extend for miles as far as the eye can reach, off to our left.

White Plains,—361 miles from San Francisco, with an elevation of 3,894 feet—the lowest point we reach in this great basin. The place—a side track, is appropriately named for it is surrounded by a white alkali desert, covered in places with salt and alkali deposits.

The evidences of volcanic action and a lava formation are everywhere visible in the hills and on the plains in this vicinity. Though the plains immediately adjoining the station are white with alkali or salty deposits, yet the ridge and uplands to the right are covered with the reddish, porous rocks and finer blackish sand which always accompany this formation. At White Plains we have reached the lowest elevation on the Central Pacific, east of the Sierras. We are, in fact, almost in the sink itself of the Humboldt and Carson Rivers. The low flats stretching away to our left, are usually more or less covered with water in the season of floods, and the two rivers virtually unite in this great valley or basin. There is no visible outlet to these streams, or rather to this basin, and the immense drainage of these two rivers sinks in the sand and is taken up by evaporation. The oldest settlers in this region of country, hold to the opinion that the water is taken up by evaporation, and say that at certain seasons of the year this process is very rapid—large bodies of land covered with water becoming thoroughly dry in a few days.

Leaving White Plains, we again begin to go up a grade. We have to cross a divide between White Plains and the Hot Spring Valley. This divide is reached at

Mirage,—355 miles from San Francisco, with an elevation of 4,247 feet. It is simply a side track with no habitation near it but a section-house—and is near the summit of the divide. This place, like many others, is named from some peculiarity of location or from some characteristic of the country. The wonderful optical delusions that are apparently seen here, have given it a suggestive name. When the conditions of the atmosphere are favorable, wonderful visions of lakes, mountains, trees, rivers, etc., can be seen. It is reported that many a weary emigrant in the days of old, was deceived by the optical illusions that here seemed so real, and wondered why he did not reach the cooling lakes and spreading shade that seemed so near and was yet so far away. The heat of summer during the day time on these plains is almost intolerable. The dust, sometimes blowing in clouds, is suffocating, and long distances add to the inconvenience of wagon travel, without water. But overland travelers on the trains have more comforts. No matter how oppressive the day, yet the moment the sun is set, a lovely cool breeze comes from the mountains, the air becomes fresh, and sleep is delightful. The heat and dust of the day is soon forgotten in the comforts of the pure, cool night atmosphere. Crossing a low divide, the end of the Antelope Range we reach

Hot Springs,—346 miles from San Francisco. with an elevation of 4,072 feet. This is a telegraph station with side track, section-houses, etc. Great efforts have been made here to sink artesian wells in order to obtain fresh water for the use of the road. First a depth of 800 feet was reached, then 1,000 feet, and lastly 1,300 feet, but all without success. In some portions of work very rapid progress would be made—95 feet having been made in one day—then some hard, flinty rock would be struck, and progress of less than one foot per day would be the result. The station is in the midst of a desert, and is named from the Hot Springs, whose rising steam can readily be seen about half a mile from the track on the left. There are quite a number of them boiling hot. They formerly extended along the base of the hill, still farther to the left, and nearer the track, but while they seem to have dried up in one locality, they have broken out in another. These springs are now owned by a German company, who have a dwelling-house, and works for producing borax, erected near by. They were badly "sold" by sharpers who induced them to believe that borax, in large quantities, could be obtained here. They sent out an expert who was induced to make a favorable report to the effect that there were inexhaustible quantities of the mineral to be found near here. As a consequence, they invested large sums of money in the purchase of the mines and in the erection of works. We believe some 60 boxes of the manufactured article was all that was ever turned out, and then the mine suddenly gave out, the production ceased, of course, and the company, after an expenditure estimated at about a quarter million of dollars, ceased operations, their property remaining idle. These springs are said to be a sovereign remedy for rheumatism and kindred diseases, and the property may yet be utilized as an infirmary or watering-place for invalids. The erection of a bathing-house would be all that is at present required. The steam from these springs can be seen for quite a distance in the

cool mornings of the winter, and in the spring and fall months. Looking off to the right, as far as the eye can reach, almost, is a valley coming in from the north-east—a dreary waste of sage brush and alkali, which extends across the track, over low hills, to the sink of the Carson. We move out through a gap in the hills, and in about two miles come to the salt works. Buildings have been erected, side track put in, and large platforms built where the salt is stored preparatory to shipping. The whole face of the country, in this vicinity, is nearly white, the saline water rising to the surface and evaporating, leaves the white incrustations to glisten in the sun. The salt obtained here is produced by solar evaporation, and is said to be nearly 99 per cent. pure. Formerly vats were tried, but they were found to be useless and unnecessary. Vats are now dug in the ground and the salt water pumped into them. It soon evaporates, and after a sufficient quantity has accumulated, it is shoveled out, drawn to the station, ground and sacked, when it is ready for the market. We are now passing over one of the most uninviting portions of the desert. The range of mountains directly in front are those through which the Truckee River comes, and the valley, both north and south, extends beyond our vision. Away off to the left we can see the mountains south of the Carson Sink and River. The aspect of the desert becomes more dreary as we approach

Desert,—335 miles from San Francisco; elevation, 4,018 feet. It is only a side track, rightly named, and passenger trains seldom stop. The winds that sweep the barren plains here heap the sand around the scattering sage brush like huge potato hills. Now we turn toward the right approaching the base of the adjoining hills, while boulders of lava, large and small, greet the eye. The hill on our right, dwindles into the plain; we round it, toward the right, and arrive at

Two-Mile,—329 miles from San Francisco; elevation, 4,156 feet. The gap, in the mountain range in front, now opens and we see where the Truckee River comes tumbling down. The valley extends, on the right, till it is lost in Pyramid Lake. We pass rapidly on, and in a short distance pitch down a steep grade into the valley of the Truckee, where green grass, green trees and flowing water, God's best gift to man, again greet our vision.

Rabbit drives and Rabbit Robes.—The Piutes have a very clever way of catching rabbits, by a method called "rabbit drives" in this country. They make some long, narrow nets like fish-seines from the bark of the willow, or from wild hemp, and hold them up on edge by means of sticks, which they fasten in the ground at intervals; the part of net next to the ground is held there by weights—just as seine is managed. These nets they spread in the shape of the letter "V," with the arms extended to receive the game when it shall be driven in. One Indian crouches in the enclosure for a purpose which will be explained hereafter. The nets are woven coarsely, so that a rabbit's head, once through the meshes, is tight. Late in the fall or early in the winter, when a light snow has covered the ground, the Indians will set their nets generally across some valley and prepare for the "drive." From twenty-five to sixty of them, the more the better, will start out and go quietly away from the net some ten or twelve miles. This company is composed of Indians, squaws, and children armed with sticks, old sacks or blankets which they can flourish in the air, and when they have arrived where they propose to commence the drive, they spread out in a semi-circular form, and begin to hoot and yell, swinging their rags around their heads, and beating the sage brush with their sticks. The rabbits, very much frightened, run in the only direction open for them, while the Indians press forward to the net and gradually draw in toward it. The rabbits continue their flight until they are fairly within the arms of the nets, with the Indians close upon them. The Indians, perhaps two or three of them—who have remained in the net perfectly still until the frightened rabbits surround them, suddenly rise up with a shout, and the frantic creatures wildly rush hither and thither and finally dash into the meshes of the net, which holds them by the neck so that they cannot escape. Then follows "the slaughter of the innocents." The Indians pass along and tap the rabbits over the head, the squaws secure the game, and the whole drive results in a big feast, wherein the course begins and ends with rabbit *ad libitum*. Our informant stated that he had known from 500 to 1,000 rabbits to be caught in this way, in one drive.

About Rabbit Robes.—The traveler has doubtless noticed the gray fur robes, which adorn the persons of a large number of the Indians seen on the road west of Ogden. These robes are a curious piece of workmanship in some respects. They are not made of whole rabbit-skins sewed together, as wolf and coonskin robes are made. When the rabbits are skinned, their hides are at once cut into narrow strips with the fur on. These strips are sewed together until the right length for a robe is secured, and then they are twisted like a rope—in fact, become fur ropes. These are used the same as "filling" in woolen or cotton cloth, as distinguished from the "warp." You can press your fingers through these robes at pleasure—the threads of the "warp" being from one to three inches apart. This warp is made from the sinews of animals, from the bark of willows, or from the wild hemp which the Indians gather for this purpose. It is very stout and very durable, and is not perceptible as you casually ex-

amine one of these robes. The Indians value a rabbit-skin robe very highly, and much prefer them to blankets, though it takes a good deal of time and patience to make one. This work, however, is all done by the squaws, and is taken as a matter of course by the "bucks" of the tribe.

Wadsworth,—328 miles from San Francisco; elevation, 4,077 feet. It is a little village of about 400 inhabitants, nestled down in the valley of the Truckee and overshadowed by the range of mountains beyond. The railroad has a twenty-stall roundhouse, 65 feet deep, with over 500 feet of circular length. The machine shop has six working stalls where engines are repaired, and is 75 by 130 feet. Engines are here entirely rebuilt. At one end of this shop a piece of ground has been fenced in, a fountain erected, trees planted, and alfalfa and blue-grass sown. It affords a refreshing sight to the mechanics here employed, and strangely contrasts with the barren desert surrounding the place. The engines used on that part of the division between Winnemucca and this place, have very large tenders, the tanks in them holding 3,800 gallons of water. They run 70 miles without taking water on the line of the road. Other shops for the convenience of the road are located near by. The huge water tank in which water is stored for use of shops and engines, has a capacity of 60,000 gallons. Hydrants have been erected, connected with it by pipes, and hose supplied by which the water may be quickly applied in case of fire, to any part of the buildings. The road passes from Wadsworth to Sacramento through a mountainous region of country, where there is plenty of timber and, hence, wood is used for fuel on the engines between these two places. Between Ogden and this place coal taken from the mines north of Evanston, on the Union Pacific Road, is used. West of Sacramento, coal from Oregon and Washington Territory is used. Between Wadsworth and Truckee some trouble has been experienced with snow, and in some places huge boulders roll down on the track which are knocked out of the way by the snow-plows on the engines. This is a novel use for snow-plows. In addition to the machine shops, there is a large freight building and other offices for the convenience of the company. The town has several large stores, hotels, saloons, with China houses, *ad libitum*, and is, altogether, the place of considerable trade. Huge freight wagons, from two to four attached together, are here loaded with freight for the mining districts south. These large wagons, with their teams attached, are quite a curiosity to eastern travelers, and fully illustrate how western men do their freighting.

The following mining districts do business at this station: Columbus, borax mines, 130 miles distant; Teal's Marsh borax Mines, 140 miles away; the Pacific Borax Works are 20 miles south-east of Columbus still; the Bellville Mining District, 140 miles distant. In this district the celebrated Northern Bell Silver Mine is located, also the General Thomas and others less prominent. Silver Peak Mining District is 110 miles distant. These districts, and others not named here, are all south of Wadsworth. Rhodes' Salt Marsh, an immense salt deposit, is about 130 miles distant. There is salt enough in this deposit to preserve the world, if reports as to its extent, etc., prove true.

there are three bodies of water which travelers will more fully understand by an explanation. Humboldt Lake proper, into which flows the Humboldt River, we pass at Brown's Station. A little south-west of this lake is the Humboldt and Carson Sink — the waters from the lake seeping through a channel or slough into the sink. The dam at the foot of the lake is across this outlet or slough. The waters from Carson Lake flowing nearly east, find their way into this sink through a similar outlet. Thus the waters of the two rivers, the Humboldt

PYRAMID LAKE.

From Wadsworth to Carson Lake, south, the distance is about 40 miles. This lake is named from the river of the same name, which flows into, or rather through it. Directly south of Carson Lake is Walker Lake into which flows Walker River. The lake last named has no visible outlet, and is one of the sinks of the great basin east of the Sierras. South of the railroad,

and Carson, each flowing through a small lake, finally meet in the same sink. To this sink there is no visible outlet, and the vast amount of water which is poured into this basin through these two rivers is undoubtedly taken up on its way, or after its arrival into this common sink, by evaporation.

The Humboldt River, though it has a length

of 500 miles, and has several tributaries constantly flowing into it, yet does not increase in volume, throughout its length, as do most rivers. After passing Winnemucca it diminishes to a small stream, finally spreads into a marsh and "sinks" out of sight.

In addition to the mining districts south of the railroad, the Soda Lakes and refining works must not be forgotten. These are now in active operation, and the results are the frequent shipments from this place.

North of Wadsworth about 21 miles is Pyramid Lake, and east of it, separated by Lake Range of Mountains, which can plainly be seen from Wadsworth,—is Winnemucca Lake, 26 miles distant. Both of them are sinks, and have no visible outlet. Both of them receive the waters of Truckee River, and the latter is said to be rising.—being several feet higher now than it was ten years ago.

Curiosities of Pyramid Lake.—In 1867 a surveying party visited this lake, which they found to be 12 miles long and 30 miles wide. The lake takes its name from a remarkable rock formation, a *pyramid* which towers above the lake to a height of more than 500 feet, and presents in its outlines the most perfect form. Upon visiting this pyramid, the party found it occupied with tenants who were capable of holding their ground against all intruders.

From every crevice there seemed to come a hiss. The rattling, too, was sharp and long-continued. The whole rock was alive with rattlesnakes. Even in the party those who had been champion snake exterminators, and had demolished them on all previous occasions, now found the combat beyond their power to carry on, and abandoned the island with all hope of victory.

The water of Pyramid Lake is clear, sparkling. In it are said to be fish, principally among which is the *couier*, very sprightly, with flesh the color of salmon. The weight of the fish ranges from 3 to 20 pounds. There is also said to be an abundance of trout.

Winnemucca Lake is also stated to be some 200 feet lower than Pyramid Lake, its basin being on the east side of Lake Range of Mountains. The Truckee River and these two lakes are great resorts for ducks, geese and pelicans. The latter abound here in large numbers in the spring. An island in Pyramid Lake is a great resort for them and there, undisturbed, they rear their young. These birds are very destructive to the fish of the river and lake. They will stand in the shallow water of the entrance to the lake for hours, and scoop up any unwary fish that may happen to pass within their reach. They are apparently harmless, and of no earthly use whatever. The huge sacks on their under jaws, are used to carry food and water to their young. These waddle around before they fly—a shapeless, uncouth mass, and easily destroyed be-

cause unable to get out of the way. A man with a club could kill thousands of them in a day, without much difficulty.

North of Pyramid Lake is Mud Lake, another sink of this great basin, and a little north-east of Winnemucca Lake is the sink of Quin's River and other streams. In fact, they lose their identity in flowing across the desert,—are swallowed up by the thirsty sands.

On the north, Pyramid Lake Mining District is 15 miles away. This is a new district, and said to contain good "prospects." Mud Lake District, similar in character, is 75 miles due north from Wadsworth. Black Butte District on the east side of Winnemucca Lake, is about 28 miles distant.

The Piute reservation, or rather one of them, begins about seven miles north of the town. The reservation house, which is supposed to be the place where the government officers reside, is 16 miles away. There is another reservation for these Indians south, on Walker River. They have some very good land near the lake, and some of them cultivate the soil,—raising good crops.

There is considerable good bottom-land on the Truckee River, between Wadsworth and Pyramid Lake. That which is not included in the Indian reservation is occupied by stockmen and farmers, much of it being cultivated and producing excellent crops of cereals and vegetables. The experiments thus far tried in fruit growing have been successful, and in a few years there will be a home supply of fruit equal to home demand.

The arrival at Wadsworth is a great relief to the tourist weary with the dull, unchanging monotony of the plains, the desert and bleak desolation which he has passed. The scenes are now to change and another miniature world is to open upon his view. There is to be variety—beauty, grandeur and sublimity. If he enters this place at night, the following day will reveal to him the green fields and magnificent landscapes of California, and in less than 24 hours, he will be able to feast his greedy eyes upon a glowing sunset on the Pacific Coast.

Leaving Wadsworth we cross the Truckee River and gaze with delight upon the trees, the green meadows, the comfortable farm-house, and well-tilled fields of the ranche on our left, just across the bridge. Like everything else lovely in this world, it soon fades from our vision, as we rapidly pass into the Truckee Cañon. The mountains now come down on either side as though they would shake hands across the silver torrent that divides them. The valley narrows as if to hasten their cordial grasp, and to remove all obstacles in their way. Now it widens a little as though it was not exactly certain whether these mountains should come together or not, and wanted to consider the matter. But

SCENES ON THE TRUCKEE RIVER.—By THOMAS MORAN.
1.—Truckee Meadows, Sierras in the distance. 2.—Pleasant Valley. 3.—Truckee River, near State Line.
4.—Red Bluff, Truckee River. 5.—Bridge at Eagle Gap. 6.—Truckee River Rapids.

leaving this question to the more practical thoughts of our readers, we hasten on, winding around promontories and in and out of "draws" and ravines, through rocky cuts, and over high embankments with the river rolling and tumbling almost beneath our feet, and the ragged peaks towering high above us, passing

Salvia,—a simple side track, six miles from Wadsworth. Now we have something to occupy our attention; there are new scenes passing by at every length of the car, and we have to look sharp and quick, or many of them will be lost forever. Soon we make a short turn to the right, and what the railroad men call "Red Rock" appears in front, then to our right, and finally over our heads. It is a huge mountain of lava that has, sometime, in the ages of the past, been vomited from the crater of some volcano now extinct; or it may have been thrown up by some mighty convulsion of nature that fairly shook the rock-ribbed earth till it trembled like an aspen leaf, and in which these huge mountain piles were thrown into their present position. Presently, amidst the grandeur of these mountains, a lovely valley bursts upon our view. We have arrived at the little meadows of the Truckee, at a station called

Clark's,—313 miles from San Francisco, with an elevation of 4,263 feet. This station is named from a former proprietor of the ranche here. It is a beautiful place with mountains all around it, and the only way you can see out, is to look up toward the heavens. The narrow bottom on either side of the river is fenced in, producing excellent crops of vegetables and hay, and affording excellent grazing for the stock that is kept here. As we arrive at this station, we pass through a cut of sand which seems just ready to become stratified, and which holds itself up in layers, in the sides of the cut. Occasionally, as we look over the nearer peaks in front, we can catch a glimpse of the snow-crowned Sierras in the distance. Now a creek comes in from a canon on our left, and through this canon is a wagon road to Virginia City, and now a butte is passed between us and the river—the river being on our left since we crossed it at Wadsworth. There are a few ranches scattered along its banks where vegetables for the 10,000 miners at Virginia City are grown. The mountains we have passed are full of variegated streaks of clay or mineral, some white, some red, some yellow, and some pale green. You will notice them as you pass

Vista,—301 miles from San Francisco; elevation, 4,403 feet. We are going up hill again. At this station we arrive at the Truckee Meadows. It is like an immense amphitheatre, and the traveler rejoices again in the presence of farm-houses and cultivated fields—in the scene of beauty that spreads out before him. Beyond the level plain, we see in front of us Peavine

Mountain and at the base of the hills to the farther side of the valley, lies Reno. To our left Mt. Rose lifts its snow-covered head; to the left of Mt. Rose is Slide Mountain.

Letters.—Throughout the Territories and the Pacific Coast,—*letter days,* when the Pony Express, Mail Coaches or Steamer arrived, the local population was wrought up to its most intense excitement, and expectation of news. In the Territory of Montana letters could not be obtained from any direction by regular mails, and the inhabitants depended upon the good offices of traders, who journeyed at long intervals back and forth, who brought with them letters and newspapers, for which, gladly, every receiver paid $2.50 gold. Letters in California were received only by steam *via* the Isthmus of Panama, fully 30 days being occupied in the trip from New York, and fully 90 days' time was necessary to send a letter from San Francisco to any point in the East, and receive a reply. Whenever the semi-monthly steamer arrived at San Francisco, the event was celebrated by the firing of guns, and the ringing of bells, and an immediate rush for the post-office. The letter deliveries from the post-office, were often from a window opening directly upon the public street, and a long line of anxious letter-seekers would quickly form—extending often half a mile in length. Here were gathered the characteristic classes of California life, the "*gray shirt brigade*" of miners, many of whom in their rugged life had not heard from home for a full year; next anxious merchants whose fate depended upon their letters and invoices, and on approaching the office, had only a feeling of dismay at the terrible length of the line, with little hope of approaching the window for hours. At last they were compelled to offer sums for purchases of place from some fortunate one *in the line.* It used to take five hours or longer, on ordinary occasions, to get to the window, and there were lots of idlers who had no friends, nor ever expected a letter, who from pure mischief, took their places in the line, and then when near the window sold out again. From $5 to $20 were the average prices for fair places, but $50 to $100 were often paid for a good position near the window. Prices were in proportion to the length of the line or the anxiety of the individual. The expression of countenance of some of those paying highest rates, when forced to leave the window without a letter, is beyond description. "*Selling out in the line,*" soon became a trade, and many a loafer made his $10 to $20—three or four times a day. Cases have even been known, where over-anxious individuals in search of letters, would take their positions at the post-office window, *one or two days* before the arrival of the expected steamer, often passing the entire night standing and watching at the window, and only leaving it when forced to seek food and drink. It often happened that while temporarily absent from their post a few minutes, the steamer's gun would fire, and with a break-neck race of a few minutes back again, their disgust was immense to be compelled to attach themselves to the extreme end of a line, from one-fourth to one-half a mile in length, so quickly had it formed.

Ah Ching's Theology: a Belief in the Devil.—A traveler encountered once Ah Ching, a Chinese laundryman, at one of the San Francisco hotels, who spoke some English and had some intellect, of whom he asked the question, whether he believed in the devil.

"Hallo, John, do you believe in him?"

"*Ah, velley, Mellica man, me believe him.*"

"All Chinamen believe in him?"

"*Oh, China like Mellica man, some believe him sahvey, some tink him all gosh damn.*"

Firing off the Devil.— At one of the Chinese festivals, conducted by the Chinese priests, a large figure representing the devil was brought forward, and at the close of the play a torch was applied to him. The figure, which was full of fire-crackers, "went off" in brilliant style till nothing was left, apparently, but the hideous head and backbone; these, then, shot upward, like a huge Roman candle, leaving a trail of blue fire, and exploded, high in the air, with a loud report followed by a shower of sparks and insufferable stench, and that was supposed to be the last of the devil for another year.

The apparent reason for paying so much attention to the devil is contained in the answer made by one of the worshipers: "*If God good, why pray? 'Tend to the devil.*" Hence the ceremony of getting rid of him at regular intervals.

Curious Names Given by Miners. — Placerville was, in 1849, called *Hangtown* because it was the first place where any person was hanged by lynch-law.

Tin Cup was so named, because the first miners there found the place so rich that they measured their gold in pint tin cups.

Pine Log is so named because there was once a pine log across the South Fork of the Stanislaus River in such a position as to offer a very convenient crossing to miners.

The following are among the other oddities which have, through miners' freaks and fancies, been used to denote settlements and camps and diggings, small or large:

Jim Crow Canon,	Gridiron Bar,
Red Dog,	Hen-Roost Camp,
Jackass Gulch,	Lousy Ravine,
Ladies' Canon,	Lazy Man's Canon,
Miller's Defeat,	Logtown,
Loafer Hill,	Git-Up-and-Git,
Rattlesnake Bar,	Gopher Flat,
Whisky Bar,	Bob Ridley Flat,
Poverty Hill,	One Eye,
Greasers' Camp,	Push Coach Hill,

Christian Flat,	Puppytown,
Rough and Ready,	Mad Canon,
Ragtown,	Happy Valley,
Sugar-Loaf Hill,	Hell's Delight,
Paper Flat,	Devil's Basin,
Wild-Cat Bar,	Dead Wood,
Dead Mule Canon,	Gouge Eye,
Wild Goose Flat,	Puke Ravine,
Brandy Flat,	Slap-Jack Bar,
Yankee Doodle,	Bloomer Hill,
Horsetown,	Grizzly Flat,
Petticoat Slide,	Rat-Trap Slide,
Chucklehead Diggings,	Pike Hill,
Plug Head Gulch,	Port Wine,
Ground Hog's Glory,	Snow Point,
Bogus Thunder,	Nary Red,
Last Chance,	Gas Hill,
Greenhorn Canon,	Ladies' Valley,
Shanghai Hill,	Graveyard Canon,
Shirt-Tail Canon,	Gospel Gulch,
Skunk Gulch,	Chicken Thief Flat,
Coon Hollow,	Hungry Camp,
Poor Man's Creek,	Mud Springs,
Humbug Canon,	Skinflint,
Quack Hill,	Pepper-Box Flat,
Nigger Hill,	Seventy-Six,
Piety Hill,	Hog's Diggings,
Brandy Gulch,	Liberty Hill,
Love-Letter Camp,	Paradise,
Blue Belly Ravine,	Sluice Fork,
Shinbone Peak,	Seven Up Ravine,
Loafer's Retreat,	Humpback Slide,
Swellhead Diggings,	Coyote Hill,
Poodletown,	American Hollow,
Gold Hill,	Pancake Ravine,
Centipede Hollow,	Nutcake Camp,
Seven-by-Nine Valley,	Paint Pot Hill.
Gospel Swamp,	

Tit for Tat.—When Hepworth Dixon was leaving California, he asked one of our newspaper men to write to him occasionally.

"Certainly," replied our knight of the pastepot and shears, whom we will call plain Smith, "how shall I address you?"

"Simply Hepworth Dixon, England," replied the modest author of "The White Conquest."

"All right, Mr. Dixon," responded Mr. Smith, choking down his risibilities by a severe effort, "I trust to have the pleasure of hearing from you in reply."

"Certainly, Mr. Smith," replied Dixon, "how shall I address you?"

"Simply John Smith, America," triumphantly replied Mr. Smith.

Reno—is 293 miles from San Francisco, situated in the Truckee Meadows, the junction of the Virginia & Truckee Railroad, the first point reached from which there are *two daily* passenger trains to San Francisco, and the *best point* of departure for tourists going west to visit Lake Tahoe. The Meadows, about 15 miles long and eight wide, are mostly covered with sage brush.

WINTER FOREST SCENE IN THE SIERRA NEVADAS.

BY THOMAS MORAN.

The numerous boulders which also strew the meadows, are built into fences, and alfalfa seed sown after digging out the sage brush, and rich pasturage results on which sheep thrive. Eight or ten tons to the acre are cut in a single season, and farms make handsome returns. The boulders are most numerous along the river.

Reno has an altitude of 4,507 feet, and a population of 2,000. A severe fire devastated it lately. It was named after General Reno the hero of South Mountain—has now 2,000 people, and is a county-seat with a $30,000 court-house, and is *the gate* to the West for all the State, and distributing point for a large portion of it. It has outrun Truckee in competing for the trade of California, east of the Sierras and among the beautiful and fertile valleys north of the railroad, for, from November to May, Truckee is shut in by deep snows, and its roads have steeper grades.

Sierra Valley, the Honey Lake Region, Long Valley, Camp Bidwell and Goose Lake Region, Surprise Valley, Indian Valley, Winnemucca Valley, the Pitt River Country, Fort Warner and South-eastern Oregon, all derive their supplies, wholly or in part, on wagons from this point. It is the healthiest place in the State and has the most stable population, being surrounded with an agricultural region.

It has five churches, Congregational, Methodist, Episcopal, Baptist and Catholic, and ground will soon be broken here for the erection of a Young Ladies' Seminary, under the care of Bishop Whitaker of the Protestant Episcopal Church, for which $10,000 were contributed by Miss Wolfe of New York City, $5,000 contributed elsewhere, and Reno has supplied the remaining $5,000 needed.

Nevada, by a State law, sets apart one-fourth of one per cent. of her tax for a building fund, out of which the Capitol was erected, at Carson City. About $100,000, since accumulated, has been spent on a State prison, the completion of which is yet in the future.

Here are the grounds of the State Agricultural Society and the finest speed-track in the State, two banks, one newspaper—the Nevada *State Journal*—and several factories, a steam fire department and a public library.

The benevolent orders are well represented, the Masons and Odd Fellows meeting in halls of their own. There are two hotels, the Railroad House, which is well kept, and the Lake House, on the bank of the Truckee River, a most desirable place for a few days' stay. A daily stage leaves for Susanville, in the California portion of the Sierra Nevadas.

The Pea Vine District is nine miles northwest, and about 1,500 feet above Reno, in which are valuable mines of dark sulphuret ore—the basest worked on the coast, and worked successfully only of late by the O'Hara process.

Virginia & Truckee Railroad.

Leaving Reno, the Red Mountain District is seen on the east, and the Washoe Range with Mount Rose, 8,200 feet high, on the west, and soon the cars pass a flume, 15 miles long, owned by Flood & O'Brien, running through a long canon to Evans Creek to convey lumber to the railroad. Huffaker's is six and one-half miles from Reno, the terminus of the Pacific Wood, Lumber and Flume Company's flume. The next stopping point is called

Brown's,—and is the terminus of the Eldorado Flume, owned by the Virginia & Truckee Railroad Company. This flume starts in White's Canon, and is about six miles long. The first important station is

Steamboat Springs, — 11 miles south of Reno. They consist of many springs in two distinct groups, those of each group apparently connected with each other. Their escaping steam may be seen near the station on the rise to the right of the road, and the fissures, through which the water of 212° Fahrenheit gurgles up, vary from a narrow crack to a foot in width. Formerly they were more active than now, yet at times they spout the water to a height of ten feet. Sulphur abounds in the water, and remarkable cures of rheumatism and cutaneous diseases have been effected, but no reliable analysis of the water has been made.

The hotel is a popular resort, kept in first-class style with accommodations for fifty guests. Steamboat Springs are fast becoming famous for mines of cinnabar and sulphur, of both of which this region seems to be full. Much of the sulphur is pure and beautifully crystallized. Cinnabar is found between strata of lava.

The railroad crosses Steamboat Creek, the outlet for Washoe Lake, and then enters Steamboat Valley, which contains about 6,000 acres of good soil with some natural meadow at the upper end.

South of Steamboat Valley is Washoe Valley, which is entered by passing through a narrow gorge with large conglomerate rocks, weather-beaten into castellated form. Emerging from the canon, one is in

Washoe City,—5 3-4 miles from Steamboat; it has a few dilapidated houses. Mount Rose, over 8,000 feet high, eternally snow-capped, is directly opposite the lower end of the valley.

On the left of the track may be seen the ruins of the old Ophir Mill—whose Superintendent was honored with a salary of $30,000 per annum, and a furnished house, while the mill employed 165 men.

On the left, at the foot of the mountains, overlooking the beautiful lake and valley, is Bower's Mansion—the favorite resort for picnics from Carson and Virginia City.

Franktown,—4 1-4 miles from Washoe, is an old Mormon colony, the terminus of another

flume, and was the first place settled in this regularly formed and picturesque valley, twelve miles
long by seven wide. The long promontories from
the mountain side are denuded of timber, but
numerous ice-cold crystal streams come down
from the mountain side, and the valley produces
considerable grain and fruit, and supports no
little stock.

Mill Station,—3 miles from Franktown, is
an old mill site at the upper end of the valley,
from which Washoe Lake, ten miles long and six
wide, may be clearly seen. Here is the end of
still another flume for lumber and wood; next is
Eagle Valley, reached by a short tunnel. At the
summit, or

Lake View,—2 miles from Mill Station,
commanding the finest view of Washoe Lake,
the railroad crosses the large water pipe which
supplies Virginia City from a lake on the western summit of the Sierras, above Lake Tahoe.
Washoe and Eagle Valleys almost join, and on
entering the latter, Carson City and the State
Capitol are seen below.

Carson City—is 21 miles from Virginia
City. It was settled in 1858, by Major Ornsby
and others, has a population of 4,000, is regularly laid out, the streets coinciding with the
cardinal points of the compass. Shade trees,
the U. S. Mint, the Capitol, Court-house, and
some neat private residences, four churches
(Presbyterian, Methodist, Episcopalian and Catholic), the best school-house in the State, and good
society, make it one of the most desirable places
for residence in Nevada. It has two daily papers,
the *Appeal* and *Tribune.* It is the center of a
large trade for all parts of South-western Nevada
and Mono and Inyo Counties of California.

It has three good hotels, the general offices and
workshops of the Virginia & Truckee Railroad.

The railroad from Carson City to Virginia
City, is often spoken of as the Crooked Railroad,
so full is it of curves and windings. There are
many curves on it of 14°, and one of 19°, and on
one portion of it for 16 miles, there is a continuous grade of 90 feet to the mile. This is believed
to be the road of which it is said that an engineer, badly frightened at the approach of a
red light, jumped from his engine and soon saw
that he had been scared by the rear end of his
own train. It is fifty-one and three-quarter miles
long, and has 35 miles of side track. Forty to
fifty trains daily pass over it, and it is probably
the best paying railroad in the country.

Proceeding through Eagle Valley to Virginia,
there may be seen—off to the right, the State
Prison, two and one-half miles from Carson, an
edifice whose architectural appearance is befitting its purpose. Adjoining, as if it was the
same building, are the Carson Warm Springs
and its hotel, one of the choicest spots for
an attractive resort. The great volume of water
boiling from the rocks, supplies a succession

of large plunge baths for a distance of 160
feet.

Stages leave Carson for points in Southern
Nevada and into California as follows: To
Monitor, 46 miles; *Silver Mountain,* 54 miles;
Bishop's Creek, 192 miles; *Benton,* 150 miles;
Sweetwater, 73 miles; *Aurora,* 105 miles; *Bodie,*
119 miles; *Mariette,* 145 miles; *Belleville,* 155
miles; *Candelaria,* 165 miles; *Columbus,* 173
miles; *Silver Peak,* 228 miles; *Independence,* 234
miles; *Lone Pine,* 252 miles; *Cerro Gordo,* 274
miles. The usual fare is 15 cents per mile. For
Lake Tahoe, Benton stage line runs to Glenbrook, and there connects with steamer across
lake, and stages thence to Truckee and Summit.

Near Carson there are a number of points of
special interest. Along the stage line to Lake
Tahoe are some new and wonderful springs of
great mineral value for healing, Soda, etc.,—
especially beneficial for rheumatism—also the
little narrow gauge railroad and the flume for
carrying timber.

North of Carson there crosses the railroad
track the Water Syphon for supplying Virginia
City with water. This syphon commences in
the Sierras west of Carson, at a place called
Dall's Creek, then crosses the mountains to a
point 2,100 feet above the valley where the railroad passes. The flume now changes and the
water pours into a pipe, which descends, passes
across the valley, is carried to another point
on the other side of the valley 1,540 feet high,
where it is poured out into another flume which
conducts it to Virginia City. Upward of two
million gallons per day of water are thus supplied. Cost $750,000. *The Sutro Tunnel* one of
the *mining wonders* of Nevada commences on the
Carson River, not far distant, and bores into the
mountains a passage 14 feet wide and 10 feet
high. The main tunnel is completed 20,000 feet,
reaching directly to the mines at Virginia City,
and affording not only a perfect outlet for the
water of the mines, but giving excellent ventilation and a cheap way of removing the ore.
Probably the greatest venture in risks of any
enterprises in the world, just opened for use.

Several stations beyond Carson attract attention principally because of quartz mills connected. *Lookout,* 2¼ miles; *Empire,* 1¼ miles;
at *Morgan,* is the Morgan Mill; at *Brunswick*
and *Merrimack* are others. The road ascends
above the river gradually and just beyond
Eureka is seen the first view of *Mount Davidson.*

Mound House—is the station for supplies
for Dayton and Sutro. Passenger and freight
now leave here, and pass across Walker Lake by
a steam ferry, and save 45 miles travel around
the head of the Lake. This is now the principal route to the Columbus and Monte Christo
country.

Gold Hill.—As the traveler approaches, he
sees evidence of mining in every direction—

abandoned shafts, puffing engines, smoke issuing from gigantic stacks, huge mounds of earth dumped from the end of high trestle-work, the capacious buildings and the posts and stones that mark the undeveloped claims, or the loaded ore, need no explanation as to their origin or purpose.

Gold Hill follows the ravine of the same name, and the street is both steep and crooked. It has a population of 6,000 and is, in all respects, like Virginia City. The two are built up so as to be without marked separation. Gold Hill has a vigorous daily paper, the "Gold Hill News," a Catholic, a Methodist, and an Episcopal Church.

a great credit to the city and the land of silver. Its narrow streets show with what difficulty sites are obtained for buildings, whether anchored to the rocks or perched in mid air, and, while in the city but little of it is visible at a time, the dwellings are mostly low, and, therefore, unstable roofs do less damage when the Washoe zephyrs blow. It appears small, but is the most densely packed of all American cities. One-third its people are underground, where lighted candles glimmer faintly in subterranean passages, by day and by night. Bedrooms do double duty for hundreds or thousands, whose work never ceases. Miners are *shifted* every eight

STREET SCENE IN VIRGINIA CITY, NEVADA.

Virginia City and Gold Hill are connected by a line of omnibusses, making four trips every hour during the day, while the frequent trains of the railroad carry also many passengers. By rail the distance to Virginia City is two miles, in which several tunnels are passed through.

Virginia City—is one of the most interesting towns on the coast. One expects streets of gold and silver, and finds dust or mud. On October 26, 1875, it was almost wholly destroyed by fire, but the burnt district has been rebuilt more handsomely than ever. Its population now exceeds 20,000. A first-class hotel, *The International*, has been erected, in all respects

hours, and the men of two shifts may occupy the same couch.

On many levels, down 2,000 feet, are thousands of busy, bustling, narrow streets, over which is the city proper. Tide-water is 6,205 feet below the banks, and perhaps it is best that it is no nearer, for now pumps are constructed to raise the water to the surface from 3,000 to 5,000 feet below, only seven of which are capable of raising 4,000 gallons every minute.

Dwellings on the side-hill overlook one another without any appearance of aristocratic pretensions, and steps and foot-ladders are continually at hand.

14

The streets present a busy appearance with men of all classes, and occasionally women, watching the indicator of the San Francisco stockmarket as anxiously as a gambler reduced to the "bed rock" watches for the playing of the hand against him.

Saloons are numerous and crowded, and profanity fearfully prevalent.

It is a city of extremes in prices, speculations, character, activity, enterprise, debauchery and home life. The rich and the penniless are side by side. Every notion and *ism* is advocated—every nation represented by the worst and best of the race—except the horrible Celestial, who is always called bad, but is even somewhat like "the Englishman of character and the Englishman of no character to speak of." The lazy Indians that lounge about the street, rich with a loaf of bread, a blanket, a string of beads and some feathers, are no poorer than hundreds who will have nothing until they sober up, and at the other end are the owners of wealth incomprehensible by any system of counting—all glittering and golden-hued in a vast firmament of riches, as great as the reality of idlest dreams. Here the world has seen, not one, but at least four, richer than Crœsus; with lamps, rings and slaves better than Aladdin's; four Bonanza kings, each with a mountain of treasure greater to carry than the horrible Old Man of the Sea, but which no modern Sinbad would shake off with delight.

One says, "The gods here worshiped are heathen deities, Mammon, Bacchus and Venus. The temples are brokers' offices, whisky shops, gambling hells and brothels. There is wonderful enterprise, much intelligence, some refinement, not a little courtesy, and a sea of sin."

The view from the city is picturesque and sorrowfully beautiful. Off to the south and east the eye ranges over a waste of sage brush, and the face of the whole country appears like the waves of an angered sea, broken the more because they can go no farther.

The Carson River can be seen stretching off toward its sinking place in arid sands, and the twenty-six mile desert will deceive the unthinking, and add a faint lake-like look to the picture, of which the Walker and Sweetwater Ranges and endless mountains' may light and heaven's blue dome, all add their beauty.

But to enjoy the best view, make the ascent of Mount Davidson, about 2,000 feet above the city, and nearly 8,000 feet high. One need not climb, but may ascend it on horseback by following up the ravine from Gold Cañon. When he reaches what seems from the street to be the top of the mountain, he sees another summit as far beyond, but the latter gained the view is magnificent.

Below, on the west, is a beautiful lake two or three miles in diameter, "glistening like the silver of the mountains which it covers." Reno, the Carson Valley, valleys, mountains, rivers,

lakes, and deserts may be seen in every direction for a hundred miles.

Or, if it is too fatiguing to ascend, whoever is the fortunate possessor of a note of introduction to some mining superintendent, may prepare for a visit to the world below. Donning brogans, woolen socks and coarse flannels, he will step on the cage, holding his breath, his heart feeling gone, and as the water drips around him down the shaft, his feeble lantern will not remove the queer sensation of the descent. Once below, there are cuts, and cross-cuts, drifts, winzes, stopes and a maze of strange words, sights and sounds. Here is explained the use of the squared timbers seen by the car load, passing from the Sierras to Virginia City. As worthless rock or treasured ore is removed, the excavation must be replaced almost as solid as the rock itself. The huge timbers are mortised and fitted to each other with the utmost precision; ladders lead from level to level. Cars convey the ore to the shaft, and up and down the busy cages are always going. Every minute a loaded car ascends from a quarter of a mile below and is replaced by another. The engineer tells by an indicator the precise location of the cage at any moment, and by varying the signals to him, he directs the movements for passengers with greatly decreased speed.

If time permits, ride over to the Sutro Tunnel, six miles from Virginia City. It once promised well, may benefit the Comstock Lode more than its friends have ever dreamed, but from present appearances the real contest concerning it, was not in Congress, nor opposition from the mines it aims to tap, but has yet to come. As a specimen of engineering it will repay a visit. With indomitable energy it is pushed forward, and has now penetrated nearly three miles. The average progress is 90 feet per week, and tunneling was never done elsewhere, more speedily or successfully.

Mines of Virginia City.—The discovery of the Comstock Lode, was made in 1857, by men in pursuit of gold placers. They came upon some mineral new to them, which a Mexican recognized as silver ore. Comstock at an early day, was a middle-man in the purchase of an interest in the lode, and his name thus became attached to it. As explorations were made, very rich ore was found near the surface, and soon a great excitement was created, and vigorous operations commenced, which were crowned with wonderful success. The Ophir Mine, and the Gould & Curry, at an early day began to pay dividends, and continued to do so without interruption for several years. The Savage and the Hale & Norcross were later in becoming known, and their period of prosperity continued after the others had gone into decline. These are all Virginia City Mines. The Kentuck, Crown Point, Yellow Jacket, Chollar Potosi, and Belcher, which have all paid dividends and others less widely known, are in Gold Hill. Neither of them became successful as early as the Ophir and Gould & Curry. The original discoverers of these mines "located" them, as miners say, that is, posted upon the property a notice of claim in writing, of which they filed a copy with the recorder of the mining district. The regulations in reference to locating claims differed slightly in different districts. Usually not over 2,000 feet along the length of a vein could be located in one claim, and no one could claim over 200 feet except the discoverer, he being usually allowed 300, and sometimes 400 feet. Under the present United States Mining Law no single claim for over 1,500 feet can be made, whatever number of persons join in it, and the discoverer is accorded no advantage over others. Feet in length along a vein, are always stated and understood to carry all its depth, spurs and angles, that is, its whole *breadth* and *depth* be they more or less, for the length claimed. Veins are usually only a few feet wide, but sometimes extend miles in length. The Comstock Lode has been traced for five miles, but its greatest breadth so far as yet known, is between 300 and 400 feet, and no other silver vein in the State of Nevada approaches it in breadth, and some are worked which do not exceed 6 inches. In early days dealings in mines were by feet, and not by shares. The Ophir Mine comprised 1,400 feet for instance, and was sold on the stock-board by the foot. An owner of 100 feet owned a fourteenth of the mine. Gradually the selling by feet was abandoned, and only shares were dealt in, and those have been divided up very small, in order to bring speculation within the compass of persons of small means. The Ophir Mine has been divided so that each original foot is represented by seventy-two shares. The incorporations of all the mining companies on the Comstock Lode, and their offices have always been in San Francisco, and the men who live immediately over and about the mine, cannot buy or sell stock in them except by letter or telegraph to "The Bay."

In the development of this mineral lode, three distinct periods may be marked. For some time after its discovery, prosperity continually attended operations on it somewhere along its length, and often at all points. All the mines named above paid dividends, and very few assessments were made. The ore lying within 800 or 900 feet of the surface was finally exhausted along the whole vein, and dividends fell off, assessments became frequent, and great depression followed. This continued until patient exploration revealed, several hundred feet deeper, a rich ore body, in the Crown Point and Belcher Mines. which produced an amount of bullion hitherto unexampled in the history of the vein, dividends amounting to a million a month com-

ing several months in succession. This body of ore was worked out in time, and depression followed again. The total yield of all the mines of Nevada for the last six years has been $176,731,150.

The Big Bonanza Mine.—For more than a year this mine divided $2,000,000 monthly, when suddenly came the end. The following figures, which were furnished at the company's office, give a fair view of the operations of this mine. During 1875, and the three first months of 1876, the bullion receipts of this company were *twenty-four million eight hundred and fifty thousand, five hundred and twenty-four dollars and eighty-four cents*, ($24,850,-524.84).

In March, 1876, were worked 24.991,800–2,000 tons of ore, which produced $3,634,218.92. The total yield of the two mines Virginia and California has exceeded *fifty million dollars*.

The bullion from this mine and others on the Comstock Lode is very pure, and on an average is about .045 fine in gold, and .950 in silver, leaving only about .005 of base metal. The proportion of gold to silver varies, and with it the value of the bullion per pound. A shipment, which represented a fair average, was of 50 bars of $186,998 stamped value, and weighing 5,741 lbs. avoirdupois, thus representing a value of $32.57 per lb. Had this been pure silver, it would have been stamped $18.81 per lb., and the excess above that, is for the gold in the bullion. It may surprise one to be told that silver bullion, carrying so large a portion of gold, shows no trace of it. A bar of gold and silver, in equal proportions, would scarcely differ in color from a pure silver bar. Its weight would, however, reveal the presence of the gold, at once. When six or seven-tenths are gold, its color begins to show.

The valuable product obtained from the ore was over seventy-two per cent. of its assay value during the month reported above. It is not usual to obtain a better result than this without roasting the ore before amalgamation. It will interest one, not familiar with mining, to notice how small in both bulk and weight the bullion product is when compared with the amount of ore handled. During the month referred to, four hundred and forty-six tons of ore, which would make a mass 10 feet high, 20 feet wide and 30 feet long, yielded only one ton of bullion, which could be melted into a solid cube 18 3-5 inches on a side, or 1,560 cubic feet of ore were worked to obtain one cubic foot of bullion.

Reduction of the Ores.—The ores at this place are worked without roasting by the pan process of American origin, first adopted on the Comstock Lode. It is suited admirably to ores which work kindly, requiring little chemical action or heat to make them part with their

LAKE ESTHER, SIERRA NEVADA MOUNTAINS.—FROM A PAINTING BY ALBERT BIERSTADT.

precious contents, to be taken up by amalgamation with quicksilver. Though it rarely yields as close a result as the Mexican patio process, or the furnace and barrel process of Freiberg, it is so much more expeditious and economical of labor, and so capable of being applied on a large scale, that, on the whole, it is unquestionably preferable. The other processes referred to have been thoroughly tried in Virginia City, and found utterly unsuited to the conditions existing there.

The first part of the process, is wet crushing of the ore, by stamps in iron mortars, a constant stream of water carrying off through a brass wire screen the pulverized portion as fast as reduced small enough. The screens are at the back of the mortar. Five stamps, weighing about 650 pounds each, are usually placed in a single mortar, and are lifted and dropped from five to eight inches about ninety times a minute. The feeder, standing in front, judges by the sound when and where to feed in the ore lying behind him. He is expected to feed two batteries of five stamps each, which are usually placed in one frame, and run by a single shaft. Some mills have twelve such batteries or sixty stamps. The amount crushed by a stamp in twenty-four hours—for work never stops day or night—varies with the fineness of the screen, the character of the ore, and the skill of the feeder, and is from one to two and a half tons a day. Automatic machinery for feeding batteries is now introduced in many mills.

The stream running constantly from the battery is received in a series of tanks and settled as much as possible, the deposit from it being coarse sand at first, and fine sediments at last. The fine sediments are called slums, and must be thoroughly mingled with the coarse sand in the after process, for though often containing the richest portion of the ore, the atoms are so impalpably fine, and adhere to one another so closely, as to elude the mechanical agencies employed to obtain the precious metal they bear, and, if worked by themselves, carry away nearly all they are worth with them. By mingling them with the sand in as nearly as possible the same proportion in which they come from the stamps, they become broken up, separated and distributed through the whole mass of pulp, and are persuaded to give up the most of the silver they hold. This silver is not in metallic form, but combined with sulphur, chlorine or antimony for the most part. Chlorides of silver easily and sulphurets more reluctantly part from the base with which they are united, and amalgamate with quicksilver.

Antimonial silver not only refuses to do this, but obstructs the process on the part of other silver compounds with which it may be associated, and is, therefore, dreaded by all silver millmen who do not roast their ores; but the compounds of silver at Virginia City, are chiefly chlorides, and antimonial silver ores, though they occur there, are found in small quantities only.

To effect this amalgamation of the silver in the ore with mercury, the crushed pulp is now placed in quantities of one to two tons, sometimes even more, in an iron pan, five or six feet in diameter and three to four feet deep, and ground and stirred by a revolving muller, till all the coarse sand is reduced fine. The muller is then raised and the grinding ceases, but the agitation is continued, and a large body of quicksilver is introduced, and steam is also let either into the body of the pulp, or a false bottom under the pan, so as to heat the whole mass, the amalgamator in charge standing by and testing it with his finger, thinning it with slums of water, thickening it with coarse sand, shutting off the steam or letting more on, as his judgment dictates, till the temperature and consistency suit. This process is continued from three to twelve hours, according to the richness and the kindly or refractory temper of the ore. Poor ores must be rushed through, that a large amount may be worked. Rich ores, after yielding handsomely, may still obstinately retain more value than some poor ones ever carried.

The pulp is kept thick enough to float minute atoms of quicksilver, and is made to roll over and over by wings on the sides of the pan and on the muller, until all the amalgamation that can be effected is accomplished, when the motion is diminished, and the charge in the pan drawn off into a large settler on a lower level, where it is diluted with a large volume of cold water, and slowly stirred, and the quicksilver atoms uniting, gather in a body at the bottom and are drawn off through a syphon. Meantime, a stream of water running through the settler, carries off the earthy contents, and finally, when quicksilver ceases to gather, the settler is drawn off nearly to the bottom and made ready for the contents of another pan. It is usual to have one settler for two pans, and give half the time to settling that is occupied in grinding and amalgamating.

The silver and gold, so far as they have been taken up, are now held by the quicksilver. This is strained through long, deep, conical, canvas bags, and the tough amalgam obtained is placed in close iron retorts, the quicksilver distilled out by fire; crude bullion results, which is melted in a crucible and poured into moulds, and when weighed, assayed and stamped with its value, is ready for market.

The discharged ore from the settler is called tailings, and is often caught in large reservoirs, and after lying months or years, as the case may be, is worked through the pans and settlers again, and this process is sometimes repeated several times, especially if ore becomes scarce. The practice of different mining companies as to the disposition of their tailings, varies exceedingly. So long as ore is plenty, no pains are taken to save them. They never have been worked so closely as not still to carry several dollars to the ton value in precious metal.

The process employed at Virginia City, is in use wherever silver is mined on the Pacific Coast, with such modifications as differences in the character of the ore demand. Some ores are so refractory as to require roasting. They are first dried thoroughly, then crushed dry, next roasted to expel sulphur, antimony, zinc, etc., and then treated in pans and settlers as if crushed wet without roasting. The process is expensive, but has some compensation in the closer percentage of assay value obtained, and smaller waste of quicksilver. The loss of this metal in amalgamating unroasted ores, amounts in various ways to from two to four pounds for each ton worked. Some of it combines with chlorine in the ore, and is converted into calomel. This is lost beyond recovery. Some of it is volatilized by the heat in the pans, and some escapes through the joints of the retorts, and this also is lost finally, and sometimes hurts workmen exposed to the fumes. Most of it is lost by not being gathered in the settler. It goes off in minute atoms, carrying gold and silver with it. This is partly recovered by working the tailings, or by running them over blankets in sluices which entrap enough of it to pay well for the cost of the process.

Sinks of the Great Nevada Basin. — One of the most wonderful natural features of that part of the Continent lying between the Wahsatch and Sierra Nevada Ranges of Mountains, is the Great Desert and its numerous sinks. The sink of the Great Salt Lake has already been alluded to. It is a great natural curiosity of itself. It receives the waters of an immense region of country, and, though gradually rising, is still confined to its banks, and gives off its surplus waters by evaporation. There is no evidence whatever that it has a subterraneous outlet. Between it and the sinks of the Nevada Desert, there is an elevated ridge and broken ranges of mountains, with gaps and valleys between them. This whole desert has evidently been a lake, or an inland sea, at some time, while the mountains have been islands in it. Passing the ridge, or low divide between the broken mountains, which separates the Great Salt Lake f om the desert beyond, and we arrive at the sinks of the Nevada Basin. The first is the Humboldt Lake, which has been described. Then the Humboldt and Carson Sink, which, unlike the Great Salt Lake, receives the waters of both the Humboldt River and Lake and the Carson River and Lake, flowing from opposite directions; and, in the hot months of summer, when evaporation is greatest, is very nearly dry. On the other hand, in the spring, when the snows of the mountains melt, or when heavy rains occur in the winter and spring

months, causing a large flow of water in the Humboldt and Carson Rivers, these lakes of the same name nearly always rise together, and the vast salty plain, in and around the sink, becomes a lake of great size. There is no evidence of any subterranean outlet to the waters that flow into this large sink. On the contrary, those who have noticed the rapidity with which water disappears from a tub or other vessel exposed to the sun and air in this region, have no difficulty in believing, in fact almost seeing, the process of evaporation going on, by which the waters are drunk up and scattered over the earth in clouds, to be again distilled in rain.

Walker Lake, which receives the flow of Walker River, is another one of these mysterious sinks. It is off to the south of Carson Lake. The river rises in the Sierra Nevadas and flows in a general easterly direction, till its waters are swallowed up by the sands of the desert, or lost through the same process mentioned elsewhere. There are also numerous streams rising in the mountains, assuming large proportions by the time they reach the valleys, but the sands of the desert soon drink them dry, and they are "lost to sight."

North of the Central Pacific, about 20 miles from Wadsworth, are the sinks of Pyramid Lake, Winnemucca Lake and Mud Lake, the latter being a considerable distance north of Pyramid Lake. These bodies of water at times quite large, are called fresh water lakes, though they are brackish and abound in fish. Northeast of Winnemucca Lake is Quin's River, quite a large stream near its source in the mountains of Idaho; but it becomes lost in the desert, on its way, apparently, to Winnemucca Lake. These lakes and the desert are the mighty sinks which drink up the water that is not evaporated, but sometimes evaporation gets the best of them. North-west of Mud Lake, over in California, is Honey Lake, another remarkable body of water. It is sometimes dry so that teams can be driven across its bed, and then again it is on the rampage. Its waters resemble soap-suds, and are admirably adapted for washing purposes. When lashed by the winds, its waters become a rolling mass of foam, and afford a magnificent spectacle to the beholder. If it only had permanent water of the character alluded to, it would be an excellent location for a huge laundry.

Stage Routes to Lake Tahoe. — A favorite route to Lake Tahoe is *via* Carson City. It may be more easily reached and seen on the westward tour, than to wait and include it on the eastward return.

After a visit to Virginia City, the tourist will return to Carson City, remain over night at a good comfortable hotel, the Ormsby House,— whose proprietor considers it *"the highest toned hotel in Nevada,"* and next morning, at 8.30 A. M., take Benton's Stage for Tahoe.

LAKE TAHOE.
BY THOMAS MORAN.

To visit and make the circuit of the lake, and return to Carson will require at least 18 hours, but most tourists will find it desirable to stop at the little hotel on the opposite side of the lake, and return *via* Truckee, thus seeing greater variety of scenery.

Tourists by this route to Virginia City, Carson and Tahoe, will be obliged to leave the Overland Western train at Reno, about 11.40 P. M., and a comfortable night's rest can be enjoyed at the Railroad Hotel. In the morning a train leaves at 7.35 A. M., and arrives at Carson at 9.00; after taking one hour for breakfast, the tourist can either proceed to Virginia City and spend the day, or take immediate departure for Lake Tahoe. Private team or special stage can be engaged at Benton's by any party, for a ride to the Lake at any special time.

On this route there is the best known of all California stage-drivers, who have reined kyuse or mustang horses,—the modest Hank Monk. His first fame was not on the platform of Faneuil Hall in oratory, but in the streets of Boston, with eight horses abreast, well trained to the voice and whip. He has driven stage in California and Nevada, since 1852, and made the distance between Carson and Virginia, 21 miles, in one hour and eight minutes. His appearance and gait do not indicate much energy, but he drove Horace Greeley 100 miles in 10 hours, fast enough toward the end of the journey, and as long as he can wake up his pets with a strong voice or far reaching whip, he will not fail to get his passengers through, "on time." But to the credit of others, it should be said, that California and Nevada have hundreds of drivers not less skillful and reliable than the favorite Monk.

The route to the lake lies first south, through the Carson Valley, toward Job's Peaks and Silver Mountain, always beautiful with snow. In the clear atmosphere, the first will appear only a few miles away, but it is still more than twenty miles distant. The stage road turns west, up Clear Creek Canon, through which comes the Twenty-one Mile (V shaped) Flume of the Carson & Tahoe Lumber Company, through which 700 cords of wood, or half a million feet of mining timber can be daily delivered at Carson City from the summits of the Sierras. Along the canon are many towering, sun-burnt rocks, weather-beaten and worn into weird and fantastic shapes, and these and the swift-descending timber, splashing the water up many feet at every turn, to sparkle in the sunlight, the Carson Valley spread out below, with the Pine Nut, Walker and Sweet-water Mountains on one side, and the Sierras opposite, always attract and delight the lover of bold mountain scenery.

At the summit, the flume connects with the Lake Tahoe N. G. Railroad, 9 miles long from summit to Glenbrook on snore of the lake. The distance is but three miles by wagon road, 6 miles less than by the R. R. The railroad is worked only in the summer months—after much of it has been sought out and found with shovels, and is exposed to damage and destruction from avalanches of snow or rock which come thundering down the steep sides with resistless force. Near the summit it has the enormous grade of 180 feet to the mile. This passage over the eastern summit of the Sierras is made where the range is depressed and the view, though beautiful, is far too contracted to fully gratify the traveler. Below, lies Lake Tahoe, girt with everlasting pine-clad hills whose snowy masses and evergreen foliage mingle with the deep blue of an inland sea, yet only a small portion of its beauty can be seen.

Lake Tahoe.—This great body of fresh water, 25 miles long, on an average ten wide, about three-fourths in California, and one-fourth in Nevada, has an elevation of a mile and a quarter, and has been sounded to a depth of 3,000 feet. Through glacial action in past ages, ice must have been piled up in the valley of this lake 3,400 feet high. It never freezes, is smooth as glass and clear as crystal, permitting the trout to be seen or pebbles counted at a depth of 80 feet. Its water changes color to a beautiful emerald or almost indigo blue according to the depth, and when disturbed by the fierce mountain winds, its waves lash the shore with foaming fury.

At Glenbrook, five steamers will be found, three of which are employed for the mills, and the others, the "Niagara" and "Stanford" will convey tourists, not exceeding 200 in number, around the lake.

Glenbrook is the business center of the whole region that borders on the lake. It has four saw-mills with an aggregate capacity of five million feet per month, running 11 1-2 hours per day, also a planing mill.

Captain Pray, the oldest settler, is a large land-owner, and much of the 200 acres in the ranche on the shores of the lake, is covered with a beautiful sod of timothy and clover. In the State there is no finer land, and as the captain and other mill-owners will rent none for saloon purposes, Glenbrook, with a summer population of 500, is a temperance town. The Glenbrook Hotel, usually kept in first-class style, is usually open each season, if not, comfortable accommodations can still be found at the Lake Shore House, for $20 a week, without extra charge for the use of boats.

Shakespeare Rock, a remarkable curiosity, is a bold, perpendicular rock on which the profile of the great poet's face is outlined with great accuracy.

From Glenbrook there is a charming drive on the old Placerville Road, past Cave Rock, and around the head of the lake to Rowlands or

Yank's. The road was constructed at great expense—a single mile near the rock, costing $10,000. The only other drive, of note, is from Tahoe City to Sugar Pine Point.

The whole of the lake is not visible until the steamer has run out a little distance from the shore. Then its generic name is rather fitting. "Tahoe," in the Indian, signifies "big water," and is the name for ocean. The shore slopes gently, in places, for two miles to a depth of from 30 to 50 feet, then breaks sometimes abruptly as at the Bluffs of Rubicon or Observatory Point, to a depth of 600 or 800 feet; and off Sugar Pine Point is the greatest depth yet found. The water is clear as crystal, and the temperature in summer, when taken from considerable depth, very near the freezing point. The fare across the lake is $2.50, and around, $5. The steamer must lie idle half the year, and reasonable fares may seem thus high. Leaving Glenbrook for a circuit around the head of the lake, the first object of interest is Cave Rock, three and one-half miles from Glenbrook, about 400 feet high. This appears in the engraving from Moran's sketch made from the point just south of Glenbrook, and looking south and west.

After passing the rock, and looking back, it resembles the Great South Dome of Yosemite, split in two, and the cavern, 30 feet in length, is seen about 100 feet above the ground. The line of solid masonry and bridge for the road can just be traced from the point where the artist stood. Leaving Cave Rock, Zephyr Cove is three miles south. Beautiful meadows afford fine pasturage, and being on the east side, the earliest vegetables are here grown. The mountain's wall shows plainly its broken but regular character. From the main ridge, a cross spur is thrown out, but this must again be broken into a succession of small canons and "divides."

Just south of the cave is the old Friday Ranche, well known by the pioneers who were "on the way to Washoe" and the Kingsbury Canon, through which the road crossed the mountain to Genoa. In other days, the toll receipts on the Kingsbury grade were $500 a day.

Rowlands,—14 miles from Glenbrook, at the head of the lake, on the Old Placerville Road, was the first place of resort on the lake and originally called the Lake House. It has greatly changed from the day when J. Ross Browne was a guest, and the host "seemed to be quite worn out with his run of customers,—from a hundred to three hundred of a night, and nowhere to stow 'em—all cussin' at him for not keepin' provisions, with but little to drink, except old fashioned tarantula-juice, warranted to kill at forty paces." It has now two stores and a post-office, with accommodations for tourists at moderate price. Lake Valley appears, from a distance, like a large, pine-covered flat. It is 14 miles long and six wide, partly covered with timber,

and having much grazing land of the best quality. The stock that pastures in these fertile valleys of the lake, is all driven out before the winter snows begin. Between Rowlands and Yank's, is the terminus of Gardner's Railroad, a successful enterprise for lumbering. It will soon be extended from six to ten miles.

Yank's—is 4 miles from Rowlands, and at the south-west end of the lake, just west of and with convenient access to Lake Valley, and is situated on a grassy sward, in a beautiful grove of tamaracks interspersed with tall pines and quaking aspens, with a pebbly beach gently sloping from Tellac Point, commanding a view of the whole lake, with convenient access to Tellac Mountain, and only two miles from Fallen Leaf Lake, another beautiful sheet of water, three miles long and one and one-half wide, at the head of which are excellent Soda Springs. Tellac Mountain is easily recognized from its long, flat summit, and may be ascended *via* Fallen Leaf Lake and a steep canon. The view from the summit is one of the finest on the Continent.

To the east, looking across Lake Valley and the beautiful Tahoe, the eastern summits do not shut out the country beyond, for Carson Valley and much of Nevada are in sight. On the west, are the great valleys of central California, beyond them the Coast Range, and scattered among the countless snow and purple peaks of the Sierras, there nestle thirty-six lakes in sight, varying from the deep, dark blue of Tahoe to the brilliancy of silver beneath a noonday sun. Horses and boats are always to be had at Yank's. Twenty dollars per week is the price of board; boats are charged for at city prices for carriages. "Yank" is a *soubriquet* to mark the Green Mountain origin of the host, Mr. E. Clement. The tourist will need no further introduction, but should be informed that Yank spends his winters at the lake and *sees* snow come down the mountains and accumulate around his buildings. Of all places on the lake, none is more truly beautiful for situation, than *Yank's* and it is a favorite resort.

Leaving Yank's, the steamer heads north and proceeds four miles to Emerald Bay, passing two well-rounded peaks at the foot of which is a beautiful valley, in which lies Cascade Lake. This, too, is accessible from Yank's and is one of its attractions. The point just north of the entrance to Emerald Bay was long the home of America's pride among the birds, and is named Eagle Point.

Emerald Bay—is a gem of beauty—entered on the south side of a narrow strait, as shown in our title-page. It is two miles long by about three-fourths of a mile wide. The entrance is shoal, but the bay deep. Near the head of the bay is a little granite island, with a few small trees and shrubs, and the unfilled tomb of an eccentric tar—Captain Dick—who prepared the island for his own mausoleum, in which he intended to place himself on the approach of death, but his drowned body became food for the fishes, and the lonely cross marked an empty tomb.

This charming bay is owned by Ben Holladay, Jr. His summer residence is surrounded by a grove of willows and a stream fed by eternal snows, pouring down in three successive lofty waterfalls, which rival in grace and beauty some of the smaller in Yosemite, keeps the grassy sward always green, and plays in a fountain before the door.

The surrounding hills are so steep that they can be climbed only with great difficulty. Just opposite the island, on the north side, there is the mark of an avalanche of snow, that carried the tall pines before it like shrubs, and has left the mountain side completely bare.

Rubicon Point and Bay, and Sugar Pine Point are next passed, going north on the way to McKinney's, ten miles from Emerald Bay.

At McKinney's, there is no large house, but 13 cottages and pleasant surroundings. The road to Tahoe City, gives this the advantage of a pleasant drive. Board may be had at $20 a week.

Continuing north, the steamer passes Blackwood Creek, where some towering rocks are seen whose height is scarcely comprehended, because the trees and mountains beyond are on so great a scale. Small as they seem, they are two hundred and fifty feet high, and the trees at their base not less than 200 feet.

Ward's Bay lies north of the Creek, and Bawker's Peak, a sharp, high point, is back in the mountains.

Tahoe City—is eight miles from McKinney's, and one of the loveliest spots on the lake. It is at the source of the Truckee River, the only outlet of the lake, and has the "Grand Central," the largest hotel on the Sierras, with accommodations for 160 guests, and kept by those excellent hosts, Bayley & Moody. This is the most convenient point of access for tourists from California. The road to Truckee is down the beautiful cañon of the Truckee River, through a noble forest of pines, invigorating and delightful at every step. Sail and row-boats of all kinds may be had at this point, and also carriages; but the prices should be agreed upon beforehand. No boats are kept for the use of the hotel.

Board at the Grand Central may be had, varying from $3.00 to $4.00 per day, according to rooms. The view of the lake from Tahoe City is not excelled, and equalled only at Yank's and the Hot Springs.

The hotel and other accommodations are superior to all others on the lake. Besides the Grand Central, there is the Tahoe House, kept by Captain Pomin.

Tourists who desire to spend only one day in visiting the lake, take stages at this point to Truckee, 12 miles down the river.

Trout.—At Tahoe City there is a trout establishment of much interest; and another, on a larger scale, on the river half way to Truckee Station. The water is admitted to a series of ponds, each pond being appropriated to trout of a different size. The eggs are taken during April, May and June, when the fish ascend the river and the creeks, to spawn. The eggs are stripped from the female and impregnated by stripping the male fish into the same vessel in which the eggs are contained, and then placed on inclined shelves or tables where about half an inch of water runs gently, but steadily over them. The temperature of the water affects the time of hatching, and the desire is to have the water as cold as possible at the expense of time to produce the hardier fish. One trout contains about 7,000 spawn. Twenty-five cents is charged for admission to the fishery, and the privilege of fishing in the ponds granted for twenty-five or fifty cents a fish, according to the size.

The fishing in the lake is done by trolling. Spoon-hooks are sometimes used, but early in the season it is necessary to have some shining device to attract attention besides a minnow on the hook. The fisheries have been quite successful in hatching fish, but not profitable. At first nearly all died; now nearly all are raised. The young fish are nourished for several days after birth by a portion of the egg from which they are hatched remaining attached to them till it is absorbed, and then are fed on mashed fish, the yolks of eggs and liver, and the large trout are fed on suckers and white fish caught in the lakes with seines. Of course no trout are caught in seines, for this is contrary to law.

After they have grown to weigh several pounds, they will increase at the rate of a pound a year. The quantity caught in a year can not be estimated. Many are never sent to market, and they are caught in both the lake and the river as well as in Donner Lake.

From the Truckee River alone, 170,000 pounds were caught last season, half of which were shipped to Virginia City.

In the lake there are at least four kinds, two of which are most commonly known. These are the silver trout and the black trout. The silver trout are most highly esteemed, are always taken in deep water, and attain a size of thirty-two pounds. The silver trout of Donner Lake grow from eight to ten pounds, and those in the river are not so large. The black trout run up the creeks sooner in the spring than the silver, but the latter can pass over greater obstacles than the former.

The white fish found in the lake are quite unlike those of the Great North American Lakes.

While the tourist who merely crosses the lake from Glenbrook to Tahoe or *vice versa*, or who desires to reach the Central Pacific Railroad, with the loss of one day only will not make the entire circuit of the lake; others will visit the north end, and some may prefer this alone. Continuing around from Tahoe City, Burton's or Island Farm is two miles from Tahoe City. It is a lovely spot, with summer green meadows and pebbly beach, and accommodates at reasonable cost, 25 or 30 people. It is a favorite resort for California clergymen needing rest.

Burton's is connected with Tahoe City by a carriage road, and is not too far to exercise at the oars of a small boat.

Passing around the north end of the lake, there is next, Observatory Point, where the great telescope of James Lick was expected to be erected, and beyond this is Carnelian Bay, and Carnelian Beach, so called from fine specimens of chalcedony here found. Here is Doctor Bournes' hygienic establishment.

Beyond this, are Agate bay and then Campbell's Hot Springs, ten miles from Glenbrook, and on Boundary Point, because it marks the dividing line between California and Nevada. The water boils out in several places in great volume. The hotel is comfortable; the charge $3 a day; the entire lake is seen from the house, and the baths are an advantage to be had nowhere else on the lake. There is a stage from this point to Truckee, and the stages from Tahoe City will also carry passengers thence to the springs.

Fishing and boating and driving can be enjoyed at pleasure, and in the hills there are a few grouse, quail, deer, and bear, but game is not plentiful.

The Lumber and Trees of the Lake Region.—The logs which are brought down to the lake at various points are towed to Glenbrook in V-shaped booms, from 50 to 70 feet wide at one end, and about 150 feet long, averaging 200,000 feet of lumber.

The sugar pine is the most valuable, then the yellow pine. The black, or "bull" pine was long despised, but is now highly prized for its strength. It reaches, in California, a diameter of 15, and height of 200 feet; about the lake, a diameter of 10 feet. The leaves are of a dark green color, but the cones are enormous—sometimes 18 inches long. The wood is fine grained and solid, soft and clear.

The yellow pine is not quite so large, seldom exceeding 10 feet in diameter, and has bark furrowed into plate-like sections, six or eight inches wide, and from 12 to 20 inches long.

The "bull" pine is a favorite with the woodpecker for storing his acorns, not in the hollow trees, but by drilling holes in the bark, and fitting an acorn into each. Old woodmen say the bird never makes a misfit, and selects, the first time, a nut which will exactly fill the hole he has drilled. In the valleys of California, nearly all large trees are utilized in this way.

There are two kinds of fir, the white and the red. The latter called also the Douglass fir, is a good strong timber; the former is the least esteemed in the market.

Other pines of the Sierras are interesting, but notice of all must be omitted except the Nut or "Digger" pine, so called from a sweet or oily seed forming a staple article of food for the Indians, but it does not grow in the high Sierras. It is dwarfish and scraggy, without one main trunk, but dividing up into several. It is said that this is so liable to "draw" while seasoning, that miners who were compelled to use it for building their cabins, were not surprised to see them turn over two or three times in the course of the summer.

As two daily passenger trains leave Reno for San Francisco, one arriving *via* Vallejo in eleven and a quarter hours, and the other *via* Stockton in seventeen and a half hours, from the time of leaving Truckee, the tourist economizing time, will take the former, leaving Truckee at midnight.

By leaving at 3 A. M., daylight will soon follow in the summer months, and the fine scenery of the Sierras be more enjoyed.

To see the mountains, the best plan is to stop at the summit, where there is another of the first-class hotels of James Cardwell, and gain the views from the peaks near by, and then descend the mountain by a freight train, leaving the summit at 5.30 A. M., and reaching Sacramento the same evening, at 7.45. For this, one must be willing to exchange the Palace car for the caboose, and accept delay in exchange for the leisurely enjoyment of the most wonderful railroad scenery in the world.

The Great Nevada Flume.
A PERILOUS RIDE.
By H. J. Ramsdell, of The N. Y. Tribune.

A 15 mile ride in a flume down the Sierra Nevada Mountains in 35 minutes, was not one of the things contemplated on my visit to Virginia City, and it is entirely within reason to say that I shall never make the trip again.

The flume cost, with its appurtenances, between $200,000 and $300,000. It was built by a company interested in the mines here, principally owners of the Consolidated Virginia, California, Hale & Norcross, Gould & Curry, Best & Belcher, and Utah Mines. The largest stockholders are J. C. Flood, James G. Fair, John Mackey, and W. S. O'Brien, who compose, without doubt, the wealthiest firm in the United States.

The mines named use 1,000,000 feet of lumber per month underground, and burn 40,000 cords of wood per year. Wood here is worth from $10 to $12 a cord, and at market prices, Messrs.

Flood & Co., would have to pay for wood alone, nearly $500,000 per year.

Virginia City is not built in a forest. From the top of Mount Davidson, which is half a mile back from the city, there is not a tree in sight, except a few shade-trees in the city.

Going into the mines the other day, and seeing the immense amount of timber used, I asked Mr. Mackey where all the wood and timber came from. "It comes," said he, "from our lands in the Sierras, 40 or 50 miles from here. We own over 12,000 acres in the vicinity of Washoe Lake, all of which is heavily timbered."

"How do you get it here?" I asked.

"It comes," said he, "in our flume down the mountain, 15 miles, and from our dumping grounds is brought by the Virginia & Truckee Railroad to this city, 16 miles. You ought to see this flume before you go back. It is really a wonderful thing."

The Journey.—When, therefore, two days afterward, I was invited to accompany Mr. Flood and Mr. Fair to the head of the flume, I did not hesitate to accept their kind offer. We started at four o'clock in the morning, in two buggies, the two gentlemen named in one buggy, and Mr. Hereford, the President and Superintendent of the company (which is known as the Pacific Wood, Lumber and Flume Company) and myself in the other.

The drive through Washoe Valley, and along the mountains, up and down for 16 miles over a road which, for picturesqueness, is without an equal in memory, can not be described. Not a tree, nor bush, nor any green vegetation was in sight. Hills and mountains, well defined and separate in character, were in every direction. Sage brush and jack rabbits were the only living things in sight. That beautiful purple atmosphere or mist, which has a dreamy, sleepy effect in the landscape, overspread the mountains and extended through the valley.

The road we traversed swung round and round the mountains, now going nearly to the summit, and now descending to their base.

Both teams employed were of the best, and in less than an hour and a half we had accomplished the first part of our journey, 10 miles. Here we breakfasted and went to the end of the flume, a quarter of a mile distant. The men were running timber 16 inches square and 10 feet long through it. The trestle-work upon which the flume rested was about 20 feet from the ground. The velocity of the movement of the timber could scarcely be credited, for it requires from only twenty-five minutes to half an hour for it to float the entire length of the flume, 15 miles.

The flume is shaped like the letter V, and is made of two-inch plank nailed together in the above shape. Across the top it is about two and one-half feet in width. The ends are very carefully fitted, so that where the planks go together there may be no unevenness; for timbers going at the rate of 15 to 60 miles per hour must have a clear coast.

In this trough the water runs from Hunter's Creek, which is situated about 20 miles from the terminus of the flume.

Some idea of the swiftness with which the timber runs through the flume, may be had when it is stated that in the flume there floats 500,000 feet of lumber every day (about ten hours), or 500 cords of wood.

Near the terminus an iron break is placed in the trough, slanting toward one side, so that when the timber comes rushing down, 50 or 100 pieces, one after the other, each piece is turned toward the side, and the men at the break, with a dexterous use of the crowbar, send them bounding to the ground.

I climbed to the top of the trestle-work, before the timber began to come. It was like the rushing of a herd of buffalo on a party of hunters, and I preferred to view the flume, in active working, from a distance.

We changed teams upon resuming our journey, taking fresh horses for the mountain ascent. Horsemen in the East who have never seen the mountains of Nevada, Colorado and California, can have no idea of the amount of work a horse can do, and of the difficult places through which he will go, and of the load he will carry or draw. How a pair of horses can pull a buggy and two men up a grade that seems half-way between the horizontal and the perpendicular, over stones and fallen trees, and through underbrush six feet high and very thick, is a question I can never hope to solve; at any rate, we reached the lower mill of the company, about 18 or 20 miles. This was several hours before noon.

The mill is situated in the lower belt of timber, and there are between 400 and 500 men at work. This number includes those engaged in cutting trees, hauling logs, and sawing the lumber. How the heavy machinery of the mills, and the engines which work them were brought from the city up the mountains and placed in position, is another mystery which I have not tried to investigate.

The amount of lumber turned out by the owner of these mills, the upper and the lower, the former being two and one-half miles farther up the mountain, is marvellous.

In five minutes' time, a log from two to four feet in diameter is reduced to lumber, planks, scantling, boards, and square timber, perhaps all from the same log, for it is cut in the most advantageous manner. Sometimes one log will give three or four different kinds of lumber. The lower mill is kept running night and day, and has a capacity of 50,000 feet per day of small stuff, and of 70,000 feet when working on large timber.

SUMMITS OF THE SIERRAS.

BY THOMAS MORAN.

The upper mill has less than half the capacity, being smaller, and being worked only 12 hours a day.

The Flume.—The flume is a wonderful piece of engineering work. It is built wholly upon trestle-work, and stringers; there is not a cut in the whole distance, and the grade is so heavy that there is little danger of a jam.

The trestle-work is very substantial, and is undoubtedly strong enough to support a narrow gauge railway. It runs over foot hills, through valleys, around mountains, and across canons.

In one place it is 70 feet high. The highest point of the flume from the plain, is 3,700 feet, and on an air line, from beginning to end, the distance is eight miles, the course thus taking up seven miles in twists and turns. The trestle-work is thoroughly braced, longitudinally and across, so that no break can extend farther than a single box, which is 16 feet; all the main supports, which are five feet apart, are firmly set in mud-sills, and the boxes or troughs rest in brackets four feet apart. These again rest upon substantial stringers. The grade of the flume is between 1,600 and 2,000 feet from the top to lower end, a distance of 15 miles.

The sharpest fall is three feet in six. There are two reservoirs from which the flume is fed. One is 1,100 feet long, and the other 600 feet. A ditch, nearly two miles long, takes the water to the first reservoir, whence it is conveyed 3 1-4 miles to the flume through a feeder capable of carrying 450 inches of water.

The whole flume was built in 10 weeks. In that time all the trestle-work, stringers and boxes were put in place. About 200 men were employed on it at one time, being divided into four gangs. It required 2,000,000 feet of lumber, but the item which astonished me most was that there were 28 tons, or 56,000 pounds of *nails*, used in the construction of this flume.

To the lower mill, as the road goes, it is about 40 miles from Virginia City. Although I had already ridden this distance, yet I mounted a horse and rode two or three miles to the top of the mountain, where I had one of the finest valley views that come to the lot of man. Miles and miles below, the valley was spread out with spots and squares of green crops growing, and barren wastes of sand and sage brush reaching in a long stretch to the base of another spur of the Sierras. The City of Reno occupied a little spot on the plain—from my mountain it seemed like a city of toy houses built on Nature's carpet.

A Ride in the Flume.—Upon my return I found that Mr. Flood and Mr. Fair had arranged for a ride in the flume, and I was challenged to go with them. Indeed, the proposition was put in the form of a challenge—they dared me to go.

I thought that if men worth $25,000,000 or $30,000,000 apiece, could afford to risk their lives, I could afford to risk mine, which was not worth half as much.

So I accepted the challenge, and two *boats* were ordered. These were nothing more than pig-troughs, with one end knocked out. The "*boat*" is built, like the flume, V shaped, and fits into the flume. It is composed of three pieces of wood—two two-inch planks, 16 feet long, and an end board which is nailed about two and one-half feet across the top.

The forward end of the boat was left open, the rear end closed with a board—against which was to come the current of water to propel us. Two narrow boards were placed in the boat for seats, and everything was made ready. Mr. Fair and myself were to go in the first boat, and Mr. Flood and Mr. Hereford in the other.

Mr. Fair thought that we had better take a third man with us who knew something about the flume. There were probably 50 men from the mill standing in the vicinity waiting to see us off, and when it was proposed to take a third man, the question was asked of them if anybody was willing to go.

Only one man, a red-faced carpenter, who takes more kindly to whisky than his bench, volunteered to go. Finally, everything was arranged. Two or three stout men held the boat over the flume, and told us to jump into it the minute it touched the water, and to "*hang on to our hats*."

The signal of "*all ready*" was given, the boat was launched, and we jumped into it as best we could, which was not very well, and away we went like the wind.

One man who helped to launch the boat, fell into it just as the water struck it, but he scampered out on the trestle, and whether he was hurt or not, we could not wait to see.

The grade of the flume at the mill is very heavy, and the water rushes through it at railroad speed. The terrors of that ride can never be blotted from the memory of one of that party. To ride upon the cow-catcher of an engine down a steep grade is simply exhilarating, for you know there is a wide track, regularly laid upon a firm foundation, that there are wheels grooved and fitted to the track, that there are trusty men at the brakes, and better than all, you know that the power that impels the train can be rendered powerless in an instant by the driver's light touch upon his lever. But a flume has no element of safety. In the first place the grade can not be regulated as it can on a railroad; you can not go fast or slow at pleasure; you are wholly at the mercy of the water. You can not stop; you can not lessen your speed; you have nothing to hold to; you have only to sit still, shut your eyes, say your prayers, take all the water that comes — filling your boat, wetting your feet, drenching you like a plunge through the surf,—and wait for eternity. It is all there is to hope for after you are launched in a flume-boat. I can not give the reader a better idea of a flume ride than to compare it to riding down an old fashioned eave-trough at an angle of 45°, hanging in midair without support of roof or house, and thus shot a distance of 15 miles.

At the start, we went at the rate of about 20 miles an hour, which is a little less than the average speed of a railroad train. The reader can have no idea of the speed we made, until he compares it to a railroad. The average time we made was 30 miles per hour—a mile in two minutes for the entire distance. This is greater than the average running time of railroads.

Incidents of the Ride.—The red-faced carpenter sat in front of our boat on the bottom, as best he could. Mr. Fair sat on a seat behind him, and I sat behind Mr. Fair in the stern, and was of great service to him in keeping the water, which broke over the end-board, from his back.

There was a great deal of water also shipped in the bows of the hog-trough, and I know Mr. Fair's broad shoulders kept me from many a wetting in that memorable trip.

At the heaviest grade the water came in so furiously in front, that it was impossible to see where we were going, or what was ahead of us; but, when the grade was light, and we were going at a three or four-minute pace, the vision was very delightful, although it was terrible.

In this ride, which fails me to describe, I was perched up in a boat no wider than a chair, sometimes 20 feet high in the air, and with the ever varying altitude of the flume, often 70 feet high. When the water would enable me to look ahead, I would see this trestle here and there for miles, so small and narrow, and apparently so fragile, that I could only compare it to a chalk-mark, upon which, high in the air, I was running at a rate unknown upon railroads.

One circumstance during the trip did more to show me the terrible rapidity with which we dashed through the flume, than anything else. We had been rushing down at a pretty lively rate of speed, when the boat suddenly struck something in the bow—a nail, or lodged stick of wood, which ought not to have been there. What was the result? The red-faced carpenter was sent whirling into the flume, 10 feet ahead. Fair was precipitated on his face, and I found a soft lodgment on Fair's back.

It seemed to me that in a second's time, Fair, himself a powerful man, had the carpenter by the scruff of the neck, and had pulled him into the boat. I did not know that, at this time, Fair had his fingers crushed between the boat and the flume.

But we sped along; minutes seemed hours. It seemed an hour before we arrived at the worst place in the flume, and yet Hereford tells me it was less than 10 minutes. The flume at the point alluded to must have very near 45° inclination.

In looking out before we reached it, I thought

the only way to get to the bottom was to fall. How our boat kept in the track is more than I know. The wind, the steamboat, the railroad never went so fast. I have been where the wind blew at the rate of 80 miles an hour, and yet my breath was not taken away. In the flume, in the bad places, it seemed as if I would suffocate.

The first bad place that we reached, and if I remember right, it was the worst, I got close against Fair. I did not know that I would survive the journey, but I wanted to see how fast we were going. So I lay close to him and placed my head between his shoulders. The water was coming into his face, like the breakers of the ocean. When we went slow, the breakers came in on my back, but when the heavy grades were reached, the breakers were in front. In one case Fair shielded me, and in the other, I shielded Fair.

In this particularly bad place I allude to, my desire was to form some judgment of the speed we were making. If the truth must be spoken, I was really scared almost out of reason; but if I was on the way to eternity, I wanted to know exactly how fast I went; so I huddled close to Fair, and turned my eyes toward the hills. Every object I placed my eye on was gone, before I could clearly see what it was. Mountains passed like visions and shadows. It was with difficulty that I could get my breath. I felt that I did not weigh an hundred pounds, although I knew, in the sharpness of intellect which one has at such a moment, that the scales turned at *two hundred.*

Mr. Flood and Mr. Hereford, although they started several minutes later than we, were close upon us. They were not so heavily loaded, and they had the full sweep of the water, while we had it rather at second hand. Their boat finally struck ours with a terrible crash.

Mr. Flood was thrown upon his face, and the waters flowed over him, leaving not a dry thread upon him. What became of Hereford I do not know, except that when he reached the terminus of the flume, he was as wet as any of us.

This only remains to be said. We made the entire distance in less time than a railroad train would ordinarily make, and a portion of the time we went faster than a railroad train ever went.

Fair said we went at least a mile a minute. Flood said we went at the rate of 100 miles an hour, and *my* deliberate belief is that we went at a rate that annihilated time and space. We were a wet lot when we reached the terminus of the flume. Flood said he would not make the trip again, for the whole *Consolidated Virginia Mine.*

Fair said that he should never again place himself on an equality with timber and wood, and Hereford said he was sorry that he ever built the flume. As for myself, I told the millionaire that

I had accepted my last challenge. When we left our boats we were more dead than alive.

We had yet 16 miles to drive to Virginia City. How we reached home, the reader will never know. I asked Flood what I was to do with my spoiled suit of English clothes. He bade me *good night*, with the remark that my clothes were good enough to give away. The next day, neither Flood nor Fair were able to leave their bed. For myself, I had only strength enough left to say, " *I have had enough of flumes.*"

RENO TO SAN FRANCISCO.

Proceeding from Reno, directly to San Francisco, the line of the railroad is along the Truckee River. The meadows grow narrower, and the mountains approach on either side, then widen again in Pleasant Valley.

Verdi—is 283 miles east of San Francisco, has three stores and a planing mill; derives its importance from the lumber trade, and its notoriety from the robbery of the express and mail cars, of an overland train.

The scenery is now becoming fine; Crystal Peak may be seen on the right, and winter moonlight nights will add charms to make the views more lovely and unique between this point and Truckee. Then the mountains, denuded at their base of all timber, and the shrubs and stumps buried in deep snow are of unbroken, silvery white, while the lofty pines, farther up the steep sides or on the rounding tops, form a veil of green, and above all irregular, fleecy clouds float fantastically by, as if a silvery mist in the valleys was rising over the dark peaks, mingling light of many shades,

SNOW SHEDS ACROSS THE SIERRAS.

while exulting clouds, glide smoothly and silently along the azure sky.

The Truckee River foams, as its rapid waters battle with the rocks, and it is crossed and recrossed on Howe truss bridges, and the mountains, often precipitous, show their volcanic origin in masses of basaltic rock.

Essex,—282 miles from San Francisco, is a side track at which passenger trains do not stop.

Bronco,—273 miles from San Francisco, is a meeting place for trains with a store and a summer station-agent. Soon after leaving the station, there will be noticed a post marked "State Line," standing on the 120th meridian west of Washington D. C., and this passed, the traveler is in the Golden State of California.

Between Bronco and Boca, at what was Camp 18, a flag station has just been located and named Dover.

Boca,—a telegraph station, is 267 miles from San Francisco, with a population of about 150. It is at the mouth of the Little Truckee River, and is the Spanish name for "mouth." The only business is that of the Boca Lumber Mill and Ice Company, and the Boca Brewery, the latter the largest on the Pacific Coast, and on account of the equable temperature, expected to produce the best lager-beer in the world. About 8,000 tons of ice are cut yearly from the pond. The cold is sometimes severely felt, the mercury standing at 22° below zero during the winter of 1875-6.

Prosser Creek—is 265 miles from San Francisco at the mouth of a creek of the same name, called from a hotel keeper in early days. It is a flag station, and the terminus of a flume for several milling stations, and the ice-field for two companies that supply San Francisco. Continuing west 3.3 miles, we reach

Proctor's,—262 miles from San Francisco, but trains do not stop On the left will be noticed a large tract of flat land covered with timber, or stumps, and a ranche or two. Across this and over the range of hills beyond, lies Lake Tahoe, but keeping to the river, 3.2 miles from Proctor's, we reach

Truckee,—259 miles from San Francisco, the dividing line between the Truckee and Sacramento divisions of the railroad, with a roundhouse for 24 engines. It has a tri-weekly newspaper, the *Republican,* and is the most important town in the Sierras, on account of the business done, as a summer resort, and because of its convenience to other favorite resorts. It is the seat of a large lumber trade, and would be benefited by the establishment of an extensive fire insurance business. The town was burned in 1868, 1869, twice in 1870, in 1874, and "ChinaTown" in 1875. The prevailing winds are west, and in summer one might think the great width of the street is designed to prevent fires from the locomotive sparks, but in winter the more probable suggestion is that it is for the convenience of piling up the snow when the people shovel out their houses. The population is about 2,000, nearly one-third of which are Chinamen. A large number of good stores are arranged on the north side of the street, and considerable trade carried on with Sierra and Pleasant Valleys on the north.

Its hotels are first-class—the "Truckee Hotel," where the train stops, and the Cardwell House across the wide street and a little removed from the noise of passing trains. Many desiring the benefit of mountain air and the convenience of the railroad, spend their summer months in

Truckee, from which Donner Lake is distant only two miles, and Tahoe 12.

Stages leave Truckee on Tuesdays, Thursdays and Saturdays for Randolph, 28 miles, time four hours, and fare $4; Sierraville, 29 miles, time four and one-fourth hours, fare $4; Sierra City, 60 miles, time ten hours, fare $8; Downieville, 72 miles, time twelve hours, fare $10; Jamison City, 55 miles, time ten hours, fare $8, and Eureka Mills, 58 miles, time ten and one-half hours, fare $8. On Mondays, Wednesdays, and Fridays for Loyalton, 30 miles, time five hours, fare $4; Beckwith, 45 miles, time seven and one-half hours, fare $5.

The stages leaving on Mondays, Wednesdays and Fridays, are also the stages for Webber Lake, 16 miles north of Truckee, and Independence Lake, about the same distance. At each of these is a good hotel.

Webber Lake is about the size of Donner, encircled by high, snow-capped mountains, but beautified by a rim of fertile meadow around its pebbly beach.

Cardwell's stages leave

GALLERY IN SNOW SHEDS, C. P. R. R.

the summit daily, passing along Donner Lake to Truckee, thence to Tahoe City on Lake Tahoe. Fare from the summit to Tahoe, $2.50. Truckee to Tahoe, $2; John F. Moody, of the Truckee Hotel, also runs an elegant open coach, of the Kimball Manufacturing Company, between Truckee and Tahoe City, daily, fare $2; and Campbell's stages leave every morning for Campbell's Hot Springs on Lake Tahoe.

Truckee was named after General Fremont's old Indian, who was engaged to guide the unfortunate Donner party across the Sierras. It is full of business and beauty in summer and winter. Here, among good hotels, is the best place in the Sierras to be snowed in, although twice as much snow may be seen falling at the summit.

15

A Snow-Storm at Truckee.—At midnight, the mountain peaks stood clear and white, with deep shadows here and there, and above, a cloudless sky ; but, at daylight, a foot of new snow lay upon many previous snows.

The one-story houses were hid from view. While the air was full of falling flakes, busy men were shoveling off the roofs of their dwellings—shoveling all the while, and half a hundred Chinamen were loading cars with snow from the railroad track to throw it down some steep mountain side. Men are coming in with their shoes in hand—not number thirteens, but—thirteen feet long, and stand them up against the wall.

These snow-shoes are about six inches wide, turned up in front like the runner of a skate, and waxed to make them slip easily over the snow. Near the middle is a leather that laces over the instep (a skeleton half-hoe), and out of which the foot will slip in case of a fall or accident.

A long pole is carried like a rope-dancer's to preserve a balance, and to straddle and sit upon for a brake, when descending a hill. They are essential to safety in these storms.

As I watched the falling snow, nothing could exceed the beauty. As it curled and shot through the air, the mountains were shut out with a gauzy veil and darker mists. Now and then I caught a glimpse of a clump of pines on the mountain side, indistinct and gray in shadow, and as the fitful snow favored the straining eye, the long white boughs seemed bending as if conscious of the enormous weight that threatened every living thing.

When the clouds broke suddenly away, a flood of golden light leaped from hill to hill. The tall pines, partly green, but now like pyramids of

snow, lift their heads above the mountain sides. But in less than fifteen minutes after the first sight of the sun, a long stratum of dark cloud came down the mountain, and the snow falls thicker and faster than ever. Its hard crystals were driven so furiously as to make one's cheeks burn, and give exquisite torture to the eyelids. I looked upon the rapid river, and around its snow-capped rocks the water played in foaming cascades.

The enormous snow-plows at length grappled with this monster of the elements.

From east and west came reports of avalanches, snow sheds down, trains wrecked and snow-bound, and soon the telegraph refused to do its bidding. The ponderous engines were thrown from the rails in the streets, before our eyes, by the hard crystals which they crushed into glacier-like ice. With five of them behind the largest snow-plow on the road, we started toward the summit. The snow flew and even the ground trembled, and every piece of the short snow sheds was welcomed with joy and misgiving. The blinding snow, I thought, will cease to fly, but suppose that, when crushed into ice like granite, it lifts the ponderous plow of 30 tons, or that we go crashing into the shed prostrate beneath twenty or forty feet of snow; or that an avalanche has come down and our way lies through the tangled trunks of these huge Sierra pines; five boilers behind that may soon be on top of us.

Never before did I realize the need of the snow sheds, but I often rebelled against the shutting out of nature's mountain charms from the weary or unoccupied traveler.

Let the discontented not forget that five feet of snow may fall in one day; that twenty and thirty feet may lie all over the ground at one

MARY'S LAKE, MIRROR VIEW.

TUNNEL NO. 12, STRONG'S CANON.

time; that forty and fifty feet are sometimes to be seen, where the road-bed is secure beneath it, and that the canons often contain a hundred feet.

These capacious reservoirs are the pledge of summer fruitfulness. A winter scene in these Sierras without even the sight of unfriendly *bruin*, will beget a fondness for the snow sheds that the summer tourist cannot imagine, and a better appreciation of the boldness and daring of the men who brave the hardships of these mountain storms, and peril their lives at every step for other's safety. Day and night I saw the servants of the public, from highest to lowest, haggard and worn, yet never ceasing in their battle against the tremendous storm, and was overwhelmed thinking of our indebtedness to their energy, skill and endurance, as well as by viewing the wonderful works of God. "The feeding of the rivers and the purifying of the winds are the least of the services appointed to the hills. To fill the thirst of the human heart with the beauty of God's working, to startle its lethargy with the deep and pure agitation of astonishment are their higher missions."

Snow Sheds.—The snow sheds, so important

to winter travel, are found east of Strong's Canon Station, and west of Emigrant Gap, wherever there is no side hill, and the removal of the snow would be difficult for the plow. Between these two stations, they are without break, except for tunnels and bridges. In all, there are about 40 miles of the sheds.

They are of two kinds, the flat roof, built to hold the weight of 25 or 30 feet of snow, or slide it down the mountain side, and those with the pitched or steep roof, and "batter brace." The massiveness of the huge pine trunks, or sawed timbers, twelve or sixteen inches on a side, may be easily seen from the cars. The cost per mile varied from $8,000 to $10,000, and where it was necessary to build heavy retaining walls of masonry, some dry and some cement walls, the cost was at the rate of $30,000 per mile. Sometimes the heavy square timbers are bolted to the solid ledge, that avalanches may be carried by, and the sheds remain.

At a distance the sheds look small, but they are high enough to insure the safety of breakmen who pass over the tops of the freight cars.

During the summer months when everything is sun-scorched, the destruction of the sheds by fire is often imminent, and great loss has been suffered in this way. To prevent fires, the greatest precaution is used, and the most effective measures adopted to extinguish a conflagration. At short intervals, both sides and roof are of corrugated iron to stop the progress of a fire, and the whole line from Strong's Canon to Emigrant Gap, provided with automatic fire-alarms, telegraphing the place of danger, and at the summit is a train with tanks, and the engine ready to become instantly a well-equipped fire-b.igade.

Near Truckee the railroad leaves the river which turns to the south, and it follows Donner Creek, the outlet of Donner Lake, for a short distance and then turns up the great and magnificent canon of Cold Stream Creek, in a direction nearly south-west. Before leaving Donner Creek, we are hard by

"Starvation Camp," where in the winter of 1846-7 a company of eighty-two persons, coming to California, were overtaken by snow, lost their cattle, and were reduced to such straits that many survivors fed on the remains of their starved companions. The company comprised eighty-two persons, of whom thirty-two were females, a large proportion of the whole being children. Thirty-six perished, of whom twenty-six were males. Of a party of thirteen, who went out for help, ten perished. Relief was sent to the company, but it was impossible to save all. Mrs. Donner, when the alternative was presented her, early in March, of leaving her husband, and going away with her children, or remaining with him and soon perishing, refused to abandon him, and when, in April, the spot was visited again, his body was found carefully dressed and laid out by her. How long she survived him is not known. The sufferings of this party were insignificant in amount when compared with the whole aggregate of misery endured in the early peopling of California by the Overland, the Cape Horn, and the Panama Route, but no other tale connected with these early days is so harrowing in its details as this, and no one thinking of Donner Lake, turns from its quiet and beauty, to think of this tragedy that gave it its name, without a shudder.

The old road across the mountains to Sutter's Fort, followed up the Cold Stream, where snows no longer forbid a passage across the dangerous summits.

Along and rounding this Cold Stream Canon are the finest views on the eastern side of the Sierras, not shut out by snow sheds from the traveler by rail. The canon is wide and long, and far above and across, the road-bed is cut on the steep mountain side, and then protected by long snow sheds till at last it enters tunnel No. 13. Looking up the canon, on the right, soon after entering, or back, after the Horse-Shoe Curve has been made, a long line of purple pyramids and jagged precipices surround the valley, and if the road is not at the bottom of everything, the enormous face of the mountain seems to forbid the most daring attempt to ascend. But upward —still looking back to the valley of the Truckee far below, and the train reaches

Strong's Canon,—252 miles from San Francisco, which,is a side track, telegraph office and turn-table, for snow-plows, principally. Cold Stream must not be confounded with Strong's Canon, for the latter will not be reached till the train has passed half-way along the lofty wall of Donner Lake. The station was originally at Strong's Canon, but was afterward moved to tunnel No. 13, the point where the road leaves Cold Stream Canon.

Donner Lake—the gem of the Sierras, is just below, and the vigilant eye will be rewarded by a sight of it through the observation holes in the snow sheds, and when the train crosses a bridge in doubling Strong's Canon. After leaving this Canon, the road-bed is cut out of rough, rugged, granite rocks; and before the summit is reached, it has passed through the seventh tunnel from Cold Stream. These are almost indistinguishable from the sombre snow sheds, and Nos. 11 and 12 and likewise 7 and 8, are almost continuous. The longest are Nos. 13 and 6, the former 870 feet, and the latter, 1,659 feet, and the longest on the line of the road. Emerging from tunnel No. 6, the

Summit,—244 miles from San Francisco, is announced, and the train is ready to descend rapidly to the valley of the Sacramento. It is a day and night telegraph station, and has an altitude of 7,017 feet—119.8 feet above Truckee—and is the highest point on the line of the road. Many of the surrounding peaks are two and three thousand feet higher.

The Summit House is the largest hotel along the line of the road, accommodates 150 guests, and is one of the most popular in the Sierras.

One who lets the train go by, to climb to the top of the ridge through which the tunnel leads, or some higher peak, will never be sorry, for an enchanting panorama will be unrolled.

Summit Valley, with its bright pastures, and warm with life, while it touches bleak rocks, and receives the shade of the inhospitable pine or the drip of the snow—one of the loveliest valleys at such an altitude—lies toward the setting sun. In the rim that shuts out the south-west wind, towers the Devil's Peak, a bold cliff rising from out of wild surroundings; and following the ridge eastward with the eye, and around toward the point of vision, there are prominent, Old Man's Peak, just across the valley, sharpened by the wintry storms of his long life, and on the main ridge, Mount Lincoln, 9,200 feet high, and Donner Peak, 2,000 feet above the railroad, and 3,200 above the lake that sleeps in quiet beauty at its base; and across the railroad

DONNER LAKE, FROM NEAR SUMMIT, NEVADA.

BY THOMAS MORAN.

the peak from which Bierstadt sketched the "Gem" beneath. Then there are a thousand other charms in the vast heights above, and vast depths below; in contrasts of light and shade, form and color; in mists hanging over the lake, and clouds clinging to the peaks; in the twilight deepening into darkness, or colossal pyres, kindled by the coming sun, and going out in the clear light of the day ; or, in the gloom of the forest mingled with the living silver of the moonlit lake.

The peaks may be ascended — some with difficulty, a n d some with moderate exertion — but persons of feeble constitution may enjoy all the varied charms.

The lake is of easy access, and has on its banks a hotel for tourists. The distance to the lake by the carriage road is 2 1-2 miles, and Truckee 9 miles. The summit divides the waters that flow east and sink amid desert sands, from those that flow west into the Sacramento river.

Summit Valley,—2 1-2 miles long and one mile wide, heads in the high peaks,

LAKE ANGELINE.

south of the hotel. It has pasturage during the summer for many cattle, and its springs and abundance of products, fresh from the dairy, make it a delightful place for camping out.

Its waters are the source of the South Fork of the South Yuba River.

The railroad descends to the foot of this valley, keeping the divide on the north to the right, then, about three miles from the summit, crosses the most southerly branch of the Yuba. A few yards before the crossing, is a summer flag station, or

Soda Springs Station.—These springs are situated on the south side of the high ridge that forms the southern wall of Summit Valley, and

are in the headwaters of the American River. They are numerous, flow abundantly, and are highly medicinal. Stages run to them both from the summit, and from Soda Station, and the ride is not surpassed, if equaled, by any in the Sierras north of Yosemite, in the number and beauty of the fine views it affords.

The hotel at the Springs is not an imposing structure, but it is kept in first-class style and is a favorite resort.

The dividing ridge, which the railroad now follows, is on the left, and on the right are great ridges and canons, which gather more water for the Yuba. Their extent alone impresses the beholder with awe, but the snow sheds allow no satisfactory view.

The first regular station after leaving the summit is 5.8 miles west, called

Cascade,— 239 miles from San Francisco. The vertical descent from the summit to this point is 498 feet, and nothing here will check one's readiness to descend farther, for it is only a signal station, and there are none to signal, except such as are employed on the road.

South of the station are Kidd's Lakes, emptying into the South Branch of the South Yuba through the Upper and Lower Cascade Ravines. The bridges over the ravines will be a grateful but short-lived relief from the restraint of the snow sheds. The time in passing is too short to take in the charms of the water-falls in summer, or the ice-clad rocks in winter, and the extended view on the right.

Kidd's Lakes are dammed so as to impound the water during the winter and spring, and when the dry season approaches. it is let out over the Cascades into the river and carried, eventually, to Dutch Flat.

SCENERY OF THE SIERRAS, NEAR SUMMIT.

Ther: is a great spur, called "Crockers" thrown out in this ridge, through which the road passes in tunnel No. 5, and thence along Stanford Bluffs to

Tamarack.—235 miles from San Francisco, another signal station. A stop will not be likely, unless to meet or pass a freight train. A small saw-mill is in operation during part of the year. Just below Tamarack, the Yuba has worn a large gorge, and the bold bluffs, which unfortunately are below the road-bed, have been called " New Hampshire Rocks," and the name may well suggest that the Granite State will soon cease to be regarded as the " Switzerland of America."

The road continues on the north or Yuba side of the divide, between the waters of the Yuba and American Rivers; and between Tamarack and Cisco, Red Spur and Trap Spur are passed by tunnels No. 4 and No. 3. Three and a half miles from Tamarack is

Cisco.—231 miles from San Francisco, a day and night telegraph station, with an elevation of 5,939 feet. It was named after John J. Cisco, the sterling, assistant treasurer of the United States, at New York City, during the late civil war. Cisco was for a year and a half the terminus of the road, and lively with business for the construction of the road, and for Nevada. It had a population of 7,000, and some dwellings erected at a cost of $5,000 ; large warehouses, and all the intensity of frontier life. After the removal of the terminus to Truckee, the deserted buildings were either taken down and removed or went fast to decay, until their destruction was hastened by a fire that left nothing for the morning sun to rise upon, but the freight house with a platform 1,000 feet long, standing alone amid the ashes and surrounding forests.

From Cisco there is a beautiful view on the north, with Red Mountain in the distance. Just back of Red Mountain is the Old Man Mountain, but hid from view until the train descends a few miles farther.

To detect in this any sharp or remote outline of the human profile, wrought in colossal proportion by the hand that moulded and chiseled the infinite shapes of nature, is probably beyond the keenness of any Yankee.

Leaving Cisco, the railroad continues on the

SCENES ACROSS THE SIERRAS.

1.—China Ranche. 2.—Looking across Blue Canon. 3.—Emigrant Gap Ridge. 4.—Bear River Valley. 5.—Prospect Hill, looking West.

north side of the divide, with the canons of the many streams that form the Yuba on the right, and a deep valley near by through hard porphyry, passing Black Butte on the left, crossing Butte Canon, around Hopkins' Bluffs and Miller's Bluffs, eight and a half miles to

Emigrant Gap,—223 miles from San Francisco, another day and night telegraph station, is almost one vertical mile above San Francisco, the altitude being 5,221 feet. Just before reaching this station, the Yuba turns abruptly to the north, and just west of the turning place, with an elevation barely perceptible to one rushing by, Bear River heads in a valley of the same name, clothed in summer with a delightful green. At Emigrant Gap the divide is crossed by means of a tunnel, and the old Emigrant Road crossed the Gap here, and is crossed by the railroad, just a few rods west of the tunnel. Here the old emigrants let their wagons down the steep mountain side by ropes, with which a turn or two were taken around the trees at the Gap. How much better are iron rails than rugged rocks, and atmospheric brakes than treacherous cords!

On the right we have now the headwaters of the Bear River, but of the valley one can have only a glimpse except by ascending the rocks above the railroad.

Once over the divide, there are on the left, the headwaters of a branch of the North Fork of the American River, and the road follows Wilson's Ravine, and the valley of the same name is in sight for some distance. A number of little ravines may be noticed emptying in Wilson's, the largest of which, called "Sailor's," is crossed where the road doubles Lost Camp Spur, from which one may look across the ravine and see tunnel No. 1 on Grizzly Hill, and continuing he will pass along and around Blue Canon.

Blue Canon,—217 miles from San Francisco, at the crossing of which, 5.2 miles from Emigrant Gap, is the hotel, a store, a shipping point for six saw-mills, and a day and night telegraph station. The elevation is now 4,693 feet. The snow sheds are unfrequent and shorter, and the traveler will become more interested in the scenery now growing most wonderfully, until it becomes the grandest on the line of the road across the Continent.

A little mining is carried on in Blue Canon, but on too small a scale to interest a stranger.

Blue Canon is the limit of the snow which remains during the winter. It is noted for the best water on the mountains — water so esteemed by the railroad men that it is carried to supply their shops at Rocklin and Sacramento.

Flumes and ditches are almost constantly in sight. The canon grows deep rapidly and seems to fall away from the railroad, so that one instinctively wonders how he is to get down so far.

This portion of the railroad has the steepest grade on the whole line—116 feet to the mile.

China Ranche.—About two miles west of Blue Canon, a side track is passed where the close-tilling Celestial gardened prior to and at the location of the road—and the fact lingers in the name, *China Ranche.* Mountains may be seen as far as the eye can reach. After passing the ranche, there is a very deep cut through Prospect Hill, the name suggesting the loss of the passenger in the cut. On the west side of Prospect Hill is Little Blue Canon, where Shady Run, a pretty little creek, is seen on the left. It was so named by engineer Guppy at the time the road was located, in honor of the good camping ground it afforded.

Shady Run,—212 miles from San Francisco, is a side track, but not even a flag-station, 4.7 miles from Blue Canon. Near it the railroad passes around Trail Spur, and, on the left is one of the finest views on the line of the road, the junction of Blue Canon Creek and the North Fork of the American River; there the great chasm, worn by glaciers to a depth of about 2,000 feet, extending a mile to the junction of the South Branch, the precipitous sides narrowing to the water's edge and forbidding ascent even on foot, through the narrow gorge—and mountain upon mountain, back toward the snow peaks left an hour and a half ago—and eastward for fifty or more miles, till they are mingled in the eye as the stars of the milky way, add to the impressiveness of the view which is enchanced by its suddenness.

Just west of Trail Spur, and after passing Serpentine Ravine, one may look down the Great American Canon into Green Valley and Giant's Gap, beyond. The view is sublime, with the bright emerald green of the terraced and rounded, black, gloomy forests, overhead, and the frowning approach of the majestic mountains, stopped where the icy torrent slowly rent the very frame-work of the Continent.

For a time the tourist will be compelled to leave the main slope of the American River and be carried across the ridge or divide at Hog's Back, across Canon Creek, to

Alta,—208 miles from San Francisco; 3,607 feet elevation. Here are several stores and the center of considerable lumber trade. Its population does not exceed a hundred. It is a day telegraph station, 4.8 miles from Shady Run. At one time soap-root, a bulb, growing like the stub of a coarse, brown mohair switch, just emerging from the ground, was gathered by the Chinamen. It has strong alkaline properties, and is used for washing and for *genuine* hair mattresses. It has become too scarce to be gathered here with profit by even the keen, mooneyed Celestial.

Below Alta we strike the slope of Bear River, and on this water-shed we travel, winding among

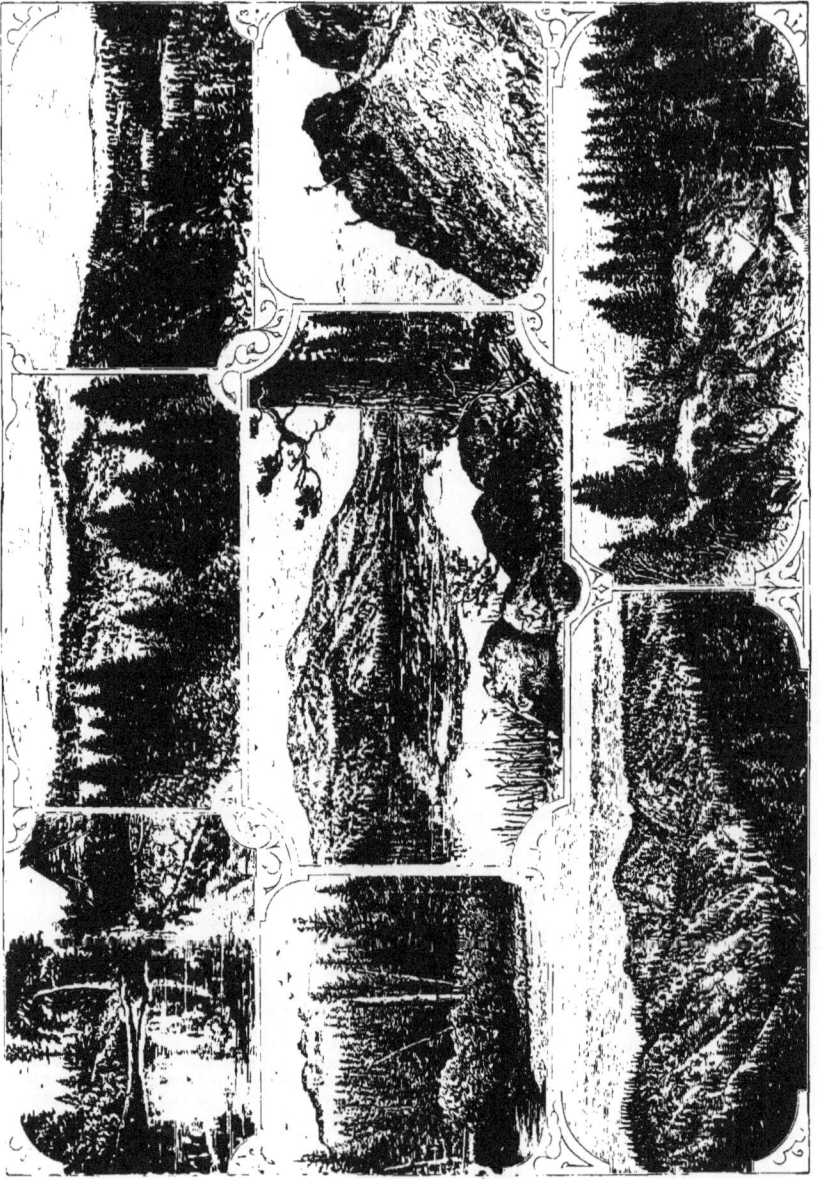

hills, until we near Cape Horn. But only 1.9 miles from Alta, we arrive at

Dutch Flat,—206 miles from San Francisco, our approach to which is heralded by the unmistakable evidences of mining, seen in the upturned face of the country.

The water that came down in advance of the cars from Summit Valley and Kidd's Lakes is now utilized. It was gathered from the East Fork of the American River, from Monumental Canon and Wilson's Ravine, and carried in Bradley's ditch around Lost Camp Spur and emptied into Blue Canon, near Blue Canon Station, and taken up again at the station and carried by ditches and flumes to Fort Point, where the railroad crosses it, and soon after one of the spurs is tunneled in two places to find an easy grade, but it cannot descend safely as fast as the cars, and at Prospect Hill passes through a tunnel 100 feet above the railroad, and is then emptied into Canon Creek, from which it is again taken up and distributed by flumes or great iron pipes to the mines we overlook at Dutch Flat and Gold Run. There are three separate ditches, the "Cedar Creek," an English company, bringing water from the American River; the "Miner's Mining and Ditch Company," with water from Bear River, and the "Yuba Ditch Company." The first two companies own and work mines, and the latter derives all its revenue from the sale of water. For hydraulic mining, this is one of the most important regions in the State.

Dutch Flat, or German Level, has an altitude of 3,395 feet. It is an old town, the mining having begun in 1851. It was once more largely populated than now, yet it boasts 1,500 inhabitants. It has a Methodist and a Congregational Church, and the finest school-house in the interior of the State. It has a tri-weekly stage to Nevada City, 16 miles, leaving every Monday, Wednesday and Friday morning. The time is three hours and the fare $3.00. The route passes through the towns of Little York, 2 1-2 miles, You Bet, 6 miles, and Red Dog, 8 miles from Dutch Flat. The town is built at the head of Dutch Flat Canon, and is very irregular and hilly. It has good stores, hotels and restaurants, and an enterprising semi-weekly newspaper.

Placer Mining.—Where the earth-carrying gold could be easily dug, and water was of ready access, and the diggings *were rich enough,* the washing out was done by hand, and this form of gold washing was called placer mining. It required no capital except the simple tools and implements used in digging and washing, with food enough to keep one till some return from labor could be obtained. Several hundred million dollars value of gold were thus washed out of the surface soil of California in early years. Little ground remains that can be made to pay by this process, and it is almost a thing of the past. It naturally led, however, to hydraulic mining

which is as flourishing as ever, and promises to continue so for many years. Placer miners came occasionally upon ground which, though carrying gold, was not rich enough to pay if worked by hand, but would pay handsomely when handled on a large scale. The device was soon adopted of providing flumes in place of cradles and rockers. Into these flumes a stream was turned and the earth shoveled in. Large quantities could thus be washed as easily as small amounts had been before.

The gold in each case, except that portion which was impalpably fine, and would even float on water, was caught by riffles on the bottom of the rocker, or the flume, and gathered up from time to time. It was found eventually that large banks sometimes hundreds of feet high, were rich enough in gold to pay for working, and the device was next adopted of directing a stream against them to wash them down. Stiff beds of cement have been found rich in gold, but too stiff to yield to any except a mighty force. Higher heads of water have been sought, until even 500 feet of head have been employed, the usual range being from 50 feet to 300, and a force obtained which nothing can resist. Such a stream issuing from a six-inch nozzle, comes out as *solid to the touch as ice,* the toughest bed of cement crumbles before it, and boulders weighing tons are tossed about as lightly as pebbles. A man struck by such a stream would never know what hurt him. The strongest iron pipe is required to carry the water to the nozzle, through which it is played. No hose can be made strong enough to bear the pressure, and the directing of the stream to the point desired is effected by two iron jointed pipes, moving in planes at right angles to each other, and thus securing a sweep in every direction. The amount of the force exerted by such a stream as has been described, it is impossible to estimate except approximately, but 1,300 pounds to the inch is not too high. To provide the water required where "hydraulicking" is done on a large scale, streams are brought long distances.

The price for selling water is graduated by the size of the opening through which it is delivered, usually under six inches pressure. Practically it is found that there is in California, more gold than water, for there are many places rich in gold, which cannot be worked for lack of water.

The season varies in length, according to the situation and the rain-fall, but nowhere is it possible to work the whole year, and probably on an average the active season does not exceed seven or eight months. There is one feature connected with hydraulic mining which no one can contemplate without regret. It leaves desolation behind it in the form of heaps of shapeless gravel and boulders, which must lie for ages before blossoming again with verdure. One of the difficult

GIANT'S GAP, AMERICAN RIVER CANON.

BY THOMAS MORAN.

problems in hydraulicking is to find room for the debris which the streams, used in washing down banks of earth, are constantly carrying along with them. The beds of streams have been filled up in some parts of the State so as to increase greatly the exposure of the cultivated regions below the mining districts to inundation and ruin. Legislation has been sought by the farmers to protect their interests, but the effort was opposed by the miners and a dead-lock followed. The muddiness which will strike the tourist as affecting all the mountain streams on the west slope of the Sierra Nevadas, is the result of this mining. Once the Sacramento River, the Feather and the American Rivers were clear as crystal, but the hunt for gold has made them like the Missouri River in high flood and even muddier, and they are not likely, while this generation and the next are on the stage of life, to resume their former clearness and purity.

Gold Run,—204 miles from San Francisco, another mining town in the famous Blue Lode. It is a day telegraph station, with an altitude of 3,220 feet. It has a population of 700, with a large number of stores, and several hotels. A mile west of Gold Run and to the right, across Bear River, may be seen You Bet, Red Dog, Little York, and other mining towns can be pointed out from the cars by those familiar with the country; but Ophir will be seen by every one, looking out on the right-hand side.

A farmer from Lancaster or Chester County, Pa., would not be impressed with the worth of the country; but the lover of nature, who does not tire of the variety in the mountain scenery, will yet feel new interest in the signs of speedily emerging into an open and cultivated country. Over the Bear River Canon, on the right, may be traced the thin outline of the basin of the Sacramento River, and, in a favorable atmosphere, the Coast Range beyond is clearly visible. Once, all the ravines in this vicinity around it, swarmed with miners. "They went to the land of Ophir for gold." The placer mines were very rich, and covered with only from one to three feet of surface. The days are long past, but every pioneer has fresh recollections of them.

" Off to the Mines."—"Hallo, Bill! where are you off to, on that mule?" [The boys all call him Bill, and so do I, but his name is William Graves.] "Wa'al, I guess I'll go'n prospect a little," says Bill, as he and his mule lazily trudge down the canon. I have known Bill these nine years, and he is a genuine prospector. I once paid him and a "pard" $5,000 in twenty-dollar gold pieces for a claim they had worked on a while. [The "pard" is not an "honest miner" any longer, but edits a one-horse paper in a little place out in the desert.] How much Bill got of the $5,000 I never knew, except that it did not long keep him from hard fare, camping out, cooking and washing for himself, and

every once in a while finding a claim to work on, locate, praise up and try to sell, and then get sick of and abandon. I would like to know how many fortunes in which his fancy and confident belief have reveled, have vanished and been forgotten, like dreams. He has never struck it rich since he made his sale to me, and I fear he never will again, but no use to tell him so. There is the "Belle Boyden," on which he is keeping up assessment work, hiring out for a while to earn something ahead, so as to buy grub and keep himself going for a few weeks.

It would be cruel to call him back now and ask him about it, but he would like nothing better, and would talk about its dip, and the rock it lies in, and how much it looks like some vein or other that has turned out well,—it is astonishing how many veins run in his head—and how many feet there are in the claim, and what he values his feet at, and how much *he wouldn't take* for it, if he only had money to open it, till he and I were both tired. Bill has gone through too many tight squeezes, and seen too much of tough life to be very emotional, but get him going on about the claim that he now holds and believes in, and his eyes brighten, and he talks with unction. He is tall and loosely hung together, and to hear him drawl out his slow speech and move draggingly around, one would not think he could do much, but give him a pick, a drill, and a sledge-hammer, and set him to running a drift, or sinking a shaft, and not many will beat him. He is cute, too. When I bought his claim he went off to Frisco and New York, and it was rich to hear him tell how the sharpers of all hues and colors were after him, thinking they never had a better chance at a greenhorn, when they were never worse mistaken. What he does not know about holding one's own in a game with the boys, whether it be at cards or banter and jokes, is not worth knowing. He is honest and kind—a whole-souled fellow, true as steel, and would doubtless take a fine polish, but his prospect is small of ever getting it. He will go on walking the mountains, camping here and there, hunting for ledges while he has grub, and working when he has not, till his hard life tells on him, and he breaks down, and it is sad to know that then he will go quick. Such as he are the men that prospect the country, penetrating its canons, exploring its gulches, climbing over and over its mountain sides, and finding the outcroppings of its mineral treasures but hardly ever are they any the richer for it themselves.

Secret Town,—and Secret Town Ravine. There is a side track but it is not now a station, and the high, curved trestle-work, at first 1,100 feet long will soon be entirely replaced by the more durable embankment. The ravine was named from its early history, to mark the efforts of a party, to conceal their discoveries of rich claims.

About a mile and half below Secret Town, there is a pretty view, where the railroad is near the edge of the side hill, and the deep ravine falls rapidly away to the American River.

A Chinese Idea of Poker.—"What's usee play poker?" remarked an almond-eyed denizen of Tueson, Nevada. the other day. " Me hold four klings and a lace; Melican man hold all same time four laces and a kling; whole week washee gone like woodbine."

Cape Horn Mills—is a side track, at which the overland trains stop on signal, but the Virginia City passenger train will no stop. It is 5.9 miles from Gold Run, and not far from Cape Horn. Before the train "doubles" the point or Cape. Robber's Ravine will be seen on the left, deepening into the great canon of the American River.

Cape Horn. —Around the Cape, the railroad clings to the precipitous bluff at a point nearly 2,000 feet above the river and far below the summit, and where the first foot-hold for the daring workman on the narrow ledge was gained by men who were let down with ropes from the summit.

When the Cape is rounded, Rice's Ravine will be on the left, and Colfax seen on the opposite side. At the head of Rice's Ravine the railroad crosses by trestle-work 113 feet high and 878 feet long, on the summit of the divide between Long's Ravine and Rice's Ravine—the waters from Long's going first northward to the Bear River,

SECRET TOWN, TRESTLE WORK.

and those in Rice's Ravine southward into the American. At the foot of the trestle-work, and climbing up both ravines to Colfax, its terminus, on a grade of 113 feet to the mile, may be seen the narrow gauge railroad just opened to Grass Valley and Nevada City—the former 16.74 and the latter 22 1-2 miles from Colfax.

At the bottom of the deep gorge around Cape Horn, and on the mountain side across the stupendous chasm, may be seen the stage road to Iowa Hill, a mining town across the river. The railroad here is an achievement of engineering skill, genius and daring on the part of its bold projectors, triumphing over natural wonders and obstacles of which ever to be proud. The view is magnificent. No one passing can afford to miss it, or he will die poorer and worse for the loss Unless it be the view at Giant's Gap, there is no railroad view to surpass it. The wonderful chasm is almost frightful to behold. The houses and even fields in the valley beneath are little things, and the buttresses to the deep water-gate are so enormous that large canons are as indistinct as the lines of masonry, and as the defying mountains open wild galleries back among the higher peaks, the mountain sculpture grows grander and grander until the rugged, but dimly outlined forms stretch away in a vast sea of pine, peak and snow,

" Though inland far we be."

The road-bed, to one looking down is apparently scooped out of perpendicular rock and overhanging the great abyss; and, to one looking up, is like a long skein of gray thread wound around the cliff.

Colfax an l the descending railroad, and the less pretentious narrow gauge toiling up to meet each other, are clearly seen across Rice's Ravine.

Skillful Cookery.—Americans who dine with the Chinese, are surprised at the perfection to which they carry their cooking. During a recent Chinese banquet in San Francisco, an orange was laid at the plate of each guest. The orange itself seemed like any other orange, but on being cut open, was found to contain within the rind five kinds of delicate jellies. One was at first puzzled to explain how the jellies got in, and giving up that train of reflection, was in a worse quandary to know how the pulpy part of the orange got out. Colored eggs were also served, in the inside of which were found nuts, jellies. meats and confectionery. When one of the Americans present, asked the interpreter to explain this legerdemain of cookery, he expanded his mouth in a hearty laugh, and shook his head and said, "*Mexican man heap smart; why he not find him out?*"

Moonlight Scenery of the Sierras.—Travelers going westward have often the pleasure of a delightful ride by moonlight across the famous scenes of the Sierras. Just at evening, when the sun casts its last glorious rays across the mountains, and lights up the peaks and snowy summits with splendor—the train arrives at Cape Horn, and the thrill of interest of the excited tourist, will never be forgotten. Take a good look from the point, westward down the grand canon of the American River. Step toward the edge of the cut, and look down the fearful precipice, which is often broken ere it reaches the lowest descent of 2,000 feet. It is a scene more famous in railroad pleasure travel, than any yet known. A few miles beyond, near Shady Run, there suddenly opens on the gaze of the expectant traveler, just before the sunlight has quite disappeared, and the evening shades com : on, the vision of

The Great American Canon,—by far the finest canon of the entire Pacific Railroad. The suddenness of approach, and the grandeur of scene are so overpowering, that no pen, picture or language can give to it adequate description. Two thousand feet below, flow the quiet waters of the American River. Westward is se.n the chasm, where height and peak and summit hang loftily over the little vale. Southward is a sea, yea an ocean of mountains—and the observer, seemingly upon the same level, is bewildered at the immensity of Nature's lavish display of mountain wonders; night comes on, and the heights catch the soft light of the moon, as it shines and twinkles across and among the tops of the pines, lighting up the open canons, and

rendering still more deep the contrast with the shady glens—the snow fields, cold, white and chilling. with ever changing turns of the railrond, make the evening ride, beyond a doubt, the most pleasurable that ever falls to the lot of the sight-seer. The tourist must stay up long—see for yourself all the beauties of the Sierras, while there is the least possible light—Emigrant Gap, Summit, Donner Lake, Blue Canon—all are delightful, and the lover of scene pleasures must not forsake his window or the platform, till the midnight hour finds him at Truckee. Travelers eastward will bear in mind that from Cape Horn to Summit, the best scenes are on south side of the train, the American River Canon on the right hand, or south side, and the Bear and the Yuba River Valleys on the north side; but from the Summit the scene changes, and the observer must find his pleasures on the north, until he reaches Truckee.

East of Truckee, the scene is again renewed, and the river and best views are mainly on the south.

Colfax,—193 miles from San Francisco. It was named in honor of the late Vice-President, has an altitude of 2,422 feet, is a day telegraph station, and the breakfast and supper station for the overland trains. Seventy-five cents, coin, are charged for meals, and 25 minutes allowed for eating them.

The old settlement was Illinoistown, but with the opening of the station, the old town was "finished." Colfax has a population of 1,000, two churches, Methodist Episcopal, and Congregational, three hotels and stores to indicate that it is the center of trade for a population of several thousand.

Nevada County Narrow Gauge Railroad.—From Colfax starts a small narrow gauge railroad twenty-two and one-half miles long. passing through scenery of the most exciting character. The tourist should spend one day over it.

Grass Valley—is 16.74 miles distant, has a population of 7,000. It is the center of the best gold quartz mining region of the State, and has the largest Protestant Church (Methodist Episcopal) in the Sierra Mountains. It has also a Congregational Church, Roman Catholic, Episcopal and Christian or Campbellite. Until recently, it had two banks, but at present has none. It is the center of large lumber, fruit and mining interests, has a daily paper, the "*Union,*" and one weekly, the "*Foothill Tidings.*"

This city as well as Nevada, is reached from Colfax by the narrow gauge railroad, on which two trains connect daily with the trains of the Central Pacific. The fare to Grass Valley is $7.07, and to Nevada City $2.25, the maximum allowed by the law of the State.

Nevada—has a population of 4,500, and is the county-seat of Nevada County. The people

CAPE HORN.

1.—View looking down the American River.   2.—View f Cape Horn and American River Canon, looking East.
3.—Point of Cape Horn.

of Truckee are compelled to attend court in this city. It is in the same mining region as Grass Valley, and was for many years the largest town in the mining regions. From an area of six miles, not less than $75,000,000 have been taken, and $2,000,000 are now produced annually. Slight snows fall in the winter. The route of the narrow gauge railroad lies through the valley of the Bear River, over which one looks in descending the Sierras. At the crossing of Bear River, where it joins the Elkhorn, there is some fine scenery, and although in the distance of 22 1-2 miles there are 16 stopping places, there are no towns or villages except at the termini and at Grass Valley. San Juan North, Comptonville, and Downieville, Sierraville, Lake City, Bloomfield, Moore's Flat and Eureka South, and Marysville are all connected with Grass Valley or Nevada by stage.

In passing along near Colfax, and in all the foot hills, the manzanita is seen, but the bushes are smaller here than in many other parts of California. It is a queer shrub, and like the madrona tree does not shed its leaf, but sheds its bark. Its small, red berry ripens in the fall and is gathered and eaten by the Indians. Crooked canes made from its wood are much esteemed. The bark is very delicate until varnished and dried, and great care should be taken in transporting them when first cut.

The foot hills are partly covered with chaparral, a low evergreen oak, which, in early days, afforded hiding places for Mexican robbers, and now accommodates, with cheap lodgings, many a "road agent" when supplied by a raid on Wells, Fargo & Co's treasure boxes or the coin and watches of stage-passengers. White blossoms load the air with fragrance in April and May.

On the right, the valley of the Sacramento is coming faster into sight, and the Coast Range growing more distinct. The next station, 5.1 miles west of Colfax, is

New England Mills,—at the west end of a plateau where there is no grade for three miles. Lumbering in the vicinity has declined, and the trains do not stop. The roadway continues on the south side of the divide between the Bear and American rivers, but this has so widened that the cars seem to be winding around among small hills far away from either river.

Water taken from Bear River, near Colfax, is quite near the railroad, on the right, for a number of miles, and will be seen crossing over at Clipper Gap.

Below New England Mills there is an opening called George's Gap, named from an early resident, George Giesendorfer, and farther west is Star House Gap, called from an old hotel; then signs of farming are again seen in Bahney's Ranche, at the foot of Bahney's Hill, and Wild-Cat Ranche farther west, where Wild-Cat Summit is crossed by a tunnel 693 feet long, and

Clipper Ravine is then found on the left-hand side.

This tunnel was made in 1873, to straighten the road, and the ends are built of solid masonry.

Across Clipper Gap Ravine, the stage road from Auburn to Georgetown may be seen winding up the mountain side.

About half-way between New England Mills and Clipper Gap, there is a side track and day telegraph station, called *Applegates,* for the running of trains and a point for shipping lime; but passenger trains run, without stopping, from Colfax 11 1-3 miles, to

Clipper Gap,—182 miles from San Francisco. The few buildings have a store and a hotel among them. It was the terminus of the road for three or four months, and then a lively place.

Hare and mountain quail abound in these foot hills. The latter roost, not on the ground, but in trees, never utter the "Bob White," so familiar to sportsmen, and fly swifter than the eastern quail.

Auburn,—175 miles from San Francisco, is a day telegraph station, 6.6 miles from Clipper Gap, with an elevation of 1,360 feet.

From Auburn Station a daily stage runs 22 miles to Forest Hill on arrival of the train from the east, fare $4.00, and to Michigan Bluffs, 30 miles, fare $6.00, and another runs daily, except Sunday, to Greenwood, 16 miles, fare $2.50, and Georgetown, 21 miles, fare $3.00, Pilot Hill, 11 miles, fare $1.50, Colma, 21 miles, fare $2.50, and Placerville, 32 miles, fare $4.00. Alabaster Cave on the route of the latter, six miles from Auburn, is an opening in a limestone formation, and the seat of the kilns in which the best lime of California is made. What little beauty the cave once possessed has been invaded and it has now no attraction for the tourist.

The town of Auburn proper is situated below the station. It has a population of 1,000, two churches, good schools, fine orchards, and is the county-seat of Placer County. It is one of the oldest towns in the State. It has three hotels, one of which is the Railroad House. Many of its buildings are constructed of brick or stone, and grapes are extensively grown in the vicinity, and with great success. The *Placer Herald* is a weekly Democratic paper, and the *Argus,* a weekly Republican paper.

From the point where the locomotive stands, the Sacramento River can be seen on the left, as also from other points as the train continues westward. Soon after leaving the station, the railroad crosses Dutch Ravine, at the head of which is Bloomer Cut, where the train passes through an interesting conglomerate, showing a well-exposed strata of boulders, sand and coarse gravel. The trestle work at Newcastle Gap Bridge is 528 feet long and 60 feet high.

16

A VISION OF THE GOLDEN COUNTRY.

BY THOMAS MORAN.

As the train nears Newcastle, the Marysville Buttes, rough, ragged peaks, are easily discerned. They are about 12 miles above the city of Marysville, and the town near the railroad, but clinging to a side hill opposite, is the decayed town of Ophir.

From the trestle work, just before reaching and also after passing Newcastle, there are fine panoramas of the Sacramento Valley, on both the right hand and the left. Mount Diablo may be seen on the left.

Newcastle,—170 miles from San Francisco, is a day telegraph station, five miles from Auburn, 956 feet above the sea. It has a hotel and several stores, every man in the place a Good Templar, and some promising quartz mines in the vicinity. It was named after an old resident and hotel-keeper called Castle. An earnest of what may be seen in the lovely valley, that has such unlimited extent before the traveler, may be seen in a flourishing orange tree, growing in the open air, in a garden only a few yards from the railroad track.

Almost every one will have noticed an evergreen of attractive hue, a shrub and a vine, always trifoliated. It is the poison oak or poison ivy, and unless one knows that he cannot be affected by it, he should avoid an intimate acquaintance.

Below Newcastle about a mile, the railroad leaves Dutch Ravine, along which it has kept its way from Auburn, and enters Antelope Ravine, by which it descends the plain.

Penryn—is a side track near a valuable granite quarry. The rock is susceptible of a high polish—probably unsurpassed in the State, and was used for building the dry dock of the U. S. Navy Yard, at Mare Island, and other public buildings. In summer, 200 men are employed in the quarries.

Pino,—161 miles from San Francisco, is about where the limit of the pines is found, in a country full of huge boulders, with quarries of granite, slightly softer than that of Penryn.

Rocklin—is 162 miles from San Francisco, a day and night telegraph station, with 249 feet of elevation, and is the point at which eastbound trains take an extra locomotive to ascend the mountain. The roundhouse of the railroad company, with 28 stalls, situated here is a most substantial structure, made from the granite quarries near the station. From these quarries, many of the streets of San Francisco are paved, public and private buildings erected, and here were cut the immense blocks used for the pavements of the Palace Hotel.

BLOOMER CUT.

Junction—is 157 miles from San Francisco. It is a day telegraph station, and 163 feet above the sea. The town is called Roseville, in honor of the belle of the country who joined an excursion here during the early history of the road, and will probably be known as Roseville Junction.

Here the Oregon division of the Central Pacific leaves the main line. On the left may be seen the abandoned grade of a road that was built to this point from Folsom on the American

River. By this road, Lincoln, Wheatland, Marysville, Chico, Tehama, Red Bluff, Redding, and intermediate points are reached. One hundred fifty-one and a half miles have been built from the junction northward. Passengers going north may use their tickets to San Francisco for passage over this division, and at Redding take stage for Portland, Or. See page 300 for full description of Railroad.

Antelope,—a side track at which passenger trains do not stop, and 6.6 miles farther on, a place of about equal importance called

Arcade. —The soil is light, much of it gravelly, but it produces considerable grass, and an abundance of wild flowers. Prominent among the latter are the Lupin and the Eschscholtzia, or California Poppy. The long fence will interest the Eastern farmer, for here is a specimen of a Mexican grant. It is the Norris Ranche, now owned by Messrs. Haggin, Tevis and others, and nearly ten miles long. When California was first settled, these plains were covered with tall, wild oats, sometimes concealing the horseback rider, and wild oats are now seen along the side of the track. No stop is made, except for passing trains, until the American River bridge is reached.

About four miles from Sacramento we reach the American River. It has none of the loveliness that charmed us when we saw it winding along the mountains. The whole river-bed has filled up, and in summer, when the water is almost wholly diverted to mining camps or for irrigation, it seems to be rather a swamp. It is approached by a long and high trestle work. After crossing the bridge, on the right, you will notice some thrifty vineyards and productive Chinese gardens in the rich deposits of the river. On the left you will obtain a fine view of the State Capitol; also you get a fine view of the grounds of the State Agricultural Society. Its speed-track, a mile in length, is unexcelled. Its advantages, including the climate of the State, make it the best training track in the United States. It was here that Occident trotted in 2.16 3-4, and is said to have made a record of 2.15 1-4 in a private trial. The grand stand was erected at a cost of $15,000.

Should you pass through the city in September or October, do not fail to see for yourself the Agricultural Park and the Pavilion, and test the marvellous stories about the beets and the pumpkins, and secure some of the beautiful and delicious fruit that is grown in the foot hills.

On the left you will also see the hospital of the Central Pacific Railroad. It contains all modern improvements for lighting, heating, ventilation and drainage, and a library of 1,200 volumes. It can accommodate 200 patients, and cost the company $65,000. Fifty cents a month is deducted from the pay of all employes for maintaining the institution. No other railroad

has made such generous provision for its faithful employes.

Railroad Works.—North of the city there was a sheet of water known as "Sutter's Lake" and "The Slough," and a succession of high knolls. The lake was granted to the city by the State, and to the railroad company by the city. Its stagnant waters have given place, at great cost, to most important industries. The high knolls have been levelled, and are also owned, in part, by the railroad company. Not less than fifty acres of land are thus made useful for side tracks and fruitful in manufactures. Six and a half acres of it are covered by the railroad shops. *Twelve hundred men* are constantly employed.

These are the chief shops of the railroad. Some you saw at Ogden, Terrace, Carlin, Wadsworth, Truckee and Rocklin, and you will find others at Lathrop and Oakland Point, and at Tulare and Caliente on the Visalia Division. At Oakland Point, 150 men are employed, but all these shops and even those of the California Pacific Road at Vallejo center here. These are the largest and best shops west of the Mississippi River, and form the most extensive manufacturing industry of the city.

The best locomotives, and the most elegant and comfortable passenger cars on the coast are built, and a large portion of the repairs for the whole road is done here. All the castings of iron and brass, and every fitting of freight and passenger cars, except the goods used in upholstering, is here produced; boilers for steamers put up, the heaviest engine shafts forged, telegraph instruments made, silver plating done, and 12,000 car wheels made every month. All the latest and best labor-saving tools and machinery used in wood, iron and brass work can here be seen in operation.

The capacity of the shops is six box-freight, and six flat cars per day, and two passenger, and one sleeping car per month. Twelve years ago, the work of the company at this point, was all done in a little wooden building 24 by 100 feet, and with less men than there are now buildings or departments.

Last year a million and a half dollars was paid out for labor in these shops alone, and 4,000 tons of iron consumed. Some of the buildings, like the roundhouse, are of brick. This has 29 pits each 60 feet long, with a circumference of 600 feet. Some of the buildings have roofs or sides of corrugated iron. Seven large under-ground tanks, 1,600 gallons each, are used for oil and 2,000 gallons of coal oil, and 400 of sperm consumed every month.

In connection with the shops, is a regularly organized and well-equipped fire-brigade, and in two minutes the water of two steam fire-engines can be directed to any point in the buildings.

Soon a rolling mill will be erected, and upon the location but lately pestilential. The whole

GARDENS AND GROVES OF CALIFORNIA.

1.—An Avenue in Oakland, California. 2.—Fountain on Hillside Garden, near Napa. 3.—Flower Garden in Oakland.

coast will be laid under further tribute to these shops for the facilities of travel and commerce.

Just before entering the depot you will cross the track of the California Pacific Railroad, and see the Sacramento River on the right.

Sacramento.—Trains stop twenty minutes in the depot. This affords ample time to get a lunch at the Palace Saloon in the depot, or to visit the City and Capitol. Take one of the "free busses" for the Capitol, Golden Eagle, Grand or Orleans Hotel, all first-class, comfortable and well patronized; or the street-cars will convey you near any of these. A new railroad depot will be finished this year, the finest in California, four hundred and sixteen feet long, and seventy feet wide, with another adjoining, thirty-five by one hundred and sixty feet.

The population of the city is about 22,000. The streets are regularly laid out, and beginning at the river or depot, with Front or First, are numbered to Thirty-first, and the cross-streets are lettered, beginning with A on the north side of the city. The stores are chiefly of brick, and residences of wood. The broad streets are shaded by trees of heavy foliage, the elm, walnut, poplar and sycamore prevailing, and in summer are almost embowered by these walls of verdure, that are ready to combat the spread of fires. It is a city of beautiful homes. Lovely cottages are surrounded by flowers, fruits and vines, while some of the most elegant mansions in the State are in the midst of grassy lawns and gardens filled with the rarest flowers. The orange, fig, lime and palm flourish, and the air is often laden with nature's choice perfumes. It is lighted with gas, and has water from the Sacramento River, supplied by the Holly system. Two million gallons are pumped up daily.

The climate is warm in summer, but the heat is tempered by the sea breeze which ascends the river, and the nights are always pleasantly cool. Notwithstanding its swampy surroundings and the luxuriance of its semi-tropical vegetation, statistics establish the fact that it is one of the healthiest cities in the State.

Among the more prominent buildings are the Court-house, Odd Fellows', Masonic, Good Templars' and Pioneer Halls; the Christian Brothers' College, the Churches, Schools and the Capitol. The grammar school building is a credit to the educational structures of the State, and attracts attention from visitors second only to the Capitol.

The Pioneers are an association of Californians who arrived prior to January, 1850. Their hall has an antiquarian value—especially in a very accurate register of important events extending back to A. D. 1650. Another association, the Sons of the Pioneers, will become the heirs of these valuable archives, and perpetuate the association. The annual business of the city exceeds *twenty-five million dollars*.

The State Capitol.—This is the most attractive object to visitors. It cost nearly $2,500,000. It stands at the west and thrice terraced end of a beautiful park of eight blocks, extending from L to N street, and from Tenth to Fourteenth street. Back of the Capitol, but within the limits of the park and its beautiful landscape gardening, are the State Printing Office and the State Armory.

The main entrance to the Capitol is opposite M street. The edifice was modeled after the old Capitol at Washington and has the same massiveness, combined with admirable proportions, and rare architectural perfection and beauty. Its front is 320 feet and height 80 feet, above which the lofty dome rises to 220 feet, and is then surmounted by the Temple of Liberty, and Powers' bronze statue of California. The lower story is of granite, the other two of brick.

Ascending by granite steps, which extend 80 feet across the front, we reach the portico with ten massive columns. Passing through this, we stand in the lofty rotunda, 72 feet in diameter. The chambers and galleries are finished and furnished in richness and elegance befitting the Golden State. The doors are of walnut and California laurel, massive and elegant. The State library has 35,000 volumes. The great dome is of iron, supported by 24 fluted Corinthian columns and 24 pilasters. Rising above this is a smaller dome supported by 12 fluted Corinthian pillars.

The beauty of the whole is equaled in but few of the public buildings in the country, and the California laurel with its high polish adds no little to the charm. The steps leading to the top of the outer dome are easy, except for persons of delicate health, and the view to be gained on a clear day, will amply repay any exertion. The extended landscape is incomparably lovely. You are in the center of the great Sacramento Valley, nearly 450 miles long by 40 wide, where fertile soil and pleasant clime have contributed to make one of the loveliest pictures to be seen from any capitol in the world.

Just beneath lies a city with many beautiful residences, half concealed in the luxuriant verdure of semi-tropical trees. Lovely gardens enlarged into highly cultivated farms—then, wide extended plains, on which feed thousands of cattle and sheep, groves of evergreen oak, long, winding rivers, and landlocked bays, white with the sails of commerce, and along the eastern horizon stretch the rugged Sierras, with their lines of arid foot hills, perpetual verdure, and snowy summits, shining like white summer clouds in a clear blue sky.

On the west the Coast Range limits the vision with its indistinct and hazy lines, out of which the round top of Mount Diablo is quite distinct. Southward, the eye takes in the valley of the San Joaquin, (pronounced, Wah-keen), with its rapidly populating plains.

In 1850, a fire left only on ˙ house standing, where are now 21 of the principal business blocks, and in 1854, a second fire nearly destroyed the city, after which lumber was scarce at $500 a thousand.

In the winter of 1851-2, a flood covered the whole city, and led to the construction of levees, which were afterward enlarged. Part of the city, too, was raised above high-water mark. Ten years later a flood occurred, with from eight to ten feet of water in all the parts of the city not raised, and flooding the first stories of all houses and stores. In the winter of 1875-6, the river was three inches higher than ever before known, yet the city was perfectly safe.

As a distributing point, the commercial advantages of the city are second only to San Francisco. Freight by the Overland route is here started north or south. Merchants of Nevada, Northern California and Utah secure their freight from this point with less charges and greater despatch than from San Francisco, and all shipments to the mountains or beyond, must go through this gate. Fruit from the foot hills, of choicer flavor than that grown in the warmer valleys, and vegetables, enormous and abundant, from the rich alluvial soil of the rivers, concentrate here to supply the dwellers from the Sierras eastward. During the summer of 1875 the average weekly shipment, of fruit alone, to the East, was 400 tons.

The industries that already give the city prominence, and not directly connected with the railroad, are more than can be mentioned. Among them are the Capital Woolen Mills, several carriage, wagon and furniture factories, several flouring-mills, one of which, the Pioneer, is the largest in the State, with capacity for producing 600 barrels of flour and 950 tons of barley per day, boiler, general iron and brass works. Wineries are permanently established and productive.

Beet Sugar—is manufactured about three miles from the city. The works were erected at a cost of $275,000, and 1,450 acres of land are in use for the factory. Ninety tons of beets can be used, per day, yielding about 13 1-2 per cent. of saccharine matter, while the refuse is mixed with other feed and used to fatten cattle.

This promises to become one of the chief industries of California, and the only occasion where the descriptive powers of Mr. Nordhoff seem to have failed him, was in the presence of the machinery of the Johnson process used in this manufacture.

The sugar-beet does not grow to enormous size, but the mangel-wurzel continues to grow, summer and winter, until it attains enormous size. Southern California is said to have produced one of 1,100 pounds, and a farmer of So-

noma County, had one (not considering the top), three feet above the ground. We believe he fenced around it, lest a cow should get inside of it and eat out the heart.

The city has a paid Fire Department, and five newspapers—the *Daily* and *Weekly Record-Union*, the *Daily* and *Weekly Bee*, *The Sacramento Valley Agriculturalist* (weekly), *Sacramento Journal* (German tri-weekly), and *The Weekly Rescue*, the organ of the I. O. G. T.

Sacramento is also an important railroad center, second only to San Francisco. Here is the practical terminus of the California and Oregon Railroad, which uses the main track of the Central Pacific Railroad to Roseville, and is completed 170 miles north, to Redding. At Redding, daily stage connection is made for Roseburg, Or., 275 miles, and thence, by the Oregon and California Railroad, 200 miles to Portland. Time, four days ; Fare, $55.00, gold.

The California Pacific runs to Vallejo, 60 miles, at the head of San Pablo Bay, immediately north of, and connected with San Francisco Bay. At Vallejo, steamers connect, twice a day, for San Francisco. The whole distance is 83 miles. Davisville, Woodland, Knight's Landing, Vacaville and the Napa Valley, are reached by this road.

Here, too, is the terminus of the Sacramento Valley Railroad, the oldest in the State. The river, also, affords a pleasant route, either to Northern California, or to San Francisco.

On the upper Sacramento, steamers of light draft ascend 240 miles to Red Bluff, or by the Feather River, from its junction with the Sacramento, 65 miles to Marysville, at the confluence of the Yuba and Feather Rivers.

Below the city an active trade is carried on with steamers and sloops. The California Steam Navigation Company have a daily line of steamers leaving Sacramento at ten o'clock A. M., and reaching San Francisco about six P. M. The distance is 108 miles. The river does not present the picturesque scenery of the Hudson, but the tourist will be interested at every point, whether as he looks out over the rich lands awaiting reclamation, or the thriving villages and fertile fields on either side, or the islands well protected by high and broad levees. The spacious bays — Suisun, San Pablo, and San Francisco — afford a series of views, in which the interest is like a good novel, increasing to the end. Mount Diablo is nearly always in view. You pass the United States Arsenal at Benicia, once the rival of San Francisco, and through the Straits of Carquinez. The United States Navy Yard, on Mare Island, overlooked by the town of Vallejo, and the beauty of the approach to San Francisco, noticed more at length in connection with the California Pacific Railroad, will amply compensate for the difference in time between the all-rail route *via* Stockton and

REPRESENTATIVE MEN OF CALIFORNIA.

1.—Senator Sargent. 2.—R. B. Woodward. 3.—Senator Sharon, (Nevada.) 4.—D. O. Mills.
5.—James C. Flood. 6.—W. C. Ralston. 7.—M. S. Latham. 8.—Gov. Irwin.

the river. The river-boats, however, are not run with the regularity of the trains, nor are they as large and comfortable as they were a few years ago.

Leaving Sacramento on the Central Pacific Railroad, formerly the Western Pacific, we reach

Brighton,—134 miles from San Francisco, where the Sacramento Valley Railroad leaves the main track. This road extends to Folsom, 22 miles, where it connects with the Sacramento Valley and Placerville Railroad, to Shingle Springs 26 miles, whence daily stages leave for Placerville, 58 miles from Sacramento. The old town of Brighton was on the Sacramento River opposite the present station, and on the old Placerville road.

California Wind-Mills. — As you pass along you notice numerous windmills, of various sizes and styles, whirling away to fill reservoirs for household wants, or irrigate the vineyards or orchards and gardens, if any there be. They are common in all the valleys and plains of California, and numerous in the cities. The sobriquet of Stockton is the " Windmill City."

About California farms there is usually no garden. Perhaps a few vegetables are raised during the winter. In some localities certain fruits or vegetables do not grow well, and the farmer who has twenty or a hundred head of horses, before his gang-plows, or harvesting his wheat or barley, has no time for gardening and prefers to depend upon the daily visits of the vegetable wagon as well as the butcher. And among our cosmopolitan people, the only class we lack is the farming women of the Mohawk Valley, or the Pennsylvania Dutch.

Florin — is 131 miles from San Francisco, a flag station — side track, store and post-office. The hard pan is near the surface, and therefore but little moisture retained from the most copious winter rains. Trees cannot send down their roots until this hard pan is broken through for them.

Elk Grove,—123 miles from San Francisco. In early days the hunter here could find large game without visiting Shasta, Tulare Lake or the mountains. At the old hotel the sign of the elk horns invited the traveler, suggesting him a dish that even then was seldom seen. Beyond, on the right hand, is some of the best soil in the State in the low lands, comprising the delta of the Sacramento, Mokelumne and San Joaquin Rivers. There are Presbyterian and Methodist Episcopal Churches in the village.

McConnell's,—119 miles from San Francisco, on the banks of the Cosumne River, a stream like all others in California, turbid in winter, and an empty channel in summer.

In California the name "ranche" (a contraction of the Spanish *rancho,* which is primarily the rude lodging-place of herdsmen, or an estab-lishment for raising horses and cattle), has almost superseded the "*hacienda,*" or farm. Mc-Connell's Ranche is, however, devoted largely to stock raising, and on it are kept the finest imported thorough-bred merino sheep. Sheep raising is among the most profitable pursuits in the State, and the woolen manufactures of California are unequaled in whatever line they have hitherto sought to excel.

Galt—is 112 miles from San Francisco. The Central Pacific Company are now building a branch road to the coal mines at Ione City, called

THE AMADORE BRANCH RAIL-ROAD.

Ione City — is in a prosperous mining and farming region, and has recently received new life from the development of large coal fields.

Sutter Creek,—on this stage route, is 31 miles from Galt, and ranks next to Grass Valley in Nevada County, as a quartz mining locality. Here is the famous Amador or Hayward Mine, where the excavations are now made several hundred feet below the level of the sea. It has been one of the richest mines in the State, and produces about $700,000 annually. With irrigation, fruit growing and agriculture succeed well.

Jackson—was formerly rich in placer mines, but the prosperous mining interests of today are in quartz. The soil and climate combine to produce fruit unexcelled in the State, and large quantities of wine and brandy are made.

Mokelumne Hill—is 41 miles from Galt, and was the county-seat of Calaveras County until 1867. It was one of the earliest mining settlements. The Gwin and other quartz mines are now successfully worked. This route to the Big Trees is traveled but little, except by those who desire to visit the towns between them and Galt. The tourist will, undoubtedly, proceed to Stockton or Lathrop.

Acampo,—only a flag station.

Lodi,—formerly called Mokelumne. A daily stage leaves Lodi at 2.20 P. M., for Mokelumne Hill, 37 miles distant; fare $5. Just before reaching the village, the Mokelumne River is crossed. Lodi is one of a flourishing trio of villages.

Woodbridge—is 2 miles north-west, and *Lockford,*—4 miles north. This is one of the best portions of the great valley, across which one now passes. The soil is a rich sandy loam, producing abundantly, and the intelligent, energetic people are surrounded with all the necessary appendages of first-class farms. The ever-green trees have given their name " Live Oaks," to a large region in this part of the valley.

Castle—is 97 miles from San Francisco—a flag station. The Calaveras River is crossed before reaching Stockton, but except in winter is only an empty channel. On either side of the road will be seen abundant crops, or unmistakable promise of them. Much of the land is so level that the large fields of 100 or more acres can be completely submerged from either of their sides.

On the right, entering the town of Stockton, stands one of the *Insane Asylums*—of the State. The other, recently opened, is located at Napa. The grounds at this place comprise 130 acres, all under a high state of cultivation. There are about 1,300 inmates. The first building passed is the largest and most imposing, has every modern convenience, and is occupied by female inmates. The male inmates occupy the other buildings.

Stockton—is 91 miles from San Francisco, and has a population of 13,000. It is 23 feet above the sea, and the county-seat of San Joaquin County. It was laid out in 1848 by Captain Webber, who named it to commemorate Commodore Stockton's part in the conquest of California. It is two miles from the San Joaquin River, at the head of Stockton Slough, which is navigable at all seasons for vessels of 250 tons.

The heart of the town was destroyed by fire in 1849 and again in 1851. It is laid out with broad streets at right angles, and has street-cars from the depot to the principal hotels and the Insane Asylum. "Free busses" also convey passengers to the Yosemite, Mansion, Grand or Central, all first-class hotels. The city was once the exclusive base of supply for a large mining and agricultural trade which is now diverted, yet the development of the country has caused a steady increase of its volume of business. It is admirably situated to control the trade of the whole San Joaquin Valley, but needs a ship canal that will enable ocean vessels to load at its wharves.

The water supply is from an artesian well, 1,002 feet deep, flowing 300,000 gallons of pure water daily, the water rising 11 feet above the surface of the ground. The city is lighted with gas and has an efficient volunteer fire department. Two daily and weekly papers, the *Stockton Independent* and *Evening Herald*, four banks and large woolen, leather, wood, iron and paper factories, wholesale and retail stores, and an extensive grain business are the foundations and measures of the prosperity of the city. The leather tanned here is considered equal to the best French, and commands as high a price.

The proximity of iron and coal should make this city the Pittsburg of the Pacific. It has fourteen organized churches, some of which have built houses of worship—Roman Catholics, Methodists, North and South, German and Colored, Episcopalians, Congregationalists, Baptists, white and colored Christians (Disciples), and Jews. Passing in the cars, nothing is seen of the better residences, of which there are many,

provided with every convenience and comfort. Excellent public and private schools are the boast of the people, for, if Californians ever boast (which they never do), they do not forget to speak of their schools. Masons, Odd Fellows, Red Men, Knights of Pythias, Hibernians, Pioneers and other societies represent social and benevolent progress. Near the depot, on the left, may be seen the grounds of the San Joaquin Valley Agricultural Society.

Heat.—The city has the best climate of the valley. The hot air of the interior is usually tempered by the sea breeze, and the nights are always cool. The hot and sickly places of California are never reached by the traveler. In Sacramento it is said to be hot in Marysville, and in Marysville, one is referred to Oroville for heat, and in Stockton, men say it is hot at Merced. The simple fact is that all parts of the Great Central Basin of California are subject to occasional north winds—the dread, at once, of man and beast. They usually lull at night, but continue, at least, three successive days. The wind having swept over hundreds of miles of dry and scorching plains, breathes as from a furnace, the mercury marking 110° to 120° in the shade. One may fancy himself in Egypt or Barbary, withered and fainting under blasts from the Sahara Desert.

The origin of the name, California, is said to be from two Spanish words, "*caliente fornalo*," meaning a "heated furnace." This seems plausible. The extreme dryness of the climate, however, enables men and animals to endure this heat surprisingly. Sunstrokes are unknown. Rapid evaporation keeps the pores open, no perspiration accumulates, the skin is dry and cool, and a heat 20 to 30 degrees above what would mark an intensely heated term, in the moister atmosphere of the Eastern States, produces little exhaustion in the dry atmosphere of this central basin. Horses travel frequently 50 to 60 miles a day without injury, the thermometer marking 100° or over. Stockton has not yet attained the importance as a railroad center, to which her position entitles her. A narrow gauge road to Ione City was commenced, but there is no prospect of its early completion. The Stockton and Copperopolis Railroad extends easterly into Calaveras and Stanislaus Counties, the main branch 30 miles to Milton, with a branch at Peters, 15 miles from Stockton, to Oakdale, 34 miles from Stockton.

To the Big Trees, Calaveras Group.— The best route to the Calaveras Grove of Big Trees is *via* Stockton and Milton. There is another grove of big trees at Mariposa, which is best reached from Lathrop and Merced. The comparative inducements to visit one or the other, will be stated hereafter, and here will be described only the route from Stockton to the Calaveras Grove. Cars leave Stockton at 12.35 P. M.,

1.—Grizzly Giant, Mariposa Grove. 2.—Three Graces, Calaveras Group. 3.—Scenes in Mariposa Grove.
4.—Trunk of Big Tree, Mariposa Grove. 5.—Natural Arch, Big Tree, Mariposa Grove. 6.—Calaveras Group, Big Trees.

for Milton; stages leave Milton at 2.15 P. M., and reach Murphy's at 7 P. M., where the first night is spent.

The Grove, 15 miles from Murphy's, is reached the next day at 11 A. M., and those who desire can leave at 3 P. M. the same day, and return to Murphy's for the second night. On the following day one may reach San Francisco, or go to Garrote, 45 miles from the Yosemite Valley. To visit the Calaveras Grove and Yosemite Valley by this route requires 145 miles of staging. This route to the Yosemite Valley via Milton, is called the Big Oak Flat, or Hutching's Route, the former name from a local point on the road, and the latter after the man who in past years did more than any other to make the Yosemite Valley known, and by whose untiring energy the stage road to it was opened. It is one of three routes by which the valley is reached without horseback riding. It is the shortest route from Stockton or San Francisco, but it requires more staging than the other two. To go directly to the valley by this route, one leaves Stockton for Milton at 12.35 P. M., and spends the night at Chinese Camp, 23 miles from Milton, reaching the valley the second day after, at 2 P. M. For the other three routes to the valley, see Lathrop, the next station. The decision whether to visit the Calaveras or the Mariposa Grove of Big Trees, substantially determines the route taken to and from the valley. The considerations that enter into this decision are as follows: There are seven known groves of big trees. Of these only the Calaveras and Mariposa have accommodations for tourists, are easily accessible and convenient to other points so as to be visited in comparatively little time and without large expense. It is true, that the Tuolumne and Merced Groves are directly on different routes to the valley, but the number of trees in these is small, and their size is not great. In the Tuolumne there are but ten, the largest only 24 feet in diameter. In both the Calaveras and Mariposa Groves are prostrate trunks one-sixth larger than the largest living trees, which enable one to realize, as cannot be done by looking at and walking round living trees, the enormous size of these forest giants. As the tourist will probably see one of these two groves it may be well to note for him that

	In the Calaveras Grove.	In the Mariposa Grove.
Number of trees	93	600
Diameter of largest,	33 feet.	33 feet.
Circumference of largest living tree, six feet above the ground,	61 feet.	90 feet.
No. of living trees between 80 and 90 feet in circumference.	0	1
No. between 70 and 80 feet,	0	6
No. between 60 and 70 feet,	1	2

The largest tree yet known in any of the groves is on King's River, 40 miles from Visalia, and is 44 feet in diameter.

The Calaveras Grove was the first discovered, the first opened to tourists, has been long and

well known, has a first-class hotel directly at the edge of the grove, where a summer vacation may be pleasantly passed; the trees all the while growing on the visitor in size and beauty, as Niagara does on him who tarries there.

Private teams for either the big trees or the valley, or both, may be had at Stockton, Milton, or Merced, but unless one's time is absolutely unlimited, the public conveyance is to be chosen. By relays of horses these hurry one over the dry plains, and once in the midst of the charming scenery of the foot hills, one can tarry at pleasure. The most notable trees in the Calaveras group are:

The Father of the Forest, which measures 435 feet in length, 110 feet in circumference.
Mother of the Forest,—321 feet high, 90 feet in circumference.
Hercules, ... 320 feet high, 95 feet circumference.
Hermit, ... 318 feet high, 60 feet circumference.
Pride of the Forest, . 276 feet high, 60 feet circumference.
Three Graces, . . . 295 feet high, 92 feet circumference.
Husband and Wife, . 252 feet high, 60 feet circumference.
Burnt Tree, ... 330 feet long, 97 feet circumference.
"Old Maid," "Old Bachelor," "Siamese Twins," "Mother and Sons," "Two Guardians."

Lathrop, 82.8 miles from San Francisco, is the junction of the San Joaquin Valley Branch, or "Visalia Division" of the Central Pacific. It extends from Lathrop to Goshen. 147 miles, where it intersects the main line of

The Southern Pacific Railroad

(For full description of which see page 279.)

San Joaquin Valley.—This great valley has the Sierra Nevada on the east, and the Coast Range on the west, is about 250 miles long, and from 20 to 150 miles wide. The area is 25,000 square miles. The greater portion of the land is a sandy loam, easily tilled. There are but a few trees, but the farmers have begun to plant extensively. Frequent patches of the black, tenacious, alluvial soil, called *adobe* are found, in which the sun cracks, visible during summer, faintly suggest earthquakes. A hundred miles of wheat fields may be seen in the valley, broken only by roads and fences.

This immense valley, with a surrounding belt of timber for lumber and fuel, coal, iron, and the precious metals bordering it, adapted for growing the grains and fruits of two zones, is destined to have a teeming population and fabulous wealth. Irrigation will supply the lack of summer rains when needed. The summer tourist will be struck with the absence of all sod, and long for the refreshing sight of it once more. As it exists in the Eastern States, it is unknown in California, except where carefully nurtured. The beautiful mantle of green that covers the earth, in winter and spring, is here turned to hay without any artificial process. The juices of the grass are stored, the seeds ripened, and the roots die, and seeds sprout again.

Alfalfa, a species of clover is however, an exception. Its roots, sometimes an inch in diameter, penetrate to a depth of 12 or more feet, and draw moisture from unseen springs. Several crops of hay may be cut from it in one season, and the quantity produced from an acre is almost fabulous. Ten years ago not a head of wheat was produced in Stanislaus County, one of the counties of this valley, and now it is the chief wheat-producing county in the State.

Wonders of California Farming and Gardening.

California is a paradise of gardens, farms and flowers, as well as of mines, scenery and health resorts. During the spring months, from April to June, the country is aglow with rural beauty. Immense patches of flowers of intensely scarlet, blue and yellow, pink colors, grow all over the valleys and sides of the hills, and the plains and valleys seem an immense garden of wild flower bloom For days in succession the traveler will pass as through a wild garden.

California would not be equal to itself were it not able to give sights to the traveler to transcend the sights of other portions of the country. Not only is the entire country a succession of beauty in the spring, but in the summer, when all the flowers have gone, comes the immense grain harvest, when the whole country is golden from the mountains to the ocean. The fields are yellow as gold with the great wheat crop, and one seems to be riding in a land whose very air smells of gold, and the eye sees gold everywhere. The gardens and farms of California are extremely rich and productive; the results are of such an astonishing size as to bewilder Eastern heads used to more moderate calculations. We have personally seen a Geranium bush with over 1,000 blossoms at one time opened, filling a mound over six feet in height and diameter. Another geranium bush clambered up the side of a garden fence, four feet high, and gracefully swung on the other side half way to the ground, and aglow with intensely red flowers. A large fence, 20 feet high and 60 feet long, we have seen filled with a few geraniums which had grown to that height in less than one year.

In a garden near Oakland we have seen a Fuchsia vine of less than three years growth, fill the piazza of a house 70 feet in length, reach to the second story, and filling the entire roof, clamber to the third. In a little garden at Los Angeles we have seen a fuchsia bend with 3,000 blossoms. In a garden near Sonoma, we have seen growing in loving company the fruit trees of both the tropics and the northern temperate zone,—the apple, peach, pear, orange, lemon, olive, hot-house grape vines, wild grape vines, crab apples, cactus, palm trees and others, as widely different as possible. California farms are of immense size, a farm of 30,000 acres is very modest, a vineyard is nothing unless it has 100,000 vines. If a grower has a fruit farm his fruit must be of huge size to attract attention. Upon the grounds of one grower near Oakland, the following is recorded as a modest fact:

Currants were half an inch in diameter, cherries one inch in diameter, and three inches around, carrots were 35 pounds each, cabbages 75 pounds, onions five pounds, water melons 95 pounds, pears 3½ pounds each, beets 200 pounds.

In the San Joaquin Valley,, crops have been raised which are perfectly astonishing. Five crops of *Alfalfa*, and 40 tons per acre per year. *Pumpkins, 250 pounds; potatoes, each 15 pounds.*

In Santa Rosa is a rose bush which produces 15,000 to 25.000 roses yearly. In Los Angeles is an orange orchard, whose crop often yields $1,500 per acre each year—worth nearly $100,000. Near San Diego, pumpkins of 350 pounds are common—one vine, from one seed, one season yielded 1,400 pounds. At San Gabriel is the largest orange orchard in California,—500 acres owned by L. J. Rose; at the San Gabriel Mission are growing over 200 varieties of cactus.

These are but a few of the productions of such a wonderful state.

Chinese Names.—Although these are becoming somewhat familiar from their signs at their wash-houses in our Eastern cities, the following list of Chinese letters advertised for a single week in San Francisco, will give a better idea of them. A correspondent says:

Ah Coon is Mr. Coon, Ah being merely a title of respect. Chinamen who have three names are of a higher rank, I am told, than those who have two only. Some of our nicknames, as Sam, Jake, Nat, etc., are very common Chinese names.

Ah Coon,	Kong Chong Ling,
Ah Chung Wo,	Quong Chung Wang,
Ah Hung,	Quong On,
Ah Lee,	Quong Son Wa,
Chang Sing,	Quong Ton Sing,
Ching Chung,	Nat Lee,
Choy Sum & Co.,	Lee Dew & Co.,
Chung Wo Tong,	Low Hing Kee,
Chong Ga,	Sam Kiam Wo,
Do Foo.	Sing Cow Wo,
Eh Da Loro,	Sing Quong On,
Tong Kee,	Si Wo Luny,
Fung Lung,	Soon Sing,
Gee Tang Hong,	San Wah,
Gee Wo Sang,	See Wo Lung,
Gum Go In,	Sen Sing,
Heng Wa Hong,	Tun San,
Ili Lo,	Way Sum Gow,
Hong Faut,	Wong Ung,
Hung Song Lung,	Yee Ching Lung,
Jake Lung,	Yen Wah Hong,
Kee Hien,	Ye Wah Sung,

SCENES IN THE YOSEMITE VALLEY.
1.—Bridal Veil Fall. 2.—Mirror Lake.

Kong Chieng,   Yen Wah Co.,
Koung Yune Ling,   Young The Keow.

California Customs. — The stage-coach from Milton was about to leave Tuttletown after changing horses. Every seat, both inside and out, was full, except one which was occupied by a tourist wrapped in his supercilious dignity and a heavy linen-duster. A resident of Tuttletown, wishing to ride to Sonora, approached the stage and inquired for a seat. "All full inside," growled the tourist spreading himself to the full extent of his dignity and duster. "But you are occupying two seats," argued the man from Jackson Hill. "I ain't going to be crowded. I pay for my comfort, and intend to keep it." "Did you pay for two seats?" "I've only secured one seat; but there is no room for another in this coach, sir!" And the tourist settled himself back, while the other passengers grunted their disgust in tones not particularly vociferous, but exceedingly deep. "You are not acting as a gentleman should, sir—not exactly in accordance with the etiquette of our rude California society," calmly replied the man on the outside, smiling the smile of his annoyance at the dog-in-the-manger-style of this boor. "I don't hold myself accountable to the society of California. I pay my way and ask odds of nobody; and your inference that I am not a gentleman might be termed, where I came from, an indication that you wish to fight." "We don't fight in this country," calmly replied the man from Tuttletown. "You don't? Then I must have been misinformed. Pray, what do you do when a man insults you?" And a sort of triumph gleamed in the eye of a stranger. "*Do?* *Why, we shoot him on the spot, and that is the end of it!* We don't waste time after we start in. *By the way, I think I can squeeze in alongside of you there, can't I?*" "Don't know but you can!" And a full half seat appeared beside the dignified fool, as if by magic.

San Joaquin Bridge,—79 miles from San Francisco, is a station at the railroad crossing of the San Joaquin River. The channel is on the west side, and in high water the country is overflowed for miles up and down the river, reaching back from it almost to Bantas, the next station.

Bantas,—74 miles from San Francisco, and 30 feet above tide-water. is named for an old family resident here. Stages leave at 10.50 A. M., for San Joaquin City, 10 miles, Grayson, 20 miles, Mahoney's. 35 miles, and Hill's Ferry, 40 miles. Through fare, $3.50. To the right of Bantas, down the San Joaquin River, or the branch called "Old River" is a vast extent of lowland, overflowed in June, by the melting snows of the Sierra Nevadas, and during most of the rainy season.

After the water passes off, flowers spring up, and the button willow blooms, affording excellent bee-pasture. From the first of July to the

first of November, a single swarm of bees will often gather 100 lbs. of honey. Those who take care of the bees also take quinine with the honey to cure the "chills." This is believed to be the extent of their acquaintance with "Bitter-sweet." Hundreds of acres of floating land here rise and fall with the water.

Tracy Junction.—Here is the junction of the two routes, the Old Overland and the New. For description of the New Route see page 297, and the following is the description of the

Old Overland Route.

Ellis,—69 miles from San Francisco, and 76 feet elevation, another village which bustles in the midst of vast wheat fields, during seasons following a wet winter, and sleeps under vast disappointments during other years.

This "West Side" of the San Joaquin River, was supposed, for many years, to be worthless. The old Spaniards left it out of their ranches except when a few square miles or leagues were taken in for the sake of securing a convenient "*loma*" as a landmark. In 1849-50, as the gold-digger urged his mule, well laden with tent, bedding, pan and rocker, and three months' provisions, his heart full of expectation of a "pile" to be speedily dug from the placers of the "Southern Mines," his eyes were often gladdened by a lake of bright water near the "trail" only a mile ahead. He saw white sails, waves chasing each other, and trees on the shores reflected from their bosom. He expected soon to camp in the grateful shade, and slake his burning thirst with the cool water. The white sails bounded away, antelope-like, across the burning plains, for alas! it was only a *mirage*— an emblem of his expected wealth. Even now many are deluded in seeing the distant water and green trees beyond.

The soil of this once desert region, now produces the best of wheat, when the rains are abundant, but from its peculiar position on the north-east of the Coast Range, the necessary rain is often wanting. A local adage is "every seven years a crop"—worse than ancient Egypt's famine. But the land-owners are moving to construct a ditch 60 feet wide and 300 miles long, to irrigate the entire valley on the west side of the river, and serve for transporting the produce to the tide-water of Suisun Bay. Once accomplished this almost desert land, will easily support a population of 3,000,000.

Fourteen miles south-west from this station is Corral Hollow or Pass, in the mountain range, at the head of which are extensive coal mines. toward which a branch railroad extends five miles. Here an extra engine is taken to overcome the steep grade of the Livermore Pass, in the Mount Diablo Range.

Medway.—The train now runs around hills,

VERNAL FALLS, YOSEMITE.

BY THOMAS MORAN.

high embankments, and through deep cuts, the engine often seen from the car window like the fiery head of a huge serpent.

The soil is coarse sand and gravel, the finer particles of which, and vegetation, too, it seems, have been blown away by the trade-winds, which, pent up by the long range, rush with concentrated fury over the summit of the pass, and sweep down with devastating force into the vacuum on the heated plains.

Suddenly the train enters a tunnel, 1,116 feet long, the only one between Sacramento and San Francisco, and is in total darkness for two minutes. Emerging, it soon arrives at

Altamont,—west of the summit of the Mount Diablo Range, 56 miles from San Francisco, and 740 feet above the level of the sea. The traveler will see numerous gray squirrels standing erect at the entrance to their homes. They are about as large as the fox-squirrel of the Eastern States, live in villages of their own, are the pest of the farmer, have increased since the land has been cultivated, and lay the grain fields under a tribute far heavier than the rent. It is a remarkable fact that both birds and squirrels have increased in variety and numbers all over the cultivated regions of the State since 1850. As the train descends into Livermore Valley, a truly picturesque scene is presented. The level valley, in form a square 12 miles across, with many narrow extensions far into the mountains, is spread out before one in full view, with rolling hills on all sides, except the west, where rises an abrupt, tree-clad mountain.

On the right, across the low hills, green with live oaks, may now be seen Mt. Diablo, not as before, a blue dome, but a real mountain, with deep gorges in its sides, covered with chaparral, and capped usually with gray mists.

It is an Indian legend that this country, west of the Sierra Nevada Mountains, was once covered with water, and the top of this mountain then a little island. At that period, says the legend, the devil was there imprisoned by the waters for a long time, and, therefore, great prosperity and quiet resulted to mankind; hence his name was given to it. However the name may have been first given, it now clings to it in Spanish form.

The western portion of this valley contains hundreds of acres of the best land in the State, much of it moist, vegetable land, in the midst of which is a lake of fresh water, near which are natural flowing wells. From these the creek derives its name "*Las Posi-as*"—i. e., little wells. Much of the eastern part of the valley is covered, to a great depth, with small, angular stones, mixed with clay, and the region was thought to be useless, but it now produces the finest of wheat.

From Altamont, it is 8.1 miles to

Livermore,—47 miles from San Francisco.

This is a live town, 485 feet above tide-water, with 1,000 inhabitants, a seminary of learning, beautifully nestled amid sturdy oaks, a Presbyterian and a Catholic church, a steam mill, newspaper, saloons, stores, and several large warehouses. Nine miles south, and at the head of Corral Hollow, are five veins of good coal yielding 100 tons per day, and six miles from the town another vein has been opened. These are probably an extension of the Mount Diablo Coal fields which have been worked for many years.

Six and one-tenth miles down the valley is

Pleasanton,—41 miles from San Francisco, 353 feet above the sea, a village of 300 inhabitants, with several stores, a large warehouse, an abundance of good water, and a rich, beautiful country on the north connecting with other valleys, and extending to Martinez at the head of the Straits of Carquinez. This region, now Livermore Valley, was formerly called Amador Valley, from its original owner, and was an inland sea. In 1836, Mr. Livermore found the bones of a whale on the surface of the ground, near the town which bears his name. The vertebræ lay in order with the ribs scattered about like the rails of a "worm" fence. Abalone shells are also found in quantities near the old ranche house. Beautiful variegated wild pansies, the lupin and California poppy have taken the place of sea weeds.

In June may be seen, near Pleasanton, high above the grain, the yellow blossoms of the black mustard. In former years it stood 12 feet high, and so thick that it was difficult to force one's way through it. To

Sunol,—(Sun-yole) 36 miles from San Francisco, the train dashes down the narrow valley of the Alasal Creek, 5.2 miles, amid pleasing scenery, and relics of the Mexican and Indian civilization of California. On the right is the Contra Costa Range of Coast Mountains, so called because opposite the Coast Range, near and north of San Francisco. It is only a few miles across to the San Jose (San Ho-zay) Valley, where the train will pass in an opposite direction. Sunol Valley, a mile wide and three miles long, is south of this station. Seven miles above this is the Calaveras Valley, containing 1,500 acres—the proposed site of a vast reservoir to supply San Francisco with water in future years. The mountains about these valleys are extensive sheep and cow pastures, covered with wild oats.

The road passes down the canon of the Alameda Creek and over three fine bridges, yet winding with the canon, steep mountains on both sides, dressed in green or parched with summer heat; the bracing sea breezes, and the knowledge that in an hour and a half the cars will reach the bay, revive the spirits of the traveler. Soon a scene of wide extended beauty is to burst on his vision—the San Jose Valley, the Bay of San Francisco, the Serrated

17

Mountains that turn back the ocean tides of 8,000 miles travel, and all around him, as he hurries on to the great city, a garden spot more and more variegated with the choicest fruits and flowers, and abundant in homes of luxury and ease. From Sunol it is 6.4 miles to

Niles,—30 miles from San Francisco, 88 feet above tide-water. Here are a store, hotel, warehouse and mill. A stage runs from all trains to Centreville, three miles distant. Here is the junction of the San Jose Branch of the Central Pacific Railroad. This branch passes through *Washington Corners,* the seat of a flourishing college, under Rev. S. S. Harmon, and a pleasant village overlooking the bay, and near the old *Mission de San Jose.*

Three miles farther are the Warm Springs, in the midst of oak and other trees near the Aqua Caliente (hot water) Creek. The minerals that increase the value of the heated water are lime, sulphur, magnesia and iron. They were formerly a popular resort, but are now the property of Governor Stanford. When his designs of building and beautifying are completed, it will be one of the most attractive of the summer resorts.

Near Niles the Alameda Creek is turned into a ditch 30 feet wide, and distributed over the valley for irrigation, for although both the land and climate are moist, irrigation promotes the growth of fruits and vegetables called for by the San Francisco market.

Adjoining the south-east end of this bay, are 20,000 acres of salt marsh, now in process of reclamation by dikes and ditches.

Through this a narrow gauge railroad has been built from deep water, at Dunbarton Point, *via* Newark to Alviso, and will run thence through Santa Clara to Santa Cruz.

Along the east side of the bay are numerous salt ponds, the sea water being let in at high tide upon a large tract of land, when the rainy season is over, and this repeated several times. The concentrated brine is then drawn off in a planked reservoir, where it slowly crystallizes.

As the train passes about 2.8 miles to Decoto, the eye is pleased, in April and May, by the mountain on the right—round, green, shaven, like a lawn, or its sides rich with fields of grain; or yellow with large patches of buttercups, blue with lupin, or deep orange with the Eschscholtzia, or California wild poppy, gathered, no doubt, far east of this point, for many a sentimental nosegay, in honor of the traveler's acquaintance. It is a flower peculiar to the north-west coast of America. Wild flowers are so numerous in California that often from twenty to a hundred varieties may be gathered from one spot.

On the left, the trees mark the Alameda Creek, flowing down to the salt land. Beyond this lies the Old San Jose Road, and the richest and best cultivated portion of the valley. At Centreville,

half-hidden in the distance, is an Alden fruit factory, convenient to large orchards, and, near by, on the farm of Rev. W. W. Brier, stands the tree from which originated the thousands of acres of Brier's Languedoc Almond, the soft-shelled almond, that no traveler has ever seen excelled in flavor.

The hill-sides from one to 500 feet above the valleys, are best adapted to its culture, because the warm air from the lowlands prevents injury from frost. At

Decoto,—27 miles from San Francisco, may be seen the Blue Gum Tree. Under favorable circumstances it will grow, in five years from the seed, to a height of 70 feet, with a circumference of four feet. The green wood splits readily, but the dry is as hard as the lignum-vitæ. They are highly prized for a supposed tendency to counteract malaria, and their cultivation is rapidly extending.

Soon after leaving Decoto, Alvarado may be seen. It was once the county-seat of Alameda County. The valley land in this vicinity sells for $150 to $250 per acre, and the mountain land from $10 to $30. It is a peculiarity of California, that the value of land is always stated separately from improvements.

Haywards,—21 miles from San Francisco, is 6.3 miles from Decoto. The town is seen a mile to the right, on the hill, at the outlet of Castro Valley—rich, rolling and beautiful, and well watered, four miles long by two wide. Castro Valley is named in honor of the original owner of the ranche, and Hayward's Hotel is a well-known resort.

On the hill, to the right, is seen a forest—that may be mistaken for evidence that these hills have been recently denuded of their timber. It is a forest of the Blue Gum Tree—200 acres, planted by James T. Stratton.

The town has churches, public schools, and the hotel, still kept by Mr. Hayward, is a popular place of resort for those who seek a good and quiet home without removing from business in the city. Stages leave this station for Alvarado at 9.20 A. M., and 4.20 P. M.; for Danville and Walnut Creek at 4.20 P. M., and from all trains to Haywards. The railroad company intend using the Eucalyptus to plant the entire length of their road.

Lorenzo,—18 miles from San Francisco, is near San Lorenzo Creek, and surrounded by a well improved country. It is a pleasant village, and contains an extensive establishment for drying fruit on the Alden process, a store, a neat church edifice and the usual places to "take a drink." The land is worth $600 per acre. The large building to the right on the mountain side, is the Poorhouse of Alameda County, with which there is a farm connected. The golden sands of California and the absence of severe winters do not keep poverty and age from every door, nor does a generous hospitality make public charity unnecessary.

This section of country is noted for its cherries and currants, but nearly every variety of fruit is extensively cultivated. One of the fine orchards on the right before reaching the station, has 100 acres of Almonds, and 200 acres of other fruits. The owner, Mr. William Meek, has constructed private water-works at an expense of $15,000.

San Leandro,—15 miles from San Francisco, was formerly a county-seat. It has a population of 1,000, a large factory for wagons and gang-plows, a Presbyterian, a Catholic and a Methodist Church, stores and saloons. In the mountains opposite, and on a creek of the same name, is located the reservoir of the Oakland water-works. The water is collected from the winter floods and is 65 feet deep.

Melrose—is 11 miles from San Francisco. Before reaching the station and after crossing the San Leandro Creek, there may be seen on the right, nestled in a beautiful vale at the foot of the mountains, the largest and best apportioned Protestant Seminary for girls of the Pacific Coast, *Mills Seminary.* The buildings were erected at a cost of about $100,000, $30,000 of which was contributed by public-spirited individuals. The 65 surrounding acres, with their oaks, sycamores, alders, willows, and laurel or bay tree; the orchards, lawns and flower-beds, the inspiring views, combining the fruitful plain, the water and the mountains beyond; a climate, always stimulating to mental effort—in short, the correspondence of attractions and advantages, without and within, make this a point of interest to all who desire to see the progress of education in one of nature's most gifted spots.

Near the race-track on the left, are several buildings with large, square chimneys, used to smelt and refine gold and silver, while on the right is a fuse factory. The town of Alameda is seen on the left, almost hidden by live oaks. A branch railroad connects it with this station, and the "local" trains of Oakland.

Between Melrose and the next station, we pass Fruit Vale, a station on the Alameda Road, and a spot of surpassing loveliness. The elegant lawns, and beautiful mansions are almost wholly concealed by the luxuriant foliage, and amid the strapping of shawls and gathering of valises, there will be no time to waste, where only a glimpse of the beauty may be had, and

Brooklyn—will be announced 2.3 miles from Melrose, and 9 miles from San Francisco. Here is the point of departure for the "local" trains that will be seen again at the Oakland wharf. It is now East Oakland, a delightful suburb of San Francisco.

The land rises gently toward the foot hills, almost from the water's edge. Since it has become a corporate part of the City of Oak-

land, it has made rapid improvement in the opening of new and well macadamized streets and the erection of fine residences. At this point there is a "local" train that passes directly through Oakland to Oakland Point. Before reaching the next station the train will cross the track of the Alameda Branch. This track is for the accommodation of local travel, and connects Alameda and Fruit Vale with Oakland and San Francisco. From the abundance of the evergreen oaks, one may quickly conclude that pleasure parties will find there a balmy retreat whether beneath the clear sky, or sheltered from the afternoon winds, and it has always been a popular picnic resort. On Sunday, the boats and trains are crowded with thousands seeking recreation and enjoyment there. Brooklyn is a splendid home resort for travelers; the comforts of so nice a hotel as Tubb's are worthy of appreciation.

Oakland—is 2 miles from Brooklyn. The train halts at the foot of Market Street, where many through passengers leave it, Oakland being really a suburb of the larger city near at hand, and the chosen residence of hundreds who do all their business and spend most of their daytime over there. It is beautiful for situation, and boasts a climate much preferred to that of San Francisco; the trade-winds from the Pacific, which are fierce and cold, and often heavy with fog there, being much softened in crossing the bay. This has attracted many to make it their residence, though obliged to do business in San Francisco, and about 10,000 passengers daily cross on the half-hourly and splendid ferry-boats, and the number of trips will be increased before long. The population of the city increases rapidly, and, in 1879, was 47,000. As measures of its enterprise and prosperity it may be stated that 2,000 new buildings are to be erected in 1879, and a quarter of a million dollars expended in building a court-house and county jail. There are three savings banks, two national gold banks, four lines of horse-cars, three flouring and four planing mills, an iron and a brass foundry, two potteries, one patent marble works, a jute bag factory, three tanneries and other establishments employing many mechanics. On the public schools, of which Oakland is justly very proud, nearly $6,000 are monthly expended, and nearly a quarter of a million dollars value in property is owned by the department. The State University is within the city limits. Its site, which has been named Berkley, is on the northern border of the city and has a direct ferry to San Francisco, and many families are planting themselves there, attracted by its natural beauty and the educational and social advantages which cluster around it. The University is open to students of both sexes, and tuition is free. The number of students exceeds 200. By special law, the

BIRD'S-EYE VIEW OF SAN FRANCISCO.

sale of intoxicating liquors is forbidden, within two miles of this University.

There are 20 churches in Oakland, of which 16 own houses of worship. Some of them are elegant and costly; the First Presbyterian Church has recently dedicated a new church building which cost them over $60,000. Seven newspapers are published, three daily, the rest weekly.

The rides in and around Oakland, for variety of attractive features, are rarely equaled. Many come over from San Francisco, in the morning, expressly to enjoy this pleasure. Lake Merritt, a beautiful sheet of water, Tubb's Hotel and the Grand Central Hotel, both spacious and admirably kept, are among the attractions which none fail to visit, and with which thousands have bright and happy memories associated.

Though incorporated as a city, Oakland is thoroughly rural. A very small portion of the business part around the chief railroad station is built up solidly, but everywhere else the houses stand detached and usually surrounded by a liberal expanse of gardens, grass-plat, and shrubbery which remind one of an eastern village. Live oaks abound, and show by their leaning over toward the east, the constancy and strength of the summer trade-winds. Geraniums, roses, fuchsias, callas, verbenas, and many tropical plants and flowers grow luxuriantly, never suffering from outdoor winter exposure, and finding a soil of surpassing richness and fertility. Fruit trees develop into bearing in a third or half the time usually required on the Atlantic Coast. The city is favored with one rare advantage. The railroad company charge no fare on their local trains, between stations within the city limits.

These trains are half-hourly, most of the day, and there are nearly five miles of railroad, and eight stations within the city limits. The convenience of thus riding freely at all hours, can hardly be understood by those who have not experienced it. The line of the local road is directly through the city, and only local trains run upon it, all other passenger trains, and all freight trains taking the main road close to the water's edge. Of all the suburbs of San Francisco, Oakland is the most popular. Its growth exceeds that of San Francisco. The time required to reach it from California Street, is less than is required to get up-town from Wall Street in New York, and once reached, the merchant, weary with the cares of the busy day, may find a home with a more tropical luxuriance of fruit and flowers, almost the same in summer and winter, and scenery scarcely less picturesque than the banks of the Hudson afford.

Oakland Point—is the last station before reaching the ferry. The stop is made to pass over the long trestle work with a light engine. Here the railroad company own about 125 acres of land, and have extensive buildings and repair shops. On their dock they remodel, or build their ferry-boats, the boats of the California Steam Navigation Company, and here the Western Development Company build all the bridges and frame all hotels, warehouses, and other buildings for the Central, California, and Southern Pacific Railroads. About 300 men are constantly employed. There is a roundhouse for 21 engines, and tracks for the extra passenger cars needed at this important terminus.

A channel has been dredged out from this yard to the bay, which shows plainly from the cars on the left hand. The train now runs out on the trestle work, which is built out into sea water farther than any other in the world, and is the largest in waters of this depth, and also the best built wooden pier in the world. It was built five years ago, and when examined a year since, a few *teredo* were found in piles without bark; but the strength of the pier was not appreciably impaired. It is 2.8 miles long.

To protect it from fire, all the engines employed on it are fitted with force pumps, and can be used as steam fire engines at a moment's notice. There are three slips and four piers, and the aggregate width of the latter is 396 feet, and over these an immense freight and passenger business is done.

Eight sea-going ships can be loaded with grain simultaneously. Nearly all the lumber for the whole treeless region in Southern California, now reached by the railroad, is loaded from vessels at this wharf. Wagons and carriages crossing between Oakland and San Francisco come over one of these piers to the ferry-boat at present; but it involves risk to horses, vehicles, and their passengers, and the company are building ferry-

boats to run by San Antonio Creek directly to Oakland, by which all teams will be ferried between the two cities, and the increasing passenger traffic have the additional tracks now needed. Freight cars cross from this wharf to the immense freight depot at the foot of Fourth Street in San Francisco, and a boat is building to carry at once 20 loaded freight cars and 20 car loads of cattle.

There is fine angling, chiefly for smelt, from these wharves. Four or five of these fish may be caught at a single cast. Within two years, eastern salmon have been placed in these waters, and occasionally these are caught. California salmon do not take the hook, because people and fish are sharp on this side of the Continent.

At Oakland wharf, passengers and baggage are transferred to the spacious and elegant ferry-boats, on which hackmen and hotel-runners will be sure to speak for themselves.

The distance from the end of the wharf across the water to the ferry-house in San Francisco is 3.4 miles, and is ordinarily made in fifteen minutes. When the wind is blowing, none but the most rugged persons should venture to stand outside the cabin; but if it is practicable to gain the view, there are many points of great interest. At night, the city itself with long rows of lights extending over hills, more than "seven," or its wide extent by day, produces at once an impression of its greatness.

Bay of San Francisco.—The bay is large enough to float the navies of the world, and beautified by a rare combination of island, mountain, city and plain. On the right, passing to San Francisco, and near the wharf, is Goat Island, a military reservation, and the subject of considerable agitation in Congress. The quarters of the officers and men are seen on the east side, and on the south end is a fog-bell and whistle that are often called into requisition. The Golden Gate proper is north, or to the right of the city—five miles long and about a mile wide.

It is strongly fortified at various points. Alcatraz, a naval station, is an island at the end of the gate and entrance to the bay, and commands the whole passage from the ocean.

Angel Island, north of Alcatraz, is another military reservation, well fortified. North-west of this may be seen the towering peak of Mount Tamalpais, the highest near the city. On the right, one may look north to the San Pablo Bay, and behind him see classic Berkley, Oakland, and Alameda, with the Coast Hills in the background. South, the view extends over the bay toward San Jose, and everywhere, except where the city stands and through the Golden Gate, it is shut in by mountains.

The trade-winds come are shut out from California by the Coast Range, the fogs not rising above 1,000 feet, and when they sweep down the coast, drive through the Golden Gate with pent-up fury. The heated interior makes a funnel of this passage and creates a demand for the lace shawl and seal-skin sacque on the same day.

The ferry-house where the trip across the Continent ends, is well arranged and provided with everything necessary for the accommodation of the throngs of passengers passing through it. The baggage department of the railroad is here, and is connected by telegraph with every station on the road, giving all possible facilities for tracing stray baggage. The loss of baggage by this railroad company is almost an unknown incident, and the Pacific Transfer Company is equally reliable.

San Francisco.—The ferry-boat lands at the foot of Market Street, which is fast becoming the leading business artery of the city. Every horse-car line, except one, either runs in or crosses it, and by direct communication or transfer, all connect with the ferry at its foot. By these cars, or by carriages in waiting, the hotels which are about a half mile away are easily reached. The Grand and the Palace Hotels are on Market, at the corner of New Montgomery Street, the Lick on Montgomery, a few steps from Market Street, the Occidental and the Russ near at hand on the same street, and the Cosmopolitan at the corner of Bush and Sansome Streets, close to Market. As to their respective merits, we must decline to make comparisons or give free advertisements. Hotel coaches charge uniformly $1.00 gold for transfer of each passenger and baggage from ferry to hotel. The Transfer Company will carry baggage alone for 50 cents. Whether the overland traveler resorts to a hotel or to the home of friends, the change from a week in the railroad cars to hospitable quarters and richly spread tables will be so grateful as at first to dispel all consciousness of fatigue; but tired nature will assert herself, and the first night especially, as the arrival is at evening, will be given to rest.

Perhaps the luxury of a Turkish bath should be had at the earliest moment. "The Hammam," erected by Senator Jones on Dupont Street, near Market, at a cost of nearly $200,000, is in truly Oriental style. The building is an ornament to the city, and in it dusty travelers will experience mingled wonder and delight at its Mohammedan architecture, perfect appointments, and complete adaptation to restore a sense of cleanliness and give solid refreshment to both body and spirit.

Thus refreshed and looking about next morning, there confronts the traveler a city, the growth of twenty-seven years, which counts 300,000 inhabitants, and covers a territory of 42 square miles. On its eastern front it extends along the bay, whose name it bears, is bounded on the north by the Golden Gate, and on the west washed by the Pacific Ocean along a beach extending five or six miles. From the Golden Gate on the

north, to the city and county-line on the south, is a distance of about seven miles, and the same from the bay across to the ocean. The surface is varied by hills, several of which have been built upon, and from whose summit commanding views may be obtained. Telegraph Hill looks down on the point where the Golden Gate leads into the bay and harbor. Clay Street Hill is farther south and west, and may be ascended in cars drawn up its steep-graded sides by an endless rope running just below the surface. This hill extends some distance southward, and makes the streets crossing Montgomery to the west, steep, and some almost impracticable for wheeled vehicles. Along its heights some of the railroad directors and others have erected, or are erecting, princely dwellings. That of Governor Stanford is perhaps unsurpassed in almost every respect. Rincon Hill is in the southern part of the city, and slopes down to the water's edge. Until a recent period, it was noted for elegant private dwellings and grounds; but these are now found in all directions, more clustering, however, around Clay Street Hill, perhaps, than elsewhere. The growth of the city is rather toward the west than the south.

Russian Hill is west and north of Telegraph Hill, and looks down toward the Golden Gate and what is called the North Beach, a portion of the city less in favor of late years than formerly. Smelting works, woolen factories, potteries, artificial stone-works and establishments of this general character, have clustered here.

San Francisco is very regularly laid out. There are two systems of streets, between which Market Street is the dividing line. North of Market the streets are mostly 70 feet wide, cross at right angles and run almost north and south, east and west, and the blocks are 150 varas or 275 feet wide, and 150 varas or 412 1-2 feet long, the length being east and west. Market Street runs about north-east and southwest. South of it the streets for over a mile from the city front, run parallel with it or at right angles. At about a mile from the city front these parallel streets gradually curve toward the south till they run almost north and south. This change of course was caused by the low Mission Hills there lifting themselves, and by the tendency of travel along the narrow peninsula toward the country beyond it. The streets south of Market are some of them very broad, and some quite narrow. This portion of the city was laid out originally with very wide streets and in blocks 200 varas or 550 feet wide, and 300 varas or 825 feet long, but these proved too large and it became necessary to cut them up by intervening streets, which have no element of regularity except parallelism with the others. The streets are all numbered from the city front, or from Market Street, one hundred numbers being allowed to each block after the first, to which only 99 are assigned, the even numbers always on the right hand as the numbers run. It is thus easy to locate any street and number. There are a few avenues, but with the exception of Van Ness, which is 125 feet wide, and built up handsomely, and Montgomery Avenue, which is laid out to provide easy access to the North Beach portion

SAN FRANCISCO MINT.

of the city, they are usually short and narrow, or in the most newly laid out portion of the city, not yet built up.

The heavy wholesale business of the city is done along the water front and, mostly north of Market Street, extending back three or four streets from the front to where banks, brokers, insurance companies and office business generally have become established, the same territory south of this street being occupied by lumber merchants, planing mills, foundries, and machine shops. Retail business of all kinds is done along Kearney, the southern part of Montgomery, the upper part of Market, and along Third and Fourth Streets. Markets are scattered through the city. The Central is near Kearney to the west on Sutter Street, and the Californian between Kearney and Montgomery Streets extending through from Pine to California. Both are worth visiting, and display everything in the market line in rich profusion and perfect neatness and order. California Street and Montgomery at their junctions, are the great resort of the crowd dealing in stocks. All sorts of men may be seen there, between 9 A. M. and 6 P. M., hovering around quotations displayed on various brokers' bulletin-boards, and talking mines, for speculation centers in mining shares. Kearney Street and the southern part of Montgomery are the favorite promenade of ladies, and especially on Saturday afternoons, the Hebrew holiday, when a profusion of them, richly dressed and bejeweled, may be met there.

The theaters are all near this region. Two of them are quite new. Wade's Opera House boasts the finest chandelier on earth, and Baldwin's Academy of Music is claimed to be unsur-

passed on this Continent, in beauty of interior decoration and finish.

Sidewalks throughout the city are wide and good. Most are of plank, many of asphaltum, which is well suited to the climate, the heat rarely being sufficient to soften it. A few are of cut stone or artificial stone. The last material is fast coming into favor for many uses. Streets are paved with cobbles, Russ pavement and plank, and off from lines of heavy business teaming, are macadamized. Wooden pavements are retained in many, but are not approved. The Nicholson pavement cannot be long kept down. It shrinks during the long dry summer, and with the first heavy rains swells and is thrown hopelessly out of place. Good paving material is not abundant, and the question is yet unanswered, what shall be the pavement of San Francisco in the future?

The water supply comes chiefly from reservoirs in the Coast Range Mountains south of the city, and is controlled by the Spring Valley Water Company. The rates are double and treble those charged in New York City, and are due monthly in advance. Many families pay more for their water than for their bread. It should be borne in mind, however, that some families use much more water for irrigating gardens and grass-plats, than for all household purposes.

The only government building in San Francisco that is finished and in use, and worth visiting, is the United States Mint, on Fifth Street, near Market. The machinery here is believed to be unapproached in perfection and efficiency. Visitors are admitted between 10 and 12 A. M.

BANK OF CALIFORNIA.

A Custom House is in process of erection, and a City Hall; but both are far from completion.

There are many fine buildings erected for business purposes. A number of new blocks of stores, on Kearney and Market Streets, combine spaciousness, solidity and elegance. The Ne-

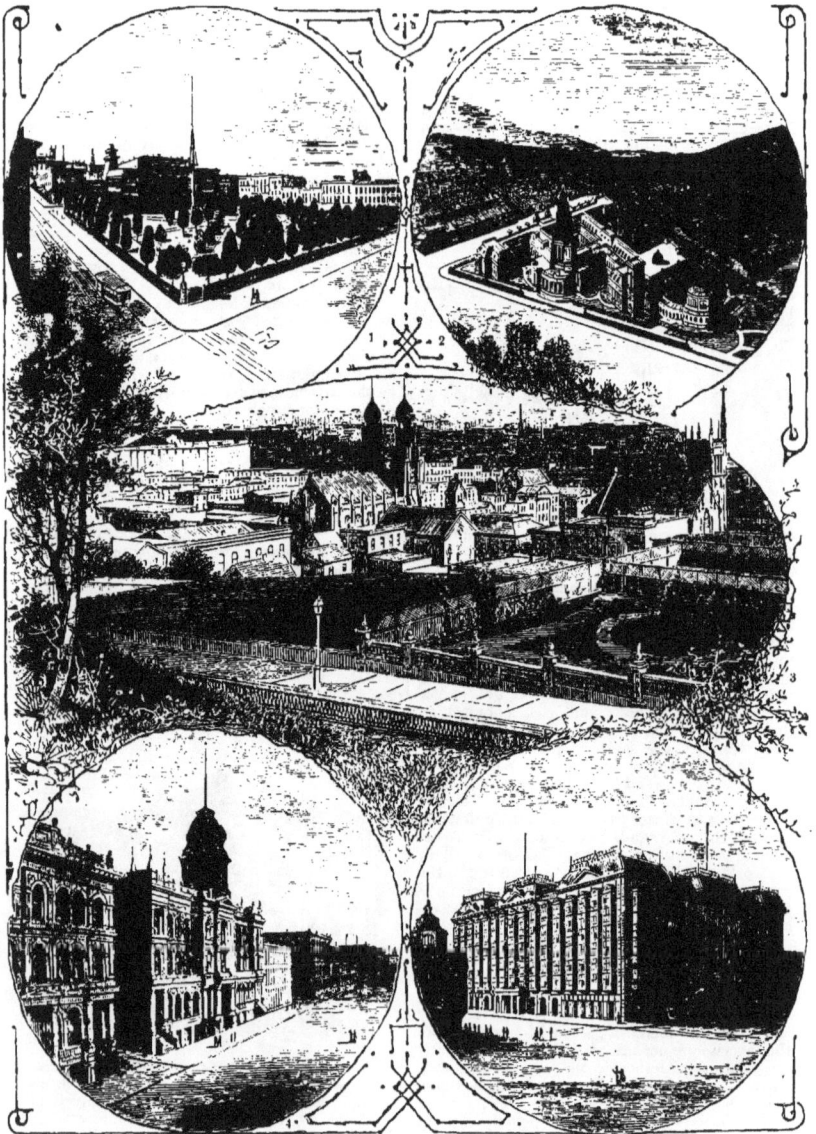

PUBLIC BUILDINGS OF SAN FRANCISCO.

1. -City Park. 2.—New City Hall. 3.—General View of City, looking towards the Bay.
4. - Merchants' Exchange. 5.—View on Market Street.

vada Block, the Safe Deposit Building, the Anglo Californian and the California Bank, the Mercantile Library and Merchants' Exchange, all combine pleasing and impressive features, and are thoroughly built and costly erections. The building, corner of California and Montgomery Streets, occupied by Wells, Fargo & Co's Express, was the first substantial erection in the city. It was imported from China, where the stone was all cut and fitted, ready for its place.

One feature of San Francisco architecture is bay-windows. Few private houses are without

proportion of the population live in lodgings and go out for their meals. The tendency to a more settled mode of life, however, increases, and a great number of private dwellings have been erected by individuals and building associations, of late years. The Real Estate Associates build and sell on an average a house a day, and have done so for three years past. They build by day's work, in thorough style, chiefly houses of six and eight rooms, and sell them for one-fifth cash, and the remainder in 72 monthly installments, based on 9 per cent. interest for the de-

" HOODLUMS."

them, and the last built hotels, the Grand, the Palace, and Baldwin's, have their whole surface studded with them, to the great comfort of their guests, and equal defacement of their external appearance. San Francisco is called the Bay City. It might well be named the "bay-window city." The mildness of the climate and the instinctive craving for sunshine, are considerations which will always make bay-windows a desirable and a favorite feature here.

A stranger will observe here the great number of restaurants and furnished lodgings. A large

ferred payment. Most of the uniformly built blocks of detached houses in the city, were built by them. They always built detached houses, which are safer in case of fires.

A great conflagration may overtake any city, but this is more secure than its wooden appearance indicates. Owing to the dampness from summer fogs and winter rains, and the liability of injury by earthquakes, wood is the only desirable material for dwellings. Nearly all used is the *sequoia*, or redwood, so abundant in the Coast Range. It burns very slowly, compared

AT THE CLIFF HOUSE

THE GOLDEN GATE

...from Russian...

GOAT ISLAND

SCENES IN THE HARBOR OF SAN FRANCISCO.

with eastern woods, and the city has a very efficient steam fire department.

The city cemeteries are yet west of the best residences, but agitation has already commenced looking to an end of interments within city limits. Lone Mountain, an isolated mound within the Roman Catholic Cemetery and surmounted by a large cross, lately blown down, has long been a noted landmark and gives its name to the region adjoining, which is devoted to burying grounds.

South from Lone Mountain lies the Golden Gate Park, in which the city justly takes great pride, and which is destined to become one of the most beautiful of city pleasure grounds in the United States. It was a waste of sand only five or six years since, but, by careful planting of the yellow lupin, the sand is subdued, and by irrigation, grass-plats have been created, and a forest of trees brought rapidly forward. The drives are fine, and, on pleasant days, thousands of carriages resort here. Driving is a Californian's weak point, and more money is expended by him on livery and private stables in proportion to his means and other expenditures, than by his brother-citizens of the "States." It is a natural result of plentiful money, long distances and few railroads. Racing is also much in vogue, and a fine race-track is laid out, near Lone Mountain, in full view from the Park.

All the religious denominations are well represented, and there are some fine buildings for worship, among which the Synagogue, on Sutter, the First Congregational Church, on Post, and St. Patrick's Cathedral, on Mission Street, are most notable.

Benevolent mutual societies and secret orders are very numerous. Particulars concerning them and the churches, may be found in the city directory. The free schools of the city are a just source of pride. They are provided for with a liberality, and conducted with a skill which make them of incalculable value to the city in all its interests.

The Mercantile Library, the Mechanic's and the Odd Fellows,' are large and valuable, and the use of them may be obtained on easy terms. Roman's bookstore, on Montgomery, and Bancroft's, on Market Street, are prominent among many good ones. Books are generally sold at publisher's prices, in gold. Bancroft is a large publisher of law books, and has erected a building in which are carried on all departments of book-making.

Excursions.—For sight-seeing in San Francisco, no plan will suit the convenience of every one, but the best for a few days is the following:

Let the morning be spent in a ride to the Cliff House, where a good breakfast may be obtained, if not had sooner. The Cliff House toll-road has been the favorite route and is unsurpassed as a drive. The shell-road of New

Orleans is no better. But the road through the Golden Gate Park, is splendidly macadamized, and should be traveled either going or returning. A drive should be taken along the beach to "Ocean House," and a return made to the city, through and over the hills. Coming into the city by this road, there bursts into view, one of the most magnificent sights on the coast. The city, the bay, Oakland and a vast extent of mountain, valley, loveliness of nature and art, are spread out below. If the Park can be reserved for a separate drive, go by the Cliff House Road, if not, go by the Park. The Cliff House may be reached also, by two lines of street-cars and omnibusses. The cost of a carriage for four persons will be $10.00 for the trip—by omnibus and cars, one dollar for each person. The trip should be made as early as possible to avoid the wind and fog.

The afternoon may be spent at Woodward's Gardens, making sure of the feeding of sea-lions at 1 or 3.30 o'clock. The aquarium is unique, suggested by one in Berlin, and has nothing like it in America. Birds, animals of various kinds, fruits, flowers, museum, art gallery and many other objects of attraction, make these gardens one of the chief attractions to tourists. They represent the Pacific Coast in its animals and curiosities, better than any other collection.

Another morning, go up Clay Street Hill in the cars, and ride to the end of the route. Fine views will be seen of the city and bay, from many points, and some handsome residences will be passed. On descending, climb Telegraph Hill on foot, the only way in which it can be done, and enjoy the view in all directions. After lunch take the Market Street cars, and ride to Twenty-first Street. At Sixteenth Street, one will be near the old Mission Church, an adobe building dedicated in 1776. Having reached Twenty-first Street, cross to Folsom, and return in the North Beach & Mission cars to the city, leaving them where they cross Market, or at the end of their route, corner of California and Montgomery. These rides will take one through the portion of the city rapidly growing and extending toward the south-west. There will be time after returning, to walk about Kearney and Montgomery Streets, near Market, also up and down Market, and see the finest retail stores, and look at new buildings, or even to climb up California Street to Highland Terrace, and see some of the finest private residences in the city, among which D. D. Colton's and Governor Stanford's are specially notable, the former on the north side of California Street, the latter fronting on Powell at the corner of California.

A pleasant place to visit is also the Mercantile Library on Bush Street, opposite the Cosmopolitan Hotel. Strangers, properly introduced, are granted the privilege of the library and reading-room free for a month, and odd hours can be put in there very pleasantly, especially in the read-

WOODWARD'S GARDENS, SAN FRANCISCO.

ing-room, which is light, cheerful, and supplied with the best papers, magazines and reviews of this and other lands.

Another day one can go to Oakland early, take a carriage at Broadway Station and ride to Berkley, Piedmont, and through Brooklyn, or East Oakland, along Lake Merritt, up and down streets and around the city at pleasure. Fine houses, beautiful grounds, good roads, flowers, shade trees and pleasant sights are everywhere. Returning to the city in season for the 4 P. M. boat up the Sacramento River, one can take it as far as Martinez, a 2 1-2 or 3 hours' ride, and see the northern part of San Francisco Bay, San Pablo Bay, Benicia and Suisun Bay, leaving the boat at Martinez and there spending the night. Early next morning a stage will take one to Mount Diablo, and three hours can be spent on its summit enjoying as fine a view as there is anywhere in California, after which the boat can be reached in season to be in San Francisco for the night, or one can stay for the night at a good hotel near the summit, see the sun rise, and return to San Francisco the next night. The fare for this round trip is ten dollars.

Most of San Francisco has now been seen. It would be well to ride through Van Ness Avenue and see the fine residences there; but one will begin to think of San Jose, Santa Cruz, the Geysers, &c. Another forenoon can be spent pleasantly in the city by taking the Central line of horse-cars (cars with white dashers) through the fast-growing western addition to the city, to the end of the route at Laurel Hill Cemetery, and walking about there for an hour. Returning by the same line in season to get off near the United States Mint, at corner of 5th and Market Streets, by 11 A. M., one can visit that institution, which is daily open for visitors until noon. In the afternoon, at 3.25, one may go to San Jose. The route leads through beautiful villages, some of which have been selected for the residence, most, if not all the year, of wealthy gentlemen of San Francisco. San Jose will be reached in season for a walk or ride about the city. The Auzerais House is a first-class hotel, and carriages can be obtained there at reasonable rates. The Court-House and State Normal School are the chief public buildings. General Naglee's grounds, which are open to visitors, except on Sunday, are well worth a visit.

If time allows, one may, by taking a private carriage, go to the New Almaden Quicksilver Mines, enjoy a fine ride, gaze upon a wide-spreading view upon the summit of the hill, in which the mines are situated, see the whole underground process of mining, provided the superintendent will grant a permit to enter them, which is not likely, and return to San Jose the same day, or if not able to afford time for this, can go over to Santa Clara by horse-car, through the shady Alameda, three miles long, laid out and

planted, in 1799, by the Padres of the mission, visit the two colleges there, one Methodist, the other Roman Catholic, and return in season for the morning train to Gilroy, Watsonville, etc., and reach Santa Cruz the same night; or, if time will not allow of doing this, he may spend a little more time at San Jose and Santa Clara, ride out to Alum Rock Springs, through the Shaded Avenue, the prettiest drive in the State, and, taking the afternoon train, reach San Francisco at 5.35 P. M.

Whoever goes to Santa Cruz will want to stay there two nights and a day, at least, and there are so many charming rides and resorts near this watering-place of the Pacific Coast, that many days can be spent there very agreeably. The trip back to the city, unless made by steamboat at night, which can be done sometimes, and is a pleasant variety for those who are not afraid of a short exposure to ocean waves and tossing, will occupy an entire day, and the arrival is at about 5.30 P. M.

The next trip will naturally be to the Geysers and Calistoga, the Petrified Forest, White Sulphur Springs at St. Helena, etc., all of which are passed in the round trip. One may go by Calistoga, or return that way, as he prefers. Steamboats start at 7 A. M. for Vallejo, and at 8 for Donahue Landing. By the first route, one connects with cars for Calistoga, and by the second, for Cloverdale, and from each place stages take one to the Geysers the same day. After seeing the Geysers, travelers usually go on so as to return to San Francisco over the route they did not take coming to them, two days being required for the round trip, if one does not go to the White Sulphur Springs, which is a delightful place to spend a half-day, nor to the Petrified Forest, which is reached by a pleasant ride by private conveyance from Calistoga, and is a very interesting and romantic spot, and also requires a half day. To visit these one must take three days for the round trip. The fare for this trip, not including the carriage to the Petrified Forest, is sixteen dollars.

As the time of tourists is variously limited, it is well to say that the time required for all the trips above described, is twelve days, allowing one day at Santa Cruz, and one day for returning from there to the city. Not all persons have so much time to spend. By omitting the visit to Santa Cruz, the Petrified Forest and White Sulphur Springs, one may save four days, and by omitting, also, the trip to Mt. Diablo, the western addition to the city, and the United States Mint, one may save three days more, starting for the Geysers, after spending three days in the city and seeing the Cliff House, Golden Gate Park, Woodward's Gardens, climbing Telegraph Hill and Clay Street Hill, seeing the Mission and south-western part of the city, and passing most of a day in Oakland. Should one do this, it would be well to fill out the day begun in Oakland, by going through Van Ness Avenue, which is, and long will be, the finest street for private residences in the city. Two days more will enable one to visit the Geysers, and thus, in five days, all that is most notable in and about San Francisco, will have been seen.

Tourists who have time enough for it will find a trip to Pescadero, very pleasant. The route is by stage from San Mateo or Redwood City, on the Southern Pacific Railroad, across the Contra Costa Range, a ride very well paying of itself for the whole cost of the trip. Pescadero is in a narrow valley, about three miles from the famous Pebble Beach, about 100 yards long, which gives it its chief attraction. Most home-like quarters and delightful cooking are found

Rain falls only in the winter half of the year, and does not much exceed one-half of the amount in the same latitude on the Atlantic shore, and the number of rainy days is very small, since it is apt to rain hard if it rains at all. The atmosphere in winter is quite moist, and though it is seemingly dry in summer, during the long absence of rain, pianos and furniture, and wood-work generally do not shrink as in many places, owing, doubtless, to the prevailing cool winds from the ocean. It is rarely cold enough for frost; plumber's work needs no protection, and hot days are equally rare, occurring only when the summer ocean winds yield for two, or at most three days, to winds from over parched and heated plains to the north. The air is rarely clear so as to reveal distinctly the outlines of hill and shore

THE OLD ONE EYED MAN
THE BEST GRINDER IN THE CITY
GET YOUR RAZORS GROUND!

STREET SCENE IN SAN FRANCISCO.

at Swanton's, and one will be taken to the beach and brought back from it at hours of his own choosing. At this beach one will linger and linger, picking up finely-polished pebbles, many of which are fit to be set as jewels. Pescadero may be reached also by stage from Santa Cruz, and the ride along the coast is wild, interesting, unique and full of interest. The time required is a day, whether coming from San Francisco or Santa Cruz, and the same to return, and no one will spend less than a day there, so that to see Pescadero means three days, and there are few more enjoyable ways to spend so much time.

Climate.—The climate of San Francisco is peculiar, and can not be described in a few words. It is equable on the whole, there being no great range of temperature, and the difference between that of winter and summer being small.

across the bay, a misty haze like that of eastern Indian summer, usually prevailing. After rains, and notably after frosts, and during the prevalence of winds from the north this sometimes vanishes, and a crystal clearness of atmosphere succeeds, in which Mount Diablo and the hills of Contra Costa and Alameda stand out mellow and clear as though just at hand. At such times, which are not frequent, and at others, more often, when it is sunshiny and the air is calm, and the haze thin, there is a spring and vitality and exhilaration in the air, and beauty in all out-door nature not often surpassed. Something of this is realized in the early part of most summer days, if fog does not hang over the city. As the day advances, the wind from the ocean rises and pours in mightily, cold and fierce—a bane and a blessing at once; a bane because it destroys all enjoyment of out-door existence, but a blessing because bearing away noxious exhalations, and securing health even to the most crowded and neglected quarters and thoroughfares.

There are few days in San Francisco when it is safe to dispense with outer wrappings, and when a fire is not needed morning and evening, both for health and comfort, and fewer yet when a room with the sun shining into it is not amply warm enough while it shines. Sunshine is therefore earnestly coveted, and many are the regrets of those who do not enjoy it. It is rare for persons to seek the shady side of the street, instinct suggests the contrary. Rooms are advertised as sunny, and many are so described which are sunny only a small part of the day. But whether the sun shines or not, it is never safe to sit by open windows or on door-steps without shawls, hats, or overcoats. Strangers do it sometimes, but never do it very long. San Francisco is not the place for out-door pleasuring. Bright and sunshiny and beautiful as it often is without doors, one prefers to look upon it from within, and if deciding to go out must wrap up almost as for a winter ride or walk in the older States.

San Francisco has few pleasure resorts. Seal Rocks, at the mouth of the Golden Gate, attract many to ride to the Cliff House, and gaze at sea-lions gamboling and snorting and basking on its sides. It is a beautiful ride thence south on the beach a couple of miles to the Ocean House, and thence back to the city by Lake Merced. Golden Gate Park is, however, the chief resort for pleasure. It is new, and its charms and beauty are still in the future, but much has been done already, and the promise for time to come is ample. The reclamation of sand wastes and dunes by planting yellow lupin and their conversion into beautiful grass-plots is a notable feature of the success already attained, which elicits the admiration of all who contrast what they see in the park with the proof of what it was once, shown in the still shifting sands around it. The park embraces about 1,100 acres, and when the thousands and ten thousands of trees planted in it have gained their growth, which they are doing almost too fast for belief, and other improvements in progress are carried out, it will rank among the most attractive and admired city parks on the Continent. It is reached by several streets leading west from Market, but most of the many drivers and riders who resort there find their way either by Turk, Tyler or McAllister Streets.

A favorite resort is also Woodward's Gardens. They are private property, and a quarter of a dollar is charged for entrance. It is a pleasant place to pass a half day visiting the collection of various living animals and birds, among which are camels born in the garden, and sea-lions caught in the Pacific, and paid for at the rate

of seventy-five cents a pound. One big fellow, a captive for seven years, has grown to weigh over a ton. Sea-lions can be better studied at Woodward's than at Seal Rock, especially at the hour they are fed, when they do some fearful leaping and splashing. There are fine collections also of stuffed birds, and other curiosities, hot-houses with tropical plants, aquaria not surpassed on this Continent, a skating rink, and many other attractive features. The grounds are spacious and well sheltered, and a pleasanter spot cannot be found within the city limits for whiling away a few hours. The city line of horse-cars leads to the gardens from Market Street Ferry by two routes for part of the distance, both joining on Mission Street, on which the gardens front. They cover over six acres, and almost every taste can be suited somewhere in them. The active and jolly can resort to the play-ground and gymnasium, and those who like quiet, will find shady nooks and walks; those fond of sights and curiosities can spend hours in the various cabinets, and those who like to study mankind, can gaze on the groups standing around, and streaming passers-by. Through the whole season, from April to November, it is always genial and sunny, and enjoyable there.

Pleasure Resorts of California.

Mineral Springs.—California possesses an abundance of hot and mineral springs. Those most numerous are sulphur, both hot and cold. Of hot springs, the most frequented are Paso Robles in S. Luis Obispo Co., 143 miles by rail-road and 99 by stage from San Francisco, Gilroy Hot Springs, 14 miles from the town of Gilroy, 81 miles south from San Francisco on the Southern Pacific Railroad, and Calistoga, at the terminus of the Napa Branch of the California Pacific Railroad, 66 miles north from San Francisco. Their waters are much used, both for drinking and bathing, with good repute for curative results. What are called mud baths are taken at Calistoga and Paso Robles, and many other places. There is nothing so muddy about them as one would fancy from the name, except at Paso Robles. They are simply baths taken in the spring itself just as it bubbles out of the ground, holding all its peculiar virtues unimpaired. At Paso Robles the mud baths are a literal plunging in thick mud. The waters of these springs, and of many others, must be used while retaining their original heat, and cannot be bottled to any purpose. The San Jose Warm Springs are only two hours from the city, but are not open to tourists.

There are three noted springs which are resorted to by health and pleasure seekers, whose waters are bottled in large quantities. These are the Napa Soda Springs, near Napa, and the Pacific Congress Springs, in the Coast Range, 10 miles from Santa Clara. They have been long

SCENE IN PARK AND PLEASURE GROUNDS AT OAK KNOLL, NAPA VALLEY, CALIFORNIA.—RESIDENCE OF R. B. WOODWARD.

known, and are very freely used on this coast, especially during the summer months. They are bottled by machinery, so as to carry their natural volume of gas, and are highly recommended by the medical faculty. The last named is on account of its natural attractions and its accessibility, being only 4 hours' ride from San Francisco, a very favorite summer retreat from the city. The water is said to resemble very closely that of the far-famed Saratoga Springs, after which it is named, and contains a larger proportion of mineral contents than either of the others. The last of these, not yet named, is that of the Litton Seltzer Springs, near Healdsburg, not long introduced to the public, but coming fast into favor, and claimed, not only to equal, but even excel the far-famed Congress water.

The analysis of these waters gives the following results :

NAPA SODA.	GRAINS IN A GALLON.
Bicarbonate Soda,	13.12
Carbonate Magnesia,	26.12
Carbonate Lime,	10.88
Chloride Sodium,	5.20
Sub-Carbon Iron,	7.84
Sulphate Soda,	1.84
Silicious Acid,	0.68
Alumina,	0.60
Loss,	2.48
	68.76

LITTON SELTZER.	GRAINS IN A GALLON.
Carbo'ic Acid (comb.),	42.76
Chlorine,	78.38
Sulphate Acid,	2.36
Silicic Acid,	2.02
Oxide Iron,	2.85
Lime,	4.41
Magnesia,	5.24
Soda,	62.19

PACIFIC CONGRESS.	
Chloride Sodium,	119.159
Sulphate Soda,	12.140
Carbonate Soda,	123.351
" Iron,	14.030
" Lime,	17.205
Silica Alumina and trace Magnesia,	49.882
	335.857

Alumina,	
Ammonia,	
Potash,	
Lithia,	27.38
Boracic Acid,	
Organic matter,	
	227.59

The quantity of *free* carbonic acid in the Litton Seltzer, *which escapes on standing,* is 383.75 grains per gallon. This large quantity of gas is very pleasant to the taste, and tests severely the strength of bottles, which sometimes explode even in a cool place.

The Paso Roble Springs (the name means Pass of Oaks) most used, have been analyzed with the following result :

MAIN HOT SULPHUR SPRING. Temperature 110,		MUD SPRING. 122 degrees.
One imperial gallon contains, Sulphurated Hydrogen Gas,	4.55	3.28 inches.
Free Carbonic Acid,	10.50	47.84 "
Sulphate Lime,	3.21	17.90 grains.
Sulphate Potash,	.88	traces.
Sulphate Soda,	7.85	41.11
Perox Iron,	36	
Alumina,	22	
Silicia,	44	1.11
Bicarbonate Magnesia,	92	Carbon. Mag., 3.10
Bicarbonate Soda,	50.74	Carbon. Soda, 5.21
Chloride Sodium,	27.18	96.48
Iodi'e and Bromide trac'e,		
Organic Matter,	64	3.47
Total solid contents,	93.44	168.38

The Mud Spring contains also alumina and protoxide of iron. There are also three cold sulphur springs and three other hot springs, the hottest of the temperature of 140 degrees. There is, also, a chalybeate spring. Paso Robles is resorted to with good results by persons suffering from rheumatism, cutaneous diseases, and some constitutional disorders. They are no place for consumptives.

There are many other springs besides those named. Near Lake Tahoe, are Soda Springs. Near Vallejo and at St. Helena, are White Sulphur Springs. In Sonoma County, are Skaggs Hot Springs, and at Santa Barbara are springs much resembling those at Paso Robles. The Bartlett Springs are a delightful resort, and will amply pay for the time and cost going to them. They are reached by stage from Calistoga on the arrival of the morning train from San Francisco, going on 35 miles to Clear Lake, which is crossed by steamer, and a ride of six miles then brings one at evening to the springs. The ride is one of the most beautiful in California.

The Geysers.—Tourists will find the trip to the Geysers, the most interesting and easy of all the short excursions in the State. It is well to go by one route and return *via* another. The North Pacific Railroad *via* steamer by Donahue City, will give a delightful sail through the bay. Neat cars will convey the passengers to Cloverdale, where stages are taken for the Geysers. The ride to the Geysers is over a splendid road, amid beautiful mountain scenery, and occasionally there are examples of fine driving of the stage-teams. One day at the Geysers is usually enough, and the visitor will find it absolutely necessary to rise as early as 5 or 6 A. M., to see the finest display of steam from the Geysers.

The ground literally boils and bubbles under the feet. There are devil's inkstands, and caldrons, and tea-kettles, and whistles enough to overwhelm eyes, ears, smell, taste and touch with horrid reminiscences. Yet so great is the curiosity it should not be missed. Neither must the traveler omit the enjoyment of the natural steam bath, the sensation on emerging from which is most delicious. From the Geysers to Calistoga, the celebrated Foss drives a crack stage, and usually has his spanking team of six-in-hand. Reports are strong as to his fearless driving, but a glance at the way he beautifully manages his leaders and wheelers, gives no one any anxiety as to safety. The stage route is over very great heights, up the side of long mountains, from the summits of which the views are glorious, probably to many, more enjoyable than the Geysers.

The tourist must not fail, as he returns to San Francisco, to stop at Calistoga and visit the Petrified Forest—the best collection we know; and even a few days' tour to Lake County and the famous soda and borax deposits will be well spent. From Calistoga to Vallejo, stop at Napa and take stage to the famous vineyards of So-

18

noma, and see grape raising in perfection; also visit the Spout Farm and the Soda Springs. From Vallejo, go to Benicia, 8 miles and visit the fort, where often there are seen charming displays of flowers. Then cross to Martinez, by ferry, and visit the fruit orchards of Dr. Strentzel, where oranges and pears and peaches and apples grow side by side, and twine their branches together,—probably the choicest fruit orchard in the State. From here ascend Mount Diablo and remain over night, witnessing the sunrise scene on all the great valleys and the bay spread out so grandly before you. Descending, the traveler will return to Vallejo, and thence by steam through the bay to San Francisco. The cost of this trip will be, for round trip ticket, $16 to Geysers and return. Extra for trip to Mount Diablo, about $8. Board per day, in absence, $3 gold. Time for whole trip, about one week.

Hints to Invalids.—California has been the scene of many remarkable recoveries of health, and of many sore disappointments to invalids who thought that coming to this coast would insure them a new lease of life. There is no doubt that a judicious availing of its peculiar climatic features is highly useful in many cases, and it is equally certain that an arbitrary resort to them may even hasten the end which one seeks to avert.

A consumptive patient should never come to San Francisco expecting benefit from its climate. Cold winds from the Pacific, often loaded with fog. prevail eight or nine months in the year, for a good part of the day, and make warm wrappings necessary for well persons. When these trade-winds cease, the rainy season then commences, variable and uncertain, often very damp and chilly, the sky sometimes clouded for days in succession. In the interval between rains and summer winds, both spring and autumn, there is a period of variable duration, when the sky is often clear, the air balmy, the sun genial, and everything in the outer world is charming and exhilarating; but this period is not sufficiently fixed to be counted on, and is liable to be inhospitably broken upon by raw winds, and chilly, foggy days.

The cause which thus unfavorably affects the climate of San Francisco in so marked a degree, spread out as it is along the Golden Gate, the only interruption for hundreds of miles to the lofty Coast Range, erected as a barrier between the cold, foggy ocean on one hand, and the spreading central basin, gleaming bright and hot with sunshine on the other, affects in some degree many other places along the sea-coast. At a sufficient distance inland, the ocean breezes are tempered. and there are places near the sea-shore where the trend of the coast and outjutting headlands break the force of the trade-winds, and give delightful shelter from them. It is this circumstance which gives to Santa Barbara its

celebrity. It lies on a bay facing to the south, the usual coast-line facing south-west, and is in the lee of Point Conception, a bold headland which turns away from it most of the cold ocean winds. San Rafael, near San Francisco, nestles under the lee of Tamalpais and adjacent hills, and is also sheltered. In a direct line, it is not over six or seven miles from San Francisco, and yet, when it is foggy or unutterably windy in the city, it is often warm, clear and still there.

The consumptive patient should carefully avoid exposure to the trade-winds by seeking some resort sheltered from them, or which they reach after being thoroughly tempered by inland travel. Neglect to heed this caution is the reason of many fatal disappointments experienced by California visitors seeking health.

In the summer season, beyond the range of the ocean trade-winds, the choice between locations for invalids in California will be governed as much by other, as their climatic advantages. Ease of access, hotel and boarding-house accommodations, social advantages, sources for amusement, comparative expense, are the considerations that will chiefly weigh in deciding the question. Sunshine will be found everywhere; the days, however hot, are always followed by cool nights; there are no storms, no sudden changes, the air is dry and clear and life-inspiring.

In winter it is desirable to go well south, where there is little rain and little cold weather, though even at San Diego. almost at the Mexican line, a fire is very comfortable sometimes, as the writer experienced one 10th of January, much to the surprise of some eastern invalids who arrived there with him. It will be wise for invalids to consult the physician best acquainted with the place they may choose, and carefully heed his advice about exposure, clothing, wrappings and the like. Every place has climatic features of its own, knowledge of which is gained only by experience and is of great value.

The following places are known as health resorts, and each has attractive and valuable features of its own: San Rafael near San Francisco, and Stockton in the San Joaquin Valley, Santa Barbara and San Diego on the southern coast, Paso Robles north from Santa Barbara, and back from the coast, a beautiful spot noted for sulphur baths; San Bernardino north-east from San Diego, and some distance from the coast, and fast coming into favor as it becomes more accessible and better known. Gilroy Hot Springs, 14 miles from Gilroy, on the Southern Pacific Railroad, 30 miles south of San Jose, is a favorite resort. It is in the hills of the Coast Range, and has good accommodations for visitors. Calistoga, at the terminus of the Napa Branch of the California Pacific Railroad, at the foot of Mount St. Helena, abounds in hot springs, and is resorted to for its baths of various kinds. On the railroad going to Calistoga the

White Sulphur Springs are passed at a distance of two miles. They are much frequented, but rather by visitors seeking summer recreation than by health seekers.

The best place for the consumptive patient is regarded by some good judges to be on an elevation among the hills of the Coast Range in summer, where the change of temperature will be only a few degrees, and in Southern California, a little back from the coast in winter. In such an equable climate, the patient can camp out, and keep in the open air, which is the best possible restorative.

The climate of San Francisco. which induces no perspiration, and by dampness aggravates rheumatic and neuralgic affections, is the most favorable in the world for mental invigoration and work.

Malaria is found in all the lowlands, and often among the foot hills, but elevated places are entirely free from it.

In short, there is such a variety of climate within a day's reach of San Francisco that the invalid may be sure of finding, somewhere on the Pacific Coast, whatever natural advantage will be most beneficial to his case.

California Pacific Railroad.

On the California Pacific Railroad two trains leave Sacramento daily for San Francisco, one at 6.30 A. M., and one 4 P. M. This is the shortest and favorite route between the capital and metropolis, and will no doubt ere long be the principal line over which the Overland Express Train will pass.

The train crosses the river by means of a "Y" and the Sacramento & Yolo bridge. Directly opposite Sacramento is the village of Washington, protected by a high levee, but retarded in growth by the toll for crossing the river. Along the river bank is a narrow strip of land sufficiently elevated for farming—but the train is soon beyond this on trestle-work, or a high embankment crossing the tules. On this narrow strip the ubiquitous pea-nut and chickory grow to perfection. No pea-nut surpasses these in size or flavor, and the chickory commands a price equal to the German. Coffee men consider it of superior quality, and the traveler will find it abundant in the pure coffee of all the hotels in the interior.

The tule land is the richest in the State—a fine vegetable mold and deposit from the winter floods. Many square miles of it up and down the river await reclamation, and much has been reclaimed. It will be difficult to reclaim the great extent of it now before the eye, because on the right of the railroad and several miles up the river, the waters of Cache Creek spread out and sink, and on the left the waters of Putah Creek are also emptied, and high levees would be required to carry off so much water. These tules are the temporary abode of some, and the perma-

nent abode of other varieties of wild fowl, and the happy hunting grounds for many a Nimrod. After the first rains come, the geese arrive, the white brant coming first and in largest numbers. Three varieties are common, the white and speckled breasted brant, and the hawnker. Acres of the ground, where the dry tule has been burned off and the young grass has sprouted are covered with the geese, and sometimes they are like a great cloud in the air, and their noise heard for a mile or more.

The varieties of the duck are many, but the mallard, sprig tail, canvas-back, and teal are most esteemed. It is an easy and pleasant task for one acquainted with the flight of the ducks to bring down from twenty to a hundred in a single day, besides more geese than he is willing to "pack." About five miles from Sacramento is an island (of a hundred acres, dry and grassy) where two or three days camping may be enjoyed by a lover of the sport.

When the Sacramento overflows its banks and the creeks are high, the tules are hidden by the water, and if the wind blows, this region is like an open sea. Frequently the road-bed has been washed away, and now it is protected by an inclined breakwater and young willows. It has been generally but erroneously supposed that hogs and the Chinamen feed on the tule roots.

The bulbous root they eat is called by the Chinese "Foo tau," and is imported largely from China, where it grows to a greater size than in this country. Across the tules at Swingle's Ranche is a side track and flag station.

Davisville—is 13 miles nearly due west of Sacramento, has a population of 300, all gathered since the building of the railroad, and has two stores, a dozen saloons, four restaurants, and a Presbyterian, a Methodist Episcopal, and a Roman Catholic Church. About the same proportion of saloons to the population holds good over California, but that of churches does not. But "Davisville is not an immoral place, for the liquor is all sold to non-residents."

In 1862 land was worth from $6 to $10 per acre, and now sells at $75 to $100.

Near Davisville are large orchards, "Brigg's" covering 400 acres, and the "Silk Ranche" orchard 250 acres, but in dry seasons the quantity and quality of the fruit, is greatly impaired by the want of irrigation.

The failure of silk culture was largely owing to the hot winds from the north, killing the worms. Attention to fruit culture, has demonstrated the necessity of allowing nothing to grow between the trees. Nor are the trees trimmed so high up as in the Eastern States. Alfalfa has yielded in one season, $55 worth of hay to the acre.

At Davisville the railroad to San Francisco, turns directly to the south, and a branch runs north to Woodland and Knight's Landing.

Woodland is a town of 1,000 inhabitants, and 9 miles from Davisville. Near Woodland the road branches to the northern part of the valley of the Sacramento, but is not yet opened for business.

Knight's Landing is on the Sacramento River, and this railroad formerly continued on northward to Marysville, until the flood of 1872 destroyed the embankment for miles.

Continuing south from Davisville, Putah Creek is crossed near Davisville, a dry channel in summer, and a torrent in winter; and 4 miles south is

Foster,—a side track, and 4.17 miles farther, *Dixon*—is reached. It has a large grain trade from the surrounding country, a Congregational, a Methodist and a Baptist Church; several hotels and a block or two of good stores. Since the completion of the railroad the town of Silveyville, about three miles distant, has been moved bodily to Dixon. Farther south 3.27 miles, is

Batavia,—a village in a promising region, with a large grain trade, a hotel and several stores, and next south 4.83 miles, is

Elmira,—formerly called Vaca Junction, the junction of the Elmira and Vacaville Railroad, extending to Vacaville five miles, and Winters 17 miles. Fare to Vacaville 50 cents, and Winters $1.70. South from Elmira 3.96 miles is

Cannon's,—a large ranche, and 6.55 miles farther is

Fairfield and Suisun City.—The former is on the right-hand side of the road, and the other on the left. Fairfield is the county-seat of Solano County, and Suisun the post-office and business center. Fairfield has a Methodist Episcopal Church, and Suisun a Protestant Episcopal, a Cumberland Presbyterian and a Methodist Episcopal. Suisun is at the head of Suisun Slough, navigable for small sloops and steamers, and on the edge of a large tract of tule land. Its streets are subject to a *slight overflow* during heavy rains, when its adobe soil is a very tenacious friend to one's feet. The hills which have been approaching closer and closer since we left Sacramento—one of the numerous ridges of the Coast Range are now not far off, and to avoid the grades in crossing them, a new road will soon be built along the edge of the "swamp and overflowed" land to Benicia, on the straits of Carquinez, and crossing these will continue along the east side of the San Pablo Bay and Bay of San Francisco, to Oakland Wharf and form part of the Overland Route.

Before reaching the next station, a small spur of the Suscol Hills is tunneled, and to the right from

Bridgeport.—5.45 miles from Suisun, and other points, may be seen fertile valleys in which the earliest fruits of the State are grown. In Green Valley—one of these, sheltered from

wind and free from fog, fruits and vegetables ripen sooner than in the paradise of Los Angeles, about 400 miles south.

The tourist will be struck with the rolling character of the farming land, when he sees the highest hill-tops covered with golden grain or thick stubble. The soil is the rich adobe, the best adapted to dry seasons, and rarely found covering such hills. The crops are brought off on sleds.

Creston,—the summit, is 3.84 miles from Bridgeport, and simply a flag station. Soon after passing it, the Napa Valley lies below on the right, but almost before one is aware of it, *Napa Junction,*—3.65 miles from Creston, is announced.

Napa Valley.

Here the road branches through Napa Valley, one of the loveliest and most fruitful of the State. It is enclosed between two ridges of the Coast Range, one of which separates it from the Sacramento and the other from the Sonoma Valley. Above Calistoga, Mount Saint Helena stands like a great sentinel across the head of the valley. The land is among the best in the State, and fruit growing extensively and successfully practiced.

The climate is well tempered and the season rare when crops fail. This branch is a part of one of the chief routes to the Geysers and other popular resorts.

The first station north from the Junction is called

Thompson,—from the owner of the ranche and orchard, which will strike the observer as closely related to the perfect arrangement and culture of the farms in Chester or Cumberland Valley of Pennsylvania, and a closer inspection would reveal one of the most convenient and complete farm-houses in the country. Suscol, a landing-place and ferry on the Napa River, is near by. The next station is 4.49 miles farther north, and called

Napa.—A town of great loveliness, with a population of 5,000, set in homes embosomed in fruits and flowers—a town not surpassed for beauty of situation in the State, and rivaled by San Jose only. It is at the head of navigation for steamers of light draft on the Napa River, and near it is located the new Branch Insane Asylum, erected at a cost of more than a million of dollars. The public schools rank high, and there are also four colleges and seminaries of high order. The *Register* is a daily and weekly newspaper, and the *Reporter,* a weekly. It has two good hotels, the "United States," and The Palace, many stores of high order, and good banking facilities. In no portion of the State is society more stable and cultivated. The churches are imposing and well attended. The Presbyterians have the largest, most convenient and tasteful house of worship outside of San Francisco and Oakland, and the Methodists, Baptists and Roman Catholics have good houses also. Daily stages connect with the morning train for Sonoma. Above Napa, 5.45 miles, is

Oak Knoll,—near which is hidden in a park of evergreen oaks, the pleasant residence of R. B. Woodward, Esq., one of the most enterprising and public-spirited men of California, near which may be seen his orchard, one of the largest and best in the county.

Yountville—is 3.45 miles farther north, a village with about 300 inhabitants, called after one of the early settlers. Near the depot is a large vinery. On the hill-sides are numerous vineyards, and in the village a Baptist and a Congregational Church.

St. Helena—is a village of about 500 inhabitants, surrounded with ranches where people of culture live in luxury, and two miles distant are the White Sulphur Springs. Stages for the Springs connect with every train, and for Knoxville in Lake County, with every morning train from San Francisco. Presbyterians, Baptists, and Methodists have churches here. The valley grows narrower until

Calistoga — is reached, with a population of about 500, and two hotels — one the "Hot Springs."

Here are hot and mud baths, and from Calistoga are numerous pleasant drives, especially to the Petrified Forest, five miles distant, on the top of the ridge lying toward the ocean, and in a sunken part of the high table-land where there was evidently a lake after trees had attained an enormous growth, and long after this the waters of the lake discharged by some sudden rupture of the surrounding wall. The mountain views, hunting, fishing and other attractions, make Calistoga a popular resort, and the recent discovery of many quicksilver and silver mines has given a fresh impetus to the business of the town. The population is about 700, but varies with the summer freighting to Lake County. Foss's line of stages leaves every morning during the summer for the Geysers, and stages leave daily on arrival of morning train from San Francisco for Bartlett's and other resorts of Lake County, continuing toward San Francisco on the main line.

Vallejo.—The pronunciation of this Spanish word is Val-yay-ho, and the town was named in honor of an old family still residing there.

Just before approaching the town, the "Orphans' Home," set upon a hill, and under the auspices of the I. O. Good Templars, attracts attention. It is on the left-hand side, and the town on the right.

At the depot, street-cars connect with all the trains, and carriages to any part of the city may be had for "four bits;" the "bit" being equivalent to the old New York shilling.

The station for the town is called North Vallejo, to distinguish it from the new town that has grown around the railroad terminus, one mile south.

Vallejo was for a while the capital of the State. It has now a population of about 5,000, and derives much of its business from the United States Navy Yard on Mare Island.

It has a Methodist, a Presbyterian, a Baptist and a Roman Catholic Church, and South Vallejo has also a Congregational Church. Vallejo has a stage to Benicia, eight miles, and the steamer Parthenius runs daily to San Francisco, in addition to the steamers that connect twice a day with the trains on the California Pacific Railroad.

Its wharves are in deep water, and at them the immense quantities of grain brought from the valleys north, are loaded direct for Liverpool and other parts. A large elevator—the only one tried on the coast, was blown down during a south-east gale. The town has two newspapers, the *Chronicle*, a weekly, and the *Independent*, a daily. At

South Vallejo,—24 miles from San Francisco, passengers are transferred to a steamer, and by it transported to the foot of Market Street, in San Francisco.

On board the steamer a good meal may be secured, for one dollar coin; and a trip to San Francisco, for which an hour and a half, or two hours will be necessary, according to steam and tide, will be delightfully occupied with the attractions of the bay and the bordering hills. As the steamer leaves the wharf, the view of the Navy Yard is fine, and when it doubles the island, the straits of Carquinez, through which the Sacramento River empties, are immediately on the left, and when fairly out on the San Pablo Bay, by looking to the north, the town of Vallejo on the hill, and the Navy Yard on the island, appear to be one city. West of Vallejo may be traced the Napa Valley, and farther west, the Sonoma Valley, so famous for its wines, and far off to the north-west the Petaluma Creek, which forms an opening to the Russian River Valley, through which the North Pacific Railroad runs to Cloverdale, and forms a pleasant route to the Geysers. These valleys are parallel to each other but separated by lofty ridges of the Coast Range.

After making this general survey of the northern end of the bay and then having breakfast or dinner, one will be in sight of the western metropolis. The city comes into view as the steamer turns to the south-east, around a point of land, off which are the "Two Brothers," corresponding to the "Two Sisters" on the west side, and enters the Bay of San Francisco. On one of the Brothers is a light-house of the fifth order, and just below is Red Rock, a bold and pretty landmark. Off to the right is Mt. Tamalpais, with a shoot for lumber, that looks like a swift road to travel, and at the foot of the mountain, nestled in a deep little cove, and overlooking the sheltered waters near by, is San Rafael, the home of some merchant princes of San Francisco, and the resort of many invalids, who are seeking a new lease of life in its genial clime. On the point of land just south of San Rafael, is San Quentin, where the State has a large boarding-house and workshop filled with unwilling inmates.

Farther south-east is Angel Island—separated from the promontory of the coast main-land by Raccoon Straits, through which one may look into the Golden Gate.

The island is a military reservation, fortified strongly on the south and south-west parts, with a road running around the entire island.

Passing the island, the Golden Gate is directly on the right, and Alcatraz, a naval station, midway across it, and directly in front, the hills of San Francisco, that ought to have been terraced.

On the east, beginning farther north are Berkley, with the buildings of the State University; and Oakland, the city of residences and gardens; Alameda, of like character, but of less extent, and more live oaks ; and in the bay the Oakland Wharf and Goat Island.

Never, except during severe winter storms, or the prevalence of heavy fog, is the navigation of the bay unpleasant, and on a calm morning when the waters are placid, the skies Italian, and the mind free from anxious care, the bay from Vallejo to San Francisco will make some of the brightest and most lasting impressions of the Golden State.

New Routes of Pleasure Travel.

By the completion of many new local railroads, so many new and delightful pleasure routes have been opened, and made easily accessible, that the tourist should not fail to visit some of the following :

Santa Cruz.—One of the most enjoyable of seaside resorts, and abounding in garden bloom and floral beauty, is now reached by three routes of travel, by *steamer* from San Francisco, usually taking a few hours or a day at utmost; by *The Southern Pacific Railroad* to *Pajaro*, and thence by *Watsonville and Narrow Gauge Railroad* along the coast, and lastly by the new *South Pacific Coast Narrow Gauge Railroad* via San Jose and over the Coast Range of Mountains. The last named is a new road of exceeding beauty. Probably there is no finer ride of a day's length equal to this. The tourist must not omit it.

Santa Barbara—is beyond question, the gem city of the Pacific Coast as a resort for tourists and invalids. It may be reached by the Southern Pacific Railroad and a stage ride of one day, or by steamer of two days. It is a city of most attractive nature embowered among gardens, fruit trees, flowers, and wonderful luxuriance of semi-tropical vegetation. This place is full of admirable conveniences of hotel life, and invalids and tourists reside the year round, in enjoyment of its balmy air. For a home residence, probably no place on the Pacific Coast is its equal in all advantages of climate, health and social privileges. It has hitherto been difficult of access, owing to prolonged stage riding or seasickness by steamer journey,—but these lessen each year by the nearer approach of the Southern Pacific Railroad. In the spring-time, when the country is in bloom, the finest route is by stage from *Soledad*. The country is then a paradise of floral loveliness the entire distance.

Paraiso Springs—are a new resort near *Soledad*, eight miles distant whose springs are of iron, soda, white sulphur, excellent for rheumatism, asthma and various skin and blood diseases.

Riverside—is a new resort near Colton, a beautiful place of residence, and a home for *asthmatics*, combining mountain air with tropical gardening, and soft balmy sunny breezes ; an *asthmatic's paradise.*

San Bernardino—has become more popular both as a place of resort and residence, and also because of the value of the *Watermin Hot Springs*, six miles north. These are said to be a sure cure for *rheumatism.* Stages four miles from Colton now reach it.

Lake County—possesses many new mineral springs. The Geysers have been made more attractive than ever ; the hotel has been thoroughly refitted and made desirable for residences. The trip to the Geysers and return can now be made in 36 hours, with time to see all the marvelous wonder of nature. Round trip tickets now cost but $13.00. Tourists will do well to extend their tour to Clear Lake, after visiting the Geysers, ascend over the mountains by the new route from Cloverdale. The scenery is delightful. The steamer ride on Clear Lake is well worth a visit. The mountain ride approaching Calistoga is thrilling.

Head Waters of the Sacramento—have been brought nearer to the public by a reduction of fares to all points as far north as *Soda Springs* and *Sissons.* Round trip tickets are now sold from San Francisco to Soda Springs for $33.80, and to Sissons for $35 40, and the U. S. Fishery on McCloud River, $24.50. The best hunting and fishing in the state for tourists is to had in this region. At *Sissons, Upper* and *Lower Soda Springs* guides and horses are provided for excursionists to the summit of Mt. Shasta, and to the salmon and trout fishing stations and " Deer Lick " on the head waters of the McCloud and Sacramento Rivers.

The Southern Pacific Railroad.

RAILROAD TRAVEL IN CALIFORNIA.

NEXT to the Central Pacific, the Southern Pacific is the great railroad enterprise of the Pacific coast. The whole length of the road (June, 1878) is 713.09 miles. It is leased, except the Northern Division, to the Central Pacific, and, in connection with the Central Pacific and its other leased roads and branches, forms one great system extending for 3150.24 miles, with 688 miles additional of steamer routes.

This harmonious system is one of the most important and successful railroad enterprises of the continent or the age. By it the whole transcontinental traffic must be performed for many years to come. And the difficulties encountered, the country opened, the wealth developed, and the wonders and curiosities of nature made accessible —all are marvelous.

From San Francisco, this giant enterprise is stretching down into the wheat-fields of the San Joaquin and the coast valleys and the orange groves of the South, and laying a fast hold on the untold mineral wealth of Arizona, New Mexico, and other lands. It was built without the aid of government bonds, when railway contractors in the East were idle and railway shops silent ; and built so rapidly that 351 miles of track over desert lands and through long tunnels were completed in the one year 1876.

In its vigorous prosecution, at enormous cost, San Francisco and the coast have already reaped many a substantial blessing. The last rail connecting San Francisco and Los Angeles was laid September 2d, 1876, and the road was opened to Fort Yuma, *via* the Central Pacific to Lathrop and Goshen, on May 5th, 1877.

When completed to an Eastern connection, it will be the shortest line from San Francisco to New Orleans and the country bordering the Gulf of Mexico, and the highway for the grain of Southern California to the European markets.

In the Southern Pacific Railroad are consolidated numerous local roads built or projected. These were the San Francisco and San José Railroad, incorporated August 18th, 1860, and built between these two cities ; the Santa Clara and Pajaro Valley Railroad, incorporated January 2d, 1868 ; and the California Southern, incorporated January 22d, 1870. All these were consolidated October 12th, 1870, into the

Southern Pacific Railroad Co.

The Southern Pacific Branch Railroad Company was incorporated December 23d, 1872, and consolidated with the Southern Pacific August 19th, 1873.

The Los Angeles and San Pedro Railroad Company was incorporated February 18th, 1868, built between Los Angeles and Wilmington, and consolidated with the Southern Pacific December 18th, 1874.

The Northern Division.—This extends southward from the corner of Fourth and Townsend streets, San Francisco, to San José, Carnadero Junction, and Tres Pinos. From Carnadero Junction there is a branch to Soledad. The route has been surveyed from Tres Pinos across the coast mountains *via* the Panoche Pass to Huron, from which point 40 miles are built to Goshen, where a junction is formed with the Visalia Division of the Central Pacific and the Tulare Division of the Southern Pacific. The 40 miles between Huron and Goshen are not traveled at present in going from San Francisco to Los Angeles, but are operated as, and called, the Goshen Division of the Southern Pacific Railroad. The branch *via* Soledad continues from Carnadero to the Pajaro (pronounced Pä-hä-ro) Valley, thence through the Salinas Valley, and is surveyed from Soledad across the coast range *via* the Polonio Pass to Posa, on the main line of the Southern Pacific, 53 miles south of Goshen.

From San Francisco Southward.

This Northern Division is the only railroad running its cars into San Francisco without the use of a ferry, the line being on the peninsula between the southern part of the Bay of San Francisco and the Pacific Ocean. It is, therefore, the most desirable line for country residences ; and when to this is added the salubrity of climate found on this peninsula in an hour's travel from the city, it is readily understood why Milbrae, San Mateo, Belmont, Redwood City, Fair Oaks, Menlo Park, etc., are chosen for the palaces of bonanza kings, senators, governors, railroad and bank presidents, and other men of culture and money who choose their locations where cost is scarcely ever considered. To these delightful country residences there are five trains each way daily, and to San José three trains ; and the tourist desiring to see the fairest and best improved portion of California must not fail to take one or more of these trains and extend his visit at least to San José.

Leaving San Francisco, you see the immense freight depots of the Central Pacific and Southern roads, and a large area of land reclaimed from Mission Bay, at a cost of nearly $400,000, owned jointly by the two companies for railroad purposes. A few minutes' ride brings you to the machine-shops of the road, and in the southern part of the city the train stops at

Valencia Street crossing, 3.4 miles, where connection is made with the horse-cars of the Market Street passenger railway.

The road will eventually skirt the bay from the Fourth Street depot, but the tourist will be pleased if he can ascend the steep grade from Valencia Street depot and thereby gain a bird's-eye view of a large part of the city. The carefully-cultivated gardens to be noticed along the road are almost exclusively in the hands of Italians and Chinamen.

Bernal, 4.6 miles, is a station at which some trains do not stop. On the right, after leaving the station, are the grounds of the House of Refuge, 130 acres, with the imposing edifices of the Industrial School and the House of Correction.

San Miguel, 6.9 miles, is also a small station, near which, on the left, is St. Mary's College, a large educational institution of the Roman Catholic Church. On the right may be seen Lake Merced, used by the Spring Valley Water Company to supply the city in part ; and across the hills is the long surf-line of the great Pacific Ocean, battling with the shifting but unyielding sand ; and still beyond is the bosom of the great deep. In a clear atmosphere, this is a magnificent view, taking in many a sail and showing the Farralone Islands and Point Reyes, north of the Golden Gate.

Colma, 9.2 miles, is a side track, at which some trains do not stop.

Baden, 12.2 miles, is of like importance. The "Twelve Mile Farm" is the residence of Charles Lux, Esq., of the firm of Lux & Miller, cattle-dealers. The firm own many and vast tracts of land in different parts of the State.

San Bruno, 14.3 miles, is on the edge of the marsh land which surrounds the bay, and the point to which the new road to avoid the hills will extend. This is the resort for more gunners than any other station in California. During the season for ducks, eighty and sometimes a hundred guns are checked to this point from San Francisco by a single train.

Targets for rifle-shooting at ranges of 200, 500, 800, and 1000 yards are erected here, and most of the practice between various military companies and societies is here enjoyed.

Milbrae, 17 miles, has the large dairy of the same name, and on the right the beautiful residence of D. O. Mills, Esq., formerly President of the Bank of California, an engraving of which may be seen on page 243.

Oak Grove, 19.2 miles, is a small station, the name indicating the change of climate.

San Mateo, 21.1 miles, is a flourishing town of nearly 2000 people, containing three churches and the elegant grounds and residences of Alvinza Hayward, the late George H. Howard, and others.

St. Matthew's Military School, for boys, under Rev. A. L. Brewer, is one of the best in the State, and about two miles from the town is Laurel Institute, for young ladies, a worthy and flourishing school. Daily stages leave for Pescadero on the arrival of the 8.30 train from San Francisco, following the lovely cañon of the San Mateo Creek through the hills four miles to Crystal Springs, and thence crossing the Sierra Morena spur of the coast range to Half-Moon Bay, or Spanish-town, 12 miles. The views are grand, overlooking on the east the Bay of San Francisco, the mountains and valleys of *Alameda* and *Contra Costa* counties, with Mt. Diablo rising over all, while near at hand are the smiling valleys of Santa Clara and San Andreas, and the lovely *Cañada del Ramundo;* and overlooking on the west the thousand peaks of the Santa Cruz Mountains and the deep blue sea.

Purissima is 23 miles from San Mateo, and Pescadero 30 miles. This is a favorite resort on account of its pebble beach, delightful drives, sea-bathing, picturesque hills, trout streams, forests abounding in game, and mild, bracing climate.

At Pescadero stages connect for Santa Cruz, 36 miles south, passing Pigeon Point, where the lighthouse has a Fresnel light of the first order, with a national history. It shone out from Cape Hatteras until, during the late war, it was packed ready for shipping to the interior by the rebels, but seized by the government and sent to this coast. This route continues mostly along the coast, passing Scott's Creek and Laurel Grove, choice resorts for fishermen and camping parties. The stages leave Pescadero Tuesdays, Thursdays, and Saturdays, and return on alternate days. Fare, $3.

Belmont, 25.1 miles, is a favorite picnic resort ; and near the station, but hidden from view, is the residence of the late William C. Ralston, now owned by Senator Sharon.

Redwood City, 28.6 miles, is the county seat of San Mateo County, and has a population of 2000, with four churches. Boats from the bay come up a small creek, and return with cargoes of redwood from the coast mountains on the west.

An artesian well supplies the city with water, and two weekly papers, the *Times* and *Gazette*, supply the local news.

A daily stage leaves for Pescadero, 30 miles, passing Scarsville, 7 miles, and La Honda, 16 miles. Fare, $3.

Fair Oaks, 30.9 miles, is in the most charming portion of the Santa Clara Valley, where the damp, chilly air of the ocean and bay is just sufficiently tempered by the heat of the interior to produce the balmy loveliness of Mentoné.

The whole region is divided into beautiful gardens, luscious orchards, and spacious parks, and set with charming homes. Among them are the country seats of Colonel Eyre, Faxon D. Atherton, and others.

There are twelve species of oak found in California, but this region is named from the number and beauty of the white oak; and on the trees the long Spanish moss will remind one of the forests in the far South. The mistletoe is also abundant.

Menlo Park, 32.1 miles, is a continuation of the attractive features of the valley. On the left, immediately after passing the station, is the residence of ex-Governor M. S. Latham, adorned with exquisite works of art and rare taste. In the park, visible from the cars, may be seen a band of California (black tailed) deer.

Further on, and on the right, is *Palo Alto*, the country seat of Governor Stanford, named in honor of the original name of the Spanish grant. This was *Rancho Palo Alto San Francisquita*, charmingly situated, but neglected when it came into the governor's hands. It is now one of the most beautiful spots in California. The race-track and breeding-farm, where Occident is at home, is perfect in its apportionments, and has also the advantage of the salubrity of climate that best produces a high development of the physical man and the horse. We may well look to this quarter, therefore, to produce some of the best stock in the world.

Mayfield, 34.9 miles, has about 1000 people and three churches, and is situated in the midst of fertile wheat-fields, and is a favorite point of departure for sportsmen seeking deer, quail, bear, and wild-cats, in the coast mountains on the right.

Mountain View, 39.1 miles, is a flourishing town of about 500 people. The original town is a quiet, unpretentious hamlet in a charming little spot a mile west of the station and present town.

The Santa Cruz range is nearer than before, and the Contra Costa grows more distant. Parties frequently start from this place to hunt deer or catch trout in the mountains on the west.

Murphy's, 41.9 miles, is named from the grant on which the side track is laid—a fair specimen of the manner in which the best parts of California were divided up in "leagues of land" and granted by the Mexican Government. As the bay receded and disappeared on the left, one must not forget that the choice, arable land is increased in extent, and around Alviso, now opposite, are numerous gardens from which twenty tons of berries have been shipped in a single day.

Lawrence's, 43.9 miles, is a station where the name of an old resident is perpetuated.

Santa Clara, 47.4 miles, is a beautiful town of nearly 4000 people. It is embowered in the most luxuriant shrubbery and surrounded with prolific orchards of choicest fruits. It is one of the oldest and most delightfully located towns in the State.

The mission was founded by Father Thomas de la Pinya in 1777, and now the imposing buildings of the large (Catholic) Santa Clara College and St. Mary's Academy will attract the first attention of the tourist. These make it a *collegiate* town. Two weekly papers are published here, the *Index* and *News*. A stage connects with the train at 3.30 P.M. from San Francisco on the Southern Pacific Railroad for the *Pacific Congress Springs*, 10 miles south-west, a fashionable and pleasant resort, with mineral waters resembling those of the famous Congress Spring at Saratoga, N. Y. Another stage line extends *via* Saratoga, Congress Springs, to Santa Cruz, and supplies a daily mail along the route. Owing to distance it is not a favorite for through travel, but on no other route crossing the mountains between San Francisco and San Luis Obispo is the scenery equal to this, and scarcely any view in California surpasses the one from the summit, looking to San Francisco, San José, and the Sierras.

On approaching the station, the train stops before crossing the track of the *South Pacific Coast* (narrow gauge) Railroad. This road forms a parallel line to San José, and is in operation from San Francisco and Alameda *via* Newark and Alviso to Los Gatos, where stage connection is made for Santa Cruz.

Santa Clara has a bank, four churches, and many beautiful homes, but no first-class hotel. The *Alameda*, a wide and beautifully-shaded avenue, connects Santa Clara with San José. The poplars and willows that meet overhead were set out in 1799 by direction of the early Catholic missionaries. A line of horse-cars runs on the avenue between the two towns, and about midway on the road is the University of the Pacific, the College of the M. E. Church, and connected with this is a seminary for young ladies. Beautiful residences have so increased that the whole Alameda is now a fashionable avenue, lined with elegant homes.

San José (San Ho-zay), 50 miles from San Francisco, is the loveliest inland city of California.

Its population is about 20,000. It contends with Sacramento for the honor of being the third city in the State. It was settled in 1777 by the Catholic missionaries, and was for a brief period the capital of the State. Without the advantages of Sacramento for wholesale trade, it commands the trade of a large portion of the State, and has a climate superior to that of the capital city. Its gardens of semi-tropical fruits and shrubs; its abundance, variety, and gracefulness of shade-trees; its well-macadamized streets; its numerous and well-supported churches, representing the Roman Catholic and every important Protestant denomination; its pure water from artesian wells and the coast mountains; its gas-works, and numerous manufactories, give it a people of the highest intelligence and industry, and ought to attract to it every tourist who desires to see what cultivation will produce in this rich and fruitful State. The city has four incorporated banks, none with a capital of less than half a million. It has a large woolen-mill, canning factories, wholesale houses, and machine-shops.

Its principal hotels are the *Auzerais*, *St. James*, New York Exchange, Hensley House, and Lick House; and outside of San Francisco, no one in the State is more popular than the Auzerais.

The city has *four routes* to San Francisco: (1) the Southern Pacific, over which goes four fifths of the travel; (2) a branch road connecting with the Central Pacific at Niles; (3) the South Pacific Coast (narrow gauge); and (4) a stage to Alviso, connecting with a steamer on the bay for San Francisco.

It has a daily stage *via* Santa Clara for Saratoga and Santa Cruz, and a daily evening stage for the new *A maden Quick-silver Mines*, ten miles distant, on Bache Mountain. The tourist visiting these should take a private carriage, or he will be compelled to spend a night at a hotel without all the comforts he may seek. These mines are open to visitors on Thursdays only. They were discovered in 1845, sought out from seeing the painted mines of the Indians, and have been exceedingly productive. Visitors may purchase specimens of the ore.

Near the Almaden mines is the Vichy Spring, celebrated for its curative properties. Its waters are bottled and sold in San Francisco, and said to be equal to those imported from France.

The Guadaloupe Quicksilver Mines are on the opposite side of a spur of the same mountains. The road to it branches westward from the road to the new Almaden mines, at a point about 7 miles from San José. The two mines are only about two miles apart. But the Almaden are the most noted for their productiveness and extent, and have yielded more than any other quicksilver mine in this country. A new drive has been made by the city, extending to the foot-hills on the east to Alum Rock Springs. This road is not

surpassed in the State outside of San Francisco and Oakland. It is of unusual width, and for the whole distance, 6 miles, it is planted on both sides with two rows of shade-trees, and will eventually surpass the noted *Alameda*.

These springs with 160 acres of ground have been set apart for a public park.

This same road forms part of that to Mt. Hamilton, constructed by Santa Clara County, to secure the location of the magnificent observatory provided for in the will of the late James Lick by a gift of $700,000. Mt. Hamilton is the highest peak in the southern part of the coast range, having an altitude of 4500 feet. The road to it ascends the hills east of San José, and may be seen from the city for a long distance; but it descends again to Smith's Creek, a lovely camping spot, before the ascent of the mountain actually begins. The grade is only five feet in a hundred, and it is one of the best mountain roads in California, and will be surpassed only by the new road to the Yosemite Valley from Madera Station.

The distance to Mt. Hamilton is 22 miles. To it there is no public conveyance, but this want will doubtless be supplied as soon as the Lick Observatory is completed.

San José has three daily newspapers, the *Mercury*, *Patriot*, and *Argus*. The *Mercury* and *Argus* have also weekly editions.

The *Court House* is a beautiful structure, and from its dome can be had a magnificent view—a panorama of the whole Santa Clara Valley, with the mountains on the east and west. The *State Normal School* is located in the center of the city in a park of six squares, and is also a large and imposing structure. *San José Institute and Business College* is well supported, and the Convent or Academy of Notre Dame, under the auspices of the Catholic Sisters, is a large and flourishing institution, and the Home Seminary (for girls) deservedly esteemed.

Fourth Street station is a mile from the principal depot, and at it all trains running south of San José stop for the accommodation of the residents in the southern part of the city.

Eden Vale, 57.3 miles,

Coyote, 62.8 miles, and

Perry's, 65.8 miles, are unimportant because near San José, or else the foot hills approach on either side, until the road passes into the valley in which Gilroy is found, and the country is best adapted for grazing purposes. Buildings to accommodate the workmen of the Almaden mines are plainly seen on the right, high up on the side of the mountain.

Madrone, 68.8 miles, and

Tennant's, 72.8 miles, are stations having no especial attraction for the tourist.

Gilroy, 80.3 miles, is an important town of 2000 inhabitants. It has six churches and a weekly newspaper, the *Advocate*. It is the only eating-station on the line of the road, and good meals are neatly served from the abundance of the farms and dairies, at 50 cents each.

The *Southern Pacific* and Williams are good hotels. The climate is warmer than that of San José.

Stages leave daily for San Felipe, 10 miles east, Los Baños, 48 miles east, and Firebaugh's Ferry on the San Joaquin River, 80 miles. The fare averages 10 cents a mile.

Stages also run every day during the summer to *Gilroy Hot Springs*, 15 miles east. The waters have proved beneficial in rheumatic affections, the hotel and cottages are attractive, and the wild mountain scenery, pine-scented air, wild game and trout-fishing have made it a favorite resort.

Old Gilroy is 3 miles south-east, and has grown none since the building of the railroad. Near the town, and on the left of the railroad, may be seen a swampy tract, which is the edge of *Soap Lake*, several miles long, around which are numerous fields of tobacco, and in which are found large numbers of wild ducks and geese. The lake is so called because soapwort is abundant, and its saponine principle so largely imparted to the water that many perform their washing without soap.

At *Carnadero*, 82.5 miles, and 2.2 miles south of Gilroy, the railroad branches ; the line to Soledad being the most important, and operated as the main branch.

At *Gilroy* passengers change cars for *Hollister* and *Tres Pinos*.

Hollister, 14 miles from Gilroy, is the county seat of Benito County, and has 1500 inhabitants. It is situated in a rich farming region, and owes its rapid growth and prosperity to the division and sale of a large land-grant owned by Colonel Hollister.

The ranch was originally 12 leagues, or about 70,000 acres, and purchased from the grantee for $20,000. The part east of the river is owned by Flint, Bixby & Co., and $60 per acre is now a fair average price for the portion divided and sold.

Tres Pinos, 20.2 miles from Gilroy, is the present terminus of this division, and the entrepot for freight to the New Idria and other quicksilver mines near the New Idria, San Carlos, and Cerro Benito peaks, from 70 to 120 miles south.

A tri-weekly stage runs through this country to San Bruno, 25 miles, and New Idria, 75 miles. Fare, about 10 cents a mile. Long's, Peach-Tree, Brown's, and Bitter Water valleys, and Slack's Cañon, are supplied partly from Tres Pinos and partly from Soledad.

North and south of Gilroy, if you find doubt as to the ownership of the land (and "grant titles" are proverbially uncertain), you may call it one of Miller & Lux's farms. They are so numerous that cattle driven to San Francisco are pastured every night on their own land.

One of the firm, Mr. Miller, resides on the *Bloomfield Ranch*, a tract of several thousand acres. But to gain a better idea of the extent of the farming of this firm, see under *Merced*, on the Visalia Division of the Central Pacific.

Branch from Carnadero to Soledad.

Sargent's, on this branch, and 86.5 miles from San Francisco, is named from J. P. Sargent, owner of the ranch a mile north. It is the station for stage to *San Juan* (pronounced San Wân), *South*. It is across the *Pajaro* (pronounced Pah-ha-ro) River, and six miles distant. Fare, 75 cents. San Juan South, is an old Spanish town, the seat of a mission located in 1787, and second best in the State in point of preservation. The town may be seen on the left a few minutes after passing the station.

The railroad now follows the course of the river, and turns westward, then crosses it from Santa Cruz to San Benito County, and then, to shorten the distance, passes through a tunnel 950 feet long and into the Pajaro Valley, 9 miles long and 5 miles wide.

On the right are the Santa Cruz (Coast Range) Mountains, and in the cañons lingering traces of the beautiful Redwoods.

Vega, 96.5 miles, is a signal station ; but

Pajaro, 99.4 miles, is an important station, receiving the freight of the valley in which it is situated, and being the junction of the Santa Cruz (narrow gauge) Railroad.

This forms an all-rail route to the most frequented seaside resort on the coast, for which see the "Santa Cruz Railroad."

Watsonville, across the Pajaro River from the station, and a mile distant, has a population of 3500, a good hotel—the Lewis House—four churches, a bank, and two weekly papers, the *Pajaronian* and the *Transcript*.

The river empties into the ocean, but furnishes no landing for vessels. Formerly there was a landing-place, "The Embarcadero," about a mile north of the river, but the wharf is now neglected and the town receives its freight either by the Southern Pacific Railroad or *via* Santa Cruz.

Watsonville Landing, on Elkhorn Slough, is about three miles south of the town, and to this point freight was formerly brought by a small stern-wheel lighter from Moss Landing, on the coast of Monterey Bay, about two miles south of the mouth of the Salinas River, and twelve miles from Watsonville.

The course of the railroad from Pajaro is now parallel with the general line of the coast, and crosses the tide-lands that skirt the eastern shore of Monterey Bay. The Santa Cruz Mountains are now behind to the left, and on the right are the Gabilan Mountains, which extend from the Pajaro River through the entire county. The range increases in height as we go south, and contains immense deposits of limestone and some quicksilver. The climate from Watsonville to Salinas is like that of San Francisco, modified because further south, and the ocean winds are less severe.

Castroville, 109.7 miles, is 4 miles from Moss Landing, and has a population of 500. The average yield of wheat in this vicinity now reaches 30 bushels to the acre, and of barley 50 bushels, although 100 bushels of the latter have been raised to the acre. Owing to the fogs and damp winds, corn and potatoes are grown in this region. Considerable game is shipped during the winter, the salt marsh affording water-fowl, and the Gabilan Mountains quail and deer.

Salinas, 117.6 miles, is the county town of Monterey County, and has a population of 3000. There are eight church organizations and about as many lodges and benevolent orders. It is the center of trade, wealth, and commerce for Monterey County, and has banks, machine-shops, foundries, flouring-mills, and factories.

I is the point of junction for the *Monterey and Salinas Valley Railroad,* for which (and the town of Monterey) see under the appropriate heading.

There is a fine hotel, the Abbott House ; two papers are published weekly, the *Index* and the *Democrat.* Stages leave daily for Natividad, a pleasant little town at the foot of the Gabilan Mountains, six miles north-east of Salinas, and for New Republic, three miles east.

Chualar, 128.5 miles, is a new town in the Salinas Valley, where a large business is done in raising cattle and sheep.

Gonzales, 134.5 miles, is another new and small but promising town.

Soledad, 142.9 miles, is the present terminus of this division, and derives its chief importance from this fact. Until the completion of the road to Los Angeles, the mails to Southern California went to Soledad by rail, and now overland passengers for San Luis Obispo and Paso Robles Hot Springs here take stages of the coast line for these points. These stages of this line run to Lowe's, 28 miles ; Solon, 40 miles; Paso Robles Hot Springs, 80 miles ; San Luis Obispo, 110 miles ; Arroyo Grande, 125 miles ; Guadaloupe, 140 miles ; Santa Barbara, 220 miles ; and there connect with stages for San Buena Ventura, 30 miles, and Newhall, 80 miles. The fare is about 8 cents a mile.

Another stage leaves daily for *Paradiso Springs,* eight miles south-west of Soledad. They are in a horseshoe-shaped plateau about 1500 feet above the level of the valley, affording a charming landscape, and with curative powers becoming quite celebrated. The four springs are of soda, sulphur, chalybeate of iron, and chloride of potassium, and vary from cold to 118° Fahrenheit. Game is abundant, the table is well supplied, the cottages neat, and every thing combines to make this as popular as the well-known and justly-celebrated Paso Robles.

To Southern California, Los Angeles, and Arizona

Via the Southern Pacific Railroad through the San Joaquin Valley.

The *Visalia Division* of the Central Pacific is operated in connection with the Southern Pacific from Goshen to Los Angeles, and forms the through line from San Francisco to Los Angeles. The train leaves San Francisco at 4 P. M., via Martinez and Antioch, reaching Lathrop for supper. At this point the Visalia Division begins, and extends southward up the San Joaquin Valley.

Morrano, 89.3 miles from San Francisco, is a side track and warehouse for shipping grain.

Ripon, 93 miles, is another side track and small station, near which the Stanislaus River is crossed.

Salida, 96 miles, is a similar station ; and *Modesto,* 102.8 miles, is the county seat of Stanislaus (pronounced Stan-is-law) County. In 1870, when the town was laid out, it was proposed to name it after the late Wm. C. Ralston, but his modesty forbade ; hence the name, the Spanish for modesty. It has a population of 1500, and is situated near the Tuolumne River.

Ceres, 107.4 miles,
Turlock, 115.9 miles,
Cressey, 126 miles, and
Atwater, 132.7 miles, are side tracks for shipping grain.

Between Turlock and Cressey the Merced River is crossed, flowing down and out of the Yosemite Valley.

Merced, 140.2 miles, was located through the exertion of Mr. C. H. Hoffman, a prominent land-owner, soon after the railroad was built, and has now become the county seat of Merced County, and the point of departure for the Yosemite Valley via Coulterville or Mariposa. See "Stage Routes to the Yosemite and Big Trees" for all information concerning travel to the valley.

The large hotel on the left of the road—the El Capitan—was erected by the railroad company to provide for the greater comfort of tourists. It is one of the most commodious structures for the purpose outside of San Francisco. The Court

THE PACIFIC TOURIST. 285

House is a credit to the town and county. It cost $75,000, and is the best in the San Joaquin Valley.

Artesian wells are numerous. In one of Mr. Hoffman's the water rises to within ten feet of the surface and is then pumped by steam, discharging at the rate of 30,000 gallons every hour.

There are two weekly papers, the *San Joaquin Valley Argus* and the *Merced Express*. The plain, especially toward the river, ten miles distant, abounds with hare, or the "jackass rabbit" (*Lepus Californicus*), and Merced is the starting-point of numerous coursing matches.

Much of the land is owned in large tracts. One of the farms of Miller & Lux is near this place. It is *ninety-seven* miles long, with an average width of fifteen miles.

In two years they built on it 780 miles of fence, costing $800 a mile. On this ranch are kept 150 saddle-horses ; and two oxen, besides calves, hogs, and sheep, are killed every other day for the workmen. It is said they can begin to drive cattle at Los Angeles and stop on their own land every night until they reach San Francisco. They send to the city 1800 oxen every month.

Leaving Merced, we cross a large number of sloughs and creeks, but all *decrease* in size as they go toward the river, and finally spread out over the plain or sink.

Plainsburg, 150.1 miles, is a small station on Deadman's Creek.

Minturn, 156.5 miles, is another small station, not far from Ash Slough.

Berenda, 166 miles, is also a new railroad town. Soon after leaving this place the Fresno River is crossed.

Madera, 173.5 miles, is a new town, started in 1876, and has a population of 400. It is the terminus of a V-shaped flume, 53 miles long, by which lumber is brought along the Fresno River from the immediate vicinity of the Fresno groves of Big Trees. It is owned by the California Lumber and Flume Company. The company have a planing-mill at Madera. The Fresno River supplies water also for extensive irrigation, and the ditches may be seen on the right of the railroad.

Madera will soon become known all over the world, because from it nearly all tourists will make their start for the Yosemite Valley. (See "Stage Routes to the Yosemite and Big Trees.") At this point a sleeping-car is detached from the train leaving San Francisco at 4 p. m., and remains upon a side track until morning, thus insuring a full night's rest and refreshment.

Borden, 176.3 miles, is a town of 200 people ; the surrounding country having the benefit of the water brought from the Fresno River. Cottonwood Creek may be noticed when filled by

the winter rains. It is crossed after leaving the station.

Sycamore, 185.3 miles, is a side track, but marks the crossing of the San Joaquin River, at the head of navigation for steamers during the high water of the winter season.

Fresno, 195.1 miles, is the county seat of Fresno County, with a population of nearly 1000. The Court House is the largest building, and cost $60,000. The soil is mostly good, but crops can be secured only by irrigation. A stage runs to Centerville, in the foot-hills, 17 miles east.

Two weekly newspapers are published here, the *Fresno Expositor* and the *Republican.*

The town has a bank, and does a large business with the surrounding country. One firm sells $120,000 per year, and the receipts for passengers and freight are $70,000 a month.

The town is located on a rich, alluvial, sandy plain, between the King and San Joaquin rivers, and the abundance of water for irrigation and the canals built and projected destine this to be one of the most fruitful portions of the whole State. There are five hotels, the principal being the Henry House.

The *Central California Colony* is located on these rich lands, where the growth of trees, shrubs, and alfalfa is astonishing. The lots are 40 acres each and are sold on small installments, and are worthy the attention of settlers with small means.

Fowler, 204.7 miles,

Kingsbury, 215.2 miles, and

Cross Creek, 223.3 miles, are small stations. King's River, which is crossed between Kingsbury and Cross Creek, rises in the high Sierras. The course of the railroad being parallel to the axis of the Sierras, the traveler has a succession of magnificent and ever-changing views.

Goshen, 229.1 miles, is where the *Southern Pacific Railroad* connects with the Visalia branch of the Central. The northern terminus of this part of the Southern Pacific is not at Goshen but at Huron, 40 miles west of Goshen. These 40 miles are the *Goshen Division* of the Southern Pacific.

On the GOSHEN *division,*

Hanford is 12.9 miles from Goshen, in what is called the Mussel Slough country, a region on the north of Tulare Lake, embracing one of the richest portions of the State. Five crops of alfalfa may be cut during the year. Corn grows to a height of twelve to eighteen feet, but the yield does not exceed sixty or seventy bushels to the acre. Pumpkins are immense.

Lemoore, 20.9 miles from Goshen, is a new and promising village.

Heinlen is 22.5 miles from Goshen, and *Huron* 40 miles. All these are in the *Mussel Slough* country. Huron is the terminus at present.

At *Goshen* there is another branch railroad to *Visalia*. It is only seven miles long, and was built by the people of Visalia, the principal and county town of Tulare County. This *Visalia Railroad* is wholly independent of the Central and Southern Pacific roads, the president and manager being R. E. Hyde, Esq., of Visalia.

Visalia is an old town, laid out shortly after the occupation of the country by the Americans. It has a population of about 2000 ; one of the best court houses in the San Joaquin Valley south of Stockton ; six hotels, three churches, a substantial bank, several mills, gas and water works, and three weekly papers—the *Delta*, *Times*, and *Iron Age*. A United States land office is located here.

Soon after leaving Goshen, there is a tangent to Lerdo—50 miles—the longest piece of straight track on the road.

Tulare, 239.6 miles from San Francisco, has a population of nearly 1000, and a round-house for the Tulare Division of the Southern Pacific Railroad.

It is an important point for shipping wood and wool. The eucalyptus-tree may be seen growing luxuriantly wherever planted.

This part of the great San Joaquin Valley is often called the Tulare Valley. It is only 327 feet above the sea-level, and is well timbered. The groves of beautiful oaks are like natural parks inviting occupancy.

Tulare Lake lies south-west, is nearly circular in form, 30 miles long. and covers an area of 700 square miles. It abounds in fish and water-fowl. After leaving Tulare, the railroad crosses Tulare River, a narrow channel, and reaches

Tipton, 250 miles from San Francisco, where the character of the land changes, the groves disappearing.

Alila, 262 miles,

Delano, 270.3 miles, and

Posa, 282 1 miles, are small stations on the great plain ; and

Lerdo, 290.1 miles, is a station of the same character, but the shipping-point for the *Buena Vista Oil Works*, about 40 miles south-west. The oil region does not bid fair to rival Pennsylvania's, but Californians are always looking for new and rich developments. Lerdo is the proposed point of junction with the branch of the Northern Division, now built to Soledad, to be extended through the Polonio Pass.

Near the next station the railroad crosses King's River, flowing from the high Sierras and the glaciers of Mounts Tyndall and Whitney, and running south in these high Sierras from these peaks directly east of Visalia until east of Sumner. After flowing a long distance to the west, the river turns to the north and flows into Tulare Lake.

Where the Kern River leaves the mountains and turns toward the plain is Walker's Pass (through the Sierras), thence a road north to Owen's Lake, into which a river of the same name flows. The lake is about 20 miles long and 10 wide.

Sumner, 302.5 miles, is a busy point, with a population of about 300. It is the depot for *Bakersfield*, the principal town in what is called the *Kern Valley*, and county town of Kern County. Kern Valley, like Tulare, is a part of the San Joaquin. The land is a rich sedimentary deposit. In this valley are the most extensive irrigating canals and ditches to be found in the State. Some are 40 miles long and 275 feet wide and 8 feet deep. A system has also been adopted to reclaim swamp lands in the valley, by which 65,000 acres will be brought into market. On all these lands water is abundant, and two crops can be raised each year. Sweet potatoes are found weighing 24 pounds each, alfalfa producing seven crops of from one to two tons each to the acre, and corn producing from 60 to 120 bushels per acre ; and the growth of cotton has been successfully tried, producing 400 pounds to the acre. On one of the farms of Mr. H. P. Livermore, of San Francisco, two artesian wells, 260 and 300 feet deep, send water 12 feet above the surface of the ground, and discharge each through a seven-inch pipe from 3000 to 4000 gallons per hour ; 3500 acres are in alfalfa. Mr. Livermore has a dairy of 300 cows, a large apiary, and 4000 stock cattle, besides horses, mules, sheep, and hogs.

One of the plows used, the "Great Western," is the largest in the world, and requires eighty oxen with a ton of chains and a ton of ox yokes to use it, and cuts a furrow five feet wide, and, if necessary, three feet deep, at the rate of eight miles a day. Another plow, "Sampson," a little smaller, requires from 30 to 40 mules for use in ditching.

Messrs. Carr & Haggin, of San Francisco, have a number of ranches in this valley, and on them 40,000 sheep.

One man raised 18,000 lbs. of sweet potatoes—350 bushels to the acre. One half acre of sweet potatoes yielded $150.

One man moved on 40 acres of land April 26th, 1877, and on November 1st, 1877, had grown and sold $2000 worth of corn, beans, and pumpkins. But it is said to be *hot* and malarious about Bakersfield, the mercury standing at 110° and 120° for days in succession.

The town of Bakersfield has a population of about 1000, good public buildings, a bank, two weekly papers, the *Courier-Californian* and the *Gazette*.

At Sumner the grade begins for ascending the Sierras, but just before reaching Pampa there is a descent of about 80 feet to cross Basin Creek (so named from Walker's Basin on the east), after which the ascent is resumed and the road soon follows Caliente Creek, crossing and recrossing it a number of times.

Pampa, 317.5 miles, is a small station.

Caliente, 324.8 miles, has an elevation of 1290 feet. It is at the junction of the Caliente and Tehachapi creeks. The axis of the Sierras runs south-west about 20 miles from Caliente to Tejon (Tay-hone) Pass. Caliente was long the southern terminus of the Tulare Division, and stages ran from this point to the railroad 20 miles north of Los Angeles. It is now the shipping-point for considerable freight.

Stages leave daily for Havilah, 25 miles, and Kernville, 45 miles, both in Kern County and north-east of this station. The population is only 100.

Tehachapi Pass.

The Tehachapi Creek flows down the mountain from the south-east, and at Caliente one can look directly up the Tehachapi Cañon for some distance.

As one approached the station, he saw the railroad on the right only a short distance away ; and on leaving the station, the train bends around the few houses and goes down the creek, but it continues and increases its steep and wonderful climb. For twenty miles the grade, including curvature, is 116 feet to the mile. So accurately and constantly are the grades and curvatures adjusted to one another, with reference to obtaining a uniform traction, that the whole is a piece of work not only unique in plan but unsurpassed in execution. A writer of world-wide travel calls it a remarkable triumph of engineering science, and says, "I know of nothing like it, unless it be the road over the Styrian Alps from Vienna to Trieste ; and even there, if I remember rightly, the track does not literally cross itself." Prof. George Davidson, of the United States Coast Survey, says it is not equaled by any railroad engineering he has seen in America or Europe. It is a marvel of genius and perfection that will give lasting honor to Colonel George E. Gray, the Chief Engineer of the road, and to his efficient assistant, William Hood, Esq., by whom all plans, suggestions, and directions were faithfully carried out.

Cape Horn, on the Central Pacific, presented no difficulty to be compared with the Tehachapi. To overcome the former was an act of courage, but requiring far less ingenuity and skill than to build successfully and economically in this defile.

But the tourist will prefer to see for himself, and his attention will be divided between the work and the scenery of the cañon. The latter is not majestic, like that on the American River, but quite picturesque and often grand.

Leaving Caliente, the Tehachapi Creek is lost sight of, and the road winds around among the hills.

Bealeville, 330.1 miles, is a small station, honoring General Beale. When approaching and at it, a pretty view may be had of the rugged hills on the left beyond Caliente. Under the morning sun on the numerous ridges and valleys, coming down from the long mountain chain, there are ever-varying lines of light and shade.

After leaving Bealeville the road passes around Clear Creek Cañon, one of the most formidable pieces of work on the mountain, having in it tunnels 3, 4, 5, and 6 ; and as you enter the cañon, you see on the left the road ascending the opposite wall of the cañon more than a hundred feet above, and it is only three or four hundred yards across the cañon !

The tunnels are numerous, there being seventeen between Caliente and the summit. The shortest is No. 11, 158.8 feet, and the longest, No. 5, 1156.3 feet. The aggregate length of the seventeen is 7683.9 feet.

On emerging from tunnel No. 6, six miles from Caliente, the Tehachapi creek and cañon are seen below, and Caliente itself only a mile away, but about six hundred feet below the train !

The old road to Havilah and Kernville appears like a trail on the hills beyond Caliente, and the new road may be seen following up the cañon of Caliente Creek.

Oaks are now becoming more numerous and beautifying the hillsides. The old stage-road to Los Angeles is far away and above on the right. And now there begins to appear the "Spanish-bayonet" (*Yucca Gloriosa*), one of the loveliest flowers that adorns the land. When it blossoms in early spring, it will attract and enthuse every one. On the top of its tall, straight, single stem is a great panicle of snow-white blossoms, and the whole air is richly laden with their most delicious fragrance. It partakes somewhat of the character of the night-blooming cereus, for the fullest bloom and sweetest fragrance are in the night. Twelve hundred blossoms may be counted on a single stalk, and in the vicinity of Los Angeles, where the stalk grows fifteen feet high, *six thousand blossoms* have been found.

The scenery now grows wilder ; the rocks in the cañon are sharper and more forbidding, and piled higher and higher. In the narrow cañon there are rocks frowning from above, and rising up from the crooked defile of the creek 700 feet below. .

On passing through Tunnel 8, one may notice how rapidly the bed of the creek is rising. The heavy cuts also indicate the difficult character of the work. The rock is granitoid, yet, solid and safe as the tunnels through it seem, the fearful may take courage, for assurance is doubly sure, all the tunnels being lined with the cedars of Oregon.

An occasional pine is now seen, and as the altitude increases they will become more numerous.

As one looks back down the cañon, he may see the top of Breckenbridge Mountain. It was hid at Caliente, but has now crawled up into view. The old stage-road is crossed and recrossed, and at length the railroad crosses the Tehachapi Creek itself. Off to the right we have a pretty view of Bear Mountain, a peak of the Sierras. It is snow-crowned late in the spring.

The track then curves, making the "Twitty Creek Bend," from which, in clear atmosphere, one may look out over the wide expanse of the San Joaquin Valley, off hundreds of miles towards San Francisco.

We recross the Tehachapi Creek, just as we approach

Keene, 338 miles. It is a small station. Around it there are many points of interest in the mountain scenery, but the view is not extensive or sublime. On the right of Keene is that familiar friend, Bear Mountain, heavily timbered. It appeared often along the road, and at Caliente seemed as near as it now does.

Then crossing and almost immediately recrossing the creek, the road makes a long curve to the right, turns again sharply to the left to pass through tunnel 9 and pass around the *Loop.*

The road-bed is no longer far above the creek, and how to ascend without expending millions for long tunnels was the problem the Loop solved. Here the cañon of the Tehachapi has widened, and in it there is a conical-shaped hill. Beneath this the train goes through tunnel 9, and emerging it curves to the left and climbs this same hill and crosses the track, with a difference in elevation of 77.46 feet. Tunnel 9 is 426.2 feet long ; the loop-line is 3794.7 feet ; the curvature, 300° 52' ; the limit of curvature, 10° ; and the radius, 573.7 feet. Then, by a fill of 150,000 cubic yards, the road passes from the peak around which it curved over to the wall of the cañon, and is again far above the bed of the creek. Or suppose one starts with the civil engineer to go down the mountain. He can not descend as rapidly as the creek tumbles over the rocks, and he reaches the narrow part of the cañon, but can not get down where his road can follow it. So he drops it down by means of the loop, and for saving money "there's millions in it."

In curving around the hill, after passing through tunnel 9, and on the north-east side of the hill, there is a heavy cut that required much blasting, and here were used the largest blasts exploded on the line of the road, and larger than any used on the Central Pacific.

The best view of the Loop is had just before entering tunnel 10, by looking back down the cañon. Five lines of railroad are crossing and recrossing the cañon. Between tunnels 10 and

11, and just before entering tunnel 11, one may see on the right the top of a lofty peak, covered with brush, but without trees. Call it after yourself, or the "enterprising newsboy," or what you choose, for it has no name.

After passing tunnel 11 the train has reached *Girard,* 343.8 miles. It is a small station. The old stage-road comes near, but it is down in the bottom of the cañon. It looks as if the summit was close at hand, but it is nearly nine miles away. The open country is an indication of its approach, but numerous spurs of troublesome rock must yet be pierced with tunnels ; and these too have all been timbered with the cedars of Oregon.

Tunnels 12 and 13 are almost continuous, and 14 only far enough distant to open your guide-book, and so you continue to alternate in light and darkness, on the solid rock and deep ravines. The creek below is gradually approaching. It is crossed and recrossed, once on a high trestle. In the tunnels and rocks and ravines we still have a country as rugged as any railroad builders need care to face.

At length the tunnels are all passed and the cañon begins to widen, showing the near approach of the summit. The road is no longer in Tehachapi Cañon, but in Tehachapi Valley.

The stage and rail road are side by side. When the hot sun of summer has burned up every thing else, here may be seen prettily-colored patches of vegetation. It is the tar-weed, and will stick to one's boots as it does to the noses of the cattle.

At last the station called

Tehachapi Summit, 350.2 miles, is reached, but the highest point, or *the* summit, is about two miles beyond, or south. This station is the nearest one to the summit. About two miles to the right is the old town of Tehachapi, with about twenty houses. It is on the old stage-road, but the new town will eventually outrival it.

On the broad top of the range and down the sides sheep find nutritious pasture. About five miles away is a marble quarry, and on this ridge there is also a little placer-mining.

The summit appears like a broad plain. The highest elevation is 4026 feet. On the broad plateau and on the right of the road there is a small lake, and it would not be worth mentioning if it was not salt. Digging down a few inches around its shores reaches rock salt.

The water has never been known to flow out of this lake and off the summit. White Rock Creek, erroneously laid down on some maps as flowing out on the plains near Mojave, empties when flowing at all into this lake.

From the little "divide," crossed just south of the lake, the road descends toward Cameron's Cañon, and follows this out of the mountain.

Cameron, 359.4 miles, is a small station. About half a mile from this the road enters the cañon, with walls from 500 to 700 feet high on the south and very much higher on the north.

This cañon is of peculiar interest, being an earthquake crack more than five miles long. Stopping to examine minutely the general slope of the mountains, the strata, or the walls would be inconvenient, but repay one who can do so. After crossing the Mojave Plains near Alpine another earthquake crack, and of recent origin, is unmistakably recorded. The Spanish-bayonet is abundant in the cañon.

Nadeau, 364.6 miles, is a small station in the cañon. A stream of water runs down the cañon, and it appears as if the winter rains would carry off the road-bed, but it is 10 or 12 feet above high water.

On leaving the cañon, the water channel continues to the left of the road a mile or two and there sinks, leaving when dry white patches of alkali and salt. Leaving the cañon, the road curves to the right and approaches the first station on the plains.

Here a new object of interest appears in the Yucca Draconis. It is peculiar to these plains, and for miles along the road will attract attention. It is palm-like, and often called a "palm" and "cactus," but *it is neither.* It is a yucca, and a remarkable tree. It is exogenous, and grows from ten to twenty feet high, has a trunk 18 or 20 inches in diameter, and terminates in stumpy branches, each having at the extreme end a tuft of dagger-shaped leaves. Out of each bunch of foliage grows a panicle of blossoms with greenish petals bearing large seed-vessels, but not remarkable for either beauty or fragrance. How often each tree blossoms is not known, but not every year, and some say once in four years. The trunk has numerous layers of fibers, which run spirally, and each layer is at an angle to the next.

The bark is removed, and the *trunk used for making paper.* It is crushed into a pulp at Ravenna, a station in the Soledad Cañon, and the pulp taken to a mill near San José and manufactured. Experts have pronounced it adapted for making a superior class of bank-note paper of great durability.

Mojave, 370.2 miles, and the terminus of the Tulare and also the Mojave Division. It is the only eating-station between the San Joaquin Valley and Los Angeles, and butter, milk, and all provisions must be transported over the mountains, and the water is carried in pipes from a spring near Cameron station, ten miles away.

Besides the hotel, there are several stores, some shops and residences. The railroad company has a round-house for fifteen engines, a machine-shop, and a large freight warehouse. Freight wagons are always on hand to unload bullion and carry supplies to Darwin, 100 miles, Lone Pine, Cerro Gordo, and Independence, 168

miles, directly north in Inyo County. The Cerro Gordo Freighting Company alone employ 700 head of horses.

Stages leave Mojave every other day for Darwin, 106 miles, Cerro Gordo, 135 miles, Lone Pine, 145 miles, and Independence, 164 miles. Stage fare, about 20 cents a mile. These plains extend eastward as far as the eye can reach, and on the west there is a semicircle of mountains. The heated sand causes the wind to rush furiously, and early in the history of the road "Mojave zephyr" was a well-fixed term. From Mojave it is only about 75 miles to Colton *via* the Cajon Pass. Mojave is the point of divergence of the proposed Thirty-fifth Parallel road, surveyed to the Colorado River at "The Needles," 254 miles east.

This survey crossed the sink of the Mojave River at an altitude of 960 feet, and crossed the Providence Mountains *via* Granite Pass at an elevation of 3935 feet.

The *Atlantic and Pacific Railroad Company* had also a charter from San Francisco to the Colorado, following the coast to the mouth of the Santa Clara River, thence east to Soledad Pass, and across the desert to the Colorado.

The course to be now followed from Mojave is nearly south. The Yucca Draconis is more abundant. Numerous buttes, hundreds of feet high, are seen. They are of soft granite and sandstone rock, showing that the country is not volcanic. The highest are on the right. It is quite probable that these are the peaks of a submerged mountain chain.

Gloster, 376.8 miles, is named a station, but there is neither house nor side-track ; and

Sand Creek, 384 miles, is also dreary. But water is only a few feet below the surface, and this peculiarity extends over nearly all the plains, and promises well for future development. Now the plains furnish a valuable stock-range, as they abound with bunch and other nutritious grasses. In the spring of the year these plains are a vast and most beautiful flower-bed, perhaps unequaled by any other gathering of colors to be found in California.

Between Sand Creek and Lancaster the road begins to ascend, the lowest elevation being 2300 feet, about six miles south of Sand Creek station. Off to the left there seems to be an ocean ; it is sand and alkali, and the well-known "mirage of the desert."

Lancaster, 395 miles, is only a side track. About half a mile north of the next station, the road passes through a cut of chalky-looking rock, and after the cut comes a fill of the same material.

This is the wave of an earthquake made in 1868, and the wave may be traced for miles. In places juniper-trees may be found half buried yet erect.

19

The Yucca Gloriosa, which disappeared in Cameron's Cañon, now reappears and is seen nearly all the way to Los Angeles.

Alpine, 405.9 miles, a side track, brings us face to face with the San Gabriel Mountains. This range directly ahead is between nine and ten thousand feet high, and the other side of these mountains will be seen from Los Angeles. This range is the Sierra Madre, or San Gabriel, Mountains, and on the west the range connects with the San Fernando Mountains at the San Fernando Pass. Ascending from Alpine to the summit, and looking back and to the left, there is a beautiful view of the Mojave Plains and the mountains we crossed.

The maximum grade is 116 feet. The summit of Soledad Pass has an elevation of 3211 feet.

Acton, 415.6 miles, is a side track. The road follows the Santa Clara, in an open valley from the summit nearly to Ravenna, where the valley narrows and continues as the Soledad Cañon to and beyond Lang. The Soledad is a wild and rugged cañon, a "Robber's Roost," but was never the home of that notorious outlaw, Tiburcio Vasquez. This murderous chief had his head-quarters near Elizabeth Lake, about 25 miles north-west of Alpine, and he ranged all over the mountains of Southern California.

Ravenna, 419.3 miles, a small station and cluster of houses occupied by Mexicans. Here is the mill in which the Yucca Draconis is crushed to a pulp preparatory to its shipment to a paper-mill near San José. No one will be likely to travel long in California and not see the California-quail (*Lophortyx Californicus*) ; but if any one has failed, he may surely see them in this cañon, for they find a secure home in these impenetrable thickets. The plume, or crest, has from three to six feathers, about an inch and a half long, and will probably be erect, though it is often lowered, falling over the bill. This quail always roosts on trees.

The plumed or "mountain quail" (*Oreortyx Pictus*), with a crest of two feathers three and a half inches long, is never found south of the Tejon (Tay-hone) Pass.

Deer and bear are also plentiful in these mountains. Before leaving Ravenna, the side hills on the right may be seen honeycombed with tunnels, built during a brief but wild mining excitement. There is a little placer-mining carried on by the Mexicans, who farm on a small scale during the summer, and mine on the same scale during the wet season.

Between Ravenna and Lang are tunnels 18 and 19, the walls of the cañon 900 feet high, the mountains much higher, and some of the crookedest and most picturesque country on the road. It was in this region, half a mile east of Lang, where the "last spike" was driven, September 5th, 1876, which completed the line between San Francisco and Los Angeles.

Lang, 427.8 miles, is a small station.

The valley grows wider, and we soon find a "stock country." As we reach Newhall, the road leaves the main Santa Clara Valley, and turns up the south fork of the Santa Clara River and follows this nearly to Andrews.

Newhall, 437.9 miles, is a stage station where stages connect daily for San Buena Ventura, 50 miles ; Santa Barbara, 80 miles, and there connecting with the coast line of stages for San Luis Obispo, Pass Robles, and Soledad. Local fares, about 10 cents a mile.

This station is in the midst of a fine grazing country.

Andrews, 441.5 miles, a small station. Here are two refineries for crude petroleum, which is found in paying quantities a few miles distant. The oil region of California may be traced in a line almost straight from Watsonville, in Monterey County, through Santa Barbara and Ventura counties into Los Angeles County at San Fernando, and thence on to San Bernardino. The road now leaves the south fork of the river and turns up the cañon, in which the north portal of the San Fernando Tunnel is situated.

The Sierra de San Fernando Mountains are now directly ahead. There was no practicable pass, hence one of the longest tunnels in America—6967 feet—in which the lamps will be needed to keep away gloomy thoughts, for nine minutes are spent by all trains in passing through it. The Hoosac is the only tunnel in America of greater length. This tunnel is approached on a maximum grade of 116 feet, and at the north end has an elevation of 1479 feet. In the tunnel the grade is 37 feet, descending southward. It is timbered from end to end, although cut through rock. At the south mouth of the tunnel we find the station called

San Fernando Tunnel, 444.4 miles.

The descending grade now increases, and we drop down as we go south 116 feet per mile for about five miles, down the San Fernando Creek, and the country opens into the San Fernando Valley.

San Fernando, 449.6 miles. Two miles east is the old mission of the same name, one of the most interesting in the State. It is well preserved, and its gardens beautifully kept. The building is locked, but the keys are under the care of the Catholic clergy in Los Angeles. The groves of orange and lemon trees are like an oasis to one who rides on horseback over the country.

Interesting specimens of cactus are on all sides. It is one of the Opuntias, sometimes called the *junl* cactus, and grows twenty feet high. Near San Fernando, at the Tehunga Wash, are beautiful specimens of the Agave Americana, the most remarkable of all the agaves. It is the *maguay* of the Mexicans, commonly called the American aloe, or century-plant. It is frequently seen in the gardens of California, but here may be seen the fleshy spiny-toothed leaves, above the Ceanothus brevifolia of the region. The flower-stalk shoots up from 20 to 30 feet.

Petroleum is found in Rice Cañon, not far away, and there is supposed to be a general diffusion of oil underlying all this San Fernando district.

Sepulveda, 462.1 miles, is a side track on the bank of the Los Angeles River, which the road crosses near the depot.

Los Angeles, 470.7 miles. Here are located, near the depot, the shops of the railroad company — quite a town of themselves. It is the metropolitan city of Southern California, with a population of about 16,000, banks, wholesale and retail stores, shops and factories, and hotels. Of the latter the Pico and the St. Charles are first class. It has many imposing edifices and blocks of fine buildings, and four daily and seven weekly papers. The dailies—the *Star, Express, Herald,* and *Republican*—circulate over all of Southern California.

The city was founded September 4th, 1781 ; is situated on the Los Angeles River, 30 miles from its mouth, and in a large valley that fronts on the Pacific Ocean ; and has two rival harbors, Wilmington and Santa Monica. The area of the city embraces six square miles. The full name of the city is *Pueblo de la Reina de los Angeles* ("Town of the Queen of the Angels"). From every point of the city the panorama is grand, especially when the Sierra Madre Mountains are in the background. It is the railroad center of Southern California, and has already roads extending in five directions.

It is the seat of a Roman Catholic bishop, and has a cathedral which is the finest church building outside of San Francisco. The several prominent Protestant denominations have organizations, including the Methodist, Presbyterian, and Episcopal. The Roman Catholics have a college located here, and the Sisters of Charity a female seminary ; and besides these there is an academic institute and good public schools.

There is also a public library, an organized fire department, and the city is supplied with gas and water, and has street railroads extending from the center in every direction. It was made a city and the capital of California by the Mexican Congress in 1836, and captured by the United States forces under Commodore Stockton and General Kearney in 1846.

It is celebrated for a mild and equable climate, fertile soil, the luxuriant growth of semi-tropical fruits and flowers, and the abundant products of its vineyards and orange groves.

Leaving Los Angeles for Arizona, about a mile south of the depot, the road turns east and re-crosses the Los Angeles River and goes into the San Gabriel Valley, and on east to San Gorgonio Pass, *Pasadena.*

San Gabriel is 9.2 miles from Los Angeles, and the station for San Gabriel Valley, which lies to the right and is watered by the San Gabriel River. It is the seat of an old mission of the same name founded September 8th, 1771. This is now dilapidated, as are all these old Spanish missions, but the ancient bells still hang in their belfry. It has the oldest orange orchard in the State.

Near this station is an orchard of 500 acres, the largest in the State—that of Mr. L. J. Rose. It has oranges, lemons, olives, figs, limes, walnuts, almonds, bananas, pineapples, and almost every variety of tropical and semi-tropical nuts and fruits.

The *Sierra Madre Villa* is a lovely spot, where stands a hotel well appointed and kept, 1800 feet above the sea, overlooking the thousands of groves in the Los Angeles Valley.

The choicest of all the " Los Angeles orange groves " are in this valley.

John Muir says : " The sun valley of San Gabriel is one of the brightest spots to be found in all our bright land, and most of its brightness is wildness—wild, south sunshine in a basin rimmed about with mountains and hills."

And Dr. Congar, his friend, says to him : " I have rambled ever since we left college, tasting innumerable climates, and trying the advantages offered by nearly every new State and Territory. Here I have made my home, and here I shall stay while I live. The geographical position is exactly right, soil and climate perfect, and every thing that heart can wish comes for our efforts—flowers, fruits, milk and honey, and plenty of money."

Mr. Muir also says persons suffering from advanced pulmonary disease are not benefited here, and too many seek these delightful regions too late and only to die.

After passing the old mission of San Gabriel, and crossing the river of the same name, the road follows a tributary of the river known as the San José Creek to the plains in the direction of San Bernardino.

Savanna, 11.7 miles from Los Angeles, is a small station with fruitful fields of corn and grain, and beautiful groves of oranges and lemons, and large vineyards around it. The San Gabriel Valley is still on the right.

Monte, 13.1 miles, is the old town of El Monte, a thriving place in a perfect garden-spot. It is almost impossible to keep the weeds from choking the corn ; but for all that, the corn is not stunted. Much of the corn is fed to hogs without being shipped.

Puente, 19.3 miles from Los Angeles, is a signal station, around which Mexicans are numerous —as, in fact, they are in all Southern California, constituting about one fourth of the whole people.

Spadra, 29.3 miles, is just 500 miles from San Francisco, and a town of a few houses.

Pomona, 32.8 miles, is a pretty town of 500 people, with luxurious vegetation. Artesian wells supply water for the town and for irrigation. A reservoir holding 3,000,000 gallons is connected with the works.

Cucamonga, 42.3 miles, is only a signal station, near a ranch of the same name famed for its wines.

Rincon settlement is ten miles south, irrigated by the Santa Ana River. This river rises in the San Bernardino Mountains, and is sometimes called the San Bernardino River. Its waters irrigate numerous colonies, among them Riverside, Santa Ana, Orange, and Anaheim.

Colton, 57.5 miles, is named after General D. D. Colton, the vice-president of the road. Trains going east stop here for supper, and coming west stop for breakfast. It has only 200 people, but a busy set, for it is the depot for San Bernardino on the north and Riverside on the south, and is itself the seat of a promising colony. Owing to the nature of the soil, it is free from all malarial influences, and has probably as desirable a climate for invalids as any place on the coast.

Colton is the seat of a new and promising colony, one having 20,000 acres of land divided into farms of 10 acres and upward. Another, the Slova Mountain Colony, adjoins the town, and has fine soil and pure water from Mix's Ranch.

The railroad company has large warehouses to accommodate the freight from San Bernardino and Riverside. Stages connect with all trains for these two towns. Fare to San Bernardino, 50 cents; to Riverside, 75 cents. Near the station on the left is Slova Mountain, from which marble is obtained.

Riverside is 7 miles south-west of Colton. It has 2000 people, three churches, and good schools, and 8000 acres of choice agricultural land supplied with abundant water for irrigation. It has all the advantages of climate that are found in the San Bernardino Valley, and its dry air gives it a claim to be called the "Asthmatic's Paradise." With mountains on nearly every side, its situation is beautiful.

Twenty miles south-west are the *Temescal Warm Springs,* on a plateau of Temescal Mountain, 1500 feet above a valley of the same name. Frost is not known at this place, owing to a belt of warm air in which the springs are found.

San Bernardino, 4 miles north of Colton, is the county town of San Bernardino County, and has a population of 6000, two banks, four churches, good hotels, two daily and two weekly newspapers. Nordhoff says it has a climate in winter preferable to that of Los Angeles, and no hotter

in summer. Two hundred artesian wells spout out pure cold water that ripples through beautiful streets, orchards, and orange groves. The valley contains 2500 square miles, with variety of climate as you ascend the mountain. It is free from the fogs of the coast, and strawberries may be picked in winter as well as summer.

Old San Bernardino is also a town in this valley near the railroad. It was the first settlement, the home of the Mormons who located in 1847. All now remaining are "Josephites." Here are the oldest orange groves in the valley, and the fruit of this region and Riverside surpasses that of San Gabriel or any part of the coast in sweetness and appearance. It is free from the black saline rust that covers so much of the golden color nearer the coast.

Crafton's Retreat, Arrowhead, and Waterman's Mineral Springs are places of resort in this vicinity, and all the valleys and mountains abound with game. Quail, deer, and rabbits are especially plentiful.

Soon after leaving Colton, the road crosses the Santa Ana River, and continues an easterly course through Old San Bernardino, and up the San Miguel Creek to the San Gorgonio Pass, where the San Bernardino and San Jacinto ranges unite.

Mound City, 60.9 miles,

El Casco, 72 miles, and

San Gorgonio, 80.6 miles, are all signal stations.

There is nothing inviting in the character of the soil, and but little for the tourist to miss while he sleeps as the train ascends to the San Gorgonio Pass, 2592 feet above the sea. Here the descent begins, the road passing down the broad open valley without following any defined watercourse until it reaches White Water River, a durable stream of water flowing out of the San Bernardino range. At this point the valley grows broader, and finally opens out into what is known as Cabazon Valley, down which the road continues to Indio.

Banning, 86.8 miles, is a signal station, and **Cabazon,** 92.7, a telegraph station. Wood from the San Jacinto Mountains on the south is brought down to the railroad at this point. Named from the Indians.

White Water, 101.2 miles, named from the creek, signifying its great importance in a dry and thirsty land. It is in the midst of the cacti, many varieties being found here. The cactus grows only in gravelly land, and the zone of it will disappear and reappear again near Mammoth Tank. There are many forms of the Mamillaria, Echinocactus, and several of the Opuntia, but none of the Cereus.

The Opuntias are with both cylindrical and elliptical stems. The spinose Opuntia the Mexicans call *Choya.*

The gigantic "nigger-head" (*Echinocactus Cy-*

lindraceus) lifts its bristling trunk sometimes four feet, and is three feet in diameter, covered with fish-hooks. The Mexicans call it *bisnaga*. It can be roasted to secure a drink that will collect in a central cavity, and its fruit can be eaten in small quantities.

Sandstorms are a noteworthy characteristic of this desert, and especially between White Water and Walters. They occur during the winter and spring. The winds come principally from the north-west, raising and carrying before them great clouds of pulverized sand and dust. The approach of the storm may be seen when it is distant several hours. The fine dust will penetrate every thing. No garments are protection against it. These storms last generally one day, sometimes three days.

Seven Palms, 108.7 miles, a signal station.

Between Seven Palms and Indio there may be seen on the north and east occasional groves of palm-trees, along the foot-slopes of the San Bernardino Mountains. This is *the only opportunity to see palm-trees* on all the road, and a good picture of them will be more satisfactory. These distant ones (*Brahia Mexicana*) are like the palmetto of South Carolina except in the extreme roughness of the serration of the leaf-stalk. They grow to a height of 60 feet. These are also the only kind of palm-trees to be found on the desert. The numerous forms of the cereus, and one of which, the candelabra, called by the Mexicans *saghuará*, sometimes two and a half feet thick and fifty feet high, are found only east of the Colorado River.

Emigrants crossing the desert from the east hailed these groves with joy, for water could be had either in springs or near the surface, wherever the palm-tree grows. About three or four miles west of Indio, the road goes below sealevel, and continues below for about 61 miles !

Indio, 129.5 miles, is a signal station, 262 feet below sea-level !

Sagebrush is nowhere found on this desert, and but little of it on the Mojave Plains. Here we find two of the species of the mesquite-tree (1) the flat pod (*Algarobia Glandulosa*), and (2) the screw-bean (*Strombocarpa Pubescens*). The flat pod is the largest, most abundant, and most valuable. The long, bean-shaped pod is greedily devoured by cattle, and highly nutritious. A gum exudes from the tree which closely resembles gum arabic in its chemical characters. The trees grow 15 or 20 feet high. The screw-bean mesquite is a smaller tree than the flat pod, in some localities much rarer, and is less valuable for food.

Walters, 142.8 miles, is where passenger trains meet. It is 135 feet below the sea-level. Eleven miles east of Walters is the lowest point reached, the *minus elevation* being 266¼ feet ! The lowest point of the valley is 287½ feet, and the whole depression is about 100 miles long and from 10

to 50 miles wide. In the lowest levels is found an immense deposit of rock salt, destined to be a source of great industry.

Dos Palmos, 160.2 miles, is a telegraph station, and the only place between Colton and Yuma at which there is local traffic.

Stages leave this point on *alternate* days for Ehrenberg, 109 miles, Wickenberg, 236 miles, and Prescott, 297 miles. Fare, about 20 cents a mile—to Ehrenberg, $20.

Dos Palmos is about 7 miles from an old stagestation where two palm-trees grew by the side of a large spring—hence its name.

Frink's Spring, 171.1 miles, a signal station. Depression, 260 feet.

Five miles south are mud springs, covering many miles. Some look like craters. Mr. Hood, who has visited and examined them, is of the opinion that the hot water dissolves and carries off the mud about the mouth, and thereby causes the ground to cave. Gases and steam issue from some of these, although no geyser action has been noticed there so extensive as Major Heintzelman reported, in November, 1852, from another locality about 4.5 miles south-west of Yuma.

Between this station and Flowing Well are some new and striking forms of vegetation that will grow more abundant. Among them are the " palo verde," the " ocotilla" (oc-co-tee'-yah), " iron-wood " tree, and the " galleta" (gah-yee'-tay) grass. *Palo verde* is the Mexican for green pole. This (*Cercidium Floridum*) resembles the willow slightly, and flowers in May. It is then almost covered with beautiful, sweet trumpetshaped flowers. In fruit it bears an abundance of beans.

From Dos Palmos to a point between Frink's Spring and Flowing Well there is no brush—nothing but complete waste and utter desolation.

Flowing Well, 188.8 miles, with an elevation of 5 feet above sea-level. Here an artesian well was bored, and at 160 feet obtained a fine flow of water, but it was " marah"—too salt to use. All the stations to Yuma are now only signal stations —*i. e.,* the train runs 88⅓ miles—we may almost say from Colton, 191 miles—without local traffic.

Between Flowing Well and the Colorado River there is an abundance of the creosote-bush (*Larrea Mexicana*). It is often included in the vague term " grease-wood." Between Mammoth Tank and Yuma it is the prevailing underbrush. The leaf is waxy-like, the bark very dark brown, almost black, and it grows about breast high. Having risen from below the level of the sea, from this point to the Colorado River bottom there may be found again the desert growths some of which were noticed at White Water and Indio.

Tortuga, 194.8 miles, has an altitude of 183 feet.

Mammoth Tank, 200.9 miles, named from a natural tank, 3¼ miles from the station, with a capacity of 10,000 gallons. Such wells are called by the Mexicans *tinajas*. Some are formed in gullies and arroyos on the sides of the mountains by dams composed of fragments of rock and sand, or worn out of the solid rock where the water falls down upon it. Between this station and Yuma may be seen the most striking plant on these wastes. The Mexicans call it *ocotilla* (oc-co-tee'yah)—the *Fouquieria Splendens*. It grows in clumps consisting of from twelve to twenty long wand-like branches, which spring from the main stem close to the ground, and rise to a height of from 10 to 15 feet. The stems are beset with rows of spines from the axils of which grow small fascicles of leaves. The whole stem is finally covered with bright green, and beneath this vivid cover are hid piercing thorns. The flower is on the top of the stem, six or eight inches long, and consists of many dark purple blossoms. Good fences are made of these poles. They continue green for years after being set in the ground. It is said they never flower if the tops are once cut off. In the bark is a green layer of chlorophyl, and through this wonderful provision of nature we have a green tree without leaves! Sometimes it looks like a dry thorny stick, but after a rain it becomes greener, and if the rain is sufficient the green leaves will appear in bunches. Sometimes it flowers without putting out a leaf! A single growth is also marked by rings around the stem.

Here also are large bunches of grass (*aristida*), called by the Mexicans *galleta* (gah-yee'-tay) grass.

Here is found also the desert willow (*Chilopsis Lineasis*), with beautiful willow-like foliage and delicate pink and white trumpet-shaped flowers. Here is also the iron-wood (*Olneya Tesota*), resembling the locust, especially in its blossom, which is pink or purple and abundant, covering the whole tree in May. The beans when roasted are quite edible—much like peanuts. This is the most common tree between Mammoth Tank and Yuma.

Mesquite, 211.9 miles.

Cactus, 225.7 miles. This station was named from the abundance of the Ocotilla, which was supposed by many to be cactus.

From Mammoth Tank the road has been ascending, and here the elevation is 396 feet. The summit is near the station, and 397 feet elevation. Adding to this the depression of 266 feet, and the whole rise is nearly equal to that in the Livermore Pass. From this point the road descends to the Colorado River, Yuma City having an elevation of 140 feet.

To the left will be noticed a prominent peak, yellowish in appearance. It has not yet been named except in the local dialect, "Cargo Muchacho."

Pilot Knob, 239.3 miles, is only a mile from a peak of the same name, seen on the right.

In the vicinity of Yuma, in the bottom of the Colorado River, are found both kinds of mesquite, and the arrow-wood (*Tessaria Borealis*), consisting of straight shoots from 4 to 8 feet high, with a silvery pubescence on the leaves. It is the principal growth of the Colorado River bottoms.

Before crossing the river, the road runs near Fort Yuma, a military post established in 1852. It is situated on a bluff, with a commanding view. The garrison is small, and with the advance of civilization promises to be withdrawn before many years.

The fort is on a butte rising about 200 feet above the river bottom, and along the river is a bold cliff of the same height. The river is about 300 yards wide at this point, and near it the Colorado and the Gila unite.

From the bluff there is a commanding view of the town across the river, of mesas, valleys, and mountains.

The Castle Dome Mountains are on the north and east, and north of this range and west are the "Purple Hills," and between these and the Castle Dome is the channel of the Colorado.

Cargo Muchaco is south-west.

Yuma, 248.7 miles from Los Angeles, and 719.4 from San Francisco, is approached by a five-span Howe truss bridge. It is an oasis to the traveler, but Colonel Hinton describes the outward aspect of the scene thus:

> "Sand-hills to right of them,
> Sand-hills to left of them,
> Sand-hills in front of them."

There are 1500 people and one principal street in the town. This is the point of departure for nearly all towns and mining districts in Arizona, and many in Mexico and New Mexico.

The *buildings* are only a story high, of sod or adobe, with walls often four feet thick, and flat roofs made of poles covered with willows, cloth, or raw hide, and one or two feet of dirt on top. Verandas from ten to twenty feet wide surround the houses on all sides.

The *climate* is excessively hot, the mercury standing for days at 120° in the shade. Sometimes it reaches 137° in the shade, and 160° in the sun. The natives wear less clothing than the negroes of the far South, and the people need no blankets for sleeping in the open air.

Visitors will notice many peculiarities. High fences, surround most of the huts, made of rawhides and stakes of irregular heights. The people sleep on the roofs of their huts eight months of the year. The only church is the Roman Catholic. *The Sentinel*, weekly, the only paper.

The South Pacific Coast Railroad.

(NARROW GAUGE.)

A. E. DAVIS, Pres.; THOS. CARTER, Supt.
General Offices, 20 and 21 Nevada Block, San Francisco.

This road connects San Francisco by ferry with Oakland and Alameda, extending thence to Santa Cruz, a distance of 8 1.8 miles. The depot in San Francisco is at the foot of Market street, adjoining the C. P. R. R. depot.

Alameda, like Oakland, is a pleasant suburb of San Francisco. For a long time the higher ground of Oakland was more attractive, but of late Alameda has grown rapidly. The soil—a light, sandy loam—and its mild climate make it a paradise for flowers; and its bathing facilities—the best in the vicinity of San Francisco—attract to it large numbers from all the surrounding towns. It has a population of about 5,000; Presbyterian, Methodist, Episcopal, Congregational, Baptist and Catholic churches, several public gardens, and many comfortable and handsome residences. The through trains stop at *Alameda Point, Pacific avenue* and *Park street.* Local trains, every hour during the day, stop at *Alameda Point, Pacific avenue, Second avenue, Third avenue, Schutzen Park, Morton street, Chestnut street, Park street, Versailles avenue* and *High street.*

West San Leandro, West San Lorenzo, Russell's and *Mount Eden* are all signal stations, and, except the last one, all are named for towns on the line of the old Overland route (Central Pacific), about a mile from which this road runs. The course is parallel to the Central Pacific and its branch from Niles to San Jose, but nearer to the bay.

Alvarado, 24.4 miles from San Francisco, is a village of about 500 people. Near it are extensive works for evaporating the water of the bay and supplying salt. Huge piles of salt may be seen below the town on the left. Another important industry is the manufacture of beet sugar. Hall's is a side-track, and

Newark, 29.6 miles from San Francisco, is a thriving village with a landing on the bay. It was laid out when the road was projected.

Mowry's is a signal station.

Alviso is a village at the southern extremity of San Francisco bay, and the center of strawberry culture, and ships by steamer to San Francisco sometimes twenty tons of berries a day. Wild fowl are abundant during the winter season

all along the bay, and Alvarado and Alviso are convenient points for hunting them. A stage connects with San Jose.

Agnew's is a signal station.

Santa Clara and *San Jose* are about four miles nearer San Francisco by this road than by the Southern Pacific northern division. For these places see pages 281–2.

Loveladv's is a signal station, about midway between San Jose and the Coast Mountains, which are sensibly near it.

Los Gatos is a village of nearly 500 people, with a flouring-mill, lime-kiln and stone-quarry furnishing the chief industries. The climate is delightful, and a slight elevation, enabling one to overlook the magnificent valley, supplies a scene of which the eye should never tire.

The route across these mountains is one of the most charming and picturesque in all the state. John Muir points out the fact that the Coast Mountains, being older than the Sierras and better finished, abound with choice bits of picturesque scenery almost wanting in the loftier range.

Leaving Los Gatos, the road follows up the cañon, through which flows a creek of the same name.

Alma, 58.3 miles from San Francisco. This is the old village of Lexington.

Wright's, 62.6 miles from San Francisco, was for a long time the terminus of the road, while the tunnel, 6,450 feet long, was being run. At this a number of Chinamen lost their lives from an explosion of coal-oil gas encountered in working.

Glenwood, 66, and *Dougherty's Mill,* 70.2 miles from San Francisco, are unimportant stations. The road, on reaching the western slope of the mountains, follows the Zayante Creek and then the San Lorenzo river to Felton, the Big Trees and Santa Cruz.

Felton, 73.7, is an admirable place from which to set out for hunting bear, deer, wild-cats and lions, or for trout-fishing. It is principally a lumbering camp.

Big Trees, 74 5 miles from San Francisco, is a charming grove of redwoods, the *sequoia sempervirens,* and was once the camp of General Fremont. Many of the trees are large specimens of the redwood, and one *is said* to be 300 feet high and 20 feet in diameter. The grove is well worth seeing.

The ride down the San Lorenzo river to Santa Cruz is one of the most charming in the state. The California Powder Works are scattered for a mile or two along the river above the town of Santa Cruz, and, combined with the wild, picturesque scenery of forest, hill and river, and ocean, the view is enchanting to every beholder. It can be most enjoyed by driving along the well-graded road from Santa Cruz to Felton.

Santa Cruz, 79.8 miles from San Francisco, is the county seat of Santa Cruz county. It is connected with Pescadero by a tri-weekly stage, and with the Southern Pacific Railroad by a narrow-gauge railroad to Pajaro. The population is about 5,000. It has long been the favorite sea-side resort for San Francisco and northern California, because of its long, clean, sandy beach, its beautiful drives, its good hunting and fishing, and its mild climate.

It is on the north side of Monterey Bay, peculiarly sheltered from wind and fog, but enjoys a fine view of the ocean, with its passing steamers and sailing craft. It has charming society, and

Congregational, Methodist Episcopal, Baptist, Catholic, and Methodist Episcopal (South) Churches. It has extensive tanneries, lime-quarries and kilns, and a variety of manufactures. Mosses in great variety may be gathered on the beach, and north of the town there are many interesting rocks, worn by the waves into fantastic shapes. On the Terry & Baldwin Ranch there is a remarkable natural bridge, formed by the encroachings of the sea.

All along the coast, from Pescadero to Santa Cruz and Monterey, there are formations of the coast that wash pebbles in great variety to the beach, and Santa Cruz boasts of one of the finest.

About nine miles north is a magnetic spring, in the midst of delightful scenery, with a well-kept cottage, and therefore a popular resort for invalids.

The Pacific House, and other hotels, are good, and in all respects Santa Cruz is a charming resort. It is less than four hours' ride from San Francisco by the South Pacific railroad.

Southern Pacific Railroad of Arizona.

During the winter and spring of 1878 and 1879 the Southern Pacific railroad of Arizona was pushed eastward from Yuma to Casa Grande, 182 miles, giving a continuous line from San Francisco of 913 miles, 18 more miles than the distance from San Francisco to Ogden.

The general course is east to Maricopa, through the Gila Valley.

Leaving Yuma, we find Castle Dome Peak and range on the left hand or north of the river. Its outline suggested its name. On the south side of the Gila river is the Sonora mesa—an extensive, hard, gravelly plain, and in about an hour's travel one reaches the Pass where the bluffs of the Gila range, cut by the river, determined the location of the road near the water. The work on the road-bed through this range was the most difficult encountered between Yuma and the present terminus at Casa Grande.

Across the river may be seen Boot Mountain, and east of this, or to the right of it, is the continuation of the Gila range, Los Floros, and

further to the right and east of Gila City, Muggin's range.

The mountains of all this region are groups of volcanic peaks, lying along an obscure axis. There seems to be an opening directly ahead of the traveler, but when he reaches it one of these rounded or irregular mountains is again in front of him and he must wind about on long curves.

The opening made by the valley of the Gila river is of the utmost importance for a trans-continental railroad. For nearly 2,000 miles of mountain after mountain, from north to south, it is the only highway prepared by nature from east to west, to connect the basin of the Mississippi and the Pacific ocean.

Gila City, 15.7 miles from Yuma, has an elevation of 149 feet. One must wonder how such an imposing name could ever have been given unless in mockery, for there is not even a side track. But once it had a thousand miners who carried sacks of gold from their "dry diggings" to wash it in the river.

The scarcity of water that strewed the territory with countless skeletons of animals and men, was encountered in the construction of the railroad, the only supply being from the river. To avoid the fate of others it was transported from the rear, like the iron and the ties. Here there is now a steam-pump that supplies a large tank for railroad purposes.

Leaving Gila City, the road runs more southerly for a few miles, and then turns eastward.

The soil of the valley is the sediment that has been washed down from the surrounding mountains and is exceedingly fertile. This silt, or fine sand, clay and earth covers volcanic rock, mostly basalt.

The mountains are usually masses of granite; but many of them are only sand and lava.

To the forms of vegetation that are local and remarkable—such as have been noticed before reaching Yuma, we must add new forms of cactus and especially the cactus candelabra (*cereus giganteus*), called by the Mexicans sahuaro (soo-war-row) and by the Indians "harsee." It has a pale green, prickly trunk, 20 or 30 and sometimes even 60 feet high, with a diameter occasionally of three feet. The prickers are in regular rows. Often it is without a single branch, standing like a pillar in the desert, but sometimes gigantic branches shoot out laterally from the trunk, and then turn upward, elbow-like, and ascend parallel to the parent stock. It is the great giant of the plains and the most interesting cactus in the world. The trunk is a mass of ribs one or two inches wide and about the same distance apart, extending from the root to the top. When green the interstices between these ribs and the hollow cavity of the trunk is filled with a dark green succulent substance somewhat like a melon. The bark is easily ignited, and in a strong wind the fire will flash quickly to the very top, but without injuring the vitality of the plant. By these fires the Apache gave their signals in time of war. The growth is slow, only a few inches a year. When the tree dies the whole of the succulent interior dries up, and is blown away like an impalpable powder. The strong and elastic ribs are then used for covering adobe houses, and many other purposes. The flower is seen in May, is of a pale yellow, appears at the extremity of both branch and trunk. The fruit appears in June and is shaped like a small pear. It is gathered by the Indians, who use for the purpose a fork on a long pole, or else is found where it falls when the birds detach it in seeking to open the outer covering to secure the dark red pulp within—a pulp sweet and delicate and rivaling any gooseberry. It is highly prized by both Indians and whites. From it the Mexicans make a syrup and agreeable preserves.

Distributed over the whole territory there is the common prickly pear cactus, producing different colored flowers and a fruit of a pleasant slightly acid taste. As many as 1,000, it is said, grow on a single bush.

One of the most useful and important plants is the celebrated Indian maguey—an agave—with a bulbous root, like a lily partly above ground, and varying in size from that of a man's head to a camel's hump. It is full of saccharine matter, and delicious when tasted. The juice of the plant is boiled down into a good syrup, and by distillation a favorite liquor is made from the plant—the strong drink of the Mexicans. The fiber of the leaves is strong and much used by the Indians and Mexicans for ropes.

Much gramma grass will be seen—valuable food for horses.

About 40 miles from Yuma, Poso Butte is opposite on the right hand or south, and on the north an old stage station called Antelope. The river is from four to ten miles distant most of the way to Gila Bend.

Mohawk Summit, 56.1 miles from Yuma, has an elevation of 540 feet. This has been overcome at a grade not exceeding one foot in a 100, and the descent eastward is on the same easy scale. The Mohawk range runs north and south, and though broken may be traced on both sides of the river. Before reaching

Texas Hill, 63.7 miles from Yuma, where trains meet at noon, the road has descended to the level of the mesa, nearly two miles from the gap. Here water is again pumped from the river, the last supply to be had until the engine reaches Gila Bend.

Stanwix is 85 miles from Yuma. At this point, one is in the midst of the great lava beds, and all around is ashes and desolation, but an intensely interesting field, both as to the past and the future. "In the rectangle contained by parallels 32 deg., 45 min., and 34 deg., 20 min., and the meridians 107 deg., 30 min., and 110 deg., more than nine-tenths of the surface is of volcanic material; and from this main body there stretch two chief arms—the one going north-east 80 miles to Mt. Taylor, and the other west-north-west 175 miles in Arizona to the San Francisco group of volcanoes."

Sentinel, 89.6 miles from Yuma, is a so-called station, with nothing that is not common to many miles of the road.

Painted Rock, 103.5 miles from Yuma, is no more important as a station, but as the name implies has much interest for the archæologist and the curious. It calls to mind the old stage station of the same name along the river, where rude hieroglyphics made upon the rocks have baffled so far all efforts to decipher them more effectually than the cuneiform inscriptions of the Assyrian kingdom or the picture-writing of ancient Egypt. These "Pedros Pintados," or painted rocks, are north of the railroad along the old stage road, and consist of huge boulders piled 40 or 50 feet high, and isolated in the great plain. How they came there is as unknown as the meaning of their grotesque carvings or paintings. It is probable that they were gathered without any direct agency of man. They are covered with rude representations of men, beasts, birds, reptiles and things imaginary and real, and some of the representations express events in human life. It is supposed that they record the battles between the Yumas, Cocopahs, Maricopas and Pinahs, or that councils were here held and recorded. The majority of those who have viewed them consider them as of recent origin, dating no farther back than the beginning of the seventeenth century, and there are those who ascribe them to the Aztec and even Toltec civilizations.

The range of mountains noticed on the north side of the railroad is the Sierra Colorado.

Gila Bend, 119.3 miles from Yuma, is where water is again pumped from the river to supply the engines on the road, and named from the bend of the river to the north. The distance by the river to Maricopa is 150 miles, and by the railroad only 45! The range of hills crossed by the road, and which has pushed the river off to the north, making the Gila Bend, is crossed at an elevation of 1,520 feet, and after crossing it the Mariposa desert extends off to the north, and on the south is bordered by high broken mountains.

Estrella, 138.1 miles from Yuma, is of no importance unless it be to mark the Sierra Estrella range, on the north or left hand side.

Maricopa, 156.3 miles from Yuma, is the first point of importance reached after leaving the Colorado river. It is situated on *a curve* in the road *five miles* long, with a radius of six and a half miles! The elevation is 1,182 feet. Six miles north is the old stage station of Maricopa Wells, two miles further north the Gila River. This is destined to become of great importance in Arizona. The Santa Cruz Valley, running north and south, and lying east of this station, has in it good land covered with a thick growth of sage brush, and added to the arable land along the Gila will form an extensive agricultural country centering around Maricopa. Water is abundant and is supplied for the railroad and temporarily for the town, from a well 60 feet deep. In digging this well at 40 feet there was encountered a strata of lava two feet thick, then a few feet of sand, and then again a strata of lava, and beneath this a copious supply of water. About five miles from Maricopa and a quarter of a mile above the plain there is a large spring

that will no doubt be utilized to supply water to the new town.

Much of the importance of the place will be derived from its being the base of supply for the Salt River Valley—a rich agricultural Valley from five to ten miles wide, and lying along the river, more than 100 miles long. The river flows through an immense salt bed, but the water is nevertheless used successfully for irrigation. In this valley Phœnix is the center of business and has a population of about 2,000. Around it are 10,000 acres of land under cultivation, mostly in farms of 160 acres. It is 30 miles from Maricopa—fare, $5.00.

North-west of Phœnix and 90 miles from Maricopa is Wickenburg, just south of the line dividing Maricopa and Yavapai counties. It is a town of about 300 inhabitants. The capital of the territory is at Prescott, 130 miles north of Maricopa (fare $25.00, time 24 hours) and is the centre of trade for the most populous region of the territory, and has about 5,000 inhabitants. It has excellent schools and churches, a promising library association and a larger volume of business than any other town in the territory, but must look to her laurels since the extension of the railroad promises many revolutions. The town was named in honor of the historian who has best studied and written the early history of the country. Leaving Maricopa, the general course of the road is southeast toward Tucson (Too-song), and the present terminus is at

Casa Grande, 182 miles from Yuma, and 913 miles from San Francisco. It is 50 miles from Florence and about 160 from Tucson. At the end of the long curve, the road strikes a tangent toward Tucson about 50 miles long, the longest part of the road without curve between Yuma and this point.

Casa Grande is named from the extensive ruins of an ancient civilization. Irrigating ditches, fragments of broken pottery, crumbling walls, even yet two and three stories in height, and all only a fragment of what was seen by the first Spanish explorers, attest the greatness of what is now so mysterious. Here is the point of departure for Florence on the north-east and Tucson in the direction in which the road is to be extended.

Florence is the county seat of Pinal county, and like all the Arizona towns is in the center of important mines. It is surrounded, too, by rich agricultural land, and has water running through its streets like Salt Lake City. The population is nearly 2,000. All the buildings are of adobe, owing to the high price of timber.

Tucson, 100 miles southeast is reached in 20 hours by stage, and connection made for Santa Fe, Texas and the East.

Casa Grande is also the point of departure by

stage for Guaymas, 350 miles from Tucson. Fare to Guaymas from Tucson is $28.00.

Picacho, 931.9 miles from San Francisco, is only a side track, near the peak of the same name. The word is the common one for an isolated peak, and this one so prominent for many miles between Tucson and Yuma has almost monopolized the name.

Red Rock, 945.8, and Rillito, 961.3 miles from San Francisco are also unimportant. But there comes into view *the oldest city in America—*

Tucson, 978.4 miles from San Francisco. This is now usually pronounced Toosön. It was supposed to be a Spanish word, but it is undoubtedly an Indian word and the correct pronunciation is Tooké-sön, and signifies good land. It is the county seat of Pima County, and situated on the Santa Cruz River, about 75 miles from the Gila River, the same distance from Sonora and 370 miles from Guaymas.

It owes its early settlement and much of its present importance to the Santa Cruz River—a river that is seen and then not seen—flowing alternately above and beneath the surface of the ground, but nearly always beneath. A few miles south of Tucson the river appears above the surface of the ground, flows past the mesa on which the town is built, and affords irrigation for several thousand acres of land.

The exact date of settlement is not known. A mile or more south-west of the town are the ruins of the old mission church built by the Jesuits. The first homes made by civilized people were on the bottom lands from the San Xavier mission toward Tucson, and in time a presidio (military camp) was established on the present site to protect the settlers, and around this the town grew. It was an important station in the Butterfield overland stage-time, and was occupied during the rebellion by a company of Texas cavalry, who were in turn driven out by California volunteers. It became an extensive military depot and has carried on a large trade with Sonora and Sinaloa.

The town lies between the railroad and the river, and to one stepping out of the cars appears to be nothing considering its age or estimated importance. But the houses are of adobe brick, and with scarce an exception, only one story high. They are flush with the narrow streets, and the streets destitute of trees or shrubbery. As in all Mexican towns, the plaza is prominent, and on it is the Catholic church. Business formerly centered around the plaza, but with the energy of the Americans the modern ways of Mexican civilization are breaking up and the principal business has left the plaza and passed to other streets.

At the western edge of the town there is a delightful park. Cottonwood trees of only a few years' growth have attained great height under the influence of irrigation, and furnish a shade and a cool retreat that every one must appreciate because the town is almost destitute in other respects of any shade. The citizens throng this park every evening, and the stranger is driven to it to enjoy the pleasant coolness.

The population of the town, now about 8,000, is steadily increasing. There are two banking-houses, Safford, Hudson & Co., and the Pima County Bank. In seven months one of these bought and sold nearly $2,800,000 in exchange.

Some of the mercantile firms do a wholesale and retail business amounting to millions of dollars per annum, and carry stocks of merchandise that one is surprised to see outside of San Francisco. But Tucson is the commercial center of a large portion of the state and parts of Mexico and New Mexico. From it are supplied the mining camps of Arivaca district, 70 miles east of south; Oro Blanco district, adjoining Arivaca on the east, and 76 miles distant; Tyndall district, 60 miles south; Aztec district, adjoining Tyndall; some mines in Sonora about 12 miles south of Oro Blanco owned by Senator Jones and others; and the Pima district about 25 miles south-west of Tucson.

It is also the center of the agriculture and stock-raising of the fertile lands along the river. Nine miles from Tucson is one of the most interesting structures on the coast—the old mission of *San Xavier Del Bac.*

One road leads past "Silver Lake" formed by damming up the waters of the river—then through groves of mesquit reminding one of the oak groves in the valley of California, then on the mesa land where the hard, gravelly, but natural, road-bed is good enough to be mistaken for a race-course or national turnpike. The mission was founded in 1654, and is now on the reservation of the Papago Indians. These are Pima Indians who are supposed to have accepted the Christian religion.

The present edifice was begun in 1768 on the ruins of a predecessor of the same name, and completed in 1798—excepting one of the towers, yet unfinished. The style of architecture is Moorish and Byzantine. The lines are wonderfully perfect. It is in the form of a cross 70 x 115 feet, and from its walls there rises a well-formed dome and two minarets. A balustrade surmounts all the walls and has 48 griffons, one at every turn. The front is covered with scroll-work, intricate, interesting and partly decayed. Over the front is a life-sized bust of Saint Francis Xavier. The interior is literally covered with frescoes, the altar adorned with gilded scroll-work, and statues are as numerous as the paintings. The tiling on the floor and roof is nearly all as perfect to-day as when laid, but its manufacture is one of the lost arts. It is marvelous that so long ago and in such a place, such architecture, ornaments, painting and sculpture were so well constructed with even patience and perseverance. No one should fail to procure tickets of admission from the priest in Tucson and visit this interesting relic.

Tucson has four newspapers. The Arizona *Citizen* and Arizona *Star* have daily and weekly editions. The Pima County *Record* is a weekly, and the Mexican population have another weekly in their own language—*El Fronteriza*.

There are two breweries, two ice machines, and two hotels, a public school, parochial (Catholic) school, a convent, a private school and a Catholic and a Presbyterian church.

Seven miles from Tucson, on the Rillito creek, and at the base of the Santa Catarina mountains, is Fort Lowell, with a capacity of one battalion. The buildings are the most attractive in the region, and it is probable that the Fort will soon be the head-quarters for Arizona.

Papago, 993 miles from San Francisco, is only a side track.

Pantano, 1,006.5 miles from San Francisco, at the Cienega creek. It is a canvas town of a dozen tents and one or two small adobe houses. While it was the terminus of the road and stages left daily for New Mexico and Tombstone, it had a lively air; but one familiar to its busy scenes will soon be unable to recognize it. Its permanence and importance will arise from its being the base of supply for Harshaw and Washington mining camps.

Stages leave Pantano daily for Harshaw 50 miles, 86; Patagonia 42 miles, 86; and Washington 51 miles, $7.50.

Mescal, 1,015.8 miles from San Francisco, keeps up the semblance of regular stations, at proper distances from each other, but why there should be a station, so far as local reasons demand it, no one can guess. As the name implies, however, there is a new form of vegetation that is important. The agáve (or mescal) plant. Its growth is so slow that it has been called the century plant. It is the American aloe. It has long, regular leaves of grayish-green color, terminating in a sharp, black needle almost as tough as whalebone. The flower stem, when the plant is ready to bloom, grows as rapidly as the plant was slow, sometimes a foot or more a day, and one can almost see it push upward. From the main stem short branches issue, and these bear a small greenish-yellow flower. From this plant is obtained the liquor, "Mescal," commonly used by the Mexicans, and sold at about $3 a gallon. The long leaves are cut off, leaving a stump like a California beet in size, and these stumps are collected and roasted in a hole in the ground or rude oven. Then raw hides strung by the corners are made a receptacle for the roasted stumps, and in a few days these ferment and form a dark, thick, pulpy mass which is distilled once or twice for the Mescal of commerce. After the stumps have been roasted they are also eaten as food and are said to be quite palatable. The ordinary brown sugar (panoche) of the Mexicans is also obtained from this plant. When the flower stalk is about ready to appear they cut away the bud and scoop out the center, and into this is poured the abundant sap that would have shot forth the panicle of flowers. This is evaporated into syrup or sugar.

Benson, 1.024.8 miles from San Francisco, is the point of departure for Tombstone mining district—Hades—and for Contention City and Charleston.

Tombstone is situated on high ground at the foot of a number of lofty hills. The mines are located in these hills at distances ranging from a few hundred yards to three or four miles. The houses are nearly all one-story and built of adobe. Some cabins are of rough lumber. California redwood is, however, making its appearance since the railroad has reached Benson.

These are all towns in Tombstone district, and this comparatively new district is the chief camp in Arizona and the rival of the Comstock. The district has a populat on of about 7,000, with a weekly paper. a bank, numerous stores, hotels, restaurants, etc.

Silver was first discovered at the old Bronco mines. six miles south-west of the town. In all 2,500 locations have been made, some of them of surpassing richness. The Tough Nut, Contention, Sunset and many of the mines produce largely. The milling facilities are limited, owing chiefly to the newness of the district and partly to the scarcity of water. The mills are on the San Pedro river, from nine to twelve miles distant from the mines.

Water for the town is supplied from wells on the stage road from Benson, about two miles from the town, and is hauled in carts and sold at two cents a gallon! Pipes are being laid from a number of springs about eight miles east of Tombstone. The water from these springs will be pumped into reservoirs to secure the necessary fall.

Richmond, about a mile and a quarter south-east of Tombstone, has three or four business houses.

Charleston is on the San Pedro river where the *Corbin* and *Tombstone* mills are located. It is a thriving village with a population of nearly a thousand.

Contention City, also on the San Pedro, nine miles below, is the seat of the Contention mills, with a few stores and good prospects, because the mills must soon increase fourfold to do the work for mines now just opened.

New Boston adjoins Tombstone town and will be the terminus of a branch railroad from Benson to Contention City, Charleston and Tombstone.

Huachuca (Wau-chu-ka) district has a few sawmills and a number of locations, and will probably be supplied from Tombstone.

Stages leave Benson daily for *Contention City*, 23 miles, fare $5; *Tombstone*, 25 miles, $5; Camp Bowie, 73 miles, $11; Shakespeare, 131 miles, $20; Silver City, 184 miles, $27.60; Messila, 300 miles, $45; and Sabinal, 482 miles, $72.30.

The front will soon be far east of Benson and the gap between the Southern Pacific and the Atchison, Topeka and Santa Fe road be closed, the work being vigorously pushed at both ends.

New Route of the Overland Pacific Trains,

VIA MARTINEZ AND SAN PABLO.

All Overland Pacific trains now leave the former line at Tracy Junction, and turning towards the river and the bay, pass over two short railroads which form a very important new connecting link in the *Overland Route*. Both are leased by the Central Pacific Railroad Company. The first is *The San Pablo and Tulare Railroad*, which is in operation from Tracy Junction to near Martinez. Here connection is made with *The Northern Railroad*, which runs from West Oakland to Benicia. It thus forms a continuous line from Tracy Junction to San Francisco, with a maximum grade of 10.5 feet to the mile, and avoids the heavy grades and curves at the Livermore Pass. The "Overland" and Los Argeles trains all use this level road, and for the accommodation of local travel a train leaves Lathrop for San Francisco after the Overland passes it going west. Passengers on the Overland, therefore going to San José, Hayward's, or any point on the main line, should change cars at Lathrop.

Tracy Junction is 3 miles west of Bantas, and 83 miles from San Francisco. The route from the junction is north-west to Antioch. On the left are the high hills of the Coast Range and Mt. Diablo, around three sides of which the road goes. On the right are the low lands of the San Joaquin River.

Bethany, 76.6 miles from San Francisco, is a small station at Wickland on Old River.

Byron, 67.8 miles from San Francisco, is near another landing on Old River.

Brentwood, 62.7 miles from San Francisco, is a small station on the Marsh (or Los Meganos) Ranch. The surrounding land is very fertile, and up in the foot-hills are large coal deposits, the quality being fair.

Antioch, 54 miles from San Francisco, is on the San Joaquin River. It is a pleasant little village of 300 people, and has a sprightly weekly paper, the *Ledger*. At Antioch, ocean vessels have taken their cargoes.

Near Antioch is the confluence of the Sacramento and San Joaquin rivers. From Antioch the road skirts the south side of Suisun Bay to Martinez, near the head of the Straits of Carquinez.

The town of Antioch may be seen about a mile distant on the right or north. Soon after leaving the station the cars pass beneath the track of the Antioch railroad, a freight road to convey coal from Mt. Diablo to tide-water; and soon beneath a similar road from Somerville to Pittsburg landing, and soon again, beneath a third road of like character from Nortonville to New York landing. At the latter is the station of *Cornwall*, etc., as reported May 20th.

Cornwall, 49.9 miles from San Francisco, a station on the "*New York ranch.*" This large tract is one of the Spanish grants, covering so much of California and called *Los Medaños*.

Bay Point, 42.2 miles from San Francisco, is the nearest approach to *Mt. Diablo*. Suisun Bay is close at hand opposite the mountains. This point is a favorite resort for shooting wild ducks and geese. Near Bay Point our road crosses a freight railroad from the coal mines of Mt. Diablo at Somerville to Pittsburg landing at tide water. Both Bay Point and

Avon, 39.1 miles are small stations at which express trains do not stop.

Near Martinez the *San Pablo and Tulare Railroad* connects with the *Northern Railway*. This Northern Railway will cross the bay to Benicia, and continue north to Suisun. A gap from Suisun to Woodland in Yolo County is supplied by the California Pacific Railroad. From a point on this last named road near Woodland, the Northern Railway is now built and operated to Willows in Colusa County. This is the quickest and most favorite route to Cooks, Allens and Bartlett's Springs in Lake County.

Martinez, 35.6 miles from San Francisco, is a pretty little town of 800 people, the county town of Contra Costa County, and the best point to take stages or carriages to ascend Mt. Diablo. The distance from Martinez is 21 miles, and Mr. Wm. Bennett's stages are of the most approved pattern. The ascent can be made by leaving San Francisco in the morning and remaining over-night on the mountain, and returning to the city at noon the next day. Sunset or sunrise or both may thus be had from the summit, and in but little more than twenty-four hours. It is the best view near the city, commanding the Sierras from Lassen's Butte on the north to the High Sierras on the south, and looking over the Coast Range out on the broad Pacific—surveying at once an area of 32,000 square miles, greatly diversified with ocean, river, city, mountain, garden, and desert. Benicia is nearly opposite, with the United States Arsenal above the town. The road passes along the south side of the Straits of Carquinez to the San Pablo Bay.

Carquinez, 32.2 miles from San Francisco is so named from the straits. At this point is a ferry connecting with Benicia, and here the overland passengers from Sacramento via the California Pacific Railroad to *Suisun*, and thence via the Northern Railway to Benicia are crossed over on a monster ferry boat to skirt the edge of the bay to Oakland. Through this narrow strait all the waters from *Mount Shasta* on the north, to *Tejon Pass* on the south about 500 miles, and from the Sierras on the east to the Coast Range on the west forces its way to the ocean. While skirting the bay of San Pablo, one may see *Vallejo* and *Mare Island* on the extreme north of the bay. (See page 277.)

Valona, 29.6 miles opposite *Vallejo* and *Mare Island* and *Towney* 26.7 miles from San Francisco are small stations for local travel. Just beyond *Valona* is a tunnel past which there bursts upon the traveler *a glorious vision of beauty of the San Pablo Bay.*

Pinole, (pronounced Pin o-lay), is a small station, a landing place on San Pablo Bay, 24 miles from San Francisco.

Sobrante, 20.8 miles from San Francisco, is a station at which express trains do not stop.

San Pablo, 17.6 miles from San Francisco,

is a mile distant from a village beautifully situated, and a promising suburb of San Francisco. It is an old Spanish town, with a population of about 300, and with Catholic and Presbyterian churches. Its prosperity has been greatly retarded by the unsettled condition of the land titles involved in the San Pablo grant. The long history of litigation in this vicinity should make every stranger careful about making his home too hastily on Spanish grants.

BARRETT, 16.1 miles from San Francisco.		
STEGE, 13.9	" " " "
POINT ISABEL, 12.8	" " "
HIGHLAND, 11.7	" " "
DELAWARE STREET, 10.4	" " and
STOCK YARDS, 8.7	" "

Are stations for local trains.

Nearing Oakland, one will find on his left, prominently situated near the foot of the Contra Costa range, the State University at Berkeley. It is controlled by regents appointed by the state, and furnishes opportunity for all who desire to obtain classical, or scientific education of the highest grade at the public expense.

On the right, across the bay, may be seen San Rafael, charmingly nestled in a deep nook, near the foot of Mt. Tamalpais, easily recognized by the long gulch washed out by the winter rains and looking like a huge shoot for logs; and further south, may be seen the Golden Gate, with Alcatraz Island, across its eastern end. Alcatraz is a naval station.

Oakland, 6.5 miles from San Francisco, is a station at 16th street, in West Oakland. At this point passengers may take carriages for any point in Oakland or Brooklyn. Or, if any one prefers, he may continue on to Oakland wharf, passing without stopping.

(For Oakland, see pages 259-262.)

West Oakland, 5.8 miles from San Francisco the terminus of the Northern Railway and its junction with the Central Pacific. It is on the edge of the bay, and at this point the cars go to sea on a pier nearly two miles long and reach.

The New Ferry Boat, now building at Benicia to accommodate the transfer of railroad trains is *the largest in the world*. Its length is 425 feet, width 116 feet. It will accommodate four tracks wide, and 24 passenger cars or twice that number of freight cars. The boat has a double end and rudder. Its boilers alone weigh 168 tons, or eight boilers of 21 tons each. The entire cost of boat, etc., is $350,000.

Distances from San Francisco.—All distances from San Francisco, over roads now described in this Guide are now rated by the *Old Overland Route* via Lathrop to Sacramento and Ogden. The present distance to Tracy Junction is 83.2 miles, via New Route, and 71.7 via Old Route, an increase of 11¼ miles. This must be added to present estimates in this Guide until further changes are announced.

The Steamers of the Colorado Steam Navigation Company

Leave Yuma weekly from January 1st to November 1st, and during November and December every alternate Saturday.

Stages leave for Camp Mojave every fifth Wednesday from January 16th, 1878, and continue to El Dorado Cañon from May 1st to November 1st if the water permits.

Yuma to Castle Dome, 35 miles, $5 ; Ehrenberg, 125 miles, $15 ; Aubrys, 220 miles, $28. Camp Mojave, 300 miles, $35 ; Hardyville, 312 miles, $35 ; El Dorado Cañon, 365 miles, $45.

All these points are on the Colorado River, 1200 miles long. For 600 miles, in Arizona, it flows through deep cañons, and receives more than 20 tributaries and falls about 3000 feet. The descent of its cañons was accomplished with peril by Colonel Powell, U.S.A., in 1869 and 1871. For more extended information on Arizona, see "Handbook to Arizona," by Richard J. Hinton.

Los Angeles and Independence Railroad.

LEASED TO THE CENTRAL PACIFIC.

This road was built by Senator Jones, and opened December 10th, 1875. It connects Los Angeles and Santa Monica, giving this southern metropolis its best seaport, and affording it and the city of San Francisco an all-rail connection with the "Long Branch" of the Pacific Coast. It was projected towards Independence, and to connect with the Utah Southern, or Union Pacific. Considerable tunnel-work was done at Cajon Pass. In 1877 the franchise and work were purchased from the original owners and leased to the Southern Pacific.

Trains leave Los Angeles for Santa Monica daily at 10 A.M. and 3.45 P.M. ; Santa Monica for Los Angeles daily at 8 A.M. and 2.25 P.M.

After leaving Los Angeles, the road passes through the beautiful orange groves in the vicinity, and soon turns directly toward the coast. There are no important stations on the line of the road, but the San Fernando Mountains in the north, and many pleasant homes, and corn growing to maturity without rain or irrigation, may be seen from the cars.

Santa Monica is a new town, begun in 1875, and has now about 1000 residents. The town site is a mile square, and has a park of five acres. It is supplied with water from the San Vincente Springs, three miles distant, and has a weekly paper, the *Santa Monica Outlook.* There are two churches and a good school-house, and one of the best hotels on the coast, the "Santa Monica House." It has ample accommodations for 200 guests.

The situation of the town is charming. It is on a horseshoe bend in the coast, that gives it a land-locked advantage for vessels, and the best surf of the ocean for bathing. From Point Dumé on the north to Point Vincent on the south is 28 miles, and a line drawn across from point to point would be ten miles from Santa Monica. But the shelter of the harbor is increased by a group of outlying islands which add picturesqueness to the lovely view from the commanding town. Point Dumas is 13 miles north-west, Point Vincent 20 miles south-west. Anacapa, Santa Cruz, Santa Rosa, and San Miguel are all islands in a line west of Point Dumé—the continuation of the Santa Monica range of mountains. Santa Rosa is 91 miles west, and San Miguel hidden behind it. On the south-west is Santa Barbara, 25 miles, and San Nicholas, 37 miles, and 40 miles south is Santa Catalina. On the north there is a beautiful background in the "saw teeth" of the San Madre range. The natural barriers of the harbor afford the best shelter on the southern coast north of San Diego, and make the gently sloping, hard sandy beach entirely free from undertow. That requisite of good bathing in the temperature is about perfect at this place.

Dr. Trask furnishes the writer various tables of temperature, out of which is taken a month too cool for bathing on the New Jersey coast—that of November.

TEMPERATURE OF AIR.

	7 A.M.	12 P.M.	7 P.M.	12 A.M.
Lowest	46	60	60	50
Highest	61	74	69	62
Average	54·6	71·4	63·4	56·5
	Total average, 61·3.			

TEMPERATURE OF WATER.

	7 A.M.	12 P.M.	7 P.M.	12 A.M.
Lowest	59	60	59	59
Highest	63	62	63	63
Average	60·8	61·2	61·2	60·9
	Total average, 61.			

The average mean temperature of the air from September, 1875, to August, 1876, inclusive, was 61.8°. In December, 1875, it was 58°. In August, 1876, the air averaged 64°, and the water 61°.

Added to these natural advantages, the bathing-house on the beach has every convenience, with fresh or salt and hot or cold water, and plunge, steam, and private baths.

The air, as modified in this region, is most agreeable and invigorating, and has proved worthy the highest praise as a resort for many persons troubled with asthma.

Besides its railroad connection with Los Angeles, it is connected with the coast towns and San Francisco by steamers. A solid and substantial wharf, 1475 feet long, is regularly visited by the steamers of the Pacific Coast Steamship Company.

The roads are peculiarly good, and in the cañons of the mountains there are many beautiful camping and picnic grounds. In the vicinity on the south are ducks, geese, and all sea-fowl in great abundance, and in the mountains on the north quail and larger game, and the ocean affords fine fishing for mackerel and smelts.

In short, Santa Monica has the climate, scenery, natural advantages, and conveniences that make it unequaled as a seaside resort.

Wilmington Division, Southern Pacific Railroad.

On this division two trains are run daily between Los Angeles and Wilmington. Leaving Los Angeles, one travels through a succession of orange groves and fruit orchards to

Florence, 6 miles from Los Angeles. This is the point of divergence of the Los Angeles and San Diego Railroad.

Compton, 11 miles from Los Angeles, is in a fertile and well-cultivated region, and is the most important settlement on the line of the road.

Dominguez and *Cerritos* are small stations.

Wilmington, 22 miles from Los Angeles. is the terminus. It has a population of only 500, and is not so favorably situated as to insure its rapid growth. Until Santa Monica became its rival as the port of Los Angeles, it had a lively aspect at times, and it derived considerable importance from the presence of the army when it was the head-quarters of the Department of Southern California and Arizona.

The harbor is not accessible to large vessels, and these are compelled to discharge by means of lighters from San Pedro, two miles below. The erection of a breakwater is in progress, and in it the government has already spent more than half a million dollars. The breakwater will be 6700 feet long. The jetty so far as completed is very strong and solid, and apparently impregnable to all assaults of the water. By confining the channel it deepens itself. Now there is only 12 feet of water at the wharf, and this gradually deepens to 22 feet at the bar. Eventually there will be at least one safe refuge for all kinds of vessels in all kinds of weather between San Diego and San Francisco, and Los Angeles will have such a harbor as its commercial importance deserves.

Firmin Point is the most prominent point on the west, and has a lighthouse on it with a light of the first order. A number of islands lie near the coast. Rattlesnake in front, Deadman's, a

rocky peak, at the end of the breakwater, and Santa Catalina 20 miles distant.

Wilmington looks like a deserted place, and changes its appearance very frequently with the sand-storms that are common to the region, often piling sand like snow in immense drifts.

The Los Angeles and San Diego Railroad.

The company which owns and has constructed this road in part was incorporated October 10th, 1876. The road is built from Florence, six miles west of Los Angeles, to Santa Ana, a distance of twenty-seven miles, and will be extended to San Diego. The Los Angeles River is crossed near Florence.

Downey, 12 miles from Los Angeles, is a small town of 500 people, but prosperous. Irrigation is essential in all this part of the State, but with abundant water, good grain, fruits, and vegetables are assured. Here there is a supply from the San Gabriel River, the river crossed soon after leaving the station.

Norwalk, 17 miles, and *Costa,* 23 miles, are both small stations.

Anaheim, 26 miles from Los Angeles, is one of the most important towns of Southern California. It was settled by a colony of Germans, and their thrift is quite apparent on every hand. Water from the Santa Ana River is used for irrigation, and along the ditches are dense rows of willows, poplars, eucalyptus, pepper, acacia, and other beautiful trees. The population is about 1500. The town has a weekly paper, the *Anaheim Gazette,* two good hotels, and many buildings quite creditable to the young and rising place.

A few miles distant is the Westminster colony, water for which is had from artesian wells and is quite abundant. It is one of the most flourishing colonies of the State. Anaheim was the first of these colonies on a large scale, deriving its water from the river, and Westminster the first deriving its water from artesian wells. Both, as well as others started since, have been eminently successful. Crops are assured without reference to seasons, and the desert lands of a few years ago are filled with plenty.

All this great valley of Southern California, near the geographical center of which Anaheim is situated, possesses a mild equable climate, and the nature of the soil—rich, sandy loam—insures freedom from malaria. Anaheim has a landing on the ocean about ten miles from the town, and to this the steamers of the Pacific Coast Steamship Company make regular trips.

Orange, 31 miles from Los Angeles, is another flourishing colony, obtaining water from the

Santa Ana River. The road crosses the river on a long bridge just before reaching the town of *Santa Ana,*—33 miles from Los Angeles. This, too, is one of the colonies in the great valley, where cactus land worth $5 an acre rises to $200 or $300 an acre soon after water has been turned upon it. Santa Ana has derived considerable importance from being the terminus of the railroad, and now has daily stages for San Juan Capistrano, 24 miles south-east (fare, $2.50); San Luis Rey, 65 miles (fare, $5); and San Diego, 100 miles (fare, $10).

San Diego,—the objective point of this road, is the oldest town in California, and well known in all lands. Its history, beautiful situation, natural advantages, and remarkable climate, which Agassiz said was "its capital"—all make it interesting and important.

It is the oldest settlement in the State, the mission having been founded in 1769. It is designated as the western terminus of the Texas and Pacific Railroad, and with its prospects and probabilities in this direction corner lots have gone up and down like a jumping-jack.

It is situated on San Diego Bay, about 12 miles long and 2 wide, with 30 feet of water at low tide, and good anchorage. It is one of the loveliest of harbors, and greatly resembles that of Liverpool. Excepting the Bay of San Francisco,

there is nothing like it between the Isthmus and Puget Sound.

For miles along the bay the land rises gently toward the interior, making a location for a city unexcelled in all the world.

Its climate has long been noted, and its reputation as a sanitarium is deservedly great The mercury never falls below 40° in winter, nor rises above 80° in summer. The sea-bathing is fine, the drives charming, and the vegetation luxuriant.

It has a population of about 5,000, is the county town of San Diego County, and has a large number of good buildings. The Horton House, a hotel erected at a cost of $175,000, is not surpassed by any house outside of San Francisco.

But with all her natural advantages and beautiful situation, others will never concede to her the importance she claims, and she will never be satisfied unless she realizes her hopes in becoming the terminus of a transcontinental railroad, and a chief gate in the highway of the nations.

San Diego is reached by the steamers of the Pacific Coast Steamship Company, and will no doubt be more largely patronized by health and pleasure seekers whenever the city enjoys railroad communication with the rest of the world.

To Australia via San Francisco.

The tour of the world is now the lot of many who of necessity must enter the Golden Gate. But some, starting from England, must decide whether they will visit Australia *via* the Suez Canal or San Francisco. It is more expensive to go from London *via* New York and San Francisco, but it has been clearly demonstrated that this is the quickest route and best adapted for the mails.

It is also the pleasantest route. By it one from England has the advantages of seeing the length and breadth of the American continent while he is *en route,* and the privilege of stopping where he pleases; and if he desires, he can turn aside and see at a trifling additional expense the great wonders of Colorado and California and the Hawaiian Islands. His journey is pleasantly broken up by having cars for a part of it,

and he will find the ocean ride from San Francisco to either Melbourne or Sydney long enough. There can be no question as to choice of route unless it should be in the winter season, and even then this route ought to be preferable; for while it breaks up a long sea voyage, the only danger of interruption from snows has proven to be comparatively little. Sometimes both Union and Central Pacific Railroads are wholly unobstructed during all the winter, and the occasional blockades are never of long duration. Passengers of this class are allowed 250 lbs. of baggage each, and leave San Francisco *every four weeks,* reckoning from June 10th or July 8th, 1878. The price of cabin passage from San Francisco to Auckland and Sidney *via* Honolulu is $200, and berths in the upper saloon are $10 extra.

20

𝔓leasure 𝔗ravel to 𝔒regon.

NORTHERN CALIFORNIA, AND WASHINGTON TERRITORY.

Some of the finest scenery on the continent is to be found in Oregon and Washington Territory. The tourist *en route* to this from San Francisco may take a steamer of the Pacific Coast Steamship Company, or the Pacific Mail Steamship Company, or the Oregon Steamship Company. There are two or three steamers a week at all seasons.

Or, if one desire to see the country and avoid the ocean, let him take the Central Pacific Railroad to Redding, and the stages of the California and Oregon Stage Company to Roseburg. The whole 275 miles of stage route is through the most beautiful, wild, and sublime scenery. The road follows the valley of the Sacramento River to its head-waters at the foot of Mt. Shasta, 14,-444 feet high, and passes along the base of this lofty, snow-capped and glacier-clad butte. (See " Head-waters of the Sacramento and Mt. Shasta.") It then crosses the Siskiyou and Rogue River Mountains, and passes over either high mountains on easy grades or through cañons and narrow valleys for its entire length.

At Roseburg the stage connects with the cars of the Oregon and California Railroad, 200 miles from Portland. The route is thence to and through the Willamette Valley—50 miles by 150 —the " garden of the north-west," pronounced by ex-Vice-President Colfax " as charming a landscape as ever painter's brush placed upon canvas."

En route to Portland one may visit Salem, the capital, and other thriving towns in the Willamette Valley, and the beautiful *Falls of the Willamette* at Oregon City ; and from Portland go to Puget Sound and British Columbia up the cañon of the Fraser River from Victoria ; or from Portland or Victoria to Alaska ; or to Astoria, near the mouth of the Columbia River ; or up the Columbia to the Dalles and Wallula, and there either take rail 30 miles to Walla Walla, or proceed up the Columbia to Priest's Rapids, or up the Snake River to Lewiston in Idaho, the head of navigation.

Portland is beautifully situated on the Willamette, the site sloping back to hills from which can be seen Mounts Hood, Adams, Ranier, and St. Helens, and four magnificent domes.

Mt. Hood is the great central figure of Oregon,
rearing his lofty head as a snow-white pyramid, and forming a pleasant background to many a charming view.

The Columbia River, the second largest volume of fresh water in the world, is mighty and beautiful in itself and its distant surroundings. No one who sees can ever forget the lands that lie at its entrance to the sea. The beauty goes far to compensate for passing over one of the roughest bars in the world. All is grand between Astoria and Portland, and from Portland to the Cascades the whole route is without any thing to equal it. From the Dalles to Celilo, it loses its beautiful green, and, although barren, it is perfectly grand.

Away up in British Columbia, near the head of navigation, it is confined within high cañons, and presents a constant succession of bold and striking views. The upper Snake, toward Lewiston in Idaho, is of the same majestic character.

The distance from Portland to the Dalles is 121 miles, and from Dalles to Wallula 121 miles, and from Wallula to Lewiston 161 miles.

Steamers leave Portland daily for the Dalles at 5 A.M., and for Wallula Mondays and Fridays at 5 A.M., connecting with 30 miles of railroad for Walla Walla. The fare from Portland to the Dalles is $5 ; to Wallula. $12 ; and from Wallula to Walla Walla, $3.

Puget Sound.

The route to " The Sound " is by the boats of the Oregon Steam Navigation Company from Portland to Kalama, thence by the Northern Pacific Railroad to Tacoma, 105 miles, and thence by steamer for all points on the sound.

" The Sound " is a most beautiful sheet of water—a succession of bays with enchanting shores on two and sometimes, apparently, on all sides, sloping up to hills and well-timbered mountains. Seattle and Olympia are the largest towns of general interest. Port Townsend and other places are extensive lumber-mills.

Victoria, in British America, is a beautiful, quiet place of 5000 people.

Passengers can leave Portland daily at 6 A.M. (except Sunday) for all points on the Sound, and for Victoria on Wednesday and Saturday at the same hour. From Portland to Kalama the fare is $1 ; to Tacoma, $7 ; and to Victoria, $13.

During the summer season, the tourist may wish to see "Clatsop Beach," the great watering-place of Oregon—her boast, and the envy of California. It is a long, wide, splendid beach from Fort Stevens, at the mouth of Columbia River, to Tilamook on the south, a distance of 20 miles. The route is via Astoria by the steamers of the Oregon Steam Navigation Company, and thence across a promontory to the ocean. Besides the splendid beach, the place has all the usual attractions of mountain, sea, and sand—meadow, grove, and stream.

Oregon, like Northern California, is a sort of sportsman's paradise. Its streams, which are everywhere, abound in trout, and the large rivers in salmon. Deer, grouse, quail, ducks, and geese, bear, elk, mountain-sheep, and cougars are in all sections of the State, although civilization has drawn the elk, mountain-sheep, and bear from the great valleys. Deer are plentiful, convenient to points reached by railroad and steamers, and grouse are found in all the valleys. The sportsman and tourist can not go amiss in any section of Oregon, Washington Territory, or Idaho.

To the emigrant its broad, unoccupied, fertile plains present a great attraction. Emigrants will find information furnished by the Oregon State Board of Immigration, or the Land Department of the Oregon and California Railroad, 504 Battery Street, San Francisco.

Oregon Division of the Central Pacific Railroad, Northern California Railroad.

All trains over the Oregon Division going north are made up at Sacramento, and leave the main line of the Central Pacific at Roseville Junction, 18.2 miles east.

The general direction of the road is north, through a grazing and wheat-growing section to the foot-hills at the head of the Sacramento Valley.

Whitney's is a signal station ; and

Lincoln, 28.7 miles from Sacramento, has a coal deposit near the village of 300 people, which supplies fuel for manufacturing purposes. The manufacture of pottery and sewer-pipe from clay convenient to the railroad is also an important industry.

The Marysville Buttes, 2030 feet high, are a landmark in every portion of the upper Sacramento Valley, and are always seen when going north, on the left-hand side of the road.

Ewing is a signal station, and

Sheridan a little village near Bear River. The soil on the south side is mostly light, and the land used for pasturing sheep and cattle.

Bear River Channel has been entirely filled with *débris* from the mines above; and from this source a great contest has arisen in the State between the agricultural and mining interests, and it is yet undecided.

Wheatland, 39.6 miles, has a population of about 800, and a weekly newspaper, the *Recorder.* The principal trade is in wheat and flour.

Reed's and

Yuba are both signal stations.

As the road approaches Marysville, it crosses the Yuba River. Like Bear River, the channel has been filled up many feet in places, and high

levees are required on each side, especially during the winter rains.

Marysville, 52.4 miles from Sacramento, is at the confluence of the Yuba and Feather rivers, is the county town of Yuba County, has a population of 5000, wide and regular streets, is the home of the Roman Catholic bishop, has large Catholic educational institutions and good Protestant schools, is lighted with gas, has water from an artesian well 300 feet deep, has six churches, banks, foundries, machine-shops, wholesale and retail stores, and numerous hotels. The Western Hotel is one of the best outside of San Francisco. There is one daily paper, the *Marysville Appeal.* Oranges and lemons grow well in and around the city, and the private residences are usually surrounded by choice fruit or shade trees and a rare wealth of roses and flowers. The prosperity of Marysville was very great when there was no railroad extending northward and the mines were yielding well, and now the city is building up again, and building solidly on the trade of the surrounding country, and especially on that of Sutter County, across the Feather River.

It has two stage-lines daily to Colusa, 28 miles west, and also stages to Grass Valley, 35 miles ; North San Juan, 38 miles ; La Porte, 65 miles ; and Downieville, 67 miles.

Marysville has been flooded several times, but is now surrounded by high and strong levees, and considered safe against any floods. Just across the Feather River is *Yuba City,* the county town of Sutter County, with a population of 800. It is at the head of steamboat navigation ; has one weekly newspaper, the *Sutter Banner.* About eight miles below the city is the "Hock Farm," the old home of General Sutter, so renowned for hospitality in the Pioneer days of California.

At Marysville passengers going north take supper, and going south take breakfast, and passengers for *Orville* (distance 28 miles), change cars, taking at the depot of the Central Pacific road those of THE NORTHERN CALIFORNIA RAILROAD, which connects closely with the Central Pacific and reaches the following stations.

Houcut is its only station, and an unimportant one.

Oroville, the northern terminus, has a population of 1500, and is the county seat of Butte County. Its placer-mines, once fabulously rich, are now worked chiefly by Chinamen, but the mining interests in the foot-hills make Oroville the seat of a considerable trade. It has stages to Cherokee Flat, 12 miles ; La Porte, 45 miles ; Susanville, 85 miles ; Chico, 25 miles ; and Bigg's Station, 12 miles. Oroville has one church—a union church. During the summer nearly all the families desert the place and take themselves to the mountains to escape the intense heat.

After leaving Marysville, on the Central Pacific, the Feather River is crossed, about two miles from the depot.

Lomo and *Live Oak* are flag stations ; and *Gridley* and *Biggs* are both new and flourishing towns, named from the owners of large ranches. From Biggs there is a stage to Oroville, 12 miles (fare, $1). Biggs has a weekly paper, the *Register,* and a population of about 1000.

All this upper Sacramento Valley is a vast wheat-field, and evidences of its productiveness are on every hand.

North of Biggs the road crosses the canal of the Cherokee Flat Mining Company, 18 miles long and 400 feet wide, but filled up like the channels of the rivers, and extending its smooth sediment over the acres on either side.

Nelson and *Durham* are small stations, but in a rich section.

Chico, 93.7 miles, is one of the best and most prosperous towns of California. Its population is 5000. It has five churches, is lighted with gas, supplied with pure water from Chico Creek, has several banks and hotels (the principal one the Chico House), has one daily paper, the *Record,* and one weekly, the *Enterprise.* The Sierra Flume and Lumber Company have constructed several V-shaped flumes from the Sierra Nevada Mountains on the east to different points on the railroad. One of these flumes terminates at Chico, and is 35 miles long.

The beautiful home of General Bidwell, who came to California prior to the "gold fever," and who has always been one of her most enterprising citizens, is just north of the town. His orchard is filled with oranges, lemons, figs, almonds, walnuts, and the choicest of other fruits, and his vegetable and flower gardens are unsurpassed in Northern California. He has 32,000 acres of the choicest land in one tract.

Chico has a daily stage to Oroville, 25 miles ; Greenville, 60 miles ; and Big Meadows, Plumas County, 65 miles ; Big Valley, Lasson County, 80 miles ; Dayton, Butler County, 6 miles ; Jacinto, 14 miles ; Germantown, 13 miles ; Willows, 56 miles ; and Colusa, 40 miles — connecting at Colusa for Williams on the Northern Railway, and for Allen and Bartlett's Springs.

Stages run Mondays, Wednesdays, and Fridays to St. John, 10 miles ; Orland, 28 miles ; Coast Range, 35 miles ; and Newville, 40 miles. The fare is from ten to fifteen cents a mile.

Nord, Anita, Cana, Soto, Vina, and *Sesma* are all small stations, but in a fertile country.

The Sacramento River is crossed on a bridge near

Tehama, 122.8 miles from Sacramento. The population of the town is nearly 1000, and the people have a daily paper, the *Tocsin.* The place was first called "Hall's Crossing." It is the terminus of a flume 40 miles long, belonging to the Sierra Flume and Lumber Company. Lassen's Peak, with an altitude, according to Prof. George Davidson, of the United States Coast Survey, of 10,650 feet, may be seen in the northwest.

Red Bluff, 134.9 miles, is the county seat of Tehama County, with 200 inhabitants. It is at the head of river navigation in the midst of rich land, and is the terminus of another flume of the Sierra Flume and Lumber Company. It has two weekly newspapers, the *Sentinel* and *People's Cause.* Mt. Shasta may be seen in fair weather, far away to the north.

Hooker and *Buckeye* are signal stations ; and

Cottonwood, 151.9 miles, on Cottonwood Creek, is a small village of 300 people ; and *Anderson's* is a village of 200 people, 158.6 miles from Sacramento ; and

Clear Creek, a small station near

Redding, the present terminus of the road. The population of Redding is about 500. It is 169.7 miles from Sacramento.

Stages leave Redding daily for Shasta, Scott's Valley, Weaverville, and Yreka, and for Campbell's Soda Springs, 69 miles ; Sisson's, at the foot of Mt. Shasta, 77 miles ; Yreka, 114 miles ; Jacksonville, 174 miles, and Roseburg, Oregon, 275 miles. The fare is fifteen cents a mile. Through fare from San Francisco to Portland, $40.

During the summer season the stage leaves Redding about midnight on arrival of the train, and runs on fast time to Roseburg. During the winter it leaves at 6 A.M.

At Roseburg connection is made with the

Oregon and California Railroad for Portland, 200 miles. On this overland route to Oregon the tourist will find one of the most attractive regions in the world, in the

Head-waters of the Sacramento and Mount Shasta.

From Redding to the Black Butte, more than 80 miles, the stage-route follows the general course of the river, leaving it occasionally and crossing it five times. At Redding the broad, fertile Sacramento Valley ends, and the foot-hills, with numerous little valleys between them, begin. The stage ride from Redding north is through these, and then across the mountains that confine the waters of the Pitt and McCloud rivers. These are the main tributaries of the Upper Sacramento. The Pitt is fed by the eternal snows of Lassen's Peak, the central and loftiest figure in a line of ancient volcanoes, and the northern extremity of the Sierra Nevada range. The McCloud is a rapid stream, rushing along at from ten to twenty miles an hour, with high cañon walls on either side, and water cold as ice and clear as crystal. It bursts from the ground in a great volume, and is probably the outlet of Mud Creek, which rises from a glacier on the east side of Mt. Shasta and then sinks in the earth. Near the crossing of the McCloud is the United States fish-hatching establishment. All these rivers abound in trout and salmon, but the best place on them for trout-fishing is the upper waters of the McCloud. The valley of the Sacramento grows narrower as one goes northward, and at last is almost a cañon. Just beyond Campbell's Soda Springs, 69 miles north of Redding, the road ascends from the river to an extensive mountain basin, walled in by yet loftier mountains—a sort of semicircular wall from Scott's Mountain on the north to Trinity on the west and Castle Rock on the south-east. On the east side of the road, and in this great basin, Mt. Shasta rears its lofty head into the dark, deep blue of heaven. This delightful region is of easy access; and while the Yosemite Valley is reckoned the most wonderful attraction of nature in California, it is surpassed in many respects by Mt. Shasta. Shasta has an elevation of 14,444 feet, according to Professor Whitney, and that of Mt. Blanc is but 15,739 feet. Mt. Whitney is the only mountain in the United States known to be higher—and that by only 500 feet. But Mt. Whitney is flanked by numerous other mountains nearly as high, while Shasta rises about 11,000 feet above the surrounding country on every side.

Mt. Whitney and Mt. Lyell have glaciers of feeble vitality, but Shasta has three, each living and accessible. It is the only mountain in America where glacial phenomena may be carefully studied with trifling exertion.

Mt. Shasta has two peaks, one called the Crater Peak, although both were active volcanoes at a former day. The Crater Peak, Professor Whitney said in 1865, was "believed by many to be quite inaccessible. Its sides appear to be covered with loose volcanic materials, probably ashes, lying at the highest angle possible without sliding down." Now it is frequently climbed, its sides being covered with blocks of trachyte of all sizes, which have broken from the crater walls above. They slip down and retard the climbing, but the footing is secure in the steepest places. Only a few feet below the summit on the main peak, and above glaciers and ice-fields, there are springs of boiling water and juts of constantly escaping steam, all strongly impregnated with sulphur. It was these that kept John Muir and his guide, Jerome Fay, from perishing when a storm overtook them on the summit and compelled them to spend a night there. They froze on one side and roasted on the other. The panorama from the summit is beyond description. The view takes in the whole of California from the Coast Range to the Sierra Nevadas, and from the Bay of San Francisco far beyond the Oregon boundary—not less than 450 miles. It is probably unsurpassed in the world. Once the writer stood upon the summit in July, and there lay around him 100 square miles of snow. Often rolling masses of fleecy clouds shut out all below, and one is left as in the very chamber of heaven. As one climbs the mountain he will hear the water gurgling through the loose rocks, fed by the melting snows, but no stream flows directly from the Butte. A journey of 100 miles around the cone may be made without crossing a stream or finding a spring. The ascent of Shasta is full of interest to every lover of nature. The flora is remarkable, and has attracted to it in person such eminent scientists as Sir Joseph Hooker and Asa Gray. The ascent of the mountain is always made from Sisson's, a charming hotel in Strawberry Valley, Siskiyou County, California, one of the best and cheapest places of resort in the State. Horses, guides, blankets, and provisions are furnished. If there are three in the party the cost will be $15 each, and $20 if only one. The trip requires 36 hours. The first night is spent camping at the upper edge of the *pinus flexilis* and the lower edge of the snow, at an elevation of about 10,000 feet. Ladies have occasionally made the ascent, and any strong able-bodied man or woman can do so. It is difficult, but not dangerous.

Besides Mt. Shasta there are hundreds of interesting places to visit or to see. The Black Butte, called the Black Cone by the Geological Survey, is a sugar-loaf mass of trachyte more than 6000 feet above the sea, with an outline in the horizon as regular as it would seem an axe could hew it. It is in striking contrast with the deep blue azure and the bright green of Strawberry Valley.

Castle Rock—seen from the stage-road—is a wonderful uplift of granite, perhaps surpassing every thing of the kind outside of Yosemite Valley, and strongly resembling the Sentinel Dome.

Castle Lake, Picayune Lake, the Big Spring, "The Falls" on the banks of the Sacramento River, and the Falls of the McCloud River are all sources of surpassing interest. No region of California is so varied in its attractions. *Yosemite is a place to see, Mt. Shasta is a place to stay.*

The hunting and fishing are unsurpassed in California. The waters are filled with trout and salmon. On the McCloud River the trout weigh from half a pound to three pounds, and the *Dolly Varden* species, with bright red spots on the side, weigh from one pound to twelve pounds. The McCloud is *a glacial stream,* and the Dolly Vardens are found only in such. Castle Lake and this river are the best trout and salmon fly-fishing places in the State.

The hunting is no less attractive than the fishing. Grizzly bears are not found in the region, but the black, the brown, and the cinnamon are numerous. The puma or cougar is sometimes found, and the lynx and two other species of wild-cats.

Deer are so numerous that a crack shot need have no difficulty in bringing down at least one every day. There are three varieties, the *mule,* black-tailed, and white-tailed. Grouse, mountain-quail, and squirrels are numerous, and mountain sheep and antelope are found at no great distance. Parties provided with guns can be fitted out for hunting elk, antelope, deer, or mountain-sheep in Oregon, and provided with competent guides by Sisson. The region is full of mineral springs, there being several in the vicinity of Sisson's, and one of the best at Campbell's—formerly Fry's—on the stage-road, 8 miles south of Sisson's. The water is ice cold, strongly effervescent, and charged with soda, iron, and salt. Campbell's hotel is excellent. Parties are fitted out for fishing in either the McCloud River or Castle Lake at both Campbell's and Sisson's, but at Sisson's only are guides to be had. Board is $10 a week at both places, saddle-horses $2 a day, and guides, with horse, $5 a day.

Those who desire a more detailed account of this wonderful region should consult Clarence King's "Mountaineering in the High Sierras," or "Californian Pictures, by Benjamin Parke Avery," or "Health and Pleasure Resorts of the Pacific Coast."

North Pacific Coast Railroad.

(NARROW GAUGE.)

This road is now completed from Saucelito, its southern terminus, in Marin County, to the north side of the Russian River. 80½ miles in length, with a branch from San Quentin to the "Junction," 17 miles from San Francisco. Nearly all passengers take the route *via* San Quentin and San Rafael, on the spacious, elegant, and fast steamers "San Rafael" and "Saucelito," from the foot of Market Street. These popular boats are owned by the railroad company.

The railroad company own barges on which they transport all their freight cars to and from San Francisco without breaking bulk, but passengers by this route take the boats of the Saucelito Land and Ferry Company. These boats also leave the foot of Market Street.

Nearly all passengers go *via* San Quentin and San Rafael.

The road passes through Marin and into Sonoma County, and the trip over it is more diversified than any other of equal length in California. From the beauty of the Golden Gate and the Bay of San Francisco, the road skirts the base of Mt. Tamalpais, and passes through a wild, picturesque mountain region, down a beautiful cañon filled with trees, babbling water, and trout, through rolling hills, the great dairy region of the coast, along the shores of Tomales Bay, through fertile grain fields, and at last ends in the dark forests of the red-woods, where the Russian River has broken asunder the coast mountains and forced its way to the ocean.

During the summer two through trains are run daily, and during the winter one train, Sundays excepted. In summer a Sunday excursion train leaves San Francisco *via* Saucelito, and returns in the evening.

Between San Francisco and San Rafael eight round trips are made daily.

Leaving San Francisco *via* San Rafael, one passes under the guns of Alcatraz Island, which stand a sentinel at the Golden Gate, and rounds Angel Island, which is separated from the mainland by Raccoon Straits, and takes in on a clear day, while passing, the cities of Oakland and Berkeley and the Contra Costa hills beyond them, and more than the eye can hold, until he reaches *San Quentin,* 11.5 miles from San Francisco. It is situated on a point of the same name on the west shore of San Pablo Bay, a division of the Bay of San Francisco. Its chief importance is derived from the fact of its being the residence of the Lieutenant-Governor of the State, who *ex-officio* has charge of the State's convicts. There are usually from 800 to 1500 of these persons kept here at hard labor. The work-shops and other buildings are on the left of the railroad ; and on the left, and directly ahead, is Mt. Tamalpais, the loftiest peak in this region. A wash-out near the summit looks like a *shute* for logs.

Here passengers exchange the steamers for the cars, neat and comfortable, but not so commodious as those of a broad-gauge road. In a few minutes' ride one will be at the town of *San Rafael* (San Ra-fell), 14 miles from San Francisco.

It is the county-seat of Marin County, and situated in a valley of the same name, about a mile in width and four in length. It is built upon the former site of the old Jesuitical mission of San Rafael, founded in 1824. The town-site is elevated, and on gently rolling ground, thus assuring fine views of the bay on the east and a favorable sewerage. As the soil is a loose gravel or sandy loam, there is no malarial influence such as renders many other favored localities unhealthy. It is completely sheltered from the ocean winds and fogs by the surrounding mountains, and the climate is mild and even, the mercury rarely falling below 40° in winter or rising above 90° in summer. The water brought from Lagunitas Creek, 750 feet above the town, on Mt. Tamalpais, is pure and soft. For location, climatic influences, and picturesque scenery, no place in this part of the State can equal it. It is quite a *sanitarium* for many in San Francisco who suffer from the cold winds and damp fogs.

Many of the residences are elegant and costly. The Court House was erected at an expense of $60,000. Two weekly newspapers are published, the *Journal* and *Herald*. The town is supplied with gas, and the roads in the vicinity are good and afford most charming drives.

This is the best point from which to make the

Ascent of Mt. Tamalpais.

It is nearer than Saucelito, the trail is better, and the variety of views greater. Horses may be procured at $2.50 and $3 per day. The start should be made as near daylight as possible, and the whole trip may be accomplished in about eight hours. The height of the western summit, the highest point, is 2600 feet. The view embraces the ocean, the Golden Gate, the bay, San Francisco, Oakland, and many other towns, and is in some respects more diversified and prettier than the view from Mt. Diablo. The latter is far more extensive.

San Rafael will also be the terminus of the San Francisco and North Pacific Railroad, now in operation from Donahue to Cloverdale.

Junction, 17 miles from San Francisco.

Here the branch unites with the main road *via* Saucelito. The distance from San Francisco is 17 miles by either route.

Saucelito is six miles from San Francisco.

The stations between Saucelito and Junction are the "shops" of the company, Lyford's, Summit, Corte, Madera, and Tamalpais. The latter is at the foot of Mt. Tamalpais, but is merely an accommodation station, without a building near except the beautiful residence of Mr. Kent, a retired merchant of Chicago. A trail leads to the summit of the mountain from his house. It was constructed at his own expense, and is not open to the public.

Fairfax, 18.5 miles, is a popular picnic resort. Leaving these grounds, the road curves to the right and begins ascending to reach the summit of White's Hill. The grade is from 90 to 120 feet to the mile, and the curves in some places 20 degrees. At one point the road doubles back upon itself, so that, after traversing three quarters of a mile, the tracks are not a hundred yards apart. At no place so near San Francisco can there be had as good an idea of the mountainous regions of California as in crossing this hill and descending to tide-water on the west. The crookedness of the road as it curves around one and another of the ravines is extremely interesting.

The railroad ascends on the north side of Ross Valley, and as one climbs up he may see on the *left,* far above him, the wagon-road from San Rafael to Olema, and directly under this wagon-road the cars pass through a tunnel 400 feet long with an altitude of 565 feet.

At the summit the road descends into the valley of San Geronimo Creek to a station of the same name, 3 miles from which is Nicasio, a small village in a dairy region. Lagunitas, another small station, marks a creek of the same name flowing from the north-west side of Mt. Tamalpais. The valley has a large variety of wild flowers in the spring, and at all seasons an abundance of California shrubbery, such as the Ceanothus, Manzanita, Madrona, Oaks, Buckeyes, and some Red-woods, but none of the Douglass spruce or firs peculiar to high altitudes.

As the cañon narrows the scenery becomes wilder, and the road follows "Paper Mill" Creek, as it is called, from the "Pioneer Paper Mill," the first mill of the kind on the Coast, at *Taylorville,* 31¼ miles from San Francisco. The creek abounds in trout. Near Taylorville is a favorite camping-ground to which hundreds go every season to exchange their close walls in the city for the freedom of the hills and woods and brooks.

Tocaloma (Grove), 33.5 miles, is a small station in a dairy region two miles from the town of Olema. A stage runs from the town to the trains. The creek is crossed and recrossed, and one embankment is 1830 feet long ; but these are soon passed, and one can look to the left and a little behind him, as the road is fairly in the valley, and see the town of

Olema, 38¼ miles from San Francisco. On the platform will be seen a large number of butter-boxes. In winter passenger trains stop for dinner. Tri-weekly stages leave for Bolinas, 13 miles south.

The general course of the road is now more northerly, to Tomales Bay, and one quickly changes from the trout streams of the mountains to enjoy a " breath of the salt sea gale."

The road passes along the northern side of the bay for about 13 miles, part of the time on the shore and part on piles. The bay is only about a mile wide, and 20 miles long, and very shallow. Oysters have been planted in it, but the water has proved too salt for their successful cultivation. The bay supplies a large number of fish, and in it are found an abundance of smooth, hard-shell clams, the only source of this variety of shell-fish for the San Francisco market. All kinds of sea fowl are abundant during the season. Along the bay are several small stations— Wharf Point, Millerton, Marshall's, and Hamlet —from which butter, fish, and game are shipped.

After passing Hamlet, the road curves to the right, crossing an arm of the bay, or Tomales Creek, and follows up the west bank of this and winds around the hills to

Tomales, 55¼ miles.

The town has a population of only 150, but the country is thickly settled by intelligent dairy-and ranch men. For a year and a half this was the northern terminus of the road, further progress being delayed by the wall of solid rock seen in the hills to the north. Here the company have a large warehouse for storing grain and freight. In clear weather Mt. St. Helena can be seen in the north-east, and east and south-east are the snow-capped Sierras.

Soon after leaving this station, the road passes through the longest tunnel on the road, 1700 feet in length, reaches *Clark Summit,* and, descending, crosses the Estero Americano, on a high trestle, and enters Sonoma County.

Valley Ford, 62¼ miles, is a pretty little village of about 300 people. Since the completion of the railroad a stage has run to Petaluma, to fulfill a contract for carrying the mails. It will probably be discontinued at an early day. Valley Ford was so named from the crossing of the old Spanish trail from the interior ranches to Tomales Bay and the coast. Up to 1857 the Indians made two or three trips a year, to procure shell-fish for eating and shells for the manufacture of money. It is a well-accredited fact that on this town site there were grown in 1854 one hundred bushels of oats to the acre.

Bodega Roads, 65 miles, is the depot for Bodega Corners on a portion of the tract formed

by the Russians, and in the midst of the potato-growing regions.

Freestone, 66.5 miles, was settled first under direction of General Vallejo to check the advance of the Russians. It is in the midst of a fertile valley and rich dairy lands.

Just beyond Freestone the road enters the belt of Red-woods (*Sequoia Sempervirens*), and ascends Salmon Creek toward the summit, where the waters flow north into Russian River and south into Bodega Bay.

On this ascent the road crosses one of the highest bridges west of the Mississippi River. The bridge crosses Brown Cañon, has two spans of Howe truss, each 150 feet long, and is at the giddy height of 137 feet above the cañon. The central pier is 110 feet high, of the kind called a cluster pier, and is a splendid piece of mechanism.

At *Howard's,* 70¼ miles, the road is at the summit and fairly in the red-wood country. To reach this timber was the first great aim of the road, and more than 200,000 feet of lumber are now shipped daily from the mills at the Russian River and along the line of the road.

The stations — *Streeten's Mills, Tyrone Mills, Russian River, Moscow Mills,* and *Duncan's Mills* — alike show the business of the country.

Duncan's Mills, the terminus, is 80¼ miles from San Francisco. The timber-land is usually held in large tracts. The Russian River Land and Lumber Company, of which ex-Governor M. S. Latham is president, owns 10,000 acres in a body, and around the terminus of this road it is estimated there are 600,000,000 feet of lumber—enough for ten years' cutting.

At the terminus of the road is Julian's Hotel, one of the best in the State. Austin Creek empties into Russian River near this point. It is one of the best streams for trout near the city. The hills abound with quail and rabbits, while deer and grouse, and even bears and wild-cats, may be occasionally found at no great distance. In the river salmon can be caught or speared, and at the mouth of the river, only six miles distant, a variety of sea-fishing may be had. Considering the unequaled variety of beautiful scenery on the line of so short a road, and the charming picturesque region in which the road terminates, the climate, game, and amusements to be had in the vicinity, no spot deserves to be more favored by the tourist who has not enough time to acquaint himself with the hunting and fishing grounds of Northern California.

The Northern Coast stages leave daily for Fort Ross, 16 miles ; Henry's, 16 miles ; Timber Cove, 20 miles ; Salt Point, 25 miles ; Fisk's Mills, 30 miles ; Stewart's Point, 34 miles ; Gualala, 44 miles ; Fish Rock, 50 miles ; Point Arena, 60 miles ; Manchester, 66 miles ; Cuffey's Cove, 80 miles ; Navarro Ridge, 86 miles ; and Mendocino City, 96 miles. Fare, about 12½ cents a mile.

San Francisco and North Pacific Railroad.

This road was built mainly by the president, Mr. Donahue, and has rapidly developed a rich section of country, and is the great highway for nearly all of Sonoma County. The road extends from Donahue to Cloverdale, and is connected with San Francisco by a ferry of thirty-four miles.

The first steamer, "James M. Donahue," leaves the Washington Street wharf, San Francisco, every day to connect with the cars at Donahue, and in summer makes two trips daily. An extension of the road from near Petaluma southward is nearly completed. This will make the southern terminus at San Rafael, San Quentin, or some point on the bay near San Francisco, and greatly shortens the time between the towns of the interior and the metropolis.

Donahue, 34 miles from San Francisco, is on Petaluma Creek, and is simply a place for the transfer of passengers and freight from cars to steamer or *vice versa.*

The route from San Francisco to Donahue is north and north-east, the steamer taking the course to Vallejo or the Sacramento River until Red Rock is passed, then heading for the north-east corner of San Pablo Bay.

Lakeville, 35 miles from San Francisco, is a small station at which passengers for Sonoma are transferred to stages. The distance is seven miles, and the fare $1.50. Sonoma Valley is celebrated for its wines and delightful climate.

Sonoma, an Indian word, means "Valley of the Moon."

The Sonoma Valley is about 25 miles long, and forms but a small part of the country. The mission of Sonoma was planted July 4th, 1823, near the present Catholic church, and was destroyed by the Indians in 1826, and rebuilt in the following year. The present town was laid out by General Vallejo in 1834, and the struggle against the Russians for possession of the country was carried on from this point for some years. Here a company of thirty-three Americans from Sutter's Fort made a prisoner of General Vallejo, the Spanish commander of California, and raised the *Bear Flag,* the standard of the pioneer societies of the State. Among those stationed at Sonoma prior to 1851 were Lieutenant Derby, Generals Hooker, Stoneman, and Sherman. This great historic town has only about 600 inhabitants.

The Sonoma Creek runs through the valley, and a small steamer runs from its mouth to San Francisco. A *Narrow Guage Railway* connects the town of Sonoma with the bay near the mouth of the creek.

Petaluma, 42 miles from San Francisco, was long the largest and principal city in the county. Its name is of Indian origin but doubtful sig-

nification. It is built on undulating ground, which affords good drainage and a fine view of the valley and mountains beyond it. Mt. St. Helena and the Geyser Peak are visible from the town. The climate is mild and pleasant, and the town one of the healthiest in the State. It was laid out in 1852, and has been the general shipping-point for the produce of Sonoma and Mendocino counties. It has a steamer running directly to the city, from a point on the creek a short distance below the city, and stages to Sonoma *via* Lakeville. It has water-works, gas, good schools, six churches, three banks, and two weekly papers.

Leaving Petaluma, the course of the road is northward through Petaluma Valley, which opens into Santa Rosa, and this into Russian River Valley. The three valleys are in fact one great valley.

Ely's, Penn's Grove, Goodwin's, Page's, Cotate Ranch, and Oak Grove are all small stations in a rich agricultural region.

Penn's Grove is near the low divide where the waters flow south into Petaluma Creek, and north into Russian River. The Cotate Ranch is four leagues in extent.

Santa Rosa, 57 miles from San Francisco, is one of the most beautifully situated towns of the State, and its inhabitants, whether natives of New Jersey or not, consider it superior to every city in the State. Its recent progress has been more rapid than any other interior town. It has a population of about 7000, is the county seat of Sonoma County, and has a street railroad, *sixty miles of streets,* water-works, gas, a daily and two weekly newspapers, two banks, eight churches, two colleges, Prof. Jones' academy for boys, Miss Chase's school for girls, and other private and public schools. One of the colleges — the Pacific Methodist—is under the control of the Methodist Episcopal Church South. The buildings and grounds are valued at $30,000. The other—the Christian College—is under the control of the Christian Church, and is valued at $35,000.

Much of the prosperity of Santa Rosa is due to these two colleges. Several hundred young of both sexes are brought by them to study in the town, and many parents, retiring from active business, make Santa Rosa their home on account of its educational advantages. Two and a half miles west of Santa Rosa are the White Sulphur Springs, a pleasant resort, and nine miles to the north-east on the road to Calistoga, *via* the Petrified Forest, are the Mark West Springs, beautifully located in a bend of the Mark West Creek.

Quite a romantic history is connected with the name of the creek, town, and valley. In brief,

Friar Amorosa, a zealous Catholic missionary, made an excursion north-east from San Rafael in 1829 and captured an Indian maiden of the Cainemeros tribe, and baptized her in the river Chocoalomi, and gave her the name of Santa Rosa, because the day of the baptism was the day of the feast of Santa Rosa de Lima. He was attacked by the natives and driven back, but the name remains and is honored to-day.

The climate of Santa Rosa is mild and pleasant, a grateful mean between the cold of the coast and the heat of the interior valleys.

Santa Rosa boasts of its exuberant vegetation, and especially its mammoth rose-bush. This is in front of the Grand Hotel, and is of the La Marque variety, with a pure white blossom. The stem measures 24 inches in circumference at the base, and grows to a height of 12 feet without branches, and in all 27 feet high, with a width of 22 feet. It was planted in 1838, and has had 4000 roses in full bloom at one time, with twice as many opening buds.

Of several good hotels in Santa Rosa, the Occidental is the best.

Fulton, 61 miles from San Francisco, is the point of divergence of the Fulton and Guerneville Branch, leading to the red-wood forests on the Russian River. The stations on this branch are Meacham's, Laguna, Forestville, Green Valley, Korbel's, and Guerneville. The length of this branch is 16 miles.

At Korbel's some of the enormous trees are preserved from cutting or injury and the grounds tastefully fitted up for picnics. Guerneville is on the Russian River, only a few miles above Duncan's Mills, the terminus of the North Pacific Coast (narrow gauge) Railroad.

A visit to the region of the red-woods will repay the tourist, for these (*Sequoia Sempervirens*) are peculiar to the coast mountains. None are found in Oregon, Washington Territory, Mexico, or the Sierra Nevadas. It is the chief material for the lumber of the State. It was used for ties for the Central Pacific Railroad, and lasts for many years in the ground. No other wood splits so true to the grain. Some of the trees are said to grow to a diameter of twenty-five feet, the largest being in Mendocino and Humboldt counties. An acre of these trees near Guerneville, on the "Big Bottom," yields 800,000 feet of lumber. The largest tree cut there was 18 feet in diameter, and made 180,000 feet of lumber. The tallest tree was 344¼ feet in height, taller than any one of the "Big Trees" (*Sequoia Gigantea*) now standing.

There are three large saw-mills near Guerneville, and others on the line of the road. In the red-wood forests there is also found an abundance of the chestnut oak (*Quercus Densiflora*), the bark of which is used for tanning, and brings from $15 to $17 a cord in San Francisco.

Mark West, Windsor, and Grant's are small stations; and

Healdsburg, 72 miles from San Francisco, is beautifully located on the west bank of the Russian River, with Dry Creek and its valley west of the town. Near the town is Sotoyome or Fitch Mountain, a butte around which Russian River winds its course. The town was laid out in 1856, and has a population of nearly 3000. It has a bank, seven churches, two weekly papers, and two academies—the Alexander Academy and the Butler Institute. The former is under the supervision of Rev. S. H. Thomas, D.D., LL.D., a Presbyterian minister, and for many years a professor in Hanover College, Indiana.

Healdsburg has a delightful climate, and is convenient to the range of mountains on either the east or west side of the valley, where trout, quail, rabbits, and deer may be found in abundance.

Near Healdsburg are several places of resort, among them "Magnolia Farm," and Mrs. Miller's, and the celebrated Litton Seltzer Springs. The station of

Litton Springs is near the hotel and spring. The buildings were erected at a cost of $80,000, and are not equaled by those connected with any mineral spring in the State.

The situation is charming, in a broad plateau overlooking Alexander Valley and the course of the Russian River for miles, and flanked on three sides by mountain peaks. The water is bottled and sold in San Francisco in large quantities, and has been carefully analyzed.

Geyserville, 80 miles from San Francisco, is the station for Skagg's Springs. The valley has become quite narrow at this point. The springs are eight miles west of Geyserville, at the head of Dry Creek Valley. There are hot sulphur springs, a soda spring, iron spring, and luxurious baths. The situation is beautiful—one of the most charming of all the mineral springs in the State.

Truett's is a small station; and

Cloverdale, the terminus, is 90 miles from San Francisco. It is at the head of the valley, and on Russian River, with romantic and picturesque scenery on every hand. It has about a dozen stores, two hotels, two churches, and one newspaper, the *Weekly Cloverdale News.* The population is about 700.

From Cloverdale there is an excellent road to the Geysers, with no grade exceeding four feet to the hundred, and the stages of Van Arnam & Kennedy are of the most approved pattern, and the distance, 16 miles, has been made in an hour and a half. The fare for the round trip is $4.50.

Stages run from Cloverdale every day to Ukiah, the county town of Mendocino County,

31 miles (fare from San Francisco, $7.75), and to Mendocino on the sea-coast, 75 miles (fare, $11.50).

Cloverdale has daily stages also to the many places of resort in Lake County—to Kelseyville,

Soda Bay, Highland Springs, Witter Springs (via Ukiah or via Upper Lake), Lakeport, Pierson's Springs, and connections for Glenbrook or Bassett's, Adams, Sulphur Banks, Howard Springs, Blue Lakes, and Bartlett's Springs.

Stage Routes to the Yosemite Valley and Big Tree Groves.

There are four all-wagon roads into the valley. One leaves the railroad at Milton, two at Merced, and one at Madera. The Big Tree groves, accessible en route to the valley, are the Calaveras, (north and south groves), the Tuolumne, the Merced, the Mariposa, and the Fresno. The first element to be taken into consideration is

1. *Distance.*—This is as follows :

BIG OAK FLAT AND CALAVERAS ROUTE—*Stages.*

San Francisco to Milton, *by rail*	133 miles.
Milton to Murphy's, *by stage*	30 "
Murphy's to North Calaveras Grove, and return to Murphy's	30 "
Murphy's to Chinese Camp *via* Sonoma	27 "
Chinese Camp to Black's Hotel	60 "
Total staging	147 "
Milton to Black's *via* Chinese Camp direct	88 miles.

COULTERVILLE ROUTE.

San Francisco to Merced, *by rail*	151 miles.
Merced to Dudley's, *by stage*	46 "
Dudley's to Merced	42 "
Total staging	88 "

MARIPOSA ROUTE.

Merced to Mariposa *via* Indian Gulch	47 miles.
Mariposa to Clark's	27 "
Clark's to Black's	23¾ "
Total staging	92 "

MADERA ROUTE.

San Francisco to Madera, *by rail*	173.5 miles.
Madera to Fresno Flat, *by stage*	35 "
Fresno Flat to Clark's	20 "
Clark's to Black's	23¾ "
Total staging	79 "

2. *Elevations, Grades, and Road-Beds.*—The bottom of the Yosemite Valley is 4000 feet above sea-level, and the roads enter it by descending the wall on either side. Therefore, the road which rises least above the bottom of the valley is most desirable, other things being equal.

The greatest elevation of the Big Oak Flat route is the summit near Tamarack Flat........................... 7040 feet.
Coulterville route, near Hazel Green.... 6085 "
Mariposa route, on Chowchilla Mountains 5750 "
Madera route, on Chowchilla Mountains. 4750 "

The low elevation of the Madera route, as well as the fact of its southern exposure nearly all the way to the Valley, will make it freer from snow in both spring and fall, and less tiresome to the weary. It may be possible to keep this route open nearly all the winter.

The *grades* vary on the different roads, the steepest being on the Big Oak Flat route, equaling 20 feet to the 100 feet, and the steep grades being unbroken for miles at a time.

On the Coulterville route, the steepest grade is near Coulterville, 4 miles in length, rising in places 18 feet to the 100 feet. Another grade of five miles in length rises on an average 10 feet to the 100 feet. On this route there are 30 miles of up grade between Coulterville and the Valley, and 20 miles of down grade.

On the Mariposa route there are numerous hills to be ascended and descended, as on the preceding routes. The steepest grade is across the Chowchilla Mountains, where the rise is 17.5 feet to the 100 feet.

Between Clark's and the Valley, the Mariposa and the Madera routes are the same, and the maximum grade is 10.5 feet to the 100 feet. On the Madera route the maximum grade between Madera and Clark's is 4 feet to the 100 feet. These grades, taken in connection with the greatest elevation, are an important element in reference to time, for on steep grades the time must be slow.

The *road-bed* will be thought bad enough whichever route one takes, if he is not accustomed to mountain roads ; but they are all good, considering the country through which they pass. In general, the greater the elevations the more rocky and rough the road-bed.

3. *Coaches and Teams.*—On these, and in some coaches on a particular seat, may depend much of the comfort of the passenger. It is well, therefore, to see a photograph of the coach, and know beforehand whether it is to be a "mud-wagon," or a "Concord coach," or an open "Kimball wagon." As there is no danger of

rain, the open Kimball wagons are to be greatly preferred. They are the most comfortable coaches ever made, and obstruct no fine view for any passenger. In these every passenger has a box-seat.

The *teams,* so far as the writer has observed, are all good ; it does not pay to have any others, and they who understand their business look well to this point.

4. *Hotels.*—These are all good. Some are excellent—as good as any in the State. Among these are the El Capitan at Merced, Dudley's, Clark's, Murphy's, and the Calaveras Big Trees. The Madera route has an unrivaled advantage in this, that a tourist can take a palace sleeping-car at 4 P.M. in San Francisco, and be undisturbed during the night, the car being placed on a side track on arrival at Madera, to remain until morning. Or, returning from the Valley, one may take the palace sleeping-car on arrival at Madera, and find himself undisturbed until he nears Lathrop for breakfast the next morning.

5. *Scenery en route.*—On every route it is beautiful. There is a general sameness in looking over the hills and taking in the great San Joaquin Valley, but there can be no two views precisely alike.

On the Big Oak Flat route, the crossing of the Tuolumne, after ascending and descending a steep mountain, is quite picturesque. On the Coulterville route there are many fine views of the mountains, and there is also Bower Cave, an interesting opening in limestone rock, into which one can descend by ladder and then pass into the main opening. It is unique and interesting, but seems not to win permanent and general interest in the midst of greater wonders. The Coulterville route descends to the cañon of the Merced before reaching the Valley proper, and passes up along the rapids, where the river roars and rushes out toward the plain. This is especially interesting, grand, and mighty in the early spring, when rains and melting snows have swollen the river to a tremendous torrent.

The Mariposa and Madera routes unite at Clark's. From Merced and Madera to Clark's the scenery is good on either route. Concerning the route from Merced *via* Mariposa, Prof. Whitney says, " The road from Bear Valley to Mariposa passes through a region which gives as good an idea as any in the State of equal extent can of the peculiar foot-hill scenery of the Sierra Nevada." Substantially this another might say of any other of the roads into the Valley. The road from Clark's to the Valley passes down the South Fork of the Merced, and at the same time ascends to the plateau between this fork and the main Merced, where the scene is continually changing, but every thing is wildly sublime. Before losing sight of the cañon of the Merced, where the river flows through it

toward the San Joaquin, the view extends to the coast mountains, and on going up and into the Yosemite, the rapids, where the Merced River leaves the Yosemite Valley and rushes through the cañon, are seen far below. But the glory of this route is the scenery, viewed from Inspiration Point. It is the best general view of the Valley. From this point the Valley was first seen by those in pursuit of the Indians in 1851, and here the most profound emotions have arisen and the most pregnant words ever uttered concerning it were conceived, and from this point Hill, Bierstadt, and others have painted it. If this view is not had by taking the route to or from Clark's, it should be had at the expense of a day, for it is not possible to have any thing comparable to it on any road entering on the north side, as the Big Oak Flat and Coulterville enter. The latter is near the bed of the river, and too low down for the grand scenic effect of Inspiration Point, and both it and the Big Oak Flat route enter below where there is a trend in the wall, and El Capitan projects its massive form and shuts out the major part of the Valley beyond. Entering on the south wall from Clark's, the tourist is directed across the lower end of the Valley, and takes in more of it than any other point can give. Whoever enters the Valley will see Inspiration Point, and many who desire to enter by one road and return by another will retrace their steps to Clark's, preferring to get the most of the Valley while they are *en route* to and from it.

6. *Time required in Traveling.*—To visit the Valley *via* Milton, the tourist must remain over night at Stockton, where he will find the " Yosemite" and other good hotels. Leaving Stockton the next morning, it will require two days to reach the Valley, arriving on the second day at six o'clock P.M.

If the road be *via* the Calaveras Big Trees, it will require four days from Stockton to the Valley.

By the Coulterville route, leaving San Francisco at 4 P.M. for Merced, arriving at 11 P.M., a few hours' sleep may be had before taking the stage early next morning. Two days are required to reach the Valley, arriving at six P.M. By the Mariposa route, one must leave Merced at the same time as if going *via* Coulterville, and would reach the Valley the second day by connecting at Clark's with the stage from Madera. On this route the time is not yet fixed.

By the *Madera* route the tourist can leave San Francisco at 4 P.M., and combine the advantage of hotel with saving of time. The rest throughout the night in the palace sleeping-car will be better than a few hours' sleep at Merced, but not so good as at the hotel at Stockton. Leaving Madera early in the morning, the Valley is reached at noon the next day. The whole time is about 44 hours, including an unbroken night's rest.

Returning from the Valley, one may leave at at 6·A.M., and reach Stockton to connect with the overland train going east the next day. This can be done only by the route *via* Big Oak Flat, and will require a ride the first day both hard and late, and an early start the second day, in order to reach the train which leaves Milton at 10.45 A.M.

7. *Big Tree Groves.*—These trees are *Sequoia Giganten*, and belong to the same genus as the Red-woods (*Sequoia Sempervirens*), found only on the Coast Range.

The King's River Grove contains the largest living tree, 44 feet in diameter. This grove, and the two groves on the north and south forks of the Tule River, are not easily accessible. In the other groves the number of the trees is about as follows : North Calaveras, 90 ; South Calaveras, 1380 ; Tuolumne, 30 ; Merced, 50 ; Mariposa, 600 ; Fresno, 1200.

The two Calaveras groves are six miles apart, connected by a trail over a wild and picturesque cañon. The hotel is located in the north grove. It is a first-class house, and the only hotel in the midst of the trees. To those who desire to linger in the shade of these giants while they grow upon him for days and weeks, this is a favorite resort. To visit the south grove requires a day, and a ride on horseback. The grove itself is four miles long and one wide. In both these groves the trees are beautiful, surpassing in symmetry and perfection those of the Mariposa, but not those of the Fresno Grove.

The Mariposa Grove is of national importance. It is *the only one* that has been set aside as a park for the nation. It was ceded by Congress to the State of California, and is cared for by the Commissioners of the State. Its trees are in two groups, and these are half a mile apart. The wagon-road now in process of construction will pass through both of these groups.

The Fresno Grove is also in two groups, a mile apart, and will be connected with the Mariposa by the Madera road, and this will pass through both groups. The trees in this grove are not only large but symmetrical, not surpassed in this respect by any grove.

As to *size*, it varies with every string that passes around them. One includes and another leaves out certain enlargements or irregularities near the ground. The writer has measured all the large trees in the Calaveras (north and south), the Mariposa, and the Fresno groves, and has followed the method and principles in all cases. The largest living tree is said to be in the King's River Grove, 40 miles from Visalia, and not of easy access to tourists. The largest tree the writer found is in the south group of the Fresno Grove, it being 96.5 feet in circumference at the ground. It is round, symmetrical, free from blemish, and the noblest specimen to be seen while visiting the Valley. Prof. Whitney says the average diameter of the trees in the Mariposa Grove exceeds that of the trees in the Calaveras Grove, and the tallest tree of these groves is in the latter. In the north Fresno group, the largest tree is near the cabin of John A. Nelder, the present owner of the group. It is 87 feet in circumference at the ground, and 72½ *feet at six feet from the ground.*

The Tuolumne group is small and somewhat scattered. The Merced group is small, but rather compact. The Calaveras, Mariposa, and Fresno groves are all similar in this respect.

The Calaveras group may be visited in connection with the Valley, by making a détour of 50 miles.

The Mariposa and Fresno groves are distant from each other about as far as the two Calaveras groves ; and as the Madera route when completed will pass through both Mariposa and Fresno groves, they may be visited without any loss of time. For this the stage coming out of the Valley will make a détour of a few miles after leaving Clark's. This détour on the "down trip" will not increase the time.

8. *Baggage and Clothing.*—Take a change of flannels, and as little else as possible. Early in the season a lap-robe or blanket besides an overcoat will be essential to comfort. Stout, well-broken shoes or boots must be worn. Ladies should wear a stout, short dress. In summer, when the rainless roads are dusty, a heavy linen or mohair coat is necessary.

9. *Guides.*—Some people need none. Almost any one can take a good map like Whitney's and read accurate descriptions, and make his own way to any point. Gentlemen need have no fear of being molested. Guides are easily procured if desired, and those who ride and are unaccustomed to the use of saddle-horses should have one to see that no accident occurs from the slipping of the saddles. A guide, including his horse, will usually cost $5 a day.

Expenses to the Yosemite Valley.

The tourist will be able to vary these in many ways, and no statement can be more than an approximation, unless it be to give *maximum* rates. These are as follows : From the railroad to the valley and return, $15.00, by any route. The additional stage fare to include the Calaveras Big Trees is $7.00, but the extra railroad fare, after leaving the main line to San Francisco is only $1.00.

To visit the Mariposa Grove there is no extra charge, but the railroad fare will be $5.75, $8.10, or $9.00 additional, according as Merced, or Madera is made the point of departure. By taking a round-trip ticket from Lathrop to Merced, and returning *via* Madera, the additional cost will be $8.10. Round-trip ticket, Lathrop to Merced, $5.75. Round-trip ticket, Lathrop to Madera, $9.00.

Board and lodging in the valley are $3.00 per day.

The time to the valley from San Francisco, *via* the Big Oak Flat Route, is two days ; and *via* the Calavaras Grove of Big Trees, four days ; and *via* Coulterville, two days ; and *via* Mariposa or Madera, one and a half days. Passengers by the Mariposa or Madera route *can return* from the valley *via* the Mariposa Big Trees by the new wagon road without loss of time.

Saddle Horses in the Valley.

The Board of Commissioners in charge of the valley and the Mariposa Big Tree Grove, have established maximum rates as follows :

1. From any hotel in the Valley to Glacier Point and Sentinel Dome and return by same route, ... $3.00
2. From Valley to Glacier Point, Sentinel Dome, Nevada Fall and Snow's (passing the night at Snow's)................................ $3.00
3. From Valley direct to Snow's and Nevada Fall, passing by Vernal Fall and returning to Valley same day,............................ $3.00
4. From Snow's to Cloud's Rest and back to Snow's, or to Valley the same day,............. $3.00
5. From Valley direct to Cloud's Rest, and back to Snow's,................................ $3.00
6. From Valley direct to Cloud's Rest and back to Valley same day,...................... $5.00
7. From Snow's to Valley,...................... $2.00
8. From Valley to Upper Yosemite Fall, Eagle Point and return,...................... $3.00
9. For use of saddle horses on the level of the Valley per day,........................ $2.50

Carriages.

(For a party of not less than four persons.)

1. To Bridal Veil Fall and return, each person, $1.00
2. To Mirror Lake and return, each person,.. $1.00
3. To the Cascades, passing by and stopping at the Bridal Veil (each person,........... $3.00
4. To the Cascades and return, each person,.. $2.00
5. To Bridal Veil and Artist's Point, each person, ... $2.00

The charge for guide (including horse) when furnished, will be $3.00 per day. The above charges do not cover feed for the horses at Snow's, nor tolls on the various trails. These latter are as follows :

To Glacier Point, each person,............... $1.00
To foot of Upper Yosemite Fall,............ $0.50
From foot of Upper Yosemite Fall to Eagle Point, ... $0.50
To Nevada Fall (including Vernal Fall),...... $0.75
To Mirror Lake in a carriage,............... $0.50
(Tourists to Mirror Lake on foot or horseback, free.)

Points in the Valley Most Attractive to Tourists.

1. South Dome, } each of these includes Vernal and
2. Clouds Rest, }   Nevada Falls.
3. Inspiration Point.
4. Glacier Point.
5. Sentinel Dome.
6. Upper Yosemite Fall and Eagle Point.
7. Mirror Lake.
8. Bridal Veil Fall.
9. Lower Yosemite Fall.
10. El Capitan.

Reference is had in the above order, to the fact that El Capitan and Bridal Veil Fall are at the entrance to the Valley and must be passed both in going in and coming out. The South Dome is difficult of access, the only way being to climb the rounded side of the Dome by holding to 975 feet of rope anchored at various points.

Time Usually Required for the Various Excursions.

From the hotels to Upper Yosemite Falls and return,......................... ....4 hours.
From the hotels to Upper Yosemite Falls and Eagle Point and return,............... 6 hours.
To Bridal Veil Falls,......................... 3 hours.
To Bridal Veil Falls and El Capitan,........ 4 hours.
To El Capitan,............................... 3 hours.
To Mirror Lake,............................. 3 hours.
To Vernal and Nevada Falls,................. 1 day.
To Mirror Lake, and Vernal and Nevada Falls,. 1 day.
To Lower Yosemite Falls, ...2½ hours.
To Mirror Lake and Lower Yosemite Falls,..½ a day.
To Glacier Point,........................... 6 hours.
To Sentinel Dome,........................... 7 hours.
To Glacier Point and Sentinel Dome,....... 8 hours.
To Cloud's Rest from Snow's Hotel to Nevada Falls,................................ 8 hours.
To South Dome from Snow's,............... 4 hours.
From Snow's to Cloud's Rest and South Dome and back to Snow's,................... 1 day.
From Snow's to Cloud's Rest, or to South Dome and back to the Valley—*possible in*.. 1 day.
From Valley to Inspiration Point and back to Hotel,............................... 1 day.

New Overland Route

SACRAMENTO AND SAN FRANCISCO.

Overland passengers were compelled for years to pass from Sacramento to San Francisco *via* Stockton and the Livermore Pass—a circuitous route of 138 miles (pages 244—260). A still longer route, but in shorter time, was made by leaving the old Western Pacific road at Tracy Junction and following the San Pablo and Tulare railroad *via* Antioch and Martinez—149 miles to San Francisco—but at last the route that must be permanent is now traveled; it is the shortest possible considering the nature of the country. After spending twenty minutes in the new depot of Sacramento, without the delay of backing on the "Y" formerly used, the train will depart for San Francisco.

This new depot is the finest west of the Missouri river, and a credit to the road for which it was constructed. In summer it is cool, and always light and cheerful.

On leaving it the train crosses the Sacramento river on a substantial wooden bridge. A draw will be noticed in the bridge for the steamers used principally in freighting along the river, or carrying passengers to points remote from the railroad. The new bridge is built a few feet above where the old bridge was located. It is a benefactor both to Sacramento City and Yolo county, for it has abolished the high tolls that almost prevented intercourse between the farmers of one and the merchants of the other.

Between Sacramento and Davisville the wide expanse of *tule* land is covered for a large part of the year with water, and whether it can ever be reclaimed without flooding Sacramento City is doubtful. During very rainy seasons the waters of the American and Sacramento rivers must find some outlet, and with such an inland sea, as one crosses between these stations, completely covering the grassy island (see page 275), and the rivers filled to the tops of the levees, and the months requisite for the water to run down so that hunters can hide in the tules to bag their game, or sheep and hogs find their feed,—it seems

probable that the Sacramento must be eventually divided and a large part carried off in a canal constructed through this tule land.

On page 275 (at Davisville) is mentioned a branch of the California Pacific railroad running north to Woodland and Knight's landing. Near Woodland the Northern Railway connects with the California Pacific, and both being leased to the Central Pacific form one continuous line northward through that portion of the Sacramento valley lying west of the river. By this route the best settled portion of Colusa county finds easy and direct access to Sacramento, San Francisco, and Bartlett and Allen Springs in Lake county, their best route to the same places. Leaving for a time the main line for overland trains, we pass Woodland, situated amid groves of oak, and reach *Yolo*, 27.53 miles, Black's 33.41 and Dunnigan 40.93 miles from Sacramento, towns in an agricultural region, each with several stores, saloons, etc., but of no general importance.

Harrington, 45.97,
Arbuckle, 51.14,
Berlin, 55.20, and
Macy, 56.13 miles from Sacramento, are all small places in an agricultural region.

Williams, 61.86 is the station for *Colusa* (City), eleven miles east, on the Sacramento river. Stages for Bartlett Springs and other points in Lake county leave Williams every morning; and stages for Colusa make close connection daily with both passenger and mixed trains.

Colusa is the county seat of Colusa county—which is one of the largest wheat-producing counties in the state. The town has a population of almost 3,000, and is connected by daily stages with Marysville; and by another line to Jacinto, Princeton and Chico. Jacinto, in this county, is the home of Dr. Glenn, the largest wheat-grower in California.

Maxwell, 70.71 miles from Sacramento,

Delavan, 75.95 miles from Sacramento,
Norman, 79.61,
Logandale, 81.97, are all unimportant stations.
Willows, 87.54 miles from Sacramento and 150.87 from San Francisco, is the present terminus of this road. It is wholly a railroad town, but has sprung up as though sure of an important future, and even aspires to rivalry of Colusa.

The extension of this road will be northward to Tehama, where the Oregon division of the Central Pacific crosses the Sacramento river. About forty miles are yet to be built to complete this connection. When this gap is closed San Francisco will have a direct line to Redding for all travel to northern California and Oregon. Leaving Davisville, the overland traveler will go southward on the California Pacific railroad (see page 276) to

Suisun.

At this point he will leave the California Pacific to take the Northern railway to Oakland.

If destined for Vallejo, or any point in the Napa Valley (see pages 276-7), he will change cars and continue on the line of the California Pacific Railroad (the old, short line between Sacramento and San Francisco), and cross the lands that skirt the western side of Suisun Bay. Numerous sloughs may be observed, and, if in the winter season, wild geese and ducks may appear, like clouds, in the air.

Across the lowlands on the left or east side are the Montezuma hills, south of which is the junction of the Sacramento and San Joaquin rivers. Almost directly ahead may be seen Mount Diablo, the sentinel of central California, a visit to the summit of which will well repay any one; the ascent can easily be made from Martinez, a town opposite Benicia (see page 298).

The difficulty of building the road across the marsh-lands cannot be comprehended as one rides comfortably in the cars; but the subsidence of the road-bed is plainly visible to the close observer. Great quantities of earth have disappeared beneath the track, and you can find many a railroad man who loves to tell how a horse and cart went down one day, "*clear out of sight,*" and were found a week afterwards carried by the current through the Strait of Carquinez into the San Pablo bay!

Teal (a name suggestive of a good meal), 44.19, and *Goodyear's,* 39.01 miles from Sacramento, are unimportant stations. When the road curves to the right and skirts the hills, with the water of Carquinez Strait close at hand on the left, the United States arsenal for the Pacific coast may be noticed on the right.

Benicia, 33.25 miles from Sacramento, was at one time the rival of San Francisco for the

commercial prominence of the state, and was the capital of the state for a short season. It is a pleasant place for residence, with educational facilities in a convent, St. Augustine's (Episcopal) College, and Mrs. Lynch's seminary for young ladies—which is one of the oldest educational institutions in the state.

Martinez, sheltered in a beautiful nook of the hills, appears across the water on the left.

At Benicia, the Strait of Carquinez is crossed by means of the ferryboat *Solano*—the largest boat of her class in the world—424 feet long and 116 wide, with two vertical beam engines, driven by eight steel boilers, each weighing 21 tons. The boilers are in pairs, and one or all may be used at pleasure. The engines are not abreast of each other, but on the center line of the boat—the whole arrangement being an ingenious method of providing for *four tracks on the deck.* At a single trip, a locomotive and 48 freight cars, or 24 palace coaches, may be transported, and when loaded the draught of the boat is only 6 feet 6 inches. The light draught is only 5 feet. Eleven water-tight, transverse bulkheads, dividing the hull into twelve compartments, make it absolutely impossible to sink the boat; and four Pratt trusses, directly under the tracks, fore and aft, and varied in size to meet the strains upon them, connect the deck and bottom of the boat, give it longitudinal stiffness, and make it, in fact, a huge floating bridge. The aprons connecting the boat with the slips at Benicia and Port Costa are each 100 feet long and 150 tons in weight, and worked by hydraulic power in a combination of pontoons and counter-weights. The cost of the boat, etc., was $350,000. Trains are run aboard without being uncoupled from the locomotive, and the whole time occupied in crossing (about a mile), including the stops for passengers, is only 25 minutes.

Port Costa (at first called *Carquinez*—see page 298), 32.17 miles from San Francisco, is the junction of the Northern Railway and the San Pablo and Tulare Railroad. Trains to and from Los Angeles and Arizona, and from Sacramento *via* Antioch and Stockton, pass this point.

Valona, 29.62 miles from San Francisco, is a side-track for local travel. After passing through a short tunnel, there bursts upon the traveler a glorious vision of beauty—the San Pablo bay and its environs.

Vallejo Junction, 29.01 miles from San Francisco, as its name implies, is on the new route from Vallejo to San Francisco. The town is to be seen on the right, situated on a sloping hill-side. Mare Island and the United States navy yard are directly between Vallejo and the bay. At the east end of the island is a small light-house. (See page 277.) Passengers from Vallejo and Napa Valley are no longer detained or perplexed by the uncertainties of a steamer from South Vallejo to San Francisco, but are ferried across to Vallejo Junction.

Tormey, 26.76, *Pinole* (a telegraph station), 24.02, and *Sobrante*, 20.82 miles from San Francisco, are unimportant local stations.

See page 298 for *San Pablo to Oakland.*

The long pier between West Oakland and Oakland Wharf (page 261) will soon be a thing of the past. The piles remain, but a solid bed of rock and earth will soon extend out into the bay for nearly two miles—a work as costly and important as a tunnel of equal length.

On arriving at the foot of Market street, San Francisco, with checks delivered to the Pacific Transfer Company, and carriages engaged through the messenger of the same company that boarded the train, one will soon reach his destination in the city. Street cars pass the principal hotels, and run to all quarters of the city. Beginning on the south, one finds the cars of the Mission-street road; next, cars through Market to Fifth, and Fifth to Townsend, to the general offices of the Central and Southern Pacific Railroads and the depot of the northern division of the Southern Pacific Railroad. These cars connect by transfer with cars for the Potrero & South San Francisco. Next are the Hayes Valley cars, running through Market street to Ninth, thence through Hayes Valley to Lone Mountain and the Golden Gate Park, and the Market and Valencia street cars, through Market to about Thirteenth street, and thence on Valencia to Twenty-sixth street. These cars connect at Valencia street by transfer to the Market street extension, running on Market to Seventeenth street.

Next are the cars of the omnibus line running up Market street a few blocks to the Grand Hotel and there transferring in one direction to Montgomery street and North Beach, and in another direction to the depot of the northern division of the Southern Pacific Railroad and the general offices of the C. & S. P. R. R., and to a third line running out of Howard street to Twenty-sixth.

Next are cars of the Central road, running along Market a few blocks to Pine, hence to Lone Mountain, crossing Montgomery and Kearney streets in the vicinity of the principal retail stores. Next are the cars of the Sutter-street road, running up Market a few blocks to Sutter, and then connecting with a cable road to Lone Mountain.

From a point on the cable road at crossing of Larkin street transfers are given to cross roads— one running north on Polk street and the other south on Larkin street.

Next are the cars of the North Beach and Mission roads, starting, like nearly all the others, on Market street, and soon turning off for California and Kearney streets, at which point trans-

fers are given to the North Beach or to the depot of the northern division of the Southern Pacific Railroad and the general offices of C. & S. P. R. R. at Fourth and Townsend streets or to cars running on Folsom street to Twenty-sixth.

Lastly, on the extreme right, is another car of the Central road, which runs past the post-office and through the vicinity of the principal retail stores, and then crosses Market street and down Sixth street to Brennan.

To many points there are several lines, but to ascertain *the most direct* is perplexing to the stranger. For such, observe the following:

For the Grand and Palace Hotels, Baldwin, Lick House (on Montgomery, near Market), and any point on Market street, take the cars of the Market-street line. For the Occidental Hotel, Brooklyn and Russ House, take the two-horse cars at the Central road. For the International or Cosmopolitan take the cars of the North Beach and Mission road.

For the general offices of the C. P. & S. P. R. R. take the Market and Fifth street (one-horse) cars of the Market-street road, or the cars of the Omnibus road; for the United States Mint, the cars of the Market and Fifth street road; for the post-office and custom-house, take the one-horse cars of the Central road; for Lone Mountain, take the cars of the Sutter-street road; for the Cliff House or Golden Gate Park, take Market-street cars to Geary street, and then the Geary-street cars; for Woodward's Gardens take the City Railroad or the Mission-street cars.

A feature of San Francisco is the cable roads. Of these there are four at present : the Clay-street Hill road, the California-street road, the Geary-street road and the Sutter-street road. None of the cables extend to the ferry, and cars of the Sutter-street road only.

The cable-roads are far preferable to any other when they run in a direction to suit the traveler. They do not wear on the nerves by compelling one to witness cruelty to animals. The cars make better speed than the horse-cars, and climb steep hills with perfect ease and descend with like safety. The cable is a wire-rope, three inches in circumference. It runs in an iron tube beneath the surface of the street, and between the rails. An open slit, three-quarters of an inch wide, is seen, allowing an iron arm to pass down from the car or "dummy." This arm is made to catch the cable by a secure grip, or is instantly released by an operator or engineer on the dummy. Of these roads, the California-street is the pride of the city. The road-bed is solid masonry or concrete, and the frame-work solid iron. The tourist should not fail to see these roads. The Clay-street road passes over the highest elevation in the city, and the California-street road passes the palatial residences of Governor Stanford, Charles Crocker, Mrs. Hopkins, and others.

:1

Recent Changes in the Principal Hotels.

The Cosmopolitan has been discontinued. The Lick House is now conducted on the European plan. The Grand has been incorporated with the Palace, and by a bridge built across New Montgomery street guests pass from one to the other, all dining at the Palace.

Other Changes of Interest

Are, that visitors driving to the Cliff House are no longer required to pay toll; Wade's Opera House (page 263) is now the Grand Opera House; every horse-car line but two (Clay street and California street), runs into or crosses Market street.

Of the United States Government buildings— at the Mint may be seen a most valuable collection of coins, including a "one cent " of 1804 for which $1,500 was paid. The Appraisers' building on Washington street adjoining the post-office, is now completed ; the post-office has lately been remodeled ; and the old Mint on Commercial street near Montgomery, has been changed into the United States sub-treasury.

Besides the libraries mentioned (page 267), a free library has been opened on Bush street between Kearney and Dupont, now Fleet street. From this, books may be taken home without charge to the borrower.

In book-stores—Roman's has been discontinued, and in the same vicinity may be found Billings and Harbourne's and C. Beach's ; and Bibles and religious books are represented by the American Tract Society and the Methodist Book Depository and Presbyterian Board of Publication.

The most imposing church edifice in the city is St. Ignatius, in connection with a college of the same name on Hayes street near Market. It is under the direction of the Jesuits.

The Army and Navy head-quarters are at the Presidio Reservation, but the Commissary and Quartermaster's offices and store-rooms are on New Montgomery street, adjoining the Palace Hotel.

Recent Changes in Popular Pleasure Resorts.

Most of these places continue open as usual. The Yosemite continues to be reached via Madeira and Mariposa Big Trees, by at least two-thirds who go thither.

The Geysers have an attractive and well-kept hotel.

Litton Springs, closed for a time, is re-opened as a resort in summer, and young men's academy during all the year.

The White Sulphur Springs and *Santa Cruz* have found more than a rival in the *Hotel Del Monte* at *Monterey,* California, and the Pacific coast has railroad trains that are as economical of the time of her business men as the fast mail trains between New York and Chicago. *Monterey* may be reached at a speed of forty miles an hour, and the tourist may extend his visit to this historic and interesting spot and take in Santa Cruz for only a trifle more than he used to pay for a trip to San Jose.

The Monterey and Salinas Valley Railroad has been purchased by the Southern Pacific and changed to a broad-gauge road. A new connection has been built from Castroville (see page 284), and the old connection via Salinas discontinued. The whole road has been relaid with the best of steel rails, and its fast trains make it the most popular road on the coast.

Monterey, 125 miles from San Francisco, the terminus, is delightfully situated on the bay of Monterey, which is 28 miles wide. This historic spot was reached in December, 1601, and possession taken in the name of the King of Spain, and named after Gaspar de Zuniga, Count of Monterey and Viceroy of Mexico at the time.

In the fall of 1769 Gaspar de Portala, governor of Lower California, came overland from San Diego with two priests and 63 soldiers and erected *Portala's Cross* (immortalized by Bret Harte), in the vicinity. In June, 1770, Father Junipero Serra, a Franciscan, erected another cross and joined in hoisting the royal standard of Spain. It was one of the most flourishing places on the coast from that time until after California became a state in the Union.

The stars and stripes were hoisted by Commodore Sloat July 7, 1846, and Monterey, long the capital of the Spanish and Mexican province, was the capital of the new state. With the removal of the capital to San Jose it entered on a Rip Van Winkle sleep, which continued until but recently.

A few years ago, the Pacific Grove Retreat was formed, designed primarily to furnish a cheap and attractive summer resort for ministers of all denominations and their families, with all the advantages of sea-bathing. But the new Hotel del Monte, the finest on the Pacific coast outside of San Francisco, and its throng of visitors, has given a new life to the place. This hotel accommodates, in first-class style, 400 guests, and has all modern conveniences and appliances. It is built in the modern Gothic or Eastlake style, is 385 by 115 feet, and three stories high—one an attic story. The house is elegantly furnished, and the grounds, consisting of 106 acres, are entirely closed, and beautifully wooded with pine, oak, cedar, cypress, English walnuts, etc.

In the town are many objects of interest, such as the Catholic church, built in 1794, with old paintings of much merit; the old block-house and fort; the Cuartel, on California street; Cotton Hall; tne old custom-house.etc.; the light-house on Point Pinos, three miles west of the town, with a Fresnal light of the third order; the Moss Beach; Seal Rocks; Cypress Point and Carmel Mission.

The last is four miles south of Monterey, on Carmel Creek, a beautiful, picturesque spot. It was founded by Father Junipero Serra, June 3, 1770. In 1825, the Mission had 90,000 cattle, 50,000 sheep, 2,000 horses, 2,000 calves, 370 yoke of oxen, $50,000 in merchandise and $40,000 in silver—all of which, ten years later, was converted to secular uses by decree of the Mexican government. The old ruins of the church are full of interest, and in the yard near it lie the remains of fifteen governors of the province and state, as well as the tomb of Junipero Serra.

Fifty miles of graveled roads afford fine drives. Hunting and fishing that cannot be excelled may be easily reached. The sea-bathing is the best on the coast north of Point Conception, and the climate equable and healthful.

The table of temperature for Monterey was kept in 1874 by Dr. E. K. Abbot, a correspondent of the United States Signal Service; that for San Francisco by many parties, and is a mean of most any three years; Los Angeles by W. H. Broedrick (for 1871), who took observations four times a day for seven years. The Santa Barbara record is for 1869,

and was kept by officers of the Coast Survey. The Santa Monica record is for 1846, and was kept by Dr. W. S. King, of the army, in 1853. The Fort Yuma record was kept by officers of the army in 1851. All others are taken from notes of travelers or from books written from friendly and sometimes enthusiastic standpoints.

The following carefully-prepared table presents the mean temperature of Monterey and many other health-resorts and places throughout the world.

PLACE.	Jan.	July.	Diff.	Latitude.	
	Degs	Degs.	Degs	Degs.	Min.
Monterey, ...	52	58	6	36	36
San Francisco, ...	49	57	8	37	48
Los Angeles, ...	55	67	12	34	04
Santa Barbara, ...	56	66	10	34	24
San Diego, ...	57	65	8	32	41
Santa Monica, ...	58	65	7	34	00
Sacramento, ...	45	73	28	38	31
Stockton, ...	49	72	23	37	56
Vallejo, ...	48	67	19	38	05
Fort Yuma, ...	56	92	36	32	43
Cincinnati, ...	30	74	44	39	06
New York, ...	31	77	46	40	37
New Orleans, ...	55	82	27	29	57
Naples, ...	46	76	30	40	52
Honolulu, ...	71	77	6	21	16
Funchal, ...	60	70	10	32	38
Mentone, ...	40	73	33	43	71
Genoa, ...	46	77	31	44	24
City of Mexico, . . .	52	63	11	19	26
Jacksonville, ...	58	80	22	30	50
St. Augustine, . . .	59	77	18	30	05
Santa Cruz, ...	50	60	10	37	00

THE HOTEL DEL MONTE AND GROUNDS AT MONTEREY, CAL.

THE

Chinese in San Francisco.

By F. E. SHEARER.

These queer looking people, with loose garments, umbrella hats, or skull-caps, rags for hose, pantaloons made ankle tight by tapes; wooden shoes, coppery skin, high cheek-bones, almond eyes, half-shaved heads, jet black hair, and dangling *pig-tails*, are the hated of the Paddy, the target of *hoodlums*; the field of the missionary, the bomb for the politician to explode, and the sinew for capital. They are called the essence of all that is vicious, villainous, and certainly are opinionated. They are everywhere; even the boys say they cannot throw stones without hitting them, but they are to be best seen in the Chinese quarters of San Francisco, from Pacific Street, the "Barbary Coast," to Sacramento Street, and from Kearney to Stockton, five squares by two, in the heart of the oldest part of the city.

Although in every block, and near every door, their special quarter is almost like a city of the "Middle Flowery Kingdom" set right down in our midst. Streets and alleys, and labyrinthian windings, not only such as we tread, are theirs; but, they live and travel under ground and over roofs, up and down, until the cunning policeman is outwitted in following them; and all their streets and by-ways are swarming with human or inhuman inhabitants, but little less numerous than the rats and the vermin. Cellars and lofts seem equally good for either lodgings, factories, shops, or laundries, and apartments of ordinary height are cut in two with a ladder to ascend to the loft, reminding us of the log-cabin days in the back-woods, or the wild frontier.

Buildings are made more capacious by rude balconies from the second stories, that almost touch over the narrow passages beneath. The Globe Hotel, corner of Jackson and Dupont Streets, three stories high, with about 60 rooms, is inhabited by about 1,500 Celestials, and the heads of the Chinamen in their bunks, must look like the cells of a honey-comb. Steamship hold, cemetery vault, Roman catacomb, or Egyptian pyramid could hardly be better packed.

Health.—The narrow streets are wide enough for hucksters, wood-piles, chicken-coops, temporary pig-pens, baskets and poles, and all sorts of foul rubbish, and just wide enough for our noses. These streets may center in open courts that reek in filth, or lead one from treading where death-dealing vapors ooze through the loose boards on which he walks, to dwellings, where the floors are easily lifted to secure sewer accommodations in pools or vats beneath; but with all this, the Chinamen seem to thrive best, and huddle closest where it is darkest and most dismal, and where sunlight never enters. Leprosy is said to exist, but if competent medical authorities have so pronounced any of their loathsome diseases, it is not generally known, or else the leprosy is not of a contagious character.

There are loathsome diseases among them, and especially among the prostitutes, by which even small boys are infected, but no wide-spread pestilence has ever been known among them, and the death-rate is not excessive.

Their funeral customs and places of burial make the concealment of the dead far more unlikely than when some victim is chopped to pieces and stowed away *a la* practices not unknown to American criminals.

Personal Habits. — Inoculation in childhood is universal, and they seem to come out of their filth as the eel from his skin, with a personal cleanliness that is marvelous, and to most, incredible. So far as the secret of their anomalous health and personal cleanliness can be detected, it is in their practice of daily ablution. They bathe as if it were a sacred duty, and in Washington Territory will cut through the winter ice to find the necessary water, and the tooth-brush is a daily companion.

The *cue* is regarded with patriotic pride. It and the tonsure were introduced into China in 1644, as a mark of acceptance of, and subjection to the Tartar rule, and enforced by the favor of the courts, to all litigants who wore the cue, and by rejecting in the literary examinations all candidates who appeared without it, and even by death in some cases, until at length the mark of derision became the badge of honor, and now every Celestial carries this flag of his country, no less dear than his own head.

It is formed by separating the unshaven hair on the crown of the head, three or four inches in diameter, into three strands and braiding with it coarse silk or false hair, until in cases of the ambitious it reaches to within three inches of the ground.

Sometimes it is worn for convenience in a coil around the head or the neck, but it is a mark of disrespect to have it coiled thus in the presence of superiors—more insulting than to enter a Fifth Avenue cathedral or orthodox church and sit with the hat on the head.

The head of those who can afford it, is shaved once in ten or fifteen days. The razor is triangular in shape, about two inches long, and an inch wide at one end, hollow ground and weighing about two ounces. The metal is of such excellent quality that the razors are often bought by Americans for the steel only.

Tonsorial operations are performed with great skill, and there are delicate instruments for swabbing the ears, pulling hairs out of the nostrils, and cleaning the eyelids on both under and upper sides. The sign of the barber-shop, is a four-legged frame—the legs painted green, and the knobs on top painted red.

As the cue is the badge of servitude to the present dynasty of China, no one can become an American citizen, or "declare his intentions" and retain this, for it proclaims that in political matters, he is not his own master, but the slave of the Emperor, and hence appears the absurdity of those who deny the sincerity of the profession of the Christian religion, made by some Chinamen who retain their cue. An English subject who unites with an American church, is not required or expected for this reason,. to renounce his allegiance to the Queen.

SCENE IN ALLEY, CHINESE QUARTERS, SAN FRANCISCO.

Chinese Quarters.—The most interesting objects to be seen in the Chinese quarters are stores, shops, restaurants and temples, or Joss houses, and opium smoking places, although some of the tourists visit viler abodes, out of curiosity.

A visit to the Chinese quarters may be made in daylight or by night, and with or without a policeman. The writer has frequently passed through the alleys and streets of Chinatown without the protection of policemen, and never experienced the least indignity. The only occasion when he failed to receive the strictest courtesy and deference was on intruding upon a company "at rice," (when they do not like to be disturbed) and introducing a large company of friends, one of whom said he came from New York, when one of the Chinamen grinned from ear to ear, exclaiming, "You foolee me—he Irishman, he Irishman."

Those desiring the protection of a policeman can secure the services of one by applying to the Chief of Police in the City Hall. Compensation should be made privately. Two dollars and a half is a sufficient fee, but visitors should pay their own admittance to the Chinese theater.

The Six Companies.—It is hard to estimate the birds of a large flock that come and go with spring and fall, and the Chinese are always traveling to and from the Celestial Empire, and no census taker, or poll tax gatherer has ever been guilty of the sin of numbering them. Whoever can be caught is squeezed for taxes, and no matter whether he has paid or not, he can pay for some one that can not be caught. The number of the people is variously estimated, but may be given as follows :

The Ming Yung Company,	63,000
Hop Wo Company,	43,000
Kong Chow Company,	13,000
Yung Wo Company,	13,000
Sam Yap Company,	11,000
Yen Wo Company,	6,000
Scattering,	1,000
Total,	130,000

Of these 65,000 are in California, and 30,000 in San Francisco. Of the whole number about 50,-000 are women, children and merchants.

Emigration is carried on through Hong Kong, a British port, the Chinese from the province of Kwangtung going *via* this port. It is not probable that it could be wholly prevented as long as the Chinamen can make money here.

At the end of the year 1851, not 4,000 had come to America. But the reports of the open country, and plenty of gold, brought 18,000 in 1852, and alarmed the Californians, so that the next year only 4,000 came, and the average of arrivals since, has not been 5,000 a year. We have often been told of "passage engaged ahead for thousands," that "enough are coming the present year to overrun us," but the prophecies are somewhat akin to those of the world's destruction.

The books of the Custom House, show the arrivals since 1868 to have been as follows, but of departures *and deaths*, there is no reliable record.

YEAR.	MALE.	FEMALE.	TOTAL.
1868,	10,024	256	10,280
1869,	11,710	1,540	13,252
1870,	9,666	645	10,318
1871,	4,864	100	4,964
1872,	8,812	565	9,377
1873,	16,605	516	17,121

YEAR.	MALE.	FEMALE.	TOTAL.
1874,	11,743	307	12,850
1875,	18,090	3,48	18,418
January, 1876,	1,170	7	1,177
February, 1876,	1,197	0	1,197
March, 1876,	1,872	0	1,872
	95,753	4,296	100,049

As to the object and power of these companies there is a difference of opinion. Some assert they are about absolute for all purposes of government, importing men and women, making and enforcing contracts for labor and passage, settling disputes, and by means of hired assassins killing at their pleasure, any one for whom they choose to offer a reward.

This and more—everything that can be said against them is believed by more than every Irishman, and on the other hand, those who have lived in China, in the service of the American or English government, and missionaries who *speak and read* the Chinese language, deny to the companies any such extent of power or purpose, and the Chinamen universally deny it.

It is certain that these organizations are *protective*, that they are practically emigration and aid societies, that they care for the sick, send some of the destitute back to China, settle disputes by arbitration, and possess such power that the officials of the companies are sometimes "bound over" for the members to keep the peace, and by an arrangement with the Pacific Mail Steamship Company, prevent the return of any one to China who has not paid his debts, and gather up and return to China the bones of all the dead belonging to the respective companies. They have no criminal power, and if American officials did not co-operate with and encourage the companies they would have much less influence and importance. Previous to coming, Chinamen have often no knowledge of the existence of the companies. A family may accumulate means to send one of their number, not from Cork, but Hong Kong, and on his arrival he usually allies himself to one of the companies for mutual assistance and protection, and the six companies may also advertise in China to induce some to emigrate.

Nearly all Chinamen in America are from the province of Kwangtung, of which Canton is the principal city, and hence only the Cantonese dialect is spoken here.

The part of the province from which they come usually determines what company each will join. No fee is exacted for membership or initiation.

A washing guild, or organization that fixes rates for washing, etc., has often been confounded with the Six Companies. It is a trades-union, independent of the companies. Trades-unions are as common in China as in America, and it is not surprising therefore that they fix here the prices of washing, and allow no new wash-house within certain limits of another, and keep wages high enough to secure the most money, and low enough to sicken the Irishman that competes with them.

The Women.—These are all of the lowest order, excepting perhaps 150 out of the thousands here. The manner of dealing with them is like that with Ah Hoe, as follows:

" An agreement to assist the woman Ah Hoe, because coming from China to San Francisco she became indebted to her mistress for passage. Ah Hoe herself asks Mr. Yee Kwan to advance for her $630, for which Ah Hoe distinctly agrees to give her body to Mr. Yee for service as a prostitute for a term of four years. There shall be no interest on the money. Ah Hoe shall receive no wages. At the expiration of four years Ah Hoe shall be her own master. Mr. Yee Kwan shall not hinder or trouble her. If Ah Hoe runs away before her time is out, her mistress shall find her and return her, and whatever expense is incurred in finding her Ah Hoe shall pay. On this day of the agreement Ah Hoe has received with her own hands $630. If Ah Hoe shall be sick at any time for more than ten days she shall make up by an extra month of service for every ten days of sickness. Now this agreement has proof. This paper received by Ah Hoe is witness.

YUNG CHEE, 12th year, 9th month, 14th day.

In October, 1873, Ah Hoe came to Mr. Gibson's school for protection, saying she had been beaten and ill-treated and gave this contract as an evidence that she had been held in slavery. The money she had held in her hands a few seconds, being compelled to pass it immediately over to her employer. She was taken to Hong Kong by her mistress and shipped to this country.

Tax Paying.—In San Francisco 324 persons or firms, are assessed for personal property, and the valuation is $531,300. Of city tax $5,012, i. e., .943 of the whole was collected last year, and of the State tax $2,896.59, i. e., .96 of the whole was collected ; a much larger proportion than the whole roll will show for other tax-payers. One of the tea-importing firms is assessed for personal property at $23,000, and another at $22,500, and six firms at $10,000 or upwards.

On real estate it is impossible to ascertain the amount of assessment, but it is certain that some of the people are so well pleased with the country as to consider it a desirable home, or else so shrewd in business as not to fear speculations in real estate, in which they often make fortunate turns. They never trouble any board of equalization for a reduction of their assessment, and if their assessments are made surprisingly low, may Allah forgive the error for such is not the intention, and strange as it may seem the names of Chinese real estate owners are never found on the delinquent tax-list. Some of the Chinamen are reputed to be worth from $100,000 to $200,000.

Striking Characteristics.—They are industrious, working early and late, are peaceable, never giving offense in the street.

They are thievish, and clannish, and have many vices, but they never garrote the belated clubman ; they will lie, but their honesty in deed and word is not a whit below any mercantile class, and their veracity is as good as the average in the same sphere of labor.

Economy—is seen in shrewd bargains, in cheap living, in picking up the gold in the tailings that slips through the fingers of the American miner, in roasting his pork by the carcass and selling it to save the services of many cooks and the cost of many fires.

The cobbler pursues his avocation on the street, reminding one of the horseback rider during the war, who was shaken heartily and awakened by a stranger who desired to know what he paid for lodgings. For the cobbler a candle-box will furnish a seat, and all his tools and stock in trade be carried about in another small box or basket.

They can live for about eight or ten cents a day, but the average cost of the working class is about thirty cents.

Skill in Imitating.—They are great imitators, and so far as known, do they not furnish a striking illustration of the truth of the theory of natural selection? Do not their caudal appendages and power of imitation show their relation to the monkey, and the link they form in the development of the race?

They are servile imitators. The sea captain who had an oil painting injured, and gave it to a Chinese artist to reproduce, was amazed to see the reproduction of the gash, and the Chinese tailor who "followed copy" in making the new coat with a patch on the elbow, needed his ideas enforced with blows, yet they never except the sticks the wheels hang on." They are more than imitators, for the ingenious headed Chinee can produce more expedients from his fertile brain than Ah Sin aces from his flowing sleeves. In the mountains John will own, drive, and care for his own team of horses, or mules.

Their value as servants or laborers is largely in this, that they do as they are shown, and have no more opinion of their own, than the miner who replied to his superintendent, when asked "what is this ore worth a ton?" "I don't know, to me it's worth four dollars a day."

Power of Control over Their Feelings,—makes their faces as unreadable as marble. They are least demonstrative of all the nationalities represented—the very opposite of the Frenchman. They rarely laugh or cry, yet they become excited, have no fear of death, and their Chinese oaths roll from them at a rapid rate.

They often express their feeling by oaths and curses, to which American profanity, it is to be hoped, will not attain by the next Centennial. They wish their enemies to be chopped into a thousand pieces,—that his bowels may rot inch by inch, and in geneal, their frequent oaths are vile, low, and most vulgar, and they use them in the consciousness that the mistress "can't sabee."

As servants many regard them as a great relief to the insolence and visiting so common to the class, and find them as reliable as any others. They are liked and hated in proportion as they are faithful and find kind mistresses. Many have tried them to their disgust, and others would have none but Chinamen.

Their language gives them no little advantage in publishing their grievances. A kind and cultured lady was greatly attached to her Chinaman, who remained in her kitchen about two years, and then returned to China to visit his relations.

His successor proved to be a surly and careless fellow, and was soon discharged. No Chinaman would then stay for more than a few days or a week, and a "Jap" was engaged but with the same mysterious result. At length some characters in the written language were discovered in the dust on the back of the mirror in the dressing bureau, and after they were effaced the trouble ceased!

Chinese Business.—Among the Chinese are pawnbrokers, money-changers and bankers, watch-makers and jewelers.

The laundries are on every block, in some of which the work is excellent, and in others miserable and destructive.

Their process of sprinkling the clothes by taking a mouthful of water and ejecting it in the form of spray is curious, but a method of sprinkling that is not surpassed for evenness.

Rag-pickers, and itinerant peddlers go about with two large baskets on the ends of a bamboo pole, and in this way burdens are usually carried and often 300 pounds are carried on a "dog-trot" from ten to twenty miles a day.

These baskets, loaded with fish, carefully picked in the markets, and vegetables selected with like care, or raised in little suburban gardens of their own, or fish and vegetables of the worst, are carried if they suit the customers. Their baskets are at the doors of all the side-streets, and supply provender to those who cry most against cheap labor.

Chinese Jewelry may be purchased for curiosity only, but the purchaser may feel easier than in buying a Connecticut clock, for the articles carved in gold and silver are of pure metal—the Chinese having not yet learned the intricacies of cheap jewelry.

Firm names are not subject to change with death or change of partners, but are often perpetuated for centuries.

Chinese Workmen.—Their employments and occupations are, in short, legion. They are adapted best to light, quick work, and engaged much in cigar making, the use of the sewing machine, gardening, mining, picking fruit, etc., but have also proved the most efficient class for building railroads and levees.

They are used almost exclusively for gathering castor-beans, strawberries and other fruits. As merchants, they prove successful, "cornering" the pea-crop and other markets, and they even charter vessels for the flour, tea and rice trade with China. Thus it is evident that the labor question wears a serious aspect on its face, but it is like the ocean disturbed most on the surface, and will be settled with some respect to the demands of capital, as such questions have always been settled.

One of the manufacturers engaged in the Mission Woolen Mills, and two other factories says: "We employ about one thousand Chinese. We pay white men wages 200 per cent. higher than that paid to the Chinese. Some of the Chinamen are equal to white men, but most of them earn from 90 cents to $1.20 a day. All the money for Chinese laborers is paid to one man. We started manufacturing with white labor, and three or four years ago came to the conclusion that we wanted to hire seventy-five white boys, and bought that many machines. The second day the boys went out on an excursion in the bay, and did not come back to work until the day after. We spoke to them about it, and said it must not happen again. Thereupon one of the boys put on his jacket and said to the others, 'Let him go to h—l,' and most of them left the factory. We could not rely on white boys. Afterward I engaged nine girls. One day I went to the factory and found no steam up. I asked 'What's the matter?' The foreman said the girls did not come, they are off on a holiday. They had too many holidays—Christmas, New Year's, Fourth of July, St. Patrick's Day, and many other holidays I never heard of. It went on from bad to worse, and when I found that the girls would rather loaf on the streets than work, I discharged them. I am not in favor of Chinese labor, mind you, but I have found out that white boys and girls of San Francisco cannot be depended upon. If we had no Chinamen, our factories would, in a measure, be hindered in their progress. If we had no manufactories of blankets here articles of that description would be bought in England. Shoes would be bought in Boston, if they were not manufactured here. Our foreman has instructions to give white labor the preference. We have offered inducements to obtain Chinese labor.

Would it be a good thing to send our raw material East, and have the articles manufactured there and sent back to us? We sell goods here as cheap as they are sold in the East, and better goods, although white labor in New England is cheaper than Chinese labor on this coast. The houses that export and sell eastern manufactured goods would put up the prices of shoes, blankets, etc., if our factories did not keep them down by competition. If our factories were closed, prices would go up at once."

And a private individual, "Chang Wo," makes a good point in public discussion, when he says, "What for the Americans have us in their houses if we are not clean and steal? You can see."

Among them are some hardened criminals, as their implements of murder to be seen in the office of the Chief of Police, or their pawnbroker's shops, will testify, and seventeen per cent. of the convicts at San Quentin are Chinese. On the one hand, it is difficult to convict them, because false witnesses are idle in the market places, but on the other hand, they need no conviction in the judgment of many, and only a pretext is sufficient to get them into prison. Guilty American criminals enjoy no fewer chances of escaping justice, but many more.

Chinese Restaurants and Food.—The restaurants are easily distinguished by their gaudy signs of red and gilt, covering the whole front of the building, and the immense round Chinese lanterns suspended from the upper stories. The higher the story, the more elaborate and costly is the rude furniture and the more aristocratic the entertainment; or like the Palace Hotel, "the high floors are the high-toned." In these high places the merchants dine their friends on a dozen different courses. They have a greater variety of food than the French or any other nation. Some of this is best seen in the provision stores, and some in the restaurants. On Jackson Street, above Dupont, is one of the oldest and best restaurants; others are on opposite sides of Dupont, near Clay. In meats, the Chinese use pork, kid, chickens, and the greatest variety of dried fish, dried oysters, gizzards, shrimps, and ducks. Beef is not a favorite meat, especially in the southern part of China. The legends concerning calamity upon those who eat so serviceable an animal are numerous.

Ducks are hatched and reared by artificial process in China, and when dried in the sun and pressed in oil, are an important article of commerce. Dried duck eggs, sometimes called "salt eggs," being first salted for three days, and then covered or coated with mud and salt, look as if they were coated with glue, and covered with black sand in stucco fashion. The Chinese call them Ham Tan, and sell them at 35 cents a dozen.

Shrimps are not only dried, but are made into a sauce that looks like an apothecary's ointment. Many Chinamen in Mexico are engaged in catching and salting shrimps. The variety of dried and salted fish is almost endless. Meat, fish and vegetables are cut up fine and cooked with rice flour and nut-oil in a variety of cakes, ornamented in various styles and colors, then sold at street stands and eaten in restaurants. Rice flour and nut-oil are used in almost all the articles of pastry. Rice is, of course, the staple article of food, and the taking of a meal is "eating rice." The Chinaman's receptivity for this, like that of the ocean, is never satisfied. He will take a bowl containing it, in the left hand, and by a dexterous use of the chop-sticks will shovel it into his mouth, and swallow it as one fish swallows another, and he seldom fails to repeat the process less than five or six times. Of teas, only the black is used in the best restaurants, and this of a superior quality, costing often several dollars a pound. It is never boiled but placed in a small cup with a cover to fit, and boiling water poured in, and then is left to steep in the presence of the guest. Tea is the common beverage, and offered on all occasions. On receiving a call from a stranger, it would be exceedingly ill-mannered not to offer some hot tea the moment after he enters. It is always taken as hot as it can be procured, and without sugar or milk. For keeping it hot they sometimes have a covered basket well-lined with some nonconductor of heat, into which the tea-pot fits, and which will retain the heat for several hours. They seldom drink water, and wine is sparingly used. At their feasts and on social occasions, they are obliged to go through the whole bill of fare, taking a little of whatever is offered.

The long, white, tapering Chinese radish, like our own winter radish, few will mistake, unless they are first cut up and boiled in oil.

One of the most delicate vegetables they call the water-chestnut, a reddish brown bulb, about as large as an Italian chestnut, and resembling the Indian turnip. They are pared or shaved with but little waste and great rapidity.

The Chinese turnip will not be readily recognized, except by its faint odor. It is oval, but quite irregular in shape.

The bean is a great favorite, and of it there are many varieties, some exceedingly small. Bean sprouts are sold in all the vegetable stores, and bean curd is a staple article of food. One might mistake it for corn-starch or milk curd. It is prepared by grinding the bean and boiling the meal. The soft, yellow-covered cakes on the stands in the street, are only bean curd.

Colt's-foot candy is not an article of food, but that which resembles it, is only the bean, cooked and drawn out into sticks, like candy; and the long, thin,—dried string-beans, one would say, are not beans at all, but—yellow blossoms to be cooked in soup with lean pork. Besides asparagus, lettuce, celery and our common articles, mustard leaves, large and small, are much used for "greens."

Pumpkins and squashes, such as the "Melican man" eats, and does not eat, and sweet potatoes, dried and prepared as potato-rice ; and yams, with fibres somewhat resembling those adhering to the cocoa-nut shell, are always seen about the stores.

Bamboo is cut into pieces about six inches in length, split and preserved in brine; and cooked with meat.

Dried olives, black, and like a three-cornered piece of dried plum, are kept in earthen jars, and cooked with meat. The abalone, a shell-fish, is dried and exported to China. A sea-weed that resembles the pulp of peaches, dried like peach-leather, is a curious article of food, and may be as good as the bird's-nests. The greasy sausages are not attractive, though evidently much sought after.

In the great variety of preserved fruits, some are food fit for Americans. The ginger root is well known, and not less pleasant are the lemon, sliced citron, small oranges, water-melons, olives, persimmons, and frozen sugar.

Of nuts there are many, some for cooking, and some for eating. The white nut is like a small almond, with a thin shell and kernel, and is used for pastry.

At the street corners are little packages of brown paper, with slices of cocoa-nut, mingled with the curious beetle nut, and the whole is daubed with some red paste, made out of lime juice and colored by the dust of the street and some foreign pinkish earth.

One of the most palatable nuts is the "Lai Che," rougher than the cup of an acorn; the meat of which is black and sweet, and the seeds of which, though hard, contain a delicate kernel. The pea-nut is found on all the stands, but the American product is far superior to the Chinese.

Water-melon seeds are eaten raw, and used in cooking. With all the variety of edibles from China, of which only a few of the most striking and common have been named, and with the new dishes adopted in this country, it may be hard for the Celestial to arrange his bill of fare, but they find rice economical, and they love it dearly; yet when the palate of one was tested by asking him, "Of all things to eat, what would you rather have?" He reflected for a time and replied deliberately, but with emphasis of tone, "Well, me likee best a nice piece of hog-meat."

Temples.—These are to be found in almost every town containing a few hundred Chinamen, but the most elaborate are in San Francisco.

No effort is made to present an attractive exterior, although much more money is expended by Chinamen in proportion to their means upon their temples than Americans spend upon their churches.

The temples are not under the control of the six companies, or in any way connected with them, nor does the relations of any one to his company affect his place, or time of worship-ing. The chief temples are

1. On Clay Street, opposite the south-west corner of the Plaza, in the building in which the Hop Wo Company has its head-quarters, and for this reason sometimes distinguished as the Hop Wo Temple.

2. The Dupont Street Temple, with entrance from Dupont near Jackson, and also from Jackson near Dupont, neither of which can be found or would be willingly entered when found by a stranger. It is reached by ascending rickety stairs to the third story.

3. The Pine Street Temple, entrance just above Kearney, in the building of the Kong Chow Asylum.

4. The Brooklyn Place Temple, off Sacramento Street near Stockton.

5. The Jackson Street Temple, on the north side of Jackson, near Stockton.

The most popular among the Chinese is the one on Brooklyn Place, but it is small, retired, with only one god, and not attractive to tourists. The most desirable to visit are the first two mentioned. The Clay Street is the newest, most elaborate and expensive, but the Dupont Street contains about four times as many gods as any other.

The temple on Jackson Street is devoted to the worship of *Ma Chu*,—the goddess of sailors, and her two assistants, on either side of her. She has had various high-sounding titles bestowed upon her, the most common of which is "Tin Ham," the Heavenly Queen, and to her the boatmen cry often, in piteous tones, "Grandmother Ma Chu!" "Grandmother Ma Chu!"

This goddess was the daughter of a sea-faring man, whose sons followed the father's uncertain and stormy life. While weaving one day she fell asleep and her weary head rested on her loom, where she saw, in a dream, her father and two brothers and their respective junks, periled in a terrific storm. She agonized to rescue them from danger, and seized her brothers' junks, one in each hand, and her father's in her mouth. As she dragged them to the shore, she heard her mother's voice calling, and, with dutiful spirit, but great forgetfulness of her father's danger, she opened her mouth to answer, and awoke from her dream; but in a few days tidings came of a dreadful storm and the loss of the father's junk and the safety of the brothers. Her dream has given her more honor than Pharaoh's gave Joseph, and the Virgin Mary has no loftier titles. Thank offerings are made to her by boatmen, after every deliverance from peril. One of her assistants is "Favorable-wind-ear," and the other, "Thousand-mile-eye."

The temple on Pine Street is devoted to *Kwan Tai*, the god of war. It is in the building of the Kong Chow Asylum, and has connected with

INTERIOR OF CHINESE TEMPLE.

it a room for ancestral worship. The asylum has a large hall for the public meetings of the company.

The stranger in San Francisco will visit the temples on Clay Street and Dupont Street, if no others. The Clay Street has taken away some of the tinsel that formerly adorned the one on Dupont Street, and is the most elaborate, having cost about $30,000, and is dedicated to the worship of Kwan Tai, and this same god occupies the central place in the Dupont Street Temple.

He is the *most popular* of all the gods, and is *always red-faced*, with a long, black beard.

On the walls of every temple and about the entrances are seen red placards—the records of the gifts made for establishing and supporting it. The "Heathen Chinee," unlike the American Christians, who *always* give their alms in secret, connect merit and worship with these gifts, sometimes burning incense before the names of the donors, while an attending priest offers prayers for blessings on them.

In the Clay Street Temple is an elaborate piece of gilt, carved wood, representing mythology and history. It cost about $3,000, and is enclosed in glass, covered with wire. Other pieces of carving, similar in character, are suspended about the room; but the significance of them is as mysterious as the ponderous classics of Confucius and Mencius.

Richly embroidered silk banners—all hand-wrought, are ready to be carried in front of or over the idol when he goes out in procession on festal days. Spears are used at the same time for his protection, and flags carried to declare his authority.

From the ceiling are suspended tablets with mottoes inscribed upon them, and some are placed vertically on the inner or outer walls, and the door-posts.

Some of the temporary ones contain good mottoes; others are thank-offerings. One of the latter, richly embroidered and fringed, (now in the Clay Street Temple,) is a thank-offering of Doctor Lai Po Tai, and has four Chinese characters, to wit: "Shing, Shan, Mo, Keung," *i. e.*, "the gods whose holy age is perpetual."

This doctor has amassed a fortune, by consummate skill in the grossest quackery, and without performing any wonderful cures, has tried his hand on many rich and noble ones, and among them even a noted professional of an eastern city, who proved in his experience the truth of the familiar adage, "never too old to learn."

The doctor lighted a match in his room, when it was filled with gas, and as a consequence had to secure himself the skill of American physicians; he barely escaped death, and then commemorated his recovery by this thank-offering, placed originally in the Dupont Street, but subsequently removed to the Clay Street Temple.

The neatest of the temples or Josh Houses is the Clay Street, but all are dirty, dingy and doleful. A heaven of such character, would be desirable to no civilized people, and the temples impress one concerning the religious taste of the Chinese, as an ignorant and irreverent hater of the Jews seemed to be impressed, when he remarked to a friend, "And you tell me that the Jews were the chosen people—God's peculiar people? I think it showed a very poor taste on God's part."

The ornamentation is of the cheapest, most miserable tinsel, gay and gaudy, smoked and begrimed with dirt, and the air laden with a nauseating odor of incense from grateful sandal-wood, mingled with the deadly fumes of the opium pipe, and the horrible smell of oil lamps and many-colored vegetable tallow candles.

Spread out before the gods there is usually roast chicken and pig, sweetmeats or cakes, and always vessels or libations of tea, and a burning lamp. Every one will be likely to wonder how the gods dispose of all the food, and why the constant and large supply of tea does not weaken the nerves, but the gods consume only the immaterial and essential parts of the offering, after which the meats, fruits, pyramids of cakes, the vermicelli of-rice flour and other articles are carried home to be eaten by the offerers.

The gods are always enthroned in an alcove, out of which their hideously extorted and repulsively daubed faces look with fiendish malignity or silly unmeaningness.

The *bell* is a fixture of every temple, and also the drum, the former curious with dragon ornamentations, and the latter with stout raw-hide and huge copper rivets. Their purpose is easily guessed, for sometimes these gods are "asleep," or "on a journey." There is also a box placed on a high stand, and carefully closed, containing the great seal, and which ought to be a better possession, than Alladin's lamp.

An oven is also a common fixture to accommodate in the burning of mock-money, or mock-clothing, or any representation, the reality of which the gods receive through the power of fire.

There are no set times for worship, except feast and festival days, such as the birthdays of the gods.

The calendar which determines these days is very abstruse, and no logarithms, differential, or integral calculus would make it intelligible. They have "big months" and "little months" of 30 or 29 days, and this year, 1876, has 13 months; i. e., a sort of leap-year, with two, fifth months.

On festival days huge paper images of the gods are made and carried in processions through the streets, and then allowed to remain in the temple for a season.

The artificial flowers are generally renewed

once a year; in fact, in no other nation, is there a more general change—so many new leaves turned over, as in the Chinese New Year.

Large urns and pewter and brass vessels of shapes and styles that the gods are supposed to appreciate, are used for burning sandal-wood sticks or incense.

There is the greatest irreverence and confusion in their worship—one never paying regard to the devotions of another. In one quarter of the room some may jabber while others are throwing the ka-pue, or shaking the bamboo splints, or consulting the spirits, or prostrating themselves to the earth.

Peacock feathers, which are "flower," "green," "one-eyed," "two-eyed," or "three-eyed," and used as marks of honor, and designate ranks like epaulets in the army, and the sinuosities of the "dragon," "the greatest benefactor of mankind," "the protecting deity of the empire," and the "national coat of arms," are used wherever possible.

One dragon, called the true dragon, is five-clawed, and this one the emperor appropriates to himself, and the whole of it is never visible in one picture—if the head is visible the tail is out of sight. It has scales but no ears, yet has two horns, through which it is said to hear.

Mode of Worshiping and Consulting the Gods.—On entering the temple, the worshiper makes the "Kow-Tow," striking the floor with his head three times.

In consulting the gods, the ka-pue, or divining sticks are used, and also bamboo slips.

The ka-pue are pieces of wood six or eight inches long, and shaped like the half of a split bean. One is held in each hand, they are then placed together, and while bowing let fall to the ground. If both flat surfaces rest on the ground, "bad luck to ye;" both flat surfaces upward mean indifference, or equivalent to "cocked" dice; and when one flat and one rounded surface rest on the ground, the favor of the god is assured. Sometimes the worshiper holds a bunch of small incense sticks in his hand, while he prostrates himself, and whenever the first effort is not successful, "the best out of three," and even the "best out of three times three," or further trial will answer as well.

The bamboo slips are contained in tin or bamboo canisters, about a foot high, and three inches in diameter. They are kept by the priest in charge of the temple, but whose services do not seem at all necessary for the ordinary worshiper. On each slip are numbers or characters corresponding to slips of paper, which contain directions or answers like boots and shoes, "ready-made and warranted to fit." After bowing thrice, the worshiper kneels, and shakes the slips till one falls to the floor. The approval of the god is sought on this lot, and the process must be repeated till a favorable answer

is obtained. Sometimes the deity does not know the circumstances of the case, and must be informed thereof by burning paper that contains the necessary information. Sometimes he must be propitiated by offerings of mock-money, white or yellow, (silver or gold) and sometimes by food.

The priest receives a fee for the slip of paper in his charge, and he is sometimes employed to write letters, and sometimes his services as a medium must be had. For this latter, he stands at a table, on which is a slight covering of sand, and there repeats his incantations until he attains the clairvoyant or mediumistic state, and then he writes with a stick, under direction of the spirits, what is intelligible to no one else, but what he never fails to interpret.

Kwan Tai is the deity of the Clay Street and the central figure in the Dupont Street Josh House. He is a great favorite. "Chinaman he likee him heap muchee, and he likee Chinaman too."

Small images of him are sometimes seen in stores and dwellings. He is the Mars of the Flowery Kingdom a "Military Sage," and is worshiped for *success in contests* of almost every character, and grows in favor from year to year. He was a distinguished officer who flourished in the later Han dynasty, and was prominent in the wars which then agitated the three States.

In the Dupont Street Temple, there are other deities, two of which will be easily recognized : *Wah Tah*, the god of medicine, who holds in his left hand the well-coated pill, and who is consulted for diseases of all sorts, and *Tsoi Pak Shing Kwun*, the god of wealth, who holds a bar of bullion. He is the patron deity of merchants, and all receivers of moneys, and, around his cabinet or throne, are pasted many mottoes or charms, such as "Protect us with Heaven's chief wealth."

Other deities here are *Nam Hai Hung Shing Tai*, the god of fire, or "the Fiery Ruler of the Southern Regions;" the local god of Canton, a "Great and Holy King."

Yun Ten Tin is the god of the sombre Heavens, able to prevent conflagrations, and eating vegetables only.

In the room on the east side of the main room, is the *Goddess of Mercy* held in great veneration by married women. She is especially worshiped on the first and fifteenth of every month. The god of the Southern Mountain, or local god of Canton, is much worshiped.

In the many gods, there is a great variety, and some confusion; but the Chinamen think they have great advantage over our religion. They have gods in the temple, and gods at home, and one of the heathen remarked to an American who reviled his polytheism :

"*Chinaman religion heap better Melican man's.*

You go church Sunday little while ; you come home, and allee week you lie and steal, and do heap muchee bad things. Chinaman, he got gods at home, see him allee time, Chinaman must be always good."

In the rear of the temple, there is a room for the sale of incense, and other articles used in worship, the profit of which goes to the priest. The candles are all of vegetable tallow, made from seeds or kernels, which grow in clusters on the tallow-tree. Beef tallow would be offensive to the gods, for the ox and buffalo are animals of merit, and the odor of burning animal fat, would be repugnant to the nostrils of the deities.

Gambling.—In this they have an advantage over our own race,—in a god of gambling, a dilapidated, seedy individual, with cue coiled around the head, and a gambling card in his hair, and also in worshiping the tiger, grasping in his mouth or paws a large cash. "His Excellency, the Grasping Cash Tiger," is usually pictured on wood or paper, and is sometimes *winged*, like pictures of another, "His Excellency the Devil.'

The Chinese are fond of gambling, and have invented many methods of playing for money.

Their dens in the business quarter are many, *always with a white sign,* and usually far back with a sentinel at the entrance from the street, to give the alarm of an approaching officer, or to turn away the "white foreign devils" who may have too great a thirst for knowledge. Sometimes as many as three doors and sentinels must be passed.

There is many an "Ah Sin" who can flatter, shame, threaten and lead on his victim. In China both gambling and lotteries are unlawful; but it is easy to bribe officials there, and here the Chinese practice these same old arts. Any and everything will be gambled away, from their money to their shoes—they gamble with bamboo slips, all held as if for drawing lots, and giving the cash to the only one which, when drawn, has a string attached to it, with defective poetry, in which the missing word is to be guessed; and with a revolving pointer, with cards, dice, and dominoes, but the most popular of all the games is that of "Fan Tan," usually contracted into "Tan," a game foreign to the Chinese, and the origin of which is more mysterious than that of chess, but which means "spread out money."

As only Chinamen are admitted in San Francisco to the sacred precincts of these resorts, the game can not be seen except by special favor. In some interior towns the Chinese are not unwilling to admit visitors. It is somewhat similar to the popular American game of faro, but so much simpler in all the appurtenances of the play, that when a lucky raid of the police is made through the quickly barred doors and winding passages,

the only implements left are a table, a few chairs, an empty bowl and a pile of beans.

The game is played on a table, around which the players sit. The sides of the table, or, of a board, which lies upon a table are numbered, "one," "two," "three," and "four." Cash, a round Chinese coin, with a square hole in the center, worth one-tenth of a cent, were formerly used, but as the seizure of money is evidence of gambling, they now use beans instead of cash. A large pile of them is laid on the table and covered wholly, or in part, by an inverted bowl, and the betting commences on either "one," "two," "three," or "four." The money may be laid on the sides corresponding to the numbers, or as is now generally practised, papers having the amount of the respective bets, written on them, are placed on the table instead of the coin.

The cover is then removed, and the beans are drawn away, *four at a time,* and the side of the table wins, according to the remainder, one, two, three, or nothing. Sometimes the bet is taken on the corners, dividing the chances of two sides. The keeper of the house receives a percentage of all the money paid, varying, it is said, from three to nine per cent.

There are nearly two hundred of these gambling houses in the city, and they furnish a rich living to the policemen, who levy black-mail on them, varying, it is said, from five to twenty dollars a week.

The Theatres.—There are two on opposite sides of Jackson Street, just below Dupont. The most popular is the oldest, the "Chinese Royal," on the north side of the street. The entrance to this is through a long passage, about five feet wide, lined with the tables of fruit and cake venders.

The auditorium has a parquette, that seats about 600 and a gallery for about 250; a smaller gallery for about 50 Chinese women, and two private boxes, void of all comfort from cushions, curtains or cleanliness, but elevated and roomy enough for six persons, near the stage and offering the only chances for securing reserved seats.

The price of admission varies with time of entrance. Early in the evening, "barbarians" are charged *four bits,* but the Celestials find open doors to the front or best seats, for two bits. After ten o'clock, the Melican man can secure an entrance for two bits, and any one going at this hour can see all he desires before the end is announced. The best parts of the play are seldom reached before 11 o'clock, and the play kept up often until 2 or 3 o'clock. For a private box, $2.50 is charged.

There are no stage-curtains, no flies, or shifting scenes, no decorations of any kind, simply a platform, at the rear of which the orchestra sits, and on either side of the musicians, is a door for

INTERIOR OF CHINESE THEATRE.

ingress or exit. As the deception is perfectly apparent, when one falls in war or passion, and is not carried off the stage, nor hidden behind the drop, but rises and trots away, there is a decided feeling that the whole thing is "too thin" for long enjoyment.

The acting is as rude as all the surroundings, yet it is often true to Chinese life. During the play of a comedy, the whole audience has been convulsed with laughter, over and over again, almost without cessation, suddenly breaking out in loud exclamations; but usually their faces are unmoved, except as they munch the pea-nuts, sugar-cane, etc., peddled throughout the room, or as they sink into dreamy contemplation, under the satisfying influence of a *pure* Havana of their own make.

The costumes are a marvel of gaudiness, but devoid of all elegance. The plays are nearly all of historic character,—rebels plotting for possession of the government, sometimes seated on the throne; messengers sent out to negotiate; and encounters between the rival factions.

Sometimes a love plot is enacted when the old man and old woman torture and rack the girl,

and *the miser* is apt to appear with his bag of gold to be stolen or wrested from him over his dead body.

In nearly every play there are acrobatic feats of a truly creditable character. The actors whirl and double up and turn somersaults, till the modern gymnast is quite put to shame.

There is no great variety of performers—no "stars" on the stage, but some plays draw more than others; and what is most striking, there are *no female performers.* Men dressed as women talk in a sing-song tone, and falsetto voice. The deception in this respect is greater than any other, and foreigners would go away fully convinced, that they had listened to female performers and heard attempts to sing, unless told to the contrary.

The music is simply horrible. While the men in the audience and the orchestra sit with hats on, the orchestra may have their coats off, working away like blacksmiths on the loud cymbals, triangles, guitar, fiddles, gongs and wind instruments, keeping up an incessant din scarcely less than infernal.

But the Chinese enjoy their theatre, and for

interesting plays, or *at intervals of a few months, when a new play begins,* the house will be crowded. In China, a company of actors is frequently hired to play at home.

Funerals and Honoring the Dead.— The funerals are conducted with great pomp. The corpse is sometimes placed on the sidewalk, with a roast hog, and innumerable other dishes of cooked food near it, when hired mourners with white sheets about them, and two or three priests as masters of ceremony, and an orchestra of their hideous music, keep up for hours such unearthly sounds as ought to frighten away all evil spirits.

The wagon-load of food precedes the corpse to the grave, and from it is strewn "cash," on paper to open an easy passage to the "happy hunting grounds" of the other world.

Ancestral Worship—is the most common of all worship among the Chinese. Tablets may be seen in stores, dwellings and rooms connected with temples. Its origin is shrouded in mystery. One account derives it from an attendant to a prince about 350 B. C. The prince while traveling, was about to perish from hunger, when he cut a piece of flesh from his thigh, and had it cooked for his master, and perished soon after. When the prince found the corpse of the devoted servant, he was moved to tears, and erected a tablet to his memory, and made daily offerings of incense before it. Other absurd stories of filial devotion are told for the same purpose.

The ancestral tablet of families, varies from two to three inches in width, and 12 to 18 in height, and some are cheap and others costly. There are usually three pieces of wood, one a pedestal and two uprights, but sometimes only two pieces are used. One of the upright pieces projects forward over the other from one to three inches.

One tablet can honor only one individual, and is worshiped for from three to five generations. To the spirit of ancestors a sacrifice of meats, vegetables, fruits, etc., is often made with magnificence and pomp, and the annual worship of ancestral dead at their tombs, is of national observance, and occurs usually in April, and always 106 days after the winter solstice.

The offerings are more plentiful than the meats at a barbecue in the Far South, carcasses of swine, ducks, chickens, wagon-loads of all sorts of food and cups of tea, are deposited at the graves; fire-crackers continually exploded, and mock money and mock clothing freely consumed. All kneel and bow in turn at the grave, from the highest to the lowest.

As in the case of the gods, the dead consume the immaterial and essential elements, and leave the coarse parts for the living. Unlike the gods, the dead consume ducks. "Idol no likee duck, likee pork, chicken, fruits."

New Year—is the great season for social pleasure—the universal holiday. All work ceases for the day, for a week or two weeks; and the stores are never closed except at this season; and the prosperity and standing of firms is measured by the length of time the store is shut. In China, stores are sometimes closed for two or three months. Every one mâkes New Year's calls, and gives himself up to enjoyment, and before New Year all debts must be paid, and accounts adjusted.

The Method of Calculating and Counting—is very rapid, and may be seen in any store. Counters are strung like beads on wires and framed, and astonishing results reached with these before "the barbarian" has written down his figures. For writing they use rice-paper, India ink and camel's-hair pencils.

Opium Smoking—is a common practice. Restaurants, the Clay Street and Dupont Street Temples, many stores and shops have the low tables or hard lounges on which these smokers recline.

A block serves for a pillow. The opium, pipe, lamp and a five-inch steel needle are all that is necessary to bind the victim in fatal fascination. The poisonous drug is boiled into a thick jellylike mass, and with the needle a small portion is scraped from the vessel containing it, rolled into a pill on the end of the needle, and placed in the flame until it swells like a soap-bubble, half an inch in diameter.

The pipe has an inverted bowl with a flat, circular top, two inches in diameter, in the center of which is a small opening, in which the heated paste is placed, and as the smoker reclines on his side he places the pipe to the flame and takes two or three short whiffs, removes the pipe, and lies back motionless, while the smoke is blown slowly through his pallid nostrils. He repeats the process till he falls back in a state of silly stupefaction, alike pitiable and disgusting. Once formed, the habit is never given up, and only three or five years will wreck the strongest constitution and noblest manhood. Exaggerated stories are told of visits to these dens by youth and women of American descent, for indulging in this vice, but they are rare and only by the lowest classes of the women.

Why Americans do not Speak the Chinese Language.—There is no alphabet, and the characters used are variously estimated at from 25,000 to 80,000.

There is one written language, but twenty or more dialects, as the natives have twenty or more ways of pronouncing the numerals 1, 2 and 3, which are alike to the eye of the Frenchman and German.

The dialects may also be written. And each of the numerous characters may have a widely different meaning by the slightest change of tone or inflection.

A teacher, with some knowledge of the language, was instructing the class in Bible truth and endeavoring to tell the interesting story of Samson slaying a lion with the jaw-bone of an ass, and perceived a strange look on the scholars' faces, and found that the slightest error of inflection had made the story run—"he killed the lion with the jaw-bone of a *louse*."

To convert them to Christianity is a difficult work, for many reasons. Besides the barrier of a language that is almost impossible to acquire, many of the characters express inadequately the ideas of the Christian religion, and the Chinese often form erroneous opinions concerning it, from other sources. One was questioned, and replied as follows:

Q. "*Jake, do you know God?*"
A. "*God? No — No sabee*," (Shaking his head and wearing a vacant look.)
Q. "*God, Melican man's Josh—you no sabee God?*"
A. "*No, me no sabee God.*"
Q. "*You sabee Jesus Christ?*"
A. "*Yes, me sabee him, Jesus Christ. Duffy call him cow.*"

The Chinese Missions.—An eminent Jesuit has said, as quoted in *The Monitor:* "These pagans, these vicious, these immoral creatures are incapable of rising to the virtue that is inculcated by the religion of Jesus Christ, the World's Redeemer and the Catholics make no attempt to instruct them in true devotion to the Virgin or the church."

The oldest and largest mission is that of the Presbyterians, at the corner of Sacramento and Stockton Streets, where an evening school is held daily except Sunday, when religious services and Sunday School are held. Two Americans who speak the Cantonese dialect, Rev. Dr. Loomis and John G. Kerr, M. D., their wives, six other Americans and three Chinese assistants, are connected with this mission and its out stations in Sacramento and San Jose. Besides the school there is a home for Chinese women, to which the superintendent and a band of Christian women seek to gather the unfortunate and degraded for instructions in sewing, embroidery, other useful occupations and moral reform.

There is a church connected with the Presbyterian Mission of 63 members, and another with the Methodist Mission of 35 members and a Chinese Young Men's Christian Association of all the churches, numbering nearly two hundred members, and a thousand have renounced idolatry.

Rev. Ira M. Condit and wife, connected with this mission for several years, have opened a new and promising mission at Los Angeles.

The Methodist Mission is on Washington Street, above Stockton, and efficiently managed under the zealous superintendency of Rev. Otis Gibson, formerly a missionary at Fuchu. This

has a branch at San Jose, schools and home for women, and several assistants like the mission before described.

On the west side of "The Plaza" opposite the City Hall, are the head-quarters of the American Missionary Association, connected with which are several schools in Oakland, Santa Barbara, and other parts of the State.

The Baptists have also a flourishing mission on Washington Street, near Dupont, and many of the churches have Sunday Schools for the Chinese, as Doctor Stone's, Mr. Hemphill's, Mr. Fiske's, Doctor Lathrop's, and others in San Francisco; and Doctor McLean's and Doctor Eell's of Oakland.

A specimen of their amusing attempts at English, is given herewith, as found at the entrance to an alley or court on Sacramento Street, just below Stockton:

☞LEE TUCK🖐
MAKE CAGE
NO UPSTIR 16 ROOMS
LIVE IN THE LANE

The meaning is, Lee Tuck makes cages, and his workshop is at No. or room 16, in the alley or court, and it can be reached without climbing long flights of rickety stairs, and this being his dwelling also, he is at home at all times.

Whether they are more successful in making poetry, the reader may determine, from the following, which has been attributed to one of their scholars, viz:

"How doth the little busy bee,
Delight to bark and bite,
And gather honey all the day,
And eat it up at night."

It is even doubtful whether it has been derived in any way from Confucius, or any of their classics.

Instances are told of their honesty to an extent that is exceedingly rare among American Christians, as of one who in purchasing a knife selected one at a dollar and a half, instead of one at half a dollar, and received a dollar too much in change, and discovered the error only after he reached his home. The next day he walked back three miles to return the money!

Castle Geyser & it's Basin

Hot Spring Cone

The Grotto

Giant Geyser

GEYSERS OF THE YELLOWSTONE.

Wonders of the Rocky Mountains.

The Yellowstone Park.

HOW TO REACH IT.

By Prof. F. V. Hayden,—U. S. Geological Survey.

THE Yellowstone Park is the grandest pleasure ground and resort for wonderful scenery on the American Continent, and doubtless the time is not far distant, when Pacific tourists will make it one of their most interesting pleasure trips. The word park, naturally brings to the mind of the reader, visions of the park as he finds it in our eastern cities, or in foreign capitals; with its beautiful drives, and its well kept walks, and neatly trimmed grass-plats. In imagination he sees the usual sign-board; with rules and regulations, and the warning, "keep off the grass." He sees them in imagination alone; for in the Yellowstone National Park, roads are few and far between. Animals untamed, sufficient to furnish innumerable zoological gardens, wander at will through the dense pine forests, or bask in the sunlight in beautiful grassy openings, whose surfaces are perfect flower gardens, resplendent with hues that rival the rainbow.

Elk, deer, antelope, and smaller game, are found in profusion; and all the streams and lakes abound in fish; large and delicious trout: making the park a paradise for the hunter and sportsman.

To the artist, and lover of nature, are presented combinations of beauty in grand panoramas and magnificent landscapes, that are seldom equaled elsewhere. Snow-capped mountains tower grandly above the valley, seeming to pierce the clouds; while at their feet are streams, that now plunge into the depths of dark and profound canons, and anon emerge into lovely meadow-like valleys through which they wind in graceful curves; often expanding into noble lakes with pine fringed shores, or breaking into picturesque falls and rapids.

To the student of science, few portions of the globe present more that is calculated to instruct or entertain. Strange phenomena are abundant.

In the crevices of rocks, which are the result of volcanic action, are found almost all the known varieties of hot springs and geysers. Geysers like those of Iceland are here seen on a grander scale. The wonderful "Te Tarata" Spring of New Zealand, has its rival in the Mammoth Hot Springs of Gardiner's River; while the mud springs and mud geysers of Java have their representatives. Sulphur and steam vents, that are usually found in similar regions, are numerous.

Captains Lewis and Clarke, in their exploration of the head waters of the Missouri, in 1805, seem to have heard nothing of the marvels at the sources of the Madison and Yellowstone. They placed Yellowstone Lake on their map, as a large body of water, having in all probability, derived their information from the Indians.

In later years, however, there began to be rumors of burning plains, boiling springs, volcanoes that ejected water and mud; great lakes, and other wonders. The imagination was freely drawn upon, and most astounding tales were told, of petrified forests, peopled with petrified Indians; and animals turned to stone. Streams were said to flow so rapidly over their rocky beds, that the water became heated

In 1859, Colonel Raynolds, of the United States Corps of Engineers, passed entirely around the Yellowstone Basin. He intended going to the head of the Yellowstone, and down the river, and across to the three forks of the Missouri, but was unable to carry out his plans. In 1869, a party under Cook and Folsom, visited Yellowstone Lake and the Geyser Basins of the Madison, but no report of their trip was published.

The first trustworthy accounts given of the region, were the result of an expedition led by General Washburn, the Surveyor-General of

Montana, and escorted by a small body of U. S. Cavalry, under Lieut. G. C. Doane, in 1870. They spent about a month in the interesting localities on the Yellowstone and Madison Rivers, and Mr. N. P. Langford made the results of the exploration known to the world, in two articles published in the second volume of *Scribner's Magazine.* Lieutenant Doane also made a report to the War Department, which was published by the government. (Ex. Doc., No. 51, 41st Congress).

In 1871, a large and thoroughly organized party made a systematic survey, under the auspices of the Department of the Interior, conducted by Dr. Hayden, United States Geologist. He was accompanied, also, by a small party, under Brevet Col. John W. Barlow, Chief Engineer of the Military Department of the Missouri, who was sent out by General Sheridan.

Through the accurate and detailed reports of that exploration, the wonders of the Yellowstone became widely known, both at home and abroad.

In February, 1872, the Congress of the United States passed an act reserving an area of about 3,400 square miles, in the north-western corner of Wyoming Territory, and intruding partially upon Montana, withdrawing it from settlement, occupancy, or sale, under the laws of the United States; dedicating and setting it apart as a public Park, or pleasuring ground, for the benefit and enjoyment of the people.

It extends from the 44th to the 45th parallel of latitude, and from the 110th meridian to a short distance beyond the 111th. Its general elevation is high; averaging about 6,000 feet; or nearly the height of Mount Washington, in the White Mountains. The Mountain Ranges have a general elevation from 9,000 to 10,000 feet above sea level, although many sharp and rugged peaks rise considerably above this. The country is so elevated that it could scarcely ever be available for agricultural purposes. The winter extends far into the spring, and it is no unusual thing to find snow covering September's flowers.

During July and August the weather is delightful; the thermometer rarely, if ever, rising higher than 70° Fahrenheit. In the early morning, however, it often records 26°; and sometimes falls as low as 10° or 12°. The air is so dry and invigorating that the cold is not felt as much as higher temperatures are, in the moister eastern climate.

Near the north-east corner of the Park, heads Clarke's Fork, of the Yellowstone. From the south-west, Snake River, or Lewis' Fork of the Columbia, starts toward the Pacific; while on the western side, the Madison and Gallatin Rivers, two of the three branches that unite to form the Missouri, have their origin.

We can climb a low ridge and see the water flowing beneath our feet; the streams on one side

destined to mingle with the mighty Pacific, and, perhaps, to lave the shores of China and Japan; while those on the other, flow down the Missouri and Mississippi Rivers, to be lost eventually in the great Atlantic. Who knows but that drops of water, starting here in opposite directions, may some day meet on an opposite quarter of the globe?

The largest mass of water in the Park is the Yellowstone Lake, which lies near the south-eastern corner of the Park, from the upper part of which the Yellowstone River flows in a northerly direction, and after a course of 1,300 miles, reaches the Missouri, having descended about 7,000 feet. Thus we have here the heads, or sources, of two of the largest rivers of the Continent, rising in close proximity to each other. The divides, or water-sheds between them, are comparatively low, and sometimes it is difficult to say in which direction the water flows; whether to the Pacific, or to the Atlantic.

Routes to the National Park.—There are several routes to the wonder-land of the National Park. The first, which is the most practicable, the pleasantest, and the one in common use, is the following, *via* Ogden:

Ogden, Utah, is reached from the East *via* the Union Pacific Railroad, and connecting lines, and from the West by the Central Pacific Railroad.

From Ogden, take the Utah Northern Railroad to Franklin in Idaho Territory, whence there is a stage line to Virginia City and Bozeman. The tourist has the choice of starting from either of these places, at both of which a complete outfit of supplies, animals and guides may be obtained.

From Bozeman, the route is up the Yellowstone River and across to the Geyser Basins, and thence by way of the Madison River to Virginia City. This is the route that will be followed in the description. There is a wagon road from Bozeman to the Mammoth Hot Springs, where there is said to be a hotel.

From Virginia City there is the choice of two roads, one of which is to cross to the Madison and follow the trail up the river through the Second Cañon to the Geyser Basins. The best, however, is to follow the wagon road which is completed to the Upper Geyser Basin. It leaves the south-eastern limit of Virginia City, and strikes the Madison near Wigwam Creek, where it crosses the river and follows it to a point just above the crossing of Lawrence Creek. Here it recrosses and closely follows the river to Driftwood or Big Bend, three miles below the Second Cañon. It then leaves the Madison Valley and crosses through Raynolds' Pass to Henry's Lake, the head water of Henry's Fork of Snake River.

From Sawtelle's Ranche, on the lake, the road follows the east shore of the lake for three miles in a southerly direction, when it turns to the north-east and passes through Tyghee or Targee Pass and down Beaver Dam Creek, over the South Fork of the Madison, and strikes the mouth of the Fire Hole Canon, 16 miles below the Lower Geyser Basin. It then follows the river closely, crossing twice before reaching the basin.

From the basins, the route is either *via* Mud Volcanoes, Shoshone Lake, or Yellowstone Lake, to the Yellowstone and Bozeman. About a month ought to be allowed for the round trip.

A second route, and one which shortens the stage ride, is to purchase an outfit at Salt Lake, or Ogden, and send it ahead to Market Lake, in Snake River Valley, joining it *via* the railroad to Franklin and stage line to Market Lake. This saves about 230 miles of staging. It is about 100 miles by a pack train trail from Market Lake to Henry's Lake from which point the Virginia City wagon road is followed to the "Geyser Basins."

Another route from Market Lake, which is long and somewhat out of the way, but more interesting, as it gives an opportunity to visit Mount Hayden and passes some magnificent scenery, is to travel with a pack train up Pierre's River, across Teton Pass, and up the main Snake River to Shoshone Lake, whence the other points of interest in the Park are readily reached. This is one of the routes followed by the Hayden Geological Survey in 1872.

Third. Camp Brown is a military post about 120 miles from Rawlins Springs Station on the Union Pacific Railroad, with which it is connected by a stage road. The trail from Camp Brown to Yellowstone Lake is said to be easy and the distance only about 140 miles. It crosses the mountains at the head of the Upper Yellowstone River, which stream it follows to the lake.

Captain Jones, in 1873, surveyed a route from Point of Rocks Station, on the Union Pacific Railroad, *via* Camp Brown, the Wind River Valley, and the head of Wind River to the Yellowstone. He claims that it saves 482 miles in reaching Yellowstone Lake. The great drawback is that it is often unsafe on account of Indians, and very much obstructed by fallen timber.

Fourth. There is the Missouri River route. The river is navigable as far as Fort Benton until late in the summer, and thence 140 miles of staging will take us to Helena, 118 miles from Bozeman.

From Bismark, the present terminus of the Northern Pacific Railroad, a trip of ten or fifteen days, will bring the traveler to Fort Benton. It will be a tedious journey,. however, over the "bad lands " of Dakotah.

Another plan is to disembark at the mouth of the Mussel Shell River, and having ordered horses to be in readiness, to take the wagon trail to the Crow Indian Agency at the Big Bend of

the Yellowstone. This would give 150 miles of land travel through a prairie country abounding in antelope and buffalo, and sometimes Indians.

The National Park may also be visited from the British Possessions, and also by a road which follows the Hell Gate and Bitter Root Rivers from the west, from Walla Walla.

Outfitting.—A few words about outfitting may be useful.

It is scarcely worth while to take wagons, as they can be taken over only a portion of the route, while a pack train may be taken anywhere. The latter is therefore preferable, and for it a saddle animal apiece, and two pack mules for every three persons, will be sufficient, if too many delicacies are not carried. A better allowance is one pack mule for every member of the party. Two packers and a cook will be required. One of the former ought to be well acquainted with the country, so as to act also in the capacity of guide. A hunter will also be a good addition to the party. Such men can easily be found at Bozeman and Virginia City.

Thick woolen clothing, stout boots, and broadbrimmed hats should be worn. Tents, plenty of blankets, and hunting and fishing tackle should not be neglected. In the way of provisions, substantials are in order; $25 per man, for a month's trip, will be a liberal allowance. Pack and saddle animals can be procured at Bozeman or Virginia City, for from $60 to $125 apiece.

The following tables of distances, are compiled principally from the reports of the United States Geological Survey:

Ogden, Utah, to Franklin, Idaho, by rail,	80¼ miles.
Franklin to Virginia City, Montana, (stage),	317 miles.
Virginia City to Bozeman, (stage),	66 miles.
Franklin to Market Lake, Snake River Valley,	152 miles.
Point of Rocks Station, Union Pacific Rn Iroad to Yellowstone Lake, by Captain Jones' route,	280 miles.

BOZEMAN TO GEYSER BASINS, *via* YELLOWSTONE RIVER.

Bozeman,	0 miles.
Fort Ellis,	3 miles.
Divide between Spring and Trail Creeks,	16 miles.
Boteler's Ranche on Yellowstone River,	39 miles.
Foot of Second Canon of the Yellowstone,	52 miles.
Devil's Slide at Cinnabar Mountain,	60 miles.
Bridge near mouth of Gardner's River,	68 miles.
Cache Valley, the mouth of East Fork of Yellowstone,	84 miles.
Crossing of Tower Creek,	88 miles.
Divide on spur from Mount Washburn,	94 miles.
Crossing of Cascade Creek,	108 n ll.es.
Mud Volcanoes,	117 miles.
Yellowstone Lake at head of River,	124 miles.
Head of Yellowstone River, to Hot Springs on South-west arm of Lake,	15 miles.
Hot Springs to Upper Geyser Basin,	15 miles.
Mud Volcanoes to Lower Geyser Basin,	24 miles.
Bridge near mouth of Gardiner's River, to Mammoth Hot Springs,	4 miles.

MARKET LAKE TO YELLOWSTONE LAKE.

Market Lake,	0 miles.
Henry's Lake,	100 miles.
Tyghee Pass,	110 miles.
Gibbon's Fork,	133 miles.
Lower Geyser Basin,	140 miles.
Upper Geyser Basin,	148 miles.
Divide,	158 miles.

Shoshone Geyser Basin,	162 miles.
Lewis Lake,	172 miles.
Hot Springs, Yellowstone Lake,	180 miles.

VIRGINIA CITY TO YELLOWSTONE LAKE, *via* WAGON ROAD TO GEYSER BASINS.

Virginia City,	0 miles.
Madison River, half mile from Wigwam Creek,	14 miles.
Driftwood or Big Bend of Madison,	42 miles.
Henry's Lake,	64 miles.
Tygheo Pass,	63 miles.
Gibbons' Fork,	86 miles.
Lower Geyser Basin,	94 miles.
Upper Geyser Basin,	101 miles.
Yellowstone Lake,	116 miles.

The Yellowstone Valley.—Starting from Bozeman, or Fort Ellis,—three miles from the former place, and one of the most important military posts in the West, protecting, as it does, the rich agricultural Gallatin Valley from the incursions of the Indians,—we follow up a small branch of the East Gallatin, through a picturesque canon, in which the road crosses and recrosses the stream many times, in the seven miles of its length.

From the head of this creek we cross a low saddle to Trail Creek, down which we proceed to the valley of the Yellowstone. Long before we reach it our eyes are greeted with the summits of one of the most symmetrical and remarkable ranges to be seen in the West; the Snowy Yellowstone Range, standing on the eastern side of the river. Sharp, jagged peaks and pyramidal masses stand out boldly against the sky, their snow-crowned heads glittering in the sunlight.

As we come into the valley, the first view is grand and picturesque The vista extends for thirty miles along the river ; on the opposite side the mountains rise magnificently. Emigrant Peak, 10,629 feet above sea level and nearly 6,000 feet above the valley, stands at the head of the range, and from its melting snows are fed numerous streams that water the hills and plains, sloping to the river.

About 40 miles from Bozeman we reach Boteler's Ranche. For a long time, the Boteler brothers were the pioneers of civilization in this region, and they have, with true liberality, entertained numerous parties on their way to the springs and lake.

From Boteler's to the Second Canon, a distance of about 10 miles, the road keeps on the west side of the river, skirting the base of low volcanic hills.

The Second Canon stands at the head of the valley we have just described. It is a gorge less than a mile in length, cut in granitic rocks, which rise precipitously on either side for a thousand feet or more. The road here i really hewn from the rock. The river, of a beautiful green color, rushes furiously through the narrow pass, broken into foam-capped waves by the rocks, which seem to dispute its right of way. One of the most agreeable features of the canon, and one also which is not confined to it, is the abundance of

trout waiting to be drawn from its pools and eddies.

Above the canon the valley widens, and we pass over a sage brush covered bottom for about ten miles, to the next point of interest, the " Devil's Slide," at Cinnabar Mountain. This curious freak of nature is somewhat like the Slide in Weber Canon, on the Union Pacific Railroad, but is on a much larger scale. Two parallel walls of rock, each 50 feet wide and 300 feet high, extend from the summit of the mountain to its base. They are separated about 150 feet ; the rock between, and on both sides, having been removed by erosion. Their sides are as even as if worked with line and plumb. On either side of the main slide are smaller ones, and in one, is a bright red band, 20 feet wide, extending from the top to the bottom, about 1,500 feet. From this red band of clay, which was mistaken for cinnabar, was given the name Cinnabar Mountain. The earlier explorers of these regions, the mountaineers and trappers, were evidently impressed with the novelty of the phenomena, and seem to have dedicated many of the localities with satanic names, which from their fitness, are not likely to be superseded. Thus we have " Devil's Slide ;" "Hell Roaring River ;" " Fire-Hole Prairie ; " " Devil's Glen," etc.

Above Cinnabar Mountain the valley is more broken ; and we cross several ridges, strewn with boulders of dark volcanic rocks, obsidian chips, and beautiful specimens of chalcedony and semi-opal.

Six miles above the slide, we come to the foot of the Third Canon, where the Yellowstone is joined by Gardiner's River, or Warm Spring Creek, as it was originally called. Here we leave the river to visit one of the crowning wonders of the region.

The Mammoth White Mountain Hot Springs.—This group of springs. is one of the most remarkable within the limits of the National Park, and as far as is known, has not its equal in grandeur in the world. The Te Tarata Spring of New Zealand. is the nearest approach to it in appearance, but the formation is of a different character; the Gardiner's River Springs depositing calcareous material, while that in New Zealand is siliceous, like the deposits in the geyser region of Iceland, and in our own geyser basins, at the head of the Madison. The exploring party of 1870, did not discover these springs, and the Hayden Exploring Expedition of 1871, was the first organized party that ever visited them.

Leaving the Yellowstone, we keep some 300 or 400 feet above the level of the river for a couple of miles. passing several small lakes, when we descend to the bank of Gardiner's River, on the eastern side of which is a high bluff of cretaceous sandstones capped with a

MTS. HAYDEN AND MORAN.

layer of volcanic rock. On the edge of the stream, we pass over a hard, calcareous crust, in which we find several warm springs. At one point we pass a considerable stream of hot water, revealed by the clouds of steam rising from it, flowing from beneath the crust into the river.

Turning to the right, we ascend the hill, made of the same calcareous deposit, which gives forth a hollow sound beneath the tread of our horses. This hill must have been the scene of active springs ages ago. Now, however, the deposit has crumbled, and is overgrown with pines. The springs once were much more numerous and far more active than at present.

Ascending the hill, and turning to the left, we come suddenly upon the marvelous scene. Before us stands one of the finest of nature's architectural efforts, in a mass of snowy white deposits, 200 feet high. It has the appearance of some grand cascade that has been suddenly arrested in its descent, and frozen. The springs are arranged on a series of terraces, that rise one above the other like steps. There are fourteen of these terraces with active springs, and others in which they are extinct.

The deposits extend from the level of Gardiner's River, to the head of a gorge 1,000 feet higher, a distance of over 5,000 feet. The area occupied by it, including the extinct basins, is about three square miles.

The lowest terrace is flat, and its basins are very shallow and destitute of water. From their midst rises the "Liberty Cap," a conical mass about 50 feet high, composed of calcareous sediment. The principal springs are contained in the mass extending from the second to the twelfth terraces, inclusive. Here the basins are most perfect, surrounded with beautiful scalloped edges. The water falls from the upper basins to the lower, becoming cooler as it descends, so that water of almost any temperature may be found in which to bathe. At the head of the gulch are several mounds, in which there are miniature geysers. The springs are changing from year to year; dying out in some places, and breaking out in others.

Toward the head of Gardiner's River are several beautiful cascades, and the scenery in the vicinity of the springs is varied and beautiful. We must wend our way up the river in search of new wonders. We can follow either of two trails; one up the Yellowstone River, and the other up Gardiner's River. Both trails eventually unite, and lead us to the mouth of the East Fork of the Yellowstone, about 20 miles from Gardiner's River. A trip up the East Fork will repay the tourist. The scenery is grand beyond description. At the extreme sources is a chaotic mass of peaks, from the water-shed between the East Fork, and Clarke's Fork. We pass by the cone of an extinct geyser, and Amethyst Mountain, on whose summit may be found beautiful amethyst crystals imbedded in volcanic rocks.

Tower Creek and Falls.—Tower Creek is about three miles above the bridge that crosses the Yellowstone, near the mouth of the East Fork. The trail keeps on the west side of the river, and reaches the creek a short distance above the fall, which is one of the most picturesque in the Park. Tower Creek is a swift mountain torrent, which, breaking into rapids, suddenly dashes over a ledge of rock and falls in one clean sweep 156 feet, to a rounded basin, cut from the solid rock, and then hurries on through a short canon, to join the Yellowstone. The rocks about the fall have been so eroded as to leave tower-like masses, from 50 to 100 feet

high. Two of them stand on either side, at the edge of the fall, like huge giants. Let us ascend one. Hold on tightly, and look down. The edge of the fall is full 100 feet below, and the foot 156 feet farther. There are a few unimportant sulphur springs on the river, and opposite the falls are Column Rocks, exposed in a bluff 346 feet high. There are three rows of basaltic columns from 15 to 30 feet high; the beds between are infiltrated with sulphur, giving them a bright yellow color. A short distance above the mouth of Tower Creek, is the lower end of the "Grand Canon" of the Yellowstone, and the trail now leaves the river to pass around the western base of Mount Washburn. This is one of the highest peaks in the neighborhood, rising 10,388 feet above sea level. An hour's ride will take the traveler to its summit, from which a view of the country in every direction is commanded, which well repays one the tedious climb. At the foot of the mountain, on the south-eastern side, is a group of mud and sulphur springs which have been called the "Hell Broth Springs." To reach them, the best way is to camp a little more than a mile from the top of the range, on a small stream which is followed for about a mile. A plain trail leads from the springs to the falls of the Yellowstone, which will be our next stopping place. The best camping places are on Cascade Creek, about 18 miles from Tower Creek. This small stream is parallel to the Yellowstone for the greater part of its course, although flowing in the opposite direction, a little over a mile from the river. It soon turns at right angles and joins the river about midway between the Upper and Lower Falls. Just before it reaches the main stream it passes through a deep and gloomy gorge, where it breaks into a cascade of exceeding beauty called "Crystal Falls." Its height is 129 feet. The water first falls but five feet, and then down it goes fifteen feet, falling into a beautiful rounded basin in which the clear water is perfectly placid. From this basin the final leap over the rocky ledges is taken.

Falls of the Yellowstone and Grand Canon.—No language can do justice to the wonderful grandeur and beauty of the Grand Canon. In some respects it is the greatest wonder of all.

It is a gorge carved by the river in volcanic rocks, to a depth increasing from nearly a thousand feet to over two thousand. Its length is about thirty miles. The walls are inclined from 45° to 80°, and in many places become vertical. They are eroded into towers, spires, and minarets. The striking feature of the remarkable view is the brilliancy of the colors. The pure whites of the decomposing feldspar are mingled with sulphur yellows, and streaked with bands of bright red, colored with iron. Dense pine forests extend to the edge of the canon. At the bottom of the chasm is the river, boiling and surging as it goes. The descent to the edge is best accomplished on the eastern side. Reaching the bottom, we hear nothing save the distant thunder of the fall and the roaring of the water as the furiously agitated waves dash against the solid rock at our feet, seeming to protest against their imprisonment. At the top, the tall pines form a green margin to the rocky walls.

On the right side near the verge of the wall, is a collection of springs, mostly mud springs, in which the mud is of varying consistency.

At the head of the canon, are the Lower or Great Falls of the Yellowstone. Long before we reach the brink, we hear the suppressed roar, resembling distant thunder. The best views are obtained from a point on the canon wall, a quarter of a mile farther down, and from the brink of the precipice over which the river plunges. Let us approach and look over. Down, down goes the whirling mass, writhing and battling with the rocks, against which it dashes with a noise like the discharge of heavy artillery. Here and there, a resisting rock is met, and the water rebounds, broken into myriads of drops, which throw back to us the sunlight resolved into its primitive colors. The bottom reached, the column breaks into an immense cloud of spray, whose moisture nourishes the vegetation on the walls near the fall. The river, before it pours over the edge, narrows to about a hundred feet. The height of the fall has been variously given. The measurement with a line in 1870, gave 350 feet as the result. Triangulation from a base line on the edge of the canon, by the Geological Survey in 1872, made it 397 feet, and a barometrical measurement in 1873, by Captain Jones, made it 328.7 feet.

The Upper Falls are about a quarter of a mile

ASCENDING THE GLACIERS OF MT. HAYDEN.

LOWER FALLS OF THE YELLOWSTONE.

above the Lower Falls. Between them, the river is in a canon whose depth is from 100 to 300 feet. Near the Lower Falls it is a succession of rapids. The two falls are very unlike, but equally interesting, the Upper perhaps not possessing as much of grandeur as the Lower. The height of the former is 110 feet. The river above is broken into rapids, and, reaching the edge, the entire volume of water seems to be hurled off the precipice with terrific force, so that the mass is broken into most beautiful snow-white drops, presenting, at a distance, the appearance of snowy foam. Midway in its descent a ledge of rock is met with, which carries it away from the vertical base of the precipice. The water has worn a circular basin in the hard rock. From any point, the view is striking and picturesque. What it lacks in sublimity is compensated for by its beauty.

Crater Hills and Mud Volcanoes.— Leaving the falls, the trail leads us up the river, and soon brings us out into a level prairie country, through which the Yellowstone flows peacefully between low, verdant banks, and over pebbly bottoms, or treacherous quicksands, giving no intimation of its struggles below. We seem to have left everything terrific and diabolic behind us. Stopping to drink at a beautiful looking creek, we find it impregnated with alum. This is Alum Creek, which has its source in the springs about Crater Hills, six miles above the falls. The best camping place will be found three miles farther on, at Mud Volcanoes, from which point the springs in this part of the valley can be visited. They are found on both sides of the river. At the head of some of the branches of Warm Spring Creek, are sulphur and mud springs, and on the eastern side of the river, numerous mud springs are found.

Crossing Alum Creek, we soon find ourselves at Crater Hills,—two high conical white hills, about 200 feet high, around the base of which are hot springs and steam jets. One of the latter is called the "Locomotive Jet" from the noise made by the escaping steam. The principal spring is the "Boiling Sulphur Spring." It is about 12 feet in diameter, and encircled by a beautifully encrusted collar-like rim. The water is constantly agitated, rising from three to four feet above the basin like some huge caldron. Crossing through a narrow belt of timber, a short distance east of this spring, we come upon a group of active mud and sulphur springs, all tasting strongly of alum. The noise made by the boiling mud, the scream of the steam jets, the plop-plop of the smaller mud-pots, the puffing and throbbing of the larger ones, and the sulphurous odors that fill the air, combined with the treacherous nature of the ground beneath us, give rise to feelings that are difficult to analyze.

At Mud Volcanoes, we find new wonders in the "Devil's Caldron," "The Grotto," "The Mud Geyser," and a host of smaller springs.

The presence of the "Caldron," is made known by the immense column of steam, which is continually rising from it. It is on the side of a low hill. The steam generally obscures the view of the seething mass of blackish mud, which is 20 feet below the surface. The trees all about the crater, are coated with mud which it is supposed has been ejected during an eruption of this mud geyser. It does not boil with an impulse like most of the mud springs, but with a constant roar that shakes the ground and may be heard at a considerable distance.

About 200 yards from the "Caldron" at the head of the rivulet, which drains the group of springs, is the "Grotto." It is a sort of cave in the rock. The orifice is about 15 feet high, and slopes gradually inward for about 20 feet. From this cavern at regular intervals of a few seconds, there bursts forth a mass of steam, with a pulsation that causes the earth to throb, while a small stream, clear as crystal, but absurdly disproportionate to the amount of noise, flows from the mouth of the cavern. The steam is so hot, that only when the breeze wafts it aside, can we look into the opening.

The "Muddy Geyser" has a funnel-shaped basin, 60 feet in diameter, which is in the midst of a basin measuring 200 feet by 150 feet—with sloping sides of clay and sand. The flow takes place at intervals of from four to six hours, lasting from twelve to sixteen minutes each. The water, mingled with mud, rises gradually until the basin is filled to the level of the brim, when a slight bubbling commences near the center. Suddenly it is thrown into violent confusion, and an irregular mass of lead colored mud and water is thrown into the air with irregular pulsations. The height attained is 15 to 40 feet. At the end of the eruption the water sinks into the funnel-shaped orifice, to go through the same operation in a few hours.

From Mud Volcanoes we can go either to the Geyser Basins of Fire Hole River, or to Yellowstone Lake. To the former, the distance is about 19 miles and to the latter, only a little over seven miles. A trail is found on both sides of the river and late in the season the river is easily forded. The trail on the eastern side will lead us to Pelican Creek, Steamboat Point, and Brimstone Basin on the eastern side of the lake, from which we can go around the southern bays to the Hot Springs, on the south-west arm of the lake, to which the trail on the western side of the river will also lead us. There are several interesting Mud Springs, opposite Mud Volcanoes, on the east side of the Yellowstone.

Yellowstone Lake.—This beautiful sheet of water is more than twenty miles in length and fifteen in width. Its form has not inaptly been compared to that of an outspread hand— the northern or main body representing the palm, while the south-western bay represents the thumb considerably swollen, the other bays corresponding to the fingers, two being small, and the others disproportionately large.

The elevation of the lake, from measurements made by the United States Geological Survey, is 7,427 feet above sea level. Its depth is from one and a half to fifty fathoms. Its shore line measures over three hundred miles, presenting some of the loveliest shore lines, especially at Mary's Bay on the east side, south of Steamboat Point. Here, also, is Diamond Beach, a broad and level sand beach extending for five miles.

The sand is composed of particles of obsidian (volcanic glass) quartz, and chalcedonies that sparkle in the sunlight.

The western side of the lake is covered with pine forests, as is the southern end, where also there are many lakelets, and considerable marshy ground. There are no high mountains in this direction, low, broad hills forming the water-shed between the lake and the sources of Snake River. One can cross almost anywhere to the Shoshone Geyser Basin. The eastern side of the lake is also well wooded, but more broken by small open prairies. The country on this side soon rises into a grand mountain range from which numerous volcanic peaks rise. Prominent among them are Mts. Stevenson and Doane. The interesting localities of the lake on the eastern side are " Brimstone Basin," "Steam Point" and " Steamboat Springs," " Turbid Lake" and the Springs of Pelican Creek and Sulphur Hills. On the south-western arm also,

characteristic. notwithstanding the name. The period of greatest activity of all the springs here is past, and they are gradually dying out.

The springs on the shore of the south-western arm of the lake, occupy an area of about three miles in length, and half a mile in width. There are no geysers. Some of the springs are found in conical, siliceous mounds, rising from the water of the lake near the shore. One of these is named the "Fish Pot," from the fact that while standing on its crater, one may extend his fishing-rod, catch trout, and turning, may cook them in the spring. About four hundred yards from the shore is a basin of boiling, pink-colored mud with conical mud craters, from which the mud is ejected. There are also a number of clear, flowing springs of hot water, and numerous springs of boiling, muddy water varying in color from white to dark yellow.

The next point of interest after Yellowstone Lake is the Geyser Region of Fire Hole River, or

YELLOWSTONE LAKE.

is an interesting group of springs. " Brimstone Basin " is south-east of Steam Point, and marks the seat of once active springs, evidenced by the deposits. The stream flowing through them is strongly impregnated with alum. At Steam Point, besides the springs, are several steam jets. From one the steam escapes with a noise resembling that made by the escape of steam from a large steamboat. Others resemble the escape of steam from the cylinders of a locomotive. Springs are found on the shore of the lake between Steam Point and Pelican Creek and along the course of the latter stream. At Turbid Lake, two miles east of the lake and back of Steam Point, the springs are mud springs and sulphur vents. The water of the lake itself is made turbid by the springs in its midst and on the shores. Sulphur Hills are between Pelican Creek and the Yellowstone. Sulphur is not

the Upper Madison. From the group of springs, a trail, striking nearly due west, will bring us to the head of the " Upper Geyser Basin," a distance of about fifteen miles. We may also keep more to the south and visit the geysers of Shoshone Lake, on the way, or we may return to Mud Volcanoes and cross to the East Fork of Fire Hole River, and visit the "Lower Geyser Basin " first, which is, perhaps, the best course, as the springs of the Lower Basin will seem less interesting after the greater wonders of the Upper Basin have been seen.

Geyser Basins of Fire Hole River.— The geyser basins of the Upper Madison include, altogether, about seventy-five square miles. In this area are thousands of springs and geysers, ranging in temperature from the boiling point to cold. Their description would occupy the space of a volume. Only the salient features can be given here. The springs are divisible into three classes: 1st. True geysers which are agitated at stated intervals, and from which the water is projected. 2d. Those which are constantly agitated or always boiling. They rarely have eruptions; most of the mud springs can also be included under this division. 3d. Those which are always tranquil. In the latter, the water is generally of a lower temperature, and has a beautiful blue color, or often a green tint like that of the beryl. In springs of the very lowest temperatures there is often a low form of gelatinous vegetable growth.

Some of the springs of the Lower Basin merit the title of small lakes. They are divided on the maps into eight groups. The first is on the East Fork; the second is about a mile farther to the south, and the third, fourth, and fifth groups still farther south on the east side of the basin. In the third group are the Fountain Geyser, and the Mud Puffs, both worthy a visit. In the fifth group is the Architectural Geyser, probably the most powerful in the "Lower Basin."

The sixth group is on the main river above the mouth of Fairy Fall Creek, the seventh is on the latter stream, and the eighth on Sentinel Creek, a stream joining the Fire Hole below Fairy Fall Creek. There are but about half a dozen real geysers in the Lower Basin, but craters are seen which must once have been active spouters. The deposits are siliceous, as is the case with the Upper Basin. There are many places where the springs are extinct, nothing remaining save the glaring white sediment. The scalloped rims extending out over the water, like cakes of ice, and the corrugated sides of the basins are exceedingly beautiful. Before leaving the Lower Basin, we must visit Fairy Falls, a very pretty miniature cascade at the head of Fairy Fall Creek. From the mouth of the latter creek, to the mouth of Iron Spring Creek, which marks the lower boundary of the Upper Basin, the distance is five miles in an air line. About midway are the Half-way Springs. The principal one is a huge caldron, 250 feet in diameter, with walls about 20 feet high. It is in constant agitation, giving off clouds of steam. On one side, the wall is broken down, and thence the surplus water flows into the river, through numerous channels whose beds are lined with scarlet, yellow, and green, which contrast boldly with the white siliceous sinter surrounding the spring. Farther back from the river, on a slight eminence, is an almost circular spring, 150 feet in diameter.

The journey from one basin to the other is suggestive of the infernal regions. The trail keeps near the river, which is warm, fed as it is by so many hot streams. The ground sounds hollow under foot. We wind in and out among holes from which steam and sulphurous odors escape, past great yawning caverns and cisterns

of bubbling, seething water and mud. The air is full of strange noises, and we feel as though we were on dangerous ground, through which we may break at any moment and descend to flames beneath. Again we pass pools of translucent water, in whose azure depths we can not see the bottom of the siliceous basins.

We also cross boiling streams which flow over hard beds colored green, yellow, and red, from the deposition of mineral ingredients by the evaporation of the water.

Upper Geyser Basin.—The Upper Geyser Basin has been called the Great Basin, because it contains the principal geysers. It is about two miles long, and will probably average half a mile in width. The best view is obtained from the crater of "Old Faithful," at the upper end. Through the Lower Basin the course of the river is almost due north, while in the upper, it flows west of north. Its banks are made of geyserite, the siliceous deposit of the springs, which is literally honeycombed with springs, pools and geysers, that are constantly gurgling, spitting, steaming, roaring, and exploding. To describe all the geysers would require more space than can be spared, and I will therefore refer only to the principal ones, hoping the reader will take the trip and see the wonders of the Yellowstone for himself, which is really the only way in which they can be appreciated, for any description must always fall short of the reality. Entering the Upper Basin from the north, we pass a series of rapids at the upper end of which we enter the gateway, as it were, guarded by two sentinel geysers, one on either side of the river; that on the left being the most active.

Following the river for about two hundred and fifty yards, we reach the "Fan Geyser," where there are several orifices from which the water radiates, the streams crossing each other and producing a fan-shaped eruption. A short distance above, on the opposite side of the river, is the "Grotto Geyser" which is easily recognized by the peculiar form of its crater, from which it takes its name. There are two orifices, the principal one being in the larger and more irregular mound, which is eight feet high, while the smaller one is only four feet high. The interval between its eruptions is unknown. It throws a column of water and steam from 40 to 60 feet above its crater. Several hundred yards farther back from the river, south-west from the "Grotto," are the "Pyramid," "Punch Bowl," "Bath Tub," and "Black Sand" Geysers.

The "Giant" is about 400 feet south-east of the "Grotto." It has a rough, cone-like crater, ten feet high, with one side broken down. The orifice from which the water is expelled is about five feet in diameter. This curious crater is near the river's edge, on a platform of deposit measuring 342 yards in circumference. It has seldom been seen in eruption. Langford gives the

SCENES IN THE YELLOWSTONE PARK.
1.—Jupiter's Baths and Soda Mountain. 2.—Valley of the Yellowstone.

height as 140 feet in 1870. It was also seen in action in 1874, but the height was not measured. Following up the river on the south-west side, we next stop at the "Castle." It is a cone, rising a little over 11 feet above an irregular platform of sinter, that measures 75 by 100 feet, and is three feet high. The orifice of the geyser tube is three feet in diameter, and circular, and its throat is lined with large orange-colored globular masses. In 1870, its eruption threw a column of water 140 feet above its crater, continuing three hours. In 1872, the maximum height observed was 93 feet and the duration fifteen minutes, after which steam escaped with a pulsating movement, the whole display lasting about an hour and twenty minutes. In 1874, the same succession of water and steam was noticed, the former lasting twenty minutes, and attaining an estimated height of 250 feet, and the latter lasting about forty minutes longer. The noise of the eruption is indescribable. Imagine a gigantic pot with a thunder-storm in its stomach, and to the noises of elemental war, add the shrieking of steam pipes and you will have a faint idea of it. After the eruption, the exhausted geyser sinks into complete repose.

Near the "Castle" is a beautiful blue hot spring, which has been given the fanciful name of "Circes Voudoir." The water is perfectly transparent, and so intensely blue that you involuntarily plunge your hand in to see if it is water. The basin is of pure white silica, looking like marble. It is about 20 feet in diameter, and has a beautiful and regular scalloped margin. The white basin slopes to a funnel-shaped opening which is 40 feet deep, and here the water is intensely blue, its temperature 180° Fahrenheit.

"Old Faithful," standing at the head of the valley, is so named from the regularity of its spouting. Its mouth is six feet by two, in a siliceous mound that rises 11 feet above the general level. On this mound are small basins whose edges are ornamented with bead-like silica. The eruptions commence with a few abortive attempts, followed by a rapid succession of jets which soon reach the maximum, and then subside, only steam escaping from the orifice. The average interval between the eruptions observed in 1872, was one hour, two and three-quarter minutes, and the average duration four minutes, fifty-three seconds. As observed by Captain Jones' party in 1873, the interval was fifty-six minutes and forty seconds, and the duration four minutes and thirty-three and one-half seconds. The height of the column was estimated at nearly 150 feet. The greatest height measured in 1872, out of seventeen eruptions, was 130 feet. The "Bee Hive" is on the opposite side of the river, nearly due north of "Old Faithful," and about 300 yards distant. It is near the river and readily recognized by its cone three feet high, and about three feet in diameter. From this cone the water is projected with great force in a steady stream. The column is fan shaped. No water falls back, but it seems to be all resolved into vapor. The length of the eruptions is from four to fifteen minutes, and the interval unknown. The column rises from 100 to 250 feet.

Two hundred yards back of the Bee Hive, is the "Giantess," which has a large basin 23 by 32 feet. It is on the summit of a gently sloping siliceous mound. Its eruptions are very irregular. They last from 8 to 18 minutes. The only eruption measured in 1872, was 60 feet. An immense mass of water was thrown up. Other estimates have given the height as 60, 200, and 250 feet.

Farther down the river and opposite the castle, from which it is distant 460 yards, is the "Grand Geyser." One would scarcely take it for an important geyser, unless he witnessed one of its spoutings; for, unlike the others, it has no raised crater. Its basin which is 52 feet in diameter, is depressed a foot below the general level. The mouth of the geyser tube in the center, measures four feet by two feet, and from this, about once in 24 hours, a column is thrown to the height of from 175 feet to 250 feet. The eruption generally consists of three periods, after each of which the water sinks completely out of sight. Near the "Grand" are the "Saw Mill" and the "Turban." The latter is only a few feet from the "Grand," and will be known by the globular masses that look like huge squashes, and are easily seen lining the sides and bottom of the crater when the water has disappeared from the basin. The eruptions are unimportant. Still farther down the river, and nearly opposite the "Grotto," is the "Riverside" which brings us back nearly to the place we started. A visit to Iron Spring Creek, is well worth taking. Near its mouth, on the north side, is the "Soda Geysers" group.

Fair camps are easily found in the "Lower Geyser Basin."

In the "Upper Basin," a good camp for a small party is in a grove near the "Castle." Another is found about a quarter of a mile higher up.

The trail to the "Shoshone Geyser Basin" leads up the Fire Hole River, and a short distance above the "Upper Basin," we pass a fall 60 feet high, that is worthy a visit from all who would see the beauties as well as the wonders of the region. It somewhat resembles the Middle Fall at Trenton, New York. Above the falls, the trail crosses the river to avoid swampy ground, and keeps on the bounding ridge of hills on the west. The narrow valley expands, and we soon enter a third geyser basin with several groups of springs, and one geyser called the "Solitary." It has a dome-shaped mound, 15 feet in diameter and 11 to 14 feet high, covered with elegant

intervals of about two hours. The elevation of this "Upper Basin," is 7,770 feet, while that of the Upper Geyser Basin, proper, is from 7,300 to 7,400. On a small stream coming into the basin from the west, about a quarter of a mile from the river, is a fine cascade 130 feet high. The river rises in a small lake to which the name Madison Lake is given. From here the trail runs due east to Shoshone Lake, which is one of the sources of Snake River, giving origin to the main stream. From the "Upper Geyser Basin" to Madison Lake, is about ten miles, and from this lake to the Shoshone Geysers, the distance is about four miles. The trail is not very good, there being considerable fallen timber through the region to be traversed.

Mount Blackmore.—This mountain, previous to 1872, was practically unnamed and unknown. It is situated in the heart of the Rocky Mountains, in Montana Territory, and at its base are the sources of the Gallatin River, which,

MT. BLACKMORE

pearly bead-work, and striped vertically with bands of white, dark green, brownish black, and various shades of orange and yellow, the white being ordinary geyserite, while the other colors are purely vegetable.

In the top of the mound are several openings, the larger about three inches in diameter, from which a stream of water is thrown 20 to 50 feet and even to 70 feet, mostly in drops, with much steam. The amount of water is small, yet is erupted with great force, reminding one of the eruptions of the "Castle." The spouting is at with the Jefferson and Madison Rivers, help form the mighty Missouri.

It was discovered by the Hayden Exploration Party of 1872, and received its name under the following circumstances: While camped at Fort Ellis, and making preparations for the explorations of the famous Yellowstone Expedition, the party was joined by Mr. William Blackmore, of London, one of England's scientific men. With him came his wife, who was anxious to see some of the beauties and wonders of our famous Yellowstone National Park. The fatigue and hardships of the journey from Corinne to Bozeman, 600 miles of staging, proved too much. On arrival at Bozeman, she was taken ill, and after a sickness of but two days, she died. Her grave lies at the foot of a mountain range, from which there rises a grand peak, standing up like a huge monument to her memory. To this peak the party gave the name of Mt. Blackmore. The height above the sea is 10,134 feet. The ascent is exceedingly difficult, and required over four days by the party who succeeded, and the scene from the summit is inexpressibly grand, and the field of vision is immense. Here a bird's-eye view is gained of the Gallatin River for over 40 miles of its course; in the distance is the Missouri. Next are the Jefferson and Madison Rivers, and southward is a country whose appearance is rough beyond imagination. Peak upon peak looms up against the horizon—the Snowy Range of the Yellowstone, with its high points, and the Madison Range with its numerous peak-capped summits. Nearly at the summit of Mt. Blackmore is the crater of an extinct volcano, and the peak itself is composed of black basalt and a brick-red lava. On the western and northern sides there is an almost perpendicular wall, too steep to hold any snow in lodgment.

PALACE BUTTE.

Palace Butte. — In ascending Mt. Blackmore, the Hayden Party passed through a lovely
little park about a quarter of a mile in length,
and almost oval in shape, bordered on all sides
by a line of grand old trees, whose symmetry
would have graced the finest artificial park in
the world. Back of these trees, on the east, rising to the height of over 3,000 feet above us,
stood an almost blank wall of volcanic rock, the
prevailing tint of which was a somber black, relieved here and there with streaks of red and
green, as though it had been painted. This wall
was surmounted by dome and spire-like points of
rock, in whose crevices lay deep banks of snow.
On the western side of the park, across the creek,
was a second wall similar in character to the
first. The effects of the weather had given curious architectural resemblances. It did not require a very vivid imagination to trace castles
and fortress walls on the face of the wall. At
the head of the park stands a monument-like
pile of rocks, to which we gave the name of
Palace Butte, and the park we call Palace Park.
The butte rises in an almost dome-shaped mass
from a blank wall, on whose sides we can distinguish narrow, silver-like lines, reaching from the
top down, until they are hidden behind the trees.
These, we afterward discovered, are waterfalls
fed by the snows above. Without any visible
means of support, they seem to cling to the rock
for protection. The scene as we came into the
park was so strikingly grand, that we could not
restrain our exclamations, and it was some time
before we became composed enough to arrange
our camp

Shoshone Lake Geysers. — In beauty the
springs of the Shoshone Basin, are probably unsurpassed although the geysers are less active
than those of the Fire Hole.

They are at the extreme western end of the
western arm of the lake, on Shoshone Creek, up
which they extend for about half a mile on both
sides.

The most important geyser is the "Union
Geyser," so called because it combines the various forms of geyseric action. It has three
vents, each of which has built up a small cone.
Its eruptions are irregular, the height being from
70 to 92 feet. Its location is on the east side of
the creek, opposite Quick Run. One hundred
yards up the stream on the same side, at the
point of a hill, are the "Minute Man" and the
"Shield Geyser." The former has a beautifully
beaded crater four feet high, and its jets reach
an altitude of from 30 to 40 feet. The shield
has an ornamented mound with a shield-shaped
opening. Between these geysers is the "Rosette
Spring" in whose shallow waters are thin leaved
rosette-shaped masses. A rocky knoll intervenes
between this and the "Bulging Spring." From
the latter, large bubbles of steam escape with a
sound like that of liquid pouring from the bung

of an overturned barrel. Forty feet beyond, is
the "Soap Kettle" in which dirty colored water
is boiling, covered with foam, looking like dirty
soapsuds. Still farther on are the "Black Sulphur Geyser," "The Twins," "The Little
Giant," "The Iron Conch," "The Coral Pool,"
and a host of smaller springs, the description of
which would be but a repetition of those already
given.

Hot springs are found also on Lewis Lake
and Heart Lake, south-east of Shoshone Lake,
and also doubtless in many localities yet undiscovered.

From the region just described, we can retrace
our steps to the Lower Fire Hole Geyser Basin
from whence we can either follow down the
Madison on the Virginia City Route, or return
to Bozeman ; or, we can follow the Snake River
passing Jackson's Lake, and the grand scenery
of the Teton Mountains, and take the trail to
Fort Hall, or crossing through Teton Pass,
go to the same place *via* Pierres River and
Snake River.

HEIGHTS ATTAINED BY THE ERUPTIONS OF THE PRINCI-
PAL GEYSERS IN FIRE HOLE BASINS, YELLOWSTONE
NATIONAL PARK.

NAME OF GEYSER.	AUTHORITY.	HEIGHT IN FEET.
Fountain, in Lower Basin,	Hayden, 1871,	30 to 60
Architectural, in Lower Basin,	Hayden, 1871,	60 to 80
Old Faithful, Upper Basin,	Hayden, 1871,	100 to 150
Old Faithful, Upper Basin,	Hayden, 1872,	*132
Old Faithful, Upper Basin,	Norton, 1872,	150
Old Faithful, Upper Basin,	Comstock, 1873,	150
Old Faithful, Upper Basin,	Dunraven, 1874,	100 to 150
Giantess, Upper Basin,	Langford, 1870,	250
Giantess, Upper Basin,	Hayden, 1872,	*39
Giantess, Upper Basin,	Norton, 1872,	100
Bee Hive, Upper Basin,	Langford, 1870,	*219
Bee Hive, Upper Basin,	Hayden, 1872,	100 to 150
Bee Hive, Upper Basin,	Norton, 1872,	100
Castle, Upper Basin,	Langford, 1870,	50
Castle, Upper Basin,	Hayden, 1871,	10 to 15
Castle, Upper Basin,	Hayden, 1872,	*93
Castle, Upper Basin,	Comstock, 1873,	30
Castle, Upper Basin,	Dunraven, 1874,	250
Grand, Upper Basin,	Hayden, 1871,	200
Grand, Upper Basin,	Hayden, 1872,	*173
Grand, Upper Basin,	Comstock, 1873,	200
Turban, Upper Basin,	Hayden, 1872,	*25
Turban, Upper Basin,	Comstock, 1873,	30
Giant, Upper Basin,	Langford, 1870,	140
Grotto, Upper Basin,	Langford, 1870,	60
Grotto, Upper Basin,	Hayden, 1872,	*41
Grotto, Upper Basin,	Comstock, 1873,	25

* Measured by triangulation, the others are estimated.

ELEVATIONS IN THE YELLOWSTONE NATIONAL PARK.

	FEET ABOVE SEA LEVEL.
Mammoth White Mountain Hot Springs,	6,278 to 7,035
Mud Volcanoes.	7,756 to 7,800
Crater Hills' Springs,	7,828 to 7,979
Sulphur Springs on divide between Yellow-	
stone and East Fork of Fire Hole River,	8,346
Lower Geyser Basin,	7,250 to 7,350
Upper Geyser Basin,	7,300 to 7,400
Third Geyser Basin,	7,772
Shoshone Lake, Geyser Basin,	7,900

LAKES.

Yellowstone Lake,	7,788
Shoshone Lake,	7,870
Lewis Lake,	7,750
Madison Lake,	8,301
Henry's Lake,	6,443

MOUNTAIN PEAKS.

	FEET ABOVE SEA LEVEL.
Mount Hayden,	13,833
Mount Washburn,	10,388
Mount Sheridan,	10,343
Mount Blackmore.	10,134
Mount Delano (Yellowstone Valley),	10,200
Mount Doane,	10,118
Electric Peak,	10,992
Emigrant Peak,	10,629
Red Mountain, south of Yellowstone Lake,	9,806
Lookout Hill, north of Shoshone Lake,	8,257
Old Baldy, near Virginia City,	9,711

PASSES AND DIVIDES.

Teton Pass,	8,464
Tyghee Pass,	7,063
Reynold's Pass. Henry's Lake north to Madison River,	6,911
Divide, Yellowstone and Gallatin, on road from Fort Ellis to Boteler's Ranche,	5,721
Divide on Mount Washburn where trail crosses,	9,155
Divide between Yellowstone and Madison, on trail from Mud Volcanoes and Geyser Basins,	8,164
Divide between Madison and Shoshone Lakes,	8,717
Divide between Yellowstone and Lewis Lakes,	8,024
Togwatee Pass, (Upper Yellowstone to Wind River,)	9,621

ANALYSIS OF DEPOSIT FROM THE HOT SPRINGS OF GARDINER'S RIVER.

Water and volatile matters,	32.10 per cent.
Lime,	57.70 per cent.
Silica,	3.32 per cent.
Ferric Oxide,	3.62 per cent.
Alumina,	3.31 per cent.
Soda and Magnesia, traces.	
	101.05

ANALYSIS OF GEYSERITE FROM LOWER GEYSER BASIN.

Water, etc.,	9.00 per cent.
Silica,	88.60 per cent.
Alumina and Iron,	1.60 per cent.
Lime,	0.95 per cent.
Magnesia, Soda, Potash and Lithia, traces.	
	100.15

ANALYSIS OF PINK MUD FROM MUD PUFFS IN LOWER GEYSER BASIN.

Water,	8.65 per cent.
Silica,	44.61 per cent.
Alumina,	45.09 per cent.
Magnesia,	2.66 per cent.
Iron,	1.86 per cent.
Lime and Soda, traces.	
	102.87

ANALYSIS OF GEYSERITE FROM UPPER GEYSER BASIN.

Water,	13.42 per cent.
Silica,	79.56 per cent.
Lime.	1.54 per cent.
Alumina,	0.46 per cent.
Magnesia,	1.78 per cent.
Iron, Chlorine and Soda, traces.	
	96.76

ANALYSIS OF GEYSERITE FROM SHOSHONE LAKE, GEYSER BASIN.

Water,	13.00 per cent.
Silica,	76.80 per cent.
Alumina,	9.46 per cent.
Lime,	1.80 per cent.
Iron, Magnesia and Soda, traces.	
	101.06

The analyses given above are from the Reports of the Hayden U. S. Geological Survey of the Territories.

Great Soda Mountain and Jupiter's Bath in the Yellowstone Region.—This natural curiosity is thus described by an artist who accompanied the Yellowstone Exploring Expedition of Doane and Washburn. It is one of the most wonderful institutions the world can afford:

"On the second day out from Boteler's Ranche —thirty-three miles—we diverge from the rocky trail on the Yellowstone, and after passing a short way up a creek called 'Gardiner's River,' we were led by an old mountaineer up quite a steep mountain.

"Near its summit an immense boiling spring spouts out, by a number of mouths and pools, the water of which, as it flows, precipitates its soda, sulphur and carbonate of lime into a succession of beautiful terraces and natural bathtubs, and like the coral insect, builds perpetually upon itself, until we have before us a hill of snowy soda and carbonate of lime, which is from 300 to 500 feet in height, and covers at least 50 acres. The water is of a deep cerulean blue, and the temperature averages 160 degrees. The process of precipitation is very rapid, and one can fairly see it deposited in beautiful strands, crystals and geodes. The elevation is a little more than 6,000 feet above the sea. No more beautiful contrast in the world of light and color can be found for the artist, than in this spot which is surrounded by dark, rugged mountains, and shades of yellow, white, amber, pink and russet on the spring-hill itself."

TOURISTS' GUIDE

≡ TO THE ≡

Scenery, Resorts and Attractions of the Pacific Coast.

California is connected with the railroad system of the Eastern States by means of the Union Pacific and Central Pacific Railroads, which together form the sole overland line of communication until the completion of the Southern Pacific Railroad, which unites with the lines, approaching it from the Mississippi river and Gulf cities.

The CENTRAL PACIFIC RAILROAD, with its branches and leased tributary lines, comprises nine-tenths of all the railroads in operation in California, Nevada and Arizona. It consists as follows:

MAIN LINE, San Francisco (via Niles) to Ogden, Utah	883.23 miles.	
OREGON DIVISION, Roseville to Redding	151.45 "	
SAN JOAQUIN DIVISION, Lathrop to Goshen	146.30 "	
SAN JOSE BRANCH, Niles to San Jose	17.54 "	
BRANCHES IN AND ABOUT OAKLAND	15.04 "	
TOTAL MILEAGE CENTRAL PACIFIC RAILROAD		1,214.06

ROADS OPERATED BY CENTRAL PACIFIC RAILROAD CO.

AMADOR BRANCH	27.20 miles.	
STOCKTON & COPPEROPOLIS	49.00 "	
BERKELEY BRANCH	3.84 "	
CALIFORNIA PACIFIC	115.44 "	
NORTHERN RAILWAY	163.65 "	
UNION PACIFIC	5.00 "	364.13

SOUTHERN PACIFIC RAILROAD (in California)	550.25 miles.	
" " " (in Arizona) in progress	300.00 "	
LOS ANGELES & SAN DIEGO	27.60 "	
" " & INDEPENDENCE	16.83 "	894.68

TOTAL MILES OPERATED BY C. P. R. R. CO.		2,472.87

Passengers going overland (East) leave San Francisco depot, foot of Market street; Express at 9.30 a.m. daily; Emigrant at 1.30 p.m., Virginia City Express at 4.30 p.m.

Passengers going overland (West) leave Ogden at 6.00 p.m. daily.

Passengers for Oregon, Washington Territory and Sacramento Valley towns, leave San Francisco (via Martinez) at 9.30 a.m. daily, and Sacramento at 2.20 p.m. daily.

Passengers for Los Angeles, Southern California, Arizona, New Mexico, Sonora, etc., leave San Francisco (via Oakland) at 4.00 p.m. daily.

Among the more notable places and features along the route of the railroad lines on the Pacific Coast are:

Salt Lake City—The chief Mormon settlement, 34 miles, by rail, south of the Ogden terminus in Utah.

Virginia City—The seat of the celebrated Comstock Silver Mines, 52 miles, by rail, south of Reno, Nevada.

Lake Tahoe—A beautiful sheet of water, 6,000 feet above sea-level, surrounded by mountains, the peaks of which rise to 10,000 feet altitude; 17 miles, by stage, south from Truckee or Summit stations, Cal. Steamboat on the Lake.

Gold Mines (Hydraulic Working) Grass Valley and Dutch Flat—Quartz mining and " Placer," or hydraulic gold mining, may be witnessed on the western slope of the Sierra Nevada, adjacent to the line of the road, on a colossal scale. Dutch Flat, 33 miles west of the Summit, is the site of extensive placer mining operations; Grass Valley, Nevada, 22½ miles north of Colfax station, by rail, are seats of both quartz mining and gold washing.

Sacramento—The State capital, contains a fine Capital Building, State Institutions, Railroad Shops and Hospital, Private Residences and displays of tropical plants.

NORTHERN CALIFORNIA, OREGON AND NORTHWEST TERRITORIES.

The line from Sacramento north passes up the broad Sacramento Valley, enclosed by high mountain ranges which consist of a succession of *wheat fields* and *fruit farms*. No such area of grain culture is elsewhere visible, unless it be in the San Joaquin Valley, the southern counterpart of this same great axial depression of California.

Mount Shasta, Pinnacle Rocks, Soda Springs—The stage route from the present terminus at Redding to the railroads in Oregon, 275 miles, crosses the beautiful McCloud river, and follows up the Sacramento or Pitt river, both of them romantic, clear streams, fed by snows and glaciers on Mount Shasta and other high ranges. About 50 miles north are passed a series of fantastic columns known as Pinnacle Rocks. About 60 miles from Redding is Fry's Soda Springs, a favorite resort for fishing and hunting sportsmen. 75 miles of staging brings one to Sisson's Hotel, at the foot of Mount Shasta. This is not like most of the protuberant points in the chains or ranges of mountains in the United States, but impresses with a singular and peculiar interest the observer, from the fact that it is an isolated " butte " or cone, standing between two ranges and overlooking the country for a hundred miles around. It has a summit altitude of 14,444 feet above the ocean, and its snow-capped sides are visible from vessels on the Pacific ocean. The ascent to the summit can be made and the glaciers studied with safety in the warmer half of the year. Taken altogether, for sublimity and massive grandeur, the spectacular interest of Mount Shasta and its environs is unrivalled in the United States, and it is justly beginning to share of late, with the Yo Semite Valley, the distinction of a world-wide wonder. A few miles north of Redding the stage passes the U. S. Salmon Hatching Establishment. Excellent salmon and trout fishing are found in the streams on this route, and also deer and other wild game at several points along this route toward Oregon, including the wild mountain sheep, a few of which still survive.

Beyond the northern boundary of California may be observed numerous snowy peaks and objects of interest, including the evidences of volcanic action on the grandest scale, extinct craters, floating pumice, sunken rivers, etc., including the memorable Mount Hood. The Columbia river itself is a remarkable stretch of fine scenery for hundreds of miles of its length.

From San Francisco, several attractions invite the tourist and sight-seer in many directions, conspicuous among these, of course, near the southern arms of the Central Pacific Railroad is:

The Yo Semite Valley—This marvel of variety and scenic effect is situated about 250 miles from the metropolis, and may be reached by either of the four routes described at length in the preceding pages.

1. By C. P. R. R. to Milton, 133 miles, and stage via the Calaveras Grove of Big Trees, 147 miles.
2. By C. P. R. R. to Milton, 133 miles, and stage via Coulterville, 88 miles.
3. By C. P. R. R. to Merced, 151 miles, and stage via Mariposa Big Trees, 92 miles.
4. By C. P. R. R. to Madera, 173½ miles, and stage via Mariposa Big Trees, 79 miles.

The time and fare by either route are about the same. Passengers by the two latter routes, however, can take sleeping cars and connect with stages, going or coming.

Further south, at a point nearly opposite Goshen Junction, upon the headwaters of King's river, is the **Hetch-hetchy Valley,** with deep chasms and precipitous cataracts, and fine specimens of the *Sequoia Gigantea* (Big Trees). Roads for wheeled vehicles have not yet penetrated it, but it is accessible by horses.

CALIFORNIA PACIFIC RAILROAD.

Next, perhaps, in scenic interest are the **Geysers and Petrified Forest.** These may be taken in the same trip by the California Pacific Railroad to Calistoga, 73 miles, and stage, 25 miles. In the Napa Valley is situated the much used Napa Natural Soda Spring. Near Saint Helena are very charming summer hotels and Sulphur Springs. At Calistoga, the famous hot and cold sulphur springs, "soup spring" and other curiosities. Both routes to the Geysers abound in extensive vineyards. At Vallejo are the government naval stations and dock-yard.

SOUTHERN PACIFIC RAILROAD.

The other great overland line from the Pacific to the Atlantic, now nearing completion, approaches San Francisco without crossing the bay. It is destined to be one of the great highways of the Continent, and is already the longest continuous stretch of main line railroad, under the same control, in the United States, and perhaps in the world. The southern portions are temporarily worked under lease to the Central Pacific.

NORTHERN DIVISION.

COAST LINE, San Francisco to Soledad..143 miles.	
TULARE VALLEY LINE, Carnadero to Tres Pinos................................ 18 "	
MONTEREY R. R. (leased)... 24 "	
	185 miles.

Monterey Sea-Side Resort and Sanitarium—The watering places of the Pacific Coast are situated at some distance south of the great central harbor, where a more equable climate and less trying atmosphere prevail. The chief of these, combining, so to speak, the Long Branch and Cape May of the west coast, since the new importance has been given to the ancient capital, is Monterey. A branch road has recently been reconstructed so as to provide direct transit to and from Monterey, and admit to its many attractions of sea-bathing, drives, parks, groves and congenial climate visitors and the population of the rest of California. An express train leaves the city in the afternoon (returning in the morning) making the trip in about three hours. Parlor cars attached to this train. Fare, $3. Excursion, $5.

Besides the new "HOTEL DEL MONTE," a wonder in its way, situated in a superb grove of live oaks, and surrounded by ornamented grounds, there are other attractions. A magnificent Beach Drive from Point Pinos to Cypress Point; Rocks, swarming with mammoth seals, groves of stupendous redwoods and a unique specimen survival of cypress, being among them. Cottages are projected for families, and a race-course for lovers of horse flesh. The conveniences and appliances for comfort of the most approved and "modern" description, are now found side by side with historic relics of the Spanish and Mexican occupation.

San Jose, 50 miles south of San Francisco, is a beautiful inland town of 20,000 inhabitants, favored in its sheltered position and climate, with several fine public buildings; and is especially noticeable for the luxuriance and taste of its private grounds and gardens, those of Gen. Naglee being justly renowned.

Along the line of the Southern Pacific are several suburbs, Millbrae, Belmont, Menlo Park and Santa Clara, distinguished for the elegance, splendor and amplitude of their private residences and grounds, some of which have no rivals in America.

SOUTHERN CALIFORNIA.

THE SOUTHERN DIVISIONS OF THE SOUTHERN PACIFIC RAILROAD connect with the Southern Arm of the Central Pacific at Goshen, 240 miles from San Francisco. They are:

HURON TO GOSHEN.. 40 miles.	
GOSHEN TO LOS ANGELES...240 "	
LOS ANGELES TO YUMA..249 "	
LOS ANGELES TO WILMINGTON HARBOR................................ 22 "	
	551 miles.

ARIZONA DIVISION (in progress).

YUMA TO BENSON......(Completed in June, 1880)...................................... 300 miles.

The Tehachapa Loop is a wonder of railroad engineering encountered about 350 miles south of San Francisco, where the railroad passes from the Tulare Basin over the Sierra Nevada range to get on the Mohave dry plains. To accomplish this feat, with the required grade, the line being shut up within a narrow and jagged defile, it became necessary at one point in the ascent to wind the road spirally round a conical hillock so as to cross itself, the only instance of the kind in the world. The elevation overcome at Tehachapa is 4,000 feet above sea level.

The portion of the line between Tehachapa and Los Angeles is not without interest to the tourist and student of nature, a tunnel of 7,000 feet in length being one feature, and the Yucca Palms of the desert another. Here are also occasional mirages and the petroleum field of California.

SEAPORTS, HEALTH RESORTS, ETC.

Los Angeles, one of many Spanish missionary settlements, has long been the chief city of Southern California, and it is now the railroad centre, as it is also the depot for the Semi-Tropical Belt, which is the seat of the most remarkable horticultural and vinicultural experiments to be found. From Santa Barbara on the north, to San Diego, an equal distance on the south, the temperature is less variable, frost and snow being rarely experienced, except on the mountains, and the winds are tempered. The use of fire is confined mainly to cooking. There are several localities which vie with each other for the pre-eminence as Sanitaria or Resorts for invalids: Santa Barbara, San Buena-venturo, Wilmington, Santa Monica, San Gabriel, San Bernardino, Anaheim, Orange and San Diego.

Santa Monica, Wilmington, Anaheim, Orange and San Bernardino are reached by railroad, the first two being directly on inlets of the Pacific Ocean, and the latter considerably elevated and inland. San Diego, the most southerly, close to the Mexican boundary, boasts of a climate of great stability, and has excellent sea fishing. The railroad is in progress to it, the staging from the present terminus at Santa Ana being about 90 miles, part of it along the beach.

Orange groves, vineyards, orchards of the almond, walnut, and also of the apple, peach, cherry, &c., are to be found in this region, frequently growing side by side with the date, banana pomegranate. Here also maize-corn is grown to perfection, and experiments are making with the coffee tree.

ARIZONA, NEW AND OLD MEXICO.

From Los Angeles the Southern Pacific Railroad takes a more decided easterly course and crosses the state of California by the shortest and most feasible route from Wilmington harbor to the Colorado River at Yuma, thus forming the western portion of the shortest rail route between the Gulf of Mexico and the Pacific on United States Territory. Between San Gorgonio Pass and Yuma the road descends for quite a long stretch below the ocean level. The region for 150 miles on either side of Yuma is the warmest to be found in this country, and on this account is recommended by some physicians for some forms of disease. The thermometer records a very high temperature at times, but the air being dry, the suffering therefrom is not proportionate.

THE SOUTHERN PACIFIC RAILROAD OF ARIZONA extends easterly, following up the Gila Valley, passing several points of interest. Among them are the Painted Rocks *Piedros Pintados*, near Casa Grande, inscriptions of human origin, not yet deciphered, and supposed to belong to a lost race. To the student of ethnology, Arizona presents much curious and instructive material.

Tucson—250 miles east of Yuma, and 980 east of San Francisco, now a city of rapidly growing proportions, has itself the distinction of being one of the oldest, if not the oldest, city in the country of European settlement, having been founded by the Spaniards in 1542. Like Los Angeles and the other Spanish named towns, it has adjacent church and military structures dating back hundreds of years, some of them of architectural pretensions, considering their remoteness and savage surroundings. The precious metals were the inspiring impulse of the original Spanish ingress ; and an influx of the same origin, but of very different character and material, is now re-occupying that country.

Along the route of the Southern Pacific, for the 400 miles in Arizona, are to be found hundreds of gold and silver mines, and every week only adds to the number of discoveries. Mining towns are springing up over two-thirds the area of the Territory, and quite a revival of this industry is springing up in the Mexican States of Sonora and Chihuahua.

The railroad is approaching the boundary of New Mexico, and is expected to reach the Rio Grande, at or near El Paso, sometime in 1881, where it will be joined by one or more of the east-and-west lines crossing Texas. El Paso is, by the route, surveyed 1,300 miles east of San Francisco, and about 1,150 miles from New Orleans. Between Galveston and either of the Los Angeles harbors on the Pacific is about 1.700 miles. From San Francisco to St. Louis, via El Paso and Sherman, Texas, will be about the same distance as by the Ogden and Omaha route.

INDEX.

	PAGE.
Overland Travel.—	
Hints and Comforts,	10
Palace Car Life,	8
Railroad Routes,	12
Sleeping Car Expenses,	13
Preparations Westward	
Trip,	18
Union Pacific R. R.	
Benefits,	6
Discouragements,	7
Fast Building,	8
History,	5
Progress,	7
NEBRASKA.—	
Adams,	60
Ames,	25
Alda,	31
Alkali,	46
Antelope,	58
Barton,	47
Big Spring,	47
Brady Island,	38
Bridge. Missouri River,	18
Brownson,	58
Brule,	47
Bennett,	58
Bushnell,	63
Chapman,	28
Chappell,	56
Clark,	28
Colton,	56
Columbus,	26
Coyote,	37
Cozad,	37
Dexter,	46
Elkhorn,	20
Elm Creek,	33
Fremont,	23
Gannett,	38
Gibbon,	32
Gilmore,	19
Grand Island,	29
Jackson,	28
Josselyn,	33
Julesburg,	47
Julesburg Incidents,	47
Kearny,	32
Kearny Junction,	32
Lockwood,	29
Lodge Pole,	56
Lone Tree,	28
McPherson,	38
Millard,	19
Nichols,	46
North Bend,	23
North Platte River,	39
North Platte,	41
O'Fallon's,	46
Ogalalla,	46
Omaha,	15
Omaha Business,	17
Overton,	33
Papillion,	19
Plum Creek,	33
Potter,	58
Richland,	21
Riverside,	21
Rogers,	25
Roscoe,	46
Schuyler,	25

	PAGE.
Shelton,	31
Sidney,	56
Silver Creek,	28
South Platte River,	39
Stevenson,	33
Summit Siding,	19
Summit Springs,	49
Valley,	20
Warren,	38
Waterloo,	20
Willow Island,	37
Wood River,	31
COLORADO.—	
Denver,	75
Denver & Rio Grande	
Railroad,	75
Denver Pacific R. R.,	73
Evans,	75
Garden of the Gods,	77
Grand Canon, Ark.,	77
Gray's Peak,	77
Greeley,	73
Life in Colorado,	77
Manitou Springs,	75
Mtn. Holy Cross,	79
Notes to Tourists,	75
Pleasure Resorts,	73
WYOMING.—	
Agate,	97
Archer,	61
Aspen,	108
Atkins,	60
Baxter,	100
Bear River City,	110
Bitter Creek,	97
Black Buttes,	99
Black Hills, Wyoming,	88
Bridger,	107
Bryan,	104
Buford,	81
Burns,	60
Carbon,	93
Carter,	107
Cheyenne,	61
Chugwater Valley,	91
Church Buttes,	105
Como,	90
Cooper's Lake,	93
Creston,	96
Dale Creek Bridge,	82
Dana,	93
Devil's Gate, Sweet-	
water,	110
Egbert,	60
Evanston,	111
Fillmore,	96
Fort Steele,	91
Granite Canon,	81
Green River,	100
Greenville,	95
Hallville,	99
Hampton,	107
Harney,	84
Hazard,	81
Hilliard,	108
Hillsdale,	60
Howell,	90
Independence Rock,	110
Laramie,	81

	PAGE.
Laramie Peak,	87
Laramie Plains,	83
Latham,	97
Lawrence,	100
Leroy,	107
Lookout,	90
Marston,	104
Medicine Bow,	91
Medicine Bow M't'ns,	88
Millis,	111
Miser,	90
Otto,	81
Percy,	93
Piedmont,	107
Pine Bluffs,	60
Point of Rocks,	99
Powder River Country,	81
Rawlins,	93
Red Buttes,	84
Red Desert,	97
Rock Creek,	90
Rock Springs,	100
Salt Wells,	99
Separation,	96
Sherman,	82
Simpson,	93
Skull Rocks,	83
Soda Springs,	109
Stock Statistics,	85
Summit,	96
St. Mary's,	94
Sweetwater River,	103
Table Rock,	97
Thayer,	99
The Siding,	83
Tipton,	97
Tongue River Country,	81
Tracy,	60
Uintah Mountains,	105
Walcott,	94
Washakie,	97
Wilcox,	90
Wind River Mountains,	87
Wyoming,	90
UTAH.—	
American Fork,	142
American Fork Canon,	143
Black Rock,	140
Blue Creek,	163
Blommeville,	162
Bovine,	172
Brigham,	162
Bromley Cathedral,	119
Castle Rock,	116
Centerville,	132
City of Rocks,	170
Coalville,	120
Corinne,	162
Deer Creek,	145
Desert, Great,	157
Devil's Gate,	126
Devil's Slide,	124
Draperville,	141
Echo Canon,	115
Echo,	119
Farmington,	132
Gardening, Irrigation,	139
Half-Way House,	160
Hanging Rock,	117
Hot Springs,	129
Junction,	141

	PAGE.
Kaysville,	132
Kelton,	167
Lake,	166
Lake Point,	149
Lehi,	142
Little Cottonwood,	141
Lucin,	172
Matlin,	172
Millstone Point,	147
Monument,	166
Mormon Fortifications,	117
Ogden,	126
Ogden Canon,	128
Ombey,	172
One Thousand Mile	
Tree,	121
Parley's Park,	122
Payson,	143
Peterson,	125
Pleasant Grove,	142
Promontory,	164
Provo,	142
Pulpit Rock,	119
Quarry,	163
Rocks Echo and We-	
ber Canons,	122, 124
Rozel,	166
Salt Lake,	155
Salt Lake City,	132, 134
Sandy,	141
Santaguin,	143
Seco,	167
Sentinel Rock,	117
Shoshone Falls,	168
Spanish Fork,	143
Springs, Salt Lake	
City,	135, 136
Springville,	142
Steamboat Rock,	117
Terrace,	172
Uintah,	126
Utah Central R. R.,	131
Utah Lake,	147
Utah Southern R. R.,	140
Utah Territory,	129
Utah Western R. R.,	147
Wahsatch,	113
Weber,	125
Weber Quarry,	125
Weber River,	120
Witches, The	119
Wood's Cross,	132
York,	143
Idaho Territory.—	
Boise City,	171
Boise Valley,	171
Rattlesnake Station,	171
Silver City,	171
Snake River,	171
MILITARY POSTS.—	
Camp Carlin,	79
Fort Laramie,	79
Fort Sanders,	84
Fort Reno,	81
Fort Casper,	79
Fort Fetterman,	79
NEVADA.—	
Argenta,	186
Austin,	186

INDEX.

	Page.
Battle Mountain,	186
Beowawe,	185
Big Bonanza Mine,	211
Bishop's,	176
Bronco,	224
Brown's,	198
Brown's,	207
Brunswick,	208
Carlin,	180
Carson City,	208
Carson Sink,	214
Chicken Soup Spring,	177
Clark's,	204
Clover Valley,	175
Cluro,	182
Coin,	189
Cornucopia Mines,	178
Dead Man's Spring,	174
Death,	176
Desert,	199
Elko,	177
Emerald Bay,	217
Empire,	208
Essex,	221
Franktown,	207
Glenbrook,	216
Golconda,	190
Gold Hill,	208
Granite Point,	198
Great Nevada Flume,	219
Halleck,	176
Hot Springs,	199
Humboldt,	194
Humboldt Lake,	201
Humboldt River,	202
Humboldt Sink,	214
Independence,	174
Iron Point,	190
Lake Tahoe,	216
Lake Tahoe—Stage Routes,	214
Lake View,	208
Lookout,	208
Loray,	173
Lovelock's,	197
Lumber,	219
Mammoth Cave,	173
Merrimac,	208
Mill City,	193
Mill Station,	208
Mines of Virginia City,	210
Mirage,	198
Moleen,	180
Montello,	179
Moore's,	174
Morgan,	208
Mount Davidson,	210
Mound House,	208
Ore—Lewis Mine,	187
Oreana,	197
Oshno,	177
Otego,	174
Palisade,	182
Peko,	176
Pequop,	174
Piute,	189
Pyramid Lake,	202
Raspberry,	193
Reno,	205
Rose Creek,	193
Rowlands,	217
Ruby Range,	176
Rye Patch,	196
Salvia,	208
Scales,	208
Silver,	208
Shoshone,	185
Shoshone Indian Village,	182
Sinks of Nevada Basin,	214
Steamboat Springs,	208
Stone House,	189
Sulphur Mines,	195
Sutro Tunnel,	210
Tahoe City,	216
Tecoma,	172
Thousand Spring Valley,	176

	Page.
Toano,	173
Trout in Lake Tahoe,	218
Truckee River,	202
Tulasco,	176
Tule,	190
Two Mile,	199
Virginia & Truckee R.R.,	207
Verdi,	224
Virginia City,	209
Vista,	204
Wadsworth,	200
Walker Lake,	214
Washoe City,	207
Wells, Humboldt,	174
White Plains,	198
Winnemucca,	191
Winnemucca Lake,	202
Yank's,	217
CALIFORNIA.—	
Alta,	233
Altamont,	237
Antelope,	244
Arcade,	244
Auburn,	241
Bantas,	255
Batavia,	276
Bay of San Francisco,	261
Beet Sugar,	247
Big Trees—Calaveras,	250
Blue Canon,	233
Boca,	224
Bridgeport,	276
Brighton,	249
Brooklyn,	259
California Pacific R. R.,	275
Calistoga,	277
Cannon's,	276
Cape Horn,	239
Cape Horn Mills,	239
Cascade,	230
Castle,	249
China Ranche,	233
Cisco,	231
Cliff House,	271
Climate,	241
Clipper Gap,	241
Colfax,	240
Creston,	276
Davisville,	275
Decoto,	258
Dixon,	276
Dutch Flat,	235
Elk Grove,	249
Ellis,	255
Elmira,	276
Emigrant Gap,	233
Excursions,	267
Fairfield,	276
Florin,	249
Foster,	276
Galt,	249
Geysers,	269, 273
Gold Run,	237
Grass Valley,	240
Great American Canon,	233
Haywards,	258
Insane Asylums,	250
Ione City,	249
Jackson,	249
Junction,	243
Kidd's Lakes,	230
Lathrop,	252
Litton Seltzer Springs,	273
Livermore,	257
Lockford,	249
Lodi,	249
Lorenzo,	258
McConnell's,	249
Medway,	255
Melrose,	259
Merced,	253
Mineral Springs,	271
Mokelumne Hill,	249
Moonlight Scenery of the Sierras,	240

	Page.
Napa,	276
Napa Junction,	276
Napa Soda Springs,	271
Napa Valley,	276
Nevada,	240
New Almaden Quicksilver Mines,	269
Newcastle,	243
New England Mills,	241
Niles,	258
Oak Knoll,	277
Oakland,	259
Oakland Point,	261
Pacific Congress Springs,	271
Penryn,	243
Pescadero,	270
Petrified Forest,	273
Pino,	243
Pleasanton,	257
Pleasure Resorts of California,	271
Procter's	225
Prosser Creek,	224
Rocklin,	243
Railroad Works—Sacramento,	244
Sacramento,	246
Sacramento Capitol,	246
San Francisco,	262
San Joaquin Bridge,	255
San Joaquin Valley,	252
San Jose,	269
San Leandro,	259
Santa Cruz,	269
Secret Town,	240
Shady Run,	233
Snow Sheds,	227
Snow Storm at Truckee,	226
Soda Springs Station,	230
South Vallejo,	277
Starvation Camp,	228
St. Helena,	277
Stockton,	250
Strong's Canon,	228
Suisun City,	276
Summit,	228
Summit Valley,	230
Sunol,	257
Sutter Creek,	249
Tamarack,	231
Thompson,	276
Truckee,	225
Vallejo,	277
Woodward's Garden,	271
Yosemite—Routes,	253
Yountville,	277
MISCELLANEOUS.—	
Ah Ching's Theology,	205
Alexis' Buffalo Hunt,	37
Alfalfa,	253
Battle with Indians,	33—37, 49
Black Hills, The	68—72
Brown's Hole,	102
Buffaloes,	62
Buffalo Grass,	46
Buffalo Robes,	26
Bullwhackers,	55
Cattle Kings,	185
Central Pacific R. R.— Discouragement,	159
Capital,	161
Expenses,	160
Chimney Rock,	42
Chinese in San Francisco,	278
Chinese Workmen,	115
Cloud Effects,	57
Coal Mine,	113
Colorado Plains,	58
Coyotes,	59
Curious Names,	205
Curiosities, Indians	91
Flaming Gorge,	103
Game—Black Hills,	72

	Page.
Giant's Club,	102
Great Plains and Desert,	188
Great Railroad Wedding,	164
Green River Rocks,	103
Hailstorms,	60
Health—Cheyenne,	66
Heat,	250
Iliff—Cattle King,	52
Indians. Astonished	64
Indian Burial Tree,	88
Indian Prayer,	64
Indian Trade,	62
Invalids. Advice to	44
Invalids, Hints to	274
Last Spike,	164
Letters,	204
Long's Peak,	61
Maiden's Grave,	184
Mormon Church,	152
Mormon Courtesies,	153
Mormon Religion,	152
Mormon Social Life,	150
Mountain on Fire,	113
Oasis in the Desert,	194
"Off to the Mines,"	237
Pike's Peak or Bust,	21
Piutes, Customs,	192
Piutes, Burial Dead,	189
Piutes, Catch Fish,	180
Placer Mining,	235
Platte Valley,	23
Poker, a Chinese Idea of,	239
Pony Express,	42
Prairie Dogs,	52
Prairie Fires,	21
Prairie Hens, Shooting	24
Precious Stones,	66
Rabbit Drives,	199
Rabbit Robes,	200
Race, Curious	93
Rainbows,	72
Rough Times, Cheyenne.	65
Scientific Explorations,	106
Sheep Raising,	84
Skillful Cookery,	237
Sporting,	142
Sporting,	112
Stock Raising,	39
Stock Raising,	68
Successful Farming,	31
Sunset Scenes,	57
The Devil, Firing off	205
Thunder Storm,	71
Tit for Tat,	205
Tree Planting,	31
Tule land,	275
Vigilance Committee Incident,	106
Windmills,	87
Yellowstone Park,	203
ILLUSTRATIONS.	
Agnes Park.	69
American Fork Canon,	144
American Fork (six scenes).	146
Ames Oakes, Portrait	22
Anderson Valley,	234
Bank, California	263
Battlement Rocks,	116
Bear River Valley,	232
Bierstadt, Albert, Portrait	30
Big Trees (six scenes),	251
Black Hills (five scenes),	67
Black Rock,	149
Bloomer Cut,	243
Blue Canon,	232
Brigham Young's Family Residence,	135
Brigham Young's Office,	136

INDEX.

	PAGE.		PAGE.		PAGE.		PAGE.
Brigham Young's New Residence,	139	Golden Gate,	266	Mt. Blackmore,	306	Shooting Ducks,	45
Bromley's Cathedral,	114	Good Bye,	19	Mts. Hayden and Moran,	297	Shoshone Falls,	168—171
Buildings San Francisco (five views).	264	Gould, Jay. Portrait	22	Needle Rocks,	118	Shoshone Indian Village,	162
Bullwhacker of the Plains,	55	Grand Duke Alexis' Buffalo Hunt,	38	Oakland Avenue,	245	Sierras, Scenery	231
Busted,	21	Gray's Peak,	63	Oakland Garden,	245	Sign Mormon Stores,	137
Cape Horn (three views),	238	Great Eastern, Echo Canon,	114	Oak Knoll,	272	Silver Palace-Car of C. P. R. R.,	161
Castle Peak,	234	Great Railroad Wedding,	165	Oakland Piazza Vines,	245	Skull Rocks,	82
Castle Rock, Echo Canon,	114	Great Salt Lake,	154	Ogden,	127	Snow Sheds, Union Pacific Railroad,	108
Castle Rock, Green River,	100	Green Bluffs,	234	Ogden Canon Narrows,	129	Snow Sheds, Central Pacific Railroad,	224
Central Pacific Railroad, Representative Men,	158	Green River (three scenes),	98	Old Mill, Am. Fork Canon,	148	Snow Sheds Gallery,	225
Chimney Rock,	42	Green River, West Bank,	102	Omaha. Scenes in (five views),	14	Snow Slide Mountains,	141
China Ranche,	232	Hanging Rock, Echo Canon,	114	Overland Stage, Indian Attack,	48	Street Scene, San Francisco,	270
Chinese Theatre, Interior	289	Hayden, Prof. F. V., Portrait	30	Palace Butte,	307	Summits of the Sierras,	221
Chinese Temple,	285	Hoodlums,	265	Palace-Car Life.	2	The Pacific Tourist,	1—5
Chinese Quarters,	279	Humboldt Canon,	184	Palisades of the Humboldt,	183	Thousand Mile Tree,	125
Church Buttes,	105	Humboldt Desert (six scenes).	181	Pappoose Scene,	195	Truckee River (six scenes).	203
Cliff House,	266	Humboldt River,	181	Pawnee Chief in Full Dress,	51	Tunnel No. 3, Weber Canon,	127
Cold Stream,	231	Humboldt Sink,	181	Petrified Fish Cut,	102	Tunnel. Strong's Canon,	227
Coyotes.	59	Humboldt Station,	193	Piute Indians,	181	Twin Sisters,	101
Custer, Gen., Portrait	30	Hunting Prairie Hens,	25	Platte River, near Fort Steele,	95	Ute Squaw and Pappoose.	163
Dale Creek Bridge,	83	Independence Rock,	110	Pony Express,	43	Uintah Mountains.	80
Deer Race with Train,	94	Indian Burial Tree,	88	Pony Express Saluting the Telegraph,	44	Virginia City, Nevada,	209
Deeth Mountain Scene,	181	Indian Costumes,	50	Pony Express Station,	43	Vision Golden Country,	242
Desert, Great American,	181	Indian Tent Scene,	27	Powell, Major J. W., Portrait,	30	Wadsworth,	181
Devil's Gate,	127	Jupiter's Baths,	304	Prairie Dog City,	53	Weber Canon, Heights,	127
Devil's Gate on Sweetwater,	111	Lake Anguline,	230	Prairie on Fire,	20	Wheeler, Lieut., Portrait	30
Devil's Slide,	126	Lake Esther,	212	Prospect Hill,	234	Wilhelmina Pass,	130
Devil's Tower,	72	Lake Lal,	112	Prospect Hill,	232	Williams' Canon,	74
Dillon, Sidney, Portrait	22	Lake Scene near Gold Hill,	40	Pulpit Rock,	119, 120	Windmill at Laramie,	87
Donner Lake,	234	Lake Tahoe,	215	Pyramid Lake,	201	Winnemucca, Indian Chief,	191
Donner Lake,	229	Laramie Plains, Morning,	86	Representative Men Union Pacific Railroad.	22	Winter Forest Scene, Sierras,	206
Durant. T. C , Portrait	22	Lightning Scene,	71	Residence D. O. Mills,	245	Witches Bottles,	118
Echo Canon Cliffs,	123	Little Blue Canon,	234	Rock Cut near Aspen,	109	Witches Rocks,	118
Echo Canon Mouth,	121	Long's Peak,	61	Ruby Range.	179	Woodward's Gardens,	268
Emigrant Gap Ridge,	232	Mary's Lake,	226	Salt Lake City,	133—137	Yellowstone Geysers (five views).	292
Eminent Explorers and Artists.	30	Medicine Bow Mtns.	89	Salt Lake at Monument Point,	167	Yellowstone Lake,	302
Egyptian Tombs,	118	Men of California, Portraits	249	San Francisco Harbor (four views).	266	Yellowstone, Lower Falls,	300
Fountain, Hillside Garden,	245	Missouri River Bridge,	14	San Francisco View,	260	Yellowstone Park Scenes,	304
Fremont, Gen., Portrait	30	Monument Point,	167	San Francisco Mint.	263	Yellowstone Valley,	304
Gardens and Groves,	245	Monument Rock,	122	Scott. Thomas A., Portrait	22	Yosemite, Bridal Veil.	254
Garden of the Gods,	76	Moore's Lake,	112	Secret Town Trestle-Work.	135	Yosemite, Mirror Lake,	254
Giant's Club,	103	Moran Thomas, Portrait	30	Sentinel Rock,	117	Yosemite, Vernal Falls,	256
Giant's Gap,	236	Mormon Tabernacle,	138	Shady Run,	234		
Giant's Tea Pot,	103	Mormon Temple,	135			Total No.	256
Gilbert's Peak,	80	Mormons (nine portraits).	151				
Glaciers, Mt. Hayden,	299	Mtn. of the Holy Cross,	78				

ADDITIONAL INDEX.

Agnew's,	295	Felton,	295	Mowry's,	295	Santa Clara,	295
Alma.	295	Geysers,	322	Mt. Eden,	295	Santa Cruz,	296
Alameda,	295	Gila City,	296	Napa Soda Springs,	271	San Leandro, west,	295
Alvarada,	295	Glenwood & Dougherty's Mill,	295	Newark,	295	San Lorenzo, west,	295
Alviso,	295			New Boston,	301	San Jose,	295
Arbuckle,	319	Harrington,	319	Norman,	320	Sobrante,	321
Atlantic City,	104	Huachuca,	301	Pacific Congress Springs,	271	South Pass City,	104
Artesian Wells,	115	Litton Springs,	322	Pantano,	300	Teal,	320
Benicia,	295	Logandale,	320	Papago,	300	Tombstone,	301
Benson,	300	Los Gatos,	295	Paso Robles,	271	Tormey,	321
Berlin,	319	Lovelady's,	295	Petrified Forest,	273	Tucson,	299
Big Trees,	295	Macy,	319	Picacho,	299	Vallejo Junction,	320
Camp Brown,	104	Martinez,	320	Pinole,	321	Valona,	320
Camp Stambough,	104	Maxwell,	319	Port Costa,	320	White Sulphur Springs,	273
Charleston,	300	Mescal,	300	Red Rock,	299	Williams,	319
Contention City,	300	Miner's Delight,	104	Richmond,	300	Willows,	320
Delavan,	320	Monterey,	322	Russell's,	295	Wright's,	295

HOTEL DEL MONTE · MONTEREY

MONTEREY, CAL.,

The Old Capital Transformed into a Fashionable Watering Place.

THE NEW HOTEL AND GROUNDS.

The Magnificent Beach and Bathing Facilities.

DESCRIPTION OF THE NEW HOTEL AND GROUNDS.

The new Hotel del Monte is one of the prettiest watering-place hotels to be found anywhere, and will have ample' and in time, lovely grounds. Indeed, no seaside house upon the Atlantic approaches its plan of exterior, while its in' terior finish, accommodations and appointments, are superior to those of any like establishment in the United States. It is built in the modern Gothic or Queen Anne style, and cost, with its furniture and other appointments, about a quarter of a million of dollars. It is 305 feet in length and 60 feet in width, with wings; it has two full stories and an attic story, and several stories in the central tower or observatory. Its ground floor, in some respects, resembles that of the Grand Union at Saratoga, and as in that and other eastern summer hotels, the lady guests have access to all the public rooms, and especially to the office, or lobby, in the front center of the building, which is 42 x 48 feet; connecting with the lobby is a reading-room, 24 x 26; then a ladies' billiard-room, 62 x 25; then a ladies' parlor, 34 x 42, and then, with a hall or covered veranda between, a ball-room, 36 x 72. There is a corridor extending the whole length of the building 12 feet wide. The dining room is 45 x 70; a children's and servants' dining-room is attached, and apartments for parties who may prefer *déjeuners à la fourchette*. The kitchen is 33 x 40 feet. There are 28 *suites* of rooms on this floor, with bath rooms and all modern improvements. There are three staircases, one at the intersection of each of the end wings, and a grand staircase leading from the lobby. In the second story there are 48 *suites*, or about 100 rooms, with bath-rooms and all other modern improvements. There is a promenade the whole length of the building 12 feet in width. In the attic story there are 13 *suites* and 29 single rooms, 65 apartments in all. The central tower, or observatory, is 25 x 30 and about 80 feet in height; there are 10 rooms in the observatory; the end tower is about 50 feet in height.

The hotel is lighted with gas throughout, and supplied with hot and cold water. The sewerage system has been made in the completest manner possible, and there are safeguards against fire in different portions of the buildings. Most of the carpets are Brussels, and the ladies' parlor and the ladies' billiard-room are each furnished in a manner suggested by the highest taste. There is a stable attached (having ample room for the accommodation of private teams) which is well stocked with reliable livery horses, and has telephonic communication with the hotel.

The grove which contains these improvements is one of the prettiest on the Pacific Coast, and is studded all over with cypress, pine and oak, and has been thoroughly cleaned of everything that would tend to impair its beauty in any way. The grounds cover 100 acres, and has swings, etc., also an archery.

The new hotel is called the "Hotel del Monte," a name suggested by the beautiful grove in the midst of which it is located.

The beach is about a third of a mile from the hotel, and is a beauty. There is a bathing-house on the beach, supplying hot and cold salt water baths.

THE CLIMATE AND HEALTHFULNESS OF MONTEREY.

The weather at Monterey is not so warm, either in summer or winter, as in other parts of California further south, but there is an even temperature that can be found nowhere else. From January to December, year in and year out, there is no summer nor winter weather. Indeed, the weather at Monterey, from one year's end to the other, partakes of that delightful interlude known in the East an I South as "Indian Summer." The same balmy zephyrs breathe a delicious atmosphere all the year round, and summer and winter, so-called, serenely face each other and exchange compliments.

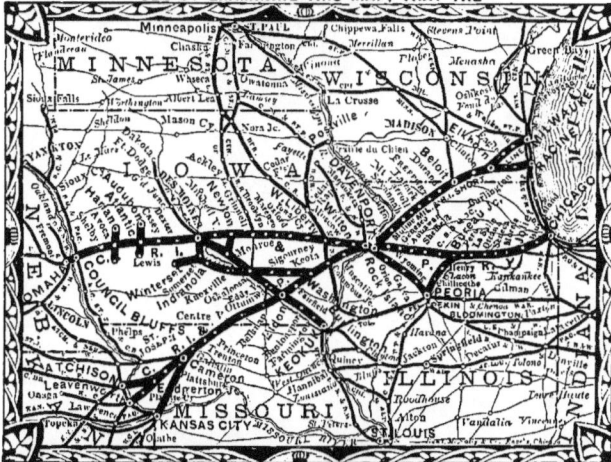

www.ingramcontent.com/pod-product-compliance
Lightning Source LLC
Chambersburg PA
CBHW030911270326
41929CB00008B/652